VITAL FORESIGHT

The Case For Active Transhumanism

By

David W. Wood
Chair, London Futurists

Dedicated

To the new generations rising in our midst
And to the older generations who might soon
Experience revitalisation as never before.

Paperback ISBN 978-0-9954942-5-1

Published by Delta Wisdom

Advance praise

"This remarkably insightful and readable book gives us an empathetic and caring view of future possibilities, offered by someone who is still actively engaged in making things better."

Kim Solez, M.D., Director of
Technology and the Future of Medicine Course at the University of Alberta

"David Wood is one of the best informed and most thoughtful people writing about the likely future impact of the exponential growth in the power of our most advanced technologies. In this book he offers practical advice about how we can all help to nudge the future in the directions we want."

Calum Chace, author of
Surviving AI, *The Economic Singularity*, *Pandora's Brain*, and *Pandora's Oracle*

"David has a rare gift for condensing insights from diverse disciplines. One could pick almost any chapter in this book and use it for generative dialogue."

Ashish Manwar, Director, FoundationsEnterprise

"In a century of accelerating scientific progress we need a balanced perspective on its promises and perils. David Wood's book offers just this in 17 well-informed chapters on how extremely advanced technology can affect all areas of society – work, environment, education, health, wealth distribution, to name a few – in the decades leading up to 2050, how society and its leaders must prepare for outcomes good and bad, and how to make the right choices. *Vital Foresight* is the must-read for any serious discussion about our future."

Catarina Lamm, independent transhumanist and cryonicist, Oxford

"David Wood, in *Vital Foresight*, has provided us with a cogent and coherent scaffold on which to move progressively toward a greater appreciation of many issues that must be resolved for our survival. It deserves serious consideration by all readers."

Gordon Silverman, Professor Emeritus,
Electrical & Computer Engineering, Manhattan College

"I consider David Wood to be the most prolific, competent, honest and dedicated technoprogressive futurist and transhumanist active today. With this book David vividly describes why and how the world could be a better place for sentient beings, what risks are involved, and what we could and should change and promote."

Didier Coeurnelle, Vice President of AFT-Technoprog
and co-chair of Heales (Healthy Life Extension Society)

"A smorgasbord of thought-stimulating insights about foresight. True to this book's title, David masterfully assists you with thoroughly thinking through all that is of vital importance to make today and tomorrow much better for all of us. A must-have companion for any serious change-agent, futurist, transhumanist, singularitarian, and humanitarian."

Philippe van Nedervelde, veteran serial NBIC tech-entrepreneur
specialized in VR & AR metaverses

"If you are a Transhumanist, Transhumanist-Curious or simply interested in the future, this is an excellent, provocative and informative must-read."

Steve Wells, Global Futurist, Informing Choices

"Transhumanist thinking is one of the few systems that directly projects itself into a technologically enhanced future in which even consciousness might be defined differently from today. In this book David Wood crosses the broadest range of areas that relate to this movement while pointing toward the need to adopt its key values. He advocates for a more active role to push for these values to avoid important civilisational risks we face. It is an inspiring book that sets up key discussion points to shape our future."

Yates Buckley, Founding Partner, UNIT9, London

"*Vital Foresight* is the masterpiece of David Wood, who has already written very insightful and thoughtful books before. This book really makes you think about the future, indeed, about different possible futures. *Vital Foresight* will help you, me and everybody, to make better decisions based on our current and expanding knowledge ahead. If you want a better future, you have to read *Vital Foresight*. It might be a matter of life or death!"

José Cordeiro, Vice Chair, Humanity+

Table of Contents

Preface

"Transhumanism"?

"Don't put that word on the cover of your book!"

That's the advice I received from a number of friends when they heard what I was writing about. They urged me to avoid "the 'T' word" – "transhumanism". That word has bad vibes, they said. It's toxic. *T for toxic.*

I understand where they're coming from. Later in this book, I'll dig into reasons why various people are uncomfortable with the whole concept. I'll explain why I nevertheless see "transhumanism" as an apt term for a set of transformational ideas that will be key to our collective wellbeing in the 2020s and beyond. *T for transformational.* And, yes, *T for timely.*

As such, it's a word that belongs on the cover of many more books, inspiring more conversations, more realisations, and more breakthroughs.

For now, in case you're wondering, here's a short definition. It's by Oxford polymath Anders Sandberg, who expressed it like this in 1997[1]:

> Transhumanism is the philosophy that we can and should develop to higher levels, physically, mentally, and socially, using rational methods.

Sandberg's 1997 webpage also features this summary from trailblazing Humanity+[2] Board member and Executive Director, Natasha Vita-More[3]:

> Transhumanism is a commitment to overcoming human limits in all their forms, including extending lifespan, augmenting intelligence, perpetually increasing knowledge, achieving complete control over our personalities and identities, and gaining the ability to leave the planet. Transhumanists seek to achieve these goals through reason, science, and technology.

In brief, transhumanism is a vision of the future: a vision of what's possible, what's desirable, and how it can be brought into reality.

In subsequent chapters, I'll have lots more to say about the strengths and weaknesses of transhumanism. I'll review the perceived threats and the remarkable opportunities that arise from it. But first, let me quickly introduce myself and how I came to be involved in the broader field of foresight (also known as futurism) within which transhumanism exists.

Smartphones and beyond

Over the twenty-five years that I held different roles within the mobile computing and smartphone industries, it was an increasingly central part of my job to think creatively and critically about future possibilities.

Back in the late 1980s and early 1990s, my work colleagues and I could see that computing technology was becoming ever more powerful. We debated long and hard, revisiting the same questions many times as forthcoming new hardware and software capabilities came to our attention. What kinds of devices should we design, to take advantage of these new capabilities? Which applications would users of these devices find most valuable? How might people feel as they interacted with different devices with small screens and compact keypads? Would the Internet ever become useful for "ordinary people"? Would our industry be dominated by powerful, self-interested corporations with monolithic visions, or would multiple streams of innovation flourish?

My initial involvement with these discussions was informal. Most of my time at work went into software engineering. But I enjoyed animated lunchtime discussions at Addison's brasserie on Old Marylebone Road in central London, where technical arguments about, for example, optimising robust access to data structures, were intermingled with broader brainstorms about how we could collectively steer the future in a positive direction.

Over time, I set down more of my own ideas in writing, in emails and documents that circulated among teammates[4]. I also had the good fortune to become involved in discussions with forward-thinking employees from giants of the mobile phone world – companies such as Nokia, Ericsson, Motorola, Panasonic, Sony, Samsung, Fujitsu, and LG, that were considering using our EPOC software (later renamed as "Symbian OS") in their new handsets. I learned a great deal from these discussions[5].

By 2004 my job title was Executive VP for Research. It was my responsibility to pay attention to potential disruptions that could transform our business, either by destroying it, or by uplifting it. I came to appreciate that, in the words of renowned management consultant Peter Drucker, "the major questions regarding technology are not technical but human questions"[6]. I also became increasingly persuaded that the disruptions of the smartphone market, significant though they were, were but a small preview of much larger disruptions to come.

As I'll explain in the pages ahead, these larger disruptions could bring about a significant uplift in human character. Another possibility, however, is the destruction of much that we regard as precious.

Accordingly, the skills of foresight are more essential today than ever. We need to strengthen our collective capabilities in thinking creatively and critically about future possibilities – and in acting on the insights arising.

Indeed, accelerating technological change threatens to shatter the human condition in multiple ways. We – all of us – face profound questions over the management, not just of smartphones, but of artificial intelligence, nanoscale computers, bio-engineering, cognitive enhancements, ubiquitous robots, drone swarms, nuclear power, planet-scale geo-engineering, and much more.

What these technologies enable is, *potentially*, a world of extraordinary creativity, unprecedented freedom, and abundant wellbeing. That's *provided* we can see clearly enough, in advance, the major disruptive opportunities we will need to seize and steer, so we can reach that destination. *And provided* we can step nimbly through a swath of treacherous landmines along the way.

That's no small undertaking. It will take all our wisdom and strength. It's going to require the very highest calibre of foresight.

That's the reason why I've spent so much of my time in recent years organising and hosting hundreds of public meetings of the London Futurists community, both offline and online – events with the general headline of "serious analysis of radical scenarios for the next three to forty years"[7].

I acknowledge, however, that foresight is widely thought to have a poor track record. Forecasts of the future, whether foretelling doom and gloom, or envisioning technological cornucopia, seem to have been wrong at least as often as they have been right. Worse, instead of helping us to see future options more clearly, past predictions have, all too frequently, imposed mental blinkers, encouraged a stubborn fatalism, or distracted us from the truly vital risks and opportunities. It's no wonder that the public reputation of futurism is scarcely better than that of shallow tabloid horoscopes[8].

To add to the challenge, our long-honed instincts about social norms and human boundaries prepare us poorly for the counterintuitive set of radical choices that emerging technology now dangles before us. We're caught in a debilitating "future shock" of both fearful panic and awestruck wonder.

Happily, assistance is at hand. What this book will demonstrate is that vital foresight from the field I call *active transhumanism* can help us all:

1. To resist unwarranted tech hype, whilst remaining aware that credible projections of today's science and engineering could enable sweeping improvements in the human condition
2. To distinguish future scenarios with only superficial attractions from those with lasting, sustainable benefits
3. To move beyond the inaction of future shock, so we can coalesce around practical initiatives that advance deeply positive outcomes.

The audience for vital foresight

I've written this book for everyone who cares about the future:

- Everyone trying to anticipate and influence the dramatic changes that may take place in their communities, organisations, and businesses over the next few years
- Everyone concerned about risks of environmental disaster, the prevalence of irrationalism and conspiracy theories, growing inequality and social alienation, bioengineered pandemics, the decline of democracy, and the escalation of a Cold War 2.0
- Everyone who has high hopes for technological solutions, but who is unsure whether key innovations can be adopted wisely enough and quickly enough
- Everyone seeking a basic set of ethical principles suited for the increasing turbulence of the 2020s and beyond – principles that preserve the best from previous ethical frameworks, but which are open to significant updates in the wake of the god-like powers being bestowed on us by new technologies.

Although it reviews some pivotal examples from my decades of experience in business, this is not a book about the future of individual businesses or individual industries.

Nor is it a "get rich quick" book, or one that promotes "positive thinking" or better self-esteem. Look elsewhere, if that is what you seek.

Instead, it's a book about the possibilities – indeed, the necessity – for radical transformation:

- Transformation of human nature
- Transformation of our social and political frameworks

- Transformation of our relations with the environment and the larger cosmos
- Transformation of our self-understanding – the narratives we use to guide all our activities[9].

Critically, this book contains practical suggestions for next steps to be taken, bearing in mind the power and pace of forces that are already remaking the world faster than was previously thought possible.

And it shows that foresight, framed well, can provide not only a stirring vision, but also the agility and resilience to cope with the many contingencies and dangers to be encountered on the journey forward.

Looking ahead

Here's my summary of the most vital piece of foresight that I can offer.

Oncoming waves of technological change are poised to deliver either global destruction or a paradise-like sustainable superabundance, with the outcome depending on the timely elevation of transhumanist vision, transhumanist politics, and transhumanist education.

You'll find that same 33-word paragraph roughly halfway through the book, in the chapter "Creativity", in the midst of a dialogue about (can you guess…?) hedgehogs and foxes. I've copied the paragraph to the beginning of the book to help you see where my analysis will lead.

The summary is short, but the analysis will take some time. The scenarios that lie ahead for humanity – whether global destruction or sustainable superabundance – involve rich interactions of multiple streams of thought and activity. There's a lot we'll need to get our heads around, including disruptions in technology, health, culture, economics, politics, education, and philosophy. Cutting corners on understanding any one of these streams could yield a seriously misleading picture of our options for the future. Indeed, if we skimp on our analysis of future possibilities, we should not be surprised if humanity falls far short of our true potential.

However, I realise that each reader of this book will bring different concerns and different prior knowledge. By all means jump over various sections of the book to reach the parts that directly address the questions that are uppermost in your mind. Let the table of contents be your guide. If need be, you can turn back the pages later, to fill in any gaps in the narrative.

Better foresight springs, in part, from better hindsight. It's particularly important to understand the differences between good foresight and bad foresight – to review past examples of each, learning from both the failures and, yes, the occasional successes of previous attempts to foresee and create the future. That's one of our key tasks in the pages ahead.

In that quest, let's move forward to an example from the rainbow nation of South Africa. Before we reach the hedgehogs and foxes, I invite you to spend some time with (can you guess…?) ostriches and flamingos.

1. Scenarios

Scenarios, defined: Visions of the future that can transform the present, and, in turn, transform the future. Exercises to strengthen the muscle of foresight and sharpen the skills of discrimination. Inspiration that can raise attention from the mundane toward real possibilities of radical change.

"I am not an ostrich."

Frederik Willem de Klerk, the seventh President of South Africa, had just seen the future. Actually, he had just seen *four* futures, named "Ostrich", "Lame Duck", "Icarus", and "Flamingos"[10]. He found much to dislike – and much to oppose – in the scenarios depicted. He was determined to choose a better future.

As we'll see, that was the reaction the scenario planners wanted.

The year was 1992. Over the preceding twelve months, a diverse multi-racial group of South Africans had been meeting on a regular basis at the Mont Fleur Conference Venue in the outskirts of Stellenbosch, thirty minutes from Cape Town International Airport. Despite the tranquil location – a quiet mountain retreat set in an area of outstanding natural beauty[11] – there was plenty of conflict in the air. South Africa was facing an abyss – a potential descent into chaos.

Decades of apartheid segregation, in which the majority black population had no voice in national elections, had prompted widespread civil unrest. International sanctions and disinvestment had caused economic stagnation. The country experienced stark inequalities of wealth and rising unemployment. Violence was escalating, not just between blacks and whites, but also between Zulu and Xhosa ethnicities.

What would happen next? How might South Africa change in the next ten years, that is, up to 2002? That was the question that the Mont Fleur meetings addressed.

The group had been assembled by a pair of professors from the University of Western Cape. The participants, numbering twenty-two in total, included activists, academics, trades unionists, and community organisers, as well as up-and-coming leaders from the worlds of business and politics. The convenors made special efforts to ensure the group contained "awkward sods" who would bring alternative perspectives to the mix[12]. Conventional thinking would *not* be sufficient for this task.

With their many differences in outlook, the meeting attendees were initially nervous about working together. However, they shared a deep concern over the turbulent situation of South Africa. Skilled facilitation by collaboration specialist Adam Kahane[13], who brought key experience from foresight exercises at Shell Oil in London, helped the group to rise to the occasion. The participants soon developed personal bonds over good-natured arguments, friendly jokes, leisurely walks, and fine food and wine.

The exercise started by brainstorming with no holds barred, suggesting possible episodes that could be part of future scenarios. An initial set of thirty ideas were gathered. As time passed, these ideas evolved into a collection of nine "preliminary stories" which were then whittled down into the four scenarios already mentioned – chosen because of their internal consistency and broad plausibility.

Before describing Ostrich – and explaining why de Klerk took actions to *prevent* that prediction of the future from being fulfilled – let me share some more context.

Two roads

De Klerk was an unlikely hero. As a government minister since 1978, he had long helped to maintain and enforce apartheid restrictions, gaining a reputation as an implacable conservative. When he succeeded PW Botha as State President in 1989, he was widely expected to continue the regime's robust opposition to any substantial reform. Witness the pessimistic comment about the new President made by veteran anti-apartheid activist Bishop Desmond Tutu[14]:

> I don't think we've got to even begin to pretend that there is any reason for thinking that we are entering a new phase. It's just musical chairs.

Leaders of the ANC – the African National Congress – likewise spoke out against de Klerk. If the past was a good predictor of the future, the future would be bleak.

But sometimes the future transcends the past, rather than merely extending it. Sometimes traits weaken, despite seemingly having stubborn roots. Sometimes, as in the case of de Klerk, a new leader has the courage and strength to establish an unexpected new direction.

Indeed, developments in the wider world were setting the scene for fresh assessments of what was possible inside South Africa. Mikhail Gorbachev of the Soviet Union was pursuing glasnost (openness) and perestroika (restructuring). The Berlin Wall fell in November 1989 and was demolished shortly afterward. The Soviet Union itself dissolved in 1991. As a result, prevailing Cold War narratives about transitions of political power lost their force – narratives that said the Soviet Union would use all methods, including subverting groups of "freedom fighters", to impose totalitarian communism throughout the continent of Africa. There was now less reason to worry about a recurrence of the pattern seen after independence in Angola, Benin, Ethiopia, Mozambique, and Zimbabwe. There was reason, instead, to believe that South Africa could fashion its own destiny – provided it could free itself from outdated mindsets.

Moreover, de Klerk had been influenced by an earlier exercise in creating future scenarios. That exercise had been conducted by personnel from the country's largest corporation: the mining company Anglo American. Originally intended purely for internal business planning purposes, the scenarios produced were increasingly shared with wider audiences. Within one year, the company had given more than 200 talks about these scenarios, to audiences totalling more than 25,000 people[15]. Such was the public hunger for foresight about the country's future.

The core of these presentations contrasted two possible futures, known as "the low road" and "the high road":

- The *low road* featured confrontation, repression, a powerful centralised state apparatus, and declining incomes, leading to what was called a "waste land"
- The *high road* featured consultation, negotiation, a willingness to share power, and a sustained economic recovery, with the country transitioning peacefully to a multi-racial democracy.

As with all good foresight, each scenario had an outer, big-picture dimension as well as an inner, local dimension. The two scenarios were set against backdrops of envisioned continuing transformation of the global situation, within which the projected evolution of South Africa was seen to make sense. Communicated vividly and clearly, the scenarios stirred the public imagination.

Even cabinet ministers could see the dangers of continuing down the low road scenario.

Accordingly, shortly after becoming president, de Klerk took actions that sent shockwaves around the world. He accelerated discussions with opposition leaders, and gave approval for anti-apartheid marches to proceed. He rescinded the official bans on the ANC and on the Communist Party. And he announced that Nelson Mandela, the iconic leader of the ANC, was to be released from prison after 27 years of incarceration.

These were bold decisions, but they raised many new questions. The release of Mandela elevated public expectations of imminent change. But could these waves of pent-up desire be channelled in positive directions? Or would the decades of accumulated resentment and bitterness explode into a torrent of destruction?

Foresight isn't something you do just once and then rest on your laurels. It's a muscle that should be exercised regularly. Each step of action resulting from foresight rewrites the situation. New options appear on the landscape and need to be fed into the next round of assessment. That need for another round of forecasting is what led to the Mont Fleur gatherings, with the aim of generating forecasts with another level of insight beyond "the low road" and "the high road".

Choosing the future

For someone in de Klerk's position, as head of the whites-only national government in 1992, the Mont Fleur Ostrich scenario might have seemed attractive.

That scenario foresaw that countries around the world would develop warmer relations with South Africa, being relieved at the steps taken toward liberalisation, even though these steps were relatively modest. The international community would reduce its support for the ANC, perceiving that organisation to be naive and overly radical. As a result, the government would be emboldened to dig in for a "moderate alliance" politics, and break off negotiations with any voices advocating full racial equality.

But when you evaluate a possible future, you need to look more than just one step ahead. You have to consider the potential longer-term developments. It was the longer-term aspects of Ostrich which made de Klerk exclaim, "I am not an ostrich":

- Increased opposition from those excluded from the "moderate alliance"
- Growing state violence to suppress that opposition
- Worsening business climate
- Economic stagnation
- Social inequalities remaining in place
- A continuing vicious cycle of conflict
- The eventual reconvening of negotiations, but from a starting point with even more bitterness and harsher economic conditions than before.[16]

Why the name "ostrich"? Because the scenario involved a head-in-sand aversion to paying serious attention to longer term consequences. And because that scenario lacked real flight.

If de Klerk recognised the risks of Ostrich and vowed not to follow that path, it was equally important that the leadership of the ANC recognised the risks of another of the scenarios – "Icarus" – and vowed not to follow *that* path. That scenario was named after the adolescent boy in the Greek myth who recklessly soared too high into the air with the wings his father had provided for him. Under the sun's heat, the wax fastenings of his wings melted, and Icarus plunged to his death in the Mediterranean below.

In the Mont Fleur Icarus scenario, negotiations between whites and blacks led to a peaceful transfer of power to the ANC, who then took advantage of a popular electoral mandate to push through a policy of rapid economic transformation:

- Food price subsidies
- Controls over business activities
- Massive spending on social programs.

The outcome for Icarus, as for Ostrich, initially looked promising for the government that would be in power:

- Improved living conditions
- A flurry of economic growth
- Increased populist support for the ANC regime.

But, again as for Ostrich, the longer-term aspects of the Icarus scenario were far less rosy:

- Large budget deficits
- Balance of payment restrictions
- A runaway surge of inflation
- Economic boom giving way to bust
- Social breakdown and political bedlam.

Icarus provided a warning that honourable intentions are insufficient to run a government. Economic forces provide their own reality which must be respected.

In between Ostrich and Icarus was Lame Duck – a scenario featuring protracted negotiations and indecisive politics. Rounding out the set of scenarios was Flamingos, featuring sustainable policies, inclusive economic growth, and, despite some lingering mistrust, democratic processes acquiring deeper roots.

Of the four scenarios, it was Flamingos that came closest to anticipating the actual subsequent events.

But to be clear, the point of the Mont Fleur exercise was not to predict what *would* happen. Instead, it was to stimulate awareness of *possible* chains of causes and effects, and to encourage creative "what if" questions. Nor was there a goal to reach any *unanimity* among all participants concerning a single correct answer. Instead, the goal was to provide everyone with a richer appreciation of matters that should be considered in any plans made for the future – including *matters which some participants initially preferred not to think about at all.*

So, whilst Mandela and de Klerk, along with many supporting figures, deserve great praise for bravely steering South Africa away from the abyss in the early 1990s, a share of the credit belongs to the practice of foresight.

That was the assessment made nearly two decades later by author and forecaster Clem Sunter. Sunter commended Mont Fleur participants for enabling, not only a peaceful national transition to full democracy, but also the sage handling of subsequent global financial recessions. It was the Icarus scenario, in Sunter's view, that had done most to change people's thinking, guiding the ANC leadership away from unsustainable policies[17]:

> Take a bow, all you who were involved in the Mont Fleur initiative. You may have changed our history at a critical juncture in the fortunes of the world.

Several members of the Mont Fleur team had gone on to hold leading positions in government and civil society, carrying in their minds and hearts the implications of the four scenarios. One of the participants, Tito Mboweni, became in 1999 the first black governor of South Africa's Reserve Bank. In his speech at the banquet marking his inauguration to that role, Mboweni offered reassurance to the assembled audience of international financiers[18]:

> The role of the Bank is to create a climate of financial stability in which sustainable economic growth and wealth creation can be achieved; an environment in which an economic boom will not be followed by an inevitable bust.

In case the point was unclear, Mboweni continued:

> We are not Icarus; there is no need to fear that we will fly too close to the sun.

Good, bad, and vital

Any race toward an *apparent* boom – toward an *apparently* attractive future – needs to be resisted if that boom would set the scene for a subsequent catastrophic bust. That's the general concept which the four scenarios of Mont Fleur turned into compelling, memorable narratives. These narratives inspired numerous practical actions to help steer South Africa away from the negative scenarios foreseen, favouring the more positive outcomes that had been identified. That's what good foresight can accomplish.

Foresight, take a bow.

This kind of foresight features no crystal ball. It provides no certainty for the scenarios it generates. Instead, it enables a richer appreciation of the landscape of potential trends and responses:

1. How various trends might grow or shrink in significance
2. How they might converge with and transform each other
3. How they might disrupt "business as usual" trajectories
4. How human action might alter the possible outcomes.

That's the kind of foresight we *particularly* need at the present time: compelling, memorable narratives that will inspire practical actions and vital transitions.

The world as a whole in the early 2020s is poised before even larger uncertainty and even greater risks than South Africa faced in 1992. Worse, whereas the challenges facing the Mont Fleur group were reasonably well understood at the time, some of the biggest challenges facing humanity in the early 2020s are ones that lie hidden from general view. They're challenges that too many of us prefer to keep pushing out of mind, whilst we sleepwalk, in effect, being preoccupied with distractions large and small.

These challenges arise from forces afoot that could, within just a few short decades, change core parts of the nature of human existence. Whether that will be for good or for ill remains to be decided.

In the pages ahead, I will take a close look at these forces, and at our options for responding to them. I'll also explain how, with the right harnessing, these forces could provide liberation, not just from unjust social structures and racial inequality, but from all manner of disease, confusion, oppression, and collective foolishness. In short, these forces could liberate us from some of the deepest dysfunctions of the human condition.

Indeed, the final human generation may already be alive, coexisting with the foundations of the first truly transhuman generation. Our future could be very bright indeed, provided we can unshackle ourselves from outdated mindsets, overcome our collective distractions, and choose wisely. But if we stick to our present trajectory, we may well plunge into the abyss.

In my view, we therefore face a new critical juncture, with new kinds of "high road" and "low road" options – where the "high" is *very* high, and the "low" is in extreme depths.

You have presumably heard similar predictions before. In recent decades, much has been foretold about, on the one hand, a high road of abundant technological progress – a road toward lands overflowing with modern-day milk and honey – and on the other hand, a low road to imminent social decay, environmental collapse, and humanitarian tragedy.

I won't blame you if these predictions have left you unconvinced. Human society may strike you as bumbling along somewhere in the middle of these polar extremes. Alongside spiralling public displays of anger, bitterness, and frequently irrational discourse, you can also see stirring examples of human generosity, collaboration, and thoughtfulness. Alongside instances of social trauma, pettiness, addiction, and alienation, there is also evidence of inventiveness, people determined to build bridges, and a focus on green, sustainable solutions. Predictions of the future, therefore, seem to be ten a penny, available in all tastes. If forecasters can predict everything, then, in effect, they can predict nothing.

My response: the excited predictions of positive technological progress have not been wrong; they've been incomplete – dangerously incomplete. What these predictions have omitted has been at least as significant as what they included. It's the same with the alternative set of predictions anticipating dramatic social decay; these predictions, likewise, contain important truths, but tell only part of the story.

Recall the warning sounded long ago by the early eighteenth-century poet Alexander Pope[19]: *A little learning is a dangerous thing.*

As with learning, so it is with foresight. Foresight that is incomplete can mislead, badly. It can provoke emotions that make matters worse. It can generate an unwarranted carefree optimism, or, just as treacherously, an unwarranted debilitating pessimism. *A little foresight is a dangerous thing.*

Of course, Pope's aphorism should lead us not to discard learning but to embrace learning more fully – to "drink deep", in the words of his poem, rather than to be content with "shallow draughts" that "intoxicate the brain"[20]. Intoxication is a poor substitute for true vitality.

Similarly, the appropriate response to shallow foresight is to embrace the discipline of foresight more fully – to bring to mind the entire picture, rather than just isolated facets. Accordingly, this book seeks to move beyond predictions that are populist and intoxicating, to elevate instead the practice of what I call "vital foresight":

- Foresight that takes full stock of the remarkable life-enhancing possibilities of emerging technologies and societal evolution
- Foresight that can connect the mind, the heart, and the soul, to enable vibrant creativity, exploration, and growth
- Foresight that is by no means short-sighted about the many dangerous landmines ahead, but which can provide a wellspring of excellent health – for individuals, societies, and the world at large.

Beyond Mont Fleur

The skilled application of vital foresight helped leaders at all levels of society take better decisions in South Africa in the years following Mont Fleur. As for the world as a whole in the 2020s, read on.

We'll proceed with the sleepwalking.

2. Sleepwalking

Sleepwalking, defined: Stepping forward without an awareness of where we are going. Dreaming that we are in one place while we're actually wandering around somewhere else. A state of real danger, if there are landmines or trip hazards underfoot, steps down which we could tumble, or open windows through which we could fall to our death.

It's my view that humanity is collectively sleepwalking toward disaster. We're paying far too little attention to critical threats in our landscape. We may tell ourselves that, all things considered, we're making good progress forward, but that assessment downplays important risks. We're oblivious to various landmines, trip hazards, downward staircases, and open windows that could, metaphorically speaking, bring our sleepwalking to a catastrophic end.

It's not just *risks of catastrophe* to which we're paying too little attention. We're failing, likewise, to attend sufficiently to *transcendental opportunities* – opportunities that could elevate humanity to a profoundly higher level of flourishing and attainment. The reason we don't see these opportunities is because they sit far outside our usual thinking patterns. It's like early critics of railways who could not conceive the human body would survive travelling at speeds faster than on a racehorse[21]. It's like early critics of home computers who could not envision the numerous uses to which such devices would be applied[22].

Except that, this time, the magnitude of the disconnect is even larger. There's a vast disparity between common expectations for the middle of this century and the likely actual outcomes. The opportunity ahead – to which most of humanity remains largely unaware – could see an increase in capability and experience on a par with the evolutionary leap from ape to human. It's as if a new species is about to be born.

Consider key human experiences that lay outside the conception of our ape ancestors – epic literature, lyrical symphonies, romantic poetry, refined humour, brilliant mathematics, scientific comprehension, legal constitutions, sports tournaments, chess gambits, medical reconstruction, astronomical journeys – but not forgetting nuclear bombs, torture chambers, concentration camps, mass-produced propaganda, products deliberately designed to be addictive, excessive financialization, hellfire preaching, and protracted wars over religious dogmas. Consider what new near-unimaginable experiences await us in the same way as technology provides us with hugely extended capabilities in both body and mind.

This is no mere "going a bit faster" or "doing things more conveniently". This is no mere reassertion of traits and abilities from a previous generation. Instead, the opportunity is for whole new dimensions of traits and abilities. The opportunity is for humanity to leave behind – to transcend – parts of our nature and culture that have cruelly constrained us throughout the entire history of our species so far. The opportunity is to become transhuman.

To be clear, this is an opportunity to which everyone is invited, even though the invitation has, so far, scarcely been noticed.

Rousing from slumber

The two sets of blindness – blindness to catastrophic risks, and blindness to transcendental opportunities – share a common cause, which the chapters ahead explore at some length: a poor understanding of the remarkable capabilities of various new technologies that are rapidly emerging.

These technologies will deliver wide-ranging powers to transform the human condition, for both good and ill. If these powers are perceived with sufficient clarity, ahead of their full arrival – and if they are assessed with sufficient objectivity – humanity will be better placed to awake from our present sleepwalking trajectory, and steer ourselves onto a far more desirable course. But if we fail to rouse from our slumber, all bets are off. If we continue sleepwalking, bitter horrors await.

This book, accordingly, highlights practical skills of:

- *Perception*: How to understand more clearly the various future scenarios that deserve our collective attention
- *Assessment*: How to move beyond unhelpful "future shock" reactions, and determine more calmly both the drawbacks and the benefits of the scenarios in question – as well as variants of these scenarios in which key elements are either added in or left out
- *Steering*: How to proactively lower the probabilities of the scenarios featuring catastrophic risks, and raise the probabilities of the scenarios bringing plentiful benefits to everyone.

These skills comprise the essentials of vital foresight.

The good news is that skills in each of these areas can indeed be improved. Professional futurists around the world[23], supported by various foresight enthusiasts[24], future studies think tanks[25], and technoprogressive activists[26], have developed insights and methods which people in all walks of life can learn to use.

An even better piece of news is that, as enhanced foresight improves our appreciation of the landscape of forthcoming scenarios, it can in consequence also lead to the future itself becoming better – as a result of wiser choices, more agile responses, and concerted action.

The first step out of the perils of sleepwalking is to rediscover the liberating power of positive vision. That's a subject with a long history. It's also a subject with plenty of disappointments. To make progress, we need to learn from these disappointments and move beyond them.

A world without foresight

Where there is no vision, the people perish.

This harsh warning from the biblical Book of Proverbs[27] echoes down the ages. When our minds are filled by mundane matters, we'll be ill-prepared for large new challenges or opportunities. We may eat and drink with happy abandon during seven years of plenty, but leave ourselves no cushion to survive seven subsequent years of lean[28]. We may enjoy a vacation in a seaside resort, oblivious to the tsunami racing across the ocean toward us. We may travel as usual on packed commuter trains to our places of work, with little thought of the risk of infection from a virulent new coronavirus. In our businesses, we may double down on "the way we do things around here", blind to the new tools or processes being adopted by competitors who are about to steal more than our lunch. In our politics, we may vote for leaders who promise to return things to how they were in a prior age of apparent greatness, without appreciating how different the future will be from the past we seem to remember. By anticipating "more of the same", we'll increase the chance that we'll end up with much *less* of what we treasure.

Where there is no vision, the people perish.

Lack of foresight doesn't just lead to a diminished appreciation of the changes that could lie ahead. It also weakens our spirit. In the absence of a compelling vision, we come to expect the ordinary, and our minds shrink. Local molehills appear to us like looming mountains. As for the true mountains, we scarcely notice them. When any bolts from the blue reach us, we shrug our shoulders and sigh to ourselves, fatalistically, that *there was nothing we could have done about that.*

So long as there is a credible vision of a better world ahead, people can endure great calamities. Because we recognise the humanity in each other, we reach out to assist strangers in distress, even when we ourselves are in distress. But when that vision fades, we become self-centred survival machines. When hope evaporates, our behaviour gets nasty.

Stated otherwise: small visions lead to small horizons, and to small circles of concern. When such a mindset prevails, few people bother to actively scan for potential incoming bolts from the blue. What's the point? *Que sera, sera.* If someone does try to expand our attention, we find it annoying, and look for reasons to return to the psychological comfort of burying our heads in the sand. We would rather be an ostrich.

Good foresight is *particularly* needed at a time when the pace of innovation is increasing, when greater global connectivity means that both good and bad ideas cascade around the world ever more quickly, when the environment might soon reach tipping points that trigger unprecedented transitions to deeply chaotic states, and when society is being ripped asunder by hostile divisions fanned by outlandish conspiracy theories and viral fake news.

In short, good foresight is particularly needed when the future is arriving faster, less predictably, and with greater tumult. We need it now, as never before.

Blinkers in place of binoculars

What's the opposite of good foresight?

One opposite is a complete lack of foresight – a life lived entirely in the present.

The first step up from that baseline is a life that spots patterns and trends. We notice that tides ebb and flow. Seasons repeat themselves, with predictable sequences of drought and flood. Royal dynasties wax and wane. Generations are born, grow up, grow old, and then die[29].

The *next* step up is to appreciate that patterns can be overturned and trends disrupted. Beyond the mechanics of everyday living dwell larger forces, that impinge on human affairs less regularly, but with huge impact.

For example, in some years, like 1816, there is no summer at all – due, we now know[30], to a huge volcanic eruption on the other side of the planet. In some palace coups, one royal family isn't just exchanged for another, but the entire monarchical system is displaced by a new, secular republic. Some generations fail to grow old, but die in vast numbers ahead of their time due to horrific circumstances, such as the arrival of Europeans in the Americas, bringing diseases to local populations with no immunity against them.

It is attempts to make sense of these larger disruptions that can result in another kind of opposite to good foresight, namely *bad* foresight.

Whereas good foresight in effect provides binoculars, so that distant mechanisms and future scenarios can be examined with greater precision, bad foresight in effect provides blinkers.

Bad foresight obsesses about factors that lack any real connection to the observed violation of previous patterns and trends. It is fascinated by phenomena such as astronomical confluences, which enthral astrologers, alleged shortcomings in religious adherence, which enthral hellfire preachers, or possible double meanings of messages on social media, which enthral incautious conspiracy mongers. Bad foresight sees occasional coincidences and jumps to the wrong conclusions.

Now there's nothing wrong with *suggesting* a possible connection between an observed effect and a potential cause, and seeking further understanding to verify or invalidate that suggestion. That mechanism – hypothesis followed by experiment – is how science proceeds. Perhaps excess deaths on maternity wards really were due to poor handwashing techniques of medical staff, as hypothesised in the 1840s and 50s by physician Ignaz Semmelweis[31]. Perhaps the similarities in shapes of coasts of far-distant continents really do point to the possibility that continents can change their positions, as hypothesised in the 1910s and 20s by astronomer Alfred Wegener[32]. Bold hypotheses have a key place in developing a richer understanding of connections in nature and society. But what is wrong – dangerously wrong – is to proclaim unproven suggestions from the pulpit, the printing press, shock radio stations, online media, or other positions of power, *as if they were incontrovertible facts.*

It's especially dangerous for the charismatic leaders of a community to prohibit or pour scorn on independent opinions. In these circumstances, with emotional disgust hampering rational assessment, the true causal connections will very likely remain unnoticed.

By vigorously limiting the ideas it is permissible to think about, bad foresight prevents us from seeing what's really happening. We become so blinkered that our eyes linger over the occasional signs that a forecast may, *perhaps*, have some truth to it. The blinkers constrain us, alas, from paying attention to any signs that the forecast has stark flaws.

Once bitten, twice shy

One unfortunate consequence of bad foresight has been to throw doubts on the whole field of foresight. In the next chapter, I'll review various examples of foresight going wrong – examples of foresight producing misperceptions rather than greater clarity. These individual incidents led to unnecessary pain, trauma, and death – or to unnecessary panic and social hostility. The set of failures, as a whole, has given rise to an understandable scepticism about visions of the future.

The line of thought runs as follows. Since visions distort perception, it's better not to have visions. Rather than attempting to speculate about matters beyond the sensory impressions of ordinary observation, it's better to stick with the plain facts of the matter. Rather than panicking as a result of dire warnings, it's psychologically more effective to remain focused on the here-and-now. Rather than foolishly raising hopes of wondrous new happenings, or fears of dreadful new enemies, let's keep ourselves well-grounded. Rather than dreaming of a fantasy future, we need to live in the present. By all means notice and anticipate cyclical patterns or linear trends, but anything beyond that is magical thinking, undeserving of our trust. Visions are throwbacks to a world dominated by superstition, and are championed by hucksters with no real credibility. *Such is the worldly wisdom about visions.*

That's not all. There's another reason why the concept of vision has been sullied. It's because of the experience many people have of "vision exercises", or similar, in their workplaces. Many businesses publish vision statements that are vague or superficial, or which seem to make no difference to the actual decisions made by management.

Consider this vision statement: "Create unprecedented value and opportunity for our customers, employees, investors, and ecosystem partners."

Or this one: "Our mission is to be a company that inspires and fulfils your curiosity."

And a third: "To be the most successful computer company in the world at delivering the best customer experience in markets we serve."

The first is from Cisco[33]. The second is from Sony[34]. And the third was used at Dell[35]. Could you have guessed? And these are by no means the vaguest of corporate vision statements.

It's little surprise, therefore, that "vision" and "mission" have a bad reputation in some circles. People have become nervous about the idea. As in the saying, once bitten, they've become twice shy.

However, although there are plenty of examples of bad vision, we would be mistaken to reject the whole idea. On the contrary, the right response is to do it better – to displace flawed vision with rational vision.

Here's a comparison. The fact that *some* scientific experiments are done badly provides no reason for us to reject science *in its entirety*. Instead, it's a reason to improve our understanding and the practice of science. It's the same with foresight and vision.

Again, the fact that *some* educational systems stunt psychological development, and in extreme cases amount to brainwashing, is no reason to reject education *in its entirety*. Instead, it's a reason to improve our educational systems. And, again, it's the same with foresight and vision. The existence of bad foresight and vision is a reason to *improve* our foresight and vision, not to allow our horizons to shrink.

Whilst some corporate vision statements can, indeed, be criticised, other examples have stood the test of time. Here's the vision of the future that Microsoft founder Bill Gates shared with employees on a regular basis since 1975[36]: "A microcomputer on every desk and in every home running Microsoft software." Or consider this vision of the future from Google's founders in 1998: "To organise the world's information and make it universally accessible and useful."[37] Tesla envisions "accelerating the world's transition to sustainable energy."[38] And after becoming CEO of General Electric in 1981, Jack Welch adopted the vision "To become #1 or #2 in every market we serve and revolutionize this company to have the speed and agility of a small enterprise."[39]

These statements have the merit of being not only memorable but specific. They make it easier to judge whether various initiatives are aligned with the company's vision, or are more likely to be distractions. They identify existing features of the various companies, and envision these features going from strength to strength.

These aren't statements of what will *definitely* happen. Instead, they're statements of what *could* happen, if the goal is given sufficient attention.

Other types of forecasts of the future are statements of what is *likely* to happen, if the possibility *fails* to receive sufficient attention. Whereas the people making the first kind of forecast *want these forecasts to come true*, people making the second kind of forecast want these forecasts *to not come true.* Examples of this second kind of forecast include the Ostrich and Icarus scenarios from Mont Fleur, covered in the previous chapter. Other examples are claims such as "if no actions are taken in the next twelve years to cut emissions of greenhouse gases, there will be significant worsening of the risks of drought, floods, extreme heat and poverty for hundreds of millions of people."[40]

In the pages ahead, I'll be offering criteria to distinguish poor forecasts from those which are more useful. I'll be pointing out how the discipline of foresight has been improving. It's like how the science of astronomy successfully emerged from a shared background with the wishful thinking of astrology – and how the science of chemistry successfully emerged from a shared background with the wishful thinking of alchemy. In the same way, rational foresight can – and must – emerge from any lingering association with fairground fortune-tellers, fast-talking know-it-all media charmers, or the ambiguity-laden quatrains of Nostradamus and his ilk.

The result of this emergence will be an increasing public trust of the power and value of rational foresight. In turn, that increased trust will give more people the confidence to break out of their present state of sleepwalking.

Beyond sleepwalking

One prerequisite for trust is being open and honest about episodes when things have gone wrong. Accordingly, it's time to look more closely at some examples when foresight failed – examples of predictions that turned out to be profound misperceptions.

There's plenty to learn from these misperceptions. In some cases, as we'll see, the predictions were right about the basics, but wrong about the timing. In other cases, the prediction grew out of a blinkered worldview. In these cases, the problem wasn't so much what *was* seen, but rather what *couldn't* be seen, on account of the misperception distorting the senses or sabotaging the emotions. Finally, in some cases, well, the real jury is still out, despite the prediction being roundly condemned in the theatre of popular opinion.

3. Misperceptions

Misperceptions, defined: Wrong conclusions drawn from imprecise observations. Items seen which do not correspond to reality, but which stem from previous fears, biases, hopes, and expectations. A dangerous basis on which to make plans. In consequence, an unfortunate cause of declining faith in the entire discipline of foresight.

Doom and gloom have long been foretold. But mainly wrongly, it appears.

In almost every generation, religious saints or mystics proclaimed that end times were nigh. In some cases, they drew support for their theories from new interpretations of texts from venerable scriptures. Various dreams and, yes, visions, seemed to lend their thinking extra authority. In other cases, it just seemed obvious that society was going downhill fast. Either way, history was about to reach a climax.

Except that it didn't. Any would-be messiah figures that appeared accomplished much less than their faithful followers had expected. History experienced some bumps and jolts, but continued running regardless.

In more recent times, religious forecasts of apocalypse are being overtaken by fearful predictions from secular sources[41]. Wide distress has arisen from the circulation of predictions that:

1. The world will become grossly overpopulated and experience horrific famine
2. Civilisation will be overrun by unstoppable diseases
3. The environment will produce floods, droughts, or other extremes of weather, as if to strike back against human callousness
4. Dangerous alien lifeforms will emerge – not from the stars, but from the software systems we humans are developing, rather carelessly, here on the earth
5. Wars will become more intense and more devastating
6. Terrorists will wreak havoc throughout society.

For each of these six categories of predictions of disaster, the predictions often ended up being *misperceptions*. Rather than increasing, famines and starvation are actually declining. Numerous potential pandemics proved relatively harmless, from a global viewpoint. The weather has varied, but hey, it has always varied. Artificial intelligence has demonstrated some impressive results, but remains pretty stupid. The world may be bristling with weapons but World War Three has been avoided. Terrorists are a darned nuisance but their incompetence means it is a mistake to give them the oxygen of publicity.

In summary, the outcome of such predictions has often been fear and panic, rather than the catastrophes foretold. No apocalypse arrived. Instead, the world had to endure a kind of hysteria. *At least, that's what conventional wisdom has to say.*

However, what I'll show in this chapter is that there's more to these examples of apparent failures of foresight than is included in the "conventional wisdom" account.

In fact, if we're not careful, our dismissal of these examples as "just bad foresight" will itself become a woeful misperception.

We shouldn't avert our eyes from these failures, with a sense of embarrassment. Instead, there's much to learn from them. What can emerge from this learning is a *more effective practice of foresight* – and a better appreciation of the seismic risks and opportunities that truly deserve our full attention.

Famine

As the human population grows, will we find ways to provide everyone with sufficient food?

Back in the mid-1960s, Stanford professor Paul Ehrlich was convinced the answer was "No". Indeed, he foresaw an imminent global humanitarian disaster. The opening words of his 1968 book *The Population Bomb* presented this stark forecast[42]:

> The battle to feed all of humanity is over. In the 1970s the world will undergo famines – hundreds of millions of people are going to starve to death in spite of any crash programs embarked upon now.

To underscore the point, the cover of the book contained this alarming message: "While you are reading these words, three children are dying of starvation – and twenty-four babies are being born".

Here are some specific predictions from the book – predictions which the passage of time has treated badly:

> I don't see how India could possibly feed two hundred million more people by 1980…

> The Green Revolution... can at the very best buy us only a decade or two in which to try to stop population growth...

The Population Bomb sold more than two million copies. As a schoolboy in the early 1970s, I remember often hearing people expressing similar views to the ones in Ehrlich's book. Sending food relief to under-developed countries in Africa or Asia was a naive idea, it was commonly said. That would just allow more children to be born, who would inevitably starve in due course. Sending aid to such countries – to "countries that are so far behind in the population-food game that there is no hope that our food aid will see them through to self-sufficiency" as Ehrlich put it – was akin to squandering scarce medical resources in a battlefield hospital by treating soldiers who were bound to die from their injuries.

A similar sentiment was expressed in a 1974 article by Garrett Hardin, the ecologist who originated the concept of "The Tragedy of the Commons". If we're crowded into a lifeboat that is already near to capacity, Hardin wrote, it makes no sense to let too many additional people clamber onboard, even if they are on the point of drowning. Extra people on board would lead to *everyone* drowning[43]: "The boat swamps, everyone drowns. Complete justice, complete catastrophe."

From that same article, here are Hardin's brutally harsh comments about the future of India:

> Every one of the 15 million new lives added to India's population puts an additional burden on the environment, and increases the economic and social costs of crowding. However humanitarian our intent, every Indian life saved through medical or nutritional assistance from abroad diminishes the quality of life for those who remain, and for subsequent generations. If rich countries make it possible, through foreign aid, for 600 million Indians to swell to 1.2 billion in a mere 28 years, as their current growth rate threatens, will future generations of Indians thank us for hastening the destruction of their environment?

Thankfully, the world failed to heed Hardin's advice. Assistance from overseas helped India toward a state of ever greater self-reliance.

Despite its overall strongly pessimistic outlook, *The Population Bomb* nevertheless contains some forecasts which it describes as having "more appeal". A "Scenario III", presented as an imagined future history looking backward to decades of great upheaval, envisions international cooperation, significant redistribution of resources from the developed to developing countries, aggressive policies to reduce birth rates around the world – keeping the global population to less than six billion – and inspirational moral leadership in support of reduced family sizes from both the pope and the first female president of the USA. But even this scenario involves "the death by starvation of as many as a billion people".

In reality, the number of people dying from starvation, although still a matter of concern, has been nothing like as high as forecast in *The Population Bomb*. India did manage to become self-sufficient in food, just a few years after the first edition of Ehrlich's book was published. This has led some critics, for example the journalist Jonathan Last, to describe *The Population Bomb* as "one of the most spectacularly foolish books ever published"[44].

I disagree with this "spectacularly foolish" description. There's plenty in *The Population Bomb* that was ahead of its time – such as its attention to the dangers of leaded petrol and other environmental concerns. Nevertheless, on reflection, it's clear that the forecasts in the book suffer from three mistaken assumptions.

First, *The Population Bomb* saw the primary cause of famines as being failures in agriculture, rather than corruption among local officials or various other political shortcomings, such as a propensity for wars and civil wars. In contrast, emphasising the political dimension, economist Jeffrey Sachs draws on the analysis of Nobel Prize winner Amartya Sen to offer what Sachs calls "Sen's Law"[45]:

> Shortfalls in food supply do not cause widespread deaths in a democracy because vote-seeking politicians will undertake relief efforts; but even modest food shortfalls can create deadly famines in authoritarian societies.

In other words, positive political reform can do a great deal to reduce threats of starvation and famine, even as the population continues to rise.

Second, *The Population Bomb* put too much emphasis on just one part of an overall equation – the number of people on the planet – rather than considering the importance of tools and lifestyles. The core assumption in Ehrlich's book is that greater population always leads to increased use of resources and worse impact on the environment. This is to disregard the ways in which technology can provide "more from less", as in the title of the recent book by MIT economist Andrew McAfee[46].

Third, *The Population Bomb* extrapolates two trends that had applied throughout history until the time the book was written:

- Population growth was accelerating exponentially
- Improvements in agricultural productivity only occurred at a modest pace.

The book did not pay enough attention to the emerging phenomenon that family sizes were already declining, due not so much to political pressures but to various sociological factors, such as lowered child mortality, increased female literacy, and greater participation by women in the job market. Nor did the book foresee the remarkable extent of the "green revolution" improvements in crop yields that innovators such as Norman Borlaug were making. In short, the book failed to foresee that one exponential trend would slow down, and that one linear trend would accelerate – namely, respectively, population growth and agricultural productivity.

As it happens, the adoption of "green revolution" agricultural practice was fiercely resisted, for a while, in some parts of the third world. Norman Borlaug later recalled some of the opposition he received to the innovations he and his colleagues were proposing[47]:

> When I asked about the need to modernize agriculture, both scientists and administrators typically replied, "Poverty is the farmers' lot; they are used to it."
>
> I was informed that the farmers were proud of their lowly status, and was assured that they wanted no change.

Borlaug's direct personal experiences with farmers around the world gave him a very different impression about the desires of those farmers to improve their living conditions. For neither the first nor the last time, those who purported to speak on behalf of people suffering poverty were allowing their own ideological prejudices to distort their perceptions.

Other reasons given by critics for resisting these innovations were that[48]:

- Innovative crops that fared well in one country, such as Mexico, would not be well adapted to the supposedly unique conditions of another country, such as Pakistan
- The new crops relied on the use of non-traditional fertilisers which would have adverse consequences on the environment
- Those farmers who happened to experience success with new crops would become unduly wealthy; the consequent increased inequality would cause adverse social tension

- The new crops would increase the dependency of third world countries on unreliable corporations based in the United States
- More fancifully, genes in the new crops might jump into cattle, sterilizing them, or even into humans, causing them to change their religion.

If this hostile resistance had prevailed, perhaps Ehrlich's predictions would have come closer to being realised.

But here's the bigger takeaway from *The Population Bomb*. Whilst the key forecasts in the book turned out to be wrong, they were not *necessarily* wrong. They turned out wrong because a number of innovations could be applied, in fields of politics, economy, and agriculture, to allow an unprecedented acceleration in the provision of food. However, there was nothing inevitable about these innovations being found and applied. Nor was it inevitable that the benefits of the innovations would outweigh the potential drawbacks which had raised concerns in the minds of critics and generated opposition to the changes.

Moreover, it would be wrong to assume the reliable continuation of that pattern, of innovation always rising to the occasion and finding good solutions to pressing social problems. To make that assumption would be to repeat the same underlying mistake of *The Population Bomb* – the assumption that trends observed in the past are bound to continue into the future. *Oops.*

On the contrary, good foresight involves examining factors that could cause trends to change – perhaps accelerating, or perhaps slowing down – and the potential consequences of these changes in tempo.

Good foresight also includes anticipating limits to what innovation can accomplish under current conditions, and exploring ways to enable more effective innovation.

In conclusion, *The Population Bomb* by no means deserves laughter and scorn. That book provides no reason to reject the discipline of foresight. Some of the scenarios it contains may still end up being fulfilled, though in ways different from originally envisioned.

Indeed, in a 2009 retrospective, Ehrlich described the language framing the scenarios in the book as being "the biggest tactical error", since incautious readers wrongly jumped from the observation that the scenarios were not fulfilled as stated, to the conclusion that the scenarios had no value and could be discarded in their entirety[49]:

> In honesty, the scenarios were way off, especially in their timing (we underestimated the resilience of the world system). But they did deal with future issues that people in 1968 should have been thinking about – famines, plagues, water shortages, armed international interventions by the United States, and nuclear winter – all events that have occurred or now still threaten.

In other words, a scenario can be useful to consider, even if it is at variance with the eventual facts of the matter. Nevertheless, keeping scenarios as credible as possible will make them more likely to receive the attention they deserve.

That thought brings us to the "Scenario II" outlined in *The Population Bomb*. That scenario featured a global pandemic.

Plagues

At first, the threat posed by the disease seemed manageable. That was the impression drawn by the scientists and politicians in the hypothetical "Scenario II" in Paul Ehrlich's 1968 book *The Population Bomb*. In that scenario, outbreaks of Lassa fever in Nigeria, whilst disturbing, initially lasted only a few months each year, before being contained by heroic measures by local doctors.

However, in the fourth year, the disease spread more widely – into Mozambique and Tanzania, before also being unintentionally released in Atlanta, Georgia, in the United States, by a medical technician who had returned from studying the disease in Africa. Shortly afterward, Lassa fever was present in India as well, presumed to have been carried by an itinerant worker from Tanzania. Due in part to the dense overcrowding in India, the disease was soon rampant there. With fatality rates of over 60% of those infected, the number of people dying from the disease soared.

Countries belatedly closed borders and imposed quarantine measures, but the infection was already widespread by then. In the scenario, the world death toll rose… to one million… to eight million… to thirty million… to 120 million… before peaking at more than one billion, in June 1974.

Meanwhile, *back in the real world*, no such outbreak took place. 1974 came and went without one billion people dying. *Does this provide grounds to ignore the details of the scenario?*

Indeed, the world seems to have grown weary from hearing predictions about deadly worldwide pandemics. The scenario depicted by Ehrlich was by no means the only one.

In the real world, in 2009, alarm bells sounded over the threat of so-called "swine flu". Deaths had been reported of several dozen people in Mexico as a result of infection by a new type of flu. Analysis of the disease showed that it was a novel strain of the same variant of flu, H1N1, that had killed perhaps 100 million people worldwide in the years 1918-1920. The virus showed close similarity to one that infects pigs worldwide – hence the "swine flu" moniker.

Influenza specialists at the WHO (World Health Organization) were concerned. They were already paying close attention to a different type of flu, namely H5N1, commonly known as "bird flu". That flu seemed to infect only a small number of humans, but it killed more than half of the people who fell ill from it.

The same specialists also remembered how two relatively recent outbreaks of flu had each led to several millions of human deaths: H2N2, also known as "Asian flu", in 1957-58, and H3N2, also known as "Hong Kong flu", in 1968-69.

Calculations at the WHO headquarters in Geneva, Switzerland, suggested that the new swine flu could kill between two and seven million people – assuming that the effects of the virus were "relatively mild" – although the forecast climbed into the tens of millions if slightly different assumptions were made[50].

News soon started arriving of fatalities from the disease in the United States, Brazil, India, China, Turkey, Russia, and numerous other countries[51]. On 25th April, 2009, the WHO declared[52] that the disease posed a "public health emergency of international concern", using that "PHEIC" designation for the first time in its history. A few weeks later, Margaret Chan, WHO Director General, raised the influenza panic alert from phase 5 to phase 6, and issued a sombre press statement[53]:

> This particular H1N1 strain has not circulated previously in humans. The virus is entirely new.
>
> The virus is contagious, spreading easily from one person to another, and from one country to another. As of today, nearly 30,000 confirmed cases have been reported in 74 countries.

Chan warned against any complacency:

> Most cases of severe and fatal infections have been in adults between the ages of 30 and 50 years.
>
> This pattern is significantly different from that seen during epidemics of seasonal influenza, when most deaths occur in frail elderly people…
>
> It is important to note that around one third to half of the severe and fatal infections are occurring in previously healthy young and middle-aged people.

Different countries took their own drastic measures to try to curb the disease. Egypt initiated a mass slaughter of pigs. Mexico banned spectators from attending football matches. The German state of Saarland passed local legislation forbidding greeting someone with a kiss[54].

The world braced for greater numbers of deaths. But rather than expanding, the disease soon seemed to contract. Rather than two to seven million people dying, the WHO's official count of fatalities reached just eighteen thousand (though it should be noted that later reassessments pushed up that estimate into the hundreds of thousands[55]).

The figure of eighteen thousand deaths was far less than the deaths each year from so-called "normal" flu. The evident discrepancy between forecast and reality brought sharp criticism to the WHO. Richard Schabas, former chief medical officer in Ontario, referred to the WHO as "the World Hysteria Organization"[56]. Schabas went on:

> They've just been [champing] at the bit waiting for a pandemic for the last 10 years and I think they dramatically overreacted.

Why might the WHO have "overreacted"?

Wolfgang Wodarg, chairman of the Health Committee of the Parliamentary Assembly of the Council of Europe, had a theory. He pointed to the influence of pharmaceutical companies[57]:

> In order to promote their patented drugs and vaccines against flu, pharmaceutical companies influenced scientists and official agencies, responsible for public health standards, to alarm governments worldwide and make them squander tight health resources for inefficient vaccine strategies and needlessly expose millions of healthy people to the risk of an unknown amount of side-effects of insufficiently tested vaccines.

Wodarg was calling for an official EU investigation into what he called a "faked pandemic":

> The "birds-flu"-campaign (2005/06) combined with the "swine-flu"-campaign seem to have caused a great deal of damage not only to some vaccinated patients and to public health-budgets, but to the credibility and accountability of important international health-agencies.
>
> The Council of Europe and its member-states should ask for immediate investigations and consequences on their national levels as well as on the international level.
>
> The definition of an alarming pandemic must not be under the influence of drug-sellers.

Reporting on the outcome of that investigation, Fiona Godlee, Editor-in-Chief of the prestigious British Medical Journal (BMJ), came down in support of the critics[58]:

> The cost has been huge… countries like France and the United Kingdom who have stockpiled drugs and vaccines are now busy unpicking vaccine contracts, selling unused vaccine to other countries, and sitting on huge piles of unused [drugs]. Meanwhile drug companies have banked vast [revenues]: $7bn to $10bn from vaccines alone…

Godlee highlighted that there were indeed conflicts of interest which had not been properly declared, and that the WHO operated with insufficient transparency.

It was not the last time such criticisms would be voiced. When news spread in early 2020 about potential dangers from a new coronavirus, COVID-19, the scepticism came thick and fast.

On 3rd March, radio talk show host Dennis Prager was quick to condemn "hysteria after hysteria"[59]. Only six people in the United States had died of the disease, Prager claimed, "most, if not all, of whom were already ill". As for the WHO, that "should be renamed the World Hysteria Organization", Prager suggested, perhaps unaware he was repeating a suggestion made ten years earlier. According to Prager, the WHO had acted hysterically in 2009 over swine fever, it had acted hysterically in 2003 over SARS, which had actually killed only 774 people, and was now acting hysterically again over COVID-19.

Allegations about conflicts of interest have been heard too. Some people were poised, it was alleged, to make financial killings from COVID-19 vaccination programmes. A variant claim was that the potency of the disease was being exaggerated for various political purposes – to alter the effect of a forthcoming election, or to inculcate a submissive attitude among the general public (by insisting that face masks be worn).

The result, in the first half of 2020, was a mix of two modes of thinking about COVID-19. On the one hand, critics acknowledged the theoretical possibility that the disease *could* become (as Prager put it) "a worldwide mass killer". But that rational assessment coexisted with an emotive hostility toward apparent doom mongers and hysteria merchants. Yes, there was a risk of people dying from COVID-19. But there was said to be an even bigger risk of an unnecessary "panic mode" caused by "breathless" newspaper reporting. The second risk dominated the minds of many opinion-formers.

The same two modes of thinking can be seen in the response by the UK government to an exercise carried out in October 2016 to assess the country's state of preparation for a possible H2N2 influenza pandemic. The exercise, codenamed "Cygnus", took place over three days, with government ministers, scientific advisers, and other officials being given the opportunity to respond to fictionalised developments.

Cygnus participants were reportedly left "ashen-faced" as they came to terms with the rapid impact of the infection[60]. Mortuaries could not cope with the number of dead bodies. Medical staff suffered from a woeful shortage of PPE (personal protective equipment). Hospitals lacked sufficient ventilators and beds. In summary, the NHS would be "stretched beyond breaking point".

That exercise brought home to participants some of the dreadful possible consequences of the NHS's lack of readiness for an influenza pandemic. That intellectual realisation could not be disputed. Nevertheless, few changes took place subsequently in pandemic preparedness planning, despite the strong recommendations in the report issued at the conclusion of the exercise. In practice, resources were actually reduced from that field, rather than being added to it.

Commenting on that subsequent lack of action, Martin Green, Chief Executive of Care England, expressed bitter surprise, during the early months of the COVID-19 outbreak[61]:

> It beggars belief. This is a report that made some really clear recommendations that haven't been implemented. If they had put in place a response to every one, we would have been in a much better place at the start of this pandemic.

Evidently, gaining good foresight of forthcoming risks is only part of the challenge. That foresight needs to be transformed into meaningful action. That foresight must spread beyond brain to heart and to hand.

It's a key goal of this book to highlight the impediments to action – the various sorts of psychological and institutional treacle that prevent society from taking advantage of foresight.

In the case of Exercise Cygnus, one of the impediments was the persistence of a sceptical frame of mind. The scenario being modelled depended on assumptions of rapid transmission of infection, and on a high proportion of the people infected becoming seriously ill. Forecasts involving high numbers for these parameters had been heard before but had been found wanting on these previous occasions, for example in the UK's response to the 2009 H1N1 swine flu, mentioned earlier.

The inaction, tragically, was a case of "ignoring the boy who cries wolf". Or in the words of another saying mentioned earlier, people were "once bitten, twice shy".

Some important takeaways deserve highlighting, from this series of predictions of forthcoming pandemics:

1. Rather than being presented with undue exactness or any false sense of certainty, predictions need to emphasise their probabilistic nature
2. In order to maintain support for any government action taken, the uncertainties involved in the decision need to be carefully explained, in a way that society as a whole is able to understand
3. Any suggestions of hidden motivations or conflict of interest can sabotage respect for a prediction
4. The bad longer-term outcomes from those forecasts of millions of deaths from 2009 H1N1 swine flu – the maddening political unreadiness in a number of countries for subsequent pandemics – were caused, not by any incorrect calculation, but by the lack of operational transparency, along with organisational incompetence and shortcomings in public communication
5. Reasons why a pandemic proved less deadly than initially feared need to be explained clearly and firmly. For example, it turned out that many people born before the H2N2 outbreak of "Asian flu" in 1957-58 were unexpectedly protected against the H1N1 outbreak in 2009 on account of having experienced a milder form of H1N1 earlier in

> their lives. Without that protection, the fatality figures would have been much higher[62]. In short, the public needs to become much more literate about pandemics.

To be clear, that improved medical literacy needs to avoid the reckless optimism which says that, because human doctors recently managed to keep a number of potential global pandemics (like Ebola) under control, these doctors will inevitably also manage to cope with forthcoming new outbreaks.

Ice ages

Famines are coming. Pandemics are coming. Have you heard the next one: an ice age is coming?

That prediction makes a change from what is more often expressed these days, which is that global warming is at hand. Yet in the 1970s, for a while, scientists apparently believed that humanity faced the peril of global cooling.

This warning was featured in a Time article in 1974 entitled "Another Ice Age?"[63]

> When meteorologists take an average of temperatures around the globe, they find that the atmosphere has been growing gradually cooler for the past three decades. The trend shows no indication of reversing. Climatological Cassandras are becoming increasingly apprehensive, for the weather aberrations they are studying may be the harbinger of another ice age.

The article provided evidence of cooling:

> Telltale signs are everywhere – from the unexpected persistence and thickness of pack ice in the waters around Iceland to the southward migration of a warmth-loving creature like the armadillo from the Midwest. Since the 1940s the mean global temperature has dropped about 2.7° F.

A 1975 article "The Cooling World" in Newsweek by journalist Peter Gwynne made similar points[64]:

> The central fact is that, after three quarters of a century of extraordinarily mild conditions, the Earth seems to be cooling down. Meteorologists disagree about the cause and extent of the cooling trend, as well as over its specific impact on local weather conditions. But they are almost unanimous in the view that the trend will reduce agricultural productivity for the rest of the century.

Gwynne raised the alarm about what could happen next:

> If the climate change is as profound as some of the pessimists fear, the resulting famines could be catastrophic.

By 2007, the editors of Newsweek referred to this article as "probably the most-cited single-page story in our history"[65].

The possibility of an impending cooling grew in plausibility because analysts could couple some theoretical ideas alongside the observational evidence:

- There's a natural ebb and flow of ice ages, caused, in part, by the changing orientation of the earth's axis relative to the sun
- That set of natural changes in climate could be accelerated by human activity that raised particulate matter high into the atmosphere – such as dust from farming or soot from burning – with the result of deflecting back into space a higher proportion of incoming sunlight.

This theory was known as "the human volcano". It is widely acknowledged that the average global temperature can be reduced for the few years following a large volcanic eruption. But the same cooling effect could be caused by side-effects of aerosols generated by agricultural or industrial practice.

Nowadays, most climate scientists support the view that average global temperatures are rising (not falling), and that ice packs are shrinking (not thickening). Does this apparent about-turn invalidate the whole enterprise of forecasting climate? *Not at all.*

There are several steps in this answer. First, the "global cooling" argument was nothing like as prominent as some critics of climate science like to suggest. Yes, the Newsweek article was widely cited, but not by scientists who were agreeing with its conclusions. The oft-repeated claim that Time ran a cover story in 1977 entitled "How to Survive the Coming Ice Age" – a claim supported by an image of that supposed front cover, depicting a penguin on top of a huge block of ice[66] – is a despicable fabrication designed to deceive: no such cover story was ever published[67].

Indeed, a detailed review[68] of all peer-reviewed articles about climate change published in academic literature between 1965 and 1979 showed that only a small number of these papers (7) predicted global cooling. A much larger number (42) predicted global warming. Moreover, five of the seven "cooling" papers had been published by 1974; the little support from actual climate scientists for that concept declined even further after that.

Second, the peer-reviewed publications that supported the idea of global cooling generally accepted that there were two sets of human pressure on the climate: particulate aerosols, which could decrease the temperature, and greenhouse gases, which could increase the temperature. As always with foresight, the point isn't just to notice trends, but to explore what might cause the trajectories of these trends to change.

One of the climate scientists who developed "the human volcano" theory, Reid Bryson of the University of Wisconsin, commented on these trends in an interview in 1976[69]:

- The Industrial Revolution led in due course to the development of pesticides and antibiotics, increasing the human population, the extent of land being farmed, and the amount of industrial activity taking place
- As a result, aerosols and greenhouse gases both entered the atmosphere at greater rates than before
- During the time period studied by Bryson, "the cooling effect caused by the first is increasing faster than the warming effect caused by the second".

However, since that time, measures to limit the emissions of aerosols like soot and dust – measures such as the 1970 Clean Air Act in the United States – have been *much* more effective than measures to limit the emissions of greenhouse gases. As a result, the former has declined significantly, whereas the latter has surged. That's why the world is becoming hotter, not colder.

Finally, we need to recognise how much the field of climate science has progressed in the decades since the 1970s. One writer who drew attention to this progress was the same Peter Gwynne whose above-mentioned 1975 "Cooling World" article in Time is still frequently cited by critics of climate science. Writing a retrospective nearly forty years later, Gwynne commented on these critics[70]:

> Certain websites and individuals that dispute, disparage and deny the science that shows that humans are causing the Earth to warm continue to quote my article. Their message: how can we believe climatologists who tell us that the Earth's atmosphere is warming when their colleagues asserted that it's actually cooling?

Gwynne's answer is a good one:

> Those that reject climate science ignore the fact that, like other fields, climatology has evolved since 1975. The certainty that our atmosphere is indeed warming stems from a series of rigorous observations and theoretical concepts that fit into computer models and an overall framework outlining the nature of Earth's climate.
>
> These capabilities were primitive or non-existent in 1975.

Just as climate science has moved forward in leaps and bounds in recent decades, so also must the discipline of foresight improve – not just in the predictions made, but in the language used to explain these predictions and to set them in their wider context. Otherwise, these predictions will become separated from the thinking that generated them, distorted in an excited retelling by hasty journalists, and result in the public in due course turning their back on the whole field, preferring to sleepwalk.

Artificial Intelligence

Another field that has been the subject of controversial predictions is the rise of artificial intelligence (AI). If you're looking for evidence that forecasters contradict each other, and therefore cannot be trusted, predictions of the development of AI will give you rich pickings.

Let's start with one of the intellectual grandfathers of AI, namely the British mathematician and wartime codebreaker Alan Turing. Turing's image appears on Bank of England £50 notes issued from 2021 onward, alongside a short quote from him, "This is only a foretaste of what is to come, and only the shadow of what is going to be"[71].

The quote is taken from an interview given by Turing to The Times in June 1949, about a new computer at Manchester University that had performed a calculation longer and more complicated than any previous calculating device could handle – a calculation that was said to have resisted a solution for 300 years. The newspaper called the device a "mechanical brain". Turing speculated about what this machine and its successors could accomplish[72]:

> We have to have some experience with the machine before we really know its capabilities. It may take years before we settle down to the new possibilities, but I do not see why it should not enter any one of the fields normally covered by the human intellect, and eventually compete on equal terms.

According to Turing, that June 1949 calculation was, potentially, a "foretaste" of a device that "could think for itself", though the *extent* of that independent thinking would be a matter for additional research to investigate.

Two years later, in a lecture given in Manchester entitled "Intelligent Machinery, A Heretical Theory", Turing stated his conclusions more boldly[73]:

> My contention is that machines can be constructed which will simulate the behaviour of the human mind very closely.

In this lecture, Turing avoided giving any specific timescale for this development, but he did offer the following thought about the likely speed of progress once an initial threshold had been reached:

> It seems probable that once the machine thinking method had started, it would not take long to outstrip our feeble powers. There would be no question of the machines dying, and they would be able to converse with each other to sharpen their wits. At some stage therefore we should have to expect the machines to take control.

This pattern, with a slow initial phase being succeeded by a transition to a faster phase and a disruption of control, is one that recurs many times in the pages of this book. It's a concept central to the practice of vital foresight.

Whenever an instance of this pattern is discussed, as a potential future scenario, two questions need to be separated:

1. Is the proposed transition mechanism plausible?
2. What is the likely timescale for this transition to take place?

The first question is often considerably easier to answer than the second one. It can be clear that an infectious pandemic could transition quickly from causing a low number of deaths to causing a much larger number of deaths, without it being predictable in advance *when* such a pandemic will occur. It can be clear that a simmering low underlying resentment against the significantly better lifestyles enjoyed by some "elite" could tip over into a furious populist revolt, without knowing *when* such a transition might be sparked. Likewise with the possibility of rapid progress in AI once software systems can improve themselves in an iterative manner – by "conversing with each other to sharpen their wits", in Turing's words.

In each case, good foresight can aspire to reach a strong answer to the first question, regarding mechanism, but only a probabilistic answer to the second question, regarding timing. Foresight goes astray when it concentrates on the second question and offers overly precise answers to it.

In one of the most famous articles in the history of computer science, Alan Turing addresses *both* questions. This article is the one that introduced the notion Turing called "The imitation game" but which is now widely known as "The Turing test". Authored in 1950, "Computing Machinery and Intelligence"[74] presents nine objections to the idea that machines will ever be able to think as well as humans, before providing in each case reasons why the objection is invalid. In this way, Turing bolsters the case that AI will, *at some time*, be able to respond as well as any human to questions it receives in an extended conversation. Indeed, this part of his article anticipates much of the discussion that many subsequent writers have raised, mistakenly imagining themselves to have found a novel refutation to the idea of AI, whereas in fact Turing had long ago refuted that refutation.

The same article also provides a prediction about timescales, albeit a rather vague one:

> I believe that in about fifty years' time it will be possible, to programme computers… to make them play the imitation game so well that an average interrogator will not have more than 70% chance of making the right identification after five minutes of questioning.

In other words, by around the year 2000, computers would be capable at least 30% of the time of leaving an interlocutor unsure, at the end of a five-minute discussion, whether they were speaking to a human or an AI.

However, in reality, even in 2021, it is all too painfully obvious to most people interacting with a chatbot that they are in fact talking to a chatbot, and not to a human. The chatbot can provide reasonable responses when the discussion stays in a narrow field, but quickly becomes confused and unhelpful when the conversation becomes more general.

If even Alan Turing failed to correctly predict the advent of AIs as smart as humans, what hope is there for anyone else to make a more reliable prediction?

Consider also the plans of the organisers of the 1956 summer workshop at Dartmouth University where the name "Artificial Intelligence" was first used. The proposal for this workshop was written the previous summer by John McCarthy, Marvin Minsky, Claude Shannon and Nathaniel Rochester[75]:

> We propose that a 2-month, 10-man study of artificial intelligence be carried out during the summer of 1956 at Dartmouth College in Hanover, New Hampshire. The study is to proceed on the basis of the conjecture that every

> aspect of learning or any other feature of intelligence can in principle be so precisely described that a machine can be made to simulate it. An attempt will be made to find how to make machines use language, form abstractions and concepts, solve kinds of problems now reserved for humans, and improve themselves.

The proposal continued with the views of the organisers about how much progress could be expected:

> We think that a significant advance can be made in one or more of these problems if a carefully selected group of scientists work on it together for a summer.

This is another example where the mechanisms proposed turned out to be generally correct – progress of the sort envisioned was *eventually* made, in the decades that followed – but where the timescales originally suggested were significantly wrong.

Two of the participants at the 1956 Dartmouth workshop, Herbert Simon and Allen Newell, summarized in a presentation in Pittsburgh the following November (1957) their assessment of the implications of what they described as the "research of the last three years into the nature of complex information processing"[76]:

> We are now poised for a great advance that will bring the digital computer and the tools of mathematics and the behavioural sciences to bear on the very core of managerial activity – on the exercise of judgement and intuition; on the processes of making complex decisions.

A new theory was emerging, they said:

> We now have the elements of a theory of heuristic… problem solving… Intuition, insight, and learning are no longer exclusive possessions of humans: any large high-speed computer can be programmed to exhibit them also.

Next, Simon and Newell gave some specific predictions, all describing events that would happen "within the next ten years" (that is, by 1967):

1. A digital computer will be the world's chess champion
2. A digital computer will discover and prove an important new mathematical theorem
3. A digital computer will write music that will be accepted by critics as possessing considerable aesthetic value

4. Most theories in psychology will take the form of computer programs, or qualitative statements about the characteristics of computer programs.

From the vantage point of 2021, the timescale elements of these predictions appear ridiculous. That's despite the fact that both Simon and Newell had distinguished academic careers. The two shared the Turing Award in 1975, bestowed by the Association of Computing Machinery (ACM) for "contributions to artificial intelligence, the psychology of human cognition, and list processing"[77], and Simon went on to win the Nobel Prize for Economics in 1978[78]. Evidently, neither of these awards guarantees the soundness of your predictions about the future.

Indeed, by 1967, humans still far outplayed the best chess computers. The same was still true in both 1975 and 1978, the years of the two grand prizes just mentioned.

Step forward to November 1981, and a gathering of computer chess enthusiasts at the 12th annual North American Computer Chess Championship, held in Los Angeles. On the final evening, marvelling at the skills shown by some of the competing programs, discussion turned to estimating when a computer would beat the human world chess champion[79]. Monroe Newborn, professor of computer science at McGill University – whose book *Computer Chess*[80] I had avidly read as a teenager in 1975 shortly after its publication – gave the most optimistic prediction: the feat would occur in less than five years. Ken Thompson, programmer of the *Belle* software that won the competition – as well as being the lead developer of the Unix operating system – thought it would take more than twenty years. Others predicted ten years into the future, or fifteen years; yet others thought the task could *never* be done.

In case you don't know the correct answer: IBM's Deep Blue beat Garry Kasparov 3½–2½ in a six-game match in May 1997, that is, 15 and a half years after the Los Angeles conversation. So, Monroe Newborn was over-optimistic by a factor of three, and Ken Thompson was mildly over-pessimistic. Arguably the worst predictions in the bunch were those declaring the feat impossible.

Arguably the *best* prediction of when computers would outperform humans at chess was made in 1994 by Peter Norvig and Stuart Russell, while writing the first edition of their highly influential book *Artificial Intelligence: A Modern Approach*[81]. The two did some research into the ELO rating – a measure of competitive strength – of the best chess computers in different years. This rating increased in almost a straight line from 1400 in 1965, adding slightly over 40 ELO points each year on average. Kasparov's ELO rating at the time was 2805. A simple calculation predicted that the computer ELO would exceed that rating by 1997. And that is what happened.

The basis for the prediction of Norvig and Russell – which, in a kind of coincidence, was essentially a duplicate of one published by supercentenarian researcher Stephen Coles in a 1994 article in the journal AI Expert[82] – was that an observed linear trend would continue to hold. That trend had already held for over thirty years, so a short extrapolation seemed reasonably safe. The only reason to reject such an extrapolation would be if factors were identified that would hinder further progress. But no limits were in sight for the speed of the hardware processors, the amount of working memory available, options to improve the software algorithms, or the number of bright engineers willing to work on the task, building on previous insights. The only conceivable limit would be some kind of mystical one, that magically prevented silicon from going beyond the capability of the human brain. Invoking such a limit would be an example of *very* bad foresight.

Step forward again to May 2014, to a survey by Wired journalist Alan Levinovitz[83] of expert opinions about when computers would be able to outperform the best humans at another board game of great skill, namely Go. Different experts broadly split into three groups. AI researchers tended to think the task would take "maybe ten years". Professional Go players were more sceptical: the full depths of Go gameplay would more likely resist AI mastery for around twenty years. A third group suggested the task would forever exceed the ability of any mechanical brain – that some kind of "wall" was about to be reached, defying further progress.

This time, however, any simple projection of previous trends was to prove misleading. A significant new disruption arrived, namely the programming methods utilised by Google's London-based DeepMind subsidiary. This disruption was no *brake* but rather an *accelerator*. Rather than needing to wait ten or even twenty years, the breakthrough took less than two years, culminating in an emphatic 4-1 victory by the AlphaGo software over human Go playing legend Lee Sedol in Seoul, South Korea[84]. All the apparent domain experts surveyed by Levinovitz just two years earlier proved to be over-pessimistic by a factor of at least five.

I have heard that some of these forecasters subsequently remarked they never expected that any one organisation would apply to this problem the vast scale of resources that Google chose to deploy. Such a possibility lay outside of what was presumed to be the landscape of plausible scenarios. That misperception is a reminder to all of us that we need to bear in mind the multiplicative effect of changed human outlook. As in a time of war, or any other major crisis, coordinated human activity can produce results that defy previous expectations.

The last word in this section belongs to Alan Turing. One of the assumptions behind the predictions that he made is that the brain of a human child has relatively little innate programming. His 1950 article "Computing Machinery and Intelligence" contains this suggestion:

> Instead of trying to produce a programme to simulate the adult mind, why not rather try to produce one which simulates the child's? If this were then subjected to an appropriate course of education one would obtain the adult brain. Presumably the child brain is something like a notebook as one buys it from the stationers. Rather little mechanism, and lots of blank sheets… Our hope is that there is so little mechanism in the child brain that something like it can be easily programmed. The amount of work in the education we can assume, as a first approximation, to be much the same as for the human child.

This was the process foreseen by Turing to obtain AI on a par with human skills:

1. Create an artificial equivalent of the brain of a newborn child
2. Provide that brain with a suitable educational environment.

If the first step was relatively easy, Turing's prediction that the whole task would be completed in fifty years sounds reasonable. But the intervening years have made it amply clear that a child's brain is far from being "lots of blank sheets". Millions of years of evolution have placed vast amounts of pre-programmed "mechanism" into the brain of even the youngest child. So, the first step in the above process would take much longer than Turing hoped.

Does this mistaken assumption invalidate the entire predictive exercise? Far from it. It merely adjusts the date at which a more rapid phase of progress – the one involving lots of "education" – is likely to start.

One glimpse of a more rapid education phase can already be seen in the performance of DeepMind's AlphaGo and its successors, when initial prowess with the game of Go transferred surprisingly quickly into unprecedented capabilities in both chess and Shogi ("Japanese chess")[85].

This means we still need to come to terms with Turing's contention that, "at some stage" the machines will "take control".

But before we delve further, later in this book, into possible future conflicts between human and machine, we should reconsider forecasts of conflicts between human and human – of wars between nation and nation.

Wars

Wars are often acknowledged to be deeply unpredictable.

The person who said it best is probably Field Marshal Helmuth von Moltke. Chief of staff of the Prussian army from 1857 to 1888, Moltke was the tactical and strategic genius behind Prussia's decisive military successes against Austria (1866) and France (1870). His writings about armed conflict have been studied by generations of military personnel around the world.

In his essay "On strategy" published in 1871, Moltke warned against any naive "layman" view that "the development of a campaign represents the strict application of a prior concept that has been worked out in every detail and followed through to the end"[86].

What military commanders must keep in mind, according to Moltke, isn't any detailed forecast, but rather the overarching objective behind the engagement:

> Certainly, the commander in chief will keep his great objective continuously in mind, undisturbed by the vicissitudes of events. But the path on which he hopes to reach it can never be firmly established in advance.

The reason that flexibility is needed is as follows:

> The material and moral consequences of every major battle are so far-reaching that they usually bring about a completely altered situation, a new basis for the adoption of new measures. One cannot be at all sure that any operational plan will survive the first encounter with the main body of the enemy.

This is often summarised by saying "No plan survives contact with the enemy".

Dwight Eisenhower, supreme commander of the Allied forces in World War Two, expressed it as follows, attributing the saying to "a statement I heard long ago in the Army"[87]:

> Plans are worthless, but planning is everything.

Winston Churchill, who like Eisenhower had military experience before becoming a politician, included the following remarks in his 1930 book *My Early Life*[88]:

> In battles… the other fellow interferes all the time and keeps up-setting things, and the best generals are those who arrive at the results of planning without being tied to plans.

But as I said, it was Moltke who probably stated it best. He did *not* say that "plans are worthless". Rather than accepting any intrinsic unpredictability of a military engagement, he urged great effort on reducing uncertainty:

> Everything depends on penetrating the uncertainty of veiled situations to evaluate the facts, to clarify the unknown, to make decisions rapidly, and then to carry them out with strength and constancy.

This advice about anticipating and conducting a military battle applies to foresight in general:

- The big picture, with its overall threats and possibilities, is more important than individual detailed scenarios
- Nevertheless, thinking through a range of different scenarios helps clarify options and increase preparedness for whatever may happen as a situation unfolds
- Rather than being content with your current level of understanding, ongoing effort should be applied to reduce uncertainties
- When surprises occur, it's important to be able to adjust perceptions and assessments promptly, rather than being stuck in a previous mindset.

That's the theory. Military commanders ever since Moltke have all been aware of this advice. How well have they fared since then?

Consider the preparations of the French military leaders in the years before World War Two, in anticipation of the invasion they expected from Hitler's Germany. Memories of the drawn-out years of trench warfare from World War One inevitably influenced thinking – too much so, it turned out.

At all costs, the French desired to avoid any repetition of the horrific World War One battles on their soil, such as Verdun, Somme, and Marne. To resist and deter any direct attack, a series of fortifications called the Maginot Line was created along the Franco-German border, from Switzerland in the south to Luxembourg in the north. Over a period of ten years, the defences were strengthened and reinforced. In places, the fortifications reached ten miles wide[89]. Films of its impressive armaments and seemingly invincible defences were viewed with national pride in cinemas throughout France. When some military and political leaders called for national investment to modernise the French armed forces, to respond to the growing militarisation of Germany, their pleas were rejected. After all, wasn't the Maginot Line already sufficient defence?

French military leaders actually knew that the country was still vulnerable to an attack via the neutral countries Holland and Belgium that lay between the northern parts of France and Germany. They had a plan for this eventuality too:

- German troops would likely take some time to break through these intervening countries
- In the meantime, French defences could be increased
- Also in the meantime, countries like the United Kingdom would likely join the conflict, in view of Germany's violation of Holland or Belgium.

In this part of their planning, French leaders drew, again, on their memory of what had happened during the previous world war.

In reality, German forces took just six weeks, from their attack on 10 May 1940 on Belgium and Holland, until the formal surrender of the French government on 22 June. Paris itself had been occupied as early as 14 June. As for Holland, such was the intensity of the attack it experienced that it surrendered after just four days.

The factor that had been missing from French military planning was an understanding of how quickly the German attack would proceed. The Luftwaffe – the German Air Force – joined the attack with great ferocity, inflicting immense psychological damage. German Panzer tanks operated relatively autonomously, adding to the sense of "blitzkrieg" ("lightning war").

This was no mere upgrade of the military capabilities of the previous war – doing the same thing as before, only faster. This was like a new species of fighting force.

It wasn't just the French who were caught unawares, misled by overconfidence in the Maginot Line defences. Leaders across the world who observed the swift turnaround were shocked.

Even Adolf Hitler is reported to have been surprised at the quick success of the attack – which he had supported, in spite of opposition from several of his own generals who thought it was reckless and would over-extend the German army. Hitler had expected around one million German soldiers to die during the invasion of France; the actual number was just 27,000[90].

With some justification, the phrase "Maginot Line" has become a shorthand for any defensive system that gives the appearance of being extensive and elaborate, but which leaves open an independent line of attack for unscrupulous hackers to exploit. "Maginot Line" neglects to prepare for a future that may involve threats or opportunities of a different character from in the past.

The rapid fall of France was by no means the only major failure of foresight during the Second World War. Other cases involved political leaders being supremely confident in their own foresight, and overlooking multiple signals that they were actually misreading the situation.

In these cases, foresight did much more harm than good.

For example, Joseph Stalin, the dominant ruler of the USSR, knew full well that Adolf Hitler had his eyes on expanding Germany far into Soviet territory, to obtain extra "living space" for a growing German population.

Hitler had openly shared his thinking in the book *Mein Kampf* which he had written in 1924 whilst imprisoned following a failed coup attempt. A key chapter in that book was entitled "Eastern Orientation or Eastern Policy"[91]. It set out the theme of "Lebensraum" ("living space"):

- Prosperous nations need room to expand, either into overseas colonies, or by displacing people of alleged lesser value on an adjacent land mass (as happened in America with repeated settler encroachment on native lands – something which Hitler applauded)

- The historic destiny of German would be to expand east, usurping the control of lands from supposedly inferior Slavic peoples, degenerate Bolshevik politicians, and hated Jews.

The Nazi invasion of Poland fitted that grand scheme. But before he could advance further east, Hitler needed to deal with opposition from Britain and France: hence the lightning strike westward described earlier.

As an opportunist, with expansionist plans of his own, Stalin had welcomed the chance of secret provisions in the August 1939 Molotov-Ribbentrop non-aggression pact between Germany and the USSR. These provisions divided up influence over various lands in between the two powers, including Finland, the Baltic states, Romania, and Poland. One week after the pact was signed, Germany invaded western Poland; two weeks later, the USSR invaded eastern Poland.

Stalin was no fool. He knew that the non-aggression pact was just a temporary expedient. But he welcomed having some extra time to build up Soviet defences in anticipation of an eventual German attack. It seems he was planning on breaking the pact himself, by launching an attack against Germany at an opportune moment[92].

Even before the pact had been signed, Soviet intelligence operatives working all over Europe had sought to warn Stalin of Hitler's plans to invade the USSR some time in 1941. As time passed, more and more reports reached Stalin, alerting him of an impending attack. Stalin would hear nothing of it. He trusted his own instincts much more than what his extensive spy network was telling him. The real enemy of the Soviet Union, Stalin was convinced, was Britain. Any messages to the contrary, therefore, were to be assumed to be British subterfuge.

After all, wouldn't Germany remember the lesson from the First World War, in which it had become horribly over-extended, fighting battles on two fronts (the west and the east) at the same time? Surely Germany wouldn't repeat the same mistake twice?

German troops massing on the border of the Soviet Union were, Stalin thought, merely keeping themselves out of reach of British bombing raids. Intrusions of Soviet airspace by German aircraft were simply due to mistakes by inexperienced German pilots. That was the information which Germany fed to Stalin, and it stoked his spectacular misperception.

Accordingly, the USSR was hopelessly ill-prepared for the sudden mass assault that Hitler unleashed on 22 June 1941: "Operation Barbarossa". With more than three million soldiers, it was the largest military invasion force in history. But in the weeks just prior to the invasion, rather than strengthening his defence forces, Stalin had conducted a purge of 300 Soviet military leaders, including many who were highly decorated – because he feared potential internal rivalry to his own diktats.

In terms of scale and ferocity, the German attack in June 1941 far exceeded what had taken place during the previous war. Within just a couple of months, around half of the USSR's agricultural and industrial capacity had been destroyed. In the years that followed, as Soviet forces regrouped and dug in and then fought back with enormous vigour, more people died in that theatre of the Second World War than in all other theatres added together[93].

If Stalin had been able to free himself of his stubborn misperception that no attack was imminent, it is likely that Hitler's attack could have been repulsed much more quickly, with many fewer casualties.

As it happens, Hitler himself was also to fall prey to a deliberate misperception. By 1944, Germany was aware that the allies would eventually mount a large invasion of territories in mainland Europe. But where would this invasion focus? And where should German defences be ready to swing into action?

British and allied intelligence carried out an elaborate operation, known as "Bodyguard", to convince Hitler that, following a prolonged distraction in the Normandy area, the main attack would take place around Calais. Related deceptions encouraged the idea that large attacks might take place in the south of France, in Norway, or in the Balkans. It took Hitler seven full weeks after the D-Day landings to realise he had been tricked, and for him to approve the transfer of reserve troops from the Calais region to intercept the allied forces that had indeed arrived in huge numbers in Normandy[94].

American General Omar Bradley later described Operation Bodyguard as the "single biggest hoax of the war"[95]. Without that deception, it's possible that the D-Day landings may have been rebuffed.

Let's note some implications:

1. Our own ideas about the future, held too tightly, can prevent us from seeing what is actually happening

2. A nation or other group that is dominated by one person with very strong opinions – such as Stalin or Hitler – is more prone to misperception than one which allows and even encourages critical thinking and diverse opinions
3. Misperceptions often involve self-deception as well as deliberate deception by others
4. The most dangerous misperceptions often imagine the future to be broadly similar to the past, instead of having radically new features
5. As Helmuth von Moltke emphasised, constant effort is needed to identify key areas of uncertainty and to reduce that uncertainty.

By the way, various optimistic predictions of the continuation of peace have proven to be as flawed as optimistic predictions for how war would proceed. Consider the views of a number of forecasters in the years ahead of the outbreak of the First World War. In the early 1910s, many trends could be observed that gave the impression of a world increasingly locked into a trajectory of growing prosperity. Remarkable economic progress was taking place in the wake of electrification, the popularisation of the motor car, the manufacturing of synthetic chemicals, and assembly-line systems of mass production. Countries had created early welfare systems with basic pension plans. Public initiatives in sanitation and vaccination were having noticeable effects on health. By many measures, life was becoming better and better.

Growing trade interdependence between nations led various analysts to conclude that major wars could no longer be contemplated. For example, in his 1910 book *The Great Illusion*[96], Norman Angell – a British journalist who was subsequently awarded the Nobel peace prize – argued that war between the great powers had become "an economic impossibility" because of "the delicate interdependence of international finance". Writing for Reuters one hundred years later, Anatole Kaletsky provides additional historical perspective[97]:

> A 1910 best-selling book, *The Great Illusion*, used economic arguments to demonstrate that territorial conquest had become unprofitable, and therefore global capitalism had removed the risk of major wars. This view… became so well established that, less than a year before the Great War broke out, the Economist reassured its readers with an editorial titled "War Becomes Impossible in Civilized World."

> "The powerful bonds of commercial interest between ourselves and Germany," the Economist insisted, "have been immensely strengthened in recent years… removing Germany from the list of our possible foes."

As late as spring 1914, Henry Noel Brailsford, a British member of the international commission reporting on the recent Balkan Wars, concurred[98]:

> In Europe the epoch of conquest is over… It is as certain as anything in politics that the frontiers of our national states are finally drawn. My own belief is that there will be no more war among the six powers.

Oops. The lesson here, to be clear, is to be cautious about similar predictions of ongoing stability made in the present time by various well-meaning apparent experts. Apparent stability and growing prosperity can coexist with deepening latent tensions, with connections that no-one fully understands, and, indeed, with disruptive innovations whose full consequences no-one fully understands. In such times, we need to beware:

1. Unfounded over-confidence: underestimates of the weaknesses in existing human psychology and the weaknesses in existing social institutions
2. Systems that are pumped up and take on a life of their own, via runaway positive feedback cycles
3. Sets of ideas that have been distorted from "hypothesis" through "ideology" to "faith" and "dogma".

It would be a brave – and foolhardy – forecaster who would maintain that the hugely complex massively interdependent systems of the present day have no shocks and surprises left to deliver to us. The kind of systemic breakdown that happened in 1914 could well happen again, all too soon. But this time, the effect will likely be even more calamitous.

Terrorism

If Hitler's Operation Barbarossa invasion of the USSR was Stalin's biggest failure to act on incoming intelligence, and if the allied D-Day landings were Hitler's biggest intelligence failure, the largest "predictable surprise" in recent US history was the 9/11 attack on the Twin Towers in New York and the Pentagon in Washington DC. That attack left US citizens in a state of utter disbelief.

Who could have imagined, in advance, that nineteen healthy young men would commandeer huge passenger airline jets, and fly them into iconic buildings to the certain deaths of themselves and all aboard?

Actually, there was plenty of evidence, in advance, that such a plan had been hatched and was being progressed. But no-one had the overall perspective to join up all the individual pieces of evidence, to be able to perceive what was about to happen.

The idea of terrorists flying a plane laden with fuel into a famous building was known to the intelligence community from 1994, when four members of the Armed Islamic Group of Algeria (GIA) had hijacked the Air France flight AF8969 shortly before its scheduled departure from Algiers for Orly, Paris. An informant within the GIA passed to authorities the disturbing news that the terrorists planned to explode dynamite on the flight as it passed by the Eiffel Tower[99]. Sadly, three members of the passengers and crew were shot dead in cold blood by the terrorists as police negotiators stalled for time. The flight was then diverted to Marseilles in the south of France, where it was stormed by members of the country's elite counter-terrorism unit, the GIGN. The case is still widely studied as a successful example of special forces intervention[100]. However, the lesson that was *not* learned, sufficiently, was the need to lookout for other terrorists with similar tactics in mind.

For another forerunner of the 9/11 attacks, consider the Bojinka plot planned in the Philippines, also in 1994, by two Kuwaiti-born Pakistani terrorists, Ramzi Yousef and Abdul Hakim Murad[101]. The plot – like 9/11 – was audacious in its scale. Indeed, the two plots had the same mastermind, Khalid Shaikh Mohammed, who was Yousef's uncle[102].

Bojinka was to involve no less than eleven airplanes being blown out of the sky at roughly the same time, over the Pacific Ocean, each as a result of a bomb being left on board with a Casio wristwatch timer attached, with the bomber having departed the plane at an intermediate stop.

The explosive mechanism had already been trialled on a bomb left by Yousef on Philippine Airlines Flight 434 on 11 December 1994[103]. Yousef boarded the flight at Manilla, assembled the bomb in a lavatory from items he had smuggled on board in his shoes and his toiletry bag, and hid the bomb in the flight jacket pouch beneath his seat before leaving the plane in Cebu, Philippines. The plane flew on over the Philippines Sea toward Japan. The bomb exploded shortly afterward, killing one passenger instantly and injuring ten others. Despite the blast opening a gaping hole in the fuselage, and damaging the aircraft control mechanisms, the pilot managed to fly the craft on an emergency route to Okinawa island. Yousef did not mind that the craft had survived the explosion: he planned to use ten times as much explosive each time in the real run.

In order to smuggle so many bombs onto so many planes, the terrorists planned to create a diversion, by assassinating Pope John Paul II during his visit to the Philippines on 15 January 1995. A suicide bomber purchased priestly clothes as a disguise, to be able to approach the Pope closely. But then the plan went wrong. While working with some explosives, Abdul Hakim Murad set off a small fire in the kitchen sink of his apartment. The instincts of an investigating police officer told her that something was amiss. This led to the capture of Murad when he returned to the apartment to try to retrieve incriminating documents. The plot quickly unravelled. It was the subsequent interrogations that provided intelligence operatives with the bigger picture:

- Murad had spent years in flight school in Dubai, in New York state, and in North Carolina, gaining a commercial pilot's licence
- The reason for that long training was to prepare him for a suicide mission: he would in the future obtain a small plane – buying it, renting it, or stealing it – pack it full of explosives, and crash it into the CIA headquarters in Langley, Virginia
- One of the documents recovered from the site of the fire was a manifesto, making the chilling claim that "we will hit all U.S. nuclear targets".

What foresight did US officials gain from this intelligence? At one level, the threat *was* taken seriously. A study released in September 1999 by the Federal Research Division of the Library of Congress highlighted the following scenarios[104]:

> Suicide bomber(s) belonging to al-Qaida's Martyrdom Battalion could crash-land an aircraft packed with high explosives (C-4 and Semtex) into the Pentagon, the headquarters of the Central Intelligence Agency (CIA), or the White House...
>
> A horrendous scenario consonant with al-Qaida's mindset would be its use of a nuclear suitcase bomb against any number of targets in the nation's

> capital. Bin Laden allegedly has already purchased a number of nuclear suitcase bombs from the Chechen Mafia.

Individual intelligence officers gathered some specific information. In July 2001, FBI agent Kenneth Williams produced an internal report for his colleagues that "warned of potential terrorists training in aviation-related fields of study in the United States"[105]. The report gave detailed reasons why Williams believed that:

> There was a coordinated effort by Usama Bin Laden to send students to the United States to attend civil aviation universities and colleges… the purpose of these students would be to one day work in the civil aviation industry around the world to conduct terrorist activity against civil aviation targets.

That same month, Richard Blee, the head of the CIA unit investigating Al Qaeda, gave a stark briefing to Condoleezza Rice, US National Security Adviser[106]:

> There will be significant terrorist attacks against the United States in the coming weeks or months. The attacks will be spectacular. They may be multiple. Al Qaeda's intention is the destruction of the United States.

One recollection of that meeting is that Rice asked, "What do you think we need to do?"

The response: a table-thumping "We need to go on a wartime footing now!"

However, in Rice's own retelling of that meeting in her memoir, she said she did not remember anything particularly unusual:

> My recollection of the meeting is not very crisp because we were discussing the threat every day… I thought we were [already] doing what needed to be done.

Either way, no new action was taken. Opportunities to prevent the 9/11 hijackings were, therefore, missed.

One month later, the Pan Am International Flight Academy in Minnesota warned the FBI about the numerous suspicious actions of one person enrolled there: Zacarias Moussaoui, who would subsequently become described as "the twentieth hijacker"[107]. Even though he had little prior experience, and even lacked a pilot's licence, Moussaoui had requested training on flying a Boeing 747, and he paid for his instruction in cash. The FBI questioned Moussaoui and arrested him for having exceeded his visa to stay in the US[108]. Agents applied for permission to search his laptop, and to search his accommodation, but the requests were turned down by more senior officials[109].

Why were the leads not followed up? Why did the many pleas for faster action – "to go to a wartime footing now!" – apparently fall on deaf ears? What were the causes of this misperception of the urgency of the threat posed?

First, an intellectual acknowledgement of the theoretical possibility of a mass attack coincided with a complacent scepticism about the capabilities of the Al Qaeda network. Cynthia Storer, a former CIA counter-terrorism analyst, summed up an impression that was widespread[110]:

> Arabs can't work together, and these guys are a bunch of ragheads who've been fighting in the mountains of Afghanistan.

Some CIA analysts who *did* take the threat seriously – such as Storer – were even advised by their superiors *not* to spend so much time focusing on Bin Laden. Signs of obsession, they were told, would hinder their career advancement.

Second, an exhausting amount of painstaking work was required to track potential suspects over months and even years of preparations for an attack. That was the kind of work that could easily be deprioritised as time passed and as overall budgets were squeezed.

Third, the suicidal fervour of Al Qaeda members defied prior experience. Politicians were more used to dealing with terrorists who had at least some regard for their own lives. Would so many people willingly end their own lives, for the sake of an other-worldly cause? Again, the idea made sense intellectually, but it offended intuition. This added to the *implausibility* of the risk.

Fourth, potential actions to improve aircraft security were resisted on grounds of costs and speed. Airlines wanted passengers to be able to pass quickly through security checks and board their planes with minimal delays. Lobbyists for the industry objected to proposed new measures that would eat into short-term profits.

Finally, the full picture of the threat could only be perceived by integrating information from multiple different viewpoints. Prior to 9/11, relations between different agencies were often cold, with limited sharing of information[111].

And that's why the Al Qaeda "ragheads" were able to pull off their devastating attack, despite many opportunities for their plans to be noticed and thwarted.

This dismal failure of foresight evidently bears many lessons. But perhaps the most important lesson is a lesson about scale. The 9/11 attacks burst into the public mindset from nowhere, and have remained high in public discussions ever since. Nevertheless, future terrorist threats might be very different from past ones. We need to be able to think "beyond 9/11". Just as Al Qaeda moved forward from "planes packed with explosives" to "planes full of fuel", other significant jumps in deadliness could take place in the future.

So far as we know, the fears that Al Qaeda might obtain and use nuclear weapons turned out to be unfounded. But the future may well be different from the past. The idea that terrorists might detonate a nuclear bomb offends our intuitions: such a development would be *too awful*. And the idea that terrorists might be *capable* of obtaining and detonating a nuclear bomb also makes us uncomfortable: they're not really that competent, we want to tell ourselves. We might even be right in these assessments, 99 times out of 100. But what about on the 100th occasion?

It's the same as with potential plagues. Most infectious diseases fall far short of killing millions. But that's no reason to dismantle centres for the control of diseases. Likewise with the possibility of a tipping point in the global climate system: most instances of extreme weather are followed by milder periods, but one day, long-standing currents in the ocean or atmosphere may move into whole new patterns, precipitating not just weeks but decades (or centuries) of life-threatening weather.

One response to these realisations is, nevertheless, to lower our gaze, and say that "we'll take our chances". After all, generations of humans have managed to survive previous perils and panics. We can't spend our lives being paralysed by fear of all sorts of existential disasters about which there's little we can do. Right?

As I'll be covering in the chapters ahead, I see such a response as being wrong in three ways:

1. There is *plenty* that can be done to reduce the threats from existential disaster

2. The background risk of disaster has been increasing in magnitude: an attitude of learned helplessness toward these disasters that made a kind of psychological sense in the past makes much less sense in the present time
3. Developing the skills of better foresight won't just reduce the risk of existential disaster; it will increase the possibility of profound positive progress.

Beyond misperceptions

Episodes from the chequered history of foresight, as reviewed above, might leave the impression that there's little that can be said with any confidence about the set of disruptive risks and opportunities facing our future.

But any such conclusion would be mistaken. Instead, foresight can follow the pattern of many other fields of study, in which understanding is gradually assembled, with practitioners building on the accomplishments of those who came before them. By learning from past failures – and also from past successes – the field of foresight can gain in reliability and usefulness. The skills of foresight can become truly essential tools, for everyone, in the 2020s and beyond.

To take things forward, I'd now like to look more systematically at the eleven risks that I have come to see, from many years studying the subject, as most deserving our collective attention. For reasons that will become clear, I'll call these risks "landmines".

4. Landmines

Landmines, defined: Explosives lurking unseen in the undergrowth, awaiting detonation by the oblivious passer-by. A scourge that maims and kills far too many people every year, severing limbs and shattering lives. Something that urgently needs detection and neutralisation, to prevent an upsurge of damage in an age where escalation can be swift and terrible.

As humanity sleepwalks, we have a dim general awareness of potential oncoming disruptions that could bring us to grief. We occasionally watch videos about these disruptions, read articles or books about them, and speculate about positive responses or negative outcomes. But when we perceive that little real progress is being made to tame these disruptions, or to harness them for beneficial results, we tend to withdraw our attention and drift back into our reveries. *After all, we're busy! – we tell ourselves.*

Breaking out of such reveries requires five factors to coalesce:

1. A stark reminder of the deep harms that are likely to ensue if the disruptions run amok – this is the *negative* part of foresight
2. A roadmap with a credible plan to tackle these disruptions – this is the *positive* part of foresight
3. The identification and formation of a coalition of participants who can work together to push the positive solutions forward – this is the *political* part of foresight
4. Agreement on some initial steps that are aligned with the overall roadmap, that can be taken quickly, and which can then be celebrated as important "small wins" to build greater momentum – this is the *creative*, *agile* part of foresight
5. The availability of systems that can nurture the practical skills needed in this work of positive transformation – this is the *educational* part of foresight.

I'll attend to the first of these five factors in this chapter, before covering the others in later chapters.

Here, accordingly, are some of the nastiest landmines, trip hazards, downward staircases, and open windows, so to speak, which deserve a great deal more attention.

I'll note in advance that they add up to a depressing list. But it's far better to have a realistic understanding of these issues than to stumble along in a state of naivety. To lessen the strain, I'll include from time to time some glimpses of the solutions to these landmines which I'll be developing in greater detail as the book unfolds.

The "left behinds"

There's ample evidence that, compared to the past, more people nowadays have access to more goods and services, more information, more opportunities, and more lifestyle choices[112]. In many ways, life is better than ever before. But how are these opportunities distributed[113]? And what should we infer about the future from various trends in the statistics of inequality?

Consider the share of national wealth that is in the hands of the richest 1% of the population. For most of the twentieth century, that share declined. Figures from the World Inequality Database show that fraction falling, in the UK[114], from a staggering 73.8% in 1901, down to 15.2% in 1984 – before starting to climb again, reaching 20.9% in 2009. Figures from the same source for the United States[115] show the same down-then-up-again pattern, albeit with a greater upward rebound: from 48.2% in 1929 down to 21.0% in 1978 ahead of a rebound up to 38.9% in 2012. *It's the rebound that's worrying.*

The Pew Research Center summarises recent trends in wealth inequality in the US as follows[116]:

> The wealth gap between upper-income and lower- and middle-income families has grown wider this century. Upper-income families were the only income tier able to build on their wealth from 2001 to 2016, adding 33% at the median. On the other hand, middle-income families saw their median net worth shrink by 20% and lower-income families experienced a loss of 45%. As of 2016, upper-income families had 7.4 times as much wealth as middle-income families and 75 times as much wealth as lower-income families. These ratios are up from 3.4 and 28 in 1983, respectively.

Given such trends, it's no surprise that greater numbers of people *perceive* themselves as being "left behind". Long-standing historical patterns of salaries rising in real terms from one generation to another are no longer being observed. Structural unemployment in many industries – worsened by automation as well as by globalisation – means that more people have difficulty in obtaining the kinds of jobs they find sufficiently rewarding and meaningful.

In the UK, former Prime Minister Theresa May spoke in 2016 about the growing number of people who were "just about managing"[117]:

> You have a job but you don't always have job security. You have your own home, but you worry about paying a mortgage. You can just about manage but you worry about the cost of living and getting your kids into a good school.

Some of these "JAMs" (to use the acronym that was briefly in vogue) are able to pull themselves up from the challenges that they face. But others find the pressures too daunting, when coupled with apparent personal misfortune and a decline in funding for social support services[118].

These personal pressures are magnified by two other factors:

1. Media of all sorts that seem to portray lots of people apparently having a high quality of life, with thrills, connections, and experiences that are denied to those who are "just about managing"
2. The circulation of theories that attribute the apparent dearth in opportunities to purportedly devious actions of various subgroups in society, such as "bankers", "immigrants", "experts", "the 1%", "welfare queens", "unbelievers", "leftists", "rightists", "deep state", "globalists", and so on.

The result isn't just that some people are *actually* left behind, but that increasing numbers of people *believe* themselves to be left behind, and fall into anger or despair as a result. They feel alienated from society as a whole.

Princeton economists Angus Deaton and Anne Case refer to increasing numbers of "deaths of despair": people dying at unprecedented rates from accumulated self-harm, liver disease exacerbated by alcohol abuse, drug overdoses, or violent forms of suicide. This trend has been worsening in recent years, causing, remarkably, a dip in life expectancy in the United States. As Deaton and Case point out[119]:

> In 2017 alone, there were 158,000 deaths of despair in the US: the equivalent of three fully loaded Boeing 737 MAX jets falling out of the sky every day for a year.

What particularly concerns many people, even if they feel they are "just about managing" at the present time, is the risk they see of their situation deteriorating. They assess their current circumstances as being insecure and precarious. As such, they belong to what the British economist Guy Standing has dubbed "the precariat… a dangerous new class"[120].

There are three reasons to pay more attention to this growing trend:

1. To lessen the numbers of individuals and families who experience this level of despair and who are inclined to self-harm as a result
2. To heal the psychic fractures in societies where neighbourhoods with abundant wealth coexist alongside neighbourhoods with significantly lower quality of life
3. To lessen the numbers of individuals and groups who are inclined to take powerful hostile action in response to their experience of inequality, their sense of victimhood, and their assessment that parts of society deserve blame or punishment as a result.

All three reasons are important. To see the full extent of the dangers arising, we need to consider the cross-over impacts of other forthcoming disruptions.

WMD proliferation

What actions do people take, when they feel outraged, cheated, taken for granted, or exploited?

Some look for ways to improve the circumstances for themselves and their families, despite their perception that society is stacked against them.

Others turn inward, harbouring resentments and depression, with various adverse impacts on their health, such as the "deaths of despair" noted earlier.

Yet others become primed to take action for revenge:

- Action to make the world "pay" for the harms it caused
- Action to strike down the sections of society that are perceived as the guilty party
- Action to obtain some kind of recognition or fame, or other compensation, as a contrast to their previous status as a nonentity.

Some of the world's most notorious political leaders – dictators and their henchmen – were likely motivated at least in part by such feelings, alongside other feelings that might be described in more positive terms.

The growing problem we face, however, is that smaller groups of disaffected people are increasingly able to get their hands on horrific WMDs

– weapons of mass destruction – and can use these weapons to cause ever larger amounts of damage.

These weapons are "the other side of the two-edged sword" provided by ongoing technological progress.

Consider jet airliners. These are marvellous at enabling mass travel around the world, at relatively low cost. But some aircraft have been turned into personal suicide machines, plunged at high speed into mountainsides, as in the tragic case of Germanwings flight 9525 on 24 March 2015[121]. Co-pilot Andreas Lubitz, aged just 27, had suffered from serious bouts of depression, though he mainly hid his condition from his employers. Fearing that a sight defect would cause him to lose his ability to pilot airplanes, he became resentful and suicidal. When the lead pilot left the cabin for a toilet break during that flight, Lubitz made perverse use of three pieces of technology:

1. A secure lock on the cabin door, designed to frustrate hijackers, which could not be opened from the outside, no matter how hard the pilot or other crew members tried
2. The GPS positioning system on the plane, which knew its position with pinpoint accuracy
3. The automated pilot system, which Lubitz set to propel the craft headlong into a nearby mountain.

All 150 people on the flight died in the resulting crash.

In this particular case, the perpetrator, Lubitz, acted alone, and without any sophisticated ideology guiding his actions. But in the case of the 9/11 hijackers, the incident went far beyond individual feelings of despair, outrage, or alienation. The 9/11 hijackers' shared membership in Al Qaeda provided them with greater strength and purpose, due to the reassurances and encouragement they received from each other. Their commitment was further augmented by the Al Qaeda creed, derived from a branch of Islam, that held out a vision:

- That "martyrs" would enjoy personal glory in an exquisite afterlife
- That any carnage these martyrs could cause had divine sanction
- That any suffering experienced by members of the American public was well deserved, as recompense for the huge damage that Americans and their forebears had inflicted in the Middle East

- That any innocents caught up in the incident would have their eternal fates looked after by divine providence.

Islam is by no means the only mainstream religion with dangerous offshoots that can motivate acts of mass destruction. Timothy McVeigh, responsible for the bombing of a federal building in Oklahoma that killed 168 people in 1995, was influenced in part by the white supremacist "Christian Identity" movement[122]. Attacks with sarin gas in the Tokyo subway, also in 1995, were carried out by members of Aum Shinrikyo, which mixed beliefs from Buddhism, Hinduism, and apocalyptic strands of Christianity[123]. Acts of terrorism are also contemplated by some adherents of groups within the broad environmentalist umbrella, such as the Earth Liberation Front and Earth First[124].

To be clear, the percentage of the overall population who are likely to want to initiate horrific acts of mass destruction remains tiny. But what's changing is the ease with which people in that tiny fraction of humanity can act on their urges. Weapons that are within their reach include not only jet airliners and semi-automatic rifles but also:

- Biologically engineered pathogens – covered in the next section
- Destructive computer malware – covered in the section after that
- Various forms of nuclear weapons – discussed in more detail in a moment.

Additional complications are that the design of these weapons can be enhanced by new forms of artificial intelligence, the manufacture of these weapons can be performed at least in part by 3D printing devices that evade centralised scrutiny, and these weapons can be delivered to their targets by autonomous drones.

Whilst the threat from small, non-state groups should not be discounted, the biggest threat may arise from political regimes that already have control of significant national resources – especially when these regimes operate outside full democratic scrutiny.

The fact that some regimes were found *not* to possess WMDs that had been widely feared – Saddam Hussain's Iraq is a prime example – provides no assurance that regimes in the future will continue to be free from WMDs. Sadly, there are already too many counter-examples.

Likewise, the fact that the world has avoided aggressive use of nuclear weapons ever since the explosions over Hiroshima and Nagasaki in August 1945, provides no assurance that military leaders will continue to keep their hands off the detonation buttons.

Indeed, there have been, over the decades, far too many "near miss" incidents where the world came perilously close to the worst kind of accident[125]. In these incidents, if military leaders had strictly complied with their agreed defence protocols, massive retaliatory strikes would have been launched. Thankfully, good human judgement prevailed in all these cases. However, factors that magnify the probability of nuclear war remain in place:

1. A growing number of countries have access to the requisite deadly technology – including the near-inscrutable "hermit kingdom" of North Korea
2. Leaders whose grip on power depends on populist rhetoric may become carried away by their own dizzying grandstanding or depressed state of mind
3. Some members of various ruling regimes seem to believe in the imminence of a "holy war" such as foretold in the biblical Book of Revelations, and that they, personally, could have pivotal roles in precipitating an "end of days" or "rapture"[126]
4. Rapidly changing local circumstances can generate confusion, in which some nuclear weapons may slip out of the supervision of national governments, into the control of fringe groups who feel less moral restraint over using devastating force
5. It's not only the weapons themselves which are vulnerable to being stolen by dissident elements; the control systems that supervise these weapons are subject to being attacked as part of cyberwarfare, with unpredictable consequences.

Biotech hazards

Although the COVID-19 coronavirus has caused havoc around the world, it's by no means the deadliest infection that can be imagined. Changes to the structure of such a virus could increase:

1. The extent to which infectious particles are expelled from someone's body, by coughing, singing, speaking, or even just breathing

2. The length of time these particles can survive in the environment, before being picked up or inhaled by someone else
3. The number of days during which someone is "asymptomatic" – spreading the infection to others in their vicinity, without noticing themselves to be ill
4. The likelihood of the virus to eventually kill someone who is infected.

So far in human history, the emergence of new infectious diseases has largely been a random process, via normal biological processes such as mutation and recombination.

It seems probable that the greater intensity of human life is increasing the rate of incidents of new infectious diseases[127]:

- Various animals are crowded together more tightly, sometimes in unhealthy conditions, in farms, in wildlife markets, or in so-called "wet markets", providing more opportunities for different diseases to combine and to jump between species[128]
- Rather than outbreaks of diseases being confined to just a single local community, the wider scale of human travel means that new pathogens can spread further before raising public attention, with more opportunity as a consequence to mutate into new variants.

However, the truly worrying threat arises from human manipulation of genetic material – something that new techniques such as CRISPR editing make increasingly straightforward. Such manipulation needn't be intrinsically malign. It may stem from a number of different motivations:

1. From the sheer intellectual quest to explore the possibilities of science and engineering
2. To investigate, ahead of time, possible cures that could be applied to variants of infections that might arise[129]
3. To consider possible new weapons that could be deployed with devastating effect – or which could bring a conflict to a rapid end simply by the threat of their use.

These manipulations could produce genetic variants that were very unlikely to arise by themselves. That's because, in any sequence of natural evolutionary changes, the DNA needs to remain viable in every intermediate stage of that process. For example, a virus that became too virulent might result in human victims dying so quickly that there was reduced opportunity for the infection to spread to other people. Thus, that infection would die out. The metaphor is that a piece of DNA cannot mutate stage by stage from one local maxima to another, distant, higher local maxima, if the intervening evolutionary landscape is significantly lower. However, human bioengineers could perform multiple manipulations in a controlled environment, reaching points in the genetic landscape that were previously inaccessible.

As well as deliberate genetic manipulation with a specific end in mind, we need to consider the possibility that mistakes will occur, or that the outcomes of experiments may vary significantly from what was anticipated. Accordingly, highly dangerous infections may arise in part by accident.

Bear in mind that organisations which are dedicated to the study of dangerous infectious diseases have a track record, sadly, of occasionally inadvertently releasing these diseases.

Consider smallpox, which was declared by the WHO in 1980 as having been eradicated. The last person to have died from this disease was Janet Parker, a 40-year-old medical photographer who worked at Birmingham Medical School in England. The same institution also contained, directly below Parker's main place of work, one of the handful of laboratories in the world that researched smallpox. In August 1978, Parker developed a rash of ugly red spots. She was subsequently identified as being ill with smallpox, and succumbed to the disease a few weeks later. Exactly how the disease escaped from its confinement is still a matter of debate. Possibilities include an air duct or contact with a contaminated piece of equipment[130].

This was not an isolated case. Small outbreaks of smallpox in the UK had also taken place in 1972, following an incident at a laboratory in the London School of Hygiene and Tropical Medicine, and in 1966, following an incident at the same Birmingham Medical School[131]. Two people died in the 1972 case. No fatalities resulted from the 1966 case, but, according to a retrospective analysis carried out years later, nor were lessons sufficiently learned.

Other biocontainment process failures have occurred at a disturbing number of locations around the world[132]. Even experienced medical scientists occasionally suffer lapses of concentration, or cut corners due to haste. In 2004, one Taiwanese scientist was in a hurry to leave work to travel to a medical conference in Singapore, and he skimped on wearing the stipulated gown and gloves while cleaning up after an experiment involving the SARS virus. He unwittingly carried that disease with him to Singapore[133]. Also in 2004, Antonina Presnyakova, a scientist carrying out research into Ebola at a lab in Novosibirsk, Siberia, accidentally injected herself with that virus when her hand slipped while holding a hypodermic syringe. Although she only pricked herself lightly, Presnyakova died of the disease two weeks later. *Accidents happen.*

Beyond the set of accidental infections, we should consider cases where malice is involved, especially when that malice is coupled to religious mania or political obsession.

In 1984, members of the Rajneesh commune in Wasco County, Oregon, were determined to influence the result of a local election. Followers of the guru Baghwan Shree Rajneesh (who later changed his name to Osho) sought to reduce the number of people who would vote in that election. They obtained salmonella bacteria from a medical supply company in Seattle, before culturing it in labs within their commune to increase its volume. Next, they explored a number of different delivery mechanisms, including poisoning parts of the water supply. They settled on sprinkling liquid containing the bacteria on food in salad bars at ten different restaurants in the region. In consequence, 751 members of the public developed chills, stomach ache, vomiting, and diarrhoea. Forty-five of them ended up being hospitalised. All but one of the restaurants targeted went out of business in the aftermath of the outbreak[134].

The goals of the Aum Shinrikyo movement in Japan were more deadly. I've already mentioned their 1995 attack on the Tokyo underground, when bombs including sarin gas were exploded on five different subway trains. Thirteen commuters died as a result. The group carried out this attack as part of what it perceived as an existential struggle for its own survival in the face of police investigations. In addition to its use of sarin gas, the group assembled traditional explosives, chemical weapons, a Russian military helicopter, hydrogen cyanide poison, and samples of Ebola and anthrax. Members of the group subsequently testified that they believed an outbreak of anthrax would catalyse a global war that would result in the group's leader, Shoko Asahara, becoming the ruler of the entire world[135].

Fortunately, it seemed that Aum Shinrikyo lacked the competence necessary to make full deadly use of the biological agents they had gathered. Next time, humanity may not be so lucky, as knowledge of engineering techniques spreads. For a foretaste of the possible future, review the incident in which operatives from North Korea used VX nerve gas to assassinate Kim Jong-nam, half-brother of the regime's leader, at Kuala Lumpur airport in February 2017[136].

As it happens, it's not just biotech that North Korea is ready to weaponize. The regime also heavily invests in the weaponization of infotech.

Infotech hazards

The increased connectivity of the modern world doesn't just provide more opportunities for biological contagions to spread. Other forms of contagion become more likely too – and potentially more deadly. This includes financial contagion, the subject of the next section, and software contagion, which we'll discuss now. Later in the chapter, we'll turn to the subject of psychological contagion.

In all four cases, what makes the contagion possible is a ubiquitous shared infrastructure:

- A common *biological infrastructure* that allows biological infections to jump from human to human, without regard for rank or status
- A common *financial infrastructure* that allows people all around the world to trade goods and to exchange tokens of money
- A common *software infrastructure* that connects everyone via Internet packets, social media, email, and other messaging systems
- A common *mental infrastructure*, with shared heuristic shortcuts, cognitive biases, and other predispositions to irrationality.

In each case, the common infrastructure delivers profound benefits, at the same time as it poses risks. In each case, the risk increases as people find cleverer ways to identify and exploit latent weaknesses in the infrastructure.

Here are some examples of the damage caused in recent years by various pieces of infotech malware[137]:

- The "WannaCry" ransomware attack that incapacitated hundreds of thousands of computers throughout over one hundred countries, in May 2017, causing many hospitals in the UK to cancel operations[138]
- The 2021 ransomware hack of the Colonial Pipeline, which halted the supply of oil and gas, prompting the US government to declare ransomware attacks as having as high a priority as terrorism[139]

- The "StuxNet" worm attack that destroyed many hundreds of fast-spinning centrifuges inside a uranium enrichment plant in Natanz, Iran, over a period of several months in 2009 and 2010[140]
- The "Shamoon" cyberattack of August 2012 that disabled 35,000 computers in use at Saudi Aramco, the enormous oil company, forcing employees to revert for a while to typewriters and fax machines to manage business operations[141]
- The 2014 "Sony-pocalypse" attack on Sony Pictures, which revealed numerous embarrassing emails, copies of forthcoming movies, and full salary details of employees, in an attack to prevent the planned Christmas Day release of the movie *The Interview* with its unflattering portrayal of North Korean leader Kim Jong-un[142]
- The publication in 2015 of over 60 GB of sensitive data stolen from Ashley Madison – a company whose website proclaims "Life is short: Have an affair… Millions of people just like you are looking for a discreet connection" – including names of users of the site and their sexual preferences; several users apparently committed suicide as a result of their names and proclivities being leaked[143]
- Data breaches at the credit reporting agency Equifax in 2017, allowing the theft of personally identifying data of hundreds of millions of consumers[144]
- Several data breaches from the Indian national ID database Aadhaar, putting at risk the personal data of up to 1.1 billion citizens of the country[145]
- The 2017 "NotPetya" attack initially targeted at the electrical grid and other elements of infrastructure within Ukraine, whose spillover effects caused damages estimated at US$10 billion at companies such as Merck, Maersk, TNT Express, Saint-Gobain, and Mondelez[146].

Groups working within several countries, often with at least semi-official support from their governments, have been identified as responsible for attacks such as the ones listed. These countries include the United States, Israel, Iran, China, Russia, and North Korea[147].

In some cases, hacks have been found to have been in place for several years prior to their discovery. In other cases, victims of malware have kept secret the fact that their systems have been compromised. It's probable that the damage actually caused by malware and cyberhacking considerably exceeds the amount that has been publicly disclosed. It's also reasonable to expect that malware and cyberhacking will increase in power and sophistication in the years ahead:

- Attackers stand to make large gains, due to scale effects of the software they deploy
- Attackers may believe their exploits will escape detection, or that no trace back to them can be established.

Indeed, a number of factors have recently increased the risks of serious harm arising from infotech malware:

1. The widespread adoption of "Internet of Things" devices with poor security – including systems for heating and air conditioning, home monitoring, connected printers, smart TVs, domestic appliances, meters to allow remote control of gas and electricity, clothing with embedded electronics, and numerous entertainment gadgets
2. The possibilities afforded by untraceable cryptocurrencies to encourage hackers to demand ransom payment from victims whose devices have suffered a malware attack
3. A booming underground community that makes available "malware for service" tools that enable more people to try their hand developing and deploying malware
4. Large groups within many countries, funded directly or indirectly by governments, that develop spyware weapons with a view to penetrating and damaging systems of potential adversaries
5. Leakage of at least some elements of these weapons to even shadier groups, who sometimes succeed in detecting and observing spyware as it operates, and reverse-engineering it, so they can copy its capabilities into their own systems
6. Fierce competition, not only between "black hackers" and "white hackers" – that is, between those broadly opposed to the rule of law and those broadly in support of it – but also between different rival groups of "black hackers" who are struggling for domination; this competition fuels innovation, and hence the creation of yet more powerful malware

7. The incorporation into malware systems of sophisticated psychological knowledge about how to manipulate individual humans into inadvertently revealing passwords or other personal information
8. Widespread availability of powerful hardware at comparatively low cost, enabling more people to experiment with new software more quickly
9. Increasing availability of AI modules that can add to the sophistication and power of malware.

Financial instabilities

It's one thing to switch on your computer and discover that all your email has vanished, or that you cannot log into your favourite sites. It's another thing to discover that there's much less money in your bank accounts than you expected, or that the money in question has plunged in value due to some kind of inflation or devaluation.

In some cases, financial losses arise from hacks of the sort mentioned in the previous section. Various sorts of miscreants can find their way into our financial systems, when we disclose information inappropriately, or when that information is part of a third-party data breach, such as at Equifax or Aadhaar. Then they remove our money.

But in other cases, financial losses arise from volatilities within complex networks of financial connections and political interactions.

Consider the drop in the value of savings held in Venezuela in the national currency, the bolivar. According to figures released by the Central Bank of Venezuela[148], the average annual rate of inflation in that country was 274% in 2016, 863% in 2017, and over 130,060% in 2018. That means savings lost more than 2/3 of their value during 2016, around 9/10 of their remaining value during 2017, and more than 99.9% of that remaining value during 2018. Ouch! (External estimates, such as by the International Monetary Fund, have even higher figures for Venezuelan inflation[149].)

The financial woes of citizens in Venezuela were, for a while, exceeded by those of citizens in Zimbabwe a few years earlier, when that country also experienced hyperinflation[150], reaching a *daily* inflation rate of 98% in November 2008.

It may be tempting to assert that the monetary problems in Venezuela and Zimbabwe are due to uniquely troubled political circumstances, and that the financial wellbeing of the majority of people in the future will be nothing like as volatile. However, a number of historical trends should be noted:

1. Financial systems regularly increase in complexity, as a result of innovations in accounting, banking, investing, insurance, currencies, and so on
2. Periods of relative financial stability and growth are accompanied by grand claims that there are good *theoretical* grounds for that stability and growth to continue: compared to earlier times, there are (it is asserted) wiser, better informed people managing our accounts, banks, investments, and so on
3. Nevertheless, each period of relative financial stability and growth in due course encounters a dramatic shock or collapse
4. The eventual collapse is often due to *different* factors than the ones from earlier periods; it arises from *new sets of connections* that were insufficiently understood.

Examples of claims that enthusiasts have made, when economies were in times of apparent boom, include "You've never had it so good", "From this point on, house prices will always rise, and never fall", and "We're now in the period of the great moderation". When their attention is drawn to prior periods of unwarranted overconfidence, the enthusiasts have one more claim: "This time is different".

That last phrase was selected by economists Carmen Reinhart and Kenneth Rogoff for the title of their 2009 book chronicling what they describe as "Eight centuries of financial folly": *This time is different*[151]. Well, yes, each time tends to lead to a different kind of financial crash.

Claims made just ahead of the Wall Street Crash of 1929 are particularly stunning[152]. One advertisement placed in New York's *Saturday Evening Post* by a long-forgotten company called Standard Statistics referred back to an earlier financial debacle – the collapse in 1720 of the Mississippi Company, which turned many investors in France from millionaires to paupers[153]. With modern methods, asserted Standard Statistics, there was no need to worry about any similar developments[154]:

> History sometimes repeats itself – but not invariably. In 1719 there was practically no way of finding out the facts about the Mississippi venture. How different the position of the investor in 1929!
>
> Today, it is inexcusable to buy a "bubble" – inexcusable because unnecessary. For now every investor – whether his capital consists of a few thousand or mounts into the millions – has at his disposal facilities for obtaining the facts. Facts which – as far as is humanly possible – eliminate the hazards of speculation and substitute in their place sound principles of investment.

Sadly, within just one month of that advertisement, formerly "sound principles of investment" had been shown to be flawed. A number of investors and bankers were so distressed that they killed themselves – by jumping from the upper floors of skyscrapers, asphyxiating themselves with kitchen gas, dousing themselves with gasoline and burning to death, self-inflicted gunshot, or drinking poison[155]. In the long financial depression that followed, the lives of millions of ordinary citizens became bitterly hard. Forget "You've never had it so good".

Claims made by apparent experts in economics before the global credit crunch of 2008 turned out to be equally unfounded. Witness this rash assertion by Economics Nobel Prize laureate Robert Lucas of the University of Chicago, in his presidential address in 2003 to the American Economic Association[156]:

> Macroeconomics was born as a distinct field in the 1940's, as a part of the intellectual response to the Great Depression. The term then referred to the body of knowledge and expertise that we hoped would prevent the recurrence of that economic disaster. My thesis in this lecture is that macroeconomics in this original sense has succeeded: Its central problem of depression prevention has been solved, for all practical purposes…

In April 2007, the chief economist at the International Monetary Fund (IMF), Simon Johnson, gave a glowing assessment of the world's economic situation[157]: "Overall risks to the outlook seem less threatening than six months ago… By and large, things look very good." Any risks from a growing wave of defaults in the US subprime mortgage market could be "withstood". Accordingly, the IMF predicted that the world economy would grow by 4.9% in 2007 and by another 4.9% in 2008.

As it happened, the forecast for 2007 was relatively close to the actual figure[158] of 4.3%. However, the growth was reduced to 1.9% in 2008, and to negative 1.7% in 2009.

As late as May 2008. Mervyn King, the governor of the Bank of England, remained bullish[159]:

> It's quite possible that at some point we may get an odd quarter or two of negative growth. But recession is not the central projection at all.

Oops. The UK economy actually shrunk for *five quarters* in a row (a recession requires only two quarters of shrinkage), and took five *years* to recover to its previous value[160]. Moreover, the fallout from the 2008 crash could have been even more drastic, were it not for exceptional actions taken by political leaders in response to the crisis.

So much for the past. What about the future?

Sadly, many potential financial hazards lurk ahead:

1. Tensions in the Eurozone: economists from diverse backgrounds – for example, Nobel laureate Paul Stiglitz[161], former Bank of England governor Mervyn King[162], and former Greek Finance Minister Yanis Varoufakis[163] – share a strong apprehension about deep-seated flaws in the design of the Euro
2. Potential new "weapons of mass financial destruction": clever bankers continue, perhaps *too* cleverly, to devise alternatives to the alphabet soup of complex financial products whose hidden interconnections hugely magnified the adverse impacts of the 2008 crash
3. Unwinding of financial regulations: various governments, under pressure from ideologues opposed to public oversight of private innovation, have relaxed the regulations put in place after the 2008 crash, increasing the likelihood of new financial misadventures
4. Growth of private debt: as economist Steve Keen has pointed out[164], financial crises tend to occur when one ratio rises, namely the ratio of private debt (money owed by individuals and businesses) to GDP (the overall size of the economy): money that is needed to cover interest payments depresses the overall economic activity unless even more loans are obtained; however, this ratio has recently reached worrying levels in dozens of countries around the world[165]

5. Chinese economic instability: as a special case of the preceding point, levels of indebtedness have risen to unprecedented levels in China[166]; coupled with the general lack of transparency into the performance of China's economy, and limited scope for independent political analysis within the country, this raises the risk of unexpected downturns, impacting the economy not just in China but worldwide[167].

Adding to the pressure, several of the above risk factors could be exacerbated by adoption of newer technology. This includes:

- Financial trading driven by superfast artificial intelligence but prone to poorly understood "flash crash" events[168]
- New coordination mechanisms involving crypto tokens and blockchain distributed ledgers, but which are vulnerable to overconfidence, scams, crashes, and general chaos[169].

Now imagine if hundreds of millions of people come to believe, at some point in the next few years, that the lion's share of their wealth has been destroyed as a result of financial chicanery – that their new-found poverty was caused by deception and subterfuge by members of a small elite that appear to be thriving economically despite the general downturn. The dispossessed will swell the ranks of what I called, earlier in this chapter, the "left behinds".

As noted earlier, some of the left behinds will suffer quietly, but others are likely to become more determined to exact a gruesome revenge upon elements of the global society that apparently sat back passively and allowed a terrible new financial crash to occur. It won't be pretty.

Environmental instabilities

Alongside the risk of growing financial instability, we should also bear in mind the risk of growing environmental instability.

Human technological inventions have a long history of changing the environment in more ways than were originally intended or foreseen. Consider the fight to overcome the disease typhus.

For hundreds of years, typhus was a feared companion of warfare[170]. Seventeen thousand soldiers out of a Spanish army of twenty-five thousand succumbed to an outbreak near Grenada in 1489. In 1527, twenty-five thousand French soldiers, out of an army of thirty-five thousand besieging

Naples, died of the disease. Some thirty thousand Prussian soldiers died of typhus during the 1741 siege of Prague. By the time Napoleon assembled his "Grand Armée" of six hundred thousand troops to invade Russia in 1812, the risks of typhus were well known. But in what we can call an act of excessively bad foresight, Napoleon seemed to be convinced his army was invincible. He ignored advice from his chief surgeon and various military commanders to delay the attack until the spring. His army was routed by a combination of extreme cold, broken supply lines, rear-guard actions from Russian forces, dysentery, and, yes, typhus. Only twenty thousand of the Grand Armée made it back to France. Typhus is thought to have killed more than half of the army. More than two hundred thousand additional French soldiers died of typhus in Western Europe in the following year, 1813. That's why it may be said that typhus was a major contributor to Napoleon's ultimate downfall.

The same miserable pattern continued until the Second World War. Two notable victims of typhus in that war were the diarist Anne Frank and her sister Margot, in literally sickening conditions in the Bergen-Belsen concentration camp[171]. In October 1943, another outbreak of the disease in Naples threatened not only the local population but also the Allied Forces that were making their way north through Italy. But this time, the army could deploy an experimental new technology: a spray containing the chemical DDT. This killed the body lice that carried the disease from person to person. The experiment was a resounding success: a few months later, the outbreak was over.

The same spray was also found to be effective at killing the mosquitoes that spread malaria. British Prime Minister Winston Churchill expressed his enthusiasm for the new treatment in a radio broadcast in September 1944[172]:

> The excellent DDT powder which had been fully experimented with and found to yield astonishing results will henceforth be used on a great scale by the British forces in Burma and by the American and Australian forces in the Pacific and India in all theatres.

As another sign of the high regard in which DDT was held, the chemist who had discovered its insecticidal properties, Paul Müller from Switzerland, was awarded the Nobel Prize for Medicine in 1948[173]. The prize was in recognition of "his discovery of the high efficiency of DDT as a contact poison against several arthropods".

However, a note added later by the Nobel Prize organisation highlighted an issue that had subsequently became apparent:

> It would turn out, however, that DDT had serious after effects. It became concentrated in the food chain and injured other animals and people.

Indeed, side-effects of the use of this so-called "magic poison"[174] include:

- The thinning of bird egg shells, leading in turn to a marked decline in populations of species such as the osprey, the bald eagle, the peregrine falcon, and the brown pelican[175]
- An increase in human male infertility[176]
- Increased miscarriages of human babies[177]
- The greater likelihood of various cancers, including testicular cancer[178] and breast cancer[179].

In this way, DDT follows a pattern that many other technological interventions also observe:

- There are both upsides and downsides of its use
- The downsides are often not obvious in advance
- People with various ideological axes to grind – including people hostile to large businesses, as well as committed supporters of various businesses who object as a matter of principle to government regulatory intervention – often clash over which pieces of apparent evidence are most reliable.

Consider CFCs (chlorofluorocarbons), the chemicals formerly used in many refrigerators and as propellants in aerosol cans. When first introduced in the 1930s, CFCs, a bit like DDT a decade later, were hailed as wonder chemicals. They were *far* safer than the chemicals which had previously been used for the same purposes: these earlier chemicals were both toxic and flammable. The inventors of CFCs received numerous prizes and accolades[180].

But, like DDT, CFCs started showing up in unexpected places in the environment. For CFCs, the location in question was high up in the stratosphere.

An appreciation of the adverse side effects of CFCs needed to wait for the invention of a detector sensitive enough to discern their presence even at very low densities. British scientist James Lovelock created such a device in the 1950s, initially for a very different purpose, but used it in the 1960s and 1970s to find CFCs all over the atmosphere. At first Lovelock was unworried by his findings: these chemicals were almost inert, that is, they would hardly take part in reactions. "The presence of these compounds constitutes no conceivable hazard", he wrote[181]. Years later, Lovelock acknowledged that "this sentence has turned out to be one of my greatest blunders".

This is an example of another pattern with the impact of technology on the environment: *the impacts often arise via unexpected mechanisms*. For CFCs, the damage took place only once these molecules had risen high into the stratosphere where they were struck by UV (ultraviolet) radiation, splitting off chlorine atoms. The chlorine atoms would then react in turn with the ozone also present at that level, triggering a chain reaction. Given that the layer of ozone prevented UV radiation from penetrating closer to the earth, the destruction of ozone could in principle lead to more cases of skin cancer among the humans dwelling miles below the atmosphere. That was the theory advanced by chemists Mario Molina and Sherwood Rowland in 1973 – work for which the pair were to earn a share of the Nobel Prize for Chemistry in 1995[182].

Once again, the case of CFCs illustrates a common pattern: many industrialists who were involved in the creation and distribution of CFCs contested the idea that their product posed a real risk. The mechanism proposed by Molina and Sherwood was speculative, whereas the many benefits of CFCs were clear and unambiguous. Even James Lovelock spoke out in defence of CFCs, testifying to the US Congress in support of chemical megacompany DuPont. Humans would cope well enough with a small increase in the amount of UV radiation reaching the earth's surface, Lovelock asserted.

What changed matters was the publication in Nature in 1985 of an article[183] by Joseph Farman and his colleagues at the British Antarctic Survey. The article reviewed data that showed that a surprisingly large hole had been developing in the ozone layer above Antarctica since around 1960[184]. Unless urgent action was taken, the hole would grow and grow, leading to a very considerable increase in UV radiation.

Politicians around the world were galvanised – helped in part by the understanding of chemistry brought to the matter by the British Prime Minister Margaret Thatcher, whose first degree was in that subject. Within two years, an international agreement known as the Montreal protocol committed to phasing out CFCs. The success of the protocol arose from the fact that alternatives to CFCs could be introduced in their place in refrigerators and aerosols. The chemical companies who at first protested that no such alternatives existed did manage to design alternatives in due course[185]. DuPont, the producer of more CFCs than any other company, flipped from demanding continued usage of CFCs to urging US President George HW Bush to champion the protocol[186].

One response to the examples of DDT and CFCs would be to observe that usage of the chemicals in question were reduced before any lasting planet-wide damage was done (although many individuals may have died). It may seem that humanity has a good track record of finding safer alternatives and putting them in place, despite some initial prevarications. A combination of engineers and entrepreneurs, guided by an overall direction established by political leaders, can design innovative solutions.

However, it would be another case of *bad foresight* to extrapolate that observation to cover all other cases when human actions are damaging the environment. Factors that can make it harder to respond in sufficient time to an emerging threat include:

1. The damage becoming more widespread and more deeply rooted before it is properly noticed
2. Analysis of the biochemical or geophysical mechanisms being less certain, with multiple conflicting theories each having some plausibility
3. Lack of comprehensive alternatives to the chemical compounds or human practices that are causing the damage
4. Politicians without any true understanding of the problem domain, who just give the matter lip service before turning their attention elsewhere
5. Business corporations wedded to current practice, that powerfully exert themselves to throw doubt on various scientific findings or to cover up awkward data points
6. Campaigning groups who noisily promote unrealistic "solutions" that have no real chance of being adopted, and which cause the rest of society to prefer to disengage from the issue
7. Feedback cycles that can accelerate problems faster than was anticipated.

Consider the way in which microplastics – tiny pieces of plastic with diameters smaller than 5 millimetres – have become widespread throughout biological systems. These microscopic particles arise from the breakdown of larger pieces of plastic waste, from fibres in waste water from laundry machines, from specks of material from car tyres, and much more besides[187]. How much harm will these microplastics cause? It seems it's too early to say[188]. There are concerns that, in oceans, populations of small fish will dwindle, which will in consequence have implications for populations of larger fish[189]. There are other concerns about damage to soil[190]. The risk is that the huge quantities of plastic already in use around the world will lead to a further accumulation of microplastics.

Along with "organic pollutants, radioactive materials, and nanomaterials", microplastics form part of a grouping described by the Stockholm Resilience Centre as "novel entities" whose accumulation over time has the potential to tip the overall network of the earth's environmental systems into a state significantly less hospitable for humans[191]. This grouping is in turn one of "Nine Planetary Boundaries" each of which has the potential to destabilise key aspects of the environment. Will Steffen, a contributor to the Stockholm Resilience Centre based in Canberra, Australia, puts it like this[192]:

> Transgressing a boundary increases the risk that human activities could inadvertently drive the Earth System into a much less hospitable state, damaging efforts to reduce poverty and leading to a deterioration of human wellbeing in many parts of the world, including wealthy countries.

Reviewing the situation in 2015, a report from the Centre assessed that four of the nine boundaries may already have been crossed: "climate change, loss of biosphere integrity, land-system change, and altered biogeochemical cycles (phosphorus and nitrogen)." Whilst the report contained positive assessments for several other boundaries – including stratospheric ozone depletion – yet others, including introduction of the "novel elements" mentioned above, were deemed as insufficiently understood to warrant any clear evaluation.

The case of climate change is particularly contentious. Broadly, four attitudes exist toward this issue:

1. The problem has been overblown[193] by people with various ulterior motives – such as climate scientists who are seeking funding for their research projects, or Chinese politicians who wish to cripple western

industry. Recently observed variations in weather are nothing out of the ordinary. There's no need to worry unduly about greenhouse gases. Society should invest more in improving the resilience of buildings and in defences against occasional storms and flood surges.

2. The problem is real, but humanity will have plenty of time in the decades ahead to introduce alternatives to industrial practices and energy usage patterns which are presently causing an accumulation of greenhouse gases in the environment[194]. Something similar to the replacement of CFCs will happen with greenhouse gases.
3. The problem is real and there are risks of it accelerating, via feedback mechanisms[195]. These mechanisms mean that humanity may have less time than expected to prepare good solutions. Accordingly, a renewed major focus on this issue is needed as a matter of priority.
4. The problem is so bad that there are no solutions available. The end is at hand of human civilisation as we know it[196]. Like someone with a fatal illness calming themselves ahead of their death, we humans should be grateful for our history, and compose a requiem for ourselves[197].

My own view is squarely in the third of these categories. Just like the hole in the ozone layer involved a self-perpetuating accelerating cycle – less ozone means less protection against UV radiation, which means more CFC molecules split up, which means less ozone – so also are there a number of feedback mechanisms whereby higher temperatures can cause environmental changes that will in turn cause yet higher rises in temperature.

A review article in Nature in 2019 gave this summary, under the ominous title "Climate tipping points – too risky to bet against"[198]:

> Politicians, economists and even some natural scientists have tended to assume that tipping points in the Earth system – such as the loss of the Amazon rainforest or the West Antarctic ice sheet – are of low probability and little understood. Yet evidence is mounting that these events could be more likely than was thought, have high impacts and are interconnected across different biophysical systems, potentially committing the world to long-term irreversible changes.

Once a tipping point is passed, the earth's average temperature could rise by several degrees in a matter of a few decades. Such changes actually took place a number of times – perhaps as many as 25 times – during the last ice age, from around 120 thousand to 11 thousand years ago. Known as Dansgaard–Oeschger (D–O) events[199], after the pair of scientists who first deduced their existence, these events several times involved an upward temperature spike of 5°C within 30-40 years, and in one case a jump of 8°C in 40 years.

In such an event, extremes of weather are likely to become much more common: floods, droughts, hurricanes, heatwaves, and wildfires, unprecedented in their ferocity in all of recorded human history.

Researchers who have studied the various mass extinction events in geological history bring to our attention an even starker concern about rapid climate change. Peter Ward, professor of geological sciences at University of Washington, put it like this in his 2007 book *Under a Green Sky*[200]:

> It's pretty clear that times of high carbon dioxide – and especially times when carbon dioxide levels rapidly rose – coincided with the mass extinctions. Here is the driver of extinction. Here is the cause of the changes in the ancient conveyer belts: short-term warming caused by increases in greenhouse gases.

Bringing the field up to date, with his review of the circumstances behind each of the five mass extinctions, *The Ends of the World*[201], science journalist Peter Brannen offers this summary[202]:

> This is the revelation of geology in recent years that presents the most worrying prospect for modern society. The five worst episodes in earth history have all been associated with violent changes to the planet's carbon cycle... Our current experiment – quickly injecting huge amounts of carbon dioxide into the atmosphere – has in fact been run many times before in the geological past, and it never ends well.

It's very hard to give any kind of objective figure for the probability of runaway climate change being triggered in the next few decades. It's probably considerably under one in ten. But that's no reason to divert our attention from the prospect. Most of us would turn back from an airplane jetty if told there was a one in a hundred chance the craft we are about to board would disintegrate whilst midway over the Atlantic. We would look to change our plans, regardless of how much inconvenience that involved.

Democracy under threat

What's the most dangerous technology ever invented? Oil wells? Artificial Intelligence? Biotech? Nuclear weapons?

Anders Sandberg, Senior Researcher at the Future of Humanity Institute at Oxford, has suggested that the answer to this question should be government[203]. Government is able to organise huge resources in pursuit of its objectives. Governments that pursue bad objectives are, therefore, a dire threat to humanitarian wellbeing.

American sociologist Charles Tilly offered this aphorism[204]: "War made the state, and the state made war". The groups of people who were best able to resist attacks from neighbours, near or far, and to collectively hold onto their possessions, were those who coordinated themselves into entities we can call "states". Within their boundaries, these states could provide an element of peace and stability, under what emerged as "the rule of law". But relations *between* states could turn violent. And in such encounters, the total amount of violence inflicted far exceeded the ravages of the smaller, pre-state battles.

Human conduct has been bloody throughout all of history, but the sheer scale of bloodiness in the twentieth century exceeded that of previous times. Consider the state-sponsored genocides of eight hundred thousand Tutsi in Rwanda in 1994[205], one and a half million Armenians in Turkey during and after the first world war[206], two million Cambodians under Pol Pot in the late 1970s[207], six million Jews at the hands of the Nazis during the second world war[208], up to seven million Ukrainians in the deliberate "Holodomor" famines arising from Stalin's policies between 1932-33[209], and up to forty-five million Chinese citizens beaten, tortured, or starved to death during Mao Zedong's catastrophically misconceived "Great Leap Forward" initiative from 1958-62[210].

That last figure, in particular, bears repeating. It is comparable to the total number of people who died in the entire second world war. Indeed, there are grounds for asserting that Mao was responsible for more deaths than either Hitler or Stalin[211]. Yet the misdeeds of Hitler and Stalin are much better known.

It's similar to how the world has gradually woken up, over the last few years, to the fact that more people died in the 1918-20 H1N1 flu pandemic than in all the fighting of the first world war. Generations of school children grew up studying the poetry of war poets like Rupert Brooke and Siegfried Sassoon, or watching epic films such as *All Quiet on the Western Front*, but heard little about the outbreak of flu. Edmund Blackadder and his fictional colleagues spent the entirety of a season, *Blackadder Goes Forth*, highlighting aspects of the futility of that war, but avoided any mention of the pandemic. The horrors of that flu were suppressed from collective memory – probably contributing to our collective unpreparedness for new pandemics.

In the same way, the powers of unconstrained political leaders are, all too often, overlooked. Instead, more and more people seem to hanker after powerful, autocratic leaders with little democratic accountability. That line of thinking has a low opinion of mechanisms that can constrain the actions of the leaders of the state – mechanisms such as an independent judiciary making their own decisions, a free press that can offer criticism and suggest alternatives to government policy, opposition parties that can organise themselves around different sets of policies, and fair elections free from government interference.

It's as if the warning raised by nineteenth century historian and politician Lord Acton has been forgotten[212]:

> Power tends to corrupt and absolute power corrupts absolutely. Great men are almost always bad men.

When the electorate lose faith in the principles of democracy, they're more inclined to accept bad behaviour from the politicians that they deem as being on their side. If their favoured politicians speak untruthfully, that's no big deal, so long as their untruths cause inconvenience or annoyance to perceived opponents. If these politicians siphon public funds for their personal purposes, that's no big deal either, since whatever strengthens these politicians will benefit their shared causes. *Right?*

A vicious cycle can develop: if normal fair-play democracy seems not to be working, more people will be inclined to disregard previous standards, leading to a race to the bottom. It's no surprise that surveys of changing attitudes toward democracy show increasing dissatisfaction.

In January 2020, the Centre for the Future of Democracy, based in Cambridge UK, issued a report entitled *Global Satisfaction with Democracy*[213]. The report surveyed data from 25 different sources, covering some 50 years in Western Europe and 25 years for the rest of the world. Here are a number of the key findings:

> In the mid-1990s, a majority of citizens in countries for which we have time-series data – in North America, Latin America, Europe, Africa, the Middle East, Asia and Australasia – were satisfied with the performance of their

> democracies. Since then, the share of individuals who are "dissatisfied" with democracy has risen by around +10% points, from 47.9 to 57.5%.
>
> After a large increase in civic dissatisfaction in the prior decade, 2019 represents the highest level of democratic discontent on record.
>
> Many large democracies are at their highest-ever recorded level for democratic dissatisfaction. These include the United States, Brazil, Mexico, the United Kingdom, South Africa, Colombia, and Australia.

The landmine here is that, out of a frustration with the perceived poor performance of democratic processes, electors may be tempted to hand over more reins of power to someone they perceive as a "benign dictator" – giving that leader more autonomy to bend or ignore the usual rules of politics. That leader may well have some remarkable qualities, but the warning from Lord Acton applies: "Great men are almost always bad men." Without democratic checks on their power, their badness may come to dominate. And their greater power will lead to greater corruption.

This is not a matter of a politician becoming *too right wing* or *too left wing*. It's simply a matter of them gaining the ability to suppress criticism or opposition. This ability will be bolstered by use of new technology:

- Technology for detailed surveillance
- Technology to manipulate what people see and even what they think
- Technology to distract and confuse people
- Technology to initiate cross-border attacks.

Citizens that show signs of dissent may find themselves with fewer privileges, being denied access to financial credit, and with family members being harassed. It will be like a combination of the worst features from the epic dystopian novels *1984* and *Brave New World*.

Unconstrained by independently-minded advisors, these leaders could embark in dangerous sabre-rattling provocations against external states. That's how World War Three could start. Alternatively, the kinds of repressive actions they take against their own citizens could surpass even the horrors of Hitler's Holocaust, Stalin's Holodomor, and Mao's Great Leap Forward.

Cancers within society

Alongside the landmine of overly powerful political leaders who are unconstrained by democratic processes, we also need to consider the landmine of overly powerful corporations who are unconstrained by political oversight.

Corporations are set up to accumulate profits. What could go wrong with that? Corporations can only make profits if they're serving customer needs, right? According to this line of thinking, once a corporation no longer serves customer needs, they will start to decline, being overtaken by competitors that are more responsive to market requirements.

But there are several problems with this picture:

1. Would-be competitors may find themselves blocked from entering the market, by patent issues or other legal obstacles, or by being unfairly excluded from key supply lines, sales locations, or marketing opportunities
2. There may be adverse side-effects of the processes by which a company achieves a low price point: it may emit unseen pollution, or disregard the health and safety of its employees
3. Customers may keep on buying a product even though it is harmful to them, or in some other way a bad choice – on account of becoming addicted, or confused, or otherwise misled
4. Interference by industry regulators, or by their political overseers, may unfairly distort a market in favour of companies who are lining their pockets behind the scenes, or who are exerting various sorts of blackmail or other pressure
5. Corporations that gain their initial market successes from an initial admirable burst of innovation may subsequently hold onto their position by an exertion of market dominance, known as monopoly power, in which they suppress or damage competitive threats.

In summary, for the world of business, a version applies of the warning originally given by Lord Acton for the world of politics. The new version runs as follows. "Market power tends to corrupt and absolute market power corrupts absolutely. Great companies are almost always bad companies."

In politics, the set of democratic processes, when they work well, are meant to guard against the tendencies of both individuals and parties to seek to hold onto power and to abuse power. These processes are meant to stop great politicians from turning into bad politicians.

Likewise in business, the operation of a free market, when it works well, is meant to guard against the tendency of companies to abuse their market power. As a result, great companies should be prevented from turning into bad companies – or, if they do go bad, they should be displaced by better alternatives.

But in both cases, the system of checks and balances can fail. Indeed, the tendencies for markets to slip into failure modes has been long known to economists[214]. Taking appropriate action to counter these failures is one of the prime roles of the political system.

In broad terms, markets can fail in two ways.

First, markets can deliver on their own objectives, that is, to generate plenty of economic activity, but without meeting key needs necessary for human flourishing. For example, companies within the pharmaceutical industry are motivated to develop drugs for diseases afflicting large numbers of patients who have enough money to pay handsomely for these treatments. Diseases that afflict small numbers of patients, or whose victims are generally poor inhabitants of low-income countries, tend to be neglected. That's in line with the frank remarks by Bayer CEO Marijn Dekkers at a Financial Times event in 2013[215], about a drug they were selling:

> We did not develop this product for the Indian market, let's be honest. I mean, you know, we developed this product for Western patients who can afford this product.

It is for this reason that political bodies around the world have cooperated to set up and support organisations like DNDi – the Drugs for Neglected Diseases initiative – which has the following mission statement[216]:

> We discover, develop, and deliver treatments for neglected patients around the world. Our treatments are affordable and patient-friendly – and have already saved millions of lives.

Second, markets can fail even to deliver their own objectives. They can move into modes in which economic progress is *far* from optimal. For the kinds of reason already mentioned, the self-interest of the different groups in the market sometimes leads to a kind of mutual destruction, rather than to the marvellous positive cooperation described in the famous "Invisible hand" metaphor by Adam Smith[217]:

> It is not from the benevolence of the butcher, the brewer, or the baker that we expect our dinner, but from their regard to their own interest…
>
> He intends only his own gain, and he is in this, as in many other cases, led by an invisible hand to promote an end which was no part of his intention… By pursuing his own interest he frequently promotes that of the society more effectually than when he really intends to promote it.

One stunning admission that the theory of the invisible hand sometimes fails to apply can be seen in the remarks made at a US congressional hearing in 2008 by Alan Greenspan, who had been chair of the US Federal Reserve from 1987 to 2006. The hearing was exploring the causes of the ongoing global financial crisis. Greenspan made the following confession[218]:

> I have found a flaw. I don't know how significant or permanent it is. But I have been very distressed by that fact…
>
> I made a mistake in presuming that the self-interests of organisations, specifically banks and others, were such that they were best capable of protecting their own shareholders and their equity in the firms.

It's an open question as to how often, and in what ways, governments and regulators should intervene to steer or constrain the self-interested operation of corporations or other entities. What is *not* in any serious question is that this kind of intervention is necessary at least occasionally.

As it happens, Adam Smith himself, in the very same book that introduced the idea of the invisible hand, also warned against the dangers of collusion between tradespeople:

> People of the same trade seldom meet together, even for merriment and diversion, but the conversation ends in a conspiracy against the public, or in some contrivance to raise prices.

For a fuller reading of Adam Smith, we can refer to the recent book *Adam Smith: What He Thought, and Why it Matters*[219] by UK Conservative MP Jesse Norman – who holds at time of writing the role of Financial Secretary to the Treasury[220]. Here's the summary from the book front matter[221]:

> Far from being simply an economist, Adam Smith emerges as one of the founders of modern social psychology and behavioural theory. Far from being a doctrinaire 'libertarian' or 'neoliberal' thinker, he offers a strikingly modern evolutionary theory of political economy, which recognises the often complementary roles of markets and the state.

And from inside Norman's book:

> Markets typically need the active cooperation of the state… to secure the rights, access, and interconnectivity for them to succeed.

When the state falls short in its duty to support and secure markets, markets can become dysfunctional, with once-great companies behaving increasingly badly. That's what happened in the lead-up to the 2008 financial crisis, in which financial institutions gambled recklessly – though probably without appreciating the extent of their recklessness – with complex new financial instruments that were poorly understood. That gambling was facilitated by governments having too little awareness of what was actually happening in the banking sector.

Lack of adequate government regulation of the fossil fuel industry has led, in a similar way, to what Sir Nicholas Stern, chief economist for the World Bank, called in 2006 "the greatest market failure the world has seen"[222]:

> The science has been our starting point. It shapes the economics. The science tells us that GHG [greenhouse gas] emissions are an externality; in other words, our emissions affect the lives of others. When people do not pay for the consequences of their actions we have market failure. This is the greatest market failure the world has seen. It is an externality that goes beyond those of ordinary congestion or pollution, although many of the same economic principles apply for its analysis.

The occasion for Stern's remarks was the launch of a 700-page report commissioned by the UK government into the economic aspects of global warming[223]. In his remarks, Stern went on to urge three policy initiatives to address this market dysfunction:

> First, we must establish a carbon price via tax, trade and regulation – without this price there is no incentive to decarbonise. Second, we must promote technology: through research and development… And third we must deal with market failure; for example problems in property and capital markets inhibit investments for energy-efficiency.

However, in the years since the Stern report was published, comparatively little progress has been made with these policy initiatives. In part, this is due to the international nature of this particular market failure. Fossil fuel corporations operate in multiple geographic jurisdictions; political responses to these corporations need, therefore, at least some elements of global coordination. I'll have more to say about that subject shortly.

Other cases of market failures perpetuated by dysfunctional political oversight have a more local nature: consider the huge costs of healthcare within the United States[224], bearing in mind the poor health outcomes in that country relative to other OECD nations[225].

The real landmine here is that some corporations are potentially becoming more powerful than ever. The problems caused by Big Finance (banking crises), Big Oil (global warming), and Big Healthcare (escalating costs without improving results), may pale in comparison to problems arising from dominance by Big Tech – the providers of the infrastructure for our social media, emails, websites, and so on.

To be clear, the companies in "Big Tech" – like those in Big Finance, Big Oil, and Big Healthcare – do provide many valuable services to people around the world. The risk, however, is with the dark underside of these services:

- Observation of people's habits (and some of their deepest secrets) by pervasive surveillance
- Manipulation of people's views by the social media they experience
- Infestation of normal thinking processes by psychological malware, also known as "fake news" and "conspiracy theories"
- Segregation of people into groups that come to perceive each other as hateful rivals who deserve to be bitterly opposed.

This risk is increased when the services provided by Big Tech are utilised by specific sectors in society, including the military, press barons, crime syndicates, the secret police, and rogue political operators. The worst combination of all may be government "Big Brother" in a shadowy partnership with Big Tech.

To recap: a healthy society involves a rich set of relationships between the different members and groups in the society. It's like the rich relationships between the different organs and subsystems of a biological animal. In each case, the overall health of the larger body is endangered when a component part takes too large a proportion of the resources available. In the biological case, we call the dysfunction a "cancer": normal limits to growth are overridden, and malignant cells reproduce uncontrollably. If the cancer cannot be cured, the overall body sooner or later has its life extinguished. Human society is vulnerable in the same way to subgroups growing disproportionately powerful and eventually destroying the health of the society – or of the environment in which the society is located.

Subgroups of society with the potential of seizing too many resources are sometimes called "complexes". This was the term used by Dwight Eisenhower in his farewell address in January 1961 at the end of his period as US President. Eisenhower drew attention to the risks of what he called "the military-industrial complex"[226]:

> In the councils of government, we must guard against the acquisition of unwarranted influence, whether sought or unsought, by the military-industrial complex. The potential for the disastrous rise of misplaced power exists and will persist.

As a distinguished former military leader – he had overseen the Allied D-Day landings – Eisenhower possessed keen insight into the ways this new complex could operate. The complex was something the American nation needed, but it had to be kept under democratic supervision, despite its inherent tendency to grow:

> Until the latest of our world conflicts, the United States had no armaments industry. American makers of ploughshares could, with time and as required, make swords as well. But now we can no longer risk emergency improvisation of national defence; we have been compelled to create a permanent armaments industry of vast proportions. Added to this, three and a half million men and women are directly engaged in the defence establishment. We annually spend on military security more than the net income of all United States corporations.
>
> This conjunction of an immense military establishment and a large arms industry is new in the American experience. The total influence – economic, political, even spiritual – is felt in every city, every Statehouse, every office of the Federal government. We recognize the imperative need for this development. Yet we must not fail to comprehend its grave implications.

Eisenhower advocated maintaining a balanced relationship, supported by careful observation:

> We must never let the weight of this combination endanger our liberties or democratic processes. We should take nothing for granted. Only an alert and knowledgeable citizenry can compel the proper meshing of the huge industrial and military machinery of defence with our peaceful methods and goals, so that security and liberty may prosper together.

The military-industrial complex is by no means unique as a potentially cancerous subgroup of society. We can point to similar dangers posed by what can be called the carbon-energy-industrial complex, the financial-industrial complex, the information technology complex, the medical-industrial complex, and, indeed, the political complex.

In all these cases, the goals of the complex are only weakly aligned with the goals of society as a whole. Without democratic vigilance and occasional incisive action, the complex might grow so powerful that it can no longer be controlled – especially if it bolsters itself by adroit use of emerging new technologies.

Reason under threat

To keep track of risks posed by various landmines – and to devise and implement sensible proactive policies in response to these threats – one key skill is supremely important: the ability to think clearly.

If minds are full of misinformation that is held too tightly, without scope for revision, we will fail to recognise the threats in sufficient time. And we might adopt foolish policies in mistaken attempts to defuse the situation. Rather than solving matters, our would-be cures might make the disease even worse.

Accordingly, the growth of irrationality acts as a kind of meta-landmine. The greater the extent of societal irrationality, the greater the likelihood of us stumbling into one of the other landmines and triggering a catastrophic explosion.

This irrationality operates at two levels. First, there's a background level of inability to clearly see and evaluate disruptive future possibilities – an inability which has persisted throughout human history, and which has deep roots in aspects of human nature. That's the subject of the next chapter, "Shortsight".

But second, there's been a surge of irrationality in our present time, taking it to a more dangerous scale than has usually operated. That's what I want to talk about now. It's the growth in popularity of bizarre theories such as[227]:

- The earth being flat
- The moon landings being faked

- Vaccination programmes being a cover for injecting everyone on the planet with a microchip
- Cures for cancer being suppressed
- Leading politicians capturing young children to drink their blood
- Royalty and senior bankers actually being lizards disguised as humans
- The 9/11 attacks being an inside job carried out by members of a "deep state" shadow regime
- Former US first lady Michelle Obama secretly being a man
- Mass-shootings such as the one at Sandy Hook Elementary School being faked by groups of trained "crisis actors" in order to discredit the right to carry guns.

The Internet used to be hailed as a prelude to everyone becoming more knowledgeable. Information would be freely available around the planet. Back in 2012, X-Prize founder Peter Diamandis offered the following striking comparison[228]:

> A Maasai tribesman in Kenya today has better mobile communications than President Reagan had 25 years ago. If they're on a smartphone, they have access to more information than President Clinton did 15 years ago. Their Google is as good as [Google founder] Larry Page's.

But since that time, it has become clear that the Internet can spread misinformation at least as easily as it can spread information. The consequences of this misinformation can be horrific.

In 2016, messages on Facebook in Myanmar whipped up hatred by the majority Buddhist population against the minority Moslem Rohingya people. These messages included graphic made-up reports of a Moslem man raping a Buddhist woman, as well as numerous inflammatory distortions of Moslem culture[229]. The result has been called genocide: at least 10,000 Rohingya massacred, and an exodus of some 700,000 Rohingya out of the country. Investigation later showed that many of the messages had been carefully planted by members of the Myanmar military, masquerading as providers of beauty advice and fans of pop groups.

Also in 2016, various made-up harmful stories about Hillary Clinton originated in posts made by members of the Internet Research Agency (IRA) based in St Petersburg, Russia. Along with scurrilous references to Clinton's health, the posts alleged financial links between Clinton and ISIS, and that funds raised for the charitable Clinton Foundation were all spent by the Clintons themselves[230]. As in the case in Myanmar, the posts *appeared* to be made by ordinary citizens of the country concerned – the USA in this case. Numerous US media celebrities, politicians, and members of Donald Trump's election campaign, appear to have taken these posts at face value, not realising their true origin, and they shared them in turn with their own social media networks[231].

Why are some social media posts shared more often than others? Is it because of their inherent truthfulness? Sadly not. It's because they have, in one or other sense, *viral qualities*. Biological viruses spread, not because they benefit their hosts, but on the contrary, because they can hijack aspects of their host's biology. Similarly, psychological viruses spread, not because they make their hosts more knowledgeable, but because they can hijack aspects of their host's psychology.

For a simple case of a psychological virus, consider the "earworm" pieces of music that we find going round and round in our head. These earworms are frequently far from being our absolute favourite pieces of music. They thrive in our minds, not because of any musical profundity, but because of their catchiness.

Of course, there's nothing new about the spread of false information. The author Jonathan Swift lamented as far back as 1710 that "Falsehood flies, and the Truth comes limping after it"[232]. Swift wryly observed that even when people subsequently learn they have been deceived, it is often "too late": the falsehood has already altered their disposition and opinions. They may have altered their loyalties, without consciously realising the factor responsible for that change. As Swift remarked, "If a lie be believed only for an hour, it has done its work, and there is no further occasion for it."

What *is* new in the present time is:

1. The speed at which misinformation can travel – literally at the speed of light
2. Methods developed in the advertising industry, with its enormous resources – an industry that rewards some of the world's cleverest individuals with huge salaries if they find better ways to capture people's attention and change their inclination

3. A deeper understanding of how minds and brains work – and of how they can be misled
4. The ease with which people with an unusual idea can find like-minded individuals online, to reinforce each other's viewpoints, rather than dropping back to conformity with more conventional thinking.

Another important change from the past is the extent to which people are willing to believe that there can be "alternative facts of the matter". This is more than appreciation that there can be two sides to a story, or a dispute about what actually happened. It's a dispute about the reliability of purported independent fact checkers, a decline in respect for information published by mainstream newspapers, and, more generally, an increase in scepticism about the authority of purported experts.

Thus, if a medical doctor makes a statement about the efficacy of a drug, they're probably in the pay of the pharmaceutical company that manufactures the drug. If a climate scientist publishes an article about accelerating global warming, why, they're probably just doing it to assist their new grant application for more funding. And if an economist makes a forecast about an impending financial downturn, why, as in the words of British cabinet minister Michael Gove, "The people of this country have had enough of experts"[233]. If you don't like what an expert has to say, it's easy to conduct an online search to find another apparent expert who says the opposite thing. If you dislike the findings of one fact-checking site, you can find another one to back you up after all.

To be clear, by no means all misinformation originates in overseas troll factories such as the Kremlin's IRA. Much of it is home grown, from state-sponsored agencies as in Myanmar, or from numerous local groupings who are seeking to change the opinions and voting intentions of people in their own region.

Moreover, not all misinformation is deliberately created as a falsehood, with the intent to deceive. Much of it originates from people honestly thinking they have discovered something true yet hitherto underappreciated. Once they find supportive echoes online, they double down on their convictions. When they also receive pushback against their ideas, the wider network of conspiracy thinking comes to their aid: they can convince themselves that their critics lack sufficient awareness, have been subjected to some kind of "false consciousness", or are in some cases being deliberately deceptive.

It is vital to appreciate that people who adopt ideas that the rest of us would assess as utterly irrational aren't necessarily being stupid. Nor can their unusual beliefs be attributed simply to them hearing deviously ingenious arguments that have overwhelmed their critical faculties. No, there's something else going on. It's a prior experience of being victimised, or cheated, or left behind. It's their *correct* observation that, in some cases, elements of society *are* conspiring against them.

Writer and activist Cory Doctorow puts it like this[234]: it is "the trauma of living through real conspiracies all around us — conspiracies among wealthy people, their lobbyists, and lawmakers to bury inconvenient facts and evidence of wrongdoing" that makes people "vulnerable to conspiracy theories".

These real conspiracies, Doctorow reminds us, "are commonly known as 'corruption'".

The examples of irrationality which I listed earlier, such as believing the 9/11 attacks were an inside job, aren't too far removed, conceptually, from other beliefs that turned out to be "true conspiracies" – beliefs concerning events that were covered up for a period of time, but where light was eventually shone.

For example, the event that led the US to enter a full-scale war with North Vietnam, in August 1964, was a skirmish in the Gulf of Tonkin with some North Vietnamese patrol boats. Details of the interaction were deliberately exaggerated in a report of the incident on US television by President Lyndon Johnson. The US Congress quickly passed the Gulf of Tonkin Resolution, effectively giving the president a free hand in escalating the conflict. The degree of systematic falsification in the reporting only became clear in documents made public more than forty years later[235]. One of the pilots involved in the event, Navy Commander James Stockdale, had commented:

> We were about to launch a war under false pretenses, in the face of the on-scene military commander's advice to the contrary.

Twenty-five years earlier, in 1939, a group of elite officers of the German SS, operating under the direction of one of Adolf Hitler's right-hand men, Reinhard Heydrich, staged a number of "false flag" attacks on German properties, whilst disguised as Polish soldiers. This included briefly taking over a radio station at Gliwice, four miles inside the German border from Poland, and shouting some words in Polish over the airwaves[236]:

> Attention! This is Gliwice. The broadcasting station is in Polish hands.

Within hours, the BBC had broadcast news of the incident:

> There have been reports of an attack on a radio station in Gliwice…
>
> Poles forced their way into the studio and began broadcasting a statement in Polish. Within a quarter of an hour, say reports, the Poles were overpowered by German police who opened fire on them. Several of the Poles were reported killed but the numbers are not yet known.

Just as the Tonkin Gulf incident provided the justification for US attacks in North Vietnam, this Gliwice incident provided Hitler with a ready-made excuse to roll his tanks into Poland. World War Two started the very next day.

A full list of "true conspiracies" would be very long indeed. Even longer is the set of incidents where the truth is still hotly debated, with serious historians reaching opposing conclusions.

Couple this with the fact that so-called experts often do make claims with more authority than the science of the matter justifies – claims which are subsequently found to be false. Serious geologists long ridiculed the plate tectonics theory that continents changed their position over millions of years[237]. Albert Einstein, along with many esteemed physicist colleagues, flatly rejected the possibility of obtaining practical amounts of energy from nuclear reactions[238]. Until Barry Marshall, at the time an obscure Australian doctor, conducted an experiment on himself, mainstream doctors were convinced that stomach ulcers were caused by stress; Marshall identified the bacteria *Helicobacter pylori* as a frequent cause too – with significantly easier treatment options[239]. And as mentioned earlier, economist forecasters have made numerous assertions which turned out to be wrong.

In short, there are plenty of reasons for people to feel suspicious of statements from apparent experts who criticise their viewpoints – plenty of reasons for people to feel justified in persisting with what others would call irrational conspiracy theories.

Such theories have the additional attraction of offering some psychological comfort: people who believe in such a theory can see themselves as uniquely privileged. It's like a religious community which perceives themselves as belonging to an "elect" group with special divine sanction – like the adepts of an esoteric initiation rite, who have glimpsed knowledge hidden from the rest of society. It makes believers feel special. In a time when so many are feeling left behind, it's no surprise that such knowledge has strong allure. To rephrase Karl Marx's famous aphorism about religion[240]: conspiracy theories are the sigh of the oppressed creature, the heart of a heartless world, and the soul of soulless conditions.

Indeed, recent research has highlighted a correlation between the prevalence of conspiracy theories and times of stressful societal change. Jan-Willem van Prooijen of VU Amsterdam and Karen Douglas of the University of Kent provide the following summary[241]:

> Societal crisis situations – defined as impactful and rapid societal change that calls established power structures, norms of conduct, or even the existence of specific people or groups into question – have stimulated belief in conspiracy theories… Evidence suggests that the aversive feelings that people experience when in crisis – fear, uncertainty, and the feeling of being out of control – stimulate a motivation to make sense of the situation, increasing the likelihood of perceiving conspiracies in social situations.

Accordingly, there's a two-way relationship between this landmine – the growth of irrationality – and all the other ones. The greater stress arising from the set of landmines as a whole, operating sometimes consciously and sometimes subconsciously, generates greater irrationality, which makes it harder to address any of the landmines. Unfortunately, this is a vicious cycle.

Worse, it's a cycle that is accelerated by the various technological and social multipliers mentioned earlier: pervasive social media technology, manipulated by people well skilled in advertising techniques, who draw on the latest findings about how the mind and brain operate. Worse again, two other accelerators need to be mentioned:

1. The rise of the phenomenon of "conspiracy entrepreneurs"[242]: people who make money from websites, radio stations, or social media channels that publicise conspiracy theories; the entrepreneur often doesn't personally believe the theories being promoted[243], but hey, there's money to be made from advertising clicks or from the sales of loosely related products such as health drinks or massage oils
2. The unprecedented endorsement of various fringe conspiracy theories by elected politicians, via retweets and other shares, giving these theories greater visibility and apparent credibility[244].

And even worse, as we'll now explore, there's an international dimension that complicates matters yet further.

Divided nations

Consider again the notion of a meta-landmine: something that increases the difficulties in devising and implementing sensible policies in response to the other landmines. Growth in irrationality isn't the only meta-landmine. A rise in international conflict has the same effect.

An example of the distorting effect of international conflict briefly arose in the discussion in Chapter 1 about impediments to progress in South Africa in the 1980s and early 1990s. Most independent observers at that time understood that the ANC (African National Congress) needed to be part of any lasting political settlement in the country. However, the ANC had long links with the Soviet Union. A former president of the ANC, Josiah Gumede, had visited the Soviet Union in 1927. On his return to South Africa, he had enthused[245]:

> I have seen the world to come, where it has already begun. I have been to the new Jerusalem.

From the 1960s onward, the Soviet Union provided increasing amounts of funding, training, and equipment to the ANC. There was no secret as to where this relationship might lead. Soviet influence in nearby Angola was evident, with their funding and support for the MPLA (Popular Movement for the Liberation of Angola). In 1976 alone, 36,000 troops from Cuba, using weapons provided by the Soviet Union, fought in Angola on the side of the MPLA[246]. This was part of an overall estimated 65,000 Cubans spread over 17 African countries – mainly soldiers, but also including civilian advisors.

The context was the Cold War – a battle between two starkly different views as to how the world should operate. Should the world respect freedom of speech and a free market of business initiatives? Or is centralised state planning more important, along with constraints on independent political parties? This was no academic dispute. Many wars had been fought between representatives of these two viewpoints – in Korea, Vietnam, Indonesia, Greece, Central America, and, yes, throughout Africa. Soviet tanks had brutally suppressed uprisings in Hungary (1956) and Czechoslovakia (1968). American CIA involvement had helped to bring down the Marxist government of Salvador Allende in Chile (1973), precipitating an era of savage military repression in that country.

The Cold War backdrop turned many local issues into potential sparring points between the two superpowers and their allies. A solution that made good sense from an abstract point of view was a risky gamble if the opposing superpower could turn that solution to its advantage. Maintaining alliances with leaders of third world countries who were brutalising their own citizens, depriving them of basic human rights, was viewed as preferable to risking a transition to another local leader who might be under the influence of the other superpower.

That sentiment was expressed by Pulitzer Prize winning political columnist Charles Krauthammer in a retrospective article in 2002 asking "How did we win the cold war?"[247]:

> We fought and won the cold war, and thus liberated tens of millions of people, precisely because we prudently, albeit reluctantly, tolerated unfreedom in certain places. Why? In order to win the larger battle for freedom on the global scale.

The article celebrated the support provided by the United States to autocratic leaders in countries such as Pakistan, Egypt, Saudi Arabia, Chile, the Philippines, Iran, and South Vietnam. Krauthammer gave this justification:

> For all their faults, they were at the time better for their own people than those who would replace them…
>
> We often need such dictators to win the larger struggle against a global threat to liberty – Nazism, communism, Islamic radicalism.

Cold War 1.0 came to an end around 1991 in the wake of the transformation of the Soviet Union under Mikhail Gorbachev. For a while, the United States had a unique degree of power in the world. Political scientist Francis Fukuyama spoke for many when he predicted (as in the title of his 1992 book) "the end of history"[248]:

> What we may be witnessing is not just the end of the Cold War, or the passing of a particular period of post-war history, but the end of history as such: that is, the end point of mankind's ideological evolution and the universalization of Western liberal democracy as the final form of human government.

Another American writer, Thomas Friedman – who has won no less than three Pulitzer Prizes – offered two optimistic predictions about the future, each of which celebrated aspects of American culture. First, in 1996, he wrote that "No two countries that both have a McDonald's have ever fought a war against each other". This was part of what he dubbed his "Golden Arches Theory of Conflict Prevention"[249]:

> When a country reaches a certain level of economic development, when it has a middle class big enough to support a McDonald's, it becomes a McDonald's country, and people in McDonald's countries don't like to fight wars; they like to wait in line for burgers.

Then in 2005 in his book *The World Is Flat* Friedman presented his "Dell Theory of Conflict Prevention"[250], referring to the PC manufacturer:

> No two countries that are both part of a major global supply chain, like Dell's, will ever fight a war against each other as long as they are both part of the same global supply chain.

Sadly, both of these theories have been overtaken and disproven by subsequent events[251]. There has been no adoption of a single unified view of the world. Different regional powers have very different fundamental assumptions about the way to organise society. And these powers seem to be prepared to use various kinds of force to extend their influence:

- Globalisation and free trade, extolled in *The World Is Flat*, are now seen to have generated many losers as well as many winners, with the result that numerous politicians have backtracked on their previous enthusiasm for the globalisation project
- Democracy, likewise, has been seen to generate some highly troubled political leadership, with the result that many countries now look more favourably than before on various models of "illiberal democracy" or "strongman government".
- Although a blossoming friendship between Russia and the West had been anticipated in the wake of glasnost and perestroika, there's been a surge of mutual criticism, with sharply divergent views over a number of military or paramilitary interventions
- The apparent trajectory of China toward adopting the same democratic political model as the West – a trajectory expected at one time to be similar to its ongoing adoption of core aspects of the

market economy – has stalled, with a one-party system remaining firmly in place, and with dissident voices being persecuted

- Countries as varied as Iran, North Korea, Israel, India, Pakistan, and Saudi Arabia have powerful weapons at their disposal, and may be tempted to use some of them in response to stresses both outside and inside their borders.

The paradox of cooperation is that everyone can benefit from mutual constraint, but only so long as everyone is confident that no cheating will take place. Without agreement on limits to actions, a race to the bottom can develop. Corporations can evade legislation levied in one part of the world by moving aspects of their operations to other regions with looser regulations. Taxes that are intended to incentivise actions to reduce negative externalities will fail, in the same way, if companies based elsewhere in the world can avoid paying corresponding taxes. And which national government will make laws to limit the capabilities of artificial intelligence used by their own military, if rival governments have no such qualms?

Vladimir Putin, President of Russia, underscored the dilemma in remarks he made in September 2017[252]:

> Artificial intelligence is the future, not only for Russia, but for all humankind. It comes with colossal opportunities, but also threats that are difficult to predict. Whoever becomes the leader in this sphere will become the ruler of the world.

In a hearing at the US Senate in 2017, Senator Gary Peters vigorously challenged General Paul Selva about what the senator feared was an unwise restriction on the capability of US autonomous weapons systems. The senator was worried that American weapons systems would be overtaken in effectiveness by those from Russia, which would utilise state-of-the-art neural networks to identify and engage targets. General Selva gave his answer[253]:

> I don't think it's reasonable for us to put robots in charge of whether or not we take a human life.

Autonomous weapons should, therefore, remain under human control. But the concern raised by Senator Peters remains on the table:

> Our adversaries often do not [pause] to consider the same moral and ethical issues that we consider each and every day.

If your adversary looks like he's about to deploy an enormously powerful new weapon that would force you to submit to all aspects of his will, what should you do? If you had a chance of developing and deploying that weapon first, to head off that threat, might you be tempted at least to consider that possibility? These were the considerations of nuclear war scenario planners during the Cold War. Thankfully, at that time, no one reached the decision to initiate a first strike. But in what we can call Cold War 2.0, with weapons of even greater power and sophistication, who can rule out a different decision this time?

Divided aging

I've left to last the landmine that is, in some ways, completely obvious – so obvious that everyone can see it, well before it explodes in our own lives. It's a landmine that people take for granted. But in the years ahead, it could acquire a disturbing new twist.

This landmine portends extinction for each and every one of us, but at different times for different people. It's the extinction that will follow the gradual weakening of our bodies as we grow older, and as our biological systems deteriorate. Eventually – assuming we don't die earlier from an accident or an infectious disease – one or more of our vital organs will fail catastrophically, and our lives will cease. This eventuality is something that each of us have been anticipating since we first learned of our mortality in early childhood.

However, what if it becomes clear to a majority of people that there's a reasonable chance, within a few decades (or perhaps a century at the most) that scientific advances could render aging optional? Every one of us who has presently reached some kind of personal reconciliation about our impending deaths will come under pressure to reconsider what we personally want to experience as the chronological years continue to pass. Our individual philosophies of life – likely including a grudging acceptance of aging and death as an unfortunate inevitability – may be thrown into tumult.

That tumult will be magnified if new leases of youthfulness might become available only to a lucky few people. If only the ultra-wealthy, or the super-elite, or people in a small number of countries, can enjoy the reversal of the effects of aging, then what will the rest of the global population think?

This would be a significant extension of an inequality that already exists: inequality in which the wealthiest members of society can access better education and better healthcare. That inequality would exceed by far the present "longevity gap" in which the life expectancy for people in well-to-do areas is some 7-9 years more than for their neighbours in poorer areas[254].

Historian Yuval Noah Harari has spoken of future scenarios in which the human species effectively splits in two, on account of differential access to new technologies that can enhance minds and bodies. The result, he said, may be "the separation of humankind into a very small class of super-humans and a massive underclass of 'useless' people"[255]. In other words, "advances in technology, genetics and artificial intelligence [could] lead to a world in which economic inequality turns into biological inequality" – with today's spectrum of different biological abilities being severely stretched.

This scenario might be called "Transhumanism for the 1%".

To be clear, there's nothing inevitable about this scenario – and the reason Harari presents it, indeed, is to help ensure it doesn't come to pass.

In broad terms, two other categories of scenario contrast with *Transhumanism for the 1%*. The first has no significant biological enhancement, beyond what is already possible. Age-reversal therapies won't be available – either to the 99% or to the 1%. The other category can be called "Transhumanism for all": age-reversal therapies, along with many other enhancements to our minds and bodies, will become available for everyone, at low cost but with high reliability. That's part of the "sustainable superabundance" vision of the future that I'll be developing in more detail as this book progresses.

There's an argument that any age-reversal treatments will be bound to become cheaper and more widely available over time. The initial costs may be high – and the quality fairly poor – but a combination of free market dynamics and democratic political oversight will bring the costs down and the quality up. That's the pattern that has been widely observed with various consumer goods, such as flat screen TVs, smartphones, and kitchen appliances.

However, I see no inevitability here. I've already talked earlier in this chapter about failure modes in both market economics and democratic politics.

Consider the sky-high pricing of many medical procedures in various parts of the world, such as the United States. For example, research by Stacie Dusetzina of the University of North Carolina at Chapel Hill highlights how the costs in the United States of treatment of cancer by the newest pills rose sixfold over a recent 14-year period[256]. *That's after taking account of inflation.* And the inflation-adjusted cost of a millilitre of insulin, used in the treatment of diabetes, increased threefold over a recent 11-year period[257].

Moreover, in questions of inequality, perceptions make a big difference. If people have witnessed harmful medical inequalities in their own lives up till now, they're more likely to assume that new health-boosting treatments will be restricted in their availability. Their scepticism will grow if they have seen well-off people expressing naive views about the causes of their own good fortunes, seemingly lacking appreciation for real-world difficulties experienced by others who have been less fortunate. This will predispose them to be suspicious when advocates for new treatments casually offer assurances that everyone will be able to benefit from these new treatments.

As mentioned earlier, people's readiness to believe outlandish conspiracy theories stems from the amount of corruption they have experienced in their lives – and from tales of corruption or exploitation passed down from generation to generation, or magnified by social media machinations. Likewise, being concerned about the possibility of "transhumanism for the 1%", as opposed to embracing the possibility of "transhumanism for all", stems from what people see happening in the world around them. If they see misfortune, or events apparently turning against them, they'll likely be on their guard about new wonder technologies that could multiply inequality.

Some of the adverse critical reactions about GMOs – genetically modified organisms – have a similar cause. Critics observe that the large companies behind GMOs are seemingly intolerant of opposition to their methods. These companies have acquired, in some corners, the reputation of being aggressive bullies. They are said to force products onto unwilling farmers, and to have few qualms about utilising the full might of the judicial system to maintain firm control of their industry. These corporations talk about themselves in glowing terms as helping to feed the world – about attending to the needs of the chronically undernourished within developing countries. But since their products are in many cases evidently targeted at consumers in countries where there is already plenty to eat, their rhetoric antagonises their critics even more. That's why these critics are often hostile to the scientific research that appears to show that GMOs are both safe and effective. These critics have already made up their minds that the companies behind GMOs deserve to be opposed.

The unhelpful irrationality of the debate over GMOs is potentially only a preview of a debate with even more inflamed irrationality, concerning the development and deployment of transhumanist technologies such as age-reversal and artificial general intelligence. Instead of GMOs we're in effect talking about GMHs – genetically modified humans – and more generally about TMHs – technologically modified humans. Many of the people who stand to benefit enormously from these technological developments will, nevertheless, oppose them vigorously, on grounds that are a mixture of rational apprehension and irrational hostility. What's foremost in their minds is the risk of adverse outcomes of these technologies, such as rejuvenated political demagogues, or octogenarian media moguls gaining a new lease of youthful vitality. These are possibilities they find especially troubling. It clouds their thinking. The bigger the stakes, the murkier the clouds.

Dispersing these clouds, and raising the level of rationality, are key steps toward defusing this landmine – and, indeed, to defusing all the other landmines mentioned in this chapter. Describing these landmines is an important initial step in that process. What's next?

Beyond landmines

In this chapter, I've indicated many ways in which society could take a profoundly bad turning in the next few decades. The outcome of these missteps could be *much* worse than the fallout from recent shocks such as 9/11, the global financial crisis, and the COVID-19 pandemic. The journey to a much better outcome – to a transhumanist sustainable superabundance – involves steering clear of any such missteps. It involves opening our eyes to the risks in the landscape, *and keeping them open* as we regularly adjust our footing. Merely wishing these risks to disappear is deeply dangerous.

I'm a big fan of optimism. Optimism triggers enthusiasm and flows of vital energy. However, it needs to be *realistic* optimism. In a world as complex as ours, the other variant of optimism, that is *wishful* optimism – a variety of magical thinking – is a recipe for ultimate disappointment.

But it's far from easy to keep disaster in mind. If we allow ourselves to become overcome with dread, we'll stop functioning well. In order to explore creative responses to these landmines, we need at least some psychological stability. Being consumed by panic is emphatically *not* the appropriate response. We need to reach and maintain a state of emotional resilience.

To keep the panic at bay, it's tempting to downplay the dangers that we face. It's no surprise that the world sees a steady stream of articles and books reassuring us with hopeful messages such as "You've never had it so good", "Don't get carried away by the doom-mongers: they've been wrong before and will be wrong again", and "Sure there are some difficulties, but nothing that can't be solved by a healthy dose of innovation and elbow grease".

It's tempting, likewise, to wish to focus on just one of the landmines that I've covered, and to exclude the others from deliberation. After all, the principle of "divide and conquer" is good general advice. However, we need to understand the risks of taking a piecemeal approach. It's far better to seek to hold in mind an integrated appreciation of the situation. Otherwise, we might *appear* to make some progress, on a single issue, ahead of that progress being undone by one of the other landmines exploding catastrophically.

Indeed, in any rush to address any one issue that may have become uppermost in the public mind, shortcuts or other careless mistakes may occur, regarding the management of other issues:

- A deadly pandemic can distract attention from the risks of accelerating climate change
- Breakdowns in financial systems can cause an underfunding or suspension of various risk management activities
- Dysfunction within political systems can allow powerful cancer-like industrial complexes to grow unchecked, distorting the flow of information and ideas
- A surge in irrationality and "magical thinking" can lead to key scientific advice being ridiculed and discarded
- Clashes between different regional power blocs can prevent society's leaders from thinking objectively, due to pressures to prioritise partisan point-scoring over any search for genuine understanding
- Flurries of extreme weather can intensify the impression of an unfair "rich versus poor" division in the world, with the well-off seemingly being spared the worst brunt of storms, floods, droughts, heatwaves, and wildfires
- The megaphones of social media provide an environment for conspiracy theories and other psychological viruses to mutate into

even more deadly forms, inciting at least some online participants to plan and conduct extreme actions

- Groups driven by an enraged sense of being left behind can use new technologies to damage or punish a world for which they feel little personal affection.

The world's response to this set of interlinked risks therefore needs to involve two sets of activities:

1. Groups of specialists analysing and tracking each of the *individual* risks of catastrophe, taking account of a broad spectrum of insights, observations, and points of view
2. Other groups of multidisciplinary thinkers and activists who analyse and track the influences and interactions *between* the various risks.

In each case, the activities include all three of the main tasks of foresight: perceiving possibilities more clearly; assessing the desirability of the various scenarios (along with creative ways in which these scenarios could be modified); and practical actions to steer toward the better outcomes that have been identified.

I claim no special novelty in these recommendations. People in various walks of life are already committed to the kinds of tasks that I have listed. This includes people in government departments, academic institutions, NGOs and think tanks, military groups undertaking strategic planning, and communities inspired by religious or spiritual visions.

The real problem, however, is that these activities have had insufficient impact on the world. The advice from these groups has, all too often, been ignored. Even though political leaders do express interest on occasion about the results of foresight studies, these leaders generally fail to back up their expression of interest with hard actions.

It's time to explore the reasons for this lack of impact. Otherwise, we might expect a few more expressions of interest but a continuing dearth of the hard actions that are actually needed.

5. Shortsight

Shortsight, defined: Focussing too much on what it is easy to see. Prioritising the short-term and the local over the long-term and the distant. Inability to anticipate how new factors can turn the present world upside down.

Why wasn't society better prepared for the shocks of the 9/11 terrorist atrocities, the 2008 global financial crash, and the COVID-19 pandemic?

Shifting the question from the past to the present: why is society *still* not taking sufficient action against risks such as: the acceleration of global warming, weapons of mass destruction falling into dangerous hands, inflammatory social media apparently ripping apart what used to be a shared sense of national and even international unity, AI-powered armament systems gaining more autonomy to inflict huge damage without direct human oversight, corporations acquiring so much power that politicians can no longer meaningfully constrain them, democracies dismantling the internal safeguards that would prevent the abuse of power by headstrong political leaders, information being spread about how to edit a biological pathogen to hugely increase its lethality, and much more besides?

Putting the question more sharply: why does foresight fail?

The simple answer to that question is: human nature. Evolutionary pressures didn't particularly care about the skills needed for successful foresight. That's why we find these skills to be counterintuitive. They go against our grain.

To be clear, *some* predictive skills did prove advantageous to our ancestors – capabilities that enabled people to notice and anticipate variations that recurred on a day-to-day and season-to-season basis. But the skills to handle more complex changes had a low priority in prehistoric times.

Happily, human nature isn't fixed. We can redesign our social systems to compensate for our weaknesses, and we can modify ourselves so that we have different instincts.

Here's a simple example. Our instinct, honed by experience, is that objects in motion tend to slow down and come to rest. We have *lots* of practical experiences of friction and air resistance. We are therefore initially uneasy when we encounter Galileo's notion that objects in motion, left to themselves, will continue to travel in straight lines at constant speed, *indefinitely*. Nevertheless, after we spend many hours in classrooms, our intuitions change. We can develop the skills to calculate with Newton's three laws of motion, and with all that follows from these laws.

It's the same with another conceptual leap that Galileo championed – the idea that the earth rotates on its axis daily, rather than the sun and moon hurtling all the way around the skies every day. *We don't feel the earth move*, critics said. And these critics seemed to have ancient authority on their side, according to verses in the Bible[258]. Nevertheless, education can again help to amend our instincts – and can point out all kinds of terrestrial phenomena (including aspects of weather) that only make sense on the basis of the earth's rotation.

What education can achieve regarding the skills of mechanics and physics – even when the ideas in these disciplines initially strike students as strange – it can likewise aid us all to improve in the practice of foresight. That's the subject of this chapter.

Misled by evolution

You will have seen pictures of Jesus in a cloud, Mother Teresa on a cinnamon bun, or an unnamed "man in the moon". What I mean is that you will have seen clouds, buns, and the lunar disk, with appearances that *remind* you of pictures of Jesus, Mother Teresa, and a generalised human face. Part of your mind will have jumped to the conclusion that you are seeing something truly interesting[259]. Outside your conscious awareness, your mind will even have filled in some of the gaps in the apparent picture, so that it causes a bigger mental impact. *Wow*, you think to yourself. *I should pay attention.*

Is that just a funny quirk of human neural circuitry?

Spotting possible similarities is a useful skill. It might help you recognise a person after many years of separation, even though their appearance has changed in the meantime. It might limit the ability of someone else to disguise themselves, so as to escape your attention. And if you jump to a false conclusion, wrongly identifying a stranger as a long-lost acquaintance, that may cause some embarrassment, but it's probably not a big deal. That explains why humans have the tendency to notice patterns that aren't really there. During humanity's long prehistory, the advantages of noticing particular sorts of patterns presumably outweighed the disadvantages of occasional mistaken conclusions.

Similarly, humans have the tendency, on noticing the movements of inanimate objects, to look for something animate that is causing the motion. If the leaves of a tree rustle, or a twig snaps, it might be the sign of a predator about to pounce on us, to consume us for their dinner. It might also be the sign of a small animal that we could capture and eat as part of *our* dinner that day. *Pay attention*, our subconscious mind tells us.

This tendency has been given the name "hyperactive agency detection device"[260]. We are prone to imagine we detect agency, that is intention, even when it doesn't exist. That tendency was useful, even though it occasionally misfired. For thousands of generations, our ancestors lived in communities as parts of environments where significant actions often *did* stem from plans and desires in the minds of others. Apparent inequities in the allocation of the products of hunting and gathering did arise on at least some occasions from jealousies, envies, grudges, score-settling, inveigling, favouritism, and so on. It was a useful skill to be able to detect and understand these mental dispositions in other minds.

But that same tendency led people all around the world to believe their environments were filled with spirits, ghosts, fairies, angels, demons, skygods, and other deities – minds with their own agencies that responded to human actions[261]. Perhaps such beliefs caused little harm for most of history. Nevertheless, before a true scientific understanding of causes and effects could flourish, these animistic beliefs needed to be supplanted – in a process that many people found deeply psychologically distressing.

The large brains in ancestral humans weren't just a home for various "hyperactive" modules that were generally useful but occasionally reached faulty conclusions. These brains also required copious amounts of energy to keep them humming along. In these bygone times, various foods were particularly useful – foods that could deliver lots of energy. Our ancestors therefore developed what we nowadays call a sweet tooth. It was advantageous for them to have an instinct to eat lots of honey, fruit, or similar nutrients whenever they could be found. But step forward to the twenty-first century, with supermarket aisles laden with sodas, cakes, chocolates, and ice creams: in *that* environment, our sweet tooth is no longer an advantage[262]. It's the cause of an epidemic of ill health. And it helps to explain why more people nowadays die from over-eating than from under-eating[263].

Our sweet tooth and our hyperactive agency detection device are but two of many inherited tendencies that mislead us humans in the very changed environment of the present day[264]. The next set of examples comes under the general heading of "cognitive biases". They're short-cuts in mental reasoning which were, on the whole, evolutionarily beneficial in the simpler times of the past, but which nowadays pose us increasing danger[265].

Wikipedia has a list of over one hundred cognitive biases[266]. Though the list contains considerable duplication, and the significance of some items can be questioned, it features plenty of substance[267]. This includes:

- *The Gambler's Fallacy*: believing that if a run of trials lacks a particular random event, such as a dice showing six, the odds of that event occurring will increase as the run continues; we tell ourselves, wrongly, that the luck needs to "balance out"
- *Anchoring Bias*: putting undue weight on the first piece of apparently relevant information encountered, including numbers heard early in a discussion, even though these numbers have no direct significance to the matter in question
- *Conjunction Fallacy*: assigning a higher probability to a compound event containing a sequence of events that seems familiar (for example, Bjorn Borg will lose the first set in a tennis match but go on to win the match) than to a single event (for example, that Bjorn Borg will lose the first set)
- *Sunk Cost Bias*: a preference to keep investing in a project, even after earlier investments have been unsuccessful – under the rationale that the money or resources already sunk into the project are somehow particularly valuable
- *Groupthink Bias*: the tendency to go along with the opinions of other people in a group
- *Authority Bias*: the tendency to trust someone in an apparent position of authority – for example, someone dressed in a white laboratory coat, or speaking in a commanding tone of voice
- *Confirmation Bias*: the tendency to look for evidence that would back up a particular belief, rather than evidence that would disconfirm it
- *Short-term Bias*: the tendency to prefer choices that have a high likelihood of a small short-term benefit, even if there is a low (but

unclear) probability of a large adverse long-term outcome, such as a miserable death from lung cancer after smoking cigarettes.

What impact do cognitive biases have on foresight? Plenty, it turns out.

Misled by exponentials

If we watch a child growing up, there's a broadly constant increase in height from year to year. It's the same when we observe the development of a puppy, or a duckling, or a tree. These are all examples of what can be called *linear* growth. The growth rate can vary from time to time, and generally stops altogether in due course. But there's no sustained *explosion* of growth.

Contrast linear growth with what can be called exponential growth – growth whose speed increases in line with the existing size of the entity. The bigger the entity, the faster the growth. Whereas linear growth looks like 2, 4, 6, 8, 10, exponential growth looks like 2, 4, 8, 16, 32. And if each sequence were to continue another five steps, the linear one would reach to 20, whereas the exponential one would reach just beyond 1,000. By the time the former sequence has reached 40, the latter one has reached over one million.

Exponential growth did take place in prehistoric times, but our ancestors rarely observed it directly. The number of cells in an embryo in a womb initially doubles on a regular basis – that is, it grows exponentially – but this growth soon slows down to a linear rate, and was in any case something outside the conscious awareness of any human observer. The number of locusts in a swarm grows exponentially with each new generation, so long as sufficient food is available, but what our ancestors would have observed was the sudden devastation that a huge migrating swarm could inflict, rather than the generation-by-generation growth in numbers.

That's why we're unused to exponential thinking. And that's why compound interest often produces results that catch us by surprise. Invest one thousand pounds, at an annual interest rate of just four percent. (To keep matters simple, let's ignore any inflation in this example.) After one year, the fund has grown by only forty pounds. The growth in the next year is almost the same: £41.60. You would be forgiven for ignoring the additional £1.60, and just thinking, *that's just another forty pounds*. How long will the fund take to double? You do some quick intuitive calculations: forty needs to be multiplied by twenty-five, to reach one thousand, so you expect that the fund will have doubled in twenty-five years. You realise that the growth will be a bit faster, because of the compound nature of interest, so you are prepared to reduce your estimate by a year or two. *Twenty-three years*, you might reply.

You would be pleasantly surprised. The fund would double in just under eighteen years. The interest on the interest adds up to more than our intuition leads us to expect.

Does a difference between twenty-three years and eighteen years really matter? Perhaps not. Which, again, helps to explain why we're disinclined to pay much attention to the possibility of exponential growth. However, the faster the doubling rate, the bigger the difference between our linearly-based intuitions and exponential reality.

For a disease in which the number of people infected can double every ten days, it doesn't take long for an initial single infection to spread to an entire population of, let's say, eight billion people. Eight billion is two doubled thirty-three times. So, everyone on the earth could have fallen ill from the disease in just 330 days. That's one month less than a year. The problem is that, initially, there doesn't seem much to be concerned about. After the first month, there's just eight people ill. Who would worry about eight people being ill? Even after three months, the outbreak only comprises 500 people. That's a tiny blip, compared to the number of people who die each year from, for example, drowning (236 thousand[268]), or road traffic accidents (1.35 million[269]).

This highlights the challenge posed by exponentials. At first, it's too early to be unduly worried about any instance of exponential growth: the absolute numbers involved are paltry. But by the time the numbers have grown large, they're on the point of becoming much larger again, and it's now too late for many kinds of preventive action.

A similar phenomenon can take place in the world of business. Imagine there are reports of some strange new product idea. It might be downloading music over the internet. It might be using a cryptocurrency like Bitcoin to purchase items. It might be switching from carbon-based energy sources to renewables such as solar or wind.

At first, only a few people seem to be interested in the new idea, and the technologies involved don't seem robust. Recall that it used to be an arduous task to maintain an internet connection, cryptocurrencies used to be mentioned alongside arcane discussions of "cooperation between byzantine generals", and renewable energy sources used to be intermittent and unreliable. Which responsible company would pay attention to what appears to be just a small market sliver of potential interest in a weird product idea? Such market segments don't look particularly profitable. But if the market growth is exponential rather than linear, so-called "responsible companies" can be caught by surprise. A market segment that was only one percent at first could double several times over, and jump from "technology geek" to "early adopter" all the way to "majority", to use terms popularised by technology marketer Geoffrey Moore[270].

Intel co-founder Gordon Moore (no relation of Geoffrey Moore) observed as long ago as 1965 that the number of transistors on an integrated circuit was growing exponentially. The doubling rate has slowed down since these early days – from around one year to closer to two years – but the overall capabilities of systems built from integrated circuits has continued to increase broadly exponentially. The consequences have included:

- Processors that can perform calculations ever more quickly
- Memory disks that can store ever larger amounts of data
- Screens that can display graphics with ever finer resolution
- Intelligent sensors that are ever more ubiquitous
- Household devices that have increasing amounts of intelligence built into them.

In parallel to Moore's Law, we should also consider Cooper's Law, which describes the persistent ongoing doubling of the communications capacity of wireless networks. In this case, the doubling rate in recent decades is around two and a half years[271].

What's remarkable about both Moore's Law and Cooper's Law is the number of generations of doublings for which the underlying growth has continued. Moore's Law describes phenomena going back to 1959, the date of the very first silicon integrated circuit, which contained only one transistor. Cooper's Law describes phenomena going back to the experiments by Guglielmo Marconi in 1895. In the former case, the total growth is in the tens of billions[272]; in the latter, in trillions[273]. Nothing in our ancestors' experience prepared us for that kind of sustained prodigious increase.

Ideally, our education should make up for that lack of instinctive appreciation of exponentials. That education should help us guard against two different mistakes:

1. Not giving exponentials sufficient attention
2. Having a naive understanding of exponentials, such as that they proceed with more regularity or greater inevitability than is actually the case.

In more detail, that education should clarify:

- The general circumstances in which exponential growth is possible – namely, when positive feedback cycles operate
- The kinds of factor that can act as *accelerators* for the rate of growth
- The kinds of factor that can act as *brakes* for the rate of growth.

For any area of technology, a total of four conditions need to hold before exponential progress can continue:

1. *Scientific possibility*: for example, velocities cannot accelerate above the speed of light, temperatures cannot be reduced below absolute zero, and the second law of thermodynamics must be respected
2. *Engineering feasibility*: mechanisms whereby engineers can take step-by-step advantage of the scientific possibilities; this usually involves improving tools alongside improving the product itself, and repeatedly learning from experience of what works and what doesn't work; this includes sufficient raw materials being available
3. *Commercial viability*: sufficient funding to cover the costs of numerous engineering experiments, more precise tooling, and larger-scale collaboration; this commercial backing is more likely to remain in place if there is a regular output of incrementally improved solutions that deliver new functionality to users
4. *Social approval*: willingness of sufficient members of society to support the ongoing development – and lack of decisive political opposition to the new products.

Unfortunately, the writers who draw most attention to exponentials often fail to emphasise the unpredictable and variable aspects of exponentials. They give the impression that it is more or less inevitable that exponential progress will continue. Unsurprisingly, this generates public excitement. But when progress falters, despite the expectations that have been raised, the public becomes disenchanted. They conclude: exponentials are overhyped. Unfortunately, they then revert to letting their linear-based intuitions govern their thinking processes. And foresight suffers.

What has gone wrong isn't just that society has an unhelpful understanding of exponentials. It's also that society has an unhelpful understanding of probabilities – of how to deal with things that are deeply uncertain. The two sets of poor understanding interact to damage foresight. Let's look more closely at this.

Misled by probabilities

Recall the gambler's fallacy. You have the chance to bet on the outcome of a dice being thrown. You can put down a stake of £25. A result of 1 to 5 means you lose your money. But if the dice lands 6, you get your stake back, plus a prize of £100.

Assuming the dice is fair, the mathematics is straightforward. Your expected winning is (5/6) times £25 subtracted from (1/6) times £100, namely minus £4.33. You would be a mug to take part, although you might bet just for the fun of things.

Instead of betting, you decide to watch proceedings for a while. After eleven throws of the dice, it still hasn't shown a six. Does this change your interest in taking part?

One line of thinking would be to revise your assessment of whether the game is actually fair. You might become suspicious whether a six will be shown as often as you initially expected, that is, one time in six. In that case, you would become even less likely to take part.

But there's another line of thinking that might tempt your brain: the thought that a six is now overdue. In twelve throws, you would expect on average to see two sixes. There's not been any yet. Surely the odds must be higher for a six on this, the twelfth throw in this sequence?

And that's the gambler's fallacy. It's one reason why the people who operate these games of chance generally make money in the long run. But not the only reason. Another reason is that sometimes the mathematics of a question is less straightforward.

A celebrated example arose from the practical experience of French writer Antoine Gombaud, who was also known as Chevalier de Méré. Gombaud often spent lots of money gambling on the outcomes of games of chance. To win one game, you needed to throw at least one six when rolling a dice four times. To win another game, you needed to throw at least one *double* six when rolling a *pair* of dice twenty-four times. At the time, in the seventeenth century, probability theory existed in only rudimentary form. Gombaud performed his own simple calculations:

- With one dice: probability of a six is (1/6); Gombaud thought that throwing the dice four times meant multiplying the probability by four, giving (2/3), which is better than (1/2), so the game was worth playing
- With two dice: the probability of a pair of sixes is (1/36); multiplying this by 24 gives the same result as before, (2/3), so Gombaud thought this game was worth playing too.

Over many repeats of the first game, Gombaud made a lot of money, which gave him confidence his calculation was correct. Subsequently, however, he lost even more money when playing the second game, no matter how long he kept trying his luck[274]. It turns out that Gombaud's intuitions about how to calculate the probabilities were wrong. Rather than simple multiplication, exponentiation is needed: the correct answers for the two games are 0.518 and 0.491. (Both figures are evidently close to 0.5. This suggests that the gamblers involved must have played these games a great number of times.)

Mistakes with probabilities are by no means restricted to the seventeenth century. They're a significant part of life in the twenty-first century.

Consider a test to determine whether someone has a particular infectious disease. For those who actually have the disease, the test gives a positive answer 90% of the time. For those without the disease, the test gives a positive answer (a "false positive") only 1% of the time. So, if someone takes the test and there's a positive result, they should be quarantined, and denied entry to any public location, right?

But suppose the disease is present in the population at a rate of one in ten thousand. Therefore, consider a group of a million people, all of whom take the test. Out of this group, roughly one hundred will have the disease, and out of these, roughly ninety will give a positive result. However, the million also contains 990,000 who do not have the disease, and out of these, roughly 9,900 will give a positive result in the test. In defiance of our intuitions, there are more than one hundred times as many false positives (9,900) than true positives (90). Accordingly, the vast majority of people that we would quarantine, denying them access to public locations, would not in fact pose any real danger to their fellow citizens.

This illustrates what is known as Bayes' Theorem. In brief: to evaluate the likelihood of a state of affairs, such as someone being ill with a given disease, or them being guilty of a particular crime, you need more than just some evidence that seems to confirm that state of affairs. You also need to know the probability of a "false positive", in which the evidence has arisen even without the state of affairs applying. That probability of a false positive depends, in turn, on assumptions about various background statistics known as "prior probabilities". In effect, people often naively assume that these prior probabilities should be split 50:50. But the case of wrongly insisting that someone should quarantine, based on what was a false positive test, shows this to be a mistake.

Because many judges and lawyers lack an understanding of Bayes' Theorem, questionable verdicts have been reached in a number of court cases[275]. It is likely that other cases feature similarly unsafe conclusions whose dubious nature has not even been noticed[276]; such is the extent of poor understanding of probabilities.

Thoughtful application of Bayes Theorem has produced some stunning results. Following the unexplained 2009 disappearance of Air France flight AF 447 while it flew over the Atlantic from Rio de Janeiro toward Paris, teams of wreckage recovery experts had failed on four occasions over the course of two years to locate the remains of the airplane. Then a team of statisticians were brought into the project, to reconsider all the information from the past failed searches. Putting the data into formulae that included Bayes Theorem, the team gave their reasons for focussing the search in a particular area of the seabed. Within two weeks of this new search, the wreckage of the flight was found – along with the black-box recorder and the critical information it included[277].

A previous application of those same search methods had discovered the wreckage of a ship that had been missing since 1857, the SS Central America. Because that ship was carrying gold worth fifty million dollars at present-day prices, numerous searches had been conducted for it over the decades. Finally, a young mathematician called Lawrence Stone used Bayes Theorem, along with results from all previous searches, to narrow down the search region, leading to the recovery in September 1988 of more than one ton of gold bars and coins[278]. It was the same researcher, Stone, that headed the team of statisticians who found AF 447. Stone has stressed the advantages of rigorous mathematical approaches over "ad hoc methods" that "delayed success" by years[279]. Our intuitions, expressed in these "ad hoc methods", are too prone to mislead us in complicated situations.

Our assessment of the credibility of forecasts of the future likewise need to move beyond ad hoc intuitions to a more rigorous basis. If the BBC weather forecast says there's a 71% probability of rain tomorrow, but the day stays dry throughout, does this mean we should stop listening to BBC weather forecasts? After all, the forecast seemed confident.

Again, if a military specialist forecasts a 15% chance of nuclear war happening in the next ten years, but no such war breaks out during that time, does this mean we should disregard any future predictions the same forecaster makes regarding an increased likelihood of nuclear war?

The Bulletin of Atomic Scientists don't give numerical probabilities for their forecasts, but instead use the metaphor of the hands on a clock. In 1947, they launched their "Doomsday Clock", with its hands set to seven minutes before midnight, apparently close to an imminent global catastrophe. In 1949, after the Soviet Union tested its first atomic bomb, the hands of the clock were advanced four minutes. Then in 1952, the Soviet Union tested a hydrogen bomb – which is much more powerful than an atomic bomb – much sooner than western-based observers had anticipated. The Korean War was still in progress, and US President Harry Truman had been considering the use of nuclear weapons[280]. The Bulletin of Atomic Scientists nudged the hands of the clock forward by another minute, leaving just two minutes before annihilation[281]. Given that no such annihilation has come to pass, can we now ignore any subsequent updates from that Bulletin?

Not so fast. This is not a matter of truth versus falsity. It's a matter of statistics. When the weather forecast predicts rain with a probability of 71%, on many different occasions, the actual number of times rain occurs is pretty close to 71%. We would be foolish to follow any instincts that told us to ignore a forecaster just because of one variant outcome. Even if there are many cases of apparently wrong predictions, that would still be compatible if the forecaster gave a low probability each time. Even if the probability is low, we should still pay attention to that forecast if:

- The predicted *impact* is high
- The forecasters have followed *appropriate processes* in reaching their prediction

- The forecasters have *updated their models* in the light of what happened since their earlier forecasts.

Consider another set of forecasts, for the outcome of the 2016 US presidential election. On the eve of polling, the highly regarded FiveThirtyEight site, run by Nate Silver, gave Hillary Clinton a 71.4% probability of winning the presidency, leaving Donald Trump a probability of only 28.6%[282]. Nevertheless, Trump gained 304 seats in the electoral college, well above the total of 227 for Clinton. Given the extent of the discrepancy between the prediction and actuality, should we stop paying any attention to future polls by FiveThirtyEight? *Not so fast.* Let's again consider the probabilities. In the long run, a set of similar predictions, favouring one candidate 71% to 29% over another, should get the prediction wrong once every three or four elections.

Again, we need to look deeper: at the methodologies involved, and at whether the polling companies have updated their processes in the light of the actual 2016 results. The retrospective analysis published two months later by Nate Silver himself makes some important points[283].

Part of Silver's analysis is that media reports on the predictions of polls failed to communicate the level of uncertainties of these predictions. The fact that most polls favoured Clinton was taken as an indication that a victory by Trump was almost unthinkable – even though FiveThirtyEight put the probability at nearly 30%.

Silver also points out that all electoral polls are subject to errors of at least 2% in assessing voters' intentions. This error rate is well-known in the industry. However, many pollsters assumed that the different errors around the country would cancel each other out. In contrast, FiveThirtyEight modelled the possibility that these errors would be correlated together. Again, that's why they gave a relatively high probability to Trump's victory, compared to other polls. In reality, it seems that Trump at the last minute gained an unexpectedly high proportion of "undecideds" and "late deciders", to use polling terminology[284]. *As we'll see later in this chapter, an incorrect assumption that individual errors will cancel each other out, being independent, is a common factor behind bad foresight.*

But Silver's most significant comments, from his January 2017 retrospective, refer to "real shortcomings" in the media analysis of politics:

> Pervasive groupthink among media elites, an unhealthy obsession with the insider's view of politics, a lack of analytical rigor, a failure to appreciate uncertainty, a sluggishness to self-correct when new evidence contradicts pre-existing beliefs, and a narrow viewpoint that lacks perspective from the longer arc of… history.

That takes me to the third major way in which evolution has prepared us badly for the task of vital foresight in the twenty-first century. Alongside our inabilities to think seriously about exponentials and probabilities, we have inherited some dangerous mental assumptions regarding the reliability of our own thinking processes. We are over-confident, insufficiently willing to seek evidence that would challenge our current ideas, and too prone to spend time exchanging self-reinforcing views with people who think the same as us.

Misled by confidence

Suppose you are disconnected from the Internet and have no access to a library or any other sources of knowledge, other than what you carry inside your head. Suppose you are asked to estimate a quantity such as "the melting point of gold, in degrees Celsius", "the year David Livingstone was located in Africa by the journalist Henry Stanley", or "the ratio of the area of Texas to that of Rhode Island". Unless you're a specialist in any of these topics, you will be reluctant to offer an exact answer. However, you might feel more confident to offer a *range* of possible answers. That's OK. In this experiment, what you're actually asked to provide is a range within which you are 90% confident the true answer lies. In other words, if you give answers of this sort to a range of twenty such questions, you might expect to be wrong on around two occasions, with the true answer in these cases lying outside what you predicted. You would expect to be correct in the vast majority of cases.

This kind of experiment has been performed on many occasions. The result is that the true answers lie outside the supplied interval more than fifty percent of the time[285].

Indeed, consultant Lee Merkhofer, after observing even poorer predictive powers over many years of interactions with attendees of his workshops, has formulated what he calls the "2/50" rule of misplaced overconfidence[286]:

> I've often repeated a well-known demonstration of what I call the "2/50 rule." Participants in my training course are asked to provide confidence intervals within which they are "98% sure" that various uncertain quantities

lie. The quantities for the questions are selected from an Almanac, for example, "What's the elevation of the highest mountain in Texas?" "Give me low and high values within which you are 98% sure that the actual value falls." When the true value is checked, up to 50% of the time it falls outside of the specified confidence interval.

This is only one of several types of overconfidence that have been studied. Another type is when we assess our personal ability as exceeding the average. Thus, when asked if their driving skills were better than that of the median (average) driver in their country, 93% of a sample of American drivers replied in the affirmative – as did 69% of a sample of Swedish drivers[287].

We may become especially vulnerable to overconfidence if we have experienced success in past tasks. Our success may actually be due to the particular skills and efforts of others in our team, or to matters outside our own control, such as the weather, random accidents, or fortunate coincidences – but we find it psychologically comforting to imagine our own contribution to be the decisive factor. In that case, our abilities must surely be above average, right?

In some cases, we might make claims about our own past contributions that, initially, we know to be exaggerated. We might do this in an attempt to mislead others, so that they offer us employment, or a contract, or some romantic attention. I have often noticed on the employee reference site LinkedIn several different people claiming decisive responsibilities for smartphone development projects in which I was involved in earlier stages of my career. The different claims were mutually incompatible. Evidently, at least some of these claims were overstated.

One problem with that kind of exaggeration is that, in order to increase the chance of us deceiving someone else about our skills and contributions, it helps if we also deceive ourselves[288]. So, again, we end up having a higher opinion about our abilities than what an objective assessment would provide.

Even when our predictions of the future prove faulty, we have an array of tricks we can use to convince ourselves that we were essentially correct, notwithstanding an outcome different from what we predicted. It was only due to a fluke that our forecast didn't come true. Our forecast *would* have come true were it not for someone lacking courage at a critical moment, or because of someone else cheating the system in a dastardly way. The underlying thinking that informed our prediction was surely correct, even though our prediction just happened to be wrong in this one instance. And in any case, we always had this different outcome in the back of our mind too. *Or so we are inclined to tell ourselves.*

This propensity toward overconfidence is magnified yet further if we do what Nate Silver describes, namely, to restrict our main sources of ideas to people that already tend to think in the same way as us. It's "pervasive groupthink..., a failure to appreciate uncertainty, a sluggishness to self-correct when new evidence contradicts pre-existing beliefs..."

But why has evolution left us with this propensity toward overconfidence? After all, overconfidence has evident drawbacks: false expectations, flawed assessments, and decisions that will lead us into danger. Well, overconfidence can lead to advantages too: fearlessness, risk-taking, winning support from others who fall into our "reality distortion zone", and intimidating potential opponents to withdraw meekly rather than entering a direct confrontation. Hence the phrase, "fortune favours the brave". Hence the common preference for optimists over pessimists.

In which circumstances will the advantages of overconfidence exceed the disadvantages? That calculation is complicated by the fact that the trait might help a group as a whole, even though it causes many individuals in that group to come to grief. Suffice it to say that evolutionary theorists have identified many circumstances in which the "prizes" for overconfidence have historically outweighed the "costs"[289]. Alas, the mere fact that the costs of overconfidence are rising, does not cause any automatic change in our tendency to be overconfident. Researchers Dominic Johnson and James Fowler put it as follows[290]:

> We predict that... overconfidence will be particularly prevalent in some very important domains that have inherently high levels of uncertainty, including international relations (where events are complex and distant and involve foreign cultures and languages), rare or unpredictable phenomena (such as natural disasters and climate change), novel or complex technologies (such as the Internet bubble and modern financial instruments) and new and untested leaders, allies and enemies.

These theorists conclude their analysis in ominous terms:

> Although overconfidence may have been adaptive in our past, and may still be adaptive in some settings today, it seems that we are likely to become overconfident in precisely the most dangerous of situations.

Misled by normalcy

In November 2008, a new building was opened at the London School of Economics (LSE). To mark the occasion, Queen Elizabeth II was invited as the guest of honour. The displays shown to the Queen included some models for "managing the credit crunch" – the global financial crisis which was in full swing at that time.

The Queen was no passive bystander. "How come nobody could foresee it?" she asked the group of professors who had assembled at the event. Why had the credit crunch taken so many apparent experts by surprise? It was a good question.

Professor Luis Garicano gave one answer, referring to social systems malfunctioning[291]:

> The main answer is that people were doing what they were paid to do, and behaved according to their incentives, but in many cases they were being paid to do the wrong things from society's perspective.

This concords with the famous observation by American writer Upton Sinclair who remarked in 1935[292] that "It is difficult to get a man to understand something, when his salary depends upon his not understanding it!" In other words, economic motivation, such as the need to earn a salary, can badly interfere with your reasoning abilities. People benefited financially, in the short term, from downplaying any risk of a major crash. Even when banking leaders suspected that an end would come in due course to the increases in values of various financial instruments, it was prudent for them to suppress these negative thoughts. Chuck Prince, the chief executive of Citigroup, used a memorable comparison in a Financial Times article published in July 2007[293]:

> When the music stops, in terms of liquidity, things will be complicated. But as long as the music is playing, you've got to get up and dance.

I'll have more to say later in this chapter about social impediments to good foresight. But for now, let's look at various other answers given by LSE professors to the question posed by Queen Elizabeth. Several months afterward, a three-page letter was sent to the queen. Signed by Professor Tim Besley of the LSE and the distinguished historian Peter Hennessy, the letter conveyed conclusions reached at a British Academy forum organised to answer the monarch's question[294].

Once again, the social dimension was identified as a key part of the problem. Objectives that it made good sense for individuals to pursue, added up in aggregate to an outcome that was bad for everyone:

> Everyone seemed to be doing their own job properly on its own merit. And according to standard measures of success, they were often doing it well. The failure was to see how collectively this added up to a series of interconnected imbalances over which no single authority had jurisdiction.

But the letter also highlighted various psychological traits:

1. A "feelgood factor", encouraged by the low cost of borrowing, which distracted attention from potential growing underlying imbalances in the world economy
2. A "psychology of denial" that praised executives for offering quick slap-down refutations to any dissident voices
3. Over-trust in "financial wizards" who used mathematical language to persuade politicians and regulators – and probably also themselves – that they had discovered ingenious mechanisms to take the sting out of any risk in financial markets.

The letter offered this summary:

> The failure to foresee the timing, extent and severity of the crisis and to head it off, while it had many causes, was principally a failure of the collective imagination of many bright people, both in this country and internationally, to understand the risks to the system as a whole.

This summary can be further condensed into just two words: "overconfidence" and "misunderstanding". In turn, the reason so many people misunderstood the severity of the risks was because of what can be called an *assumption of normalcy*. This "normalcy" refers to the well-known bell-shaped curve that many data distributions follow.

The Normal Distribution arises for data, such as heights, weights, or blood pressure, in which the outcome is influenced by many small individual causes. Why is a given individual a bit higher than the average person? There's not just one reason, such as a single genetic variation, but rather a host of contributing factors spanning both nature and nurture.

A Normal Distribution is characterised by its mean, that is its average, and its sigma, that is, its standard deviation. The bigger the sigma, the bigger the spread of the data around the mean. However, in a Normal Distribution, it's rare to see an individual data point that is more than three sigmas higher (or lower) than the mean. It's *exceptionally* rare to see a data point that is more than four sigmas from the mean. The probabilities for that kind of deviation are 1/370 (for exceeding three sigmas) and 1/15,787 (for exceeding four sigmas). Stated otherwise, if you took one sample each day, you'd expect to wait more than a year before seeing even a single deviation of the first type, and *more than forty years* for a single deviation of the second type[295].

The probability of a variation exceeding *twenty-five* sigmas is truly miniscule. Yet that kind of variation was mentioned in August 2007 by David Viniar, the Chief Financial Officer for Goldman Sachs, as the reason for a significant reversal of fortune in the bank's Global Alpha investment fund. This was no ordinary fund: it used what was described as "sophisticated computer models" to identify very small differences in market prices, and to buy or sell securities as a result. The fund had good financial results for a number of years, before experiencing a major setback as the global financial crash gathered pace. Viniar's comment[296]: "We were seeing things that were 25-standard deviation moves, *several days in a row*".

Viniar was by no means alone, as a banking executive, at being caught out by the scale of deviations which occurred in the prices of key financial instruments. John Taylor of Stanford and John Williams of the Federal Reserve Bank of San Francisco have documented that[297]:

> On Thursday, August 9, 2007, traders in New York, London, and other financial centers around the world suddenly faced a dramatic change in conditions in the money markets where they buy and sell short-term securities. The interest rate on overnight loans between banks – the effective federal funds rate – jumped to unusually high levels…

Taylor and Williams calculated some stunning "before and after" statistics for the so-called "spread" between the overnight interbank lending rate and the London interbank offer rates (Libor). The baseline statistics covered the period from December 2001 to July 2007, that is, the period before the financial crisis. However, the spread on 9th August 2007 exceeded the previous mean by *seven* standard deviations of the baseline statistics. By 20th March 2008, the spread exceeded the previous mean by *sixteen* standard deviations.

The Normal Distribution applies in cases when numerous small events tend to cancel each other. For example, consider the number of mortgages where the house owner defaults on a payment. This figure will vary from month to month, and from region to region. These variations mostly balance out: a few extra people becoming financially overstretched in one part of the country is likely to be balanced by a small reduction in the number of financially overstretched people elsewhere in the country. Of course, the numbers don't cancel exactly, but nor do the variations all point in the same direction. At least, that's what happens ordinarily.

However, these diverse events sometimes do become strongly coupled, and the assumption of independence breaks down. That's when more extreme outcomes can occur. Factors causing stronger coupling include:

- The rise of so-called shadow banking, in which dependencies between different bank accounts were deliberately hidden
- Public sentiment, also known as "animal spirits", in which feelings of panic can spread far and wide.

In such cases, normalcy no longer applies. Instead, so-called "fat tails" come into consideration, and the worst reasonably likely outcome moves beyond "harm" to "ruin"[298]. Risks that it made sense to embrace, when the worst that could happen was "harm", become intolerable gambles when the possibility of "ruin" enters the picture.

It's not just in the world of finance where this question of potential ruin arises. This kind of catastrophic risk exists whenever strong links can be formed between factors that previously seemed to be independent – whenever an apparently diverse population actually has some characteristics of being a monoculture. In such a case, the shared characteristic can turn into a shared vulnerability. It's similar to the way in which, over the last few decades, fungal pathogens with names such as "wheat leaf rust" and "southern corn leaf blight" have devastated large areas of farmland planted with monocultures of corn or wheat[299]. Diversity in the farming methods employed are of little significance when a pathogen can spread quickly from location to location.

Education, therefore, needs to spread greater awareness, not only of the possibilities of exponentials, the importance of probabilities, and the factors causing dangerous overconfidence, but also of the circumstances in which apparently normal variations can be rapidly overtaken by much larger swings and deviations.

The possibility of these larger swings and deviations has an important implication for society's preoccupation with finding ever more efficient ways to get things done. As we'll see next, these larger swings and deviations convert our desire for efficiency, away from being an instinct that is generally valuable, into one that can prove seriously destructive.

Misled by efficiency

A great deal of the progress made throughout human history has involved improvements in efficiency. The same amount of human effort exerted has resulted in ever greater amounts of work accomplished.

For example, the number of people working in agriculture in the United States shrank from 11.68 million in 1900 to 1.92 million in 2012[300]. Despite this six-fold reduction in agricultural labourers, the industry in 2012 fed a total national population four times larger than in 1900[301]. Similar trends continue worldwide: in 1991, nearly 44% of total employment was in agriculture, but that figure had fallen to 26% by 2020[302].

Travel has also become much more efficient. Trips that would have taken weeks in previous decades can now be completed within hours.

Similar speed-ups apply throughout the retail chain. Goods ordered online can be delivered to homes within hours, whereas, not so many years ago, people might have waited weeks.

A competitive marketplace drives this kind of improvement in innovation. When a company finds a way to deliver a good or service at the same quality as before but at a lower price – or more quickly – the competitors of that company will go out of business unless they find a way to respond. In practical terms, there are numerous ways to improve efficiency:

- Applying resources more skilfully or more effectively
- Changing the design to use lower-priced materials
- Changing the design to have *fewer* features than before – removing features that customers judge to be less important
- Finding suppliers able to provide component goods and services more cheaply
- Taking advantage of scale effects
- Eliminating variability
- Reducing the amount of wastage

- Minimising the amount of capital tied up in inventory – items in an incomplete form, or which are awaiting distribution or sales orders
- Applying better technology, and so on.

Sometimes these improvements are obtained *deliberately*, as a result of conscious forethought and planning. On many other occasions, these improvements arise *fortuitously*, as a result of serendipitous observation, tangential experiment, and the dawning of insight.

However, there are many casualties when a market puts a special premium on efficiency. It's not only that the companies who lose out in the competitive struggle may cease trading, with employees losing their jobs. It's that the companies who win particular competitive bids may find they have committed themselves to processes where they end up spending more money than they can gain from the project. This phenomenon has been named "The Winner's Curse" by economists[303]. It's a reason why the choice of a supplier for a particular project needs to take into consideration more than simply the bottom-line price being charged. Our natural human instinct to select the lowest ticket price can lead us astray in such circumstances: the chosen contractor may discover they have bitten off a lot more than they can chew, and the overall costs of the project may skyrocket as a result. That's particularly likely to happen when variables estimated during the planning process to have a certain range of likely outcomes, end up significantly outside that range.

Worse, a focus on efficiency can blind us to undesirable side-effects of selecting a given product or supplier. The low costs – or fast delivery times – may involve, behind the scenes, harsh working conditions, poor health and safety for the employees involved, reliance on goods that are stolen or counterfeited, unreliable service warranties, or inadequate handling of the waste products arising.

In principle, we realise that, whenever we are making a purchasing decision, we should weigh up a lot more than the visible features such as price and delivery schedule. We appreciate that there are a number of less visible features of the supply process that we should also take into account. However, purchasers are often the victim of what is called "information asymmetry", and they can end up purchasing what is known as a "lemon" – something that fails to perform in the way they expected[304].

Economist George Akerlof, who coined the term "Market for Lemons", and who was awarded the 2001 Nobel Prize for these insights, argued that markets in which lemons arise regularly – such as the market that trades used cars – risk failing entirely, unless this problem of information asymmetry is addressed[305]. Hence the importance of mechanisms such as:

- Warranties and guarantees, backed up by legal enforcement
- Published standards for goods of a particular type
- External product certification
- Protection of brand assets against imitation or infringement
- Community-wide sharing of customer satisfaction ratings
- Transparent access into the supply chains in use.

Without at least a number of these mechanisms being in place, protecting customers and steering the operation of the free market, the market is likely to fail to deliver the gains in efficiency that it promises.

This takes us to perhaps the most dangerous drawback of our quest for greater efficiency. Even when mechanisms are in place as described above – even when purchasers have full sight of how products are being assembled behind the scenes – bad choices can still take place. Whilst these choices make good sense in the kinds of situations with which we are accustomed, they may serve us poorly if "non-normal" events arise, that is, when large disruptions occur.

It's like the case of a biological monoculture, already mentioned. A novel variant of a plant may be well suited to usual circumstances, but fail catastrophically if a new kind of disease afflicts it. As an example, the dreadful tragedy of the famine in Ireland in the late 1840s arose following the widespread adoption of one variety of potato, known as the lumper. The lumper had the dual attraction of low cost and high yield in the wet climate that prevailed in Ireland. However, the lumper turned out to be particularly vulnerable to an airborne fungal potato blight. Lacking any resistance to this blight, potatoes all over the country turned into an inedible black pulp, resulting in mass starvation. In a reversal of a previous vibrant upward trend, the population of Ireland plummeted by around 25% in a few short years[306].

We might look back condescendingly on the past political leaders who failed to prepare adequately for the onset of that potato blight. We might wonder to ourselves: *what were they thinking?* However, we fare little better in modern times. We allow modern-day supply chains to become highly optimised for "business as usual". That "business as usual" includes scope for limited variation in demand from week to week and from year to year. However, it does *not* cater for the kinds of larger, dramatic, disruptive changes which are the subject of this book. Modern-day upward trends in aspects of human flourishing could be reversed just as decisively as occurred in Ireland in the late 1840s.

For this reason, initiatives to improve efficiency need to sit alongside initiatives to improve *resilience* – initiatives that will enable society to respond in a timely manner to larger deviations from "business as usual".

In part, this means maintaining reserve stockpiles of key goods – contrary to the emphasis, mentioned earlier, about always minimising inventory. In other words, the modern embrace of "just in time" supply chains needs to be partially unwound.

In part, greater resilience also means being ready to quickly reconfigure manufacturing systems to create items differing from their normal produce – items that have unexpectedly become scarce. In other words, the modern tendency to overspecialisation should, again, be partially unwound. Instead of seeking to minimise variation, our goal should be to maximise agility.

However, two obstacles lie in the path of such changes being made: two additional instinctive biases, with roots dating back to prehistoric times. These two biases are the subjects to the concluding sections of this chapter:

1. Our bias toward the short-term, rather than the long-term
2. Our bias toward supporting our local group, rather than sharing control with groups with traditions very different from our own.

Misled by immediacy

Whatever plans we may have for the future, we first need to survive in the present, in order to have a chance to carry out these plans in due course. Our short-term needs demand immediate attention. Longer-term needs can, well, wait until tomorrow.

Every student knows the issue. An assignment needs to be written within two weeks. Just as you are settling down to work on the task, a friend invites you out to eat, drink, and be merry. You tell yourself: there's plenty of time to write the assignment later.

In the absence of all control over short-term impulses, human society would not be possible. There is some evidence that when people suffer brain injuries, they can become dominated by immediate desires. Consider a passage published in 1868 by Dr John Harlow about a famous patient of his, Phineas Gage. As a result of a premature explosion during the excavation of the path for a new railway, Gage had suffered the extreme misfortune of an iron bar being propelled at high speed straight through his skull and out of his head[307]. Gage recovered physically – indeed, remaining conscious throughout the accident and its aftermath – but, for a while at least, his character was decisively changed:

> The equilibrium or balance, so to speak, between his intellectual faculties and animal propensities, seems to have been destroyed. He is fitful, irreverent, indulging at times in the grossest profanity (which was not previously his custom), manifesting but little deference for his fellows, impatient of restraint or advice when it conflicts with his desires, at times pertinaciously obstinate, yet capricious and vacillating, devising many plans of future operations, which are no sooner arranged than they are abandoned in turn for others appearing more feasible. A child in his intellectual capacity and manifestations, he has the animal passions of a strong man.
>
> Previous to his injury, although untrained in the schools, he possessed a well-balanced mind, and was looked upon by those who knew him as a shrewd, smart business man, very energetic and persistent in executing all his plans of operation.

Thankfully, few of us experience the extent of mental disequilibrium that afflicted Phineas Gage. Nevertheless, aspects of procrastination do intrude in our plans from time to time. Given a choice between starting a diet today or next week, leaving it until next week strikes us as a safe decision. We delay submitting our tax return, booking a dental check-up, repairing the barn roof, or commencing payments into a pension.

Writers throughout the centuries have lamented this tendency. Here's Britain's Samuel Johnson from 1751[308]:

> The folly of allowing ourselves to delay what we know cannot be finally escaped is one of the general weaknesses which, in spite of the instruction of moralists, and the remonstrances of reason, prevail to a greater or lesser degree in every mind; even they who most steadily withstand it find it, if not the most violent, the most pertinacious of their passions, always renewing its attacks, and, though often vanquished, never destroyed.

And the Greek poet Hesiod from around 800 BCE[309]:

> Do not put your work off till tomorrow and the day after; for a sluggish worker does not fill his barn, nor one who puts off his work: industry makes work go well, but a man who puts off work is always at hand-grips with ruin.

Evolutionary biologists have explained our tendency for procrastination as having advantages in at least some circumstances[310]. People prone to act on immediate impulse can amass more resources. People who, on the other hand, are preoccupied with far-off possibilities, may be wasting their mental energy on matters that never transpire. A proverb that summarises this worldly wisdom of procrastinating is "A bird in the hand is worth two in the bush". Let's not unduly worry about what we might track down in the bush. Let's enjoy what's already at hand.

Nevertheless, the more complex our network of relationships and social obligations, the greater the importance of forming and following longer-term plans. That's why society has developed many mechanisms, both informal and formal, to place a higher priority on longer-term issues. We structure children's schedules, so that youngsters gain many skills that might serve them well in later life. We ritualise the public commitment of marriage, to encourage long-term fidelity of partners to each other. We share narratives in which the heroes and heroines are conscientious, deferring their own pleasures. And, like Hesiod and Samuel Johnson, we regularly remind ourselves of the drawbacks of procrastination.

Despite these mechanisms, various pernicious short-term biases still remain:

- Companies need to keep on creating and reporting positive short-term results, to keep their investors happy by issuing dividends and raising the share price
- Politicians need to concentrate on winning the next election, lest they lose power and therefore the ability to continue implementing their longer-term plans.

For this reason, business leaders frequently find themselves pressurised to concentrate on the next few months, and political leaders find themselves pressurised to concentrate on the next few years. *Address climate change?* That can wait until the next election – though some short-term "greenwashing" gestures might be made. *Plan ahead for business disruption by next generation artificial intelligence?* Let's concentrate on milking the current cash cows. If anything does come of next generation artificial intelligence in due course, the company can hope to make up ground quickly as a "fast follower". *Introduce a new carbon tax that will encourage more responsible energy policy?* Not until after the current round of bonuses have been paid out, for meeting the previously agreed short-term targets, thank you! *Diversify a monoculture to make it more resilient against possible surprise infections?* Maybe in a few years' time, after reaping good harvests from the current crops.

In principle, the answer to these remaining short-term biases is straightforward: we need to evolve the structures under which business and politics is carried out.

After all, there are already many constraints that lead both politicians and business people to keep broader considerations in their minds – to pay attention to birds in the bush as well as those already in hand. Legal officers play a key role, highlighting any instance where actions would violate agreed rules. Companies that publish misleading financial accounts are subject to significant fines, their executives may be prohibited from holding office again, and their directors may be put in jail. Legal systems also provide protection, in theory at least, for whistle-blowers inside organisations who bring to public attention aspects of these organisations that will have adverse longer-term consequences.

Alongside lawyers and courts, who take action when explicit laws are violated, another major role is played by journalists and the press. They can take action when issues are less clear cut, but where there are grounds to question actions taken by businesses and politicians. Of course, newspapers have their own short-term agendas too, such as boosting circulation figures and attracting advertisers. Nevertheless, they form part of a larger network of different components in society that, collectively, can protect future issues from being submerged in shorter-term distractions.

We can, and should, go further. Governments throughout the world should appoint senior ministers with explicit responsibility for future generations. Whereas many voices around the cabinet table will be calculating how the party can win the next election, the Minister for the Future will be speaking up on behalf of the needs of people who will be voting in ten years' time, twenty years' time, and later[311]. Further, these ministers should regularly provide updates to parliament, and to the wider public, about matters of vital foresight. This includes the latest thinking about:

- Disruptive trends that may be accelerating – or slowing down

- Scenarios that have been receiving more attention – and those that imminently deserve more attention
- Coalitions and partnerships that can cooperate to increase the likelihood of various desirable future scenarios
- Instances in which groups in society are, perhaps inadvertently, increasing the likelihood of various *undesirable* future scenarios
- How the desirability of various scenarios can be altered by suitable modifications – adding in new elements, or removing others
- New educational programmes covering the skills needed for effective foresight.

Businesses, likewise, need to be strongly encouraged to prioritise foresight, rather than merely considering the financial results expected in the next few quarters. Some of this encouragement can come from activist shareholders who emphasise longer timescales rather than immediate returns on investment. Other encouragement can come through changes in what is recognised as best practice in the statement of financial accounts. Specifically, more prominence needs to be given to credible longer-term forecasts – forecasts that go beyond mere linear extrapolation of present trends, and which consider the probabilities of disruptions.

Bear in mind that legal regulations governing financial accounts have changed many times in the past decades. In the United States, GAAP – the set of Generally Accepted Accounting Principles – was established by legislation as recently as 1933 (the Securities Act) and 1934 (the Securities Exchange Act). These acts were responses to a wide perception that the market crash of 1929 and the subsequent Great Depression were caused at least in part by companies providing misleading financial reports[312]. A set of more recent revisions to GAAP include[313]:

- Clarifications on what non-profit organisations need to disclose about management of funds for day-to-day purposes
- Changes in the rules about when revenues can be included in accounts even though these payments have not yet been received
- Restrictions on which assets can be hidden from the public accounts by them being placed instead on "off-balance-sheet" accounts.

Further changes need to be prioritised in GAAP and in related standards such as the IFRS (International Financial Reporting Standards), so that organisations will no longer be able to wave their hands vaguely regarding the sustainability of their activities, or about adverse external impacts of these activities.

One ground for opposition to any such changes is the claim that they would put companies at a disadvantage to competitors from other countries where regulations are more flexible. That brings us to the final piece of this complex jigsaw puzzle: our bias toward maintaining control on a local level, rather than acquiescing to agreements overseen by a remote power.

Misled by sovereignty

Evolution has placed two contrasting sets of instincts deep into our human nature:

1. An instinct to *compete* – to obtain for ourselves or our families a greater share of the resources that are available
2. An instinct to *cooperate* – to share with others the fruits of our own activities, or whatever resources we have already accumulated.

Related to the first of these instincts is the tendency to *distrust* others. We need to watch people carefully, since they may be inclined to deprive us of what we would consider a fair share of the community's resources.

Related to the second of these instincts is the converse tendency to *trust* others, and more generally, to trust the wider community. Rather than hoarding resources for our own use, we trust that members of the community as a whole will take care of us when the need arises in the future, just as we are presently taking care of some of them.

Societies all around the world developed norms and traditions to prevent our competitive, distrusting instincts from becoming too dominant. Ethical frameworks frequently entreat everyone to "treat others as you would like to be treated", or include some other version of the so-called golden rule of morality[314]. This is sometimes expressed along lines such as "You shall love your neighbour as yourself" – as formulated in the Old Testament book of Leviticus[315].

But who is our neighbour? How widely should our cooperative instincts be applied? The phrase preceding the verse just quoted from Leviticus refers to "any of your people". The same ethical frameworks that advocate cooperation within "your people" often display a more hostile attitude toward outsiders. These frameworks warn against loss of purity or loss of identity, as can happen when outsiders are mixed into your community. Thus, the very next verse of the book of Leviticus issues a commandment that sounds strange to many modern ears:

> You shall not let your cattle breed with a different kind. You shall not sow your field with two kinds of seed, nor shall you wear a garment of cloth made of two kinds of material.

Ancient codes of conduct, such as the earliest books of the Old Testament, frequently assign lower sets of rights to outsiders who live alongside "our people". People with decidedly lesser status included the slaves who were part of the spoils of war and who were now subordinate to "our people". This is from the book of Exodus – which precedes Leviticus in the Old Testament[316]:

> Anyone who beats their male or female slave with a rod must be punished if the slave dies as a direct result, but they are not to be punished if the slave recovers after a day or two, since the slave is their property.

In other words, slaves needed to be treated with *some* respect, but not with as much respect as a full "neighbour". With this and various similar commandments, the Old Testament broadly matches the dual-level of concern found in other ancient middle east legal codes[317].

As for members of tribes with which "our people" are at war, the Old Testament displays on occasion a frightful *lack* of neighbourliness:

- "The people of Samaria… will fall by the sword; their little ones will be dashed to the ground, their pregnant women ripped open" – Hosea 13:16
- "Daughter Babylon, doomed to destruction, happy is the one who repays you according to what you have done to us. Happy is the one who seizes your infants and dashes them against the rocks" – Psalms 137:8-9 (this is the conclusion of the psalm that starts with the words sung by pop group Boney M, "By the rivers of Babylon"[318])
- "Now go, attack the Amalekites and totally destroy all that belongs to them. Do not spare them; put to death men and women, children and infants, cattle and sheep, camels and donkeys" – 1 Samuel 15:3.

Some commentators have suggested that the language in such passages should be treated as poetic, hyperbolic, or rhetorical – as when sports enthusiasts might talk about their team having "totally slaughtered" their opposition in a "massacre"[319]. I am ready to concede that these age-old tales have likely been exaggerated in the retelling. But that misses the point. What's at issue isn't whether the moral code in these age-old scriptures is somehow perfect. The point, instead, is that it can make *good evolutionary sense* for a clan or tribe of people to have, simultaneously, strong neighbourly ties within their group, and strong latent hostility to external clans or tribes that might threaten their identity or collective wellbeing.

Accordingly, evolution has given us two senses of moral outrage:

1. Outrage against any free-riders within our group who shirk their share of collective responsibility – people who take a full helping of the rewards but without making appropriate efforts in shared tasks
2. Outrage against any outsiders who advocate different customs, unfamiliar rituals, or novel methods for making decisions – outsiders whose influence challenges the stability and integrity of our group.

This outrage goes far beyond an intellectual observation. It can stir up, in both cases, intense feelings of disgust.

Our fear of the alien – sometimes called xenophobia – probably has at least two sorts of roots. First, people who we recognise as part of our extended community will likely be interested in approval or disapproval from the rest of our community. That will motivate them to behave in a positive neighbourly way toward us. However, outsiders will be more likely to be motivated by approval or disapproval from a quite different community, with much less concern for the wellbeing of members of the first group (to which we belong). Therefore, when we contemplate outsiders, we need to raise our vigilance.

Second, there may be a biological root. Distinct tribes are likely to have developed different levels of immunity to pathogens that they carry with them. An extreme example was when Europeans from Christopher Columbus onward brought infections such as smallpox, typhus, cholera, and measles to the Americas, leading to enormous fatalities in native populations that lacked any prior immunity to these diseases. It has been estimated that deaths reached 80% in many regions[320]. A psychological aversion to intermingling with people who look different to us may well have provided a positive survival aid – reducing the chance of us catching infections beyond those to which our group has already acquired some defences. That's the theory of a "Behavioural Immune System" as proposed by researchers Lene Aarøe and colleagues[321]:

> ...a theoretical framework that connects disgust, a powerful basic human emotion, to political attitudes through psychological mechanisms designed to protect humans from disease. These mechanisms work outside of conscious awareness, and in modern environments, they can motivate individuals to avoid intergroup contact by opposing immigration.

For example, we might, subconsciously, interpret differences in skin colour as being signs of people carrying a dangerous infectious disease. Differences in diet might lead us, were we to adopt the same custom, to fall foul of a perilous new form of food poisoning. The very thought, therefore, can make us gag. *It's disgusting*, we exclaim.

Rather than trusting groups of outsiders that we hardly know, it's far better, we tell ourselves, to stick to our own rules of local sovereignty.

Alongside the various psychological reasons why we are biased toward local sovereignty – and why we fear people that appear alien – we also need to consider some reasons rooted in logic itself. That brings us to the topic of game theory.

Suppose there's only a limited quantity of fish that can be caught from a lake each year – otherwise there will be none left to repopulate the lake for subsequent years. Should each group of fishermen try to take as many fish from the lake as is physically possible for them? Should they try hard to create more effective nets, and to stay out longer in the lake in their fishing boats? Up to a point, that may be a sensible strategy. But when more groups of fishermen improve their capabilities in this way, the lake may become overfished, with bad consequences for everyone. Provided all groups of fishermen coordinate their activities and agree various limits, the danger passes. But if you suspect that some groups might be cheating – taking more than their fair share – your own motivation to cheat grows too.

What I've just described is an example of a problem known as "the tragedy of the commons"[322]. Other examples of commons include shared grazing land, shared supplies of fresh water, shared space on the beach, shared fresh air, shared wireless spectrum (as used by mobile phones and other devices), and so on. In each case, as the population grows, and as heavier use is made of the shared resource, the greater the need for *some kind of coordination mechanism*, to prevent spiralling overuse of that resource.

In principle, various solutions are possible. Where all the fishermen know each other (directly or indirectly), and feel a joint sense of loyalty to the same group, they may be inclined to self-police mutually agreed limits. This agreement can be reinforced by shared narratives that extol the virtue of observing rules on how many resources each person can use, and which vilify anyone who is tempted to pursue a narrow self-interest. But this kind of mechanism faces challenges as the community becomes larger, as personal knowledge of the participants for each other diminishes, and as the community includes subgroups that regard each other as alien. In these cases, to restrict the actions of each participant, other kinds of enforcement become necessary.

One mechanism involves parcelling out licences, which are then available for resale to the highest bidder. In principle, the licenses permit catching fish in numbers only up to the safe limit. But how will it be checked that no-one cheats, and catches more fish than their licenses permit? The mechanism needs to be backed up by some kind of police force, armed unit, or security team.

Provided people can be confident that the overall limits will be enforced, they can accept some restrictions on their own freedom. The restriction hinders what each one person can do in the short-term, but makes it more likely that their longer-term livelihood is preserved.

For example, in order to enjoy the benefits of driving vehicles on a shared set of highways – an instance of a "commons" – each driver or potential driver needs to agree to give up some liberties:

- The liberty to drive faster than the limit generally agreed to be safe
- The liberty to drive without having passed a test that verifies their driving capabilities
- The liberty to make their own decision on how much alcohol they can have in their blood while driving.

Many drivers may feel that a speed limit of, say, 20 miles per hour in a built-up area, is an awkward restriction, which they personally would like to ignore. However, if everyone acted on such an impulse, there would be a spike in the number of accidents with bad consequences, such as a fatality.

Accordingly, we accept the surveillance of traffic police, the imposition of fines for offenders, and the removal of the driving licenses of repeat offenders. We surrender some elements of our personal freedom in order to gain the freedom of roads with fewer dangerous accidents.

This is the solution described as long ago as 1651 by English philosopher Thomas Hobbes in his pioneering work on political philosophy, *Leviathan*. According to Hobbes, in the absence of mechanisms to ensure good cooperation, the natural state of human affairs would be a state of war "of every man against every man"[323]. We would never be sure who we could trust. Accordingly, we would need to be ready for combat at any time. This would be a truly dismal situation, providing people little incentive to work hard and build up resources – since these resources could be stolen at any time. In consequence, there would be no development of trade, knowledge, technology, art, or culture:

> In such condition there is no place for industry, because the fruit thereof is uncertain, and consequently no culture of the earth, no navigation nor use of the commodities that may be imported by sea, no commodious building, no instruments of moving and removing such things as require much force, no knowledge of the face of the earth; no account of time, no arts, no letters, no society, and, which is worst of all, continual fear and danger of violent death, and the life of man solitary, poor, nasty, brutish, and short.

Hobbes seems to have underestimated the potential for groups of people to cooperate locally without warfare. As I mentioned above, biology has given us instincts for cooperation alongside our instincts for competition. However, the problems identified by Hobbes become more forceful when larger groups of people are involved.

The solution advocated by Hobbes was the emergence of a so-called "commonwealth", namely a system of law and order with the purpose of maintaining peace. Any such commonwealth involves members of society giving up some of their own rights. As Hobbes remarks, it is as if each person in the commonwealth makes a covenant, saying to each other[324],

> I… give up my right of governing myself to… this assembly of men, on this condition, that thou give up thy right… in like manner.

To be successful, according to Hobbes, the commonwealth needs to be headed by a person we could describe as a "sovereign":

> …one person, of whose acts a great multitude, by mutual covenants one with another, have made themselves every one the author, to the end he may use the strength and means of them all as he shall think expedient for their peace and common defence.
>
> And… this person is called sovereign, and said to have sovereign power.

This "commonwealth" headed by a "sovereign" – something we might nowadays call a "government" – can ensure that various things will happen in defiance of the tragedy of the commons:

- Shared resources can be protected against individual misuse
- People who violate the agreed laws can be fined or imprisoned, to put an end to their unlawful activity, and to serve as an example to deter others from following in their footsteps.

When they function well, governments can ensure that sufficient investment is made into what are known as "public goods" – initiatives that will benefit society as a whole, but where individuals or companies are loath to make personal investments since there is no guarantee that any financial rewards arising will apply particularly to them. Examples of public goods include general education, fundamental scientific research, the development of treatments for diseases afflicting poor people (the kinds of diseases tackled by the DND initiative mentioned in the previous chapter), cleaning up the environment, and constructing and maintaining infrastructure for transport or communications in areas where, again, a commercial case cannot attract sufficient private investment.

Many aspects of foresight also fall into this category of public good. From a short-term perspective, there's little commercial merit in investments to create stockpiles of goods just in case a disaster strikes, or to earmark some manufacturing capacity so that it can be quickly reassigned to produce different kinds of goods. Likewise for efforts to study potential new infectious pathogens in advance of any actual outbreak. To be clear, in all these cases the initiatives would likely benefit society as a whole, but there's no business case for any individuals to make the necessary investments. That's where governments need to step in, collecting money via various taxation systems, and then making requisite public investments.

Nevertheless, there are many ways in which this model can go wrong – failure modes for the Hobbesian scheme in which individuals give up some of their personal liberty for the sake of a stronger commonwealth in which everyone ought to end up better off. Once it has obtained its own power, the government can end up harming individuals even more than they were previously likely to harm each other. The government might apply the law unfairly, or devise laws in the first place that disproportionately favour only a part of the commonwealth. Individuals within these societies will regret and resent being obliged to sacrifice many liberties.

According to political scientists Daron Acemoğlu and James Robinson, most societies throughout most of history shied away from allowing leaders to acquire too much power. The general view was that would-be strong leaders need to be brought down to size, lest they end up dominating society for selfish purposes. That's the thesis Acemoğlu and Robinson advance in their 2019 book *The Narrow Corridor: States, Societies, and the Fate of Liberty*[325]. The only kind of "leviathan" that is ultimately good for society, they say, referring back to the title of the 1651 book by Hobbes, is a "shackled leviathan": one in which the powers of a government are constrained by the powers of multiple other sections of society.

The story of social history, as Acemoğlu and Robinson tell it, is the story of leviathans emerging in various parts of the world – often despite initial apprehensions from the people in these regions – and being shackled to greater or lesser extents by institutions such as independent courts, free press, and regular democratic elections. These shackled leviathans enable people in various countries to collaborate together at a scale that could otherwise not have been possible. The result is countries with a relatively strong government alongside relatively strong social infrastructure. In these countries, people may complain about aspects of their government, but they tend to feel a kind of overall pride in their national traditions.

If you ask citizens in these countries to give up some of their hard-won national sovereignty to even larger international bodies, you'll often find resistance to the idea. Any supranational bodies are likely to be the bad kind of leviathan, these citizens might say – though not in these exact words. These bodies are run by people with alien characteristics. It would be a big mistake to share sovereignty with them.

However, the most dangerous instances of tragedies of the commons have a fundamentally multinational angle. Problems such as the hole in the ozone layer, escalating climate change, or new infectious pandemics don't simply stop at borders between countries.

That fact has long been understood by political leaders and their advisors. That's why, for example, countries have acknowledged in principle the benefits of notifying each other of any outbreaks of any so-called "communicable diseases" occurring within their jurisdiction.

Indeed, following the devastating spread throughout Europe of cholera in preceding decades, twelve European states sent delegates in 1851 to Paris to attend the world's first International Sanitary Conference[326]. The intent was to share knowledge and to agree common quarantine standards in order to control the further spread of the much-feared disease. Yellow fever and the plague were added to the set of diseases in the scope of that conference and a series of follow-ups held over subsequent years. Progress was slow, and provisional agreements reached at the conferences generally failed to be backed up by legislation within national parliaments. Part of the reason was due to ongoing debates about the scientific principles of transmission of the various diseases. Eventually, at the seventh conference in the series, held in Venice in 1892, the first International Sanitary Convention was signed. A similar agreement, the Inter-American Sanitary Convention, was agreed in Washington DC in 1905, covering cooperation between eleven countries in the Americas. That convention was the first to require each country to notify the others of any outbreaks of cholera, plague, and yellow fever.

Although clear in principle, this obligation has proved troublesome in practice. Many countries have preferred to retain full control of any news of potential infectious outbreaks within their borders. They don't want panic spreading, with adverse impact on business. On many occasions, countries have taken the decision that a particular outbreak likely involves no person-to-person transmission: humans are catching the disease only by direct contact with various animals, such as birds, pigs, or bats, they say. Even when global health bodies such as the WHO have suspected otherwise, they have been obliged to await a formal notification from the countries involved before stepping up their own communications. In this way, opportunities have been lost to restrict transmissions at early phases of pandemics[327].

Even though all countries would in principle benefit from faster reporting of early signs of transnational threats – and from stronger cooperation to address these threats – the question of national sovereignty, therefore, causes complication. National governments distrust transnational bodies, for both psychological and logical reasons. After all, every transnational body – such as the European Union, the World Health

Organization, or the United Nations General Assembly – takes decisions that can be criticised from various viewpoints. Such is the nature of international compromise. Critics who have their own reasons to oppose a given transnational organisation can, therefore, find and highlight actions that show the organisation in questionable light. The sternest critics go on to argue, moreover, that these questionable decisions reflect fundamental issues with the setup of the transnational organisation. They allege that these organisations are incapable of evolving in ways to make them truly fair. It would be better, therefore, to minimise engagement, and to take as many decisions as possible on a local basis.

It was that kind of thinking that led the United States to decline involvement in 1920 with the League of Nations that had been set up after the First World War. In defiance of the recommendations by President Woodrow Wilson, the US Senate in 1919 rejected the verification of the Treaty of Versailles, including admission of the USA to that newly formed international body[328]. Reasons for non-participation included adherence to the principles of the Monroe Doctrine articulated in 1823 by a previous US President, James Monroe – principles that sought to reduce control by European powers in the American hemisphere.

The absence of the United States from the League of Nations left that organisation weaker, unable to prevent the growth of international hostilities between major powers. Italian dictator Benito Mussolini provided a scornful but accurate summary of the limitations of the organisation in 1935 following its inaction when Italian troops openly used poison gas in Ethiopia[329]: "the League is very good when sparrows shout, but no good at all when eagles fall out."

However, the shortcomings of the League of Nations were in everyone's minds when, at the conclusion of the Second World War, a new organisation was designed that would have a greater likelihood of succeeding in the same purpose, namely, the United Nations:

- Some of the criticisms of the design of the League of Nations voiced by the US Senate in 1919 were addressed by the design of the United Nations, via the veto it gave to the United States along with other permanent members of the Security Council
- Twenty-five additional years of history had impressed on everyone the imperative of finding mechanisms to subordinate at least some

aspects of national sovereignty for the sake of preserving international peace.

This demonstrates a pattern which can be extended in the future, to improve the speed and effectiveness of international cooperation in the face of major transnational threats and opportunities:

- The starker the threat, the greater the incentive to find and follow new mechanisms
- The design of these mechanisms needs to take into account the legitimate worries and concerns of the countries who have to give up some of their sovereignty in order for the cooperation to work.

In parallel, the message of the "Narrow Corridor" analysis of Acemoğlu and Robinson needs to be borne in mind: successful transnational governance depends upon the mutually constraining operation of *multiple* connections. Delegation of executive power needs to be accompanied by the growth of other international links that are, broadly, independent of each other:

- International legal systems
- International financial systems
- International journalists and a free press
- International sharing of academic research
- International liaison between practitioners of vital foresight
- International gatherings of citizens, in addition to gatherings of official representatives of governments.

In all these liaisons, there is one more bias that needs to be resisted. That's the bias toward loyalty *at all cost* to our original local grouping.

Misled by loyalty

It is said to take a whole village to raise a child[330]. Compared to infants in other animal species, human infants are particularly weak. An innate tendency to learn from those around us, to trust what they teach us, and to stick with them despite behaviour we cannot understand, serves us well as children. But as evolutionary scientist Richard Dawkins points out in his 1998 book *Unweaving the Rainbow*, the attributes that serve us well at one stage in our development sometimes fail to serve us well at a later stage. As Dawkins says, the characteristics of a good caterpillar differ from those of a good butterfly.

Dawkins uses the metaphor of an "automatically credulous" caterpillar transitioning into a "constructively sceptical" butterfly, to describe some key aspects of the passage of a human child to a human adult[331]:

> Not to grow up properly is to retain our 'caterpillar' quality from childhood (where it is a virtue) into adulthood (where it becomes a vice). In childhood our credulity serves us well. It helps us to pack, with extraordinary rapidity, our skulls full of the wisdom of our parents and our ancestors. But if we don't grow out of it in the fullness of time, our caterpillar nature makes us a sitting target for astrologers, mediums, gurus, evangelists and quacks.
>
> The genius of the human child, mental caterpillar extraordinary, is for soaking up information and ideas, not for criticizing them. If critical faculties later grow it will be in spite of, not because of, the inclinations of childhood. The blotting paper of the child's brain is the unpromising seedbed, the base upon which later the sceptical attitude, like a struggling mustard plant, may possibly grow. We need to replace the automatic credulity of childhood with the constructive scepticism of adult science.

In times of great distress, it's tempting to seek comfort and support from the community around us, rather than facing hardships in a solitary manner. To deepen our connections to that community, we may adjust our style of speaking, our dress, and our habits – and we may fall in line with whatever narrative ideas seem to be important in the community. It's of lesser concern to us whether there is any good evidence in favour of these narrative ideas. What's of more concern to us is whether we fit in, and are seen to fit in.

Sometimes the dissonance is too large. Many of us find ourselves alienated from members of the groups in which we find ourselves located. We cannot reconcile ourselves to their attitudes, their prejudices, and their prevailing worldview.

Nevertheless, even if we're ill-at-ease within our current community, our innate social tendencies remain. These tendencies push us to seek a new community where we can feel more at home. Social media makes it easy to find such communities nowadays – including ones that are geographically dispersed. What draws us to these new groups might be a perception that they'll help us economically; just as likely a draw is that they give us a sense of belonging, that overrides the estrangement we felt from the people in our original surroundings. They help us find meaning in life, and validate us, satisfying our inner needs. They make us feel cool, or part of a vanguard.

In this way, our loyalty attaches to a new community. As before, we might find *some* aspects of the narratives prevailing in that group to be strange; but in this case, we're happier to swallow our doubts and to press on regardless. We might not have 100% faith in these new narratives, but we do have faith that it's good to *display* faith in these new narratives.

Because we value these new groups, we want to secure our bonds to them. It's not sufficient that we happen, for a while, to be part of such a group. Loose connections are subject to unravelling. Instead, we have profound human desires for *status* in the groups that matter most to us. With increased status, our longer-term security has deeper roots:

- We're less likely to be driven out of these groups
- We're more likely to benefit from whatever fruits can be shared in these groups – physical rewards, social relations, intimacies, privileged knowledge, and control over the evolution of the group.

Our actions, therefore, often have the purpose of heightening our status in the groups that matter most to us. If we have a choice of banners to hold high – or a choice of which messages to publicise on social media – we reach a decision based, not on whether a particular message strikes us as being *true*. Instead, what matters is the *usefulness* of a message *as a signal*. Will that message mark us as a valuable member of the group where we care to have good status? If so, then our subconscious mind will get to work, and the rational parts of our brains will adapt to these messages.

With a heightened sense of the importance of group identity, we cheer on pro-group "blue lies" rather than respecting objective analysis[332]. It's like the way we applaud the crafty chicanery of the secret agents working for "our side" in any movie. The untruths confuse the enemy, and make it easier for "our side" to win. That end justifies the means. *Hoorah!* – says evolution.

Accordingly, if you see it as really important for candidate A to defeat candidate B in an election, you'll be inclined to spread any messages that discredit candidate B, regardless of whether these messages are fair.

It's as one of my friends-of-a-friend said on Facebook, explaining why she passed on a particular photograph seemingly validating a rumour concerning past homosexual preferences of VP-elect Mike Pence:

I have not verified this, but wouldn't be surprised....

Sharing just because even if fake it would piss this f*cker off.

A cursory online check quickly indicated that the photo in question had nothing to do with Pence[333]. The photo featured a gay porn actor, Brad Patton, who bore only a passing resemblance to the politician. Nevertheless, sharing the photo served the dual purpose of:

- Annoying members of political tribes disliked by my friend-of-a-friend
- Drumming up excitement and approval in the tribe she identified with – the tribe objecting to the election of Pence and Trump.

This is only one of very many examples of "striking below the belt" in recent political discussions. In such encounters, truthfulness limps far behind the fast-flying falsehoods. By the time any retraction might appear, confusion has multiplied, and the various tribes despise each other even more than before. Perversely, people felt good that they had strengthened their status within their own favoured tribes.

But there are many downsides to preferring loyalty to truthfulness. First, this loyalty may blind us to recognising when we're probably on the wrong side of an important debate. Second, even if our general position can be justified, our unflinching loyalty to it may prevent us appreciating a significant problem – a problem which, if we continue to ignore it, will end up undermining our whole approach.

For example, an overly loyal commitment to the European Union (EU), as opposed to your country separating from it, might leave you short-sighted to genuine design problems within the EU, such as dangerous tensions in the architecture of the Eurozone. Conversely, an overly loyal commitment to national sovereignty might leave you short-sighted to the need to sacrifice *some* elements of that sovereignty to address a particular transnational dilemma.

The best solutions often arise from combining the most important insights from conflicting perspectives. It can take some time to reach the right combination. If we're too biased by loyalty, we'll never see the whole picture, and we'll never find the best solutions.

Here are some steps forward to counteract this destructive tendency:

1. Spread awareness of examples of problems arising from excess loyalty, blue lies, and other motivated falsehoods
2. Reflect carefully whether the messages and ideas we're distributing do have an objective basis
3. Take advantage of independent fact-checkers, including those powered by AIs
4. Also take advantage of friendly "red team" adversarial exercises, to uncover possible shortcomings in positions we previously convinced ourselves were fully sound[334]
5. Be ready to acknowledge areas of uncertainty within our worldviews, rather than pretending that everything is rock solid
6. Document the dependencies between ideas clearly and fairly, in an accessible way – for example, in an open-access wiki
7. Respond in a polite, constructive way to people who sincerely express views that differ from ours
8. Keep conversations as free from stress and antagonism as possible, to reduce the pressure for people to revert to pro-tribal instincts.

The larger the network of people who are taking one or more of the above steps, the greater the chance for all of us to counteract the shortsight of tribal loyalty.

Nevertheless, a person's willingness to prioritise objective truth higher than tribal loyalty depends on whether they believe the objective truth really will back up their hopes and visions. If they suspect that reality will turn out to be opposed to these views, they may prefer to stick with their illusions. If they think that loss of faith will result in dissolute behaviour, in that case the possibility of loss of faith must be opposed at all costs, even if it means all sorts of cognitive trickery. If people need to be deceived in order for them to do what's best for them, let's keep the deception engines running. Better a comforting distortion than an unpleasant truth. Right?

That may be your view of life, but it's not mine. It's my judgement that the vision of transhumanist sustainable abundance is one that is objectively feasible. As I'll argue in the chapters that follow, this vision can be achieved without any cognitive trickery or engines of deception. Indeed, cognitive trickery or engines of deception would *prevent* us from seeing matters sufficiently clearly.

Beyond shortsight

Many of the causes of shortsight I've described in this chapter have the same solution: education. That's education about the pitfalls of insufficient understanding of evolution, exponentials, probabilities, confidence, normalcy, efficiency, immediacy, sovereignty, and loyalty. In view of their vital importance to building a better future, these topics need to be part of the core syllabus.

Alongside the pitfalls, education also needs to highlight reliable mechanisms for positive change. These mechanisms can transform the forces of disruption from being dangerous and destructive to being wonderfully constructive. Accordingly, let's take a closer look at disruption.

In the next chapter, I'll share some observations from the development of computers and smartphones – an industry that experienced considerable turbulence, with once-great companies mishandling (or *almost* mishandling) difficult transitions. In subsequent chapters, we'll deepen the understanding by reflecting on similar patterns in other areas of life.

6. Disruptions

Disruptions, defined: Violations of linear expectations. Existing patterns being usurped by new possibilities. The causes of failure of great businesses, movements, and empires – but also the means by which new businesses, movements, and empires can rise from obscurity to prominence.

"There's no chance that the iPhone is going to get any significant market share. No chance."

Steve Ballmer had joined Microsoft in 1980, as its 24th employee, and had helped steer that company from strength to strength. By 2000 he had taken over the CEO role from co-founder Bill Gates. Seven years into his tenure running the software giant, Ballmer was asked by USA Today senior media reporter David Lieberman to compare the fortunes of Microsoft and their long-time rival Apple[335].

The interview took place in April 2007, three months after Steve Jobs, Apple's CEO, had announced the iPhone in an electrifying stage performance, but two months before that device had started shipping. Alongside the adulation the new device had received, it was already clear that it would have unusually expensive hardware. Few phone users could afford such a device, Ballmer reasoned. He therefore gave his emphatic forecast about poor iPhone sales, quoted above. The forecast has since gone down in history as an infamous example of a bad prediction.

To his credit, Ballmer did more than just gesture. Living up to his reputation as a "numbers guy"[336], Ballmer went on, in his answer to David Lieberman, to make a more precise statement about the relative market share he expected for Apple phones versus phones running Microsoft software:

> If you actually take a look at the 1.3 billion phones that get sold, I'd prefer to have our software in 60% or 70% or 80% of them, than I would to have 2% or 3%, which is what Apple might get.

Step forward five years, to the second quarter of 2012. Consider the total of 406 million mobile phones that were sold worldwide in these three months[337]. Apple had a 6.4% share of that market, more than double the high end of the range predicted by Ballmer. Microsoft's Windows Phone software lagged far behind, featuring in just a small fraction of the smartphones shipped that quarter by the previously high-flying Nokia. The majority of

Nokia's smartphones at that time were still running Symbian OS, about which I'll say more below. By that stage, Nokia's smartphones comprised just 2.5% of global mobile phones sales. Both Nokia and Apple in turn lagged some way behind the smartphone market leader, Samsung, whose Android handsets already made up 12.4% of the entire phone market.

Step forward another five years, to April 2017. Ballmer's prediction now fares even worse. By this stage, Apple iPhones made up a chunky 19.9% of the entire phone market[338]. A few months later, Microsoft threw in the towel in the competition for smartphone market share, discontinuing the development of any new features for Windows Phone[339]. As a mark of the failure of that operating system, Bill Gates had stopped using Windows Phone on his personal handset, switching to Google's Android[340]. On the back of the very significant revenues from iPhone sales, Apple was already well on the way to becoming (in August 2018) the world's first publicly traded company with a valuation in excess of one trillion US dollars – and (in August 2020) the first with a valuation in excess of *two* trillion dollars.

If Steve Ballmer could misperceive the future so badly, despite his long experience at the helm of the world's premier software company, what hope is there for anyone else to make reliable predictions about the future of technology?

It turns out there is *plenty* of hope for better foresight. The key is to gain a fuller understanding of the phenomenon of *disruption*. That's my subject in this chapter – which I'll be connecting back to the book's broader discussion of both existential risks and existential opportunities.

It also turns out that many misleading things have been said by pundits about the relative trajectories of the various mobile operating systems. These misstatements are an example of a wider set of misleading assertions about disruption that are often heard. At the start of this book, I suggested that *a little foresight is a dangerous thing*. I'll now add: *A little learning about disruption is a dangerous thing.*

Indeed, something that prevents a proper appreciation of both the risks and opportunities of disruptions is an attitude that can be called "disruption worship". Going beyond respect for disruption to worshipping it, is a move fraught with hazard. That's something we need to learn to resist.

Changing games

Disruption is no ordinary kind of change. It's *not* about finding ways to deliver existing products more quickly, or at a lower price, or with additional features or improved quality. It's not about finding ways to play an existing game better. Instead, it's like switching to a new game, where the old rules lose their importance, and where the criteria for success are different from before. Hence the phrase "game-changing".

The terms "disruption" and "game-changer" share the feature that both are overused. Every little change in a product or service can be hyped as a game-changer. But the fact that these terms are overused doesn't mean they are devoid of value. On the contrary, disruptions are an important cause of companies losing their market power. In the political space, disruptions can be a cause of major changes in voter sentiment. And for sustainable solutions to the landmines among which humanity is currently sleepwalking, understanding and managing disruptions will be vital.

In these disruptions, the reason for the change in power – with formerly dominant companies or political regimes losing their support – isn't because the one-time leaders have lost their touch. Indeed, these one-time leaders generally keep on applying the same kinds of processes, ideas, and values that *previously* brought them success. But because the game has changed, these efforts now have less impact.

Consider, again, the manner in which Apple's iPhone disrupted the previous smartphone industry. By the way, I speak here with considerable feeling, since I witnessed at close quarters the emergence of the iPhone, and the reactions to it from numerous industry executives. I was no unbiased observer. My role on the senior leadership team at smartphone operating system pioneer Symbian – a position I held from 1998 until 2009 – meant that Apple's entry to this space posed an existential risk to my own business. In due course, indeed, Symbian was dissolved into its largest customer (and leading investor), Nokia, with all Symbian development activity being wound down a few years later. Like Microsoft's Windows Phone operating system, Symbian OS ultimately failed to survive the market disruption of the joint rise in prominence of both Apple's iPhone and Google's Android[341].

Ballmer was far from alone in predicting a lame future for the iPhone. Many other commentators had similar views. Indeed, as a phone, the iPhone wasn't particularly good. In attributes such as maintaining a cellular wireless connection, having clear voice audio, being robust when dropped, and its battery having a long lifespan, it fared poorly in comparisons with devices from longer-established phone manufacturers, such as Nokia, Motorola, Sony Ericsson, and Samsung. On these devices, the most important app was the one for making and receiving phone calls. The second most important app was SMS – text messaging. Yet the SMS app on the first iPhone lacked some basic functionality that other phones took for granted, such as being able to copy an SMS, or being able to send a single SMS to multiple recipients.

But that's only the start of the ways in which the first iPhone lagged its competitors. The 3G wireless standard was common on advanced phones when the iPhone was launched, but the iPhone didn't support it. As for camera functionality, the iPhone had no front-facing camera (hence no support for "selfies"), and its rear-facing camera lacked the handy auto-focus capabilities of competing devices. As for recording video, forget it: that feature was absent too. Yet another thing the first iPhone lacked was GPS – the ability to know its own position by picking up signals from satellites[342].

And let's not forget a couple of features that Microsoft's Steve Ballmer highlighted at the time[343]:

- Many business customers would be uninterested in the iPhone, since it lacked a physical keyboard – "which makes it not a very good email machine"
- The $500 price point exceeded by some margin what most users of phones would be willing to pay to purchase their device.

In summary, in terms of the existing competitive landscape, the iPhone was badly outgunned. However, the iPhone transformed that landscape:

1. Although "phone" was part of its name, for the iPhone, the phone app was no longer the most important piece of functionality
2. The iPhone performed brilliantly, instead, as an attractive mobile graphical interface to the world wide web – and to music
3. Whereas the old competitive game was to make devices smaller and lighter, the iPhone was surprisingly large – something users loved
4. Whereas the old competitive game was to create devices that were cheaper, the iPhone was packed full of expensive processors and built-in memory

5. The iPhone utilised a new kind of touch interface – in technical terms, the screen used "capacitive touch" rather than "resistive touch" – which delighted users by supporting two-fingered manipulation such as stretch, squeeze, and turn.

One more change in approach was at least as significant: a change in what can be called the "route to market". The other phone manufacturers all viewed the mobile network operators as their direct customers – companies such as Vodafone, AT&T, Orange, and T-Mobile. The support of these companies was critical for a phone to reach the market. Therefore, phone manufacturers needed to accept the key specification requests from leading network operators. This included the focus already mentioned on making devices that were smaller, lighter, and cheaper. In contrast, Apple saw individual phone users as their customers. If these phone users had a strong enough demand for handsets with particular features, the network operators would be obliged, Apple thought, to allow these devices onto their networks.

How did Apple succeed in this new game, despite all the competitive disadvantages when assessing the iPhone from the standpoint of the old game?

First, Apple made the old evaluative criteria less important. The old criteria were championed by gatekeepers in the old route-to-market, namely the network operators. But the opinions of these gatekeepers mattered less due to Apple's strong direct links to phone purchasers.

Second, Apple, along with users of their phones, developed or took advantage of some practical workarounds to the limitations of the device. For example, weak cellular signal management – including lack of 3G capabilities – mattered less in locations where wi-fi was available. And many users developed the unexpected habit of carrying *two* phones with them – a cheap, robust Nokia, for voice calls, and an expensive, sparkly Apple, for music, enhanced graphics, and web access.

Third, Apple took full advantage of a subsidy system which was already in place, whereby the purchase price of a phone was in effect covered by an initial loan from the network operator, which was repaid as part of increased data usage charges spread out over the next year or so. In a 2016 retrospective on his infamous 2007 prediction, Steve Ballmer chided himself for not having considered that option[344]:

> I wish I'd thought about the model of subsidizing phones through the operators. You know, people like to point to this quote where I said iPhones will never sell because the price at $600 or $700 was too high. And there was business model innovation by Apple to get it essentially built into the monthly cell phone bill.

The broader principle here is that technological innovation – in this case, using hardware with much higher specification – often needs to be accompanied by a business model innovation, or else it will fail to find a route to market. An *extension* of that principle, to which I'll return shortly, is that a successful disruption generally involves a *combination* of a number of different breakthroughs, that are applied at the same time.

It's at around this point that discussions of disruption often veer off into a set of recommendations that are actually misleading. The most important aspect of being a successful game-changer, we're often told, is to "think different", and to be ready to disregard the usual principles of effective business management. In this analysis, the previous giants of the mobile phone business were too wedded to their legacy ideas. They wanted to keep on doing what had already made them successful, rather than being ready to embrace innovation. They should have created nimble innovation teams instead.

My objection to this set of recommendations is that it significantly understates the actual effort required to successfully manage a disruption. Yes, being able to think differently is, indeed, a vital skill. But as we'll see, it's only a small part of the skillset needed.

Integrating trends

The *outcome* of a disruption is the phenomenon I've described above: a visible change in the landscape of expectations. Something has become important which was previously unimportant. Criteria for success have been displaced. People who continue competing according to the old rules no longer receive the same positive market response as before.

This *external* change generally arises from products or services being created using components or processes that are in some way novel. It's tempting to imagine that these components or processes must be brand new. However, what's more likely is that these components or processes have themselves followed a lengthy path of improvement. The hard task is to combine these individual improvement trends into an integrated whole.

Apple's iPhone successfully integrated at least *seven* such improvement trends – some of which Apple had already been nurturing inside the company, and some of which were adopted from outside. That's a pattern which applies, in general terms, to many other disruptions. It's worth taking a few moments to appreciate the scale of Apple's accomplishment, lest anyone is still tempted to attribute their success simply to "embracing innovation" or "thinking differently".

First, the iPhone extended a long line of previous products, namely Apple's iPod music playback devices. The iPod had gained market success because users found it easy – and enjoyable – to load up their device with music that they loved, and to listen to that music as they were on the move. These devices made it clear that many consumers were more interested in good user experience than in low product cost. Technology journalist Stephen Levy summed up the enthusiasm of millions of ardent iPod owners in October 2006 when he released a book entitled "The Perfect Thing" that was glowing with praise about the "coolness" of the device.[345]

Indeed, the growth of sales of the iPod had refuted another infamous "bad prediction", this time from British computer industry veteran Alan Sugar – founder of the company Amstrad. Sugar had spoken to the Daily Telegraph in February 2005, to promote his appearance on the UK's version of the TV show "The Apprentice". When the journalist raised the topic of the increasing global success of the iPod, Sugar had been scornful about the continuing prospects for the device:[346]

> Nah, bollocks! There's nothing in it. Every Chinese manufacturer has got one. Next Christmas the iPod will be dead, finished, gone, kaput.

Sugar's forecast was based on the assumption that portable music players were already a commodity: the greatest market share would go to manufacturers who could produce the lowest cost devices. That was a shallow analysis. Compared to its competitors, one task the iPods did particularly well was to enable a fast transfer of music from desktop computers, via cable, to the device. Apple had realised that slow music transfers posed a significant usability problem, and they had applied focused engineering effort to fix it. That feature, among others, made the device stand out in comparison to cheaper competitors. Ten months after Sugar's forecast – that is, by Christmas 2005 – iPod sales, far from being "dead, finished, gone, kaput", had grown fivefold.

Perhaps Sugar could have warned Steve Ballmer, two years later, that low cost was the wrong criteria to use when predicting sales of a new Apple device family. He might have added that it would be wiser to pay attention to the calibre of Apple's skills in both design and engineering – skills that Apple transferred from the iPod project to the iPhone project.

However, the prior project that many critics of the iPhone had in mind, back in 2007, wasn't the iPod; it was the Rokr project jointly conducted in 2005 by Apple and phone manufacturer Motorola. The Rokr included various pieces of iPod software inside hardware based on Motorola's highly popular Razr flip-phone. With total sales of around 130 million units, the Razr was the best-selling flip-phone ever[347]. Combining features of the Razr and the iPod seemed like a great idea. However, the Rokr had been dogged by problems. It was a worse phone than the Razr and a worse music playback device than the iPod.[348] Users who purchased the device reportedly returned it in droves.[349] The CEOs of Apple and Motorola, Steve Jobs and Ed Zander, exchanged public barbs as to the cause of this debacle.[350]

On the surface, the Rokr episode might have suggested that Apple would be unable to successfully integrate its iPod music experience into a mobile phone. But, again, that was the wrong conclusion to draw.

Apple's own conclusion from the Rokr project was that the integration of the two sets of technology should be handled by themselves, rather than being left to a phone manufacturer. That raised the question of where they could obtain suitable phone technology – the technology to interface with wireless cellular networks, and to conduct voice calls. And that takes us to the second trend which fed into the iPhone project: the trend that phone functionality was becoming available from independent technology suppliers.

As mentioned earlier, that phone functionality wasn't of the same high quality as the versions developed and incorporated by the leading phone manufacturers. However, Apple's judgement was that it was "good enough", and would become even better over time. It proved to be a shrewd decision.

A third trend that Apple integrated into the iPhone project was the emergence of a new kind of touch screen, namely capacitive touch. Compared to the touch screens on other phones at the time, capacitive displays enabled more intuitive operations such dragging, pinching, and stretching. Whereas the other smartphones with touch-sensitive screens were designed to be operated by a pen, the iPhone could be operated by a finger

– or thumb. In particular, this enabled one-handed operation: the user could use a single hand both to hold the device and to interact with its screen.

As it happens, up to this point, Nokia had been sceptical about the merit of including touch functionality in their smartphones. In their view, a touch screen would add to the cost of the device, reduce the sharpness of the display, and lead to the screen being covered with unsightly smudges. Worse, the need for one hand to hold a pen whilst the other held the device would rule out important use cases when the user already had one hand occupied carrying a shopping bag or pushing a trolley. It was the innovation of capacitive screens that altered the balance of that thinking.

But what could users do, by pressing and sliding their fingers and thumbs on the iPhone screen? They could interact with websites more easily, and with less delays, than on any previous smartphone. One reason for this improved browsing experience was Apple's choice of web browsing application for the iPhone: a modified version of the "Safari" browser that had already been in development for four years, and which had featured on Apple's desktop and laptop computers. Safari itself benefited from open source web-browsing software known as "Webkit". Safari therefore counts as the fourth component trend to be integrated into the iPhone.

That takes us to the question of the operating system that would connect together all the software necessary for the device. In an essay I had written back in August 2001 and circulated at that time within Symbian, "Towards the 100 millionth Symbian OS phone"[351], I had described the following as "the one billion-dollar question":

> What kind of software is going to be able to power increasing numbers of… phones with the latest high-end features?

That essay – which incorporated key insights from a number of my colleagues at Symbian – had been written at a time when the total number of smartphones sold was around only one million. It looked ahead some six years to a time when 100 million Symbian smartphones would have been sold. The essay includes much that I still consider good foresight[352]. However, one aspect of that essay can now be seen as decidedly short-sighted. Instead of the operating system question being "the one billion-dollar question", it turned into "the one *trillion*-dollar question" – seeing the impact on Apple's share price valuation from their success with the iPhone.

Just as Apple chose a modified version of their desktop web browser, Safari, for the iPhone, they also chose a modified version of their desktop operating system, macOS, as the basis for what became the iOS operating system inside the iPhone. Because of the significant hardware demands made by this operating system, it was an audacious choice. It would need extra memory and a powerful set of processors. However, Apple's calculation was that ongoing exponential improvements in semiconductors, as described by Moore's Law, had reduced the cost of that additional hardware by a sufficient amount. Yes, the device would be notably more expensive than competing smartphones. But this difference was within the range that the market could bear, on account of the advantages it brought. One of these advantages was that the close similarity in operating system meant that software originally written for desktop or laptop Macs – including the Safari web browser app – could be adapted relatively quickly for the iPhone.

The extra processing power did have another drawback: reduced battery lifetime. According to the previous prevailing wisdom, shorter battery life would be a fatal impediment for a smartphone. The iPhone would frequently run out of charge midway through a day. But this was another way in which the device disrupted the old rules. Owners of the iPhone quickly converted to charging up their devices more than once a day – and heavy users started carrying around portable recharging packs. *The game had changed.*

As a sixth component to be integrated, Apple took advantage of an evolution of their iTunes online music purchase network. Millions of users had already entrusted that network with their credit card information. Apple evolved that software into an iPhone management system, handling functionality such as backup, synchronisation, and enterprise configuration.

And that brings us to the seventh component: the iPhone app store, along with the systems whereby: developers could write apps, Apple would verify them, and users could find them, purchase them, and install them on their devices – with Apple receiving a 30% cut of the revenues. Before long, the extensive stock of apps was part of the reason why people preferred the iPhone.

Apple was by no means the inventor of the concept of mobile apps. Apps had already been available for a number of years for installation on mobile devices running Palm OS, Microsoft Windows Mobile, and Symbian OS, among other operating systems. Other phones supported apps written in frameworks such as Java or Brew. Nevertheless, Apple deserves special credit for an excellent implementation of the idea. Indeed, several aspects of Apple's systems for apps copied what was available for these other platforms, including Nokia's "Ovi" app store and the underlying "Symbian Signed" application certification initiative. However, Apple invested many times more resources in its versions of these systems. The difference showed.

To recap, Apple's disruption of the smartphone market was based on their successful integration of features from:

1. Their iPod family of music devices
2. Independently available phone functionality
3. Capacitive touch
4. The Safari web browser
5. The macOS operating system
6. The iTunes music distribution system
7. App creation, verification, and distribution.

Note in particular that this integration was far from being a single event. On the contrary, Apple followed the release of the original iPhone with a regular heartbeat of new releases. Each new release brought incremental improvements for the device, as well as the introduction of yet more features. Areas where the iPhone had previously fared poorly in competition, such as camera, map navigation, and support for 3G and later wireless cellular networks, saw considerable catch up. Before long, the iPhone was out-performing its competitors, not just according to the new criteria, but also according to many of the older criteria.

That's another important characteristic of disruption. The disruptive new platform may at first be dismissed by observers – especially those with vested interests in the current leading platforms – because it only outperforms these current platforms in what are seen as fringe areas. For example, consider the idea of downloading music over the Internet, as opposed to buying copies of music on physical media such as vinyl, tapes, or CDs. This disruption was at first thought to be relevant only to people who had little disposable income, and who didn't mind the awkwardness of connecting over modems to painfully slow websites – this was in the days when it was often said that "www" stood for "world wide wait". However, as Internet connectivity improved, a larger and larger segment of the population grew comfortable with using it to obtain their music. Stores such as HMV saw a decline in their customer numbers, moving from an initial slow trickle, to a larger reduction that in due course caused the company to declare bankruptcy[353].

In the general case, improvements within the disruptive platform can enable it to outperform previous platforms in a greater number of areas. Accordingly, the disruption moves from being an interesting curiosity with limited market significance, to posing an existential threat to companies or organisations who are overly wedded to the older platform.

Shifting gears

In a way, the story of the bankruptcy of music chain HMV was foretold by an exchange between two characters in Ernest Hemingway's 1926 novel *The Sun Also Rises*[354]:

> "How did you go bankrupt?" Bill asked.
>
> "Two ways," Mike said. "Gradually and then suddenly."

Disruptions typically pass through a phase in which little change is evident to any casual observer, before apparently shifting gear into a much more dramatic phase. The first phase can be characterised as "disappointing", from the point of view of people who had been expecting a bigger impact. The second phase can be characterised as "devastating". During the first phase, when forecasters draw attention to the trend in question, and warn of large impending consequences, critics tend to complain, "Oh not this again – it's *so* over-hyped". But during the second phase, when the world is in the process of being turned upside down, the complaint that is heard is "Why did no-one warn us about this?"

A simple model of this apparent shift in gear involves two upward-sloping curves. These curves represent the capabilities of, respectively, an existing dominant platform, and a disruptive new one. The first curve has a higher starting point, but a slower rate of growth. The second curve has a lower starting point but a faster rate of growth. If the trendlines continue on these trajectories, the second one eventually overtakes the first. When the public notices this has happened, it can lead to more people jumping on board the new platform – writing applications, or providing auxiliary services such as training, consultancy, and tools. This extra wave of support can cause an additional surge in the capabilities of the disruptive platform. Provided there is no matching uptick in the capabilities of the previous dominant platform, a market transition can occur, faster than what was previously thought possible.

Well, this model is *too* simple. Most trends that point upward for a while eventually run out of steam. Most would-be disruptions never make it out of the disappointing phase into a devastating phase. Recall from the section "Misled by exponentials" in the previous chapter that ongoing improvements in a field depend upon four conditions continuing to hold true:

1. The *scientific possibility* of further improvements
2. The *engineering feasibility* of relevant mechanisms to take advantage of these scientific possibilities
3. The *commercial viability* of the investments needed to achieve these engineering breakthroughs
4. Sufficient *social approval* of the necessary developments.

Accordingly, whether or not a trend actually becomes part of a disruption – as well as the timing of when this eventually happens – can be strongly influenced by

1. Breakthroughs in scientific understanding
2. Breakthroughs in the application of engineering – such as more capable teams focusing on that task, or teams applying new tools or new methodologies
3. The emergence of investors who take a longer-term view about paybacks from their support for an innovative idea, or who invest for reasons other than their own financial returns
4. Changes in the public mood regarding which matters have greater significance, and which others are seen as less important.

Changes of the above types can impact potential disruptions in two different ways:

1. Greater support for an innovation might cause that innovation to break through more quickly
2. A reduction in support for the management of the current dominant platform might cause that platform to become more vulnerable to shocks and disruptions.

For all these reasons, any modelling of disruptions as the interplay of two smooth curves can be at best only a first order approximation. There is no inevitability in the actual trajectories of progress. Real life is more fitful.

Consider the disruption that can be experienced by an existing financial system, as underlying instabilities accumulate beyond a tipping point. Mervyn King, who was the Governor of the Bank of England throughout the financial crisis of 2007-2009, has proposed "two laws of financial crisis"[355], which he attributes to the MIT economist Rudiger Dornbusch[356]:

> It is always surprising how many bricks can be piled one on top of another without their collapsing. This truth is embodied in the first law of financial crises: an unsustainable position can continue for far longer than you would believe possible. That was true for the duration of the Great Stability [the period starting in the mid-1980s which saw reduced volatility of business cycle fluctuations]. What happened in 2008 illustrated the second law of financial crises: when an unsustainable position ends it happens faster than you could imagine.

In other words: financial systems can continue for a long time in a state of intrinsic instability. During this period, most observers are misled by the outward signs of stability, and draw the wrong conclusions about likely future developments. These observers are then comprehensively surprised when the system actually breaks down. Such breakdowns arise from a combination of:

- Increased debts, reduced liquidity, excess interconnections, and other internal imbalances
- Stumbles by the authorities who are meant to be overseeing the system, but who may direct their attention instead at other *issues du jour*
- A wave of "animal spirits" – adverse sentiment regarding the future, leading to a decline in trust, and a desire to claw back investments to perceived safer formats, which further reduces the liquidity of the system.

But conversely, with a higher calibre of management, potential disruptions can be held at bay, and can even be integrated into existing dominant platforms to give these platforms greater vitality. A good example of this type involves one of the companies that featured at the start of this chapter: Microsoft. Although Microsoft failed to handle the disruption of smarter technology in mobile phones, they did succeed, around a decade earlier, in handling the disruption of the world wide web. That response also involved a dramatic shifting of gears.

Evolving understanding

The story of Microsoft and the world wide web starts with what looks like another piece of bad foresight.

The book *The Road Ahead* was published in November 1995[357]. The cover featured a photo of the principal author of the book, Bill Gates, CEO and co-founder of Microsoft, standing in the forefront of a road that stretched toward a distant horizon. The publishers gave this short summary of the book:

> The pioneering founder of Microsoft presents a visionary, jargon-free look at how the tools and emerging technologies of the future – especially the "Information Highway" – will transform the way we live and work.

Much of the content of *The Road Ahead* has passed the test of time well[358]. Online connectivity and distributed computing have, indeed, significantly transformed shopping, business, entertainment, and education. Digitisation has brought down costs to remarkable degrees. Easier access to information has led to the decline of professions such as travel agents or stockbrokers that previously acted as intermediaries or gatekeepers to information. Social communities keep in touch via displays on screens. Video conversations have become convenient and ubiquitous[359]. Gates was right on all these counts.

Another merit of the book was its willingness to be serious about future timescales. Many of the use cases described by Gates wouldn't be possible "for at least a decade", he foresaw. This delay was primarily due to the time that would be required to provide broadband connectivity to houses throughout the country. As some readers may remember, most connectivity to the Internet in 1995 took place over "narrowband" provided by dial-up modem links, with their whistling start-up negotiations that often dragged on for minutes, and with the line frequently being dropped partway through an exchange of data. For the video services that Gates saw as the eventual "killer app" for the Internet, faster connectivity would be needed. To emphasise this point, Gates stated,

> Today's Internet is not the information highway I imagine, although you can think of it as the beginning of the highway.

Gates pointed to the frustrations experienced by users of narrowband Internet:

> It's important that expectations don't get cranked too high. The total number of users of the Internet is still a small part of the population. And

> the attrition rate is high – many subscribers drop off, disappointed, after less than a year.

This is in line with a forecast Gates is reported to have made at the Comdex tradeshow in Las Vegas in the previous year, 1994[360]:

> I see little commercial potential for the Internet for the next 10 years.

Even the earliest reviews of *The Road Ahead* picked up on its lack of coverage of the topic of the world wide web. Here's an extract from a November 1995 review by Seattle Times writer Paul Andrews[361]:

> I found Gates' observations on the Internet weakest of all. The World Wide Web receives just four index citations and is treated as a functional appendage of the Internet (rather than its driving force).

One reason the book's omission of any serious discussion of the world wide web was particularly surprising was the public prominence, three months earlier, of the IPO (Initial Public Offering) of Netscape. Netscape's web browser, codenamed "Mozilla", had quickly taken three quarters of the market for web browsing. I personally remember being stunned when the graphics capabilities of that browser were pointed out to me by a student intern at Psion where I worked at the time.

On the day of their IPO, Netscape's valuation surged to nearly three billion dollars[362]. By the time *The Road Ahead* was published, that valuation had almost tripled. Alongside investment from major banks, what drove the growth in Netscape's share price was the large numbers of users of the web browser who were enchanted by what it could accomplish, and who decided they wanted a share in that company's future.

With the success of companies like Yahoo and Amazon as well as Netscape, the Internet developed huge commercial significance much sooner than the ten-year delay forecast by Gates.

The lack of analysis of the world wide web in *The Road Ahead* wasn't simply due to a blind spot by Bill Gates. The book had two additional authors: Peter Rinearson, a Pulitzer Prize winning journalist and entrepreneur, and Nathan Myrvhold, who had founded Microsoft Research in 1991 and who was appointed as Microsoft's first Chief Technology Officer. With all the superstar brainpower behind the book, how did such a startling omission happen?

Part of the answer involves a phenomenon I'll explore in more depth in the next section: inertia. It takes time to make changes. In this case, it took many months to prepare the book for publication. The book was accompanied by a CD ROM of additional "companion" material; this added to the time elapsed between the content being finalised and the product reaching shops. One more complication stretched out this delay even further: Microsoft's decision to launch the book simultaneously in multiple countries, for maximum market impact.

Even before the first version was available for sale, the team behind the book were already working on some significant rewrites. These would be included in the second edition of the book, published in September 1996, which was described as "Completely revised and up-to-date".

Even before work had started on these revisions – in fact, back in May 1995 – Gates had amended his own views on the importance of the Internet, including the growing number of applications that utilised narrowband access. He announced his latest understanding in a memo circulated to his executive staff. The title of the memo set the tone: "The Internet Tidal Wave"[363]. What happened with the Internet "over the next several years", Gates wrote, would "set the course of our industry for a long time to come". He then clarified how his thinking had changed:

> Perhaps you have already seen memos from me or others here about the importance of the Internet. I have gone through several stages of increasing my views of its importance. Now I assign the Internet the highest level of importance. In this memo I want to make clear that our focus on the Internet is crucial to every part of our business. The Internet is the most important single development to come along since the IBM PC was introduced in 1981. It is even more important than the arrival of the graphical user interface (GUI).

Gates recognised that content on the web benefited from positive feedback loops:

> The Internet has bootstrapped itself as a place to publish content. It has enough users that it is benefiting from the positive feedback loop of the more users it gets, the more content it gets, and the more content it gets, the more users it gets.

The more Gates had looked at what was already possible on the web, the more serious he had become:

> Amazingly it is easier to find information on the Web than it is to find information on the Microsoft Corporate Network. This inversion where a

> public network solves a problem better than a private network is quite stunning.

He anticipated some "scary" scenarios, in which the PC – software for which provided most of Microsoft's revenues – would lose its significance as the main access route for consumers to connect to wider networks:

> One scary possibility being discussed by Internet fans is whether they should get together and create something far less expensive than a PC which is powerful enough for Web browsing.

But the memo was more than an expression of surprise – and more than an exhortation to think differently from before. The memo was full of technical details, and spelt out many existing trends and initiatives that Microsoft should now move urgently to prioritise. The overall result would have the same characteristic as many important disruptions: a step-by-step integration of diverse components and processes.

In this way, Gates led a remarkable refocusing of Microsoft: the world wide web would no longer be a kind of afterthought; from now on, mastery of this emerging new field would be central to the company's plans. By September 1998, Microsoft Internet Explorer had overtaken Netscape Navigator as the most widely used web browser[364]. And Microsoft continued to move from strength to strength.

A number of key factors enabled Microsoft to manage this powerful disruption in a way that brought the company additional success. When considering future disruptions, in fields including politics and society as well as business, the outcome may well depend on whether similar factors apply:

1. The executives running Microsoft had a good grasp of the essentials of the company's products and technologies, rather than trotting out empty buzzwords or weighing up decisions at purely a financial accounting level
2. The same executives were committed to re-evaluating their strategy on a regular basis, rather than viewing it as something fixed and unchanging
3. When strategic initiatives changed in priority, the company's engineering teams could be redirected relatively easily from their previous tasks
4. Where new components could not be developed quickly enough in-house, the company was able to spend money, decisively, to acquire

solutions from outside itself and them integrate these solutions into its own systems, where they could be evolved further

5. The company had a culture of openly sharing via email ideas that were creative and even controversial
6. The company was able to accept input from relatively junior members of staff that ran at variance to prevailing internal wisdom.

As an illustration of the last of these points, consider an email written by a manager at an early stage in his career at Microsoft, on returning from a trip to Cornell University to conduct recruitment interviews. During his time on campus, he had observed students making wide use of the web, for tasks such as managing their schedules. Netscape was everywhere, he had realised. Accordingly, he fired up a report, which various colleagues remember as a "sky is falling" memo. The manager pleaded for attention: "Microsoft will go out of business" unless it pays attention to this disruption, he wrote. Because others in the company were already starting to have similar thoughts, the different lines of analysis dovetailed in positive ways, helping to spur Gates himself to change his mind.

Accumulating treacle

If Microsoft could pivot itself relatively quickly to transform the threat of web disruption into a positive advantage, why did it fail to make a similar transformation regarding the threat of smartphones? Why did it end up losing the smartphone operating system war, whereas it fared well in the browser wars?

And just as important, why were other companies, such as Nokia, unable to respond sufficiently to the threats to their livelihoods posed by the dual disruption of Apple iPhone and Google Android?

Was it that these companies lost the desire to be innovative, and were overly committed to outdated modes of operation?

That's the kind of analysis that is often raised. But I see that answer as misleading. Instead, the answer I offer is "treacle"[365]. Or in different words, "debt", or "inertia".

In physics, inertia measures the tendency to keep going in the same direction as before. The bigger the inertia, the bigger the force needed to cause a change of direction. According to a common metaphor, ocean liners are particularly hard to turn around quickly. They've got enormous inertia.

For organisations that do similar tasks again and again, and which are good at carrying out these tasks, there can be advantages to having a large inertia. This prevents the organisation from wasting energy by introducing errors or other deviations from a pathway that has a proven track record. But when the game changes – when different types of action are needed – that inertia can prevent the necessary changes from taking place.

Rather than an ocean liner which is steaming along by itself in the open ocean, consider one that is moving in close formation with a flotilla of other ships. Each vessel constrains the movement of the others: any movement in a new direction needs to be choreographed at a group level. But if the crew on any one of these ships is preoccupied with continuing along their "business as usual" route, it makes it even harder for the group as a whole to manoeuvre. That describes the situation where a large company works in close alignment with a complicated logistics chain of suppliers and partners. If the logistics have been optimised, with little slack, that restricts the agility of the company. As covered in the previous discussion "Misled by efficiency", initiatives to improve efficiency need to sit alongside initiatives to improve resilience, that is, to improve the capability to respond in constructive ways to shocks and blows.

One cause of having restricted freedom of movement is being burdened by debt. This debt might be financial, technical, strategic, or behavioural.

Financial debt is when you have paid insufficient attention to savings or income, so you don't have enough money available to let you make the changes that you have in mind. Technical debt is when you have paid insufficient attention to the quality of your technology platform or its accompanying tools, so your technology lacks the flexibility to operate in the new ways that you have in mind. Strategic debt is when you've failed to take *and implement* hard choices about the future direction of your company or organisation, and the resulting tensions and conflicts prevent effective internal cooperation. Behavioural debt is when you've treated potential partners badly in the past, diminishing their willingness to cooperate with you in new projects; once again, you end up unable to make the changes that you have in mind.

Technical debt was a primary cause of Nokia's inability to adapt sufficiently quickly to the challenges posed to its smartphone business by Apple and Google. As a company, Nokia was full of innovative ideas, which arose from its research division with its many links to leading universities around the world, as well as from feedback it received from hundreds of millions of users of its products. However, these ideas took longer and longer to add into their phone line-up.

In principle, with software, anything is possible. That's what the "soft" in the word "software" implies. However, as software increases in its complexity, changes in one piece of functionality tend to break other pieces of functionality. That's because of the interconnectedness and re-use of many parts of the software system. Worse, unless a comprehensive test suite is in place and is run on a regular basis, changes in one piece of functionality may cause problems with other pieces of functionality that aren't detected until much later.

Things become even more complicated when an underlying piece of platform software supports a range of different products and product families. A company's desire to release products quickly can lead to short-cuts in the maintenance of the platform. After all, the products are visible to end users, and need to sparkle. The platform is much less visible. Short-cuts made in the platform therefore tend to accumulate. And that's how technical debt grows. Like financial debt, it may not seem dangerous in the beginning. But once it grows larger, it tends to expand more quickly.

By around 2004, there was a growing degree of technical debt at all layers of the software included in Nokia phones: the Symbian operating system, the hardware adaptations that connected the operating system to different types of phone hardware, and the S60 ("Series 60") user interface and app framework. As a result, changes that Nokia wanted to implement – changes in the UI or in the functionality of devices – frequently took longer than expected. One truly painful example is that the addition of pen (touch) capability to S60, first announced by Nokia managers in November 2004 as being expected in less than 18 months, ended up taking more than two and a half times as long: 48 months[366]. That's despite the underlying Symbian OS having supported touch since 1997.

Nokia also suffered from a growth of strategic debt. Different executives had conflicting views on the relative importance of matters such as:

1. The "wild west" phone market of the United States – compared to other regions of the world where sales were much larger and where wireless cellular standards were more uniform

2. The inclusion of touch – as opposed to relying on physical buttons and keypads
3. Switching from Symbian OS to one or more new software platforms based on Linux
4. Business users, with their own special requirements
5. Phones containing expensive high-powered hardware – similar to the strategy adopted by Apple – compared to phones with lower price points and therefore greater unit sales.

For a number of years, Nokia in effect selected "all of the above", demonstrating an impressive ability to pursue multiple market segments in parallel. Over time, however, as the technical debt of their platforms grew in scale, a greater focus may well have served the company as a better strategy.

While Nokia was still creating scores of different phone models each with distinctive features, Apple had a dramatically simpler line-up of products. What's more, Apple raised the issue of user experience right to the top of their hierarchy of priorities. To be fair to Nokia, there were many employees inside that company who were passionate – and highly knowledgeable – about the design of user experience. But the contrast with Apple is that designers had much greater influence inside Apple than their counterparts had within Nokia. Indeed, Apple's lead designer, Jonathan Ive, reported directly to their CEO, Steve Jobs, and wielded enormous power over product decisions[367]. Nokia's designers, on the other hand, had to operate in an environment more akin to treacle.

The treacle of strategic debt can in similar ways hinder society's responses to major disruptive threats and opportunities. As a result of conflicting underlying strategic inclinations, key influencers within society may fight rearguard actions against policies that are actually good choices. These underlying inclinations might include profound distrust:

- Of major corporations
- Of particular industries
- Of anything that might be described as "socialist"
- Of anything that might be seen as "international government"
- Of anything that might look like a religion
- Of people from particular countries or with particular ethnicities

- Of particular technologies – such as nuclear, genetic modification, algorithmic analysis of big data, or surveillance tech.

The way to overcome strategic debt is to bring the various underlying tensions and conflicts out into the open, to make the case that specific actions offer the best prospects for advancing shared goals, and – with some care – utilising a number of cognotech solutions to be described in later chapters of this book.

The way to address technical debt is to not let it grow in the first place, or if it has grown, to deploy engineering teams of sufficient calibre to undo the damage. In some cases, the best action will be to switch platforms altogether – but bear in mind that the project to select and develop a new platform will often be significantly more difficult than suggested by enthusiasts for the various platforms under consideration. Let's just say on this point that platform engineering is a profoundly important skill.

Incurring debt

Back in 1999, Microsoft employed many engineers with world class capabilities in the design and delivery of platform technologies. Microsoft's subsequent poor performance with smartphones cannot be attributed to any shortage of platform engineering skills. The cause instead involved both strategic debt and behavioural debt. Once again, vital lessons can be learned.

1999 was also the year in which Microsoft faced, and arguably flunked, a key strategic decision about operating systems for smart mobile devices. The company's established viewpoint, as set out in the book *The Road Ahead*, was that mobile access to online services would largely take place through various devices that were each, in their own way, miniature PCs – and each running reduced versions of Microsoft Windows. *The Road Ahead* enthused about an envisaged "Wallet PC"[368]:

> Wallet PCs with the proper equipment will be able to tell you where you are anyplace on the face of the Earth. GPS receivers… will be built into many wallet PCs. The wallet PC will connect you to the information highway while you travel a real highway and tell you where you are. Its built-in speaker will be able to dictate directions to you to let you know that a freeway exit is coming up or that the next intersection has frequent accidents. It will monitor digital traffic reports and warn you that you'd better leave for the airport early or suggest an alternate route…

> Some wallet PCs will be simple and elegant and offer only the essentials such as a small screen, a microphone, a secure way to transact business with digital money, and the capability to read or otherwise use basic information. Others will bristle with all kinds of gadgets, including cameras, scanners that will be able to read printed text or handwriting, and receivers with the global-positioning capability. Most will have a panic button for you to press when you need emergency help. Some models will include thermometers, barometers, altimeters, and heart-rate sensors.

These wallet PCs evidently have much in common with today's smartphones. However, as we know, today's smartphones are typically *not* viewed as miniature PCs, and they don't run versions of Microsoft Windows.

For Bill Gates, Microsoft Windows was the strategic centre of the company's technology future. Under his direction, Microsoft developed a "compact edition" ("CE") of Windows, named Windows CE, for use in "companion" products. Windows CE presented developers with a similar programming interface to that of the PC's version of Windows. It also presented users with a similar user interface to that of PC's Windows, including a pruned-back "start" button. But the leader of Microsoft's Consumer Appliances group, Harel Kodesh, grew increasingly concerned about these decisions.

Before joining Microsoft, Kodesh had worked in the mobile data division of phone manufacturer Motorola, where he was responsible for new technology in wireless radio modems and handsets. The Microsoft press release announcing Kodesh's promotion to the position of VP (Vice President) had extolled his achievements[369]:

> We are delighted to recognize the truly valuable contributions that Harel Kodesh … [has] made to Microsoft. Harel has overseen the development and introduction of our Windows-CE based products, and the success that these products are now enjoying is in large part owing to his skill, enthusiasm and hard work.

The same press release described Kodesh's new role:

> Kodesh, vice president of consumer appliances, manages the development and marketing of the Microsoft Windows CE operating system and its embedded development kits as well as categories of information appliances that run on Windows CE, such as the Handheld PC, Palm-size PC, Auto PC and Sega Dreamcast.

However, within a year, Kodesh had undergone what Wall Street Journal writer David Bank called "an almost religious epiphany". Bank covered Kodesh's change of heart as an important episode in his 2001 book *Breaking Windows: How Bill Gates Fumbled the Future of Microsoft*[370]. As you can tell from that book's subtitle, its author took a dim view of several of the actions of Bill Gates. The general story in that book follows a familiar pattern: the genius and tactics that enabled a company to outperform its competitors during its rise to dominance often serve it badly once that company has become dominant. Without appropriate reinvention, the company can lose its vitality, and become bogged down in a kind of treacle.

A partial reinvention was what Kodesh proposed – and what Gates rejected[371]. Initially, Kodesh accepted the "Windows Everywhere" philosophy. As described by Bank, that philosophy was as follows:

> As with PCs, a uniform operating system across many different electronic devices would attract software developers, who generally target their efforts on the highest-volume platform. Because Windows CE used the same tools and Win32 interfaces as Windows for the PC, Microsoft's dominance in the PC market would give it additional leverage in the non-PC world. Windows CE was a key element in the Windows Everywhere strategy.

But despite the optimistic note in the press release mentioned earlier – that talked about "the success" that Windows CE products "are now enjoying" – Kodesh knew that these products were actually faring poorly in the marketplace:

> Microsoft seemed permanently behind in the handheld market, where Palm was established as the software of choice for "personal digital assistants." And Microsoft was being outflanked by a consortium of cell phone makers, led by Nokia, which established the Symbian joint venture with a British software maker, Psion, to create a specialized operating system for Web-connected cell phones, a potentially huge market.

After discussing the general theory of disruption with its intellectual pioneer, Professor Clayton Christensen of Harvard[372], Kodesh developed the radical proposal that these new types of devices needed a new approach for the technology platform they contained. He wrote his proposals in a memo to Bill Gates and Steve Ballmer entitled "Starting from Scratch":

> Microsoft should start from scratch on new software for cell phones and all other non-PC devices.

The Windows CE platform was unsuited for those categories of device, Kodesh argued. The constraint of keeping the Win32 interfaces overly complicated the design. Rather than this similarity being an advantage, it was "a tax on device design". Kodesh proposed building an autonomous new team as a "company within a company" who would "work solely on developing the best software for information appliances, unconstrained by the needs of the rest of the company".

The answer given by Gates:

> It's very disappointing you feel that way. We don't have time to start from scratch.

Kodesh left Microsoft a few months later, and went on to enjoy a distinguished career in a number of major tech companies, including Amdocs, EMC, and GE Digital. In parallel, Windows CE and its successors, Windows Mobile and Windows Phone, continued to struggle against its competitors, including Palm OS, Symbian OS, RIM BlackBerry, Apple iOS, and Google Android.

A key objection raised by Kodesh was to the idea that "Microsoft knows best". In his view, the company was wrong to pressurise device manufacturers to shoehorn PC applications such as Excel and Word into their products, regardless of the design ideas of these manufacturers:

> Microsoft should start from the other direction, asking manufacturers what they could build for, say, ninety-nine dollars and offering to give them the software they needed, rather than only the software the company already had.

It was a perceptive comment. Over my years working with companies who produced smartphones from more than one OS provider, I heard similar complaints on many occasions: Microsoft was too much of a bully in its relationships, controlling too closely what manufacturers could do with their software, and seeking to take what seemed an excessive share of the profits from the relationship. In other words, they accumulated behavioural debt.

On more than one occasion during these discussions comparing different OS providers, the fable of the scorpion and the frog arose. The fable seems to have originated in a Russian folk story[373]:

> A scorpion, which cannot swim, asks a frog to carry it across a river on the frog's back. The frog hesitates, afraid of being stung by the scorpion, but the scorpion argues that if it did that, they would both drown. The frog

considers this argument sensible and agrees to transport the scorpion. Midway across the river, the scorpion stings the frog anyway, dooming them both. The dying frog asks the scorpion why it stung despite knowing the consequence, to which the scorpion replies: "I couldn't help it. It's in my nature."

What made this fable resonate with people on the rough end of Microsoft's dominating behaviour was the happenstance that the name chosen by Microsoft for a version of Windows CE targeted at smartphones was – wait for it – "Stinger"[374]. Microsoft had proclaimed that they had changed their style of partnering from the domineering way they interacted with PC manufacturers. Their relationship with phone manufacturers would, instead, be mutually beneficial, they said. But when so much of a company culture has been based on a particular philosophy, it's hard to change it. Words are easier than deeds. One phone manufacturer, the British-based Sendo, felt so aggrieved at Microsoft's actions that they tabled a 27-page court filing alleging theft of trade secrets and proprietary technology[375]. The case was settled out of court a couple of years later. Seeing what was happening, other phone manufacturers gingerly maintained collaborations with Microsoft, holding their nose in the process, and refraining from putting their hearts into the relationship. In this way, behavioural debt impeded Microsoft's ability to fully capitalise on the disruptions of smartphones.

Enabling multitudes

There's one final lesson that should be learned from the ups and downs of smartphone operating systems – one more insight applicable to the general case of anticipating and managing disruptions. This lesson arises from the example of the rise of open source software within smartphones. That was a trend which spent many years proceeding slowly, before shifting gears into something much faster and wider. The outcome was that the dominant operating system for smartphones in the early 2020s, as measured by the number of smartphones using the platform, isn't Apple's iOS, despite the huge profile of the iPhone, but Google's Android.

When software is open source, the source code is publicly available on the Internet. No-one needs to pay any license fees to use that software, or to copy it or to modify it for their own purposes. In contrast, for closed source software, the source code is hidden behind protective barriers, and cannot be viewed, copied, or modified, except on payment of a license fee.

I've already mentioned two important ways in which Bill Gates' book *The Road Ahead* failed to foresee future developments: lack of anticipation of:

1. Extensive adoption of the world wide web over narrowband connections
2. Mobile phones gaining capabilities and becoming the vehicle for many services Gates envisioned as being delivered by "wallet PCs".

It's time to add a third omission: the growth in significance of open source software. Gates had a long track record of criticising open source software. This criticism went all the way back to 1976, when Microsoft was still styled as "Micro-Soft" and was based in Albuquerque, New Mexico, and when the company's twenty-year-old co-founder referred to himself as "William Henry Gates III". In that year, Gates had published a letter complaining about the open distribution of software source code. Without mincing words, Gates had decried that practice as a kind of robbery[376]:

> As the majority of hobbyists must be aware, most of you steal your software. Hardware must be paid for, but software is something to share. Who cares if the people who worked on it get paid?

The young Gates argued that the only way significant software could be written is if people are paid as a result:

> Who can afford to do professional work for nothing? What hobbyist can put three man-years into programming, finding all bugs, documenting his product and distribute for free?

Someone with a different view was Linus Torvalds, the lead developer behind the open source operating system Linux. As a twenty-one-year old student at the University of Helsinki, Torvalds had released a prototype version of Linux in 1991. In asking members of the newsgroup comp.os.minix for feedback on features he should include, Torvalds declared that[377]:

> I'm doing a (free) operating system (just a hobby, won't be big and professional...)

By 1993, over 100 developers were making contributions to Linux – without anyone being paid for these contributions. By 1995, versions of the platform ran on two families of minicomputers: the DEC Alpha and the Sun Sparc. Support for Linux from major computing companies such as Compaq, Hewlett Packard, IBM, and Oracle would follow shortly.

Linux was by no means the only open source project that was becoming significant by 1995. The Apache web server software was also being developed and distributed collaboratively by this time[378], with the software freely available to anyone who wished to study it or help improve it. Richard Stallman had created the Free Software Foundation ten years earlier, and by 1989 had released the first version of the GNU GPL licence which was designed to strengthen positive collaboration between advocates and users of "free software" (an earlier name for some types of open source). A compiler – a piece of software central to the development of new software – known as GNU GCC was available soon afterward, and became used increasingly widely throughout the software industry. Indeed, by early 1995, GNU GCC became part of the toolchain used to create what would become Symbian OS.

Yet there are no references in *The Road Ahead* (published in 1995) to Linux, Apache, or "open source", and only fleeting references to "free software". The book assumed that the software industry would continue to be dominated by software written for profit, rather than software written and distributed for free.

By 1998, Microsoft was paying more serious attention to the threat that open source might pose to its business. A leaked series of internal Microsoft articles that became known as "The Halloween Documents" highlighted the competitive strengths of open source, including Linux, and reviewed tactics by which Microsoft might hinder or neutralise the growth of open source[379]. The tactics reviewed included[380]:

- "Fear, uncertainty, and doubt" – announcing new Microsoft products as "forthcoming", with appealing feature sets, even though they don't exist
- "Embrace, extend, and extinguish" – adopting the same communications protocols and file standards as are used by open source software, but then extending and modifying them in ways that favour Microsoft products and break the open source software.

One effect of these documents was to spur the open source community to greater efforts. Eric Raymond, the free software advocate to whom the Halloween Documents had been leaked, had already written an essay on why open source methods could be so powerful[381]. The title of the essay, "The

Cathedral and the Bazaar", reflected Raymond's realisation that two different approaches were possible for the creation of large, complex software systems:

> I [previously] believed there was a certain critical complexity above which a more centralized, a priori approach was required. I believed that the most important software… needed to be built like cathedrals, carefully crafted by individual wizards or small bands of mages working in splendid isolation, with no beta to be released before its time.
>
> Linus Torvalds's style of development – release early and often, delegate everything you can, be open to the point of promiscuity – came as a surprise. No quiet, reverent cathedral-building here – rather, the Linux community seemed to resemble a great babbling bazaar of differing agendas and approaches… out of which a coherent and stable system could seemingly emerge only by a succession of miracles.

Raymond noted his "distinct shock" that "this bazaar style seemed to work, and work well". But the essay went on to offer a theoretical explanation for the productivity of the bazaar approach, as led by Torvalds:

> While coding remains an essentially solitary activity, the really great hacks come from harnessing the attention and brainpower of entire communities. The developer who uses only his or her own brain in a closed project is going to fall behind the developer who knows how to create an open, evolutionary context in which bug-spotting and improvements get done by hundreds of people.

Raymond therefore proposed what he called "Linus' Law":

> Linus was keeping his hacker/users constantly stimulated and rewarded – stimulated by the prospect of having an ego-satisfying piece of the action, rewarded by the sight of constant (even daily) improvement in their work.
>
> Linus was directly aiming to maximize the number of person-hours thrown at debugging and development, even at the possible cost of instability in the code and user-base burnout if any serious bug proved intractable. Linus was behaving as though he believed something like this:
>
> *Given a large enough beta-tester and co-developer base, almost every problem will be characterized quickly and the fix obvious to someone.*
>
> Or, less formally, "Given enough eyeballs, all bugs are shallow." I dub this: "Linus' Law".

As Raymond explains, the division of contributions within an engaged community goes further than simply many people all trying to do the same thing:

> My original formulation was that every problem "will be transparent to somebody". Linus demurred that the person who understands and fixes the problem is not necessarily or even usually the person who first characterizes it. "Somebody finds the problem", he says, "and *somebody else* understands it. And I'll go on record as saying that finding it is the bigger challenge." But the point is that both things tend to happen quickly.

The growing success of Linux itself exemplifies the principles of convergence and integration that I have been describing. As Raymond comments, Torvalds was able to take advantage of something that previously didn't exist:

> Linux was the first project to make a conscious and successful effort to use the entire world as its talent pool. I don't think it's a coincidence that the gestation period of Linux coincided with the birth of the World Wide Web, and that Linux left its infancy during the same period in 1993-1994 that saw the takeoff of the ISP [Internet Service Provider] industry and the explosion of mainstream interest in the Internet. Linus was the first person who learned how to play by the new rules that pervasive Internet made possible.

It seems that Torvalds himself was stung by the negativity toward free and open software exhibited by Microsoft's Hollywood Documents. During his keynote address at the Linux World event in Spring 1999 in San Jose, California, Torvalds gave a number of tongue-in-cheek forecasts about the future[382] in a slide headed "What our grandchildren will say":

> My dog rejected her chip implant. What should I do?
>
> My 12-year old son hacked the toaster, and changed the root password. Now it only does peanut butter and jelly sandwiches. Do I need to buy a new toaster, or can I use remote administration for Linux v7.1 to reset it?

Then came a prediction with more venom:

> MicroSoft? They used to do computers, right?

And in his next slide, Torvalds said the answer to the question "Wouldn't you like to be Bill Gates?" was to ask in return, "Bill who?"

Referring to the picture on the cover of *The Road Ahead*, Torvalds used even more hostile language:

> People standing in the middle of the road look like road kill to me.

But could Linux, or any other open source software, really displace operating systems written by large commercial companies, in the majority of PCs, or in the majority of smartphones?

That question was on my own mind in 2001 while I was writing the essay "Towards the 100 millionth Symbian OS phone"[383] that I mentioned earlier in this chapter. In that essay, I reviewed the strengths and weaknesses of various operating systems. I acknowledged the capabilities of open source:

> What about Linux? Hasn't the open source development model at last found the counter-example to the mythical man month maxim? Yes, the open source community has produced some remarkable software. But it's not a miracle worker.

I offered two reasons why Linux would pose only a limited threat to Symbian OS. First, the source code for Symbian OS could be shared within the community of companies that created devices based on that platform. It was not "open source" as such but "community source". Therefore, the same benefit that applied to Linux also applied to Symbian: a multitude of different developers could become involved and help to improve the software.

Second, Linux was too heavyweight for the requirements of smartphones:

> Like Microsoft CE, Linux comes from a heritage that is far removed from mobile phones. In mobile phones, efficient power management is a necessity. That didn't feature in the requirements for Windows, nor for Linux. Likewise for a close focus on efficient use of memory, for avoiding memory leaks even in low memory situations, and so on.

For most of the remainder of that decade, that assessment seemed to be prescient. Numerous companies *tried* to use Linux in various ways as the basis for smartphones, but achieved very limited market success. Sales of Symbian-powered smartphones far exceeded their Linux-based competitors, reaching a cumulative total of 100 million by November 2006[384], 200 million by April 2008[385], and 500 million by January 2012[386].

That's an impressive upward curve, with the appearance of exponential growth. As we now know, that upward curve was about to be overtaken – disrupted – by two other upward curves that had started later and, initially, slower. Android, based on Linux, reached a cumulative total of 500 million by September 2012[387], and Apple reached that same milestone with the iPhone by March 2014[388]. And both these upward trajectories have continued rising ever since, whereas Symbian sales had stalled by 2012. But neither of these upcoming transitions were particularly obvious during the early days of these newer smartphone platforms.

Google had announced its plans for Android in November 2007: a phone platform based on the Linux operating system[389]. Andy Rubin, the leader of the initiative inside Google – who had first conceived of the idea of Android four years earlier – emphasised that

> We are not building a GPhone; we are enabling 1,000 people to build a GPhone.

Rubin forecast that Google's open-source strategy would lower the barrier for new companies to create smart mobile devices and enable rapid innovation by multiple manufacturers.

Backing up these statements was the announcement of an "Open Handset Alliance" containing thirty-four different companies.

The American press, in particular, gave the news extensive coverage, including a lengthy New York Times spread about Andy Rubin[390].

The Symbian executive team had been expecting that news for some time, and had rebuttals ready. Nigel Clifford, Symbian's CEO, referred to the wide range of existing Linux-based mobile phone platforms[391]:

> It's another Linux platform. There's 10, 15, 20, maybe 25 different Linux platforms out there. It sometimes appears that Linux is fragmenting faster than it unifies… I probably would say there is no such thing as free software… We're no stranger to competing with big brands… We're the market leader, and we aim to remain the market leader.

John Forsyth, VP of Strategy at Symbian, shared his analysis that the "rocket science" of building and supporting an integrated smartphone platform was altogether different from the "rocket science" of building the world's premier search engine. Just because Google had succeeded in the latter was no reason to suppose it would succeed in the former too[392]:

> Search and a mobile phone platform are completely different things.
>
> It's costly, arduous and at times a deeply unsexy job of supporting customers day by day in launching phones. That's something there's very little experience of in Google's environment.
>
> If you are a serious phone maker and you are asked to bet your handsets on somebody, you would want to bet on someone with a track record of delivery and support.

Forsyth offered his own analogy:

> About every three months this year there has been a mobile Linux initiative of some sort launched. It's a bit like the common cold. It keeps coming

> round and then we go back to business. We don't participate in these, full stop. We make our own platform and we are focused on driving that into the mobile phone market at large ever more aggressively.

In other words, a potential Linux disruption of the smartphone business had been hyped many times before, so there was little reason to pay too much attention to the new Android wave of hype.

But with Google, things really were different. They succeeded in enabling a multitude of partners and customers in ways that no previous Linux-based platform provider could manage. They succeeded in this task because – just like Apple, discussed earlier in this chapter – they had both the imagination *and the skills* to integrate a number of different trends into a single platform.

For example, rather than including the cut-down J2ME "mobile edition" of the Java programming language and its associated libraries, similar to what was available on other smartphones, Android featured a version of "standard edition Java", making it considerably easier for developers to write sophisticated apps and services for Android devices. Symbian researchers who looked at that aspect of Android enthused about smart design choices made by the Google engineers.

How was such an implementation possible, in face of prevailing opinion that standard Java would be burdensome on smartphones with limited resources? In part by the clever design choices just mentioned, and in part by recognising that, roughly every 18 months, phone hardware was approximately doubling in capability whilst having the same cost as before.

Indeed, the first few Android phones produced were underwhelming. By February 2009, fourteen months after the public announcement of Android, only one commercial Android device was on show at the Mobile World Congress in Barcelona, the T-Mobile G1 from HTC. Even the Android enthusiast site Android Central published a despondent report[393]:

> We had expected a HUGE Android turnout at the show but at the moment, the biggest news coming out of MWC is the complete lack of Android Devices – Android is just nowhere to be found.
>
> We're quite obviously disappointed because as great as we think the T-Mobile G1 is, the appeal of Android is in its potential – not its current performance. We knew that the bigwigs like Samsung and Motorola weren't ready to showcase their devices but we expected a heck of a lot more from other companies that could definitely use some of the press. HTC announced all Windows Mobile devices. Nokia is sticking with Symbian.

> Huawei is just showing off a non-working prototype. And honestly, we're starting to worry…
>
> After a solid launch of the T-Mobile G1, Android could have gained a ton of momentum with official announcements of upcoming devices. Sadly, the opposite happened. We got nothing.

Google themselves had already indicated that disrupting the phone industry was proving harder than they had expected. The Wall Street Journal had carried an article entitled "Google's Mobile-Handset Plans Are Slowed: Android Launch Is Being Delayed As Carriers Struggle"[394]. Executives at Symbian particularly enjoyed reading a quote in that article attributed to Andy Rubin:

> Andy Rubin, director of mobile platforms at Google, says managing the software-development effort while giving its partners the opportunity to lobby for new features takes time. "This is where the pain happens," he says.

Yes, responding to conflicting feature requests from multiple partners was difficult. Yes, the initial phone models produced using Android were lacklustre, and several were scrapped before ever going on sale. Nevertheless, Google continued to deploy a team of world class software engineers, backed up by the might of the company's financial resources. And in time, these efforts produced more impressive outcomes. In addition to the points already mentioned, these outcomes were due to three more factors that Google succeeded in integrating together:

1. Users found that their favourite Google services worked particularly well on Android phones – services such as Google Mail, Google Calendar, Google Maps, and Google Search
2. Device manufacturers found it relatively easy to start work on a new Android phone project, because adaptations were readily available for whichever choice of semiconductor hardware they wanted to use; in turn, these adaptations were available because of the maturity and wide distribution of the Linux operating system upon which Android was based
3. Although device manufacturers had considerable freedom about the design of their phones, these devices needed to pass a conformance test suite, before Google permitted them to include Android in commercial products; this conformance increased the likelihood that

apps written by developers for one Android phone would run on all other Android phones.

Although many Android devices were market disappointments, a sufficient number of them stood out from the crowd and became best sellers. In this way, overall Android unit sales rose and rose.

In parallel, one hope I had expressed back in 2001 for the future of the Symbian platform was ultimately proved over optimistic: the idea that a large community of developers could share Symbian platform code as productively as happened within the community of open source Linux developers. Various legal impediments, functioning like treacle, complicated such transfers of Symbian OS source code:

- Due to restrictive licences applicable to parts of the platform that had been purchased from third parties
- Due to some key parts of the source code being deliberately kept secret, out of a fear that phone manufacturers might copy these ideas into non-Symbian phones, or would modify these parts to wrest control of the platform away from Symbian.

In short, openness of source code needs to be designed into a platform in advance, and cannot easily be added in afterward. As a more general principle, mechanisms for collaboration likewise need careful forethought. Without such forethought, a platform is burdened with technical debt.

Crossing chasms

As just reviewed, the adoption of an innovative trend can be driven by the involvement of greater numbers of engineers, designers, and entrepreneurs in the improvement and distribution of products and services incorporating that innovation. Once the community of solution-builders has reached a critical mass, many hands can make light work.

But as well as considering the growth of the community of people who are improving and distributing these products and services, we should also consider the growth of the community who are *investigating and using* these solutions. That growth can follow its own pattern of slow, slow, slow, followed, in suitable circumstances, by fast, faster, and extremely fast.

In other words, as well as a potential exponential growth on the supply side of innovation, there can be potential exponential growth on the demand side. The two sets of growth are related, but aren't the same.

In each case, the growth can be stalled, at an early phase, and fail to shift gears into the faster phase. In the case of an inability to move into the faster phase with a larger community of users, the innovation is said to have failed in "crossing the chasm", in the terminology of technology marketer Geoffrey Moore, who drew attention to the phenomenon in his 1991 book with that name[395].

Let's consider the spread of an innovation throughout a society. It might be the innovation of replacing a petrol-powered car with an electric car – that was an example featured in Moore's book. It might be lots of other types of innovation in product usage, social attitude, or personal determination:

- Replacing a simple mobile phone with a smartphone
- Installing and using a smart home hub, such as Amazon Alexa
- Switching eating habits to incorporate lab-grown synthetic meat
- Supporting the proposition that marriage should be available to same-sex couples
- Making a determined personal resolution that serious action is needed to reduce the threat of accelerating climate change
- Campaigning for a greater share of public resources to be allocated to investigating and reversing the causes of human biological aging.

For any such innovation, the population can be split into a number of different sections, depending on the factors governing whether they will adopt the innovation:

1. The first group can be called "Innovation enthusiasts". They are attracted to ideas by their novelty, and are willing to adopt the innovation purely from intellectual curiosity, or in order to stand out from the crowd, as some kind of fashion statement or expression of personal identity
2. The second group can be called "Early adopters" or "Visionaries". They are interested in the innovation on account of practical benefits it could deliver, such as the apps on a smartphone or smart home hub, or the reduction in numbers of animals being slaughtered for their meat. They are willing to adopt the innovation even though it doesn't work very well, since they are prepared to put in additional effort by themselves to obtain the potential benefits.

3. The third group can be called "Early majority" or "Pragmatists". They are also interested in the benefits arising from an innovation, but are less interested in making special effort to work around limitations and problems that arise. They want a solution that works out of the box.
4. Fourth comes the "Late majority" or "Conservatives", whose instincts are to push back against the innovation and oppose it, but who are willing to change their mind once the majority of society endorses it.
5. Finally, the "Laggards" or "Skeptics" avoid the innovation until no alternatives are available – for example, until petrol-powered cars have been made illegal.

According to research by University of New Mexico Professor Everett Rogers[396], populations typically split among these sections in proportions 2.5%, 13.5%, 34%, 34%, and 16%[397]. Of course, the relative numbers depend on how radical or surprising the innovation is. But regardless of the absolute numbers, it's the case that the majority of potential adopters need a *different kind of encouragement*, before they will change their habits or disposition, than does the much smaller group of people who are ready to embrace novelty more instinctively.

That core insight of Geoffrey Moore's *Crossing the Chasm* can be summarised as follows:

- A new product can gain some initial market interest, merely on account of its novelty, or on account of underlying technical merit
- The early adopter proportion of the market will be ready to engage with a product, just by seeing its technical feature set
- This early surge of interest can mislead the creators of the product, who think that they simply need to deliver "more of the same" to expand their market penetration
- However, the mainstream market operates by different criteria, and is positioned on the other side of a "chasm" from the early market
- Adopters on the other side of the chasm seek complete solutions, reliability, and convenience
- Pre-chasm adopters are willing to put up with poor usability, and make do with some compromises and workarounds; not so the post-

chasm adopters, who want solutions with minimal friction or inconvenience

- Pre-chasm adopters are ready to walk a solitary path; post-chasm adopters require social validation that their choice makes sense.

That final distinction deserves emphasis: members of the visionary early adopter community are looking for ways to "get ahead of the herd", as Moore puts it, whereas members of the pragmatic early majority community are more inclined to "stick with the herd". Their decisions about adoption are strongly influenced by what they perceive their peers are doing. If they see "people like them" adopting the innovation, it will bolster their own inclination to follow suit. But if the only people they can see using or advocating the innovation are in some ways "strange" or "not like us", it will deter them: members of the early majority are reluctant to be seen as sticking out from their community.

This tendency is another aspect of the attribute of human nature that I covered in the previous chapter under the heading "Misled by loyalty". The instinct to follow the practice of the others in our local tribe served, usually, to strengthen community bonds. But as noted in that chapter, that instinct can leave the community stranded in a mistaken view of the world or an unhelpful set of practices.

So how do innovations cross this chasm? Moore refines his metaphor from "crossing the chasm" to "crossing the channel", referring to the D-Day landings of allied forces across the English Channel in northern France in June 1944. Rather than spreading out the invasion force all throughout the territory controlled by enemy forces, the attack focussed massive strength in a small number of landing areas. Only once these landing areas had been successfully controlled did the invasion force start to spread out. In contrast, Moore warns, most innovation effort is wasted. In effect, innovation initiatives tend to scatter effort all over a large domain, without reaching a critical mass in any one area. That kind of effort may be sufficient to inspire members of the early adopter market, but it's *not* sufficient to convince members of the early majority to change their ways. That's why most innovations lose their momentum. That's why most start-up companies die in the "valley of death" – another name for the chasm between early market excitement and actual commercial impact. And that's why potential disruptions frequently fail to live up to their potential.

The equivalent of finding and securing a suitable landing region, on the other side of a channel of water, is to find a "killer app" for a platform – a reason why at least a portion of the early majority of potential users will pay more attention to what the platform can provide. This "killer app" must be something that can deliver real value with minimal effort by the user.

The idea of a killer app has its origins in the world of software but, as we'll see, it extends into wider kinds of innovation.

In the world of software, something can be described as a killer app if enough people say about it, "I need this software and something that runs it".

For example, the world's first spreadsheet application, VisiCalc, was at first only available on the Apple II computer. This was in 1979, two years before IBM released their Personal Computer – the device that introduced the term "PC" to the world. VisiCalc is credited with transforming the Apple II from being of interest only to hobbyists, into a device used for serious business purposes. The device was apparently bought in thousands by professionals who used VisiCalc to assist them with financial planning.

Another killer app was a later spreadsheet application, Lotus 1-2-3, which, from 1983 onward, was the application that gave many people a reason to buy an IBM PC.

For the Apple MacIntosh, it was the 1985 introduction of the desktop publishing application PageMaker, by Aldus, that made the device especially popular among creative arts professionals.

Games consoles also had killer apps – better termed "killer games" in this case: Space Invaders for the Atari 2600 console, Tetris and Pokemon for the Game Boy, Sonic the Hedgehog for Sega, Super Mario Brothers for Ninento consoles, Final Fantasy VII for the PlayStation, Grand Theft Auto III for the PS2, and so on.

Discussions within Symbian often looked back in time at two applications that had, in the same way, done wonders for sales of Psion handheld computers: the Data application which had been the hallmark application for the Psion Organiser II, from 1986 onward, and the Agenda application which was the standout feature of the Psion Series 3a from 1991. We also ruefully acknowledged the significance of the HotSync "one button synchronisation" feature on Palm handsets. That was a killer app for one of our rivals.

In order to capture and hold the attention of early majority users, the killer app needs to work extremely well within its particular domain. It needn't be all-singing and all-dancing. But it should perform a number of core tasks in a reliable, appealing manner.

I had a humbling experience of the power of a killer app in October 2007, when I was visiting San Francisco for the CTIA tradeshow. It was a chance for me to make the acquaintance of someone with whom I had previously exchanged emails – James Clement, recently appointed as the new Executive Director of the WTA (World Transhumanist Association). We agreed to meet at the Waterfront, to share views about the future of the WTA. However, our discussion quickly became side-tracked to the topic of the iPhone.

Our conversation had raised a question whose answer neither of us knew immediately. Without saying a word, we both instinctively reached for our smartphones. I took out my then favourite Nokia E61i, typed a few words into the web-browser, and started waiting. But James had the answer almost immediately, so it seemed, on the Safari browser on his iPhone.

I felt embarrassed; I was someone who had spent decades in the mobile computing business, but I was being out-gunned by someone whose business card said "attorney and serial entrepreneur". The example was no flash in the pan; as James and I did a few more simple experiments, the iPhone browser seemed to beat the browser on my Nokia phone every time.

To be clear, the iPhone web browser had some limitations. It would not load web pages that used Adobe Flash technology. But what it did handle, it handled very well indeed. In contrast, on my Nokia phone, the web browser was just one app of many. It was a great app for technology enthusiasts, like me, who were prepared to put in the effort to get the best out of it. But the iPhone experience reached a much larger audience.

Also to be clear, engineers and product managers in both Nokia and their operating system provider, Symbian, realised the strategic importance of web browsing, and wanted to deliver an excellent web browsing experience to as large a market of users as possible. However, for the reasons explained earlier in this chapter, that aspiration was frustrated by layers of what I called treacle, including various sorts of technical debt.

A later version of the iPhone involved a new killer app, namely the App Store. Here the terminology might be a bit confusing: the "killer app" was actually a means whereby ordinary users could easily discover, purchase, and download new applications for their iPhone.

Again, this thought was not new to Apple: Nokia also recognised the importance of users discovering, purchasing, and downloading apps. However, once again, Apple outdid Nokia in terms of execution. They applied their resources more skilfully and more decisively, putting in place a huge team to verify apps before they were made available on the App Store. In contrast, Nokia worked with numerous partners in their equivalent of the App Store, none of whom were able to live up to management expectations[398].

One more action by Apple in support of their App Store deserves commendation. They produced and ran primetime TV adverts depicting normal-looking people finding and downloading apps on their iPhones. In this way, they popularised the slogan "There's an app for that". These adverts also convinced members of the early majority that other people, similar to them, were already enjoying benefits from the iPhone. In this way, Apple recognised and took advantage of the important angle of social validation for wider market growth.

Once members of the early majority have become enthusiasts for an innovation, they can become its most effective advocates. And that's how an initial period of slow market growth can start to surge forward more quickly. But it depends upon the existence of something akin to a killer app.

How does this apply for innovations involving changes in thinking, or practical changes in behaviour? Consider again two of the examples I gave earlier: making a determined personal resolution that serious action is needed to reduce the threat of accelerating climate change, and campaigning for a greater share of public resources to be allocated to investigating and reversing the causes of human biological aging. In such cases, the "killer app" can be something that:

- Is easily understood and easily communicated
- Involves a clear set of actions
- Appears to make a real difference for the goal in mind
- Grows in its impact as larger numbers of people adopt it
- Leads to a permanent change in attitude and behaviour, rather than just a flash in the pan.

Designing and supporting such a package can be just as hard as designing and supporting a killer app for a new software platform. Having the idea is just the beginning. Making it stick is the truly hard part – especially in a world where, as forthcoming chapters will review, so much is uncertain.

Beyond disruptions

To recap this chapter: four keys to the successful anticipation and management of disruptions are:

1. The anticipation and management of *trends*
2. The anticipation and management of *convergences* – where trends overlap with and influence each other
3. The anticipation and management of *shifts in gear* of the pace of change – shifts in the supply side and/or the demand side
4. The avoidance of becoming bogged down in *debt* – financial debt, technical debt, strategic debt, or behavioural debt.

In the next chapter, I'll look at some additional practical examples of these points, including instances of both good and bad predictions. In the process, one more key skill will come to the fore: the anticipation and management of *contingency*.

7. Contingency

Contingency, defined: Items that cannot be predicted with any confidence. Provision that is made in anticipation of unexpected changes in circumstance. A source of major problems in the management of plans, unless systems are designed to include suitable agility and resilience.

At around midday on 30th June 1954, the chickens in my grandparents' farm in North East Scotland scurried back to their hen house, and prepared to sleep. The sky had become exceptionally dark, as if night-time was fast approaching. The reason for the darkness was a near total eclipse of the sun by the moon. Just a few minutes later, normal daylight started to resume, presumably leaving the chickens even more surprised.

That episode was something I heard about from my father during my childhood in the 1960s. I was intrigued to hear that forthcoming occurrences of total solar eclipses could be foretold with precision, decades and even centuries ahead. The next one visible from the UK, apparently, would be on 11th August 1999 – a date that seemed to me like aeons in the future.

Much nearer to that date, I started planning a family holiday, to witness that long-anticipated eclipse. My wife and I, accompanied by our own son, and by my parents, decided to travel to Luxembourg in mainland Europe for what we hoped would be a good vantage point to observe the heavens.

When the day arrived, the sky was overcast, but winds were moving clouds around briskly, causing occasional breaks in the cover. Even five minutes before the start of the total portion of the eclipse, no-one could be sure whether the relevant portion of the sky would clear.

Two separate branches of physics were involved in predicting what we would observe that day:

1. Astronomical theories, which picked out the precise time of the eclipse many decades in advance, completely accurately
2. Meteorological theories, which tried to forecast whether the sight of the eclipse would be obscured by clouds.

As it happened, the sky did turn unusually dark, but the clouds blocked any direct visual access to the overlap of the two celestial discs. It was a memorable event, though not quite as memorable as we had hoped.

Similarly, whilst practitioners of foresight might from time to time prove remarkably prescient in their predictions of long-distant events, there are inherent limitations in any such predictions. Recognising these limitations, and managing them, is a key step in transitioning from shallow foresight to vital foresight.

Chaotic amplification

Predicting gaps in cloud cover – along with predicting the severity of many other weather events – remains an imprecise task even to this day. In some circumstances, specific predictions of rain or shine are indeed possible; but in others, the chains of causes and effects are too finely balanced. In these cases, the best forecast involves statements of probability. In these cases, even small changes in initial conditions can escalate into huge changes in subsequent conditions. The likely course of a hurricane once it reaches land can be plotted in advance, but it remains subject to unforeseen deviations. And whether a storm will decrease or increase in power is, again, often a matter of probability, rather than something that can be known for sure.

The phrase is well known: the flap of a butterfly's wing in the Brazilian jungle could give rise to a tornado in Texas. That particular example may be an exaggeration: a larger initial push may be needed, to have a longer-term noticeable effect on the subsequent weather[399]. But the phenomenon of *chaotic amplification* is real. It was discovered in the 1960s by Edward Lorenz, a mathematically-minded weather forecaster. Lorenz found that minute variations in the data input to his calculations would result in very different weather forecasts[400]. Lorenz initially used the metaphor of a seagull flapping its wings, rather than a butterfly, though his ideas reached a larger audience once a more delicate creature featured in the description.

The weather is by no means the only unpredictable contingency that complicates forecasts that might initially seem clean and reliable. The prediction of what my family and I would observe in the heavens on 11th August 1999 – the date of the long-anticipated total solar eclipse – was also subject to complications arising from potential traffic jams, road accidents, or illnesses that might have kept all of us indoors.

Around four centuries earlier, in 1504, the explorer Christopher Columbus faced a similar split in predictive capabilities. He was on his fourth voyage westward, and his ship had been marooned for six months on the island of Jamaica. Initial friendly relations with the local population had turned sour due to members of his crew mistreating the islanders – robbing and even murdering some of them. The islanders, understandably, stopped supplying food to the visitors. With starvation looming, Columbus came across a piece of unexpected fortune[401].

A vital part of every ship's inventory in those days was a printed copy of an Almanac created in 1475 by German mathematician Johannes Müller von Königsberg, also known as Regiomontanus[402]. The Almanac contained dates and times of different phases of the moon – and lunar eclipses – for the years up to 1506. The main value of the Almanac was that it allowed navigators to determine their position, by comparing their own observations with those in the book. Consulting the Almanac, Columbus saw that a full lunar eclipse was forecast as taking place on the last day of February. He knew this meant the lunar disk would appear as reddened and darkened. A few days before that occurrence, Columbus declared to the natives what would be observed, couching his predictions in apocalyptic, religious terms. As Columbus put it, the Christian god with whom he communed was angered by the lack of respect shown by the natives. Accordingly, the moon would shortly be "inflamed with wrath" and "obliterated".

When his forecast appeared to be fulfilled, the natives pledged to resume providing sufficient food to Columbus and his entourage. Columbus gained even more respect from the natives by foretelling, with precision, the end of the period in which the moon was covered in blood, some forty-eight minutes later. His god was no longer displeased. Or so he said.

But no consultation with any Almanac could help Columbus anticipate when support would arrive for him from the colony which he had founded ten years earlier on the nearby island of Hispaniola. The small group of sailors that had set out from Jamaica in a canoe to request such assistance had experienced all sorts of delays – due in part to adverse weather, but mainly due to personality conflicts. Indeed, the governor of the colony detested Columbus. Columbus had to wait another four months before assistance finally arrived in the form of two ships[403].

The renowned seafarer was soon on his way back to Spain. He would never sail westward again. It was an anti-climactic end to a trailblazing set of discoveries.

I'm reminded of the lament of one of the most distinguished mathematicians from history: Isaac Newton. Newton had lost the equivalent of three million pounds in today's money in the South Sea Bubble investment craze of the 1720s[404]. Newton is said to have remarked[405], "I can calculate the movement of stars, but not the madness of men." In contrast to the predictability of celestial bodies, human behaviour frequently defies expectations, especially when lots of investors are making their own assessments of whether or not public sentiment will remain upbeat or turn sour. That's the kind of circumstance when chaotic amplification applies, magnifying uncertainties.

Moonshot management

Despite their tendency to behave chaotically, people can, sometimes, be predicted. And even when they can't be predicted, they can be managed.

With his ploy of pretending to commune with a deity who might devour the moon, Columbus anticipated how the islanders would react. His prediction of the lunar eclipse had, therefore, two outcomes in mind:

1. The eclipse which would be seen in the sky
2. The islanders resuming supplying food to Columbus.

It was the same with a celebrated declaration issued by US President John Kennedy. That declaration, likewise, had a celestial outcome in mind as well as a human outcome. I expect you already know the content of that declaration[406]:

> This nation should commit itself to achieving the goal, before this decade is out, of landing a man on the moon and returning him safely to the Earth.

The occasion was a speech given by Kennedy to a joint session of the US Congress on 25th May 1961. Eight years and two months later, in July 1969, astronauts Neil Armstrong and Buzz Aldrin landed on the moon, walked on the lunar surface and collected some rocks from it, before launching back into space to rendezvous with a lunar orbiter vehicle piloted by Michael Collins, and then returning, safely, to the Earth. Before the decade was out. The entire journey was watched in real time on television screens around the world. This culmination of the decade-long Apollo project was visibly spectacular.

Since that time, the word "moonshot" has, like the words "game-changer" and "disruption", become overused. People with a big idea in their mind often seek to bask in glory reflected from the accomplishments of the

Apollo team, by describing their project as a moonshot in its own right. But, again like these other words, there's more to the concept than first appears.

To be successful, a moonshot needs to involve more than just a large vision – a glorious accomplishment at the end of the project. It also needs at least an outline plan for:

1. Step-by-step progress that can be taken toward that vision
2. The sort of engineering solutions that will be developed and used
3. The resources that could be marshalled to support the project
4. The management of any contingencies that may arise.

Without such a plan, the would-be moonshot is likely to remain wishful thinking. *With* such a plan, the initiative has more chance of capturing *and sustaining* the imagination of a broad community of potential supporters – people whose actions can make all the difference between the initiative succeeding or failing. The interest of that larger community will in turn be maintained by the enthusiasm of the smaller community of relevant experts who can assess and review the plan as it unfolds.

Before Kennedy asked Congress to approve the Apollo project, NASA had conducted a number of careful preliminary investigations. Engineers and designers had already conceived in basic terms what might be involved by a mission to the moon and back. General awareness of the possibilities had been raised by[407]:

- A 1950 movie with wide cinema distribution, *Destination Moon*[408]
- Books written by futurist and science fiction author Arthur C. Clarke, including *Interplanetary Flight: An Introduction to Astronautics* (1950) and *The Exploration of the Moon* (1954)
- Presentations and reports by the British Interplanetary Society, dating back to its formation in 1933[409].

US interest in space exploration accelerated when the Soviet Union unexpectedly launched the Sputnik satellite in October 1957. One month later, Sputnik 2 contained a passenger: Laika, a stray dog, who survived for several orbits around the earth before the capsule apparently overheated[410].

The Sputnik flights produced some strong reactions[411]. Arthur C. Clarke declared that the day of Sputnik's launch was the day "the United States became a second-rate power". The scientist Edward Teller, known as the father of the hydrogen bomb, said that Sputnik was a greater defeat for the

United States than Pearl Harbour. Reporter Paul Dickson described Sputnik as "the shock of the century", in his book of the same name[412].

How might the United States respond to this shock – and to the fear that control of space would allow the Soviet Union to impose its will on the rest of the world? One person who helped define the response was Wernher von Braun, who had designed rocket missiles for Nazi Germany during World War Two before surrendering to the Allies and eventually gaining key responsibilities in NASA.

Von Braun had long been fascinated with the idea of space flight. Aged just eighteen, he had approached a famous pioneering high-altitude balloonist after a public lecture in Berlin in 1930, and told him "You know, I plan on travelling to the Moon at some time." By 1950 he was leading a research team in Huntsville, Alabama. A story in the city's Huntsville Times newspaper on May 14th that year was headlined "Dr. von Braun Says Rocket Flights Possible to Moon"[413]. After the shocks of Sputnik, the US government raised its level of interest in what von Braun proposed. By January of 1959 he submitted a proposal to the House Select Committee on Astronautics and Space Exploration. A manned flight around the dark side of the moon and back to earth should be possible within eight to ten years, he suggested, followed a few years after by a manned landing on the lunar surface. Apollo 8, in 1968, and Apollo 11, in 1969, were to fulfil the two stages of that forecast with impressive accuracy.

But it was by no means clear in 1959 whether von Braun's forecast was an over-excited fantasy, or something that could prove realistic. The mere fact that von Braun had successfully designed the V2 supersonic rocket missile during World War Two was insufficient, by itself, to provide confidence for the much grander vision of the lunar landing. It's hazardous to extrapolate from prior successes into future projects with significantly larger scale. That's like saying because humans can train for the task of swimming across the English Channel, and succeed in it, it can't be that much harder to swim all the way across the Atlantic.

That's why the US administration, first under President Eisenhower, and then under his successor President Kennedy, performed its own evaluations of the ideas that enthusiasts such as von Braun were proposing. In September 1960 NASA published a "Request for Proposal" asking engineering companies to submit their own designs for spacecrafts for a number of missions, including flights to the moon[414]. Out of fourteen bids received,

NASA selected three to receive grants of 250 thousand dollars each to carry out six-month research projects: Convair/Astronautics of San Diego, General Electric of Philadelphia, and the Martin Company of Baltimore. At the same time, as another check on the sanity of what was being proposed, an internal NASA team ran its own research. It was the combined positive outcomes of these four independent research projects that gave Kennedy the confidence to bring his proposal to the joint session of Congress in May 1961, mentioned earlier.

In that speech, Kennedy acknowledged that aspects of the project were still far from certain. He therefore explained that different design options would continue to be investigated in parallel:

> We propose to develop alternate liquid and solid fuel boosters, much larger than any now being developed, until certain which is superior.

Kennedy also emphasised that the project would require long-term commitments, including significant ongoing budgetary support:

> Let it be clear that I am asking the Congress and the country to accept a firm commitment to a new course of action, a course which will last for many years and carry very heavy costs… If we are to go only half way, or reduce our sights in the face of difficulty, in my judgment it would be better not to go at all…
>
> This decision demands a major national commitment of scientific and technical manpower, materiel and facilities, and the possibility of their diversion from other important activities where they are already thinly spread. It means a degree of dedication, organization and discipline which have not always characterized our research and development efforts.

The initial reaction to Kennedy's proposals was subdued, as can be seen from archive video footage from his presentation[415]. Many people even in NASA were unconvinced by the ambitious timescale Kennedy had outlined. Whilst welcoming the official support from the President, NASA engineers were still wrestling over what became an increasingly contentious design decision. What was unclear was whether two spacecraft could successfully rendezvous in lunar orbit, or, indeed, anywhere else on the journey between the earth and the moon. Such a manoeuvre appeared fraught with danger – especially if carried out at a distance of 240 thousand miles from any potential rescue vehicle. Over a number of months, three different methods for the mission were vigorously debated[416]:

1. "Direct ascent", avoiding any need for a potentially hazardous rendezvous, but requiring an enormous initial rocket
2. "Earth-orbit rendezvous", in which a large lunar landing craft would be assembled from pieces delivered by separate rockets from the ground into orbit around the earth, before travelling to the moon and back
3. "Lunar-orbit rendezvous", with a smaller lunar landing craft reconnecting with its parent lunar orbiting module.

For a while, a fourth concept was entertained as well, in which a manned lunar landing craft would combine on the moon's surface with some resources that had previously been deposited there by an earlier unmanned craft. That option was known as "Lunar surface rendezvous".

The debate ran and ran, until June 1962, when von Braun came down in favour of lunar-orbit rendezvous, supporting the option that had previously been widely viewed as irresponsibly dangerous. It was to prove to be an inspired decision. From that time, the programme could proceed more quickly.

In September that year, 1962, Kennedy gave another public speech about his moonshot vision, at Rice Stadium in Houston, Texas[417]. It's a speech that is, understandably, more famous than his 1961 presentation to Congress: it has richer oratory, and Kennedy's growing confidence about the initiative shines through. It's worth quoting at some length:

> This city of Houston, this State of Texas, this country of the United States was not built by those who waited and rested and wished to look behind them. This country was conquered by those who moved forward – and so will space…
>
> We set sail on this new sea because there is new knowledge to be gained, and new rights to be won, and they must be won and used for the progress of all people…
>
> We choose to go to the moon. We choose to go to the moon in this decade and do the other things, not because they are easy, but because they are hard, because that goal will serve to organize and measure the best of our energies and skills, because that challenge is one that we are willing to accept, one we are unwilling to postpone, and one which we intend to win, and the others, too.

> It is for these reasons that I regard the decision last year to shift our efforts in space from low to high gear as among the most important decisions that will be made during my incumbency in the office of the Presidency.

Once again, Kennedy highlighted the fact that the project involved much that was unpredictable, and which would require skill and resolve to handle:

> If I were to say, my fellow citizens, that we shall send to the moon, 240,000 miles away from the control station in Houston, a giant rocket more than 300 feet tall, the length of this football field, made of new metal alloys, some of which have not yet been invented, capable of standing heat and stresses several times more than have ever been experienced, fitted together with a precision better than the finest watch, carrying all the equipment needed for propulsion, guidance, control, communications, food and survival, on an untried mission, to an unknown celestial body, and then return it safely to earth, re-entering the atmosphere at speeds of over 25,000 miles per hour, causing heat about half that of the temperature of the sun… and do all this, and do it right, and do it first before this decade is out – then we must be bold.

Kennedy knew well what he was doing. His vision encompassed not only the voyage of an Apollo capsule to the moon and back, but also an unprecedented human collaboration – a collaboration with sufficient resilience to withstand shocks and crises in the years to come. That collaboration would be created by people holding in their minds the vision that Kennedy proclaimed.

And the project, indeed, did experience some bitter shocks and crises. Just two months later, Kennedy was felled by an assassin's bullet in Dallas, Texas. His successor as president, Lyndon Johnson, picked up the mantle of the project. In January 1967, an intense fire broke out in the Apollo 1 module during a launch rehearsal test[418]. All three of the astronauts on board died: Ed White, Roger Chaffee, and Virgil "Gus" Grissom – who had been tipped to become the first man to walk on the moon (the role subsequently fulfilled by Neil Armstrong)[419]. Apollo flights were put on hold for twenty months until NASA was confident the problems were fully understood and would not recur.

Contingency planning continued during the Apollo 11 flight too. Richard Nixon, the US President by the time of the moon landing, had an announcement ready in case the lunar module was unable to take off from the moon, to return the astronauts earthward[420]:

> Fate has ordained that the men who went to the moon to explore in peace will stay on the moon to rest in peace.
>
> These brave men, Neil Armstrong and Edwin Aldrin, know that there is no hope for their recovery. But they also know that there is hope for mankind in their sacrifice.
>
> These two men are laying down their lives in mankind's most noble goal: the search for truth and understanding. They will be mourned by their families and friends; they will be mourned by their nation; they will be mourned by the people of the world; they will be mourned by a Mother Earth that dared send two of her sons into the unknown.
>
> In their exploration, they stirred the people of the world to feel as one; in their sacrifice, they bind more tightly the brotherhood of man.
>
> In ancient days, men looked at stars and saw their heroes in the constellations. In modern times, we do much the same, but our heroes are epic men of flesh and blood.
>
> Others will follow, and surely find their way home. Man's search will not be denied. But these men were the first, and they will remain the foremost in our hearts.

Thankfully, that contingency did not arise. Instead, when it was clear that the Apollo 11 mission had succeeded, Wernher von Braun turned to John Houbolt, the NASA engineer who had fought hardest and believed strongest in the idea of lunar-orbit rendezvous, even when several layers of his management had rejected that idea. Houbolt, by that time retired from NASA, was seated in the area of the mission control room viewing area reserved for guest dignitaries. Von Braun signalled him a thumbs up congratulation and said, "John, it worked beautifully"[421].

Cancer complications

Just as John Kennedy is fondly remembered for his bold Apollo moonshot, Richard Nixon wanted to be remembered for a moonshot of his own.

The date was 23rd December 1971. Nixon was speaking, like Kennedy ten years earlier, to members of both the Senate and the House of Representatives. He indicated his sense of the occasion as follows[422]:

> I hope that in the years ahead that we may look back on this day and this action as being the most significant action taken during this Administration.

At the end of his speech, Nixon signed the National Cancer Act. Nixon explained why he saw the Act as momentous:

> When we consider what cancer does each year in the United States, we find that more people each year die of cancer in the United States than all the Americans who lost their lives in World War II.

Nixon's language was emphatic:

> We have set up a procedure for the purpose of making a total national commitment… The Congress is totally committed to provide the funds that are necessary, whatever is necessary, for the conquest of cancer.

The set of organisations who would be part of this new national commitment was impressive:

- The National Institutes of Health
- The department of Health, Education, and Welfare
- The American Cancer Society
- "Other volunteer organisations".

Earlier that year, Nixon had explicitly compared this effort to that of the lunar landing[423]:

> The time has come in America when the same kind of concentrated effort that split the atom and took man to the moon should be turned toward conquering this dread disease. Let us make a total national commitment to achieve this goal.

The President of the American Cancer Society, Alva Letton, also saw the act as having singular importance. He assessed it as follows[424]:

> This bill has the possibility of doing more for humanity than any other single act the US has ever undertaken.

Journalists liked to use the metaphor of "war on cancer". Here's Walter Cronkite commenting on the signing of the National Cancer Act:

> President Nixon signed into law today the bill committing more than one and a half billion dollars to a War on Cancer. The 3-year program involves research, diagnosis, prevention and treatment.

In the year 1970, shortly before Nixon's commencement of this war on cancer, 162.8 people out of every 100,000 in the United States died of cancer. Twenty years later, in 1990, instead of falling as Nixon had hoped, that rate had actually increased, to 203.2. By 1997 the figure had increased again, to 210.0[425]. Nixon had died three years earlier, disgraced as a result of the

Watergate scandal. The rising cancer death statistics meant he could take no solace from the outcome of his intended moonshot.

What went wrong? Why was the United States the loser in this war, despite the huge coalition assembled by Nixon?

Just as Kennedy's moonshot took advantage of many prior initiatives – a succession of rockets and spacecraft that were increasingly powerful and capable – so did Nixon's moonshot aim to stand on the shoulders of prior medical advances. These advances had tamed other diseases that previously scourged the population – diseases such as tuberculosis, smallpox, polio, diphtheria, measles, pneumonia, and gastrointestinal infections. Cancer was at one time thought to be a different category of disease – so much so that news of a cancer diagnosis was often hushed up. Childhood leukaemia, a type of blood cancer, was a particularly feared disease. But pioneering treatment with chemotherapy in 1947, led by young Boston doctor Sidney Farber, changed opinions[426].

Unlike many of his medical colleagues at that time, Farber refused to accept "the incurability of cancer". His breakthrough results with chemotherapy were to earn him the sobriquet "the father of modern chemotherapy"[427]. Farber also proved to be an effective public advocate for increased funding for cancer research. His testimony to the US Congress in 1954 secured an additional three million dollars of funding in support of chemotherapy[428], and he was to return on several occasions in the following years. Richard Nixon, Vice President at that time, observed Ferber's advocacy at first hand, and was to appoint him to the National Cancer Advisory Board he set up after signing the National Cancer Act[429].

In the 1950s and 1960s, Ferber was part of a growing pressure movement that raised public interest in the idea of curing cancer. Husband and wife Albert and Mary Lasker played an important role too, utilising the public relations expertise Albert Lasker had acquired in the advertising industry, as well as the considerable wealth earned by the company he owned – the largest advertising agency in the country at the time. Mary Lasker was a successful saleswoman and entrepreneur in her own right. The two used their influence to arrange for educational articles about cancer to appear in widely read publications such as *Readers Digest* and on popular radio channels. They also set up a substantial prize fund, with over eighty winners of Lasker Awards going on to subsequently win a Nobel Prize[430].

After her husband's own death from bowel cancer in 1952, Mary Lasker redoubled her lobbying efforts. She explained her rationale for why more money should be applied to the field[431]:

> I thought that if a toothpaste, which [my husband] owned or had an interest in, deserved advertising at the rate of two or three or four million dollars a year, then research against disease maiming and crippling people in the United States and in the rest of the world deserved hundreds of millions of dollars. It seemed perfectly simple and natural to me.

By 1969, one of her organisations, the Citizens Committee for the Conquest of Cancer, placed full-page advertisements in the Washington Post and the New York Times, with the striking headline "Mr Nixon: You can cure cancer"[432]. The messages in the advert were crisp and clear:

> We spend more each day on military matters than each *year* on cancer research. And last year, more than 21 times as much on space research as on cancer research…
>
> There is not a doubt in the minds of our top cancer researchers that the final answer to cancer can be found. Already, 4 out of about 200 types of cancer can be cured with drugs. And 37 other drugs can cause temporary remission in 17 other types of cancer.
>
> Dr Sidney Farber, Past President of the American Cancer Society, believes: "We are so close to a cure for cancer. We lack only the will and the kind of money and comprehensive planning that went into putting a man on the moon".

The advert proposed a bold timeline:

> Why don't we try to conquer cancer by America's 200th birthday [1976]?

The closing text had echoes of language that John F. Kennedy might have used:

> Our nation has the money on the one hand and the skills on the other. We must, under your leadership, put our hands together and get this thing done.
>
> Surely, the war against cancer has the support of 100% of the people. It is a war in which we lost 21 times more lives last year than we lost in Vietnam last year. A war we can win and put the entire human race in our debt.

Encouraged by a call-to-action in the advertisement, and in other publications that amplified the message, readers mailed in upward of one million letters to US government officials. The letters arrived in truckloads, according to one observer, the journalist Barbara Walters[433].

President Nixon heard the message, loud and clear – hence his own actions to put America onto a kind of war footing against cancer.

Nevertheless, as already mentioned, progress proved disappointingly slow. Cancer turned out to be a much more complex problem than was anticipated. Contrary to expectations, no single underlying cause was uncovered, amenable to a single approach that would solve all variants of the disease. Nor is there just one genetic mutation which gives rise to all cancers of a given type.

Some researchers had supposed cancer to be mainly a modern disease, caused by the unnatural stresses of living in a consumerist, competitive society – in which case, the disease might be avoided by adopting a simpler style of living. That line of thinking might have some truth to it, but it became clear that cancer has many other causes. Other researchers thought that, since a number of cancers had already been cured, it would only be a matter of time until the remaining types of cancer were cured too. However, that view also proved to be over-optimistic.

Right from the beginning, a number of distinguished cancer researchers had been worried by the optimism of the Nixon moonshot. Sol Spiegelman, professor of human genetics at Columbia University, who was also director of the Institute of Cancer Research, commented that[434]

> An all-out effort at this time would be like trying to land a man on the moon without knowing Newton's laws of gravity.

Physician Philip Lee, who served as assistant secretary of health under two different US presidents, had a similar objection[435]:

> Cancer is not simply an island waiting in isolation for a crash program to wipe it out. It is in no way comparable to a moon shot – to… an Apollo program – which requires mainly the mobilization of money, men, and facilities to put together in one imposing package the scientific knowledge we already possess.

In the five decades since 1971, our understanding of the science underlying cancer has made substantial progress, though much still remains unclear[436]. Given what we now know, it's no surprise that the optimism of Mary Lasker and others she inspired, that a cure for cancer could be found by 1976, or in a timescale comparable to that of the Apollo program, turned out to be ill-founded. The understanding of cancer possessed by scientists in the 1970s had far too many gaps in it.

In some cases, the discipline of engineering can produce wonders, even when the underlying science is poorly understood. The earliest steam engines preceded the development of the science of thermodynamics. The reason why various medicines work often remains mysterious – but enterprising medical professionals can see that they work in some circumstances, and they manage to extend their applicability to new circumstances too, without being able to explain what is actually happening at the molecular or biochemical levels. Some of the earliest treatments for cancers fitted that pattern. It seemed reasonable to anticipate, therefore, that huge additional research effort would extend that set of treatments, whether or not a complete scientific understanding accompanied these treatments.

But in other cases, no amount of diligent engineering can make up for shortcomings in fundamental understanding. Many forms of cancer fall into this category. Various therapies can extend lives of cancer sufferers for months, and sometimes even years, but malignant cancers all too often return, with greater vigour.

As a veteran of four decades of research on cancer, Dr. Benjamin Neel, Director of the Perlmutter Cancer Center in New York, offered this harsh assessment of Nixon's moonshot ambitions[437]: they were "like Kennedy trying to put a man on the moon in the 1600s". But Neel emphasised that the initiative had, nevertheless, been deeply worthwhile:

> I don't think there has been a single better, more efficient expenditure of public money. Far from being embarrassed, we should be trumpeting those successes.

Although research into cancer has hit obstacles time and again in the decades since Richard Nixon threw his weight behind it, researchers have been able to respond to these obstacles by adapting their approaches, considering new biochemical pathways, and conceptualising various cancers in new ways. In due course, more refined, precise tools are likely to become available. Underlying biological causes will be more fully understood. In this way, the waves of contingencies of fighting cancer can be tamed, stage by stage – although for the time being, plenty of new contingencies keep cropping up, even as the previous ones are falling under control.

I'll return to options for a comprehensive cure for cancer in later chapters, when I offer my own forecasts for the progress of medical technology. But first, there's more to be said about contingencies, and about the role of forecasts in anticipating and managing these contingencies.

Fusion delays

"I venture to predict that a method will be found for liberating fusion energy in a controlled manner within the next two decades".

The year was 1955. The occasion was the first "Atoms for Peace" conference, held in Geneva, Switzerland[438]. The speaker was the chair of the conference, Homi Bhabha, a former researcher at the Cambridge University Cavendish Laboratory who worked closely with pioneers of quantum physics such as Paul Dirac and Niels Bohr, and who became known as "the father of India's nuclear programme"[439]. Via his remark, quoted above, was born the barb that nuclear fusion is always twenty years in the future[440]: it was thought to be twenty years in the future in the 1950s, but remains twenty years in the future, seventy years later, in the 2020s.

Conceived as a theoretical possibility in the 1920s by the British physicists Francis Aston and Arthur Eddington, nuclear fusion reactors have the potential to duplicate on the earth key aspects of the reactions that take place in the sun, with atomic particles crashing into each other at huge temperatures, creating new elements, and thereby emitting surplus energy. If such reactions could be arranged in a sustainable, controllable way, the result would be enormous flows of energy from readily available fuel sources, with little waste product, no emission of greenhouse gases, and quantities of radioactivity that are low and easy to manage. It is little wonder that nuclear fusion has been compared to the "holy grail" of sources of energy[441].

Containing hydrogen at temperatures over 100 million degrees Centigrade in a fusion reactor poses numerous engineering difficulties. Whilst some physicists, such as Homi Bhabha, mentioned above, believed these challenges would likely be solved within a couple of decades, other pioneers of the field expressed uncertainty, particularly at the second "Atoms for Peace" conference, held once more in Geneva, three years after the first one. Edward Teller from the United States, who had previously been deeply involved in the design of the hydrogen (fusion) bomb, said that the situation at that time, 1958, with controlled nuclear fusion, was "similar to the stage at which flying was about 100 years ago"[442]. Teller's conclusion was that the difficulties were so substantial that "an economic exploitation of controlled thermonuclear reactions may not turn out to be possible before the end of the twentieth century". In other words, Teller put nuclear fusion forty years into the future.

We now know that even this forecast would be too optimistic. More recent forecasts continue the pattern of covering a spread of different dates. The EUROfusion consortium published a roadmap in 2012 that predicted successful demonstrations of nuclear fusion in the early 2040s, with energy being supplied on a commercial basis to the electrical grid by 2050. However, the consortium updated these forecasts in 2017, revising the first of these dates to 2054[443]. So commercially significant nuclear fusion, in this view, was still *forty* years in the future. However, researchers from MIT who are working on a more compact "SPARC" design predicted in September 2020 that their product could be generating commercially significant quantities of electricity within just ten years[444]. And two small British companies, each in Oxfordshire, Tokamak Energy and First Light Fusion, have both provided reasons for believing their systems could be operational within a similar timescale, that is, by 2030[445].

As with the examples from earlier in this chapter, these forecasts are all subject to at three main sources of uncertainty:

1. Uncertainties in the science involved, such as the physics of plasmas
2. Uncertainties with engineering – ways to take advantage of the best understanding of science in order to achieve the desired aims
3. Uncertainties with human cooperation – ways to encourage application of sufficient insights and resources from different teams.

In the case of curing cancer, the uncertainties with the underlying science have proven the most problematic. But in the case of nuclear fusion, the other two categories have proved more significant. The joint ITER project involves thirty-five countries cooperating to construct a massive fusion reactor in Saint Paul-lez-Durance, southern France. Bernard Bigot, the Director-General of ITER, has described himself as "quite confident" that the technical challenges facing the project can be solved, but he expressed less assurance about handling the politicians from the various countries involved. These politicians are "more uncontrollable", he said, in view of the particular complications of "the political world"[446]. In contrast, smaller projects, such as MIT's SPARC and the solutions of Tokamak Energy and First Light Fusion, have much simpler political structures, and can change course more nimbly when required.

The reason why ITER became such a large project was because the engineering design from the 1980s strongly recommended the creation of a single huge fusion reactor[447]. In more recent years, however, a number of developments have increased the credibility of smaller designs[448]:

1. Superconductors that can operate at high temperature
2. New geometries for the reaction vessels
3. Use of liquid metal
4. Improved artificial intelligence that can suggest new designs and assist with real-time monitoring.

For these reasons, the forecasts of many advocates of nuclear fusion, made over the last sixty years, that the technology will start yielding enormous amounts of clean energy within just a few decades, appear to be within our grasp as never before. The long years of fusion being frustratingly elusive may be coming to an end. The right conclusion to draw from a series of past delays isn't always that the future will bring more delays.

Surprise anticipation

It's time to highlight some general lessons from the preceding examples in this and previous chapters:

1. *No guarantees*: Raising public desire for a major technological breakthrough can help focus the minds of politicians, and result in the allocation of greater amounts of both private and public funds in support of relevant research and development, but cannot by itself guarantee that the breakthrough will happen in any specified timescale
2. *No bullshit*: If the public perceive that apparent experts have misled them over potential timescales for technological breakthrough, they may lose their interest in the field, and even start to agitate against it. What's needed is ongoing communications that explain the uncertainties involved, treat members of the public with respect, and keep them informed about setbacks and other project changes
3. *No undue despair*: Just because an expected outcome is taking longer than previously expected – such as a cure for cancer, or progress with nuclear fusion, or an open source software smartphone platform – that's no reason to jump to a despairing conclusion that

the outcome will forever lie out of reach. The outcome may simply require more ingenuity, more patience, and additional sheer effort

4. *No blind optimism*: To follow on from the previous point: if an outcome is taking longer than previously expected, careful reviews should take place of the factors that might be responsible for the delay, to determine which changes may be needed in project activity, or indeed if the project should be put on hold
5. *No moonshot-worship*: World-class outcomes don't arise merely because project leaders have set audacious goals and urged project members to be willing to "break free" from established norms and methods. A great deal of old-fashioned hard work is almost certainly needed too, with careful attention to principles such as usability, performance, security, safety, interoperability, accountability, maintenance, and sustainability
6. *No blinkers*: Eyes should be kept open for unexpected developments, new risks, and new opportunities, that are different from what the project previously assumed. Be ready to investigate more than one option in parallel
7. *No monoliths*: The larger the project structure, the harder it will be to adapt promptly to new insights. The project should beware any of the types of "treacle" discussed in the previous chapter – the debts or inertia which will limit its room for manoeuvre.

One consequence is that any large project of this sort needs two sorts of activity: "doing" and "reviewing". The former involves progressing the plan as previously agreed. The latter involves reflecting on questions such as: What is going well? What is going badly? What blockages need special attention? What new opportunities deserve special attention?

As a result of these reflections, the plan may well be updated. *Being open to changing the plan, when a better understanding has been obtained, is far preferable to a policy of invariably sticking to the plan.*

The importance of doing regular project retrospectives is a key insight of the "Agile" movement in software and product development. It's a vital skill in handling contingency – in learning from both successes and failures.

This learning shouldn't be confined to a single project, regardless of how large that project is. Instead, insights from the management of contingency should be shared across different projects, as part of an ongoing collective education in the principles of vital foresight. Of course, the book you now hold in your hands is intended as a catalyst to increase that type of education.

The learning that should be shared isn't just a set of operating principles. It's also any update of the sets of relevant trends, canaries, and scenarios, that a project has found to be useful:

- *Trends* are factors that might develop additional momentum, and shift gears from being "interesting but probably unimportant" to "important after all"
- *Canaries* are indicators that should be selected ahead of time, and monitored regularly, in order to alert observers of forthcoming gear shifts in the relevance of various trends that might otherwise pass unnoticed
- *Scenarios* are creative combinations of different trends – combinations where the interactions can give extra significance to the individual trends involved.

For each trend that a project is considering, the key question is: how likely is it that the trend will develop sufficiently that it will lead to a significant change in the plans of the project? To help answer that question, it's a good idea to look into potential accelerators or brakes for the trend – influences that could lead the trend to speed up, or to slow down. And it's advisable, as just mentioned, to decide in advance what canary signals you will be checking, on a regular basis, to let you know if a key threshold is about to be reached, or if your basic assumptions about the trend are about to be invalidated.

The term "canary" refers to the caged birds that human miners used to bring with them, as they worked in badly ventilated underground tunnels[449]. Canaries had heightened sensitivity to carbon monoxide and other toxic gases. Shows of distress from these birds alerted many a miner to alter their course quickly, lest they succumb to an otherwise undetectable change in the atmosphere. Becoming engrossed in work without regularly checking the vigour of the canary could prove fatal. As for mining, so also for foresight.

If you're super-confident about the future, you won't bother checking any canary signals. But that would likely be a big mistake. Indeed, an openness to refutation – a willingness to notice developments that were contrary to your expectation – is a vital aspect of managing contingency, managing risk, and managing opportunity.

Canary selection

"All who drink of this treatment recover in a short time, except those whom it does not help, who all die. It is obvious, therefore, that it fails only in incurable cases."

With these words, the renowned physician Galen (129-210 CE) indicated a strong self-confidence in his own medical judgement[450]. Regardless of whether a patient was cured by the potion in question, or instead died from drinking it, Galen remained convinced that the treatment was good. Does that vigorous self-confidence trouble you? *It should.*

In Vienna in the 1910s and 1920s, the young philosopher Karl Popper found himself troubled in the same way by the explanations for human behaviour that he heard from friends of his who were advocates for various branches of psychoanalysis[451].

Popper observed that these friends could draw upon diverse concepts in their favoured theories to seemingly interpret all sorts of contradictory aspects of human behaviour. Since these theories, apparently, could explain even diametrically opposite actions, Popper judged them as being non-scientific.

Popper reached the same assessment regarding the Marxists he knew from his membership, for a while, of an Austrian political party that fully supported Marxism. Regardless of which political or social ups-and-downs occurred, these thinkers could find ideas within their elaborate ideology that somehow described the outcome. A theory that could explain everything, Popper reasoned, actually didn't explain anything. The mere fact that adherents of these theories insisted on calling them scientific – as in "scientific Marxism" or "scientific psychoanalysis" – did not make these theories actually scientific. A better name for them would be *pseudoscientific*.

This led Popper to suggest the following distinction. The difference between science (good science) and pseudoscience (bad science) is that pseudoscience takes all outcomes in its stride without blushing, whereas science from time to time encounters experimental results that it cannot explain, and which therefore trigger a re-evaluation of its current theories. Indeed, good science should identify ahead of time critical experiments where these theories make clear predictions as to the outcome, and where any different outcome indicates a shortcoming of these theories.

That distinction is one of the foundational ideas of the discipline known as the philosophy of science, which regards Karl Popper as one of its key influencers[452].

I offer a similar distinction between good foresight and bad foresight: good foresight accepts the possibility of refutation, whereas bad foresight carries on regardless, denying that any assumption needs to be changed. With bad foresight, it's only when the project has gone horribly, visibly wrong, that there's any admission of surprise. By then, it's too late.

By this criterion, the management of the Apollo moonshot fares well. Recall how the project selected one out of four possible options for the overall journey to the moon, namely "Lunar-orbit rendezvous", as opposed to "Direct ascent", "Earth-orbit rendezvous", and "Lunar surface rendezvous". That decision had been reached in 1962, following lots of intense debate. It became the project's prevailing theory for the best mode of flight. But it remained subject to refutation by experiment. Six times during 1965 and 1966, two spacecraft docked, as part of the Gemini sequence of spaceflights, confirming the basic principles of space rendezvous. In March 1969, the full set of manoeuvres between the lunar landing module and the lunar orbiting module were rehearsed during the Apollo 9 flight, which took place in orbit around the earth. Two months later, a more demanding rehearsal took place during the Apollo 10 flight, this time in lunar orbit, but without the landing module actually touching down on the moon. Only when all these experiments were completed and data from them thoroughly analysed, was approval given for Apollo 11 to actually land on the moon[453].

For a different kind of example, consider a set of forecasts given in 2002 to the UK management board of HMV, the music retailer. The forecasts were presented by Philip Beeching, a marketing and advertising consultant who had been working closely with HMV since 1982. The occasion of the presentation was the arrival of a new managing director, who wished to undertake a review of the company's partnerships. Beeching reviewed the remarkable past history of the company – which had in 1986 opened in Oxford Street what was described as "the largest record store in the world". But he cautioned his audience that, sooner or later, change would arise[454]:

> The three greatest threats to HMV are, online retailers, downloadable music and supermarkets discounting loss leader product.

The managing director did not like that message. He interrupted the presentation with the following objections:

> I have never heard such rubbish. I accept that supermarkets are a thorn in our side but not for the serious music, games or film buyer and as for the other two, I don't ever see them being a real threat, downloadable music is just a fad and people will always want the atmosphere and experience of a music store rather than online shopping.

Determining whether or not a trend is "just a fad" is far from easy. Bear in mind that Beeching gave his presentation shortly after the dot com crash, when many companies had gone out of business after promising that they would transform the world with various online services. Bear in mind, too, that internet speeds were still slow in 2002, and that online shopping was a much less pleasant experience at that time, compared to how it evolved in subsequent years. Finally recall that Apple's iTunes did not appear as a competitor until April of the following year, 2003. Accordingly, the managing director had considerable logic behind his stance. He can hardly be blamed for disagreeing with the forecasts presented. However, where he can be blamed is for having a closed mind. Rather than rejecting the forecasts in their entirety, he should have said something like this:

> The trends you've described seem unlikely to me. But I'm going to assign a small team to check them on a regular basis. We'll keep an eye on the progress of download speeds, on the usability of online shopping, on the emergence of any new types of competitor, and on the type of people who are purchasing and downloading music online.
>
> In the meantime, we'll also investigate scenarios for how we might react to these trends gaining momentum. We'll consider ways to develop or acquire the new skills and processes that will become important in these scenarios. And we'll review options at least once every six months. That way, we'll be ready to move fast, if need be.

Someone else who disliked a forecast that he heard, but who refrained from looking for more information that would throw light on the likelihood of the outcome predicted, was Harry R. Truman, who came to media prominence for a couple of months in 1980. Truman – who is not to be confused with his near namesake, the 33rd US president, Harry S. Truman – was the caretaker of a lodge near Spirit Lake just below the timberline of Mount St Helens in Washington State. He had lived in that lodge for fifty-four years, and was in no hurry to change his ways.

Throughout March to May, 1980, Mount St Helens showed signs of a possible volcanic eruption. Nearby residents were urged to evacuate their homes, out of caution. Truman would hear nothing of it. A flurry of small earthquakes did nothing to damp his self-reliance. If these shakes knocked him out of his bed onto the floor as he slept, as apparently happened, so what? He refused to pack his belongings and move, and scorned the threat posed by a potential larger earthquake. He told a reporter[455]:

> This area is heavily timbered, Spirit Lake is in between me and the mountain, and the mountain is a mile away, the mountain ain't gonna hurt me… boy.

He seemed convinced that his own intuitions, formed by six decades of coexistence with the mountain, were superior to the book knowledge of "goddam" long-haired academics:

> The mountain has shot its wad and it hasn't hurt my place a bit, but those goddamn geologists with their hair down to their butts wouldn't pay no attention to old Truman.

When I saw "old Truman" on live TV news reports, transmitted all the way from Washington State to the United Kingdom, I felt a surge of admiration for his bravado and folk-hero status. It seemed heart-warming that someone had the spunk to stand up to interfering authorities.

However, that bravado was misplaced. On the morning of 18th May, Mount St Helens suffered the most destructive eruption in the recorded history of the United States. Almost immediately, Truman's lodge was buried under 150 feet of volcanic debris, from a landslide that had hurtled downhill at around 110-155 miles per hour. More than fifty people were killed, in most cases presumably instantly, including journalists, photographers, and volcanologists, as well as Truman himself[456].

In partial defence of Truman, the mountain had shown no signs of increased activities in the last few days leading up to the full eruption. We might call this the lull before the storm. However, the preceding two months had provided geologists with what they saw as ample indications of major trouble ahead. Metaphorically, canaries were dying all over the place.

The explosion of Mount St Helens is noteworthy for its brutal suddenness. But it is part of a wider general pattern, in which a disruptive trend passes through a phase of slow change before a dramatic acceleration occurs. By the time of the second phase, it's often too late to act on the advice that was given – but rejected or ignored – during the first phase.

Here's another question that the Mount St Helens example highlights: who do we believe, when they tell us they are seeing canaries keeling over? Maybe these observers are mistaken, or biased. If an academic has attributes that make us personally uncomfortable – long hair, or particular political allegiances, or whatever – should that influence whether we listen to their warnings? If newspapers carry forecasts of impending danger – coronavirus infections, extreme changes in weather, election malfeasance – does our dislike of previous messages carried in these same newspapers justify us in turning a blind eye to these forecasts?

In other words, it's not just a question of which canary signals we choose to monitor. It's also a question of which canary signal *observers* we choose to trust. It's a question not just of "what" but of "who".

Ever since Karl Popper advocated his famous distinction between science and pseudoscience, described above, philosophers and scientists have been highlighting complications with that idea. If an experiment appears to disprove a favoured theory, it's not necessarily the theory which is at fault: perhaps the experiment is mistaken. The equipment being used may be unreliable. An observation might be recorded incorrectly. Or an assumption connecting the theory to the experiment may be questioned.

For example, suppose someone has a theory that the air in a particular set of underground tunnels is free from toxic gases. To test the theory, a caged canary is brought into the tunnel. If an observer reports that the canary has fallen off its perch and expired, does this disprove the theory? You can see the scope for other explanations. Perhaps the canary became ill for some other reason. Perhaps the canary was jolted off the perch by a careless sudden movement by the person carrying the cage, and didn't actually die, but is just stunned. And so on.

These alternative explanations each have some plausibility. However, what would be dangerous, on hearing a report that a canary is distressed, is to simply shrug your shoulders and say, "well, there's doubtless some weird anomaly, so we can ignore this result".

Consider again the experiments conducted by the Gemini and Apollo projects between 1965 and 1969 regarding the rendezvous of crafts in space. Suppose that one of these experiments had gone wrong, and that two craft had failed to connect as expected. In principle, this would have raised questions over the viability of the Apollo project's chosen plan for lunar-orbit rendezvous. We can imagine a number of possible responses to such a failure:

1. "There's doubtless been some weird anomaly, so we can ignore this experiment, and carry on with our plans regardless"
2. "This failure refutes the theory of lunar-orbit rendezvous, which we must now discard, and pick one of the other theories instead"
3. "This failure means we need to alter some of the details of our plans before conducting an updated version of the experiment".

The first of these responses is an under-reaction, laden with danger. The second is probably an over-reaction, although it might turn out to be the best course of action if subsequent similar experiments fail as well. The third fits what is known as "normal science" – to use a term popularized by another key influencer in the philosophy of science, Thomas Kuhn[457] – in which aspects of the prevailing theory are refined in the light of the new findings.

The third of these responses matches the actions taken by the Apollo project following the greatest setback in that project, namely the tragic 1967 fire in the capsule of Apollo 1 in which three astronauts died. That fire did not lead to any sweeping reconfiguration in strategy for the project, but it did cause changes in many details of the project design.

As in many other aspects, the Apollo moonshot thereby acts as a model from which other would-be moonshot projects can learn – provided we are able to move beyond naïve "moonshot worship", in order to appreciate the depths of skills that the team brought to bear on all the uncertainties and contingencies they encountered.

One of these skills was a shared commitment to objective vigilance – a commitment to pay attention to any potentially anomalous results, regardless of whether these results were aligned with prevailing theories.

Let's now look more closely at what that commitment involves. The next examples will help us answer the "who" question: who should we trust as monitors of canary signals? The answer will be that we should not trust any one individual. Instead, it is the considered opinion of the scientific community as a whole that we *ought* to be able to trust.

Cholera disputes

A commitment to objective vigilance is one of the cornerstones of the scientific method. Although individual scientists may have their own biases and blind spots – and they may be in thrall to their own cherished theories or ideologies – the scientific community as a whole operates, in principle, under the norm of independent verification:

1. Scientists publish their results openly, along with a description of the methods used to obtain them
2. Other scientists take the time to check if they can repeat the methods, and reach the same results
3. These independent checks are required, even if the original scientists are highly distinguished and have impressive track records
4. Discrepancies between outcomes are the subject of further investigation, including additional experiments
5. Scientists who change their mind, as a result of new findings, are admired for their objectivity, rather than being criticized for apparent feeble-mindedness.

Consider the debate in London in the middle decades of the nineteenth century as to why people became infected during outbreaks of cholera. This was a debate with enormous practical implications: tens of thousands of people died from the disease in four major outbreaks between 1832 and 1866[458]. The leading epidemiologist of the era, William Farr[459], was one of many champions of what was called the "miasma" theory: the disease was caused by contaminants carried in the air. Venerable doctors from the classical period, such as Hippocrates (active around 400 BCE) and Galen (active around 200 CE), had warned long ago about the dangers of bad air. The evident foul smell from decaying matter made this notion seem intuitively plausible. The distinguished social reformer Edwin Chadwick expressed that viewpoint in his remarks to a committee of the UK parliament in 1846[460]:

> All smell is, if it be intense, immediate acute disease; and eventually we may say that, by depressing the system and rendering it susceptible to the action of other causes, all smell is disease.

In the following year, Farr referred to a "disease mist… like an angel of death"[461]:

> This disease mist, arising from the breath of two millions of people, from open sewers and cesspools, graves and slaughter-houses, is continually kept up and undergoing changes; in one season it was pervaded by cholera, in another by influenza; at one time it bears smallpox, measles, scarlatina and

whooping cough among your children; at another it carries fever on its wings. Like an angel of death it has hovered for centuries over London.

An alternative theory was that contaminants were carried in water. That was the view of John Snow, whose main medical specialty was in the emerging field of anaesthesiology. Snow reasoned that an airborne disease would impact the lungs, rather than (as with cholera) the digestive system.

Part of what happened next is reasonably well known. A cholera outbreak in 1854 was particularly deadly in the central London region of Soho. Snow observed that families who drew water from one particular pump in the area, in Broad Street, suffered disproportionate numbers of infections. In contrast, only five of the 530 inhabitants of a nearby workhouse fell ill, but Snow determined that the workhouse received water from a different source. Workers at an adjacent brewery were also unaffected by the disease: Snow observed that these workers drank beer instead of water, and that the water in the beer was boiled as part of the fermentation process.

These findings were sufficient to persuade the local authorities to remove the handle of the Broad Street pump, disabling it. Almost immediately, new cases of infection stopped in the neighbourhood. The experiment seemed to confirm that cholera was transmitted by water rather than by air. That view was supported by a plethora of other observations that Snow painstakingly collected and documented. He is, rightly, celebrated as a pioneer of public health research[462]. But he is by no means the only hero of this episode. The reason that the scientific understanding of the disease could advance was that people who were formerly strong advocates of the miasma theory were prepared to revise their position, publicly, after scrutinizing evidence shown to them.

One person who changed his mind on this subject was Reverend Henry Whitehead, the Oxford-educated assistant priest at one of the churches near the heart of the Soho outbreak. Keenly interested in the course of the outbreak, on account of his frequent visits to parishioners, Whitehead at first shared the long-standing prevailing view that the disease was transmitted by bad vapours. He was unconvinced by any impact of removing the handle of the Broad Street water pump, seeing this as coincidental rather than definitive[463]. Next, he sought evidence that would back up his view. He visited numerous households in the area, often several times over, and travelled to meet former residents in their new locations in other parts of London, collecting information about the circumstances of each person who had died from the disease. What he learned persuaded him, "slowly and… reluctantly", that Snow was right after all. Part of what he discovered was disturbing information about leakages from a cesspool into the underground water source of the Broad Street pump[464]. He documented his change of opinion in a widely read ten-page article in Macmillan's Magazine[465]. His advocacy was to lead to significant improvements in the treatment of sewage throughout London[466].

Someone else who in due course changed his mind in the light of evidence was William Farr, the pioneering epidemiologist mentioned earlier. Farr had collected and analysed substantial information of his own. That seemed to show, for example, that incidence of cholera diminished in line with the elevation of the ground above the high-water mark of the River Thames. That appeared to support the idea of aerial disease transmission. John Snow acknowledged that relationship but suggested it was a mere coincidence – just as critics of his own views saw the decline of the 1854 epidemic after the removal of the Broad Street pump handle as likewise being a coincidence. How was the conflict of opinion between the two theories to be resolved? *By collecting and reviewing more data, with an open mind.*

By the time of a new outbreak of cholera in London in 1866, Farr had made a thorough study of Snow's notebooks and observations. As the outbreak intensified, Farr made his own investigations of the sources of water used by the communities most impacted by the disease. For example, he discovered evidence that one water company, East London Waterworks, had been flouting the law on the treatment of waste, and was moreover taking steps to obscure that fact.

Farr's conclusion was decisive: a small number of cases of cholera might be due to airborne transmission, but the vast majority were due to the consumption of contaminated water[467]. The improvement of drainage systems should, therefore, take the highest priority. His declarations helped accelerate a kind of nineteenth century moonshot project: the modernization of London's system of sewers. Under the leadership of civil engineer Joseph Bazalgette, that project was with good reason described at the time by the Observer newspaper as "the most extensive and wonderful work of modern times"[468]. It involved a widespread network of new sewers under the streets of the capital, requiring the construction of over one thousand miles of new drains. Twenty-two acres of land were cleared on the banks of the Thames, creating the Victoria, Albert, and Chelsea Embankments. So that the system would be long-lived, Bazalgette had the excellent foresight to insist on the use of the latest type of water-resistant cement, and to build tunnels considerably wider than the current needs required[469].

Bazalgette's new waste disposal system was already partly in place by the time of the 1866 cholera outbreak. William Farr pointed out that the regions of London where the disease struck were those which had not yet been connected to the new system. It was a powerful vindication for Bazalgette's project, and also a reason for it to speed up. By 1892, after the system had been completed, a particularly nasty outbreak of cholera struck one of London's closest trading partners, Hamburg. Nearly nine thousand people died in that city. Understandably, Londoners feared the disease would strike them next. Nevertheless, despite frequent contacts between the two cities – and despite an ongoing stench in the air in London – no such cholera outbreak took place[470].

Some historians have nominated Joseph Bazalgette as the person who "made probably the single biggest contribution to the health of Victorian Londoners"[471]. It may be surprising that this honour would fall, not to a medical practitioner, but to a civil engineer. However, doctors themselves emphasise the importance of prevention rather than cure. What better prevention than systematic improvements in hygiene?

In any case, the merit needs to be shared. The inspiration and increasingly broad public support for the bold initiatives of engineers such as Bazalgette came from publications by scientists – both professional and amateur – such as John Snow, Henry Whitehead, and William Farr.

Before moving on to look at other examples of "objective vigilance", let me briefly highlight five other takeaways from the example of the disputes over the causes of cholera.

First, the free exchange of data between Farr and Snow is exemplary, not only because of what Farr learned from Snow, but also because of insight flowing in the other direction. Despite their opposing theories, they both saw the value of sharing their observations. Indeed, it was data from Farr in the early 1850s that led Snow to understand more fully the implications of his own theories, and to refine these theories.

Second, by no means everyone is motivated to share what they know. Recall how East London Waterworks Company took steps to hide how their processes risked waste products contaminating the water they supplied to households. In more recent times, many other corporations have taken steps to hide what their own scientists have told them about dangerous side-effects of their products or processes:

- From 1953 onward, following a secret meeting in New York of executives of the country's six largest cigarette companies, the tobacco industry pursued a policy to deliberately distort or throw doubt on the findings of scientists about the adverse health consequences of their products[472]
- Oil companies such as Exxon and Mobil have painstakingly covered up information about the damaging changes to climate caused by greenhouse gas emissions – information understood and acknowledged by their own in-house experts[473]
- Companies active in biochemical engineering, such as Monsanto, have communicated in evasive or misleading ways about research into the safety of their products, including the weedkiller Roundup and various GMOs (genetically modified organisms)[474].

It's not just these companies that have been selective with the truth when discussing evidence about their products. Many of the critics of these companies have their own blind spots. For example, they rush to find reasons to disregard any evidence of positive safety and efficacy of GMOs, without taking the time to assess that evidence more carefully.

That brings me to the third takeaway from the cholera disputes: there were important elements of truth in both sides of the debate. Whereas cholera is a disease in which transmission usually takes place via water, there are many other diseases in which transmission takes place through the air. Reality is usually more complicated than any single model would suggest. It's likely the same for many ongoing controversies, such as the right mix of energy sources (potentially including nuclear energy) to head off chaotic climate change, or the measures appropriate to ensuring beneficial applications from technologies such as GMOs and AI. In all these cases, the best solutions are likely to incorporate insights from people that come from different backgrounds. What's needed, therefore, is a commitment from as many people as possible:

- To listen carefully to questions raised in good faith by critics of their favoured viewpoints

- To avoid over-emphasising material that is suspect, even though it appears to bolster their favoured viewpoints
- To point out any problems or queries with observations
- To seek to disentangle the emotional passion behind a claim from the evidence for or against that claim; after all, the emotion often hinders participants from reviewing matters objectively.

Fourth, one reason why many people opposed the water-transmission theory was because it was literally disgusting that drinking water might contain pollution such as faeces. Understandably, it was preferable not to have to think about that possibility. It was less psychologically disturbing to suppose that existing hygiene measures were already sufficient to render water safe to drink. Instead of keeping an open mind to other possibilities, people preferred to push the whole area of thought out of their conscious awareness. That's a pattern which recurs with many other disruptive forces, including the various landmines this book reviews. These landmines are sometimes deeply upsetting.

Fifth, one additional breakthrough helped to raise the prominence of the theory of water-borne infection, making it harder to deny, regardless of questions of psychological preference. That breakthrough was progress with what we now call the germ theory of disease. Experiments by Louis Pasteur in France from 1860 onward, and subsequently by Robert Koch in Germany, made it clearer that various diseases were caused by microscopic organisms – different microorganisms for different diseases. In 1883 Koch identified a particular comma-shaped bacillus as being responsible for cholera.

Some scientists resisted this conclusion for a few years, but the results of the cholera outbreak in 1892 led to increasing consensus[475]. As already mentioned, that outbreak was devastating in some cities, such as Hamburg, but left other cities untouched, including London, but also Altona, which is adjacent to Hamburg. The difference was that cities with good water filtration systems avoided the disease.

The wider takeaway here is that people are more likely to accept an uncomfortable proposition if they also see a solution at hand to help manage the undesirable consequences of the proposition. Drawing attention to landmines is only the start of providing vital foresight. What's also needed is a credible vision for a positive outcome. But that vision needs to be able to withstand scrutiny and vigilance. It cannot be based simply on someone's prior reputation, no matter how distinguished that reputation is.

That thought brings us to the remarkable example of Linus Pauling.

Community vigilance

American scientist Linus Pauling (1901-1994) is the only person to have twice won an undivided Nobel Prize. He won the chemistry prize in 1954, "for his research into the nature of the chemical bond and its application to the elucidation of the structure of complex substances", and the peace prize in 1962, "for his fight against the nuclear arms race between East and West"[476]. Other work that he did on the three-dimensional structure of proteins, on the genetic basis of the disease sickle-cell anaemia, and on comparing the DNA in the blood of different species to determine when these species diverged from each other on the evolutionary tree, arguably also reached Nobel Prize standards. The 1996 book *Scientific 100: A Ranking of the Most Influential Scientists, Past and Present* by science writer John Simmons placed Pauling at number 16 in that all-time top 100 ranking, just behind Werner Heisenberg, but ahead of Erwin Schrödinger, Ernest Rutherford, Marie Curie, and Francis Crick, along with many other household names[477].

You might think, therefore, that if Pauling published a suite of articles and books supporting a particular way of combatting cancer, the rest of the scientific community would quickly fall into line behind him. But, *thankfully*, that's not the way science works.

It was vitamin C that Pauling thought provided the basis to cure many types of cancer. Based on advice from a biochemist who had corresponded with him, Pauling had at the age of sixty-five started taking a daily dose of three grams of vitamin C[478]. That's far in excess of the usual daily recommended intake, which is 65 to 80 milligrams; anything in excess of one gram[479] is said to be prone to cause various kinds of negative reactions, including stomach pain, diarrhoea, or (at even larger doses)[480] vomiting, heartburn, headache, and insomnia. But Pauling reported a very different response. He described his experience as following in his book *Vitamin C, the Common Cold and the Flu*[481]:

> I began to feel livelier and healthier. In particular, the severe colds I had suffered several times a year all my life no longer occurred. After a few years, I increased my intake of vitamin C to… 18,000 milligrams per day.

The more that Pauling spoke and wrote about vitamin C, also known as ascorbic acid, the more he was contacted by people with their own stories to tell about apparently wonderful things that the vitamin could do. Pauling did his own investigations, and came out in favour of many of these theories. Not only would sufficient usage of vitamin C completely eradicate the common cold; it could cure schizophrenia, snakebites, detached retinas, and, potentially, AIDS[482].

One industry that loved what Pauling had to say about vitamins was the supplements industry. Sales of vitamin C tablets sky-rocketed. Extracts from articles written by Pauling, between the 1970s and 1990s, continue to be featured in newsletters circulated by that industry to this day.

A Scottish surgeon called Ewan Cameron persuaded Pauling that the restorative potential of vitamin C extended to cancer. Cancer patients who had taken daily doses of ten grams of the vitamin had, Cameron claimed, fared significantly better than those not receiving that treatment. Pauling was soon convinced. By 1977, he was writing the following[483]:

> My present estimate is that a decrease [in deaths from cancer] of 75 percent can be achieved with vitamin C alone, and a further decrease by use of other nutritional supplements.

He went on to predict:

> Life expectancy will be 100 to 110 years, and in the course of time, the maximum age might be 150 years.

Sadly, Linus Pauling was to watch his wife of sixty years, Ava, battle stomach cancer for five years, before succumbing to the disease in 1981 – despite taking lots of vitamin C in the process. Pauling himself died of prostate cancer fourteen years later, proclaiming to the end that he would have lived an even longer life if he had started taking vitamin C earlier.

Four questions arise from this case:

1. What led Pauling to reach his unusual ideas?
2. Why has the vast majority of the scientific community nevertheless rejected his claims?
3. What are the implications for curing cancer – and for lifespans of up to 150 years?
4. What are the broader implications for forecasting radical improvements in medicine?

Let's address these questions one by one.

Pauling's disruptive theories on vitamin C confirm to the general pattern described in the previous chapter: they extend and integrate ideas from several different perspectives:

- Vitamin C had played a vital role in curing a disease which had, earlier in history, killed millions of sailors, namely scurvy. Adding oranges and lemons – sources of vitamin C – to their diet made a huge difference to sailors' health. Since vitamin C could evidently cure some diseases, perhaps higher doses could cure more diseases.
- A particular theory of the causes of aging and diseases had grown in popularity from the 1950s onward. It stated that cells were damaged by highly reactive molecules known as "free radicals". Other molecules known as antioxidants can neutralise these free radicals. Since vitamin C is an antioxidant, that could explain beneficial results from it[484].
- Whereas many other animals can synthesise vitamin C internally, the line of apes leading up to humans lost that ability, perhaps by an accidental genetic mutation, millions of years ago[485]. That might explain why humans experience many diseases.
- The pharmaceutical industry has a reason to dispute information about the ways in which vitamins can prevent or cure diseases, since their profits depend on people becoming ill and buying expensive drugs.

Pauling could also point to a number of scientific trials, including those of the Scottish doctor Ewan Cameron. Finally, many people *felt better* as a result of taking vitamins, and some did recover from various diseases.

However, none of the above arguments are decisive; at most, they are suggestive. There is no reliable basis to extrapolate from one disease, such as scurvy, to another, such as cancer. The free radical theory of aging has fallen out of favour, and it is now recognised that the body has plenty of innate mechanisms to deal with the adverse side-effects of these molecules[486]. And whilst the pharmaceutical industry might not be able to make large profits from selling vitamins, that's no reason to conclude that all criticisms of Pauling's theories are motivated by commercial concerns. Instead, we have to look more objectively at these criticisms.

And of course, the fact that someone recovers from a disease – the common cold, or something else – after taking a treatment, does not prove that the latter was the cause of the former. People recover from diseases all the time, for all kinds of reason. That's why science requires, as far as possible, the performance of controlled, randomised trials. In these trials, patients don't know whether they are taking the actual compound under investigation, or an inert substitute known as a placebo. And the assignment of patients into two groups – the group receiving the actual treatment, and the group receiving the placebo – needs to be random.

When other scientists looked at the trials of the efficacy of vitamin C carried out by Linus Pauling and his co-workers, such as Ewan Cameron, they found these trials fell far short of the principles of randomisation. For example, the cancer patients who received the vitamin C were less ill *at the start of the trial* than the other patients[487].

When a trial is found to have shortcomings, the next thing to be done is for other groups to seek to repeat the trial, but with improvements in its design or administration. When that happened, other researchers were unable to obtain the results that Pauling predicted. Pauling objected that the new experiments were unfair in various ways: the vitamin C should have been administered at an earlier stage of the patient's treatment, and so on. That's the kind of to-and-fro which characterises a healthy scientific debate. But over time, more and more concerns emerged about the claims being made by Pauling.

Indeed, rather than vitamin C curing cancer, it emerged that it could *accelerate* cancer in some cases. A former long-time colleague of Pauling, Arthur Robinson – who was the first president of the Linus Pauling Institute created to carry out additional research into Pauling's ideas on medicine[488] – raised concerns about the results he was finding. This led to Robinson being fired from his position and Pauling publicly criticising the calibre of Robinson's research. Robinson sued for slander and libel, and received $575,000 in an out-of-court settlement. Robinson subsequently described the break-up as follows[489]:

> The results of these experiments caused an argument between Linus and me, which ended our 16-year period of work together. He was not willing to accept the experimentally proven fact that vitamin C in ordinary doses accelerated the growth rate of squamous cell carcinoma in these mice.

It may be psychologically comforting to turn a blind eye to unwelcome experimental findings, but that's hardly the way to advance a full understanding of any complex system. Just because someone, such as Linus Pauling, performs outstanding work in one area of investigation – or even in multiple different areas – that's no guarantee of the quality of their work in any new area. Each time, the results need to be reviewed by the scientific community as a whole.

That's why my answer to the question, who do we trust to monitor potential canary signals, is not that we simply pick one person with a good track record. It's that we should involve *a diverse group of observers*, who, regardless of their various differences, are each committed to principles of objectivity and openness.

That's also why it's particularly important for a society to have:

- *A free press*, which is able to investigate from several different points of view any reports of actions which challenge prevailing opinions
- *A multiplicity of responsible political parties*, able to constructively challenge decisions being made by political leadership
- *A tradition of scholastic academia*, which collectively prioritises the quest for truth over the quest for power.

What about Pauling's predictions that human lifespan might one day reach to 150 years, on account of new medical interventions that undo the kind of bodily damage that will in due course lead to diseases such as cancer?

Even though the particular interventions advocated by Pauling do not work in the way he hoped, I believe his overall intuitions remain valid in this case. Evolution did leave the human metabolism with many awkward compromises. Advances in scientific understanding and medical engineering prowess will in due course allow the systematic reversal of the biological damage that arises from these compromises. As a result, we humans will become able, if we wish, to live for 150 years – or even longer. However, the interventions will be substantially more complicated than merely taking vitamin tablets. Vitamins are natural compounds, whereas the interventions I envision will likely involve brand new creations.

Landmine indicators

I wouldn't blame you for being sceptical about some of the claims I'm making in this book:

- Claims about the possibility of radical enhancement of the human condition, including the option to live in a healthy state for 150 years or more
- Claims about a number of landmines that could plunge civilisation into something akin to a new dark age – or worse.

But how will you go about deciding if these claims might prove true?

Will you be like "old Harry Truman", whose fifty-four years of life in his lodge on Mount St Helens made him sceptical that the lodge faced an existential threat from the mountain?

Will you be like the HMV UK managing director and declare you "have never heard such rubbish"?

Will you be like the leaders of the NASA Apollo project and take steps to experimentally verify concepts about which some doubt has been raised?

Will you be like nineteenth century researchers William Farr and Henry Whitehead, able to change your mind as you find new pieces of evidence?

Ideally, you'll say to yourself (and mean it) something like the sentences I suggested earlier the HMV managing director *should* have said:

> The trends you've described seem (a bit) unlikely to me. But I'm going to forge links with a community that checks these trends on a regular basis. I'll keep an eye on appropriate canary signal indicators.
>
> In the meantime, I'll also investigate scenarios for how society might react to these trends gaining momentum. I'll consider ways to develop or acquire the new skills and processes that will become important in these scenarios. And I'll review options at least once every six months. That way, I'll be ready to move fast, if need be.

To help with the first of these tasks, let me offer some potential canary signals for each of the eleven landmines that I introduced in Chapter 4. In case a landmine is moving closer to the point of deadly explosion, these signals can provide at least some advance warning.

Landmine 1: *The "left behinds"*:

- The share of national wealth in the hands of the richest 1%

- Changes in the inflation-adjusted median household income
- The proportion of working-age people who have given up looking for paid employment
- Ratios of employee-performed tasks to robot-automated tasks
- Other measures of technological unemployment or technological underemployment
- Numbers of "deaths of despairs"
- Other indicators of widespread mental illness.

Landmine 2: *WMD proliferation*:

- Actual uses of chemical or biological weapons
- The proliferation of nuclear weapons
- Instances where suicidal individuals arranged for many other people to die in the act that ended their own lives
- Plots by terrorist organisations or other groups of disaffected individuals involving the use of WMDs
- The availability of 3D printed weapons, or other ways to manufacture weapons away from centralised scrutiny
- The use of autonomous drones to deliver deadly payloads
- Instances of accidental near use (or actual use) of WMDs, perhaps due to malfunctioning information technology.

Landmine 3: *Biotech hazards*:

- Cases where viruses evolve in the wild into more dangerous forms
- The emergence of new strains of bacteria that are resistant to existing antibacterial treatments
- The frequency of accidental releases of deadly viruses due to failures of biocontainment processes
- Cases when genetic editing using methods such as CRISPR have unanticipated detrimental consequences
- Publication of research that would assist people with inflammatory intent to create more deadly versions of existing viruses

- The availability of "bio-malware-as-a-service" on the dark web.

Landmine 4: *Infotech hazards*:

- The growing availability of "info-malware-as-a-service" on the dark web
- Measurements of financial losses due to malware attacks
- Usage of untraceable money exchange systems by people seeking financial gains from conducting cyberattacks
- Assessments of the quality of security in "Internet of Things" devices in wide usage
- Instances of cyberattacks between nation states
- Publication of information that would assist people with inflammatory intent to create more deadly versions of existing info malware
- Examples of malware incorporating sophisticated artificial intelligence to attain more dangerous capability.

Landmine 5: *Financial instabilities*:

- Measurements of national economic distress caused by widespread theft of money by cybercriminals
- Measurements of national economic distress caused by the instability of shared currencies, such as the Euro
- Measurements of dangerous underlying connections between different financial instruments that are nominally independent
- The ratio of private debt to the overall size of the economy
- Other measurements of growing financial instabilities in major economies, such as China
- Instances of "flash crashes" involving automated stock trading systems, especially where these crashes lack a clear explanation
- The vulnerability of economies to major problems emerging within cryptocurrencies, such as a failure of bitcoin security mechanisms.

Landmine 6: *Environmental instabilities*:

- New examples of chemicals being discovered to have dangerous side effects, many years after having first been introduced to the environment
- Measurements of harm arising from the distribution of microplastics, organic pollutants, radioactive materials, or nanomaterials
- Reductions in populations of plants or animals (including insects) that are unexpected and unexplained
- Updates on the state of the "Nine Planetary Boundaries" as being monitored by the Stockholm Resilience Centre
- Growing severity of extreme weather – as opposed to what could be considered ordinary statistical variation
- Instances where ongoing adverse weather is a significant multiplier of other stresses, such as increasing pressures on migration, or making violent conflict more likely
- The approach of climate change feedback cycles toward potential tipping points
- Any limitations that might prevent renewable energy sources from scaling up in the way optimists like to forecast.

Landmine 7: *Democracy under threat*:

- Surveys of the degree of importance placed by citizens on their government being fully democratic
- Surveys of the extent of popular satisfaction with national political systems
- Measurements of government corruption around the world
- Use of technology by governments to undermine freedoms which citizens previously took for granted
- The extent to which citizens self-censor out of fear of political repercussions.

Landmine 8: *Cancers within society*:

- Abuses of the monopoly power possessed by dominant corporations

- Loss of independence of industry regulators, with these bodies falling under the control of forces they are meant to be regulating
- Instances where companies diminish overall human flourishing whilst nevertheless boosting measures such as GDP that are *meant* to represent the health of the economy
- Objective measures of market failure – instances when the self-interested pursuit of objectives by a number of different parties adds up to collective harm rather than the expected mutual benefit
- Changes in the inflation-adjusted costs for various medical treatments (as an indication of potential dysfunction within the healthcare industry)
- The dominance of information systems and media platforms by a small number of companies that take key decisions free from democratic oversight
- Assessments of the size and influence on society as a whole of various "complexes", such as the military-industrial complex, the carbon-energy-industrial complex, the financial-industrial complex, the information technology complex, and the medical-industrial complex.

Landmine 9: *Reason under threat*:

- Instances of real-world riots, pogroms, vigilante justice, or even genocide, whipped up by false reports circulating on social media
- Measures of the resources allocated by governments to create false narratives that deliberately foment social chaos, either at home or abroad
- The proportion of statements by political leaders that are fact-checked as being misleading or unreliable
- Measures of the activities of "conspiracy entrepreneurs" – people who circulate misleading information, not for political reasons, but in order to benefit financially from associated advertising clicks
- Assessments of the ability of citizens to think rationally and critically, even about topics where they have strong feelings

- Assessments of the general knowledge of citizens, covering basic facts of science, geography, and history
- Assessments of the numeracy of citizens, covering matters such as exponentials and probabilities.

Landmine 10: *Divided nations*:

- Measures of the effectiveness of international bodies such as the UN, the World Bank, the International Monetary Fund, and the World Health Organization
- Growing barriers to freedom of movement and freedom of international trade
- The adoption of autonomous weapons system that can operate outside of direct human oversight
- The proportion of national funds that are allocated to military purposes
- Occasions where relations with obnoxious political leaders – leaders who degrade human flourishing inside their own country – are defended on account of the need to maintain alliances in perceived global conflicts
- Measures of inequality between nations
- The growth of ideologies or movements that fan criticism of particular nations or ethnicities – encouraging sentiments that are, for example, anti-Chinese, anti-Arab, anti-Jew, anti-Russian, or anti-American.

Landmine 11: *Divided aging*:

- Increases in the "longevity gap" – the difference in life expectancy between people in rich areas and people in neighbouring poor areas
- Indications of a growing two-tier healthcare system, potentially tending (in the extreme) toward something like that portrayed in the dystopian movie *Elysium*, in which whole-body repairs are available to the wealthy inhabitants of a large satellite that orbits the earth, whereas everyone living on the earth's surface receives only limited medical treatments

- Signs of growing popular hostility to technologies such as genetic modification, body augmentation, life extension, sensory enhancement, or AIs that act as always-on personal assistants
- The emergence of any anti-transhumanist ideologies or movements, that uphold "natural" modes of living and oppose lifestyles involving "non-natural" technological intervention
- Media narratives about AI that emphasise detrimental outcomes, without highlighting the routes to extremely beneficial outcomes.

Beyond contingency

Out of the several score landmine indicators that I've just listed, it's likely that a reasonable fraction will remain quiescent over the next few years. In those cases, rather than any signal of major impending trouble, the signal may, instead, be that things are becoming calmer.

Nevertheless, I also believe that a reasonable fraction of the above indicators – a different subset – will over the same timescale show that civilisation is approaching a major detonation. In these cases, we should accelerate the corresponding action plans that are already under preparation.

The problem, of course, is that it's by no means clear in advance which indicators will end up in the quiescent group, and which in the volcanic group. That's why genuine vigilance is so vital.

What's more, we need to avoid restricting our attention just to an initially suggested set of potential canary signals. The future will likely produce surprises outside of the set we already have in mind.

If we take seriously the idea that the future is uncertain – that the landscape ahead includes many contingencies – then we should be collectively asking ourselves this question on a regular basis: *do we need to add new indicators to the list that we are observing?* Are there new kinds of interactions – new convergences or new disruptions – whose possibilities are just starting to become apparent?

Alongside new fears, at least some of these new convergences and new disruptions can bring powerful new hope. Let's pick up that thought in the next chapter, as we move from the *observing, predictive* side of foresight to its *creative, constructive* side.

8. Creativity

Creativity, defined: Imaging possibilities that are different from the present. Considering additions, or subtractions, that can alter the attractiveness of potential scenarios. The steps taken to add colour or shape to a provisional idea, and to transform it from an abstract hypothesis to something that can actually change the world.

"To create peace, we have to prepare scenarios involving war."

That's not exactly what Publius Flavius Vegetius Renatus said in his book *De re militari* written around the year 390 CE. But it's close.

The book summarised the practice of warfare as conducted by the Romans as they extended and defended their empire. For more than a thousand years afterward, military commanders carried copies of the book with them, to consult it for advice on how to prepare for and conduct war[490]. Here's one of the gems of wisdom it contains:

> The main and principal point in war is to secure plenty of provisions for oneself and to destroy the enemy by famine. Famine is more terrible than the sword.

Perhaps the most famous maxim in that book is "If you want peace, prepare for war" – though a more precise translation from the original Latin is "Let him who desires peace prepare for war". That's the maxim which I've restated in a tweaked form at the start of this chapter.

The version I gave was core to the thinking of the person who helped popularise the idea of scenario thinking from the 1960s onward, the military strategist Herman Kahn.

Kahn was consumed by the question of how to avoid a terrible nuclear war. He developed his ideas in the 1950s, when both the USA and the USSR had conducted tests of hydrogen bombs, when US military commanders had sought permission to use nuclear bombs during the Korean War, and when the Bulletin of Atomic Scientists had moved the hands of their famous "Doomsday Clock" to just two minutes before midnight. Not long after, the USSR seemed to leap ahead of American capabilities by launching several Sputnik spacecraft into orbit. Might a bellicose Soviet Union, emboldened by its advantages in rocketry, launch a pre-emptive nuclear attack on America, in line with the "we will bury you" warnings of shoe-banging Soviet premier Nikita Khrushchev?

Kahn's conclusion, in effect, was "To create nuclear peace, we have to prepare scenarios involving nuclear war."

Specifically, Kahn created detailed scenarios involving a retaliatory "second strike" response to any attempt by one side to disable the missiles of the other side via a surprise first-strike[491]. To deter any such first strike, Kahn argued, there had to be a credible case that:

1. Sufficient weapons would survive any first-strike attack
2. Military commanders of the side attacked would be prepared to launch a massive second-strike in these circumstances.

The scenario became known by the acronym MAD, meaning Mutual Assured Destruction. Most people who heard about the idea hated it. They objected that it was deeply immoral. But Kahn's response was that arguments over morality would not be sufficient to avoid a war. When a disaster is at hand, it can't be deterred merely by expressions of disgust. A cooler head is required.

Accordingly, the idea was developed of a *strategic triad* of systems each capable of providing a terrible nuclear response[492]: airborne missiles in craft such as the B-52 bomber, intercontinental missiles launched from hardened silos controlled by underground monitoring centres, and another set of intercontinental missiles carried around the seven seas by underwater submarines. An incoming strike might disable large parts of that triad of response capabilities, but it would likely leave at least some elements able to inflict a devastating counterpunch.

Further thinking along the same lines led to a redesign of intercontinental missiles to incorporate multiple independently-targetable reentry vehicles (MIRVs). A single missile from a submarine, therefore, could split up high in the atmosphere into as many as sixteen different warheads, which could explode over sixteen different cities[493].

This kind of thinking probably makes you uneasy. It *should* make you uneasy. But there's an argument that these ideas have indeed helped to deter political leaders from approaching any brink from which a descent into nuclear conflict might follow. Despite the fears expressed by the Bulletin of Atomic Scientists – and many others – the world has avoided any offensive use of nuclear weapons since 1945.

When thinking about future scenarios, cool heads are needed, not just to try to avoid nuclear holocaust, but also to determine the best responses to all kinds of other existential transformations. Our initial emotional reactions can mislead us, fatally, since they are grounded in past experiences which may be very different from future occurrences. Whether these reactions involve the three-letter word "yuk" or its near opposite, another three-letter word, "wow", we need to be able to keep these emotions on hold whilst we think through the options available to us.

Either way, we need to be able to move beyond what futurist Alvin Toffler dubbed "future shock"[494]. This detachment can allow us to perceive ways in which the "wow" scenarios can go terribly wrong – in which case, we need to avoid being seduced by what seemed so attractive about them. This detachment can also allow us to perceive ways in which the "yuk" scenarios needn't be so terrible after all.

Thinking the unthinkable

Herman Kahn is a controversial figure. He argued that society needed to become skilled in "thinking about the unthinkable", as in the title of the book he wrote in 1962[495]. The nuclear deterrent would succeed in its goal of creating and maintaining peace only if using these nuclear weapons in a second-strike retaliation was at least partially credible. Therefore, there needed to be positive answers that were at least partially credible to questions such as:

1. Could food be grown in soil that had been contaminated by nuclear fallout?
2. Could shelters be built that would protect at least some of the population against incoming missiles?
3. Could society adapt – as it had following the Black Death in Europe in the Middle Ages – to the loss of a significant fraction of the population?

Kahn developed scenarios covering all these cases. Life would go on, he insisted. And such a thought was critical, in his view, to persuading potential adversaries *not* to launch any nuclear attack.

One person who was struck by Kahn's work was the filmmaker Stanley Kubrick. Seeing the dramatic potential, Kubrick devised the idea for his much-praised 1964 film *Dr. Strangelove* – subtitled *How I Learned to Stop*

Worrying and Love the Bomb. It starred the comic genius Peter Sellers, who played multiple different characters with aplomb. As a sign of the influence of the film, in 1998 the American Film Institute put it at #26 in its list of America's greatest movies over the preceding one hundred years, collating the viewpoints of "more than 1,500 leaders of the American movie community"[496].

Spoiler alert, in case you haven't seen the film: it doesn't end well. The clever stratagems of the nuclear war theorists in the film, including the eponymous Dr Strangelove, turned out to be *too* clever.

Another spoiler: the character of Dr Strangelove is described as an amalgam of four people in real life[497]: Herman Kahn, two who have featured in preceding pages of this book – Edward Teller and Wernher von Braun – and one other person who will appear in the final chapter, John von Neumann. All four of these people are famed for their prodigious intellects. One message of Dr Strangelove, therefore, is that cleverness isn't enough.

I concur with that message. Intelligence is an important *part* of good foresight, but it needs to be coupled with other key skills. One of these additional skills is that of vivid communications – communications that use more than mere logic in order to break through preconceived mindsets. In this sense, the artistic skills deployed by Stanley Kubrick and his colleagues, along with the mesmeric acting skills of Peter Sellers, created a positive result that Kahn's logical reasoning, by itself, could not achieve. Generations of viewers of the film came away from the experience viscerally determined to avoid the ultimate scenario it portrayed.

Both Kubrick and Kahn can be seen as vindicated: they both outlined scenarios they passionately wished would not come to pass. The reason the scenarios didn't transpire was because they were given sufficient attention beforehand. The "unthinkable" was not only thought; it was dramatized.

Whether Herman Kahn is best seen as a villain of this story or as a hero, we cannot deny an important influence that he exerted, beyond the field of nuclear strategy, into the wider field of foresight analysis. As I'll now describe, his ideas about scenario planning were to pass from the military theatre into the world of business.

Disrupting flows of oil

Here's another variant on the maxim from the start of this chapter, "To create peace, we have to prepare scenarios involving war." The variant emphasises economic scenarios rather than military ones: *"To create prosperity, we have to prepare scenarios involving adversity."*

For seven large companies that dominated the oil industry, the period from the 1920s to the 1970s saw prosperity followed by more prosperity. Nicknamed "the seven sisters", these companies maintained lucrative control over huge flows of oil from oilfields around the world[498]. For Exxon, Mobil, Chevron, Texaco, Gulf Oil, BP, and Shell – to use names by which these companies might be recognised today (although different names were used at different times) – it seemed that the future was likely to be bright. Despite the many international upheavals that took place between 1936 and 1970, the cost of a barrel of crude oil remained between one and two US dollars throughout that period[499]. What *did* change over that timescale was the *demand* for oil, as more people in more countries around the world found more reasons to use the substance. One pattern that emerged is that the actual demand regularly exceeded what forecasters had predicted just a few years previously.

One measure of the dominance of these seven companies is that a listing in Fortune magazine in 1973 of the world's twelve largest manufacturing companies, ranked by the value of their assets, included all seven of the sisters – in positions 1, 2, 4, 7, 8, 11, and 12[500]. (The other five companies on that list, since you ask, were General Motors, Ford, IBM, Nippon Steel, and ITT.)

Of course, the ongoing successes of the seven sisters could not be taken for granted. First, they needed to keep on managing complex processes of exploration, drilling, extraction, and distribution. Second, they needed to handle local variations and surprises. For example, in 1967, Saudi Arabia stemmed the flow of oil from refineries in that country, being angered by Israel's decisive victory in the Six Day War against Egypt, Syria, and Jordan. But the oil giants could balance that shortfall by rapidly increasing production elsewhere in the world, such as in Texas, Venezuela, and Iran.

Political leaders in countries with large oil deposits were far from happy that so much of the profit in that industry was being taken by companies headquartered in the United States or Europe. From as early as 1960, representatives from five of these countries – Iran, Iraq, Kuwait, Saudi

Arabia, and Venezuela – had joined together to create OPEC, the Organization of the Petroleum Exporting Countries[501]. Over the next few years, they were joined by Qatar, Indonesia, Libya, the United Arab Emirates, Algeria, Nigeria, Ecuador, and others. Might this alliance disrupt the profits being generated by the seven sisters?

As is often the case with potential disruptions, the early indications looked weak. Oil industry executives scorned the idea that the OPEC countries could transcend their individual short-term goals in order to cooperate. It was like the idea that the Internet would disrupt the sales of music. "Arabs will never get it together" was one comment written in response to a report highlighting the potential challenge posed by OPEC.

But for those who were watching more carefully, there were canary signals to be seen. Muammar Gaddafi had seized power in Libya in September 1969. Four months later, he declared that international oil companies should be paying a higher price for Libyan oil, and that the Libyan state should retain a larger share of the profits made by these companies in the country. Otherwise, all oil flow from the country would be halted. Gaddafi's negotiation tactics were successful: the price rose 30%, and the profit share retained by his regime rose from 50% to 55%[502].

Of the companies making up the seven sisters, Shell was described (in a Forbes article in 1972) as "the ugly sister". Compared to the others, it had smaller oil reserves, and weaker relations with various Arab governments. Senior managers in Shell therefore felt more vulnerable to any winds of change than the corresponding personnel in their competitors.

It has also been said that Shell's corporate culture was less visceral and more imbued with "understated, pragmatic intellectualism" than the culture of the other oil giants. Here's an observation shared by a writer on strategic affairs, Art Kleiner[503]:

> An observer of several meetings between the British government and oil company representatives during the 1970s noticed that men from Exxon, Texaco, BP, and Gulf tended to blurt out angry reactions on the spot. The Shell man would wait quietly, watchful and attentive, his position prepared. He would have talked over Shell's stance several times that week with colleagues back at the office. If he had to denounce someone or block a plan, he struck "not with a bludgeon, but with a rapier," the observer recalled. Shell men were like representatives of a secret service, he had decided – not people to oppose lightly.

Out of that "pragmatic intellectualism", and the perception of being particularly vulnerable to shocks, arose a greater openness to exploring alternative futures. Perhaps the company would be struck by disruptions with a greater magnitude than those it had successfully weathered in the preceding decades. But how could Shell prepare for such disruptions?

The task of thinking about unthinkable futures was given to a London-based manager, Ted Newland. Newland was both an insider and an outsider – a Shell veteran with a diverse background. He had been a Royal Air Force pilot during the Second World War, and frequently vacationed on a farmstead in Argentina he had inherited from family connections there. His assignments in Shell had included time in Venezuela and Nigeria. He was prepared to think differently. Looking around the world for people who might help him in that task, he noticed the writings of Herman Kahn.

By this time, Kahn was running his own company, the Hudson Institute[504], offering consultancy on the scenario analysis methods he had developed when considering nuclear deterrence. He had also developed a rich range of forecasts for how the world would change in the decades up to the year 2000, many of which he published in book form in 1967[505]. Some of Kahn's predictions were to prove to be accurate: widespread use of computers in business, direct broadcasts from satellites to home receivers, two-way "pocket phones", the collapse of Soviet communism, and the rise in significance of Japanese companies[506]. Other predictions failed to come true by 2000: undersea cities, control over the weather, humans hibernating for months or even years, pre-programmed dreams during sleep, and wide use of robots as "slaves" inside family homes[507]. Perhaps the most important point where Kahn was correct was his forecast of an increase in economic growth – and a corresponding increase in the global demand for energy.

Newland concluded from his discussions with Kahn that "business as usual" would no longer apply. Shell would probably not be able to adapt to new waves of change in a reactive manner. They needed to get ahead of developments, to anticipate transformations before they arose.

Other people were added to Newland's scenario planning team, including the Frenchman Pierre Wack, chosen on account of his excellent communication skills. Before joining Shell in France, Wack had been a magazine publisher; his professional background also included government administration. Thus, like Newland, he was both an insider and an outsider. Perhaps most significant, Wack was keenly interested in how to inspire people to take unconventional ideas seriously. He had spent time in the 1940s in Paris with the Russian mystic Georges Gurdjieff; and he used to visit India for several weeks each year to meditate[508]. He was familiar with Japanese mystic traditions too[509].

A simple account of what happened next would be that Newland and Wack absorbed scenario planning methods from Herman Kahn, developed scenarios applicable to the future of the oil industry, presented the results to Shell executives, and the company was therefore uniquely prepared to handle the disruptive forces which subsequently changed the world. But that account skips over the fact that Shell's scenario initiative almost died before it was successful.

The first major output from Newland and Wack's team was a set of four scenarios for the year 1976, presented to higher management in 1971[510]:

1. A "surprise-free" future, extending long-established patterns, with events playing out in the way senior management tended to assume
2. A "high-take" future, in which the governments of Arab nations demanded – and received – a larger share of oil revenues, causing a significant decline in oil industry profits
3. A "low-demand" future, featuring a decline in international trade, an economic depression, and consumers becoming more interested in leisure than in industry
4. An "energy alternatives" future, in which coal and nuclear displaced oil.

The managers were underwhelmed. "So what?" they asked. "What do I do with these scenarios?"

Wack later offered this assessment of the shortcomings of what he called "first generation scenarios":

> When the set was presented to Shell's top management, the problem was [that]… no strategic thinking or action could be taken from considering this material… The first-generation scenarios presented the raw uncertainties but they offered no basis on which managers could exercise their judgment. Our next task was to provide that basis so that executives could understand the nature of these uncertainties and come to grips with them.

If scenarios lack actionable takeaways, they are likely to pass quickly out of mind. Executives have plenty of other challenges that need their attention – all the many difficult tasks of "business as usual". And scenario forecasters might find themselves out of a job. But Shell's executives let Newland and Wack continue their work. The first four scenarios were not the end of the exercise, but rather a beginning. They provided a basis for further discussion. Pierre Wack sought out feedback from people all throughout Shell, and the scenarios evolved in the process.

In September 1972, Wack presented a set of second-generation scenarios, in a half-day workshop with Shell managing directors. Those who attended later recalled the experience as being an "enthralling three-hour performance"[511]. In contrast to the initial presentation, the scenarios in the new set:

- Involved the attendees emotionally as well as intellectually
- Wove engaging narratives involving potential sequences of causes and effects
- Explored reactions that might be taken by figures like US President Richard Nixon, the Shah of Iran, members of the Saudi royal family, Libya's Gaddafi, and Shell's competitors such as Exxon
- Highlighted potential actions the executives could undertake in anticipation of future developments.

This workshop involved three variations on each of two families of scenarios, making a total of six scenarios. The first family involved disruption in the supply of oil, whereas the second involved variants of business-as-usual. What particularly impressed attendees was the way Wack seemed to have anticipated their own favoured solutions, as different members of the second family of scenarios. As the workshop proceeded, attendees increasingly saw scenarios in that second family as losing plausibility: for them to remain on course, too many "miracles" would need to take place.

In the wake of that workshop, the company decided on four steps forward:

1. Wack would present his analysis to managers of divisions of the company around the world; these managers would be asked to prepare operational responses in case the disruptive scenarios would come to pass
2. Wack would share these scenarios with Shell's contacts in governments in Europe and North America, so that they, too, would be prepared to take fast action – in particular, being ready to reduce

usage of oil, and to coordinate their actions in the face of a growing assertiveness by OPEC

3. Decisions about future investments would include more flexibility; for example, new refineries should be designed to be able to process more than one kind of oil
4. Profligate expenses would be cut back, and be replaced by more frugal policies, in anticipation of the need to tighten belts.

Governments were sceptical. The disruptions described might happen some time in the 1980s, or later, they thought, rather than in the second half of the 1970s as Pierre Wack suggested. After all, the price of oil had hardly changed in four decades – whereas Shell was daring to suggest it might triple to as high as six dollars a barrel.

What happened next was different from what any of the scenarios had proposed. Rather than the oil price rising from 1975 onward, it surged as early as 1973. And never mind six dollars; it reached thirteen dollars within a year – *on route to tripling again later in the decade.*

As is often the case, the cause of the acceleration of the disruption was an external event – actually the confluence of a couple of external events.

The main event was the Yom Kippur War of October 1973. Egypt and Syria launched a surprise attack against Israel, and initially seemed to have the upper hand in the conflict. But the Israelis quickly reversed the situation, securing territorial gains. The Arabs felt humiliated. They saw Israel's military success as being dependent on support from the United States. As it happens, negotiations on oil prices were taking place at that very same time in Vienna. Just as happened after the Six Day War in 1967, Saudi Arabia led the calls to raise the price of oil. This time, the OPEC countries were much more unified. In a resulting embargo, the volume of oil shipped to the west would be tightly restricted. And the price of what *was* shipped would rise, and rise.

The second external event was that Richard Nixon was highly distracted at that same time by his growing problems with the Watergate scandal. That partly explains the lack of a unified response by oil consuming countries to the new demands from OPEC.

All seven companies of the "seven sisters" were thrown into turmoil. But Shell managers were uniquely ready for this disruption. Three of the other sisters were eventually acquired by competitors and consolidated. Shell was never again viewed as "the ugly sister".

In later years, Shell was to credit its practice of scenario planning in helping them to be better prepared for other disruptions, such as the Iranian revolution of 1979 and the decline of the Soviet bloc in the 1980s[512]. By that time, many of Shell's scenario planners had moved on, to apply the ideas of scenario planning in yet other sectors.

Destino Colombia

"Telling new stories enables us to create new futures."

That's how Adam Kahane describes the purpose of scenarios[513]. A Canadian by birth and upbringing, Kahane held for a number of years the role of "Head of Social, Political, Economic, and Technological Scenarios" for Shell in London[514]. Stepping beyond that role, Kahane facilitated foresight exercises in various troubled circumstances around the world – including the Mont Fleur exercise in South Africa that featured in the opening chapter of this book.

We humans live our lives under the influence of stories we tell ourselves: stories about heroes and villains, about destinations and distractions, and about what really matters. These stories often serve us well, for a while at least – which is why we keep them in our minds. But they can remain lodged in our minds long after they have outlived their true usefulness, a bit like the way a biological virus can inhabit our body even though it does us no good. As Kahane puts it[515]:

> We are addicted to our old stories. We need new stories…
>
> If we keep telling the same stories, and keep doing the same things, we will stay where we are.

How do we break these addictions? How can we find better stories, to displace those which serve us badly?

Consider the example of Kahane's work in one of the world's most troubled countries, Colombia. That country experienced two bitter civil wars in the first half of the twentieth century, before becoming immersed in another series of conflicts from the 1960s onward. Protagonists in that latter struggle included two separate left-wing guerrilla organisations (the FARC and the ELN), drug cartels, right-wing paramilitary groups, and the national military – all of which were heavily armed. Kidnappings, massacres, and extra-judicial executions were all-too-common. Many parts of the country lay outside the rule of law. Despite all this, democratic votes took place from time to time, and many businesses prospered[516].

Taking inspiration from the positive changes they had seen happening in South Africa, a number of Colombian entrepreneurs and politicians wondered if a similar process might take place in their country. They set the goal of creating useful scenarios for what might happen in Colombia over the following sixteen years. A young politician with a background in economics and journalism, Juan Manuel Santos, travelled to South Africa in 1996 where he met with President Nelson Mandela[517], who spoke warmly of the beneficial impact in his country of the Mont Fleur scenarios project.

Santos and his colleagues had already tried the previous year, 1995, to commence a scenarios project of their own, involving Adam Kahane, the facilitator of Mont Fleur. An initial meeting had included participation by telephone from guerrilla representatives dialling in from a remote location. Participants in the main room were so fearful of these guerrillas that they gave the speaker phones a wide berth when they walked past them. The room itself contained fierce enemies. Apparently one city councillor, with Communist Party allegiance, complained to Santos about the presence of a warlord from a paramilitary organisation: "Do you really expect me to sit down with this man, who has tried to have me killed five times?" But Santos responded, "It is precisely so that he does not do so a sixth time that I am inviting you to take your seat".

That indicates the level of distrust – but also the hope of discovering a better way of cooperating – that marked the start of what became known as "Destino Colombia", which is Spanish for "Destination Colombia".

The initial meeting succeeded in breaking some ice and establishing some grudging respect between long-bitter foes. But as often happens in such projects, progress was fitful. Addictive mindsets cannot be wished away overnight. Without the positive encouragement that Santos received from Mandela the following year, the whole initiative might have been abandoned. Here's the summary from Kahane of the history of the project:

> The Destino Colombia scenario project was conceived in 1995 but was almost stillborn; in 1996 it suddenly came to life; in 1997 the scenario team held three energetic workshops; in 1998 and 1999 they disseminated their results to the whole country; in 2004 the project was pronounced dormant or dead; in 2007 I heard stories about the project's continued influence; and

in 2012 the president of Colombia announced that it had always been alive and was now the leitmotif of the policies of his new government.

That kind of pattern often occurs, in projects that seek to establish new visions of the future. As the participants spend some time together, they start to appreciate each other's perspectives. They may not like each other, and they still distrust each other, but they learn what the world looks like from another point of view. New relationships begin to form. But after the workshop finishes, previous modes of thinking – previous stories – reassert themselves. Once participants are back in their "normal" roles, surrounded once again by people who broadly think alike, familiar judgements tend to drive out the unfamiliar new ones that were tentatively starting to form. Ideas that had seemed promising in the workshop setting, and commitments that it had seemed sensible to make at that time, come to seem strange, or otherworldly, once participants are removed from that location.

That helps to explain why many transformational projects of this type fail to achieve their objectives. Kahane's books about his experiences – *Transformational Scenario Planning* (2012) and *Collaborating with the Enemy* (2017) – are to be commended for candidly reviewing the projects that halted partway through, incomplete, as well as those which were successful.

But good scenarios can take on a life of their own, influencing thinking long afterward – even if it seems, for a while at least, that they have been discarded. That's what happened with Destino Colombia.

In 1997, building on previous ideas, the project participants had jointly elaborated four scenarios for the future of their country:

1. *"When the sun rises, we'll see"* – in which matters would be left to evolve along their current trajectory; without any collective will to confront the challenges being faced, the result in due course would be a collapse of the country into chaos
2. *"A bird in the hand is worth two in the bush"* – with a compromise being negotiated between the government and the guerrillas; even though no side would be truly satisfied by this outcome, it would be preferable to continuing a downward spiral
3. *"Forward march"* – with the government gaining sufficient public support for taking an aggressive military stance against the guerrillas, imposing a kind of national peace via force

4. *"In unity lies strength"* – featuring a bottom-up adoption of greater mutual respect and cooperation between different groups, in which differences were respected but a greater unity achieved.

As with the Mont Fleur scenarios in South Africa, this set of scenarios had been illustrated with cartoons, and described in six-page inserts in newspapers published around the country. A video summary was broadcast on national television. In addition, the ideas were presented at public meetings in major towns.

But despite an initial flurry of public interest, it seemed that business-as-usual thinking soon reasserted itself. In effect, the country was choosing the first of the four scenarios – the "do nothing different" approach.

By 2000, a report at a United Nations Development Programme (UNDP) workshop summarised the output of Destino Colombia as "a treasure to be revealed", that is, the potential of the project had not yet been fulfilled. Basically, it had failed. However, lessons could be learned from it.

Drawing on retrospective comments from project participants, the UNDP report raised the following issues[518]:

> The group Destino Colombia did not keep on meeting once the scenarios had been constructed. As a result, in some cases the initial enthusiasm and cohesion of group members was reduced…
>
> Destino Colombia did not have a managerial team contracted fulltime for this project…
>
> The group needed the participation of more young people and women, as well as influential leaders in public decision-making…
>
> Governments and politicians have not shown interest in knowing, assuming responsibility or accepting the results of Destino Colombia, therefore the incidence of the project on public decision-making has been very limited.

It seemed like the end of the road. But as often happens with disruptive changes, the disappointment was a prelude to a longer-term transformation. The creative ideas of the Destino scenarios needed more time to spread their influence – to transition from "interesting but impractical" to "vital".

Kahane explains that he was pleasantly surprised when he heard in 2007 from one of his Colombian contacts that the ideas from the four scenarios were still very much in the public mind, and were influencing the actions being taken by successive governments. The contact, Antanas Mockus, was twice mayor of Bogota, the capital city of Colombia, and was preparing his candidacy for the position of President of Colombia in forthcoming national elections. In the view of Mockus:

- From 1998 onward, the policy of the government had been to pursue the kind of negotiated agreement with guerrilla groups as described in "A bird in the hand is worth two in the bush" – but that effort had failed, largely for reasons anticipated in the narrative description of that scenario
- From 2002 onward, the next president had sought to achieve the enforced pacification of the country described in "Forward march" – but that effort had failed too, for (again) reasons largely anticipated in the Destino Colombia work
- It was therefore approaching the time for yet another new president to attempt the national reconciliation of the "In unity lies strength" scenario.

Evidently, the impact of a compelling set of scenario narratives sometimes has to wait until the full relevance of these scenarios has become clearer.

As it happens, Mockus failed in his own bid to become Colombia's president. He was defeated in a run-off race by someone else who had a long association with the Destino Colombia project, namely Juan Manuel Santos – the politician who had, more than ten years earlier, taken inspiration from Nelson Mandela about the value of a foresight project. Santos set to work reducing the power of the armed wings of the guerrilla movements whilst simultaneously winning respect from the leadership of these organisations.

In 2016, the Nobel Prize committee decided to award Santos the Nobel Peace Prize. Here's an extract from their official commendation[519]:

> The Norwegian Nobel Committee has decided to award the Nobel Peace Prize for 2016 to Colombian President Juan Manuel Santos for his resolute efforts to bring the country's more than 50-year-long civil war to an end, a war that has cost the lives of at least 220,000 Colombians and displaced close to six million people…
>
> President Santos initiated the negotiations that culminated in the peace accord between the Colombian government and the FARC guerrillas, and he has consistently sought to move the peace process forward…
>
> The Norwegian Nobel Committee emphasizes the importance of the fact that President Santos is now inviting all parties to participate in a broad-

> based national dialogue aimed at advancing the peace process. Even those who opposed the peace accord have welcomed such a dialogue…
>
> The civil war in Colombia is one of the longest civil wars in modern times and the sole remaining armed conflict in the Americas. It is the Norwegian Nobel Committee's firm belief that President Santos… has brought the bloody conflict significantly closer to a peaceful solution, and that much of the groundwork has been laid for both the verifiable disarmament of the FARC guerrillas and a historic process of national fraternity and reconciliation.

Later that same year, both houses of the Colombian parliament approved a version of Santos' peace plan, signalling an end to decades of bloody conflict.

Santos himself attributed a considerable share of the credit for progress to the Destino Colombia initiative, and to its facilitator, Adam Kahane. He contributed a prologue to the Spanish language edition of Kahane's book *Collaborating with the Enemy*[520]:

> I met Adam Kahane many years ago… I invited him to come to our country, which at that time was going through a very difficult situation, plunged into political instability and violence.
>
> Kahane helped us with a very interesting exercise. We managed to gather representatives from all sectors of Colombian society: from the government and the opposition; peasants and large landowners; trade unionists and industrialists; academics, politicians and retired military; even members of the self-defence groups and guerrilla leaders, who participated by telephone.
>
> That meeting, which seemed unlikely, gave way to a process of discussion, reflection, and analysis never before seen in Colombia. Following the methodology proposed by Kahane, this diverse and complex group discussed in depth the reality of the country and the paths it could take in the future.
>
> From there came the document Destino Colombia, in which four possible scenarios were contemplated…
>
> Little by little… the destinies of Destino Colombia were fulfilled: from the loss of the authority of the state, the territorial fragmentation, the resurgence of violence, and the increase of poverty and social inequity contemplated in "When the sun rises, we'll see"; going through the attempts – unfortunately unsuccessful – to seek peace through a negotiation alluded to in "A bird in the hand is worth two in the bush"; following the clamour of the Colombian people for a strong and determined leadership against the violent ones that

> privileged the military option spoken of in "Forward march"; up until "In unity lies strength" the road that we have begun to take, where the joint work of political and social forces enabled us to successfully achieve the negotiation of peace and to open the doors to reconciliation and progress.

Santos gave the following conclusion:

> After so many years we can say that the exercise had an almost prophetic clarity.

But to be clear, the merit of the scenarios was not just that they predicted key actions and reactions that took place in subsequent years. It was that they helped to bring about the national reconciliation vividly described in the "In unity lies strength" scenario. We can all take inspiration from that example.

When change fails

Change is hard – particularly when:

- There is no firm agreement on the steps that need to be taken
- Large gulfs need to be bridged between differing perceptions, especially when the roots of these perceptions diverged long ago
- People key to progressing the change have set their minds on other tasks, including other ways to evolve the current situation, or even to maintain the status quo
- People key to progressing the change actively dislike each other or distrust each other.

Hence the examples in Adam Kahane's books, mentioned above, in which scenario exercises failed to have the desired impact, despite significant effort being invested, and despite initially encouraging meetings. These meetings, indeed, sometimes produced a set of scenarios, but they were unable to create long-lasting changes of mind.

I am reminded of a profound piece of analysis to which I often referred during my career in the mobile computing and smartphone industry – analysis by Harvard professor John Kotter as to the causes of failure of the majority of large change initiatives within corporations or organisations[521].

The research presented by Kotter indicates how these change initiatives can falter at eight different points along the journey of transformation:

1. *Lack of a sufficient sense of urgency*: The suggested new path forward is perceived as being more painful and unpleasant than sticking for the

time being with the current trajectory, however awkward that may be; any ideas of far-reaching change are, therefore, put off until another time

2. *Lack of an effective guiding coalition*: The team of people interested in the change have insufficient power or overall influence to drive the initiative forward
3. *Lack of a credible appealing vision of the desired new state of affairs*: The envisioned positive scenarios are too vague, have too many unanswered questions, and fail to engage participants both emotionally and intellectually
4. *Lack of ongoing communication for buy-in*: Without being engaged by regular updates, people lose track of the importance of the change; their attention becomes diverted elsewhere
5. *Lack of empowerment of the people who could implement the change*: People lack sufficient skills or coaching, are subject to conflicting incentives (for example, for bonus payments or career advancement), or are hampered by unnecessary bureaucracy or a stifling organisational hierarchy
6. *Lack of celebration of early small wins*: No sense of positive momentum is established
7. *Lack of follow through*: Gains that are made are not consolidated, and are subsequently unmade, or just linger as isolated special cases
8. *Lack of embedding the change at the cultural level*: Changes in management personnel or focus can lead to previous progress being unravelled, as older habits reassert themselves.

With so many points of possible failure, the idea of managing a disruptive transition is daunting. However, forewarned is forearmed. A number of the solutions offered by Kotter have already been illustrated by the positive examples of change from earlier in this book. These solutions split into three categories. The first category is *creating a positive climate for change*, and addresses failure points 1.-3. above:

- Increase the sense of urgency, by clarifying the risks if disruptions accelerate in an unmanaged way
- Strengthen the guiding coalition, by forging greater mutual trust, and by noticing and filling gaps in it

- Sharpen the positive vision, so that it is arresting, challenging, plausible, and memorable.

The second category, *engaging and enabling the whole organisation*, addresses failure points 4.-6. above:

- Communicate often, using multiple media formats, and listening as well as speaking, deepening a sense of shared ownership
- Empower others to contribute, by acting quickly to address any personal or structural blockages that are observed to be hindering progress
- Produce and highlight short-term wins, via a series of quick "sprints" as described by the discipline of agile development.

Finally, the third category, *sustaining change*, addresses failure points 7.-8. above:

- Don't let up: consolidate gains, via (if need be) wave after wave of follow-up
- Make it stick: manage the creation and adoption of new elements of organisational culture.

Each of these eight pieces of positive advice can, in different circumstances, make all the difference between the success or failure of a major change initiative. Each piece of advice is important, and the skills to carry it out should be a central part of everyone's education. Critically, this includes so-called "soft skills" (human skills), alongside familiarity with relevant processes, tools, and technologies.

But one area of failure deserves our particular attention. It's when there are shortcomings in the main analysis of future possibilities – when potential major risks or major opportunities fail to receive sufficient attention. In a time when change is both unusually rapid and unusually diverse – as at the present – such failures of analysis grow in significance. In such cases, any change initiative risks being overtaken by events beyond those which the guiding team chose to consider. Let's look at some examples.

When analysis fails

Despite its famous prowess in scenario planning, the oil giant Shell was sometimes caught by surprise – by a *bad* surprise – which *they should have seen coming*.

Indeed, in the year 1995, Shell's planners failed to anticipate two sets of actions – one in the North Sea, and the other in Nigeria – each of which were to have a large negative impact, not only on the company's public image, but also on its finances.

The issue in the North Sea was over the disposal of the Brent Spar oil platform. This was a massive floating structure roughly the same size as the Big Ben clock tower: 150 metres high and 30 metres in diameter. It could store up to 300,000 barrels of crude oil from nearby drilling rigs before that oil was collected by tankers. The platform helped Shell earn vast revenues from its construction in 1976 until being rendered redundant in 1991 by the establishment of a pipeline to the Shetland Islands north of mainland Scotland. Next came the question: now that it was no longer needed, what should be done with this huge hulk of metal, along with the waste chemicals it still contained[522]?

The two main options were:

1. Tow the platform into a shallow-water location, where it could be broken up, with some portions being recycled
2. Tow the platform into deep waters in the Atlantic, 150 miles to the west of Scotland, where it could be sunk onto the sea bed.

Shell's engineering experts reviewed the costs and safety issues of each approach. Taking into account the precautions needed in each case to avoid the platform breaking up prematurely and discharging contaminants, the first option was costed at around £41 million, which was more than double the figure of £17 million estimated for the second option. The company's analysis was cross-checked by the UK's Fisheries Research Services, who agreed with the assessment that "the environmental impact of the disposal of the Brent Spar in the deep Atlantic Ocean would [be] negligible"[523]. By 1995, Shell had received approval for its plans from the UK government, and was ready to move forward with the deep-sea disposal option.

What this analysis failed to incorporate, however, was the potential coordination of public outrage about Shell's intentions. When members of the campaigning organisation Greenpeace heard about these plans, they hurried into action. For Greenpeace, the deep-sea disposal of the Brent Spar could not be seen as simply an isolated incident. If it were allowed to happen, it would set the precedent for similar disposals of many other aging oil platforms from offshore locations.

Greenpeace activists also had in mind the horrific environmental damage that had been caused a few years earlier when the Exxon Valdez oil tanker struck a reef in Prince William Sound, Alaska, and had disgorged more than a quarter of a million barrels of crude oil. Here are some of the conclusions Greenpeace drew from that incident[524]:

> Officials habitually understate spill risk, size, and impact. Government and industry officials always downplay the risk, size, and impact of spills. We should not trust official assertions of the "low risk" of offshore drilling, tankers, or pipelines, nor should we trust industry assertions regarding size and impact of a spill…
>
> Oil money corrupts democracy. Big oil is big business, and its concentrated wealth distorts democratic governance the world over. Oil money flows freely into political campaigns, lobbying, bribes, advertising, and results in self-serving, perverse public policy, such as the billions of dollars in subsidies the global fossil fuel industry receives each year.

In other words, even though Shell management declared their plans as being safe and cost-effective, and even though the UK government had approved their plans, these decisions could not be trusted, in the view of Greenpeace.

To be fair to Shell, their managers did anticipate that activist groups would try to stir up adverse sentiment, and might even try to board the Brent Spar platform as a publicity stunt. Shell's security experts were well aware of previous examples when Greenpeace personnel had placed themselves into environmentally sensitive locations[525], such as the sites of intended nuclear weapons tests, or where culls of seal populations were planned. Greenpeace dinghies had also harried commercial whaling ships[526].

Shell managers were, likewise, aware of negativity about their plans from other companies in the oil industry, whose preference was to avoid any new public antagonism against their industry.

Nevertheless, Shell managers were confident in their calculations. If a protest occurred, they could remove protesters easily enough, and would find legal support from court judgements. Shell had, on its side, the backing of scientific expertise, government approval, legal endorsement, and financial calculations. What could go wrong?

It was the *scale* of the human reaction which Shell failed to foresee – a reaction that was cleverly nurtured by Greenpeace and which amplified a number of pre-existing sentiments latent within the public mood.

Shortly after noon on the 30th of April, 1995, four members of Greenpeace clambered onto the Brent Spar, having arrived in two different boats – one bringing people from Scotland, and the other from Germany. They placed a huge banner on the top of the platform, with its message easily readable from low-flying aircraft[527]: "Save the North Sea. Stop Shell". They intended to stay: they brought supplies of food with them, alongside communications equipment. Passengers on the accompanying boats included photographers and journalists. News of the occupation soon spread far and wide, including via the home page of the webpage for Greenpeace – something few other organisations possessed at that time.

Over the next four weeks, more than twenty different activists and journalists spent time on the Brent Spar. Greenpeace members back on dry land kept up a steady spate of press releases. According to the organisation, measurements carried out by their activists on the Brent Spar indicated that the contents were much more dangerous than Shell was telling people.

Shell's use of water cannons against Greenpeace dinghies and personnel on the Spar was seen by many members of the public as heavy-handed. Parallels were drawn to the biblical conflict between plucky young shepherd boy David and the towering Goliath.

The fact some of the waste was radioactive added to public apprehension. Shell's experts argued that the waste was entirely within limits that the ocean could easily absorb. Sinking the Brent Spar would be similar to an ordinary shipwreck: the ocean would take it in its stride. However, the public became concerned, not about the hazards which seemed to be known and quantifiable, but about potential *unanticipated risks*, and about the prior bad track environmental record of the oil giants who, it was claimed, put short-term financial measures ahead of all other concerns.

All this was taking place at a time of growing interest in various European countries, such as Germany, in recycling household waste, and, more generally, in lessening the impact of human activity on the environment[528].

Greenpeace had cleverly timed their actions to take place in the run-up to a G7 summit in Canada. Echoing increasing disquiet among members of the public, Germany's Chancellor Helmut Kohl complained to the British Prime Minister, John Major, about what Shell was doing. A young Angela Merkel, Government Minister for the Environment, Nature Conservation and Nuclear Safety, declared that the oil platform should not be dumped[529].

Motorists in Germany started to boycott Shell petrol stations. Sales were soon down by an unprecedented 30%.

Greenpeace kept up the media pressure. Two of their activists arrived back on the Brent Spar via ropes from a helicopter, despite Shell firing water cannons at the helicopters. Footage of such episodes were broadcast widely on televisions around the world. Employees of Shell in mainland European countries found themselves ostracised – for example, no-one would talk to them when they attended local church services. Alarmingly, some Shell petrol stations were fire-bombed and some had shots fired at them. Boycotts of Shell oil spread to other countries. National heads of the company in Holland, Belgium, Austria, and Scandinavia joined the head of the German company in complaining bitterly to their UK counterpart. Finally, Shell reversed its decision – and literally reversed the direction in which the Brent Spar was being towed. In due course it ended up in a Norwegian fjord where it was disassembled, with part of the material forming the base of a new ferry quay.

Reporters in the Wall Street Journal gave their summary of the episode[530]:

> There's no question that Shell was caught by surprise…
>
> The Brent Spar shows that high-profile cases, properly framed and easily explained, can ignite widespread public interest, especially if the news media get plenty of good photo opportunities. It also shows that economic warfare may be the best way to wage eco-warfare. The attention-grabbing tactics helped spark a boycott against Shell that cut sharply into gasoline sales and pushed the company to reverse course.

Shell spokesperson Rainer Winzenried highlighted this lesson which the company had learned[531]:

> We have learned to bring new projects into the public sphere for discussion, so we can take public concerns into consideration during the planning phases. We do this via so-called "shareholder forums".

Other lessons that Winzenried emphasised were that:

- Just because an action is legal, this does not mean the public will accept it
- Just because an action takes place inside territory under the control of one country (for example, the United Kingdom), this does not mean that opinions from other countries can be ignored.

From the point of view of Greenpeace, the whole episode was an inspiring example of the creation of a desirable new future. From Shell's point of view, however, it was an example of the devastating consequences of an incomplete analysis of the forces at play.

Shell's experience in Nigeria that same year had consequences that were even deadlier. Shell had been extracting oil from the Niger delta since 1958, in the face of growing opposition from members of the Ogoni people who lived in that area. The tribespeople objected to what they saw as the destruction of their environment. Ken Saro-Wiwa, a novelist and television producer who headed the Movement for the Survival of the Ogoni People (MOSOP), put it like this in an interview recorded in 1991[532]:

> The Ogoni country has been completely destroyed by the search for oil… Oil blow-outs, spillages, oil slicks, and general pollution accompany the search for oil… Oil companies have flared gas in Nigeria for the past thirty-three years causing acid rain… What used to be the bread basket of the delta has now become totally infertile.

MOSOP tried to organise non-violent protests against Shell's activities in the region. These protests were often met with violent responses from the military police. According to documents submitted to a New York court many years later, in 2009, Shell officials in the country collaborated with members of the government to repress the protests and to have key activists arrested[533]. The government fabricated charges of murder against nine defendants, including Saro-Wiwa, and bribed alleged witnesses to give testimony against the defendants. Shell tried to intervene at this stage to request clemency, but matters had escalated beyond their control. The nine defendants were executed by hanging on 10th November 1995[534].

Even the hanging was botched. Four attempts to operate the hastily assembled gallows failed. It was only after the fifth hanging attempt that Saro-Wiwa's body finally went limp[535].

An international outcry ensued. Nigeria was suspended from the Commonwealth. The condemnation targeted Shell too: it became, for a while, one of the world's most despised companies.

With support from various NGOs, relatives of the executed men eventually managed to bring a court case against Shell in New York. The company was accused of crimes against humanity, and complicity with torture and arbitrary detention. Just before formal evidence was presented in front of the world's media, Shell agreed to an out-of-court settlement, paying members of the Ogoni people a total of $15.5 million.

It was another case of inadequate foresight by Shell, the company who had, perhaps, done more than any other until that time to advance the practice of scenario forecasting. Their interactions with the Nigerian government had consequences that spiralled out of their control. In the years that followed, they had to work triply hard to restore their reputation.

Superforecasters

You'll have noticed the pattern. Individuals and companies that have some good track record in predicting or steering the future nevertheless also experience failures in these activities from time to time.

As the examples in this chapter indicate, that pattern applies to individuals such as Herman Kahn and Adam Kahane as well as to companies such as Shell. Previous chapters had other examples, including the scientist Linus Pauling, the writers Thomas Friedman and Francis Fukuyama, and the corporations Microsoft and Nokia.

But please don't conclude that the success or failure of predictions is, therefore, random. A top-rank football team may occasionally lose to weaker competitors, but that doesn't annul the value of acquiring and practising good football skills. It's a reason for the team in question to develop these skills more fully, and to apply them more systematically.

Conversely, the mere fact of someone making a forecast that turns out to be true, cannot be taken as a sign that any new forecasts from that person will be reliable. Anybody can get lucky on occasion.

We need to distinguish *methods* from *results*. And rather than looking at just a small number of results, it's better to look at *the statistics of performance* over a range of different forecasts.

Someone who has devoted many years – indeed, decades – to such a study is Philip Tetlock, a professor of psychology and political science at the University of Pennsylvania[536]. Tetlock summarised his findings in his pathbreaking 2015 book *Superforecasting*[537].

Tetlock's research revolves around a large set of predictive challenges about events that might, or might not, happen a short time into the future. Some examples:

- "In the next year, will any country withdraw from the eurozone?"

- "Will India or Brazil become a permanent member of the UN Security Council in the next two years?"
- "When will the NYC public schools resume in-person instruction for at least some students?"
- "When will enough doses of FDA-approved Covid-19 vaccine(s) to inoculate 200 million people be distributed in the United States?"

A group of several thousand volunteers provide answers on a regular basis to these questions. These forecasters are asked to provide in each case, not only their predictions, but also the confidence with which they make these predictions. For example, if a challenge question offers three possible date ranges as answers, a forecaster might assign 5% probability to the first date range, 15% probability to the second, and 80% to the third.

The accuracy of an individual forecast can be calculated by something known as the "Brier score"[538]. It's the average of the squares of the errors. In the above example, if the correct answer turns out to be the third option, the accuracy is calculated as $(0.05\text{-}0)^2+(0.15\text{-}0)^2+(0.8\text{-}1)^2$, divided by 3, that is 0.022. If the correct answer had been the second option, the accuracy would have been $(0.05\text{-}0)^2+(0.15\text{-}1)^2+(0.8\text{-}0)^2$, divided by 3, that is 0.755. Evidently, lower scores indicate a better forecast. The smallest possible score is 0, and the largest is 1.

In this setup, forecasters are able – and indeed are encouraged – to revise their forecasts in the light of new information received. For example, a forecast about the likelihood of a country exiting the eurozone could be updated in the light of comments from a country's finance minister. The assessment of a forecaster's performance takes into account their predictions throughout the period of time the question remained open.

Some predictive challenges turn out to be easier than others. What's of particular interest is how well the scores of a forecaster compare with the median (average) score of the overall community of forecasters. This is known as their *relative* Brier score.

If you want to try your own hand at this task, you can sign into the open version of the "Good Judgement Project"[539].

The first important finding from this project is that some forecasters are systematically better than the crowd. They're not just accurate on occasion;

they tend to make better forecasts nearly all of the time. Tetlock calls these individuals "superforecasters".

The second important finding – actually a set of findings – is that these superforecasters are characterised by a number of personal attributes. These are attributes which can be studied and learned – which is good news for those of us who aspire to improve our forecasting abilities.

Tetlock summarises this finding as follows:

> Broadly speaking, superforecasting demands thinking that is open-minded, careful, curious, and – above all – self-critical. It also demands focus. The kind of thinking that produces superior judgment does not come effortlessly. Only the determined can deliver it reasonably consistently, which is why our analyses have consistently found commitment to self-improvement to be the strongest predictor of performance.

Some of the characteristic attributes of superforecasters have already featured in earlier sections of this book:

1. Rather than insisting on seeing things in binary ("black and white") terms, superforecasters are comfortable with probabilistic reasoning
2. They prefer precise numerical language over vague terms (such as "might") whose apparent meaning can change with hindsight
3. Rather than "fate" or "inevitability", they can accept contingency, such as the chaotic amplification of the flapping of a seagull's wing, as often being the factor responsible for an outcome
4. They consider hypotheses about the potential influences on outcomes, and then seek out evidence that would either confirm or refute these hypotheses
5. They are ready to incrementally adjust their forecasts in the light of new evidence, and they avoid investing emotional energy in defence of a prior forecast out of some misplaced sense of loyalty
6. Critically, they prioritise looking for evidence that would *disprove* their current favoured hypothesis, rather than just trying to accumulate more data points that are compatible with it
7. Rather than accepting an argument merely on the say-so of a fellow forecaster who has a good track record, they subject that argument to their own scrutiny, thereby avoiding the perils of groupthink

8. They believe their forecasting abilities are by no means fixed or innate, but can be improved via a combination of practice and review
9. Accordingly, they regularly reflect on what they can learn from their past forecasting experiences – both successes and failures.

One more characteristic attribute of superforecasters deserves particular attention. This attribute is whether someone is a big idea "hedgehog" thinker or a pragmatist "fox" thinker. This terminology, by the way, was borrowed from the philosopher Isaiah Berlin[540], who had in turn adapted it from this stanza by the Greek lyric-poet Archilochus:

The fox knows many things; the hedgehog one big thing.

The "big idea" of someone in the hedgehog category was a core belief around which they sought to organise all the rest of their thinking. The belief in question varied from hedgehog to hedgehog. It might be socialism, with its preference for state control of the economy. It might be free-market fundamentalism, with its desire to reduce regulation. It might be a pessimism about the environment, or an optimism about the potential of technology to fix every problem, or so on. Members of this category tended to disregard as irrelevant potential evidence that lay outside their preferred filters. The best understanding, they assumed, would come from remaining focused on the most important principles.

In contrast, forecasters in the fox category were each willing to embrace a wide variety of different analytical styles, conceptual tools, and procedural methods. Evidence from multiple sources was equally welcome. They had no "sacred dogmas" that constrained their thinking. Rather than being ideological purists, they were open-minded about the best approach to each individual forecast challenge.

Of the two categories, hedgehogs and foxes, which do you suppose proved to be the better forecasters?

I confess that, when I first came across this piece of analysis by Philip Tetlock, I had strong sympathies for the hedgehog. That was on account of being impressed a few years earlier by a different writer, the business management expert Jim Collins, whose 2001 book *From Good to Great* had also utilised the fox versus hedgehog contrast[541]. In that book, Collins asserted that one factor distinguishing truly great companies from merely good also-rans was the single-mindedness of their strategic vision.

As Collins saw things, foxes pursue many ends at the same time. They perceive the world in all its complexity, but their attention is scattered over many levels. They never integrate their thinking into one transcendent concept or unifying vision. In contrast, hedgehogs simplify the complexities of the world into a single organising idea, a basic concept or principle that unifies and guides everything. Despite the greater cunning of the fox, the hedgehog always wins the vital battles between the two, because it is able to curl up into an unassailable formation.

In *From Good to Great*, Collins had a recommendation for the leadership teams of companies who aspired to greatness. They should invest the time to develop a single hedgehog concept, and then implement that concept "with almost fanatical simplicity". The hedgehog concept was what the leadership team could discover at "the intersection of three circles"[542]:

1. What the company has a deep passion about
2. What the company can do as well as any other in the world
3. What the company can earn money by doing.

As Collins clarifies:

> A Hedgehog Concept is not a goal to be the best, a strategy to be the best, an intention to be the best, a plan to be the best. It is an *understanding* of what you can be the best at.

That notion had appealed to me, and influenced many discussions over the years among members of the Symbian executive leadership team.

That notion also matched the recommendation of Geoffrey Moore, the writer of *Crossing the Chasm* whose ideas I outlined in the previous chapter. You may recall Moore's contention that most innovation is wasted – that innovation initiatives tend to scatter effort all over a large domain, without reaching a critical mass in any one area. Without deliberate focus, most companies will die in the chasm before mass-market adoption of their products or services. Without finding a suitably crisp and compelling form, most potential disruptions will stay at the level of "quaint idea", rather than transforming the world.

Nevertheless, the evidence from Philip Tetlock's research was emphatic. Forecasting foxes consistently outperformed forecasting hedgehogs. For better forecasts, ideology is a hindrance, rather than an enabler. Being self-assured may win you a crowd of followers who are impressed by what they see as charisma, but it will hinder your ability to pay proper attention to countervailing evidence or to reach a deeper understanding of particular circumstances. Having simple answers ready to deploy in all situations may result in repeat invitations to talk shows or keynote presentations, but the predictions you make at such events will likely turn out to be wrong – or to be couched in such vague language as to be without value.

Hedgehogs, good, bad, and vital

Despite my admiration for the work of *Superforecasting* researcher Philip Tetlock, I'm going to disagree with one of his conclusions. That's his conclusion that foresight is served better by foxes than by hedgehogs.

As I see it, what's needed is not people who are *either* foxes or hedgehogs. Instead, what's needed is people who are *both* foxes and hedgehogs: people who can approach questions from multiple different angles and who are open to multiple different techniques, but who, nevertheless, put a high priority on a small number of core insights.

After all, the full purpose of foresight isn't just prediction. It is the creative transformation of the future. For successful transformation, a strong hedgehog-like sense of compelling purpose is needed alongside strong fox-like skills in perceiving diverse signals.

What's particularly important is the choice of the ideas at the heart of the hedgehog's thinking. Danger arises when someone is preoccupied by an idea that is only partially valid. In that case, the person might be called a *bad* hedgehog.

I believe that Jim Collin, author of *From Good to Great*, would agree with me here. Recall that his advice to leadership teams was to pick their hedgehog concept very carefully – from the intersection of three circles of demanding requirements – before organising their whole company in the pursuit of that concept.

I would go further. Rather than simply having two stages in this model – selection of concept followed by vigorous pursuit of that concept – I envision a spiral, iterative approach:

1. Selection of hedgehog concept(s) as deserving paramount attention
2. Pursuit of these concepts, in a period of focused activities
3. Review of what has happened and what has been learned in the previous phase

4. Open-minded reconsideration of the ongoing validity of the choice of hedgehog concepts, by returning to step 1 before iterating again.

I offer a similar response to the observation by Geoffrey Moore, author of *Crossing the Chasm*, that most innovation is wasted, and that successful companies focus their innovation activities into a small number of "beachhead" target areas. The challenge is that it is hard to know, in advance, what these beachhead target areas should be. Therefore, some agile experimentation is needed:

1. After initial analysis, select a few possible activities, to form what is sometimes known as a "backlog"
2. Conduct a few quick experiments – known as "sprints"
3. Based on feedback, select areas for further development, and set aside the options that seem less promising
4. Minimise distractions during any one sprint
5. At the end of each sprint, conduct a review ("retrospective") before commencing the next sprint
6. Be prepared to alter direction ("pivot") in case priorities need to be changed.

Accordingly, periods of hedgehog-like singlemindedness are interspersed with periods of fox-like open exploration. Your project team therefore needs a constructive collaboration between good foxes and good hedgehogs.

If your analysis is deficient, and you become psychologically locked into it, you may become long-term single-minded about the wrong concept, and do a lot more harm than good.

Collins recommended considering three different circles of requirements. In a similar way, professional foresight practitioners sometimes follow what is known as the "PESTEL" method, where each of the six letters represents an area of factors that could prove significant in influencing the future[543]:

- 'P': *Political factors*, such as government interventions, electoral cycles, alliances or splits of political parties, the growth of populism, legislative logjams, amendments to constitutions, international alliances, and international conflict

- 'E': *Economic factors*, such as inflation, unemployment, debt, banking stability, exchange rates, booms and busts, behaviour of monopolies and cartels, and changes in stock market prices
- 'S': *Social factors*, such as inequalities, crime rates, cultural norms, demographics, intergenerational dynamics, sex and gender roles, migration, dominant religious and philosophical ideas, and other attitudes and expectations of members of the public
- 'T': *Technological factors*, such as automation, communications, data storage, medicines, virtual and augmented reality, sources of energy, enablers of recycling, and modes of travel or manufacture
- 'E': *Environmental factors*, such as pollution, deforestation, loss of biodiversity, water scarcity, pandemics, biohazards, and extreme weather events
- 'L': *Legal factors*, such as health and safety regulations, consumer protection laws, employee protection laws, copyrights and patents, discrimination laws, and laws constraining monopolies.

In this method, it is recommended that before any predictions or scenarios are formulated, a survey should be conducted covering all six of these areas, for influences that could prove unexpectedly relevant. Potential interactions between various influences should be considered too, since it is these interactions that can produce the biggest surprises.

All this requires *both analysis and imagination*:

- Analysis of what is possible, and imagination to suggest what *might* be possible
- Analysis of what is desirable, and imagination to suggest what *might* be desirable
- Analysis of what can be done, and imagination to suggest what *might* be done.

In each case, analysis is needed both before and after the imagination step, so that the flights of imagination start from a good foundation, and are subsequently evaluated afresh to see how they stand up.

Does this whole task strike you as daunting? Did that long list of PESTEL considerations make you want to turn the page quickly?

With so much to consider, it's no wonder that people are tempted to take shortcuts. But as I've said, these shortcuts – if they become locked in – would blind people to the fuller picture. As a result, key risks and key opportunities would fail to be noticed.

Thus, here are some examples of "bad hedgehog" core beliefs that I frequently encounter in my discussions with groups of people about creating a better future – core beliefs that:

- The market mechanism *invariably* creates distress and polarisation, in some kind of zero-sum competition; therefore, the dismantlement of capitalism has to take the highest priority
- The market mechanism is *always* the best system for encouraging creativity and determining the allocation of resources; therefore, the highest priority is to protect the market from interference by politicians or regulators
- Technological enhancement of human capability is an *intrinsically* dangerous activity, and should be fervently resisted
- Technological enhancement of human capability will *inevitably* lead to a world that is better for everyone, and should be accelerated.

In all these cases, the belief in question has *some* validity. Market mechanisms *sometimes* do cause distress and alienation; in some other circumstances they do result in magnificent creativity. Human enhancement *sometimes* does have monstrous consequences; in some other circumstances the results are truly beneficial. But giving any of these beliefs a fundamentalist status would be doubly dangerous: it would be unbalanced, and it would be one-dimensional.

Instead of the above "bad hedgehog" core beliefs, I offer a set that I consider to be "good hedgehog" core beliefs. These propositions arise from the numerous PESTEL studies I have in effect carried out or witnessed over the last two decades – iterative studies involving many different groups of people around the world.

Accordingly, read on for my considered summary of the most vital change factors for the next few decades. Keeping them firmly in mind could make all the difference whether we successfully steer the major disruptions ahead, or fall as dejected victims of these forces.

Transhumanist creativity

First things first. Technological changes over the next few decades will place vast new power in billions of human hands. Rather than focusing on the implications of today's technology – significant though they are – we need to raise our attention to the even larger implications of the technology of the near future. That's the argument I develop in the following two chapters, "Technology" and "NBIC".

Second, these technologies will magnify the risks of humanitarian disaster that I covered in Chapter 4, "Landmines". If we are already worried about these risks today (as we should be), we should be even more worried about how these risks will develop in the near future.

Third, the same set of technologies, handled more wisely, and vigorously steered, can result in a very different outcome: a sustainable superabundance of clean energy, healthy nutrition, material goods, excellent health, all-round intelligence, dynamic creativity, and profound collaboration. That possibility, and the contrast with the deeply negative scenarios, comes to the fore in Chapter 16, "Juncture".

Fourth, what will make the biggest difference for which outcome is realised, is the widespread adoption of transhumanism. This in turn involves three activities:

- The advocacy of the transhumanist philosophy[544], as an overarching worldview that encourages and inspires everyone to join the next leap upward on life's grand evolutionary ladder. That's described further in Chapters 11 and 12, "Transhumanism" and "Antitheses".
- The extension of transhumanist ideas into real-world political activities, to counter very destructive trends in that field. That's covered in Chapters 13 and 14, "Politics" and "Geopolitics".
- The underpinning of all the above initiatives by a transformation of the world of education, to provide everyone with skills suited to the very different circumstances of the near future, rather than the needs of the past. That's the subject of Chapter 15, "Education".

Finally, overhanging the momentous transition that I've just described is the potential of an *even larger change*, in which technology moves ahead yet more quickly, with the advent of self-improving artificial intelligence with superhuman levels of capability in all aspects of thinking. I'll return to that topic in Chapter 17, "Singularity".

As you can see, that description of the core transhumanist assertions runs to eight paragraphs. To be a true candidate hedgehog belief, it needs to be expressible in a much shorter form. Here goes:

Oncoming waves of technological change are poised to deliver either global destruction or a paradise-like sustainable superabundance, with the outcome depending on the timely elevation of transhumanist vision, transhumanist politics, and transhumanist education.

To be clear, the point of this assertion is *not* to expel all alternative thoughts, or to force all considerations to fit into that single pattern. Fox-like tangential exploration needs to be practised on a continuous basis.

Nevertheless, until such time as these explorations highlight any major shortcoming in that assertion, I will uphold it as the best starting point for ensuring the creation of a world that is full of human flourishing.

Accelerating returns

Can we simplify the simplification? Can various parts of that 33-word assertion be removed, while still preserving its essential meaning?

How about the following?

Accelerating technological change will deliver sustainable superabundance.

This formulation is similar to statements made by perhaps the world's most famous living futurist, Ray Kurzweil. In contrast to the 33-word version, this 7-word formulation (and others like it):

- Emphasises positive possibilities, and gives little attention to negative ones
- Expresses certainty (with the word "will") and avoids suggestions of contingency
- Makes no mention of specific activities that are needed to bring about this positive outcome.

Consider how Kurzweil explains his views of the impact of accelerating technological change in his 2005 book *The Singularity Is Near*. Here's how he introduces the concept of "the Singularity" in the opening chapter of that book[545]:

> The key idea underlying the impending Singularity is that the pace of change of our human-created technology is accelerating and its powers are expanding at an exponential pace…
>
> What, then, is the Singularity? It's a future period during which the pace of technological change will be so rapid, its impact so deep, that human life will be irreversibly transformed.

Kurzweil goes on to describe the nature of the transformation as humans overcoming the "severe limitations" of our present "version 1.0 biological bodies":

> Although impressive in many respects, the brain suffers from severe limitations… Our thinking is extremely slow: the basic neural transactions are several million times slower than contemporary electronic circuits. That makes our physiological bandwidth for processing new information extremely limited compared to the exponential growth of the overall human knowledge base.
>
> Our version 1.0 biological bodies are likewise frail and subject to a myriad of failure modes, not to mention the cumbersome maintenance rituals they require. While human intelligence is sometimes capable of soaring in its creativity and expressiveness, much human thought is derivative, petty, and circumscribed.
>
> The Singularity will allow us to transcend these limitations of our biological bodies and brains.

The result will be something that "vastly exceeds" even "the best of [current] human traits":

> We will gain power over our fates. Our mortality will be in our own hands. We will be able to live as long as we want (a subtly different statement from saying we will live forever). We will fully understand human thinking and will vastly extend and expand its reach…
>
> The Singularity will represent the culmination of the merger of our biological thinking and existence with our technology, resulting in a world that is still human but that transcends our biological roots…
>
> Our technology will match and then vastly exceed the refinement and suppleness of what we regard as the best of human traits.

Observe: no 'if's and no 'but's. Instead, there are plenty of 'will's.

Indeed, the word "inevitable" appears frequently throughout both *The Singularity Is Near* and Kurzweil's earlier (1999) book covering similar themes, *The Age of Spiritual Machines*[546]. In Kurzweil's grand conception of the evolution of the cosmos, once the big bang has set things in motion, the subsequent development of intelligence is "inevitable". The development of technology is "inevitable". The development of computation is "inevitable". And, to quote from the Epilogue at the end of *The Age of Spiritual Machines*:

> The accelerating pace of change is inexorable. The emergence of machine intelligence that far exceeds human intelligences in all its broad diversity is inevitable…
>
> Once computation emerges… we see the exponential increase in power of the computational technology over time… Both the species [humanity] and the computational technology will progress at an exponential rate, but the exponent of growth is vastly higher for the technology than it is for the species. Thus the computational technology inevitably and rapidly overtakes the species that invented it.

Kurzweil interweaves occasional notes of caution into his overall upbeat narrative. Passages in his writing address criticisms of his thinking[547].

For example, Kurzweil concedes that skills in genetic manipulation will in due course enable terrorist groups to bioengineer new viruses with deadly results – viruses with a long incubation period in which infected people show no outward designs of being ill, and during which the virus spreads to many more people, before killing huge numbers. Kurzweil's response:

> Ultimately… nanotechnology will provide a completely effective defence against biological viruses.

But won't nanotechnology itself pose problems? Perhaps nanoscale replicators might inadvertently eat their way through vast amounts of biological matter? Indeed, might terrorists with skills in nanotechnology seek to deploy horrific new weapons based on that possibility? Kurzweil's response:

> Ultimately… strong AI will provide a completely effective defence against self-replicating nanotechnology.

As for risks from strong AI developing beyond human control and losing any interest in human wellbeing? What if a future AI shows as little regard for human welfare as we humans often show for the welfare of insect colonies as we repurpose blocks of land for our own purposes? Kurzweil's answer: "a yet more intelligent AI" would defend humanity from any missteps of the type just described.

Underlying Kurzweil's analysis is his concept of "accelerating returns". At its simplest level, the idea is that progress enables more progress.

For example, in order to create technology, tools are needed. But as technology improves, it allows the creation of better tools – tools that are more powerful, more precise, more adaptable, more programmable, easier to use, and so on. In turn, these improved tools enable the creation of yet better technology. It's the same with the production of synthetic chemicals – chemicals different from the ones we find in nature. Chemicals are created in reactions that involve different reagents and catalysts. But once new chemicals have been created, they can be fed into yet more new reactions, as reagents or catalysts. It's the same with computers: each new generation of computers can help with the design and manufacture of yet another generation of computers. It's the same with software: software tools such as compilers, debuggers, profilers, and optimisers assist the creation of even better generations of software. Critically, it's the same with AI too: each new breakthrough in AI capability can become the input for the creation of even better AI: AI can assist with the refinement and cleaning of training data, with the review of feedback architectures, with the adaptation of machine learning results from one field for use in another field, and with the assembly of networks of less powerful algorithms into systems with greater levels of emergent intelligence.

It's well worth reading Kurzweil at first hand. His writing contains a host of interesting ideas and data points. But it's more than just factual or even conceptual: it's visionary. It's a vision that goes beyond science and engineering, into the fields that are usually described as "spiritual" or even "religious". In director Barry Ptolemy's 2011 film *Transcendent Man* about Kurzweil's life, Kurzweil muses[548]:

> Does God exist? I would say, "Not yet".

From where will such a deity emerge? Kurzweil offers a compelling retelling of cosmic history into what he calls "six epochs":

1. *Physics and chemistry*: information in atomic structures, leading to the evolution of DNA
2. *Biology*: information in DNA, leading to the evolution of brains
3. *Brains*: information in neural patterns, leading to the evolution of technology

4. *Technology*: information in hardware and software designs, leading to mimicry then mastery by technology of the methods of biology
5. *The merger of technology with biology*: the methods of biology are integrated into the exponentially expanding human technology base, leading to the spread of human intelligence (predominantly in non-biological form) through the universe
6. *The universe wakes up*: matter and energy throughout the cosmos become "saturated with intelligent processes and knowledge".

Filmmaker Jason Silva challenges viewers, at the end of his own whirlwind video presentation of Kurzweil's conception of the six epochs[549]:

> Tell me that that is not an *intoxicating* idea.

I, for one, was swept along by the ideas in *The Age of Spiritual Machines* when I first encountered them around twenty years ago. I found myself persuaded that machines sometime later this century would be not just "intelligent" (as in the title of Kurzweil's preceding book, published in 1990, *The Age of Intelligent Machines*) but "spiritual" – having all the attributes that we humans sometimes think make us unique.

I'm by no means alone in having had my personal worldview transformed by Ray Kurzweil. Many other people that I encounter in the worlds of transhumanism and futurism can offer similar accounts. In this way, Kurzweil's writings have been powerfully creative. They have tilted the life trajectories of, probably, tens of thousands of people around the globe, awakening us to the possibility that much greater change could take place over the next few decades than we were previously contemplating – a change not just in degree but in kind; a change in which consciousness will transcend the biological framework that gave it life. Alerted to the possibility of such changes, we readers of Kurzweil's books have redoubled our efforts to study more deeply the nature and implications of these changes.

Nevertheless, what that extra study shows is that we need, in turn, to transcend the single-track narrative that Kurzweil highlights.

Shortcomings of that single-track narrative are in any case clear from any review of the numerous predictions that Kurzweil includes throughout his writings: things that he predicted would take place by 2000, by 2010, by 2020, and so on.

Yes, in some cases, these predictions have proved prescient. In 1990 he predicted that computer software would outplay the human chess world champion "by 2000" – it happened in 1997.

But consider these predictions from *The Singularity Is Near* (2005) regarding what could be expected by 2010:

> Computers arriving at the beginning of the next decade will become essentially invisible: woven into our clothing, embedded in our furniture and environment… Displays will be built into our eyeglasses and contact lenses and images projected directly onto our retinas…
>
> These resources will provide high-resolution, full-immersion visual-auditory virtual reality at any time. We will also have augmented reality with displays overlaying the real world to provide real-time guidance and explanations. For example, your retinal display might remind us, "That's Dr. John Smith, director of the ABC Institute".

Even by 2021, ten years later than predicted, these forecasts are far from being widely fulfilled. Whilst many computing chips are embedded into devices that look nothing like traditional computers, visible laptops and other computing terminals remain ubiquitous. Face recognition software and augmented reality headsets exist, but aren't in wide consumer use. Full-immersion virtual reality remains a minority experience.

Other predictions fare even worse[550]:

- By 2010, car accidents on newly built highways will almost be eliminated, as a result of self-driving cars that are guided by sensors built into these highways
- By 2010 (or, at the outside, 2015), drugs will be available that allow people to eat as much as they want, without gaining weight
- By 2010, miniaturised autonomous drones no larger than dust particles will be able to carry out reconnaissance missions
- By 2010, "going to a website" will mean entering a virtual reality environment, where users interact with visual and auditory simulations of people such as sales assistants and reservation clerks, and haptic (tactile) feedback will enable users to "touch" both products and people.

One response is that Kurzweil's predictions can be interpreted, with some charity, as being correct more often than they are wrong. Indeed, it's possible to spend considerable time picking over the many individual forecasts, debating exactly what was meant by various bits of imprecise language, and how much "wiggle room" should be granted in the interpretation of these forecasts – for example, whether a prediction stated as happening in 2010 still counts as prescient if the outcomes described happen in 2020.

If you're interested in that kind of analysis, you can review the conclusions reached in 2013 by a team of volunteers in the Less Wrong rationality community, coordinated by Oxford philosopher Stuart Armstrong[551]. These volunteers were set the task of assessing each of 172 predictions from *The Age of Spiritual Machines* about what would happen by 2009 or earlier. The first conclusion they reached is that many of the predictions were expressed in language that made it difficult to assess categorically whether the prediction had come true. Predictions therefore needed to be assessed as one of "true", "weakly true", "impossible to decide", "weakly false", and "false". One subgroup of nine volunteers reached this collective assessment:

- Only 31% of the predictions could be evaluated as either "true" or "false"
- 42% were evaluated as true or weakly true
- 46% were evaluated as false or weakly false.

A different subgroup, carrying out their analysis independently, evaluated only 30% as true or weakly true, and a whopping 57% as false or weakly false.

What is undeniable is that at least some of his predictions did not come to pass. The writings of Ray Kurzweil therefore cannot be taken as any kind of infallible guide to future occurrences.

Beyond creativity

The many shortcomings of the predictions that Ray Kurzweil has made over the years do not negate the fact that his insights about "accelerating returns" are profound. Although progress often deviates from a smooth exponential trajectory, it does have the potential to accelerate via positive feedback mechanisms of the sort Kurzweil describes:

- Better technology enables better tools, and vice versa
- Better technology enables better education, for more people around the world, leading to more people having the skills needed to

improve technology yet further: more scientists, more engineers, more entrepreneurs, more designers, and, yes, more educators

- Better technology enables better networking, allowing ideas to travel more quickly around extended communities, being improved and refined in the process, leading to yet more technology improvements
- Better technology makes available new sources of energy, more cheaply and more reliably, powering further rounds of progress.

But it's not a one-way street. Alongside these positive feedback cycles, various negative factors can slow down progress:

- Unhelpful bureaucracies, regulations, and vested interests
- Loss of public interest in particular types of enhancement
- Resources being diverted into projects that promise short-term returns, depriving longer-term research of the more patient capital which it needs in order to stimulate fundamental breakthroughs
- The spread of misunderstandings or distractions, with the result that brainpower is deployed unproductively
- Shortages of resources which had previously fuelled key processes within a society – as might happen due to environmental contamination or exhaustion.

There's no law of nature that guarantees that the first set of forces will always win out over the second set. Rather than any inexorable rise in human flourishing, the future could well witness a catastrophic collapse.

Indeed, in past centuries, many once-proud societies were brought to their knees[552]. In these previous cases, the consequences were local: other civilisations in other parts of the world continued, albeit often from a lower starting point. But if a new collapse takes place in the coming decades, the consequences could be total in this case.

The most important task of all, therefore, is to develop sufficiently robust positive solutions ahead of any impending civilisational collapse. Kurzweil's insight is correct that technology can provide the means for comprehensive solutions. However, it won't get there on any auto-pilot.

For more details of the potential for rapid technological change – and how that change can be steered – read on.

9. Technology

Technology, defined: The practical application of science and engineering in order to augment human capability. Systems of tools and machines that take on a life of their own due to positive feedback and accelerating performance. The forces that have made the biggest difference to the human condition, and which are poised to make even larger differences in just a few additional decades.

For most of history – that is, until relatively recent times – the life circumstances of the average person saw little change. The general social conditions prevailing at the end of someone's life were pretty similar to those prevailing at the beginning. The career options and life course trajectories available to someone tended to match those that had been available to their grandparents – and, indeed, *to their grandparents' grandparents.*

Consider how long someone could expect to live. In countries where local parish records include death statistics, it's possible to estimate the average life expectancy of people at different times. James Riley, Distinguished Professor of History at Indiana University, has collated demographic material from over 700 sources in his own research into changes of life expectancy[553]. The longest available sequence of estimates is for the United Kingdom, and dates back to 1543[554]. In that year, life expectancy was 33.9 years. One hundred and twenty years later, in 1663, the figure was 33.3. After another century, the figure for 1763 was 35.4. As I said, little changed.

Actually, the estimates range up and down in intervening decades, but the overall trend is flat[555]. The highest figure in any year prior to 1800 was in 1583, namely 42.7, but that looks like a statistical outlier. It took until 1850 for that value to be matched, and until the 1880s before it was regularly surpassed. It's from around 1860 that a steady increase is observed. To pick out dates with ten-yearly gaps: life expectancy was 39.6 in 1864, 42.1 in 1874, 43.6 in 1884, 48.3 in 1894, 48.1 in 1904, 53.2 in 1914, 58.1 in 1924, 61.3 in 1934, 64.8 in 1944, 69.9 in 1954, 71.3 in 1964, 72.4 in 1974, 74.5 in 1984, 76.5 in 1994, 78.8 in 2004, and 80.1 in 2014.

Various questions arise from these numbers:

1. Why was there little overall variation during the first 300 years of this data? (Short answer: this fits the observation that, for most of history, there was little sustained change in the human condition.)
2. What led to the trend of marked increase, from around the 1860s – with a jump of 13.6 years from 1864 to 1914, and another 18.1 years from 1914 to 1964? (Short answer: it was a by-product of the Industrial Revolution – something to be discussed later in this chapter.)
3. What caused the slowdown in the increase since then – with a jump of only 8.8 years from 1964 to 2014? (Short answer: countervailing forces blocked a straightforward continuation of the previous trend.)
4. And what can we anticipate about *future* changes in this metric? (Short answer: there are *no* simple conclusions to be drawn from this data alone!)

Data from the second longest set of life expectancy statistics, from Sweden, shows the same pattern[556]: little change from the start of that series, 1750, up until the 1860s; then a significant rise until around 1950, followed by a slower rise. It's similar, too, for both Finland and Denmark.

Before looking more closely into the question of *why the speed up*, a quick word about the subsequent slowdown in more recent times – a phenomenon which, by the way, is being repeated in countries all over the world. Indeed, within the last few years, life expectancy in a number of countries has stopped increasing, or is even going into reverse, as in the United States[557] (in a trend that predated the Covid pandemic).

The quick word I offer here is that this decrease flies in the face of what a straightforward reading of Ray Kurzweil's writing would imply. As reviewed at the end of the previous chapter, Kurzweil repeatedly refers to the inevitable acceleration of progress. Evidently, that's not what's happening in the case of increased lifespans.

But there's an important additional twist to this discussion. The twist is the insight that acceleration can undergo some backward steps ahead of picking up pace again in new circumstances. This backward-before-forward theme is a common idea when considering the phenomenon of disruption. Let's look at this more closely.

Epochs and revolutions

Let's recall the notion of a series of epochs. As mentioned in the previous chapter, the universe as a whole seems to be progressing through a series of different phases: first physics and chemistry, then biology, then brains, then technology, and so on. As another example, Kurzweil draws attention to a similar sequence for the progression of computing[558]:

1. Mechanical calculators and tabulators, as used to process data collected in the 1890 national census in the United States
2. Systems incorporating electrical relays, as used in telephone switchboard equipment
3. Replacement of relays with electronic valves – as in the secret code-breaking computers at Bletchley Park during World War Two
4. Replacement of valves with individual transistors
5. Computers incorporating integrated circuits formed from ever larger numbers of ever smaller transistors
6. Integrated circuits might shortly change from two-dimensional to three-dimensional – or computer architectures might undergo other fundamental transformations.

In this way, when considering technological progress over an extended period of time, a simple notion of a single exponential curve often needs to give way to a richer model. This new model features an overlay of multiple different S-shaped curves – one curve for each epoch in the overall sequence[559]. (The shape of these curves is akin to an *old-style* S, as in the integral sign used in mathematics, '∫', slanted-forward.) Progress along any one of these S curves tends to be slow at first: that's the lead-in part at the bottom of the letter 'S'. It subsequently accelerates, but can then slow down again, once the full potential of this particular epoch has been reached. At this stage, further progress depends on making a jump to the next S curve in the sequence. The S curves in aggregate trace out a shape resembling an upward exponential curve, but with more jumps and jerks involved.

As alternatives to the term "epoch", other words that are often used instead are "paradigm", "architecture", and "wave". Moving from one S curve to another is therefore a matter of "adopting a new paradigm", "switching architecture", or "jumping to a new wave". Yet other ways to describe such a move is as a "revolution" as opposed to the "evolution" of progress that sticks within a single S curve, and as a "disruption" as opposed to "incremental" progress.

Overall progress depends, therefore, not only on harvesting the potential of individual waves of technology, but on managing the disruptive transitions between successive waves.

For a number of reasons, these disruptive transitions are often delayed. This can happen because of lack of financial investment, an over-focus on short-term monetary returns (which favours sticking with tried-and-tested incremental approaches, despite the diminishing returns), philosophical opposition that insists "that's not how we do things around here", concerns over risks of unintended consequences of a new technological platform, and social or political opposition from vested interests who perceive themselves as doing well from the status quo.

Worse, this opposition can do more than *delay* the jump to a new wave of technology. It can cause the jump to be *flunked altogether*. The revolution can be stopped in its tracks.

That's another reason to query any assumptions that technological progress is inevitable. As we've seen, life expectancy can stop increasing and can even decline. It's my personal view that it can start rising again, rapidly – but only when society embraces technological possibilities that are still at a relatively early phase of development. But there's nothing inevitable about that embrace.

What caused the trend of increase in life expectancy from around the 1860s? Unsurprisingly, given the previous discussion, a number of overlapping waves of improvement can be discerned[560]:

- Reduction in deaths in childbirth, infancy and early childhood, due to better hygiene and sanitation, including the pasteurisation of milk and cleaner sources of water
- A decline in the significance of infectious diseases, due the discovery and application of vaccinations and antibiotics
- Other breakthroughs in medical understanding and practice, such as x-rays and biopsies, and surgery that more patients could survive due to sterilisation, antibiotics, and anaesthesia
- General improvements in health due to a wider choice of food being available and housing being less crowded and better ventilated

- Reductions in the numbers of people being killed in accidents, due to health and safety regulations at work, as well as improvements in the design and management of automobile transport
- A decline in smoking
- A reduction in pollutants such as fumes from leaded petrol.

What's particularly interesting, however, is that this broad trend of improved *health* was accompanied by a number of other important demographic changes:

- Growth in the *wealth* of the average person
- Growth in the *educational level* of the average person
- Growth in the amount of *energy* used by the average person.

In each case, the pattern is the same: little change for most of history, followed by an acceleration from, roughly, around the year 1800.

Let's look more closely at the interactions between these changes.

Interacting changes

Statistics for the wealth of the average person in England exist all the way back to the year 1270[561]. These statistics tabulate estimates of the "GDP per capita in England" – namely, the monetary value of all the products produced within the country, divided by the population, and adjusted for inflation. For 1270, that worked out as £806, expressed in the equivalent of pound sterling of 2013. By 1659, nearly four centuries later, the figure was only £974. That's an average compound growth rate of only 5% per century. The figures varied up and down in individual years – as for the life expectancy figures covered earlier – but the basic trend was a very slight upward increase.

It took until 1690 until the GDP per capita, at £1614, was double the 1270 starting point. The first time it exceeded £2,000 was in 1760; and it took another 35 years (until 1795) to add another 10% (exceeding £2,200 for the first time). But from then onward, the pace of growth increased. £3,000 was reached in 1846; £4,000 in 1871; £5,000 in 1906; £6,000 in 1937; £7,000 in 1940; £8,000 in 1953; £9,000 in 1959; £10,000 in 1961; £12,000 in 1968; £14,000 in 1973; £16,000 in 1983; £18,000 in 1987; £20,000 in 1993; £24,000 in 2000; and £28,000 in 2007.

Reliable estimates for the average number of years people spent in education don't go back so far in time, but a similar general trend can be observed[562]. For most of history, most people worked in agriculture, and had minimal formal schooling. Girls in particular received almost zero schooling. In 1870, people in the UK received on average 0.8 years of formal tuition. This reached 1.96 in 1900, 3.03 in 1910, 4.13 in 1920, 5.07 in 1930, 5.71 in 1940, 6.11 in 1950, 6.49 in 1960, 7.54 in 1970, 8.13 in 1980, 8.88 in 1990, 11.7 in 2000, and 13.2 in 2010.

As for the increase in the amount of energy used by the average person, that's another case where waves of new usage overlap[563]:

- Energy used to come primarily from burning wood or harnessing animals
- Some additional energy was supplied from windmills and waterwheels
- Peat and coal were collected and burned, with mines being dug ever deeper into the ground
- The production of oil led to rapid expansion in energy usage
- Natural gas provided another source of energy, as did hydroelectric
- In more recent decades, increasing amounts of energy have been delivered from solar, wind, wave, geothermal, and nuclear.

Overall, these different sources of energy add up to a lengthy period of comparatively little change, followed by an acceleration of usage once systems were in place to extract first coal and then oil from below the surface of the earth.

These fuel extraction systems were outgrowths of yet another trend: increasing mastery of engineering and technology. Underground coalmines were often filled with water, making them difficult or impractical to exploit. Mining was, therefore, accompanied by systems of water pumps operated by the movement of horses. During the eighteenth century, these horse-powered pumps were gradually replaced by steam-powered alternatives. Taking advantage of the insights of seventeenth century scientists including Evangelista Torricelli, Blaise Pascal, Robert Boyle, and Robert Hooke, into the subjects of air pressure and vacuums, pioneering engineers such as Thomas Savery and Thomas Newcomen developed the first practical steam engines. Savery described his invention as "The Miner's Friend"[564]. Adoption was slow at first since these systems were only barely better than well-established horse-powered pumps. However, a series of decisive design enhancements made by James Watt from 1765 onward transformed the effectiveness of the invention.

A few short years after Watt's innovations, steam engines were at work not only in coalmines but also tin mines and copper mines; they were, moreover, revolutionising the operation of mills producing flour, cotton, paper, and iron, as well as distilleries that produced alcohol. It's for good reason that the start of the industrial revolution is often dated to the 1760s[565].

The various trends described above evidently influenced each other:

- Greater mastery of engineering allowed for easier access to long-buried sources of energy
- Growth in engineering capability, coupled with widespread low-cost energy sources, led to improvements in agriculture and manufacturing, which in turn created more wealth, raising the average economic wellbeing
- Greater economic wellbeing provided an opportunity for more people to spend more time gaining a wider education, since there was less need for everyone to be fully occupied from an early age working in farms or factories
- With more people gaining a better education, innovations in science, engineering, and medicine came more quickly, with people building on each other's insights; therefore, health and lifespan improved, for the reasons given earlier in this chapter
- A healthier workforce in turn further raised the performance of industry and generated more economic wellbeing.

There's scope to debate which of these trends acts as a primary cause, and which are effects. MIT economist Andrew McAfee gives priority to the influence of technology, writing that[566]:

> History teaches us that nothing changes the world like technology.

He backs up that claim as follows:

> For thousands of years, until the middle of the 18th century, there were only glacial rates of population growth, economic expansion, and social development. Then an industrial revolution happened, centred around James Watt's improved steam engine, and humanity's trajectory bent sharply and permanently upward.

Developing his theme, he continues:

> Great wars and empires, despots and democrats, the insights of science and the revelations of religion – none of them transformed lives and civilizations as much as a few practical inventions.

Of course, these "practical inventions" – the steam engine, the locomotive, the telephone, the Ford Model T automobile, the washing machine, synthetic fabrics, the contraceptive pill, and so on – owed their success to a number of wider factors: the insights of science, the ability of people to defy prevailing orthodoxy, the possibilities of free association between inventors (like James Watt) and investors (like Watt's long-time business partner Matthew Boulton), a legal system that offered protection to intellectual property, and society being sufficiently stable to provide time for inventions to develop and take root. Technology cannot work its wonders in a vacuum.

Nevertheless, there's a deeper insight in the point that McAfee is making. Having being developed with one purpose in mind – such as removing water from subterranean mines – a piece of technology can find many new uses, beyond those considered by its original inventors.

That brings us to the subject of "overhang". It's overhang that can turn an individual invention into the basis for an industrial revolution, with world-changing consequences.

Technology overhang

Inventions sometimes turn out to be surprisingly fruitful. Mathematical ideas developed to solve individual problems have often turned out to be applicable in apparently far-distant domains. Consider the utility of the concept of "imaginary numbers" (square roots of negative "real numbers") in fields as disparate as electrical engineering, data compression, signal analysis, and basic theories of physics like quantum mechanics. Consider also the remarkable fecundity of the ideas of calculus, from the insight by Isaac Newton that force causes a proportional change in the second derivative of position (that is, acceleration). Once formulae are available that describe particular forces – such as gravity varying inversely with the square of the distance between two objects – this allows the calculation of paths of motion. Newton used these ideas to *deduce* the three laws of planetary orbits that had previously been *observed* by the astronomer Johannes Kepler, such as the elliptical path taken by each planet around the sun. But in the decades that followed, the same principles were applied to explain dynamical motion in numerous other circumstances, when different sets of forces applied.

Many a physicist, in contemplative moments, has expressed wonder at the widespread successes of mathematics within their discipline. Thus, Eugene Wigner wrote a famous article in 1960 entitled "The Unreasonable Effectiveness of Mathematics in the Natural Sciences"[567]. As Wigner observed:

> The mathematical formulation of the physicist's often crude experience leads in an uncanny number of cases to an amazingly accurate description of a large class of phenomena.

Of course, by no means all mathematical inventions produce leaps in understanding of the physical world. Most mathematical curiosities remain just that – a set of abstract ideas of interest only to determined mathematicians. On the other hand, some mathematical concepts make the jump from pure to applied after a lengthy incubation period. That was the case with the study of prime numbers, which found unexpected utility in the 1970s in the emerging field of public key cryptography[568] – something that underpins huge amounts of online business in the modern world.

As with breakthroughs in mathematics, so also with breakthroughs in science. A single breakthrough can lead to a torrent of discoveries. Once physicists Werner Heisenberg and Erwin Schrodinger had established the basics of quantum mechanics in 1925 and 1926, a flood of new results came thick and fast in the next few years. Another pioneer of that subject, Paul Dirac, later referred to this period as a "golden age in theoretical physics"[569]:

> For a few years after that it was easy for any second rate student to do first rate work.

In biology, a similar status is held by the principle of evolution via natural selection – although it took considerable time from the original formulation of that principle by Charles Darwin before its full explanatory significance was widely understood. Prominent geneticist Theodosius Dobzhansky put it like this in an essay in 1973[570]:

> Nothing in biology makes sense except in the light of evolution.

As with breakthroughs in mathematics and science, so also with breakthroughs in technology. We've already seen how steam power found multiple applications throughout industry, once it was understood how to create engines that operated with sufficient efficiency. Steam engines gained a further lease of life once they were built into railway locomotives and paddle ships. Increasing prevalence of steam power, rail transport, and mechanisation characterises the historical phenomenon known as the first wave of the industrial revolution – or, expressed more simply, as the first industrial revolution. Steam railways were initially used to transport goods, such as iron and coal, before increasing numbers of human passengers adopted that mode of carriage too. Railways were carrying soldiers as early as the 1840s in Prussia and the 1850s for the Crimean War, before playing a significant role in the American Civil War of the 1860s.

To be clear, there's nothing preordained about the social adoption of a new technology such as the railways. Sometimes the existing rulers of a country anticipate the potential social disruption that the new technology might bring, and oppose the technology on that account. They wish, instead, to preserve the status quo. Thus, Emperor Francis I of Austria rejected proposals in the 1830s that steam-powered railways should be built within the Austro-Hungarian empire – even though railways were spreading quickly in many other European countries. Francis gave this response[571]:

> No, no, I will have nothing to do with it, lest the revolution might come into the country.

Greater mobility might spread radical ideas more quickly, Francis thought – with some justification. Similar fears prevailed in Russia too, leading to resistance against steam-powered railways until the 1860s. Countries such as the United States, the United Kingdom, France, and Germany, which gave the new technology a warmer welcome, indeed saw a faster pace of steady social evolution.

The social changes in the wake of the first industrial revolution, significant as they were, are eclipsed by a greater set of changes resulting from a second wave of breakthrough technological innovation from around the 1870s onward[572]:

- Mastery of electricity, including the generation and distribution of ever larger amounts of energy to the electrical engines that increasingly displaced steam engines
- Transformation of domestic life as a result of equipment that used electricity, such as the washing machine and refrigerators
- Successful application of the Bessemer process for the mass production of steel

- New designs for large buildings, taking advantage of steel structures and elevators
- Increasing usage of petrol (gasoline) and other derivatives of oil
- The invention of the first practical pneumatic rubber tyre
- Alfred Nobel's invention of dynamite
- Other breakthroughs with industrial-scale chemistry, such as synthetic fertilisers, synthetic fabrics, and synthetic plastics
- Improved communications via telephones and radios
- New entertainment systems, including the storage and playback of both music and film
- Enhancements to manufacturing processes by the assembly line system pioneered by Henry Ford.

These changes, in combination, produced even larger technology overhang – more areas of life were to be impacted than were imagined during the initial stages of these inventions.

Even more was to come. But first, a word about counting.

Counting revolutions

Historians can reasonably disagree whether the above list of breakthrough technological innovations – from mastery of electricity to Henry Ford's introduction of the assembly line – should be analysed together under a unified concept such as "the second industrial revolution", or if, instead, they simply form part of a wider *single* industrial revolution that spans all the way from the 1760s to near the present day.

In this book, I'm going to follow the vocabulary championed by Klaus Schwab, the founder and executive chairman of the World Economic Forum, which hosts meetings in Davos every January. Schwab finds it useful to refer to a total (so far) of *four* industrial revolutions[573].

A somewhat different view is taken by eminent British-Venezuelan scholar Carlota Perez, who speaks instead of there having been *five* distinct periods of revolutionary technological innovation so far, with a sixth one starting in the present time[574]:

1. "The industrial revolution", from 1771
2. "The age of steam, coal, iron, and railways", from 1829

3. "The age of steel, electricity, and heavy engineering", from 1875
4. "The age of oil, automobiles, and mass production", from 1908
5. "The age of information and telecommunications", from 1971
6. An as-yet unnamed new age, from around the present-day, potentially involving biotech and nanotech.

Perez stresses that each of these periods of revolutionary technological innovation has a double nature:

> *Radical new technologies*: A powerful cluster of new and dynamic technologies, products, industries, and infrastructures – with explosive growth and structural change;
>
> *New techno-economic paradigm*: An interrelated set of organisational principles capable of upgrading mature industries and enabling widespread innovation – resulting in a quantum jump in attainable productivity.

Perez also points out that the largest boosts in productivity are likely to become apparent only some way into a given technological revolution:

- Once suitable infrastructure and processes have been created around the new technologies, and once people have learned how best to take advantage of the resulting combinations
- Once metrics for measurement have been adjusted, to take into full account all the benefits arising from the new systems, rather than just focusing on metrics that made good sense in a previous epoch
- Once social and political frameworks have been adjusted to ensure wide access to the benefits of the new technology, strengthening public support for the new ways of doing things.

Ahead of these wider changes being established – in what Perez describes as a phase of "creative construction" in contrast to the initial phase of "creative destruction" – there are major risks of social unrest, alienation, collapses of exuberant investment bubbles, and the rise of populism. Typically, the first phase of a technological revolution sees a worsening of inequality, whereas the second phase sees a reduction again.

The framework proposed by Perez draws upon older analysis by the Soviet economist Nikolai Kondratiev. According to Kondratiev, the global economy follows long-term cycles of boom-and-bust every 50-60 years. His analysis has the merit of claiming as its starting point data about actual economic growth and slowdowns. The resulting theory of "Kondratiev waves" has given rise to considerable debate[575]. Most researchers accept that the periods of boom-and-bust do *not* neatly reflect any predetermined time schedule. One scathing assessment, by the economist Murray Rothbard, puts it like this, in a section entitled "Torturing the Data" in his 1984 essay "The Kondratieff Cycle: Real or Fabricated?"[576]:

> For the nineteenth century – the "first two Kondratieffs" – there was never any depression as we know it: not in production, nor in employment or living standards. The "Kondratieff depression" is based on (a) statistical fallacies bordering on chicanery; and (b) the mistaken view that a price fall must mean depression. To the contrary, prices naturally tend to fall in a capitalist society. Furthermore, the "Kondratieff booms" were not long booms at all, but short inflationary spurts brought on by the creation of a great deal of money to finance major wars.

That's harsh, but it's not the end of the discussion. As I see it, Nikolai Kondratiev has some key similarities to – wait for it – futurist Ray Kurzweil:

- In both cases, the historical patterns they identify fail to respect the actual complications and variations in real-world data: their patterns apply only as a first approximation
- Nevertheless, both writers have perceived some profound truths about historical progress.

Accordingly, there's much to admire about the recommendations given by Perez, probably the most astute of modern researchers within the broad Kondratiev school:

- Revolutionary technological change can take a long time to build real momentum, but once it does so, the consequences generally extend far beyond what was in the minds of the original innovators
- Each period of revolutionary change is complicated by the interaction of multiple parallel developments
- These parallel developments involve, not only several different technological areas, but also innovations in manufacturing processes, the allocation of finance, transport infrastructure, knowledge management, and social welfare support
- A phase of "creative *construction*" generally lags some time behind the initial "creative *destruction*" phase of the technological revolution, meaning that social cohesion is particularly vulnerable as the

technology becomes more potent ahead of social and political changes catching up.

In this sense, the technological component of such a revolution exists as an overhang in *two* related ways:

1. Once it has reached a sufficient level of maturity, a general-purpose technological innovation, such as steam or electricity, can quickly transform many existing industries, and even enable the creation of whole new industries which previously lacked viability
2. The associated changes typically run far ahead of appropriate adjustments in legal, ethical, social, philosophical, and political systems, generating a public sense of great unease.

These insights hold true, whichever system you want to use to count and divide up the waves of breakthrough innovations of the last few centuries.

A counting framework that I do *not* support, however, is to say that there is just one industrial revolution, proceeding more or less smoothly from the eighteenth century onward. On the contrary, it's vital to appreciate how periods of renewed technological change are intermixed with periods of slow down and stagnation– and how the slowdowns and speedups are critically influenced by social factors as well as by technology.

Eating the world

If steam power was the primary general-purpose technology of the first wave of the industrial revolution, and electrical power took that role for the second wave, the corresponding honour in the third phase (to revert to the numbering scheme proposed by Karl Schwab of the World Economic Forum) is computing power.

The first practical computers were introduced to solve a number of specific problems: tabulating census data, plotting missile trajectories, and cracking secret codes. However, as Alan Turing had foreseen in his 1936 paper "On computable numbers"[577], a computer with a certain straightforward architecture would be "a *universal* computing machine". Indeed, from the time that computers attained reasonable performance and reliability, they have been applied to an ever-wider number of tasks – including, as part of a feedback loop, assisting with the design and manufacture of subsequent new generations of computers.

Computers in the 1940s were limited by their reliance on vacuum tubes, which took up considerable space, used a lot of energy, and frequently needed replacing. Following the invention of the semiconductor transistor in 1947, computer design switched from vacuum tubes to sets of individual transistors. However, computers remained constrained, due to the arduous nature of the task of assembling large numbers of transistors together.

Significant acceleration of the design of computers needed to wait for the invention of the integrated circuit in 1958 by Jack Kilby of Texas Instruments. Kilby's product used germanium. That innovation was quickly followed, in 1959, by the first silicon integrated circuit – created by Robert Noyce, who went on to co-found Intel. Integrated circuits soon combined together increasing numbers of transistors in small, power-efficient packages.

At around the same time, the first widely used high level computer programming languages were made available[578]: Fortran in 1957, Algol in 1958, LISP also in 1958, and Cobol in 1959.

For these reasons, the start of this third wave of the industrial revolution can be dated around 1960. Features contributing to an increasing technological overhang in the years that followed included:

- Computers used in businesses and, in due course, in homes too
- Numerous items of consumer electronics, that took advantage of silicon components
- Systems for programming software, allowing ever greater numbers of people to create more elaborate applications more quickly
- Systems for storing and accessing data electronically, including, from 1969 onward, the "network of networks" that came to be known as the Internet
- The invention and deployment of cellular wireless communication, as realised in first generation mobile phones from the 1980s, 2G mobile phones in the 1990s, 3G phones in the 2000s, 4G phones in the 2010s, and 5G phones in the 2020s
- Creative combinations of all the above, including web browsing, mobile applications, and social media.

One expression of the impact of this wave of change is in the phrase "Software is eating the world", coined in 2011 by prominent VC (venture capitalist) Marc Andreessen[579] – who, while younger, had played a leading role in developing the first commercial web browser at Netscape. It's an evocative statement. Here's how Andreessen explained its meaning:

> We are in the middle of a dramatic and broad technological and economic shift in which software companies are poised to take over large swathes of the economy.
>
> More and more major businesses and industries are being run on software and delivered as online services – from movies to agriculture to national defence. Many of the winners are Silicon Valley-style entrepreneurial technology companies that are invading and overturning established industry structures. Over the next 10 years, I expect many more industries to be disrupted by software, with new world-beating Silicon Valley companies doing the disruption in more cases than not.

In his 2011 essay, Andreessen enumerated example after example:

- The world's leading bookseller is a software company: Amazon
- The world's leading video store is a software company: Netflix
- The world's leading music retailers are software companies: Apple (iTunes), Spotify, and Pandora
- The world's fastest growing entertainment companies are software companies, including makers of graphical video games
- The world's leading animation company is a software company: Pixar (subsequently purchased by Disney)
- The world's leading direct marketing company is a software company: Google
- The world's fastest growing recruitment company is a software company: LinkedIn.

What had happened in these industries would likely be followed, Andreessen predicted, by similar transformations in other industries: oil and gas exploration, financial services, agriculture, retail, education, healthcare, and the armed forces.

Significantly, the underlying technology had passed through a phase of being expensive, unreliable, and difficult to configure, into a phase of being much more affordable, dependable, and easily adaptable:

> Six decades into the computer revolution, four decades since the invention of the microprocessor, and two decades into the rise of the modern Internet,

> all of the technology required to transform industries through software finally works and can be widely delivered at global scale…
>
> With lower start-up costs and a vastly expanded market for online services, the result is a global economy that for the first time will be fully digitally wired — the dream of every cyber-visionary of the early 1990s, finally delivered, a full generation later.

From the standpoint of the early 2020s, Andreessen's analysis seems prescient – perhaps almost obvious in retrospect. Some of the companies he mentioned have faded from public attention – the game creator Zynga and the location data platform Foursquare – but even in these cases, the companies still exist[580], and could have bright futures ahead of them[581]. On the whole, the companies listed by Andreessen have gone from strength to strength. Share prices that in 2011 already seemed sky-high, for Apple, Microsoft, Amazon, Google, and Facebook – have grown and grown and grown since then.

Whilst the increasing financial and political dominance of these Internet and software companies seems, as I said, "almost obvious" in retrospect, such an outcome was by no means obvious beforehand.

Predicting ghosts

Let's wind back to 1995, a year after the public release of Marc Andreessen's web browser Netscape. Many people who experienced these first releases were enchanted, and started imagining radical consequences of the new technology.

One person who was deeply *unconvinced* by such exuberance was Robert Metcalfe. Metcalfe had in 1973 co-invented the Ethernet standard for wired connections between networked computers. He even has an important law named after him[582]: the value of a communications network is proportional to the square of the number of connected users in the network. Since the cost of a network is proportional to the number of connected users, it follows that the financial significance of a network can explode once it reaches a certain "critical mass crossover", as Metcalfe put it in 1980.

By 1995, Metcalfe was a distinguished columnist in InfoWorld magazine, a publication I regularly read at that time in paper format. Given his appreciation of the potential tipping points that a new network could experience, Metcalfe's judgement on the potential for the world wide web commanded a lot of attention. His assessment[583]:

> The Internet… will soon go spectacularly supernova and in 1996 catastrophically collapse… There soon will be only World Wide Web ghost pages.

Metcalfe marshalled eleven arguments in support of his dire conclusion. Here is a selection:

- Whatever good content that exists on the Internet would soon become impossibly difficult to find, due to search engines being swamped by multitudes of low-grade content
- The public Internet would be subject to an increasing number of security problems, prompting companies to move their most valuable and interesting content behind firewalls into less accessible "intranets"
- Ordinary members of the public who were tempted by glitzy advertising to take a look at the Internet would soon tire of that experience, and would revert to watching television instead
- Adverse publicity surrounding privacy violations would frighten yet more people away from using the Internet
- The web would become "fatally constipated" as a result of the high costs users would need to pay for data transfer over local telephone lines, with these inertia-bound telephone companies being more interested in revenues from long-distance voice calls than providing high-speed Internet access
- The standards defining communication over the Internet would soon fragment, due to different companies and organisations having conflicting visions for how the Internet should evolve; in particular, contrary ideas about video transmission would prove to be fatal
- The large sums of money being invested into Internet companies were failing to produce matching revenues; accordingly, such investment would soon be curtailed.

On the question of a business model for Internet companies, Metcalfe did foresee the *possibility* of "some" revenue from advertising, but he asserted that would "probably not" happen. He also considered the potential of "digital money", but predicted that "transaction costs" of an increasing number of "middlepersons" would stymie any such "Internet commerce". For the foreseeable future, therefore, there would be *no* viable business model for any Internet company. As for Metcalfe's eponymous law: he insisted that would *not* apply in this case, due to the immaturity and instability of the protocols for web traffic and connections.

Hence Metcalfe's concluding forecast, laden with irony:

> In 1996, CD-ROMs through Federal Express will emerge as the information superhighway. Instead of an Internet brimming with Web pages under construction, too few of us will haunt ghost pages.

Metcalfe was far from being the only sceptic of the potential of the Web. Consider Clifford Stoll, the author of the famous 1989 book *The Cuckoo's Egg* about the painstaking investigation he had conducted of the hacking in 1986 of the computer systems at the Lawrence Berkeley National Laboratory[584]. That book was the first to bring the ideas of cyberhacking and cybersecurity to broad public attention. Stoll's powers of close observation and critical thinking arguably put him in a good situation to assess the world wide web during its early days. Here's what he wrote in 1995, originally under the headline "The Internet? Bah"[585], though editors later revised the title to "Why the Web Won't Be Nirvana"[586]:

> After two decades online, I'm perplexed. It's not that I haven't had a gas of a good time on the Internet. I've met great people and even caught a hacker or two. But today, I'm uneasy about this most trendy and oversold community. Visionaries see a future of telecommuting workers, interactive libraries and multimedia classrooms. They speak of electronic town meetings and virtual communities. Commerce and business will shift from offices and malls to networks and modems. And the freedom of digital networks will make government more democratic.
>
> Baloney. Do our computer pundits lack all common sense? The truth is no online database will replace your daily newspaper, no CD-ROM can take the place of a competent teacher and no computer network will change the way government works…
>
> How about electronic publishing? Try reading a book on disc. At best, it's an unpleasant chore: the myopic glow of a clunky computer replaces the friendly pages of a book. And you can't tote that laptop to the beach. Yet Nicholas Negroponte, director of the MIT Media Lab, predicts that we'll soon buy books and newspapers straight over the Internet. Uh, sure.

One piece of shortsight that afflicted both Metcalfe and Stoll concerned the improvements possible in web search engines. Here's Stoll's complaint about his failure to find useful material on the web:

> What the Internet hucksters won't tell you is that the Internet is one big ocean of unedited data, without any pretence of completeness. Lacking editors, reviewers or critics, the Internet has become a wasteland of unfiltered data. You don't know what to ignore and what's worth reading. Logged onto the World Wide Web, I hunt for the date of the Battle of Trafalgar. Hundreds of files show up, and it takes 15 minutes to unravel them – one's a biography written by an eighth grader, the second is a computer game that doesn't work and the third is an image of a London monument. None answers my question…

Rather than assuming that web engines could never improve, Metcalfe and Stoll would have done better to keep a more open mind. It was the same with their observations about the slow and erratic access to the web in 1995. Here's the end of Stoll's complaint about web search:

> … and my search is periodically interrupted by messages like, "Too many connections, try again later."

Again, there was no acknowledgment of the potential for access to improve, via better hardware, better software, better connectivity – and the prospect for innovative companies to earn more revenues by enabling these improvements.

Another error – obvious in retrospect, but which beguiled people at the time – was to take a snapshot of current usage figures, and to assume that no substantial ramp-up from these figures would be possible. One example by Stoll referred to the level of public interest in online copies of political press releases:

> When Andy Spano ran for county executive in Westchester County, N.Y., he put every press release and position paper onto a bulletin board. In that affluent county, with plenty of computer companies, how many voters logged in? Fewer than 30. Not a good omen.

For a second example, also by Stoll, here's his dismissal of the potential for online shopping:

> We're promised instant catalogue shopping – just point and click for great deals. We'll order airline tickets over the network, make restaurant reservations and negotiate sales contracts. Stores will become obsolete. So how come my local mall does more business in an afternoon than the entire Internet handles in a month?

Stoll offered two arguments why significant growth would not be possible. The first, mirroring a criticism we saw from Metcalfe, was that there could be no trustworthy way to send money over the Internet (a problem that was in reality solved not long afterward by credit card companies, PayPal, and consumer credit protection legislation). The second was more philosophical: potential purchasers would not want to buy any items unless they had real world interactions with human salespeople:

> The network is missing a most essential ingredient of capitalism: salespeople.
>
> What's missing from this electronic wonderland? Human contact. Discount the fawning techno-burble about virtual communities. Computers and networks isolate us from one another. A network chat line is a limp substitute for meeting friends over coffee. No interactive multimedia display comes close to the excitement of a live concert. And who'd prefer cybersex to the real thing?
>
> While the Internet beckons brightly, seductively flashing an icon of knowledge-as-power, this nonplace lures us to surrender our time on earth. A poor substitute it is, this virtual reality where frustration is legion and where – in the holy names of Education and Progress – important aspects of human interactions are relentlessly devalued.

Both Metcalfe[587] and Stoll[588] were later obliged to acknowledge that their 1995 forecasts were seriously shortsighted. Metcalfe even ate his words, literally, grinding a paper copy of his offending article in a blender before consuming the resulting drink live on stage.

As you may anticipate, my purpose in looking at their forecasts at some length is as a preparation to considering, in the pages that follow, similarly shortsighted pessimistic forecasts from the present-day – forecasts about the potential of technologies that are, today, at a similar state of immaturity as the Internet was in 1995. These present-day criticisms repeat many of the same mistakes:

- Assuming that human interaction is essential to various tasks, whereas in fact improved hardware and software can turn users' expectations upside down
- Fixating on present-day obstacles, while failing to conceive that innovative solutions might be produced by the many dynamic companies (both small and large) that apply their attention to these obstacles – similar to how Google transformed web search and PayPal transformed online payments

- Extrapolating from the visible failures of *some* companies in an emerging space, to the conclusion that *all* companies in that space will be bound to fail in the same way
- Reacting, with some justification, against overly rosy optimistic assessments by some enthusiasts for the latest technology, but jumping to the false supposition that the entire field is therefore doomed
- Suffering from a lack of imagination: critics cannot think of any new ideas for solving the problems they have identified; therefore, no other ideas are possible!

The productivity paradox

The two authors of the forecasts that I have just been discussing, Robert Metcalfe and Clifford Stoll, are technology specialists with broad interests in general topics – including economics and history. I turn now to two writers who approach the same questions from the opposite angle: they are specialists in economics and history, with broad interests in technology.

Let's start with the veteran economist Robert Solow, who became a professor at MIT in 1949 and who remains to this day an emeritus member of faculty there. In 1987, Solow expressed some exasperation with writers who took it for granted that computer and automation technology would enable a decisive jump in productivity. What productivity statistics actually showed, Solow asserted, was an awkward embarrassment for these technology enthusiasts[589]:

> What everyone feels to have been a technological revolution, a drastic change in our productive lives, has been accompanied everywhere, including Japan, by a slowing down of productivity growth, not by a step up.

It's his next sentence that is frequently quoted:

> You can see the computer age everywhere but in the productivity statistics.

That same year, 1987, Solow received the Nobel Prize in Economics, for his contributions to "the theory of economic growth"[590]. So, he was speaking from a strong vantage point that year, when he assessed the contribution of computer technology to economic growth as being dismal.

Solow was no Luddite, opposed to the introduction of technology. On the contrary, he was deeply aware of the contribution that technology can bring to economic wellbeing. Recall the discussion from earlier in this chapter about the historic growth of GDP per capita, that is, the economic output of the average citizen. What causes the GDP to grow? Classical theories of economics saw two factors at work:

1. How much *labour* was applied – how many people worked in production, and for how long
2. How much *capital* was invested – enabling the purchase and operation of factories, tools, and input materials.

Solow's research showed that these two factors, by themselves, were insufficient to explain the variations in economic productivity that existed both geographically and historically. Other factors also contribute to overall productivity – and indeed are responsible, by some calculations, for as much as seven eighths of productivity growth. These other factors have come to be known as the "Solow residual", although Solow used the term "technical change"[591] or sometimes just the single word "technology".

Briefly, what matters isn't just the *quantity* of labour and capital, but also their *quality*:

- The infrastructure within which companies operate
- The skills of the workforce
- The processes followed
- The particular tools adopted.

Accordingly, the way to boost the productivity of the economy is to make smart investments in the above areas:

- Enhancing transport systems, regulatory frameworks, legal support, sources of finance, the provision of insurance, networks of just-in-time suppliers, and systems for public relations and business development
- Improving the education received by the workforce – boosting their expertise in domain-specific skills as well as in the "soft skills" that improve human interactions
- Taking advantage of process innovations, such as "Taylor Scientific Management", quality control, agile development, lean manufacturing, and Kaizen continuous improvement – as well as numerous innovations specific to particular industries

- Deploying new technologies, including steam engines, electrical engines, protective clothing, enzymes for chemical reactions, microscopes, scanners, telephone switchboards, fax machines, filing systems, calculators, and, yes, computers.

In its issue published on 3rd January 1983, Time Magazine broke from its tradition stretching back to 1927 of announcing a "Man of the Year". Instead, in picking the most decisive contribution for the year that had just ended, 1982, Time selected a "Machine of the Year", namely the computer. They explained their decision as follows[592]:

> There are some occasions… when the most significant force in a year's news is not a single individual but a process, and a widespread recognition by a whole society that this process is changing the course of all other processes. That is why, after weighing the ebb and flow of events around the world, TIME has decided that 1982 is the year of the computer.

As that Time article noted[593], sales of personal computers in the United States were on an upward trajectory: 724 thousand sold in 1980, 1.4 million in 1981, and double that number again in 1982. A survey held that year indicated that 80% of Americans already expected that "in the fairly near future, home computers will be as commonplace as television sets or dishwashers".

Why, therefore, were computers having such little impact, five years later, on the Solow residual, that is, on the overall growth of the economy? Why was the economy growing more slowly, in the 1970s and 1980s, than in the preceding decades? Had the promise of computing technology been oversold by overexcited hype merchants?

During the early years of the 1990s, MIT economist Erik Brynjolfsson paid special attention to what he called "The Productivity Paradox of Information Technology". His research addressed issues raised in more than a score of empirical studies into the relationship between IT (Information Technology) and productivity. These studies had published conclusions such as the following[594]:

- "IT investments added nothing to output"
- "IT marginal benefit is 80 cents per dollar invested"
- "IT improved intermediate outputs, if not necessarily final output"
- "No correlation between various IT ratios and performance measures"

- "Vast increase in IT capital per information worker while measured output decreased"
- "IT coefficient in translog production function small and often negative"

Brynjolfsson also cited an Economist article from 1990:

"No, computers do not boost productivity, at least not most of the time."

In summary:

Delivered computing-power in the US economy has increased by more than two orders of magnitude since 1970, yet productivity, especially in the service sector, seems to have stagnated.

Having drawn attention to the paradox, Brynjolfsson proceeded to explain it. He has returned to this field many times in the following years, and his explanations remain deeply pertinent[595]. As we'll see, similar explanations apply to the timing of impacts of the technological changes that are accelerating in the present time.

The basic answer is that there can be significant delays between investments in new technology and consequent gains in productivity. Not only does the technology take time to mature, but companies also take time to learn how to adopt that technology in fruitful ways.

In more detail:

1. Many well-known technology vendors may *talk* in grand ways about the capabilities of the solutions they are selling, but the vendors of the solutions that *actually* boost productivity are often companies that are, initially, smaller and lesser-known. It takes time for purchasers to sort out the vendors with truly valuable solutions from those that only *sound* like they know what they are talking about.
2. To take real advantage of a technological innovation, management practices may need to change. New technology enables not only a duplication of previous management practice, but the adoption of new methods with greater effectiveness. Managers who are set in their ways may find these process changes to be disruptive and may resist them, especially in the interim period before the new practices have demonstrated their value.

3. Companies often need to change, not only their internal management practices, but also how they connect into the wider infrastructure of industry and society.

There is also the sheer difficulty in measuring productivity. A modern car may retail for around the same price, in inflation-adjusted terms, as its predecessors from half a century earlier. Does that mean there has been no improvement in the productivity of the automobile industry? On the contrary, the modern vehicle has large numbers of new features and capabilities. But an overly simple measurement will provide a misleading result.

In any case, some industries can experience economic downturns for external reasons unconnected with underlying technological innovation. This was the case with the oil industry during the 1970s, as a result of the OPEC oil embargo discussed in the previous chapter. Given the prominence at that time (and for decades to come) of the oil industry within the overall economy, this factor complicated the detection of the positive impact of computers on productivity.

Finally, even as some companies learn how to take good advantage of new technologies, others struggle; however, aggregate industry metrics involve an average of both the successful and unsuccessful companies – until such time as the latter either amend their ways or drop out of business. That's another way in which an inadequate measurement can obscure, for a while, what is really happening.

Stepping forward in time: an updated graph of the GDP per capita in the United States from 1870 to 2016 shows only a modest slowdown in the 1970s and 1980s. It resumes a fast upward curve from 1983 onward, which was interrupted only by the financial crash of 2007[596]. Since Solow made his famous remarks, it has become abundantly clear that computer technology *can* make a huge difference to the health of the economy. Indeed, as per the observation of Marc Andreessen noted earlier, a lack of proficiency with computer technology is, nowadays, likely to prove fatal to companies in almost every industry. It just took more time than many tech enthusiasts had initially expected, for that state of affairs to become a reality.

Tellingly, a similar lag in impact in productivity can be seen, in retrospect, earlier in history, with the adoption of the technologies of the second industrial revolution. Switching from steam-power to electricity involved lots more than disconnecting a large steam engine and connecting a single electrical engine in its place.

Writing about the delays in industry gaining real benefits from electricity, Stanford Economist Paul David analysed what he called "the pronounced slowdown in industrial and aggregate productivity growth experienced during the 1890-1913 era by the two leading industrial countries, Britain and the United States". He light-heartedly remarked[597]:

> In 1900, contemporary observers well might have remarked that the electric dynamos were to be seen "everywhere but in the productivity statistics!"

After all, by 1900, roughly twenty years had already passed since key breakthroughs with electricity:

> The introduction of the carbon filament incandescent lamp by Edison, and Swann (1879), and… the Edison central generating station in New York and London (1881).

By 1900, however:

- Electric lights were in use in only 3% of homes in the United States; even in cities, only 8% of homes had such lighting
- Manufacturing facilities in the United States received only 5% of their power from electricity.

It was to take until the 1920s that electricity was in wide use, with the companies that used it having by that time an undeniable advantage over competitors still wedded to earlier forms of power.

To be fair to Robert Solow, he did not say that computer technology was intrinsically incapable of causing the kinds of transformations of the economy that its boosters had predicted. The objection he raised in 1987 was, instead, to any claim that such a transformation was already material. The promise would take longer to be delivered.

That puts Solow in a different camp from the sceptics Robert Metcalfe and Clifford Stoll already mentioned. It puts Solow in the same broad camp as the economist Carlota Perez who, as we reviewed, sees each wave of technological revolution as passing through a phase of "creative destruction", with mixed results, before it reaches the phase of "creative construction" in which wider societal benefit is evident.

One more critic deserves to have his case presented. This is Robert Gordon, perhaps the most thorough chronicler of the second industrial revolution. What Gordon has to say about the *third* industrial revolution will usefully set the stage for a deeper look in the next chapter into the *fourth* industrial revolution that is presently gathering pace.

The special century?

"Does the 'New Economy' measure up to the Great Inventions of the past?"

That was the question addressed in a 69-page essay published in 2000 by economist Robert Gordon[598].

In using the term "New Economy", Gordon was following common parlance of that time, referring to "the Internet and the accompanying acceleration of technical changes in computers and telecommunications". Gordon noted that it was often claimed that this New Economy was "an Industrial Revolution equal in importance, or even more important, than the Second Industrial Revolution of 1860-1900". However, Gordon argued that the comparison was exaggerated. After all, the "Great Inventions" from that period covered diverse life-transforming fields such as electricity, motor transport, air transport, motion pictures, radio, and indoor plumbing. Could the Internet really be compared to these previous breakthroughs? Consider two choices Gordon presented to readers:

> We might gather together a group of Houston residents and ask them, "if you could choose only one of the following two inventions, air conditioning or the Internet, which would you choose?"
>
> A parallel question might be asked in Minneapolis: "If you could choose only one of the following two inventions, indoor plumbing or the Internet, which would you choose?"

Nearly two decades later, in 2016, Gordon published a magisterial book that expanded on the argument of that original 69-page essay. Weighing in at over 700 pages, that book is one of the thickest on my home bookshelves. Entitled *The Rise and Fall of American Growth: The U.S. Standard of Living Since the Civil War*[599], it is packed with examples of how the lives of ordinary men and women were changed enormously during what Gordon calls "The special century"[600]:

> The 100 years after 1870 witnessed an economic revolution, freeing households from an unremitting daily grind of painful manual labour, household drudgery, darkness, isolation, and early death. Only 100 years later, daily life had changed beyond recognition. Manual outdoor jobs were replaced by work in air-conditioned environments, housework was

> increasingly performed by electric appliances, darkness was replaced by light, and isolation was replaced not just by travel, but also by colour television images bringing the world into the living room. Most important, a newborn infant could expect to live not to age 45, but to age 72.

Hence Gordon's conclusion:

> The economic revolution of 1870 to 1970 was unique in human history.

What happened *after* 1970, as Gordon sees things, was less stellar:

> Advances since 1970 have tended to be channelled into a narrow sphere of human activity involving entertainment, communication, and the collection and processing of information...
>
> For the rest of what humans care about – food, clothing, shelter, transportation, health, and working conditions both inside and outside the home – progress slowed down both qualitatively and quantitatively after 1970.

Gordon predicts that although technological development will continue, it will cause less of an impact in the future than it did in the past.

Gordon is fully aware that technological revolutions can take many decades to reach their full potential. He is far too good a scholar to miss the pattern of slow ramp-up which characterises technological revolutions. Nevertheless, he expects only modest changes as the computing age unfolds further. His view is that the really big inventions have already taken place; accordingly, what remains to be invented will be less significant.

I offer four responses.

First, the choice is not *either/or*. We don't have to pick either air conditioning or the Internet. The point is that both technologies are available to us. They address different levels of the human hierarchy of needs. Once we have secure access to food, shelter, and a comfortable ambient temperature, we care more deeply about other levels of the hierarchy, including social reputations, communications, entertainment, knowledge, meaning, and self-mastery. It's wrong to say that one level of needs is somehow more important than another.

Second, Gordon is wrong to say computing will have little impact on "working conditions". For example, the profession of secretary used to be the single most common occupation in numerous states of America. That profession has been deeply transformed by computing, with many fewer people holding that job title. As computing continues to improve, other professions which are among the most common ones today – including driving and food preparation – stand to be transformed just as deeply.

Likewise, computing has transformed the performance of supermarkets, improving supply chain logistics, providing customers with a wider choice of both food and clothing than at any previous time in history.

As for healthcare, large changes are pending, following improvements in the creation and management of electronic medical records – something which has taken longer than expected, but which remains full of promise[601]. And that's before we introduce the topic of biotech.

That brings me to the third of my four responses: the computer age is starting to change in an even more significant way. Although the potential of the third industrial revolution is far from being fully developed, a fourth industrial revolution is already afoot. Indeed, changes are gathering pace which justify talking about a *quadrant* of new technological revolutions, known as NBIC for brevity:

- *Nanotech ('N')*: New types of computing chips, computing sensors, and computing actuators
- *Biotech ('B')*: The use of software methods not just in silicon but in biology, allowing reprogramming of our genetics, epigenetics, cellular dynamics, and much more
- *Infotech ('I')*: Software that is no longer written by humans, but which is written by software (artificial intelligence), thanks to machine learning that operates upon "big data"
- *Cognotech ('C')*: The use of the above three sets of technology to radically enhance not only the biology of life but also the psychology of life, via the transformation and augmentation of brains and minds.

I'll have more to say in the next chapter about these four quadrants. For now, I'll simply say that it is presumptuous in the extreme to say that all the really big inventions have already taken place. On the contrary, inventions from each of these quadrants could put even the marvels of past industrial revolutions into shade. Some examples:

- *Nanobots*: Swarms of nanoscale programmable molecules which can utterly transform tasks of recycling, repairing, and reconstruction
- *Synbio organs*: The manufacture of synthetic bodily organs which can supplement or replace the organs with which we were born – not

just new hips and knees but new hearts and lungs, significantly extending our healthspan

- *AI-driven science*: Software systems that can create new scientific theories that resolve long-standing problems in physics, chemistry, and engineering – and which can lead in turn to fundamental advances in fields such as drug design, renewable energy, and climate management
- *Smart helmets*: Neurofeedback methods that can raise both IQ (rational intelligence) and EQ (emotional intelligence), reliably and substantially, without any adverse side-effects.

Beyond technology

The last of my four responses to Robert Gordon is to express vigorous *agreement* with a number of the key concerns he raises:

1. There's no *automatic* connection between investment in technological innovation and a notable increase in the standard of living – even if that investment is continued for years or even decades
2. Some types of technological innovation turn out to have a decreasing marginal utility: as time passes, the improvements they provide over what was previously available can shrink ever smaller
3. The mere fact that an industry can generate a huge amount of publicity and apparent excitement is no guarantee that human wellbeing is actually being advanced in any significant way
4. Just because an innovation can be imagined, it by no means follows that it can actually be created and deployed
5. Just because more research findings are being published than ever before, it by no means follows that the research has greater quality[602]
6. Even if there are benefits from a technological innovation, these benefits may be divided in very uneven ways, creating social inequalities that result, overall, in a *worsening* of the human condition.

Indeed, Gordon forecasts that, unless significant changes are made to how society manages technological innovation, social progress will be:

> …held back by the headwinds of rising inequality, stagnating education, an aging population, and the rising debt of college students and the federal government.

Changes that Gordon recommends (and with which I concur) include:

- Improvements in both the content and the teaching methods of education – see Chapter 15 of this book
- Political changes, to ensure a wider spread of the benefits from new technologies – see Chapter 13
- Clearer thinking about what's truly important, to enable many more people to focus on the challenges that will genuinely boost wellbeing – see Chapters 11 and 12.

With these changes adopted, the hundred years from 1870 to 1970 will no longer be the time period seeing the greatest improvements in the standard of living. Rather than talking about "a special century", we'll more likely talk about the forthcoming twenty or thirty years as being "the special decades", when a powerful set of interconnected changes accelerated.

Indeed, if the summary of the previous three decades – the 1990s, 2000s, and 2010s – has been increasing conformance to Marc Andreessen's observation that "software is eating the world", a potential summary of the *next* three decades – the 2020s, 2030s, and 2040s – is increasing conformance to a variant of that same observation. This time, it will be "software written by AI is eating the world" – or, more simply, "AI is eating the world". Companies that fall behind in understanding and applying the latest techniques of artificial intelligence will be at an increasing disadvantage, regardless of the field in which they operate.

And if society as a whole fails to understand and apply these techniques wisely, all bets are off regarding the kind of future that will arrive.

10. NBIC

NBIC, defined: Nanotech, Biotech, Infotech, Cognotech. Increasing understanding of – and the ability to systematically manipulate and enhance – (1) matter at the molecular level, (2) the biological building blocks of life, (3) the sets of information that exist at all levels of nature and human life, (4) the components of human minds. Four quadrants that, via their accelerating interactions and convergence, drive the fourth industrial revolution.

The first and second industrial revolutions saw an increasing transcendence of human *muscle-power* by machines that were powered first by steam and then by electricity (with significant assistance from oil too). The third and fourth industrial revolutions – "3IR" and "4IR" for short – are seeing, similarly, an increasing transcendence of human *brain-power* by machines with ever-greater all-round intelligence.

Three factors distinguish these latter two revolutions. The first of these factors is the nature of the machine intelligence involved:

- In 3IR, the machine intelligence was programmed by human experts
- In 4IR, the machine intelligence will increasingly be self-programmed, that is, by "machine learning" operating on "big data".

A second distinguishing factor is where machine intelligence operates:

- In 3IR, computing was largely confined to devices that were recognisably "computers" – including handheld smartphones
- In 4IR, computing is taking place everywhere, in parallel, in a pervasive "Internet of Things", including ever smaller devices.

A third factor is the accelerating importance, in 4IR, of biology:

- Software nowadays is increasingly able to *understand* biology – both the body as a whole and the brain as a particularly important organ
- The techniques of software will increasingly be able to *modify* and *improve* that biology – both the body as a whole and the brain
- The techniques of software will, in turn, increasingly themselves be improved by learnings from biology, putting in place a two-way positive feedback loop.

Bringing the above points together, we can identify two dimensions in which breakthrough improvements are happening: hardware/software and physics/biology. These two dimensions define four quadrants in total, known as the NBIC quadrants: nanotech, biotech, infotech, and cognotech:

- Broadly speaking, 'N' and 'B' concern the domain of hardware, whereas 'I' and 'C' concern the domain of software
- Again broadly speaking, 'N' and 'I' concern the domain of physics, whereas 'B' and 'C' concern the domain of biology.

What's particularly important is not the distinctions between these different quadrants, but rather the potential for profound interactions between them. A couple of examples:

- Improvements in nanotech enable better sensors. Better sensors can analyse what's happening inside human brains without needing invasive surgery. A better understanding of human brain mechanisms that underpin rationality, creativity, intuition, and so forth, can feed into improvements in artificial intelligence. These improvements in artificial intelligence can support numerous improvements in medicine[603].
- Artificial intelligence can be accelerated by innovations in semiconductor chip design. In turn, improved artificial intelligence can lead to breakthroughs in the layout of semiconductor chips, enabling them to deliver more computation whilst using less power – as reported in an MIT Technology article headlined "Google is using AI to design chips that will accelerate AI"[604].

These are just the start of the interactions arising. Pull up a chair.

Foundations

There's no exact science to identifying the start dates of the various industrial revolutions. After all, the starts are generally inauspicious: the full significance of various breakthroughs usually only becomes clear in retrospect. And as mentioned, different historians can use different systems to divide up the various phases of innovation. Nevertheless, just as the first industrial revolution can be dated from around 1760, the second from around 1870, and the third from around 1960, there are reasons to suggest 2010 as the rough start date of the fourth industrial revolution.

For example, 2012 was the year in which image recognition software based on neural network techniques first surged ahead of the capabilities of traditional AI systems. The idea of AI learning from the structure of relationships between neurons in the human brain dates back decades – to the research of Walter Pitts and Warren McCulloch in the 1940s[605], and that of Frank Rosenblatt in the 1950s[606]. However, it was only in 2012 that an artificial system based on these ideas outperformed handcrafted "expert" image recognition systems in the annual "Large Scale Visual Recognition Challenge" contest.

AlexNet, the system that won the contest that year, was designed by researchers from the University of Toronto: Alex Krizhevsky, Ilya Sutskever, and long-time advocate of neural networks, Geoffrey Hinton[607]. Previous winners of the contest had utilised lots of specific logical formulae. However, AlexNet was trained by means of adjustments being automatically made to numerous internal parameters based simply on feedback on whether it had correctly identified sample pictures.

To distinguish these two types of AI, consider how a human might learn to distinguish pictures of different people:

- One method involves explicit rules, and might include attention to hair colour, eye colour, the distance between specific points on a face, and so on. As an experiment, you could try to think of a set of rules to identify a picture as one of your mother. You can imagine that these rules could become very complicated, since lots of exceptions will need to be noted.
- The other method involves feedback in response to random guesses. The guesses are the output of a vast matrix of numbers, arranged into layers with signals passing between adjacent layers, a bit like neurons in a human brain communicating via synapses. Depending on how close the guesses are to the correct answers, the numbers in this matrix are adjusted: "up a bit, left a bit, down a bit..." and so on, with the changes taking place over thousands of dimensions.

In 2011, the best performing system in the contest had an error rate of 25%. However, in 2012, AlexNet achieved a dramatically smaller error rate: 15.3%, compared to the 26.2% score of the next best system that year. Observers were stunned. In subsequent years, all participants in the conference switched to the same basic system – a so-called convolutional deep neural network – and found ways to improve it further. By 2015, the winning system had an error rate of just 4% – which was better than the 5% score of humans who attempted the same image classification tasks.

Related ideas were quickly adopted in other computer science tasks, including speech recognition and language translation. A blogpost in 2016 by the product lead for Google Translate extolled the virtues of "neural machine translation" methods on top of "statistical models"[608]:

> With this update, Google Translate is improving more in a single leap than we've seen in the last ten years combined.

Expert system models for translation involve large numbers of rules for grammar and meaning, including exceptions, special cases, and exceptions to special cases. Neural network methods involve pointing software at existing translations of texts, such as those produced by human translators at the EU or UN, and training them with much the same automated multidimensional "up a bit, left a bit, down a bit…" feedback.

Three developments enabled this 2012 breakthrough:

1. The availability of huge sets of labelled data, or matching translations, that could be used for training purposes
2. Clever modifications in the methods used to automate training, including the "back propagation" mechanism, and variants of rules between different layers in the overall deep neural network
3. New hardware which allowed the training to take place much faster than previously possible: the GPU graphics processing chips which were initially developed to support enchanting animated displays during games, but which turned out to enable huge numbers of parallel calculations (matrix arithmetic).

These practical breakthroughs with deep neural networks were by no means the only NBIC accomplishments in or around 2012. That same year saw landmark publications about the usage of the CRISPR gene-editing technique, including the potential for altering the DNA in human cells. From that time onward, Google searches for "CRISPR" jumped upward[609]. Two of the key pioneers of the field, Emmanuelle Charpentier and Jennifer Doudna, received the Nobel Prize for Chemistry in 2020 in recognition of this work. As the Nobel Prize committee explained[610]:

> Emmanuelle Charpentier and Jennifer Doudna are awarded the Nobel Prize in Chemistry 2020 for discovering one of gene technology's sharpest tools:

> the CRISPR/Cas9 genetic scissors. Researchers can use these to change the DNA of animals, plants and microorganisms with extremely high precision. This technology has revolutionised the molecular life sciences, brought new opportunities for plant breeding, is contributing to innovative cancer therapies and may make the dream of curing inherited diseases come true.

2011 had seen another biological breakthrough – less heralded at the time, but it may come to be appreciated in due course as having fundamental significance. It was the demonstration by a number of researchers from the Mayo Clinic that removal of senescent cells can extend healthspan. Senescent cells are a by-product of aging: these cells stop working properly, yet are unable to be absorbed and recycled by the body's normal damage-repair mechanisms. Instead, they remain in place, leaking hazardous chemicals, and causing further damage in that vicinity of the body. For this reason, they are sometimes nicknamed as "zombie cells". What the Mayo Clinic researchers showed, in this pioneering experiment involving genetically altered mice, was that particular drugs could cause the body to absorb these senescent cells after all. The result: compared to controls, the mice who were treated were stronger, fitter, better looking, and had longer healthspans[611]. In this way, a significant boost was given to senolytics, confirming it as one of the most promising lines of treatment in the anti-aging field.

Senolytics was just one of many subjects discussed at a breakthrough conference in London the previous year, 2010, "The new science of ageing", organised and hosted by the venerable Royal Society[612]. For the first time in such a conference, leading academics from all over the world shared their research into "the scientific challenges and the prospects for a broad-spectrum, preventative medicine for age-related disease". Repercussions from the ideas shared at that conference continue to the present day, as new researchers join this field in ever greater numbers.

Slightly earlier, in 2009, an event took place that could come to be seen as a pivotal moment in the development of the field of artificial emotional intelligence – sometimes also called "affective computing". I refer to the founding of the company Affectiva, which spun out of MIT Media Lab, co-founded by two pioneers of the field, Rana el Kaliouby and Rosalind Picard[613]. El Kaliouby has declared that her personal quest is[614]:

> To make technology emotionally intelligent – and change the way we interact forever.

El Kaliouby looks ahead to a time when all mobile computers have an emotion-processing chip that is at least as central to their operation as the GPS navigation chip is today:

> I think that, ten years down the line, we won't remember what it was like when we couldn't just frown at our device, and our device would say, "Oh, you didn't like that, did you?"

Affectiva has a suite of competitors. It is by no means certain that it will retain its prominence as artificial emotional intelligence moves increasingly into the mainstream. However, the field is gathering pace, and provides another component of NBIC convergence.

In the previous chapter, I spoke of "overhang" – the way in which technological developments can in due course spring ahead of the expectations of their original pioneers, and place many new opportunities (both good and bad) into human hands before there has been adequate time to evaluate these opportunities. In the four following sections, I'll give some examples of potential future overhang in each of the four NBIC quadrants. The methods we should use to evaluate these opportunities – as good, bad, or vital – will be the subject of the *following* chapter, "Transhumanism".

Nanotech

By nanotech I mean increasing understanding of – and the ability to systematically manipulate and enhance – matter at the molecular level.

The semiconductor industry has long measured its progress by the number of nanometres that defines the dimensions of the individual transistors in chipsets. Until around the year 2000, that measurement was still generally expressed in micrometres (µm), for example "0.18µm" or "0.15µm"[615]. But for designs with characteristic length 0.09µm, reached around 2002[616], a switch was made to nanometres. Bearing in mind that there are 1000 nanometres to a micrometre, the expression "90nm" was used instead of "0.09µm". From that time, the architecture moved to smaller dimensions roughly once every two years: 65nm, 45nm, 32nm, 22nm, 14nm, 10nm, 7nm, and, most recent at the time of writing, 5nm. The Taiwanese semiconductor fabricator TSMC is planning commercial production of chips with 3nm architecture in 2022-2023, and with 2nm architecture around 2025[617]. A slide of Intel's roadmap for future designs has included chips with 1.4nm architecture in 2029[618].

This regular shrinkage in size bears testimony to the ongoing validation of Moore's Law – first expressed (though not in exactly the same language) by Gordon Moore in 1965[619]. Initially roughly every single year, but later roughly every two years, double the preceding number of transistors could be assembled into a commercially practical integrated circuit. (The words Moore used in his 1965 article were "cramming" and "squeezing".)

The longevity of Moore's Law has been central to the ongoing impact of the third industrial revolution. For roughly the same cost, devices in each new silicon architecture provide around double the output power, and around double the processing speed. With around five generations each decade, that amounts to at least a 32-fold improvement every decade, and a thousand-fold improvement every twenty years. Over the sixty years from the first data point on Gordon Moore's graph, 1959, to 2019, that means a performance improvement of one thousand times one thousand times one thousand, which is to say, one billion. *Remarkable.*

There's nothing mystical or absolute about Moore's Law. It's not a law of nature on a par with Newton's Laws of Motion or Maxwell's equations of electromagnetism. Reaching ever smaller architectures requires three things to continue to exist:

1. Scientific possibilities that can be investigated
2. The willingness and capability of companies to invest growing numbers of highly skilled resources in research to incrementally improve their engineering grasp of the scientific possibilities
3. The desire of the marketplace to purchase goods which take advantage of improved technology.

An individual silicon atom is about 0.2nm in width. A transistor that is 1.4nm in size therefore is about seven silicon atoms thick. It might appear there's not much scope for further downsizing. Accordingly, it's common to hear predictions that Moore's Law is coming to an end within a few more years. As it happens, for about as long as I have personally been paying attention to Moore's Law – over twenty years – it has been commonly said that semiconductor industry insiders can foresee only ten more years of improvements ahead. That makes for a kind of "Meta Moore's Law".

I wouldn't rule out more than ten additional years of improvements along the same trajectory. Rather than putting extra transistors onto an ever more crowded flat chip, 3D configurations have interesting potential[620].

Other engineers consider using light beams in place of flows of electrons, that is, photonics instead of electronics[621]. And there are plenty of other ideas in play: Jim Keller, head of silicon engineering at Intel in 2020, spoke of there probably being[622] "more than a hundred variables involved in keeping Moore's Law going, each of which provides different benefits and faces its own limits". Whilst the time for each additional round of performance doubling may extend longer than two years, there's still life left in this aspect of the third industrial revolution.

However, that line of performance improvement is increasingly being side-lined. For the fourth industrial revolution, new factors are becoming more important.

The first change is that new types of chip are gaining importance, alongside the CPU (central processing unit) which has been so pivotal over the early decades of personal computers. What sets these new chips apart is their ability to carry out huge numbers of calculations in parallel, rather than everything taking place in sequential computations. I've already mentioned GPUs. That term was first used in the 1990s for a chip in Sony's PlayStation games console. Among other companies, Nvidia produced a series of GPUs with increased performance in the 2000s, still focusing on supporting enhanced visual displays on computers, including laptops. Their use during the training of deep neural networks helped transform AI from 2012 onward. Modifications of the design of GPUs – with some features being removed that were less useful for machine learning – led to the creation of various chips known as TPUs (created by Google), IPUs (created by startup Graphcore), and, as a more general heading, "AI accelerators".

A second new direction in computing chips is the forthcoming vast field of quantum computing. In a way, quantum computing takes parallel computing to an entirely new level. There are certain types of calculation which can be accelerated if hardware is able to operate in what's known as a "superposition" of different configurations. Thus, rather than being definitely "on" (binary '1') or definitely "off" (binary '0') – as in classical computing chips – bits in quantum computing can take combinations of intermediate values. As the calculation proceeds, a single quantum chip explores multiple options simultaneously in different parallel branches. Branches that fail to find answers cancel each other out, leaving only the branch in which an answer is found.

To be clear, only certain types of calculation can be speeded up by using this technique. However, there are sufficiently many uses of quantum computers to give the field a huge potential. Examples include[623]:

- Computational chemistry: Simulations that allow the properties of complex new chemicals to be explored ahead of these compounds actually being created
- Drug discovery: An application of computational chemistry in which the compounds involved have biochemical interactions
- Finding solutions in cases of "unstructured search", when a huge set of candidate answers needs to be searched, but where there are no hints as to whereabouts in that set to start looking, nor any feedback from near misses
- Process optimisation, where there are too many options for classical computers to find solutions in a timely manner
- Forecasting weather – and forecasting climate change.

Moreover, quantum computing could accelerate the training of deep neural networks, and will likely also enable completely new models for machine learning[624].

However, all these applications depend upon various hard engineering problems being solved, so that a larger number of quantum bits (qubits) can remain in an entangled state of superposition for long enough to carry out useful calculations.

In the last few years, the number of qubits in individual quantum computers has moved from single figures (prior to 2000) into double figures, and is expected to reach triple figures in shortly. IBM have presented a roadmap in which their quantum computers will have 127 qubits in 2021, 433 qubits in 2022, and 1,000 in 2023[625]. Many other companies have similar plans – including several in China[626].

One thing that makes the future of quantum computers hard to predict is that many different physical models are being used. It's like the early days of the semiconductor industry, when it wasn't clear whether silicon or germanium would prove to be the best choice for transistors – except that the range of choices for quantum computing chips is much wider[627]. Given the sheer variety of ideas in play, it's unlikely that they will all fail.

Accordingly, the odds are good that quantum computing, of at least one sort, will be changing the world within the next couple of decades.

A third new direction within nanotech involves molecules that not only store and process information, but also change their physical shape and location on account of their computations, and interact with other molecules in the environment. They're not just computers but robots. But given their nanoscale size, the name "molecular machine" is appropriate. Other terms in use include "nanobots", "nanomachines", and, with a nod to their use in manufacturing, "nanofactories".

One type of molecular machine has been operating inside biological cells for billions of years. In what we might call "natural nanotechnology", a marvellous choreography of chemical reactions reliably assembles various different proteins, molecule by molecule, following codes stored in DNA and RNA. These reactions take place via the help of cell organelles known as ribosomes[628].

The idea of "synthetic nanotechnology" is that specially designed nanofactories will be able, in a broadly similar way, to utilise atomically precise engineering to construct numerous kinds of new material products, molecule by molecule. But whereas natural nanotechnology involves processes that evolved by blind evolution, synthetic nanotechnology will involve processes intelligently designed by human scientists. These scientists will take inspiration from biological templates, but they can look forward to reaching results far transcending those of nature.

The revolutionary potential of synthetic nanotechnology was popularised by Eric Drexler in his 1986 book *Engines of Creation: The Coming Era of Nanotechnology*[629]. That book fired the imagination of a surge of readers around the world, and, as it happened, helped to fuel the early growth of the transhumanist movement. Since that time, however, progress with many of the ideas Drexler envisioned has proven disappointingly slow.

It's my judgement that the long period of disappointing progress with molecular machines can soon give way to a period of much swifter accomplishment. We can look forward to increasing use of nanofactories, designed by human ingenuity (aided by AI), that can build a range of products with similar atomic precision. These products could include ultra-efficient solar energy arrays, materials that combine ultra-resilience with extraordinary strength, fabrics that never need to be cleaned, and swarms of nanobots that can roam in the bloodstream to identify and eliminate cancer cells.

One sign of progress with nanomachines was the award of the Nobel Prize for Chemistry in 2016[630]. This prize was jointly received by Fraser Stoddart from Scotland, Bernard Feringa from the Netherlands, and Jean-Pierre Sauvage from France, in recognition of their pioneering work in this field, such as finding ways to convert chemical energy into purposeful mechanical motion.

As the Nobel committee remarked, the nanomachines of 2016 can be seen as being in a roughly similar situation to electrical motors of the 1830s: the basic principles of the manufacture and operation of these machines are just becoming clear. The scientists in the 1830s who demonstrated a variety of spinning cranks and wheels, powered by electricity, could hardly have foreseen the subsequent wide incorporation of improved motors in consumer goods such as food processors, air conditioning fans, and washing machines. Likewise, as nanomachines gain more utility, they can be expected to revolutionise manufacturing, healthcare, and the treatment of waste.

Some critics have argued that synthetic nanomachines are simply too difficult to create. Here are some objections raised by Richard Jones, Professor of Materials Physics at the University of Manchester[631]:

> The first difficulty relates to the question of whether the "machine parts" of molecular nanotechnology (MNT) – the cogs and gears so familiar from MNT illustrations – are actually stable...
>
> The second problem relates to the importance of thermal noise and Brownian motion on the nanoscale at room temperature. The issue is that the mechanical engineering paradigm that underlies MNT depends on close dimensional tolerances. But at the nanoscale, at room temperature, Brownian motion and thermal noise mean that parts are constantly flexing and fluctuating in size, making the effective "thermal tolerance" much worse than the mechanical tolerances that we rely on in macroscopic engineering.

These arguments remind me of the many objections that used to be raised against the viability of neural networks. As mentioned earlier, more than fifty years passed between the original vision of neural networks, and their practical usage in commercial settings. The three people sometimes called the "godfathers of deep learning" – Yoshua Bengio, Geoffrey Hinton, and Yann LeCun – endured decades of hostility and criticism before finally attaining wide interest for their work in the 2010s. Hinton recalls a rejection letter he received on submitting an article to the Association for the Advancement of Artificial Intelligence (AAAI)[632]:

> The last time I submitted a paper to AAAI, it got the worst review I've ever got, and it was mean. It said, Hinton's been working on this idea for seven years and nobody's interested, it's time to move on.

The arguments raised against nanomachines by Richard Jones and others are by no means showstoppers. Instead, they should be seen as lists of engineering problems that still need to be solved – problems which will probably require solutions that differ from those initially in the minds of the field's pioneers. Indeed, later on in his account of nanomachines, Jones acknowledges that possibility:

> Will there be progress towards some, at least, of the more radical goals of nanotechnology, by routes quite different from those foreseen by the proponents of molecular nanotechnology?
>
> I think the answer to this is quite possibly yes; developments in synthetic biology (understood in its broadest sense) and in making systems in which quantum computing is possible may well have far reaching consequences…
>
> What are beginning to take shape are new paradigms for radical nanotechnologies; in place of a mechanical paradigm, inspired by macroscopic engineering, we are seeing the development of biological paradigms and quantum paradigms, which acknowledge the different physics that dominates the nanoscale world and makes the best of the opportunities this offers.

Jones even ends with a note of partial applause for Eric Drexler:

> Perhaps we should applaud Drexler for alerting us to the exciting general possibilities of nanotechnology, while recognising that the trajectories of new technologies rarely run smoothly along the paths foreseen by their pioneers.

I also point to the recent comprehensive survey by Oxford Professor Sonia Contera, *Nano Comes to Life: How Nanotechnology Is Transforming Medicine and the Future of Biology*[633].

What will determine the speed of breakthroughs in this field is the same three factors as apply in other areas of potential exponential progress:

1. Scientific possibilities that can be investigated

2. The willingness and capability of companies to invest growing numbers of highly skilled resources in research to incrementally improve their engineering grasp of the scientific possibilities
3. The desire of the marketplace to purchase goods which take advantage of improved technology.

The main obstacle in the case of nanomachines has been the second one. That's often the case with platform technologies that will likely require significant long-term investment before paybacks become possible. In such cases, it's the attitude of governments that can make all the difference, as they allocate public funds into different categories of research. In turn, these public investments are strongly influenced by the general opinion in the country as to the desirability of various outcomes. We'll come back to this topic in later chapters.

The two areas of nanotech that will lead to the largest overhangs – quantum computing and nanomachines – still need considerable work before they start to reach their potential. As you will realise, there's likely a positive feedback loop between these two areas: improvements in quantum computing are likely to accelerate progress with nanomachines, and vice versa.

Even before that improvement takes place, however, it's worth briefly noting other aspects to the nanotech quadrant of NBIC:

- Superconductors that can operate at room temperatures[634]
- Progress with finer-scaled 3D printing – and the 4D printing variant, in which the items created are designed to change their layout over time, in response to external signals
- Wider use of so-called nanomaterials, including various nanowires, nanoshells, and nanoparticles; one example is graphene, for which Andre Geim and Konstantin Novoselov, two Russian-born physicists working at the University of Manchester in England, won the 2010 Nobel Prize in Physics, in recognition of their "groundbreaking experiments"[635]
- Low-powered sensors, sometimes called nanosensors, that operate on the nanoscale[636]
- DNA-based methods of data storage that enable orders of magnitude increases in the density of information handled[637]

- Early successes with the field known as nanosurgery, documented in Sonia Contera's book; this includes "DNA origami"[638].

Mention of nanosurgery and DNA-based data storage takes us from the 'N' quadrant of NBIC to the 'B' quadrant.

Biotech

By biotech I mean increasing understanding of – and the ability to systematically manipulate and enhance – the biological building blocks of life.

The structure of DNA – the carrier of genes (genetic information) – has been known since 1953. Francis Crick and James Watson deduced that this enormous molecule consists of two long polymer chains, helically wrapped around each other. The two chains are connected by bonds linking four possible nucleobases: adenine ('A') always bonds with thymine ('T') on the other strand, and likewise for guanine ('G') and cytosine ('C').

How did various different sequences of As, Ts, Gs and Cs give rise to all the proteins which cells assemble? That so-called "genetic code" remained obscure for a number of additional years.

In 1961, a team led by Marshall Nirenberg at the National Institutes of Health demonstrated that a sequence of three Ts in DNA would select the amino acid phenylalanine to be added to the protein currently under construction[639]. They next showed that a sequence of three As would select lysine, and three Cs would select proline. By 1968 the code was fully understood, with each of the 64 triplet combinations of the four letters being mapped to one of the 20 amino acids (with some duplications), or, in three cases (TAG, TAA, and TGA) to an instruction to terminate the manufacture of the current protein. That same year, Nirenberg won a share of the Nobel Prize in Physiology or Medicine[640].

The profound importance of Nirenberg's work had already been recognised back in 1961. In December that year, the New York Times announced that, thanks to these ongoing breakthroughs[641],

> The science of biology has reached a new frontier… a revolution far greater in its potential significance than the atomic or hydrogen bomb.

Not content with comparing these breakthroughs to the vast explosive power of nuclear weapons, the article continued with other grand metaphors:

- The cracking of the biological code by Nirenberg and his colleagues, in 1961, would prove to be more significant in the long run than Yuri Gagarin's Sputnik orbital flight around the earth that same year
- It would provide the same kind of added impetus for biology as Newton's work had provided for physics in the seventeenth century.

Nirenberg himself was well aware of the radical applications that might follow from mastery of the genetic code. A draft of his Nobel Prize speech contained these thoughts:

> Man eventually will ... influence his own biological evolution. One can predict that a new area of research will emerge during the next twenty-five years, that of molecular evolution, in which the effects of synthetic genes upon the economy of the cell will be explored in a systematic fashion.

As with many of the predictions reviewed in this book, the vision seems to me to be largely correct, but the timescales for the realisation of that vision differed from what was initially suggested. It turned out that several large steps are required, before humanity gains the ability to change the behaviour of cells with newly synthesised genes (new sequences of nucleobases), and thereby take charge of our future biological evolution:

1. Methods needed to be developed to identify, quickly and reliably, the sequences of nucleobases on given strands of DNA
2. An understanding was needed of *epigenetics* – the circumstances in which various genes in DNA are disabled or enabled, depending on which cell in the body the DNA finds itself
3. An understanding was needed of how biological traits, far from being determined by single genes, typically arise from a combination of different genes *and* a combination of non-genetic factors
4. Methods needed to be developed to create genes with desired properties, and to insert them into cells in appropriate locations
5. Finally, an understanding was needed of when genetic synthesis, of the type just mentioned, would be the most effective way to obtain a desired biological characteristic – and when other biological interventions would be a better choice to obtain the same effect.

Let's consider progress with the first of these steps. The well-known writer on evolution, Richard Dawkins, drew attention in an essay in 2002 to what he called "The Son of Moore's Law"[642].

As I described earlier in this chapter, Gordon Moore had noticed a trend in which the number of semiconductors on a chip doubled on a regular basis – roughly once a year, from 1959 to 1975, and roughly once every two years, from 1975 onward. Richard Dawkins noticed something similar, regarding the number of nucleotide base-pairs that could be identified ("sequenced") for a given cost. Moore's original 1965 article had a graph with five data points, illustrating the trend; Dawkins' 2002 article had a graph with four data points: a cost of around £1,000 per base-pair in 1965 declined to about £10 per base-pair in 1975, £1 in 1995, and £0.1 in 2000. Once these figures are adjusted for inflation and plotted on a graph with a vertical log axis, the result is a pleasing straight line – at least as convincing as the one in Moore's original article. The conclusion: the time it takes to double the number of base-pairs that can be identified for the same cost – equivalently, the time for the cost to half, to sequence an entire human genome – works out at twenty-seven months. That's just slightly slower than the two-year doubling time for the later versions of Moore's Law.

Just as Moore had extrapolated forward, at the end of his 1965 article, Dawkins imagined that the trend he had noted (dubbing it "The Son of Moore's Law") would continue forward into the future. How long would it take before an entire human genome could be sequenced for £100? Dawkins gave the answer: 2050. The rest of his essay consisted of some implications of full genetic sequences being available for such a low cost.

Why, then, is the terminology "Son of Moore's Law" – or perhaps "Dawkins' Law" – not better known? Two reasons:

1. Scientists are approaching the £100 target *much more quickly* than simple extrapolation had predicted
2. Scientists also realised that many other parts of the genetic jigsaw puzzle would need to be solved – the items I listed as points 2. through 5. above – before genetic analysis would be widely useful.

The unexpected acceleration in cost-reduction can be seen from graphs published on the US government's website for the National Human Genome Research Institute[643]. That website points out

> The sudden and profound out-pacing of Moore's Law beginning in January 2008. The latter represents the time when the sequencing centres transitioned from Sanger-based (dideoxy chain termination sequencing) to 'second generation' (or 'next-generation') DNA sequencing technologies.

A cost of $95.3 million to sequence an entire human genome in September 2001 had reduced to $7.1 million by October 2006, equivalent to a halving of the cost every 16 months – somewhat faster than Richard Dawkins had predicted. But step forward another three years to October 2009, and the cost had plummeted to $70.3 *thousand* – equivalent to halving the cost every five and a half months. That dizzying progress slowed down slightly in subsequent years, but not by much. By May 2019, the cost was comfortably less than one thousand dollars: $606.

Key to this speed-up was something similar to the transformation of AI covered earlier in this chapter: the ability to conduct huge numbers of operations in parallel. Just as GPUs enabled much faster training of deep neural networks, "next generation" sequencing machines could analyse many parts of a strand of DNA at the same time. Here's a description from Nick McCooke, who led the team at the startup Solexa that developed these new machines[644]:

> The initial idea came from a couple of guys at Cambridge University. The concept of next-generation sequencing is basically to massively parallelize the sequencing process. [Existing sequencers were] processing 96 strands of DNA in parallel – highly accurately, actually, but only 96 lanes. Our first instrument had something like 40 million interrogation sites on the array. We realized it could impact speed and cost by several orders of magnitude.

Solexa struggled for five years to convert that basic idea into a practical reality. McCooke talks candidly about "a complete dead end" and "lots of ups and downs". But by 2005 the proof of principle was complete. Solexa was acquired shortly afterward by the US company Illumina. Illumina remains to this day one of the world leaders in genetic sequencing techniques, in what is a fast-moving market with companies exploring a range of potential breakthrough ideas[645]. These alternative next generation sequence methods have names such as massively parallel signature sequencing, polony sequencing, 454 sequencing, ion torrent technology, SOLiD DNA sequencing technology, and DNA nanoball sequencing. I am reminded of the wide range of ideas that the semiconductor industry keeps pursuing as potential ways to keep improving the performance of chipsets.

The remarkable speed up in the performance of genetic sequencing depended not only on the availability of new scientific ideas to be investigated, but also – perhaps more crucially – on the growing commercial interest in this whole field. The potential was becoming clear for faster genetic sequencing to deliver improvements in plant agriculture, animal husbandry, ecosystem monitoring, food safety, personalised medicine, tracking the development of cancers, the treatment of so-called "rare" genetic diseases, and so on. These improvements could be considered no longer as some far-off pipedream, but as potential near-term successes.

The kind of speedup of techniques for genetic sequencing has been mirrored, a few years later, by a speedup in techniques for genetic synthesis. That is, prowess in *reading* DNA has been followed by prowess in *writing* DNA – either by editing existing DNA, using mechanisms such as CRISPR, or by creating brand new chromosome sections.

Accordingly, something that happened during the second industrial revolution – a dramatic surge in the capabilities of *synthetic chemistry* – will be mirrored as the fourth industrial revolution progresses: a dramatic surge in the capabilities of *synthetic biology*. What was seen during the so-called "green revolution" in agriculture, thanks to innovations by Norman Borlaug and others, may be dwarfed by new sets of enhancements enabled by greater precision in synthetic biology:

- Food with greater nutritional value
- Food that uses less land, less water, and less pesticide
- Food that is more robust against extremes in climate
- Food without adverse health implications.

As a particularly important example, various sorts of meat may be grown without needing to breed and slaughter live mammals, birds, or fish. Present-day solutions known as "cultured meat" or "clean meat" fall short of "traditional meat" in terms of taste and cost, but these differences are fast being eroded. Huge areas of land will no longer be tied up growing plants to feed animals that are destined to be slaughtered to provide meat for human consumption.

A different kind of genetic manipulation involves stem cells – cells that can replenish the body's stock of blood cells, muscle cells, nerve cells, gut cells, skin cells, and so on. As the body ages, many of its ailments arise from declining performance of the remaining population of stem cells. However, infusion of new stem cells has the potential to address and even reverse these ailments. Japanese researcher Shinya Yamanaka received the 2012 Nobel Prize in Physiology or Medicine for work he had done in 2006 demonstrating that old cells, taken from the skin, can be genetically reprogrammed back into the state of a youthful stem cell – one, indeed, that can give rise to numerous different types of cell[646].

Stem cell therapies share an important attribute with the senolytic therapies mentioned earlier in this chapter: both address aspects of the biological aging that underpins a growing severity of diseases of aging. Ailments such as cancer, heart disease, stroke, dementia, and diabetes, as well as many infectious diseases, become more prevalent – and more deadly – as people's bodies grow old and lose their former powers of self-repair. An idea that is likely to become increasingly mainstream, as the biotech revolution continues, is that the most effective way to tackle these diseases is to undo the characteristics of bodily aging (also known sometimes as the "hallmarks of aging"[647]). These characteristics include[648]:

1. An accumulation of senescent cells – which can be treated by senolytics
2. Loss of performance of the population of stem cells – which can be treated by various stem cell therapies
3. Malfunctions of the immune system
4. Malfunctions of the microbiome, that is, the population of microorganisms that exist in our gut, on our skin, and elsewhere in our bodies
5. Proteins that are misfolded or which aggregate together with crosslinks that hinder their usual functionality
6. Damage to the mitochondria "power houses" inside cells
7. Damage to the DNA in the cell nucleus
8. Damage to the set of epigenetic markers that determine which parts of the DNA in a cell are operational, and which are quiescent
9. The inability of cells to divide further, due to shortening of the "telomere" tips at the end of chromosomes
10. Growing confusion in the sets of signals exchanged between different subsystems of the body.

It's still early days with senolytics and with stem cell therapies. Potentially adverse side-effects of various treatment mechanisms need to become better understood. Further research will clarify how to safely apply these therapies with beneficial consequences for overall health.

As for the other types of biological damage mentioned, there are a growing number of potential interventions that are being researched. Until around 2010, the whole idea of treating chronic diseases by reversing or repairing the various kinds of biological damage was generally viewed as impractical or even deluded. However, as more researchers are demonstrating the viability of some of their ideas in proofs of concept, attitudes are changing. For that reason, I do see it as plausible that the extension of healthy human longevity, as reviewed in the previous chapter, can become significant again, rather than slowing down (as has happened recently).

It's possible, indeed, that by around 2040, low-cost suites of therapies will have become widely available that enable people to remain in a biologically youthful state for as long as they wish. As a side-effect of these therapies, the underlying causes of diseases such as cancer and dementia will be kept under control. That's a development I call "the abolition of aging"[649].

Before such therapies are widely available for human usage, it's likely that people will be trialling similar therapies on some of their favourite pets, whose (normal) lifespans are typically considerably less than their own. Visible success with extending the healthspan of beloved cats and dogs will help transform the mindset of the public concerning the desirability of similar treatments in humans.

A comprehensive solution to the chronic diseases of aging may strike some readers as being science fiction. But bear in mind the impact that infectious diseases used to have on populations around the world. The leading causes of death in 1900 were influenza, pneumonia, tuberculosis, and gastrointestinal infections[650]. As the germ theory of disease grew in maturity, systematic methods for addressing and preventing infectious diseases became more common: better hygiene (including sterilisation), vaccinations, antibiotics, and anti-viral treatments. Accordingly, the rates of deaths from infectious diseases shrunk dramatically over the course of the twentieth century. That was after the germ theory of diseases had faced considerable opposition in earlier decades, from people who preferred alternative theories of disease and health, including miasmas (bad air), the need for blood-letting, the importance of a balance of various elements of life, and the centrality of religious faith.

What can be called the aging theory of disease has faced similar opposition in recent decades. Nevertheless, the tide is turning: greater numbers of researchers are studying potential hallmarks of aging and are making encouraging progress with interventions against these hallmarks. These researchers are being backed by major initiatives inside some of the world's largest companies, and also by a steadily increasing flow of private investment[651]. The projects benefiting from these investments are taking advantage of accelerating progress in all four of the NBIC quadrants: the nanotech and biotech quadrants that I've just described, and the infotech and cognotech quadrants to which I turn next.

Infotech

By infotech I mean increasing understanding of – and the ability to systematically manipulate and enhance – the sets of information that exist at all levels of nature and human life.

Infotech is not just about *storing* information, *communicating* information, and *performing computations* using that information. More than that, the infotech of the fourth industrial revolution involves *drawing conclusions* from that information: observing patterns and finding meaning.

It used to be widely held that the ability to find meaning in data was unique to humans. Whereas machines might calculate, they had no intuition. They might follow instructions, but they could not create anything new. A statement by the Spanish artist Pablo Picasso has often been quoted approvingly[652]:

> Computers are useless. They can only give you answers.

That was broadly true of the computers that existed when Picasso first expressed that sentiment, back in 1964. Since then, however, computers have acquired broader capabilities. A portrait generated by a piece of artificial intelligence software sold at auction at Christies in December 2018 for $432,500 – far exceeding the figure of $10,000 that the auctioneers had expected it to fetch[653]. Admittedly, that picture is not in the same cost league as a portrait by Picasso; moreover, the outputs of that AI need to be selected by human overseers, so humans remain in this creative loop for the time being. Nevertheless, the picture is a pointer to what more powerful AIs might produce in the near future. Other AIs are producing music that matches the creativity of human composers in at least some limited genres – elevator music and the audio backing tracks of YouTube videos[654]. OpenAI Jukebox shows what is becoming increasingly possible, with its creation of "An album in the style of The Beatles"[655]. A particularly impressive demonstration of creativity from AI is the game playing style of the AlphaZero software from Google's DeepMind subsidiary. Demis Hassibis, the founder of DeepMind, summarises feedback from world-class human players who have analysed the performance of AlphaZero while playing chess[656]:

> It doesn't play like a human, and it doesn't play like a program. It plays in a third, almost alien, way… It's like chess from another dimension.

A sceptic might respond that all this software is doing is mimicking what it has already observed humans doing. That comment might have been partially true for earlier versions of the DeepMind software, which indeed did benefit from having huge numbers of games played by human experts fed into its training system. However, the 'Zero' in the name "AlphaZero" is a reminder that *zero* human input was provided to this version of the software. Instead, the software attained such a high level of skill simply by playing itself, over and over again, and observing which methods of play were the most effective.

This *description* of how AlphaZero improved is simple, but the *reality* of the process was much more complicated, at two levels:

1. The software to "observe which methods of play were the most effective", namely an implementation of "Deep Reinforcement Learning", embodies some very clever algorithms
2. The actual output of the learning process is, in effect, a vast matrix of billions of different numbers, which presently defies attempts to analyse it into concepts that can be easily explained.

We can ask the question: what made the software decide to select a particular move at a given point in a game? But we are likely to be dissatisfied by the answer. The selection arose from an interplay of these billions of different numbers. What do these numbers mean? *They're just numbers.*

It's like an expert human player explaining their decision in a game of skill. On some occasions, they can list a number of tactical and strategic principles. But on other occasions, they are at a loss to articulate why they preferred one more to another. They might say, "It just felt right". These players have developed powerful intuitions about different types of positions in their game – intuitions which can operate under the level of conscious introspection. It's now the same with software like AlphaZero: it selects moves for reasons which cannot always be reduced to tactical or strategic principles. For this reason, we can speak of "Artificial Intuition" as being a powerful component of modern Artificial Intelligence[657].

A list of the interesting things being enabled by AI could well be the longest list in this book – with the examples just mentioned, of game-playing, music-composing, and portrait-drawing, being just the tip of a very large iceberg. In the same way, the number of new books that are being published about AI probably exceeds that of books about any other future-related topic. The potential applications of AI range across many fields where participants are looking for a decisive competitive advantage:

- Algorithmic stock-trading
- Games that feature novel AI-powered characters
- Customer support, with chatbots handling more complicated queries
- Modifications to the user interface of software applications, to tailor them more precisely to the needs of individual users
- Faster healthcare research and development
- New creative directions in music, visual art, poetry, and fashion
- Better engineering designs
- Optimisation of resource usage
- Detecting malware and cyberhacking
- Autonomous weaponry – both offensive and defensive.

Understandably, much that is being written about AI raises questions about shortcomings in today's state-of-the-art solutions:

- Unintended biases built into algorithms, or present in the data used to train these algorithms
- Ways in which algorithms can be misled, by specially concocted "adversarial" input
- The potential for AI to magnify social inequalities, by increasing the profits of the companies that use the best AI solutions, and driving their less successful competitors out of business
- The potential for AI to displace many employees from the workforce, or to leave employees with jobs that require less skill (such as Uber drivers) and therefore provide lower income

- Risks from inadvertent errors that are contained in algorithms, and which are noticed only after some catastrophic malfunction – this includes malfunctions in autonomous weapons systems, as dramatized in the film *Dr. Strangelove*
- The potential for AI to empower people to inflict harm on society – people such as cybercriminals, trolls, international adversaries, and religious fundamentalists eagerly anticipating apocalypse.

The potential advantages are real, as are the shortcomings listed. To that extent, it's appropriate that so many books are being written about AI.

Nevertheless, it's my observation that many of these books suffer from either of two drawbacks. In combination, these drawbacks seriously distract public attention from the main issues and opportunities in the infotech quadrant over the next couple of decades.

The first drawback is an over-emphasis on the issues and opportunities of AI as it already exists, or as it might evolve in straightforward extensions of existing capabilities. This analysis fails to give sufficient attention to the many ways in which AI could evolve in more disruptive ways over the next 5-10 years. Accordingly, the risk is of society being blindsided by emerging new issues and opportunities that will be, in many ways, even larger than the ones that are often featured in today's public discussions about AI.

The second drawback is that, when writers do consider the possibility of more powerful future variants of AI, their discussion becomes preoccupied by just one such variant, namely AGI (artificial general intelligence), which is AI that matches or exceeds human intellectual abilities in every field of thought. AGI differs from today's AI in that the latter outperforms humans in numerous specific areas, but is unable to function properly when the domain changes. For example, chatbots can conduct reasonably intelligent conversations if the topic is narrowly constrained, but are horribly inept when the conversation moves outside these boundaries. This difference can be expressed by saying that AIs presently lack *general knowledge*. Equivalently, AIs presently lack *common sense*. Today's AIs therefore need assistance from human overseers. However, once the status of AGI is reached, the resulting software will be capable of wide self-improvement *without any further assistance by humans*.

I have no objection to discussing AGI. Indeed, I'll return to that topic at some length in the final chapter of this book, "Singularity". I'll argue in that chapter that most of what is said about AGI by mainstream commentators – and, indeed, by some professors of AI – is misleading. I see the probability of AGI being created by mid-century as around 50% – a figure much higher than is often suggested. Absolutely, AGI deserves lots of our attention, well before it is brought into existence.

But ahead of the creation of AGI, there are likely to be many other disruptions within AI – disruptions that form part of the unfolding fourth industrial revolution. In contrast, AGI will be so significant that it can be described as providing the core of a *fifth* industrial revolution.

However, we're not going to reach or manage that outcome – the creation of AGI – unless we are successful in managing the disruptions of the fourth industrial revolution. Let me therefore list fifteen ways in which AI could change over the next 5-10 years. These are ways which would still leave AI short of AGI, but which could open up considerable AI overhang.

1. *Synthetic data sets*: So far, the data sets which are used to train Deep Learning systems have generally been assembled from real-world data. Progress has been restricted by the effort required to label items in the training sets – for example, with human volunteers giving their assessments of the content of each picture in the set. However, new training sets can be created synthetically, with a vast diversity of pictures being created *and labelled* by one AI (which knows what it has put in each picture, so the labelling is trivially easy) before being passed to another AI to strengthen its skills in recognition.
2. *Cleaned data sets*: Existing training sets have been limited by quality as well as by quantity. A solution for quantity has just been described: synthetic data sets. The quality problem is where a proportion of some real-world data may have been mislabelled, as a result of limitations in how that data was collected and categorised. However, once again, a division of AI responsibility can come to the rescue. A specialist AI can be tasked with checking the labels on the data set, using a variety of clues. Once the data has been cleaned up in this way – with portions that remain uncertain having been removed – it can be passed to the main AI to train it more effectively.
3. *Transfer learning*: Systems that have been trained with one task in mind can sometimes be repurposed, relatively quickly, to handle another task as well. For this new task, only small amounts of training data

are required, since learning transfers over from the previous task. This is similar to how evolution creates brains in a state ready to learn new tasks with limited numbers of input examples. For real breakthroughs with transfer learning, it is likely that changes will be needed in how the initial training is done. As with many of the items on this list, the speed of progress cannot be predicted in advance.

4. *Self-learning of natural language*: Systems that explore vast quantities of text have gained more prominence due to the surprising results from the GPT-3 text prediction tool released by OpenAI in May 2020[658]. The training of GPT-3 involved scanning 45 terabytes of text – equivalent to more than a hundred million average-length books – and the consequent fine-tuning of a vast matrix of 175 billion numbers ("parameters"). When presented with some new text, GPT-3 generates sentences of text in response, based on its internal model of what flows of text tend to look like. It lacks any genuine understanding, but parts of the text generated do resemble what an intelligent human might have typed in response to the prompt. It even generates some passable humour[659]. Variations of these methods – perhaps with names of the form "GPT-n", but possibly using some new mechanisms – may increase the degree to which the output text appears to possess "common sense" knowledge.
5. *Generative Adversarial Networks*: Another area of AI where progress has taken observers by surprise is the output of GANs (Generative Adversarial Networks). These involve an arms race between one deep network that aims to create new examples conforming to a general pattern, and another deep network that aims to identify which examples have been generated, and which belong to the original data set. Like an arms race between coin counterfeiters and authorities wishing to spot counterfeits in circulation, the competition between the two networks can produce results that increasingly look indistinguishable from genuine examples. The first applications of GANs included the generation of realistic photographs from given specifications, showing what someone's face would look like at a different age, altering the clothing in a photograph, predicting subsequent frames in a video, and improving the resolution of blurry images or videos[660]. Wider uses of GANs

have been explored subsequently, in fields such as chemistry and drug discovery[661].

6. *Evolutionary algorithms*: The arms race aspect of GANs is an example of the wider possibilities in which AIs could be improved by copying methods from biological evolution. An idea that has been explored since the 1950s is to include "genetic algorithms", in which decisions are based on the combinations of small "genes". Much as in biological evolution, sets of genes that result in greater algorithmic fitness are preferentially used as the basis for the next generation of algorithms, obtained from previous ones by a mixture of random mutation and recombination. Until now, genetic algorithms have had limited success. That's a bit like the situation with neural networks until around 2012. It's an open question as to what kinds of changes in genetic algorithms might result in similar kinds of dramatic breakthrough as for neural networks.
7. *Learning from neuroscience*: Do neurons in the brain actually operate in ways similar to neurons in deep neural networks? Can the differences in operating modes be ignored? Or might a deeper appreciation of what actually happens in brains lead to new directions in AI? Significant fractions of the researchers in large AI companies have done research, not just in the computer science departments of universities, but in their neuroscience departments. One example is Demis Hassabis, founder of DeepMind, who studied neuroscience at Harvard, MIT, and the Gatsby Computational Neuroscience Unit of UCL – where Shane Legg, another DeepMind co-founder, also studied[662]. On their website, DeepMind declare that "better understanding biological brains could play a vital role in building intelligent machines"[663]. Consider also Jeff Hawkins, inventor of the Palm Pilot, who moved on from his ground-breaking career in the mobile computing and smartphone industry to lead teams carrying out brain research at his new company Numenta; Hawkins has recently explained his theories for significantly improving AI in his thought-provoking book *A Thousand Brains*[664].
8. *Neuromorphic computing*: It's not only the software systems of AI that could be improved by studying what happens in human brains. In their use of energy, brains are much more efficient than their silicon equivalents. A typical laptop computer consumes energy at the rate

of around 100W, whereas a human brain operates at around 10W[665]. Companies such as IBM have dedicated units looking at what they call "neuromorphic computing", to see if novel hardware structures inspired by the biology of brains could enable leaps forward in AI capability[666].

9. *Quantum computing*: As already mentioned in the section on nanotech, the novel capabilities of quantum computers could enable new sorts of AI algorithms, and could radically speed up existing algorithms that are presently too slow to be useful. For example, quantum computers can accelerate the machine-learning task of "feature matching"[667], as well as "dimensionality reduction algorithms" as used in non-supervised learning[668]. Given that quantum computing is such a new field, it's likely that further applications for AI will come to mind as the field matures.

10. *Affective computing*: What will happen to AI systems as they gain a richer understanding of human emotion? Research in affective computing, already mentioned earlier with the example of the company Affectiva, looks for ways to make software notice and understand human expressions of emotion, to add apparent emotion into interactions with humans, and to influence the emotional states of humans. Such software possesses emotional intelligence, even though it need have no intrinsic emotional feelings of its own. This will surely alter the dynamics of interactions between humans and computers – though it remains to be seen whether these changes will truly benefit humans, or instead manipulate us into actions different from our actual best interests.

11. *Sentient computing*: A different approach to computers with emotional intelligence is to try to understand which aspects of biology give rise to inner sensations – sentience – and then to duplicate these relationships in computer hardware. Sentience is a subject that is more elusive and controversial than intelligence, and it is unclear whether any real progress with sentient computing can be expected any time soon. Nevertheless, a growing number of researchers are interested in this subject[669], and we should keep an open mind[670].

12. *Algorithms that understand not just correlation but causation*: Much of machine learning is about spotting patterns: data with such-and-such a characteristic is usually correlated with such-and-such an output.

However, humans have a strong intuition that there is a difference between correlation – when two events, A and B, are associated with each other – and causation – when event A is understood to be the cause of event B. In a case of causation, if we want B to happen, we can arrange for A to happen; and if we want to reduce the chance of B happening, we can stop A from happening. Thus, stopping smoking is recommended as a way to decrease the chance of catching lung cancer. However, the correlation in a city between rising ice cream sales and greater deaths from drowning accidents provides no reason to reduce ice cream sales as an attempt to reduce the number of drowning accidents; instead, both these events likely have a common cause: the weather being hotter. The computer scientist Judea Pearl argues that software that can reliably detect causation will embody a significant step forward in intelligence[671]. Breakthroughs here may come by applying methods from the field known as "Probabilistic Programming"[672] which has recently been generating considerable interest[673].

13. *Decentralised network intelligence*: The human brain can be considered as a network of modular components with a division of responsibilities. Various parts of the brain are specialised in recognising faces, in recognising music, in preventing the body from falling over, in consolidating memories, and so on. It's the same with organisations: they draw their capabilities from relationships between the different people in the organisation who have different skills and responsibilities. AI systems often embody similar modularity: decisions are taken as the outcome of multiple sub-units performing individual calculations whose results are then integrated. One approach to building better AI is to take that idea further: allow vast numbers of different AI modules to discover each other and interact with each other in a decentralised manner, without any predetermined hierarchy. Higher levels of intelligence might emerge from this kind of relationship. That's the driving thought behind, for example, the SingularityNET "AI marketplace"[674].

14. *Provably safe AI*: Most AI development regards safety as a secondary consideration. Yes, software might have bugs, but these bugs can be found and removed later, once they prove troublesome. Yes, software might behave unexpectedly when placed into a new

environment – for example, one in which other novel software algorithms have been placed. But, again, these interactions can be reconfigured later, if the need arises. At least, that's the dominant practice behind much of the industry. AI developers might shy away from the infamous mantra from the early days of Facebook, "Move fast and break things"[675], but they seem to be guided by that slogan in practice. However, a minority movement puts the issue of safety at the heart of its research. It's possible that the new designs for AI that arise from this different focus will, as well as being safer, attain new capabilities[676].

15. *Combination approaches*: To the fourteen items already on this list, we should add two more that are straightforward: improvements with classical-style AI expert systems, and improvements with deep neural networks. That takes the count to sixteen. Next consider combinations of at least two of these sixteen items: that makes a total of 120 approaches to consider. Adding ideas from a third item into the mix raises the number yet higher (over five thousand). OK, many of these combinations could provide little additional value, but in other cases, who knows in advance what disruptive new insights might arise?

In summary, there are many potential avenues whereby AI could be significantly advanced. The *supply side* of innovation in AI is extensive. Ideas abound. At the same time, the *demand side* is powerful too, given:

- The commercial benefits for the companies who own or utilise these breakthroughs in their lines of business
- The political benefits for the countries who can utilise these breakthroughs in defensive or offensive weapons systems – including cyberweapons and tools for psychological manipulation.

I cannot predict with any confidence *which* of the many lines of research will prove most significant. That would be like trying to predict, in 1970, which types of app would be the most widely used on personal computers in the year 2000. Again, it would be like trying to predict in 1900 the layouts of cities in 1970, ahead of the creation of interstate highways, airports, suburbs, and out-of-town shopping malls. What I *do* predict, however, is:

- That at least some major breakthroughs in AI capability will occur, in as little as ten years

- That these breakthroughs will take many casual observers by surprise – in terms of the new functionality demonstrated, and the impact on people's daily lives
- That the general pace of improvements in AI will be faster than the pace of technological change in earlier industrial revolutions: that's because of improved education, improved mobility, improved networking, and improved flows of capital these days.

Cognotech

By cognotech I mean increasing understanding of – and the ability to systematically manipulate and enhance – the components of human minds.

Just as one key goal of biotech is to radically improve physical health – not only undoing the damage of biological aging, but allowing people to become "better than well" – a key goal of cognotech is to radically improve mental health. This will not only undo the damage of mental rigidity or forgetfulness, but also allow people to have mental experiences far exceeding in quality those that are typical of most human life up to the present time.

Seeking to understand and change minds is one of the very oldest traits of the human species. It's the primary focus of the field of psychology. Much of religion has the same purpose; likewise for education, advertising, and marketing. Numerous practices have been recommended in various ways for their ability to provide insight and control over the mind: meditation, yoga, prayer, confessionals, counselling, music, dance, immersion in nature, immersion in art, hypnotism, and imbibing various "magical" mind-altering substances, such as hallucinogens.

Where cognotech goes beyond these traditional methods is as follows:

1. A more systematic understanding of what's actually happening inside people's brains
2. Scientific experiments to find out which practices tend to work, and in which circumstances
3. Biomonitoring tools that can provide reliable feedback in real time as to the state of the brain
4. Technologies that go beyond monitoring to actually alter the state of the brain.

Here are some examples of cogno-technologies that are presently at an early stage, but which could gain more capability in the years ahead:

- Virtual reality headsets, along with enveloping clothing, which provide ongoing vivid experiences that seem to the perceiver to be "at least as real" as ordinary sensations
- Selected psychedelics, as are being investigated by the Centre for Psychedelics Research at Imperial College, and by the Multidisciplinary Association for Psychedelic Studies (MAPS)
- Nootropics: psychoactive substances that are intended to boost concentration, creativity, memory, or vitality
- So-called "smart helmets" that deliver tDCS (transcranial direct current stimulation), or other electromagnetic stimulation
- Guided lucid dreaming, guided hypnotism, and guided meditation – where the guidance takes account of biomonitoring measurements
- Personalised "intelligent assistants" which can coach people regarding actions likely to affect their mental health or their personal relationships
- Improved brain-computer interfaces, which can infer user intention without the user needing to type it, write it, or speak it
- Synthetic extensions of the nervous system, as being explored in the Neuralink company founded by Elon Musk, and by the Kernel company founded by Bryan Johnson
- The possible addition of new brain cells, by methods explored by Jean Hebert of the Albert Einstein College of Medicine[677].

The power of these technological interventions will likely increase if researchers and practitioners are also aware of ongoing advances in theories of how the mind operates. These theoretical insights include:

- An understanding, developed by, for example, the Search Inside Yourself Leadership Institute, of how and when various mindfulness practices work
- The ideas behind Cognitive Behavioural Therapy – psychological interventions that can be delivered via face-to-face interactions, or (increasingly) via online sessions and dedicated mobile applications

- An appreciation of the harmful effects of social media, and how to counter these effects
- Growing insights regarding the evolutionary background of our cognitive biases and "wilful irrationality", and about how to rise above these self-sabotaging traits
- Awareness of which methods of critical thinking work best, to inoculate us all against our minds being hijacked by ideas that are enticing but false.

As with all the technologies discussed in this chapter, their rate of improvement will be influenced by the importance that society attaches to the benefits which these technologies are expected to deliver.

On that point, there has recently been a large rise in public awareness of the significance of mental health. It is being increasingly acknowledged that far too many people are experiencing a debilitating overload of stress, depression, obsessive ideas, mood swings, or other mental disorders – and that, as a result, there's a growing pandemic of suicide, self-harm, and general self-sabotage. Even when we appear to be in control of our mental health most of the time, we often damage our own wellbeing by short periods of unwise behaviour, emotional spasms, or self-deception. Just being clever is no assurance of avoiding stupidity or self-destruction. It's *all-round* intelligence that is needed – badly.

The need for better all-round intelligence is clear. What is less clear is the extent to which various cognotech innovations can actually deliver improvements in all-round intelligence. Without such demonstrations, most people will prefer to rely on traditional methods (meditation, yoga, and prayer, etc) in their attempts to increase mental wellbeing. But as more examples of practical cognotech are demonstrated in the years ahead, there's likely to be a switch in public mood.

It could be like the example mentioned earlier of biotech interventions that improve the healthspans of pet cats and dogs; once these interventions are seen to be effective in some of our closest animal friends, it will intensify clamour for them to become available for human usage too. Likewise, once long-lasting benefits are demonstrated for at least some cognotech interventions, beyond what used to be available by traditional methods, the progress of cognotech could tip over from a slow phase to more rapid expansion.

Once cognotech that addresses mental ill-health has become available, variants of it will likely also be used to raise mental wellbeing beyond the levels that normally exist. The consequences will surely be profound.

Beyond NBIC

The four NBIC quadrants are each full of remarkable possibilities. Nevertheless, to appreciate the full extent of the potential of the fourth industrial revolution, we need to add three more considerations.

The first of these extra considerations involves potential technological breakthroughs that depend on combinations of NBIC, but which impact other areas of human life. These include:

- Factories that operate with less and less human involvement
- Driverless trucks and cars
- Swarms of drones, used, for example, for military purposes
- Transport via low-pressure low-friction "hyperloop" tubes that could be placed, at least part of the way, in underground tunnels
- Improvements in sources of renewable energy
- New methods of nuclear fission or nuclear fusion
- Geoengineering methods to transform the world's climate
- Better methods to travel to other planets, to mine asteroids, or to spend more time living in outer space.

There's no established term, alongside nanotech, biotech, infotech, and cognotech, to collectively refer to these technologies. Perhaps "planetary tech" ('P') will do.

The second additional consideration is potential enhancements in the *social infrastructure* within which technologies are developed and used. In particular, these enhancements can themselves take advantage of technological innovations. I call this set "social tech". It includes methods to:

- Allocate finance to projects that deserve funding
- Store vast amounts of data securely in the cloud
- Record transactions in tamperproof ways in distributed ledgers
- Assist the operation of markets – to guard against market failures, and to promote openness and fair competition

- Streamline the creation, operation, and updating of regulations
- Ensure people can keep sensitive material private
- Combat risks of cyberhacking or cybertheft
- Combat risks of damaging psychological malware
- Improve the effectiveness of education
- Improve the effectiveness of politics.

Getting social tech ('S') right should increase the chance that the technologies of NBIC – and P – will ultimately prove beneficial to humanity, rather than detrimental.

Speaking broadly and loosely, if nanotech concerns *atoms*, biotech concerns *genes*, infotech concerns *bits*, and cognotech concerns *neurons*, then social tech concerns *values*. These values include:

- Fair access to resources such as finance, storage, and computing power
- Transparency – sharing information openly by default, avoiding exclusions
- Privacy – allowing selected information *not* to be shared
- Security – protection against theft, damage, or subversion
- Personal growth – via good access to information and education
- Social wellbeing – via politics that guards against undue dominance of society by factions or complexes
- The generation of abundance – via a well-functioning economy with protection against market failures.

But are these the right values? Or are key points missing? And in any case, how do we resolve clashes between these different values?

That brings us to the third additional consideration. Just because we *could* do something, and even *want* to do it, does that mean we *should* do it? And to what extent should we be placing limits on what each other can do, in areas where (again) there is both potential and desire?

I'm a strong believer in liberty. But the fullest liberty, and the greatest flourishing, comes via the willing acceptance of thoughtfully agreed mutual constraints. That's the subject of the next chapter.

11. Transhumanism

Transhumanism, defined: The recognition that humanity is at a relatively early stage in the progress of conscious life. The observation that there are deep flaws in human nature which, when coupled with emerging new technological capabilities, could cause catastrophic damage. The call to take urgent collective action to steer the intelligent design of the transhumans and posthumans who are on the point of emerging, and the redesign of the humans who are alive today. A movement that can be seen as the culmination of many previous historical forces, including both religion and humanism.

Science can tell us *how* to do lots of things. But it can't tell us *whether* we should be doing these things.

For example, science can enable a woman to terminate a pregnancy, in a way that poses herself minimal medical risk. It can enable a couple to avoid conceiving a child, for a period of time, by means of using contraceptives. It can allow, sometime later, the selection of the gender of an embryo to be implanted in the woman's womb, following in-vitro fertilisation. It's not possible yet, but another choice that some couples might prefer in the future is for their baby to grow from an embryo to full term, not in any natural womb inside a biological mother, but in an external synthetic womb, in a process known as ectogenesis.

Science can tell us how to do all of the above things, but it cannot tell us whether it is *right* to terminate a given pregnancy, or to use a particular method of contraception, or to select only male (or only female) embryos for a particular implantation, or to bypass the experience of natural pregnancy in favour of ectogenesis.

Likewise, science can tell us how to strengthen our muscles, or improve our concentration, by taking various stimulants, but it cannot tell us whether these stimulants should in fact be used. Science is on the point of telling us how to significantly extend our healthspans, but, again, cannot tell us whether such extensions should be embraced or shunned. And it's the same with questions over:

- The use of hallucinogenic substances that can lead to profound out-of-the-body experiences

- The release of particles high in the stratosphere to reduce global temperatures
- Improving the processing powers of AI in ways that will utterly disrupt core aspects of how humans spend their working hours.

If science cannot answer such questions, where else can we turn?

Let's consider various potential sources of such answers.

Sources of morality

For many people throughout most of history, it seemed relatively obvious how moral dilemmas should be resolved. You should consult the wise elders of your community, who in turn had access to transcendental wisdom via the intermediation of prophets and seers. Over time, much of that wisdom was written down in holy books and commentaries, and was shared in sermons by priests. These priests would let you know, for example:

- The general methods of conduct that deserve praise, and those which should be condemned as "cheating" or even "sinful"
- The particular methods of contraception which were allowed and which were forbidden[678]
- The circumstances in which killing a person could or could not be justified
- The best ways to discipline children, including recommendations on corporal punishment – "spare the rod and spoil the child"[679]
- The delicious foods that, despite being delicious, should not be eaten (except, perhaps, on special occasions)
- The types of sexual relations that should be encouraged, and those which (despite being pleasurable) should be vigorously opposed
- The restrictions on rights applicable to slaves or to people from supposedly lesser castes or tribes.

In cases when priestly rulings clashed with human intelligibility, the religious commandment took priority – even when there seemed no rational justification for what a priest was asking. "God moves in mysterious ways" was often the best answer that could be expected. Given human limitations – and presumed human sinfulness – our incomprehension of the divine realm seemed unsurprising. Accordingly, reason would have to take second place to faith.

The first problem with this methodology, of course, is that different priests from different traditions, consulting different holy books, give conflicting answers. Catholics were forbidden to use condoms or contraceptive pills, but Protestants had no problem with them. Items of food (or drink) that were permitted by some religious traditions were sacrilegious to others. Some religious traditions took the social institutions of slavery and castes for granted, whereas others – a minority – asserted that all people should be treated equally. And rules varied regarding the number of wives someone could have, the roles in society open to women, the appropriate treatment of dead bodies, and so on.

How could we decide between the conflicting demands of different faiths? Why, we would need, after all, to use our human reason.

The second problem arose in response to trying to make sense of the first problem. People started to appreciate that the rules that were so dear to various religious communities might reflect, not some transcendent absolutes, but rather a set of human responses to particular historical circumstances. The way to make sense of these different rules wasn't by theological contortions but by the disciplines of sociology and psychology. If someone claimed they had received a revelation from a divine realm, there was no need to debate whether they had, instead, been misled by a mischievous imp or a treacherous devil. Rather, a humanistic assessment could be made: the supposedly divine messages the person was passing on arose at least in part from factors inside their subconscious that were, in turn, sculpted by their personal and social situation.

But once you invoke the disciplines of psychology and sociology to analyse the rules in diverse religious traditions, the same disciplines throw doubt on any infallible authority in your own favourite religious tradition. The American sociologist and theologian Peter Berger drew attention to this trend, writing the following in 1969[680]:

> A good deal of the work in the sociology of religion begins as market research undertaken on behalf of religious organizations. The lesson, perhaps, is that one calls on the sociologist at one's peril. One may do so, initially, for the most pragmatic reasons, simply wanting to get information that will be useful in the planning and execution of institutional policies. One may find that, without anyone's (including the sociologist's) desiring it,

> the information that emerges subverts some basic presuppositions of the institution itself…
>
> It was historical scholarship, especially as it developed in the nineteenth century, that first threatened to undermine theology at its very roots. Its challenge… began with details that could more or less plausibly be dismissed as trivial – the discovery of different sources for biblical books that had been canonized as unities, or of inconsistencies in the several accounts of the life of Jesus. All these details, however, came to add up to something much more serious – a pervasive sense of the historical character of all elements of the tradition, which significantly weakened the latter's claims to uniqueness and authority. Put simply, historical scholarship led to a perspective in which even the most sacrosanct elements of religious tradition came to be seen as human products.

In summary, whilst there may still be considerable merit in various religious traditions, it was increasingly difficult to accept the messages of these traditions in any absolute way. Rather, human skills of interpretation need be brought to any discussion of religious instructions:

- Various parts of the tradition might reasonably be interpreted in a poetic or allegorical manner – a disobedient prophet living three days inside the belly of a fish, stars falling from the heavens onto the earth, a cunning serpent talking to a primordial woman, etc
- Other parts might be rationalised as being directly relevant in the different times of the past, but as being less applicable in the present – such as the abrupt Old Testament declaration that "Anyone who curses their father or mother is to be put to death"[681].

However, decisions on which parts of the tradition belong in which category inevitably involve human judgement at both collective and individual levels. Attempts to give some parts of holy scripture a foundational role, free from human interpretation, fall flat – because of evident variations of opinion between different readers of these scriptures. In summary, these religious codes inevitably arise from human construal of human experiences. *That's no bad thing.*

Inspired by nature

Alongside attempts to answer moral enquiries by referring to religious authorities, another grand tradition emphasised systems of natural balance. According to this viewpoint, humans should live in harmony with nature and with one another, avoiding excesses, accepting responsibilities, and thereby embodying relationships that conform to fundamental archetypes.

For example, the concept of yin-yang balance features in many branches of oriental thought. Nature involves both brightness and darkness, both summer and winter, both hills and valleys, both male and female, both integration and disintegration, both predator and prey, both life and death, and so on. The ancient Chinese tradition of Confucianism emphasises maintenance of appropriate relationships and responsibilities: ruler and ruled, parents and children, teacher and students, husband and wife, elder sibling and younger sibling, friend and friend. Hippocrates, known as "the father of medicine", opined that good health involves appropriate relations between four kinds of body fluid: blood, yellow bile, black bile, and phlegm. Many cultures teach that plants in nature can be found to address all human ailments, bringing relief, if not always a return to full vitality. Disney's *The Lion King* tells us there's a "circle of life": deaths give rise to new life. Perhaps this saying attributed to Mahatma Gandhi summarises this general philosophy best[682]:

> The world has enough for everyone's needs, but not everyone's greed.

These are all fine sentiments, but there are three major reasons why they cannot serve as the basis for hard moral choices in today's world.

First, just as with the difficulties in trying to ground moral principles from religious traditions that offer conflicting advice, there are fundamental disagreements between different claims about what's "balanced" – and about what's "natural", and about what's "responsible". Given these different claims, human judgement needs to be supplied.

Second, a system of social roles and responsibilities that preserved societal stability during past circumstances is often found wanting in times of rapid change. Supposedly timeless requirements for women to stay at home and look after children were deemed less fundamental, after all, when there were many vacancies in factories and farms on account of menfolk being called away to war. The requirement to have large families, to raise the probability that at least some children would live long enough to take care of their parents in old age, became less pressing once healthcare improvements had reduced childhood mortality rates. A philosophy of passively accepting illness and aging as an inevitable aspect of nature makes less sense once medicine has the ability to combat illness and, probably, aging as well.

Third, the more we study nature, the more we recognise it has many aspects that can hardly be elevated as examples for humans to emulate. Nature is full of wanton cruelty – being "red in tooth and claw" in the evocative words of the poet Alfred Tennyson[683]. Charles Darwin drew attention to examples of pain inflicted by parasitic wasps "feeding within the living bodies of caterpillars" and by cats playing with mice before killing them[684]. The comedians of Monty Python highlighted additional examples in the lyrics of their mischievous song *All Things Dull and Ugly* (sung to the tune of the classic hymn *All Things Bright and Beautiful*)[685]:

> Each little snake that poisons,
> Each little wasp that stings…
> All things sick and cancerous,
> All evil great and small,
> All things foul and dangerous…
> All things scabbed and ulcerous,
> All pox both great and small,
> Putrid, foul and gangrenous,
> The Lord God made them all.

In summary, whilst nature contains many marvels, there cannot be any useful moral principle that simply states humans should "copy nature" or "align with nature". Nor is it sufficient to request that humans should "respect balance" and "promote harmony". These principles leave unresolved the questions of *which aspects* of nature should be copied, which kinds of balance should be pursued, and which harmonies to preserve.

The discussions of *religious authority*, on the one hand, and *natural balance*, on the other, both lead to the same conclusion, which is a third potential source of answers to moral questions. In this third approach, the principle to uphold and advance is that of *human wellbeing*. In this approach, insights from religious traditions, and insights from studying nature, retain value to the extent that they can clarify methods to uphold and improve human wellbeing. However, we should avoid putting religious tradition onto any pedestal; likewise, we should avoid putting nature onto a pedestal.

Humanism

The points I've just outlined in the previous paragraph are among the core principles of the philosophy of humanism.

Humanists International, founded in Amsterdam in 1952, and described as "the global representative body of the humanist movement"[686], gives the following definition of the term "humanism"[687]:

> Humanism… affirms that human beings have the right and responsibility to give meaning and shape to their own lives. Humanism stands for the building of a more humane society through an ethics based on human and other natural values in a spirit of reason and free inquiry through human capabilities…
>
> A humanist bases their ethical decisions… on reason, with the input of empathy, and aiming toward the welfare and fulfilment of living things.

That page goes on to cover a number of "aspects of humanism", including the following:

> *We learn about the world using conjecture, reason and experience.*
>
> Humanists agree that we can learn about the world through the use of reason and scientific method, or conjecture tested against logic and empirical evidence. In other words, the world is amenable to rational investigation. This position is sometimes called rationalism.
>
> As rationalists, humanists value free inquiry, in that they reject artificial limits on investigation. Rationalism also embodies freethought: it focuses on knowledge which people can share and test as one community, rather than the acceptance of authority, tradition, or dogma.
>
> *We must make the most of the one life we have.*
>
> We give our lives meaning and purpose. Not believing in an afterlife, or any "divine purpose" for the universe, humanists focus on making meaning and purpose for themselves, on living a good life in the here and now.
>
> *Morality arises from human nature and culture.*
>
> Human beings were not suddenly blessed with love and reason at some point in the past by an external power! Rather, our nature as deliberating, social beings evolved over time. We are able to empathise with others, and reason about fairness and justice and how societies work.

Some of the same problems that faced the two other potential sources of moral guidance I mentioned, religious authority and natural balance, might seem to apply to humanism as well. After all, different humanists differ in their conclusions. Just as the concepts of "balance" and "harmony" mean different things to different people, it's the same with the concepts highlighted by the definition of humanism: "a more humane society", "the welfare and fulfilment of living things", "a good life in the here and now", "fairness and justice", and "human wellbeing". Once again, there's scope for differences of opinion.

At one level, that's no problem. The cardinal principle of humanism is that humans decide values. If different humans have different ideas on how best to achieve human wellbeing, that's something for these humans (and the wider community) to address. It's no blow to the notion that, yes, values are decided by human reference to human wellbeing. So, there's a key difference in this third case from each of the two preceding ones – cases where the fundamental answers were meant to be obtained from sources beyond the human sphere.

In practice, however, the diversity of interpretations means there's a fragmentation within humanism. As pointed out by the social psychologist Jonathan Haidt, different humanists put different degrees of emphasis on various so-called "moral foundations"[688]:

1. Minimising harm, by caring for yourself and others
2. Treating people fairly, by respecting shared rules without cheating
3. Maintaining loyalty to family, colleagues, friends, or group
4. Respecting authority, rather than subverting it
5. Avoiding actions or items that provoke disgust
6. Upholding liberty, and avoiding people being suppressed.

Further, there are hard questions over *whose* wellbeing: to what extent should attention be given to yourself, to your family, to people you know, to people you don't know, to people in future generations, to unborn children, and to non-human animals?

None of these questions mean the humanist enterprise is flawed. They just mean that it faces significant challenges, and that humanists form a diverse community.

The diversity is to be welcomed – up to a point. The diversity can be considered as a helpful division of responsibility, with some humanists giving particular attention to local issues, some to global issues, others to matters of fairness, others to matters of liberation, and so on. That's a positive outcome, provided the different groups avoid unnecessary hostility or conflict. But only up to a point. As philosopher Sam Harris emphasises in his 2010 book *The Moral Landscape*[689], the fact that there can be different emphases within humanism does not mean that every set of humanist choices deserves equal respect.

This can be compared, Harris points out, to choices of diet. We can accept that there are multiple possible choices of good diet, without conceding that *all* choices of diet are equally good. As progress with science enhances our understanding of how various foods impact our health, we can gain more confidence in asserting that certain diets are bad for us, and certain other diets are better for us. It's the same with analysis of how various moral principles tend to impact human wellbeing. As science teaches us more about the development of brain states, we can gain more confidence in asserting, for example, that enforced strict respect for authorities can damage human wellbeing in many circumstances.

In both cases – the impact of diet on health, and the impact of moral principles on wellbeing – we can be justified in holding opinions even though we don't, yet, have a *complete* understanding of health or wellbeing. As more scientific findings are established, we may alter some of our previous views, and gain confidence about assertions where, previously, we held off from offering a strong opinion. In other words, humanism is a work in progress, rather than being a completed theory.

Let's rewind to some of the sample questions posed at the start of this chapter. Is humanism in a state to be able to give clear answers to these questions?

1. Should parents be permitted to choose the sex of their child?
2. Should mothers be supported, if they wish to bypass the experience of natural pregnancy in favour of ectogenesis?
3. Should we welcome hallucinogenic substances that can give people profound out-of-the-body experiences?
4. Should the pursuit of significant extensions of healthspans be embraced, rather than shunned?
5. Should we impose constraints on geoengineering experimentation with stratospheric particles?
6. Should improvements in the processing powers of AI be welcomed, even if many humans will be made redundant from the workforce as a result?

My own observation is that different humanists will give a variety of different answers to these questions, with a variety of different degrees of confidence. Some humanists favour giving individual people as much freedom of choice as possible: if people want to use technology in new ways, it's wrong to stand in their way. Others are more worried about unequal access to the benefits of new technologies: their concern is that greater wellbeing for a number of well-off individuals will fail to compensate for drawbacks of greater inequality. Yet others are moved by a sense of distaste or even disgust about radical new ways of living. Finally, another factor on some minds is a general concern about harm that may arise, probably unintentionally, from the adoption of new technology in place of more familiar methods that have passed the test of time.

None of this is to say that humanism is the wrong basis for resolving moral dilemmas. However, it leads me to introduce a fourth potential source of answers to moral questions. This fourth approach takes humanism as a starting point, but goes further. It can be called "Humanism+", since it adds extra features on top of humanism; that's one reason for the abbreviation 'H+' that is sometimes used. As we'll see, another name for this approach is "transhumanism", because it looks beyond the current circumstances of humanity to a situation which *transcends* many of the limitations of human experience.

Humanism+

How is human wellbeing to be maximised?

Religious viewpoints generally point to conceptions of ideal men and women. The greatest fulfilment, they say, is when people approach that kind of lifestyle – lifestyles of faith and service.

Naturalistic viewpoints generally uphold the notion of life in harmony with the ebb and flow of nature. The greatest fulfilment, they say, is when people are aligned with these natural principles of rhythm and balance.

Humanist viewpoints generally imagine that the most desirable outcome is when the vast majority of people have a quality of life broadly akin to that of the highest level of fulfilment and contentment enjoyed by anyone at the present moment – or in a previous period of history.

Compared to these three viewpoints, transhumanism has much greater ambitions. Forget pictures based on what is possible today, or idealised versions of historical experiences. These are just in the foothills of future possibilities.

Here's how Oxford philosopher Nick Bostrom introduced the concept of transhumanism, at the start of an extended "FAQ" essay in 2003[690]:

> Transhumanism is a way of thinking about the future that is based on the premise that the human species in its current form does not represent the end of our development but rather a comparatively early phase.

Summarising the collective views of the world transhumanist community at that time, Bostrom went on to give this two-fold definition of transhumanism:

> 1. The intellectual and cultural movement that affirms the possibility and desirability of fundamentally improving the human condition through applied reason, especially by developing and making widely available technologies to eliminate aging and to greatly enhance human intellectual, physical, and psychological capacities.
> 2. The study of the ramifications, promises, and potential dangers of technologies that will enable us to overcome fundamental human limitations, and the related study of the ethical matters involved in developing and using such technologies.

Next, Bostrom highlights how transhumanism builds upon humanism, and moves beyond it:

> Transhumanism can be viewed as an extension of humanism, from which it is partially derived. Humanists believe that humans matter, that individuals matter. We might not be perfect, but we can make things better by promoting rational thinking, freedom, tolerance, democracy, and concern for our fellow human beings.
>
> Transhumanists agree with this but also emphasize what we have the potential to become. Just as we use rational means to improve the human condition and the external world, we can also use such means to improve ourselves, the human organism. In doing so, we are not limited to traditional humanistic methods, such as education and cultural development. We can also use technological means that will eventually enable us to move beyond what some would think of as "human".

In an accompanying essay also published in 2003, "Transhumanist Values", Bostrom again emphasises the possibilities for states of wellbeing far beyond those presently experienced[691]:

> Transhumanists view human nature as a work-in-progress, a half-baked beginning that we can learn to remould in desirable ways. Current humanity need not be the endpoint of evolution. Transhumanists hope that by responsible use of science, technology, and other rational means we shall eventually manage to become posthuman, beings with vastly greater capacities than present human beings have.

The gulf between future "posthuman" and present-day human wellbeing might exceed that of the gulf between humans and our evolutionary cousins, the chimpanzees:

> The range of thoughts, feelings, experiences, and activities accessible to human organisms presumably constitute only a tiny part of what is possible. There is no reason to think that the human mode of being is any more free of limitations imposed by our biological nature than are those of other animals.
>
> In much the same way as chimpanzees lack the cognitive wherewithal to understand what it is like to be human – the ambitions we humans have, our philosophies, the complexities of human society, or the subtleties of our relationships with one another – so we humans may lack the capacity to form a realistic intuitive understanding of what it would be like to be a radically enhanced human (a "posthuman") and of the thoughts, concerns, aspirations, and social relations that such humans may have.
>
> Our own current mode of being, therefore, spans but a minute subspace of what is possible or permitted by the physical constraints of the universe. It is not farfetched to suppose that there are parts of this larger space that represent extremely valuable ways of living, relating, feeling, and thinking.

But why should present-day humans care about the wellbeing of future posthuman beings? After all, it's common to discount the importance of future events compared to ones taking place in the present time. There's a strong argument to focus on matters that we can directly influence, here and now, as opposed to far-distant scenarios over which we have little control, and whose details are vague. Future generations can look after themselves, right? Shouldn't we prioritise the low-hanging fruit of improving the wellbeing of countless people already alive, who lack basic amenities such as hygiene, sanitation, and protection from infection by mosquitoes?

Transhumanists answer these queries by pointing out the possibility that billions of people alive today could become posthumans. This is not some far distant speculation. It's a consequence of the acceleration of technological development, as covered in the previous chapter, "NBIC".

Even for those people presently alive who are likely to die before the NBIC technologies approach their full potential, there's a good reason to care about what will happen in the following decades: many of their family members are likely to be alive at that time – children, grandchildren, nieces, nephews, etc – as well as many of their friends and acquaintances.

Wait, does this mean a disregard for present-day suffering?

Not at all. Indeed, reaching the higher peaks of experience and wellbeing of the near-future is dependent upon the sage management of present-day issues. That's required in order for humanity to collectively survive what would otherwise be a set of increasingly intense problems – as covered in the earlier chapter, "Landmines".

But transhumanism frames present-day suffering, intense though it is for numerous individuals, as being at a lower overall scale than either of two potential near-future outcomes:

- The paradise-like sustainable superabundance that can arise from wise management of NBIC technologies
- The global destruction that can follow from the *mismanagement* of these same technologies.

Questions answered

What about the six sample questions we looked at earlier, where humanism could give no clear, unified answers? Can transhumanism offer stronger guidance?

To my view, transhumanism would give the answer "yes, but" to all six of these questions. Let me explain.

To start with, transhumanism urges that we *reduce* the level of attention given to a couple of the candidate moral foundations from the earlier list from Jonathan Haidt:

- Assessing actions by whether they "provoke disgust" gives too much priority to intuitions that are founded in historical or present-day conditions. Yes, we need to dig into the sources of the intuitions involved in those feelings of disgust, to understand them better. But, no, we shouldn't put these intuitions onto any pedestal. We need to learn how to move beyond future shock. Indeed, if need be, we can learn to reprogramme our intuitions.

- It's the same with assessing actions by whether they "respect authority" versus subverting it. Transhumanism regards traditional authority structures as overrated. Authority structures that made sense for past circumstances should not be allowed to constrain our options for radically new configurations.

Further, we should avoid becoming preoccupied over questions of equal access to new products and technologies. Our moral instincts about the importance of fairness are sound. But those instincts shouldn't be allowed to obstruct the roll-out of new products and technologies. Here's why. As NBIC technologies progress, there really *will* be enough for everyone's needs – not just basic needs, but also needs for higher levels of experiences in all areas of life. That's because of:

- More than enough clean energy reaching the earth from the sun, and being gathered and channelled to wherever it is needed
- The production of ample nutritious food by synthetic biology (including "cultured meat"), vertical farming, and other methods
- The generation of sufficient fresh water by desalination plants powered by solar energy
- The provision of excellent education, healthcare, and all kinds of entertainment at ever lower costs, using AI and VR (Virtual Reality)
- The breakdown and recycling of waste, thanks to nanotechnology.

It's true that, in a transitional period, some products and services will, for a while, remain expensive and rare. It's also true that political pressures will be required, during that transitional period, to combat the tendencies for subgroups of society to commandeer the main benefits of these technologies. Nevertheless, with good politics (the subject of Chapter 13), these technologies will transform *all* lives for the better.

This possibility of superabundance transforms many previously vexed moral questions about trade-offs. When there are limited healthcare facilities available, which patients should receive preferential treatment? When there are limited educational scholarships available, which students should receive them? But with the availability of abundant high-quality healthcare and education for everyone, these questions will lose their relevance.

There's likewise no reason for any special concern about potential overpopulation arising from longer lifespans. With wise management of all the energy and other resources of the environment, and with the help of transformational NBIC technologies, the earth can house and feed many more people than the present population[692]. We can anticipate the migration, over time, of more people into huge ecologically-sound skyscrapers, into space satellites, and, eventually, beyond the earth to other planets. Experiences in low-footprint VR worlds that feature magnificent simulations of gardens, landscapes, and other aspects of nature, will defuse any conflicts over access to limited real-world equivalents.

Superabundance also transforms ideas about the centrality of paid employment in human life. Should we worry that AI will remove opportunities for people to earn a living, by taking over many tasks for which they are presently receiving an income? Transhumanism answers that people will no longer need to receive large incomes, since the goods and services necessary for high quality lifestyles will be abundant. To be clear, people will likely still be inspired to apply themselves diligently on a range of tasks, including what we might call "hobbies" or "passions". But the motivation behind such diligence will no longer be to earn a salary. Instead, the motivation will be the pleasure of the task in its own right.

Accordingly, various trade-offs that have proved hard to resolve in the past – between different groups of potential recipients of welfare, between the benefits of automation and the drawbacks of workplace disruption, and between economic progress and environmental protection – can be anticipated to become less critical in the future.

Nevertheless, hard choices *do* remain for how to manage *the transitional period* between the present-day and the full flowering of NBIC technologies. The hardest of these choices is in the area of freedom versus harm. It's for that reason that I said the answer to each of the six sample questions above was "yes, *but*".

Transhumanist advocacy of liberty, as a fundamental component of wellbeing, might seem to lead to a simple answer "yes" to questions such as the first three of the set:

1. Should parents be permitted to choose the sex of their child?
2. Should mothers be supported, if they wish to bypass the experience of natural pregnancy in favour of ectogenesis?
3. Should we welcome hallucinogenic substances that can give people profound out-of-the-body experiences?

In contrast, someone from a traditional humanist background might be anxious about allowing parental choice over aspects of the genetics of their child – such as the child's sex, appearance, and other attributes which are subject to genetic influence. Might the world become full up of boys – boys that all look like popular celebrities such as the footballer David Beckham, the golfer Tiger Woods, or the tennis player Roger Federer?

In this case, the risk applies only if large numbers of parents are likely to take decisions in a simple-minded way, being overly influenced by one dimensional notions of the ideal child. Parents who appreciate a wider diversity of options are unlikely to all choose exactly the same genetic makeup for their children. So long as parents are freed from any tyranny of stereotypical notions about how children should look – notions that might have been prevalent, once upon a time, in some traditional cultures – this risk diminishes. The "but" in this case is the requirement to ensure that people are freed, as they grow up, from any restrictive sense of loyalty to such traditional norms. Loosening inappropriate cultural bonds is one of the tasks of transhumanist education – the subject of Chapter 15.

A larger "but" concerns wider risks from experimenting with new technologies. Edits of the human genome might unwittingly lose some important element of resilience, resulting in a monoculture that is vulnerable to unanticipated new external shocks. Hallucinogenic substances could give people profound out-of-the-body experiences but nevertheless weaken their personal autonomy, rendering them passive and quiescent. Geoengineering with stratospheric particles might plunge the planet into an unstable state, cooling regions far below what was expected. More powerful AI might have other unforeseen consequences, beyond merely displacing humans from the workforce. New nanoparticles might end up lodging themselves in parts of biological organisms with results worse than those from misplaced DDT, asbestos, or microplastics. New virtual reality headsets that prove particularly alluring, so that vast numbers of people spend more time inside VR games, could be vulnerable to some mass malfunction (or hacking) that permanently damages the brains of billions of users. And so on.

In other words, new technologies are associated with so-called "existential risks", meaning that human society could be plunged into a much lower state of existence, or even be rendered extinct.

Such risks feature heavily in the nearest thing that transhumanism has to a canonical document, namely the "Transhumanist Declaration", which consists of the following eight clauses[693]:

1. Humanity stands to be profoundly affected by science and technology in the future. We envision the possibility of broadening human potential by overcoming aging, cognitive shortcomings, involuntary suffering, and our confinement to planet Earth.
2. We believe that humanity's potential is still mostly unrealized. There are possible scenarios that lead to wonderful and exceedingly worthwhile enhanced human conditions.
3. We recognize that humanity faces serious risks, especially from the misuse of new technologies. There are possible realistic scenarios that lead to the loss of most, or even all, of what we hold valuable. Some of these scenarios are drastic, others are subtle. Although all progress is change, not all change is progress.
4. Research effort needs to be invested into understanding these prospects. We need to carefully deliberate how best to reduce risks and expedite beneficial applications. We also need forums where people can constructively discuss what should be done, and a social order where responsible decisions can be implemented.
5. Reduction of existential risks, and development of means for the preservation of life and health, the alleviation of grave suffering, and the improvement of human foresight and wisdom should be pursued as urgent priorities, and heavily funded.
6. Policy making ought to be guided by responsible and inclusive moral vision, taking seriously both opportunities and risks, respecting autonomy and individual rights, and showing solidarity with and concern for the interests and dignity of all people around the globe. We must also consider our moral responsibilities towards generations that will exist in the future.
7. We advocate the well-being of all sentience, including humans, non-human animals, and any future artificial intellects, modified life forms, or other intelligences to which technological and scientific advance may give rise.
8. We favour allowing individuals wide personal choice over how they enable their lives. This includes use of techniques that may be developed to assist memory, concentration, and mental energy; life extension therapies; reproductive choice technologies; cryonics

procedures; and many other possible human modification and enhancement technologies.

In particular, you'll notice the equivalent of "yes, but" sentiments in clauses 3, 4, 5, and 6 of this Declaration. Yes, there are many incredible possibilities. But, there are also profound risks.

Let's look closer at this "yes, but" landscape.

Transcending human nature

Human nature is wonderful, but also flawed. These flaws – along with our wonderful qualities – arose from the long processes that gave rise to the human condition: biological evolution through natural selection, and, more recently, cultural evolution. Evolution prepared us to survive in particular circumstances, in which our flaws might have been troublesome, and even fatal to individuals and to groups, but on the whole, they served us well. That was my message in the "Shortsight" chapter of this book.

The problem is that these flaws are now being magnified in powerful ways by the technologies that are the output of wave after wave of industrial revolution. If human nature remains unchanged, there's a significant likelihood that our instincts will lead us into collective ruin – perhaps within the next few decades. Our flaws will no longer just destroy groups of us; they could bring to an end the entirety of humanity. That was my message in the "Landmines" chapter.

However, the same technologies which could lead to our destruction also have the potential to enable us to transform our own nature – to alter our core dispositions. Being transformed, we will no longer follow the sad trajectory described long ago by Lord Acton – that power will tend to make us corrupt, and that absolute power will corrupt us absolutely. Instead, with greater power, we'll demonstrate greater generosity, greater compassion, and greater benevolence. And with greater intelligence, rather than behaving with greater cunning and more skilful duplicity, we'll demonstrate deeper wisdom.

This new phase of the development of human nature will take place differently from our historical development. Our nature was largely crafted by blind forces that operated throughout countless millennia; now it can be changed via conscious, intelligent design, within just a few decades.

In broad terms, five areas of human character await transformation. The outcomes can be called "the five supers":

1. *Superlongevity*: Transcending current human tendencies toward physical decay and decrepitude; enabling dramatically improved biological health, including the abolition of aging
2. *Superintelligence*: Transcending current human tendencies toward mental blind spots and collective stupidity (cognitive biases); enabling dramatically improved all-round thinking capabilities
3. *Superhappiness*: Transcending current human tendencies toward egotism, depression, alienation, self-loathing, and needless internal suffering; enabling dramatically improved states of consciousness
4. *Superdemocracy*: Transcending current human tendencies toward xenophobia, divisiveness, deception, and the abuse of power; enabling dramatically improved social inclusion and resilience, whilst upholding diversity and liberty
5. *Supernarrative*: Transcending current human tendencies toward small-mindedness or naive fantasies; enabling dramatically improved engagement and collaboration on a credible, compelling transformational journey.

These transformations could also be called "the five rejuvenations": the rejuvenation of physical health, the rejuvenation of all-round intelligence, the rejuvenation of emotional health, the rejuvenation of social relationships, and the rejuvenation of vision. However, to be clear, the transformations I'm describing won't simply *restore* a previous state of health and wellbeing. *They'll result in levels of health and wellbeing never before possible.*

The challenge, of course, will be to preserve the parts of human nature that are truly wonderful, at the same time as we reengineer ourselves to constrain or remove our flaws. That's no small task. It's not something that any small group of people are going to be able to accomplish. Indeed, it is probably the hardest task in the history of humanity.

To succeed in that task, we'll need to gather together and apply the very best of present-day human skills and resources:

- The best scientific understanding of both the actuality and the possibilities for biology, psychology, sociology, and so on
- The best insights from multiple different cultural streams within worldwide human society

- An appreciation of both the strengths and drawbacks of different types of diversity
- A far-seeing creative imagination, to consider not just what is, but what might be
- A thoughtful critical evaluation of these imaginative possibilities, to assess which deserve the most attention, and which should be set aside – as infeasible, dangerous, or fantastical
- Stage-by-stage implementation methods, coupled with careful monitoring and agile interventions.

This collective wisdom needs to be nurtured and developed, by an expanding community of supporters and campaigners. It needs to be shared widely and vividly – that's the task of transhumanist education. And it needs to move from the status of "interesting idea" into that of actual projects – that's the task of transhumanist politics.

Along the way, there will be many profound obstacles, as well as some fresh new ideas. To prevent us from becoming distracted or side-tracked, we're going to have to keep on putting "first things first".

But what are these "first things", from a transhumanist point of view?

Transhumanist values

To guide us in the hard, hard task of the intelligent redesign of human nature, I nominate a number of principles to be kept in mind as fundamental priorities.

These principles can be called the thirteen core transhumanist values. They split into:

- Four statements highlighting the present *context*
- Three foundational principles for *goals* to be pursued
- Three principles about the *means* adopted in pursuit of these ends
- Three key *generalisations and extensions*.

The context:

1. *Radical opportunity*: The near future can be *much* better than the present situation. The human condition can be radically improved, compared to what we've inherited from evolution and history.

2. *Existential danger*: The near future can be much *worse* than the present situation. Misuse of powerful technology can have catastrophic consequences.
3. *Human agency*: The difference between these two radical future options depends critically on human agency: wise human thinking and concerted human action.
4. *No easy options*: If humanity gives too little attention to these radical future options, on account of distraction, incomprehension, or intimidation, there's a high likelihood of a radically bad outcome.

Goals promoted:

5. *Human wellbeing*: In all decisions, actions should be preferred that lead to the increase of human wellbeing. As for what wellbeing involves, how to measure it, and how to improve it, these are enquiries that remain open and ongoing. Wellbeing involves vitality, liberty, creativity, health, intelligence, awareness, happiness, collaboration, and bliss – but extends beyond these separate traits. Over time, our understanding of the conditions and possible expression of human wellbeing will surely evolve and improve. That's as it should be.
6. *Individual wellbeing*: Individual wellbeing should never be sacrificed or subordinated in favour of collectivist goals. Individuals should never become cannon-fodder in service of some tribal, national, ethnic, religious, or ideological quest. In short, individuals are ends not means.
7. *Mutual responsibility*: It's in our mutual interest to protect and elevate all members of society. Rather than keeping quiet about impending dangers about to befall someone, or major opportunities they are about to miss, we should find ways to speak up, just as we would ourselves like to be alerted to such dangers or opportunities in an equivalent circumstance. We're stronger together, rather than in isolation or a state of war.

Means to be adopted in pursuit of these goals:

8. *Science and data*: To improve our decisions, it's important to seek, publish, and review objective data, respecting the best scientific principles, rather than accepting the say-so of would-be pundits or celebrities.

9. *Openness*: In deliberations between conflicting insights, no book, thinker, or tradition should be given any absolute priority. Society needs to remain open to the possibility that our current favoured ideas and methods will be superseded. Of course, respect can be shown to books, thinkers, or traditions with good track records as sources of insight. But that respect should be tempered with caution. Runs of success can come to an end – especially in new circumstances or new contexts.
10. *Proactive vigilance*: We need to expect the unexpected – in other words, to keep monitoring for new risks and new opportunities. Where possible, actions should be preferred that are reversible, lest surprises arise. In anticipation of the possibility of changes in plan, we should design for change, rather than with certainty in mind.

Finally, the key generalisations and extensions:

11. *Sustainability* (generalising from the present into the future): Our plans need to enable, not only wellbeing today, but also wellbeing tomorrow – and the days and years that follow. Hence the need to avoid actions that reduce the possibilities for future wellbeing.
12. *Consciousness* (generalising the previous principles beyond present-day humans): In all decisions, actions should be preferred that lead to the increase of the wellbeing of consciousness. To the extent that animal or artificial minds possess core attributes of consciousness, these minds deserve at least some of the same care and support as human minds. This care includes possibilities for growth and development, and the reduction in needless suffering.
13. *Diversity*: These above principles leave many questions unanswered. They define a broad envelope that can accommodate a multiplicity of different viewpoints. That diversity is, itself, something to embrace. Hence the final core principle: within the overall transhumanist framework, diverse opinions and lifestyles should be cherished and nurtured. It's from interactions between diverse subcultures that some of the most important insights and experiences are likely to arise.

I offer the above description of transhumanism as an *advocate* – someone who wishes to see the philosophy flourish – but also as an *interpreter* –

someone who sees the need to describe the movement in new ways, in order that it can grow more quickly in influence and effectiveness.

I also count myself as a *critic* of transhumanism. Part of my interpretation is to draw attention to the problems arising for the movement owing to various transhumanist enthusiasts apparently disregarding a number of the core values I have just listed. On account of what these enthusiasts have said and done at various times, issues have arisen which cause some analysts to view the overall transhumanist project with suspicion and alarm. The public perception of the movement has, accordingly, become confused.

It's tempting to try to draw a veil over these issues, and to focus on the positive accomplishments of the movement rather than any sources of embarrassment. "Boys will be boys", we might chuckle, half-heartedly, and try to move on quickly to another topic. But that would be a mistake. We have to face up to the shadow that accompanies transhumanism. Out of a better self-understanding, we have better chances for self-healing.

Transhumanist shadow

Every movement has a shadow – a dark underbelly which can cause it problems. Transhumanism is no exception.

One reason why some analysts have a lukewarm or even hostile attitude toward transhumanism is because they focus on the attitudes and practices of various people or subgroups within the shadow of transhumanism. Unfortunately, these analysts take those attitudes and practices as being emblematic of the wider movement.

Accordingly, let's look into this shadow. I see eight areas in it.

The first area is *technological determinism*: the view that technological development will control what happens in the future, more or less regardless of the actions of individual humans. In this view, bigger forces of history are at play, dictating outcomes, ensuring the ultimate transcendence of humanity. Transhumanists therefore are reduced to cheering from the sidelines, awaiting what has been heralded as "the inevitable victory of transhumanism". This cheerleading sees itself as potentially speeding matters up slightly, but not as changing any overall direction of history.

As an example, the Facebook group "Scientific Transhumanism" displayed for several years on its front page a banner that proclaimed "Victory of transhumanism is inevitable"[694].

This mindset has some similarities with Marxist determinism, which foresaw as inevitable the rise of the working class and the overthrow of capitalism. There are similarities, too, with religious visions of forthcoming messianic interventions and apocalyptic vindication for the faithful.

This mindset receives encouragement from a plain reading of the books of Ray Kurzweil, as reviewed in Chapter 8. I often see transhumanist enthusiasts apparently trying to convince themselves that Kurzweil's forecasts remain on track, and that, therefore, his predictions for the "singularity" by 2045 can be trusted[695]. As I indicated during that review, any such trust is misplaced.

In contrast, there are no firm dates given in the Transhumanist FAQ document[696], nor any guarantees of how NBIC technologies will develop within stated timeframes. The outcomes will depend critically on numerous human actions. The uncertainty is at two levels:

1. The *pace* at which key breakthroughs are made, governing when new products and services become available
2. The *use* to which these new products and services are put – that is, whether the impact is beneficial or deleterious.

It may be psychologically appealing to deny the relevance of human action, and to indulge in wishful "rah-rah" thinking regarding the smooth arrival of sustainable superabundance. It's understandable that people who arrive in the transhumanist community with battered psyches, on account of their personal histories, may be attracted to that kind of vision. But any such "hands off" mentality makes it more likely that the trajectory of technological development will lead us to a dreadful landmine encounter. The only way to navigate through these landmines is to remain vigilant and active. Cheerleading is *not* what is needed.

A second area within the transhumanist shadow concerns various sorts of *solution dogmatism*. Examples include *genetic determinism* – the view that the most important changes in our biology will necessarily result from altering our genes. An example from another extreme is *anti-capitalist fundamentalism* – the view that progress toward transhumanist goals will be held up until the capitalist system is overthrown. Yet another example is *anti-money fundamentalism*, which insists that the first thing that needs to be done is to abolish money (or, perhaps, to abolish the ability of banks to issue new "fiat" money).

Whilst there's definitely room to evaluate some interventions as more significant than others, it's important to keep an open mind. Dogmatism and fundamentalism shutter perceptions, and make it more likely – again – that technological development will go off the rails in unexpected ways.

Whilst genes clearly do influence biological wellbeing, they're by no means the only factor in play. To improve human wellbeing, interventions at many other levels of biology should be considered too – alongside interventions at social, political, or mindset levels. It's the same with the pros and cons of capitalist economics, and with the operation of banks and currencies. In all these cases, having closed minds could cause us to miss the best opportunity to achieve the future we desire.

A third area of the transhumanist shadow is a special case of the second one. It's *anti-regulation fundamentalism*: the idea that all regulation of the economy should be resisted. In this view, entrepreneurs and engineers should be allowed a free rein to make progress as fast as they would like.

This view arises from a dual assessment of competencies:

1. Entrepreneurs and engineers are assessed as being the great heroes of societal progress, creating and applying new technologies
2. Politicians and regulators are assessed, in contrast, as being the villains of this story, hindering progress for their own short-sighted reasons, such as preserving a status quo from which they benefit.

Accordingly, some members of the transhumanist community blame regulatory organisations such as the FDA (Food and Drug Administration) for what is described as "hundreds of thousands" of "needless and preventable" deaths, due the slow approval of new treatments[697].

However, a fuller assessment would show that:

- Some public health initiatives, driven by visionary politicians, have actually saved millions of lives[698]
- Products introduced by entrepreneurs and engineers often have significant safety issues, especially when quality has been sacrificed, or when users have been deliberately misled – hence there's a positive role for regulators, to curtail misleading marketing
- Powerful companies, if left to their own trajectory, often eliminate competitors, and then move from a mode when they frequently introduce innovations into one that restricts disruptions – hence,

again, there's a positive role for regulators, this time to ensure market competitiveness

- The most effective way to solve various problems isn't always by applying new technology; instead, political changes can sometimes prove much more applicable.

In other words, there are two problems with anti-regulation fundamentalism:

1. It is in thrall to *techno-solutionism*, always expecting technical fixes, whereas non-technical changes are sometimes a better solution
2. Even when a technological change would be the best solution, sometimes the best way to ensure such a solution is developed is via positive political direction of the economy, via *industrial strategy*[699].

As I see things, transhumanism aims to elevate the operating methods of entrepreneurs and engineers, *and* the operating methods of politicians and regulators. To be clear, I am not advocating *more politics* or *more regulation.* Instead, I am advocating *better politics* and *better regulation.* That's what I meant by the term "superdemocracy" introduced above. That will be the subject of Chapter 13.

A fourth area of the transhumanist shadow takes an overly rosy attitude toward entrepreneurs one step further. This problem, *solution hyping*, is when unwarranted marketing claims are tolerated, or even promoted. The issue arises when people seek to make money from particular products, without any reliable evidence of the efficacy and safety of what they are selling. Examples include various pills or potions supposed to help extend lifespan, increase intelligence, sharpen concentration, or strengthen emotional bonds.

To be clear, it's my belief that various pills and other treatments *can* deliver the kinds of results claimed, and that they have a good evidence base. These products are not the problem. Nor is there a problem when a treatment is made available even though the experimental evidence for it remains unclear, so long as the people who choose to take part in a trial of it are fully aware of the product's uncertain status. The problem, instead, is with rogue products, and when some transhumanists fail to demand appropriate levels of rigour and evidence before endorsing a product.

In some cases, the over-selling is deliberate: the people involved understand that they are over-stating their claims, but they proceed regardless. In other cases, the over-selling arises from naivety and lack of sufficient knowledge by the vendors and their supporters. In all cases, lots of damage can arise:

- To people who purchase the goods or services and suffer actual health problems as a result
- To people who squander lots of money on ineffectual goods or services
- To the reputation of the transhumanist community as a whole, for apparently tolerating, or even praising, the products involved or the people who were pushing them.

Incidentally, it's possible to question the underlying motivation of some of the people in this area of the transhumanist shadow. They may only be *simulating* an enthusiasm for transhumanism, on account of courting a potential market for the products and services they hope to sell. There may also be grounds to assess a number of people within the overall shadow as being duplicitous or mal-intentioned – as being interlopers who actually wish to bring harm to the movement or to some of its prominent representatives. In other words, part of the damage to the reputation of transhumanism has been caused by people who were just feigning support.

Part of the damage is also due to things said or done by people who make *no* claims to being transhumanist, but who are nonetheless associated with the movement by careless or excitable reporters. But to be clear, part of the damage arises from people who honestly see themselves as good representatives of the philosophy.

That takes us to a fifth area of the transhumanist shadow, namely, a lack of concern for unequal access to the fruits of technology. This can be described as *egocentric transhumanism*: the transhumanist enthusiast celebrates his or her own opportunities for better health and better intelligence, etc, but shows little practical concern regarding whether others also share these benefits. When explicitly asked, the enthusiast might indicate that others should be able to benefit too, but this topic seems to be far from their mind most of the time.

This lack of concern may be accompanied by what might be called a "trickle down" theory of transhumanism: the belief that once technological benefits are available for a vanguard set of early adopters, they will in due course become available to everyone who is sufficiently interested in them.

I have already given *some* support for that kind of thinking, earlier in this chapter, when I said that the consequence of a superabundance of goods and services is that there will be sufficient for everyone to enjoy a high quality of life. However, you will recall that I was careful to qualify that remark by saying that different considerations apply in the lead-up to the achievement of that superabundance. During the extreme stress and turmoil of the next decades, if groups of people perceive that they are falling behind from the wave of benefits that other people are receiving – people who seem, perhaps, to be more grasping and self-seeking – the resulting anguish and hostility will magnify the challenges in steering humanity away from major landmines.

Related to egocentric transhumanism is *monoculture transhumanism* – a sixth area of transhumanist shadow – in which individual enthusiasts show concerns for other people who are sufficiently similar to themselves, but they are disinterested, or even antagonistic, to other potential supporters of transhumanist principles who have different backgrounds, different primary or secondary aspirations, or different ways of expressing themselves.

So long as any one transhumanist monoculture dominates:

- The movement is weaker, because it fails to take advantage of the experience, insights, and talents from more diverse sources
- The growth of the movement is stymied, because of alienating and deterring potential new supporters with different backgrounds and desires.

A seventh area of transhumanist shadow is *loathing of biology*. These transhumanist enthusiasts find aspects of their biological existence so distasteful or limiting that they concentrate on ideas for transferring their minds as soon as possible out of biology into alternative hardware substrates, such as a cloud of silicon computers. These transhumanists show less interest in options to repair and augment their existing physical bodies, and they speak contemptuously about their bodies as being "meat sacks".

Although that view represents, in my experience, only a small minority of the overall transhumanist community, it has been selected by some researchers as somehow providing the core definition of transhumanism. In this view, transhumanism is all about "uploading minds to the cloud". Thus, in the 2019 BBC/HBO series *Years and Years*, one teenage character, Bethany, comes out to her parents as being "trans", meaning "transhumanist". What shocks Bethany's parents most is her expressed desire to "live forever as information"[700].

An eighth area of transhumanist shadow is *risk complacency* – a focus on the potential large upsides of NBIC technologies, whilst giving only lip service to their potential large downsides. It's worth taking some time to explore this final shadow area more fully.

In this case, the transhumanist enthusiasts in question may accept intellectually that new technologies do bring some risks, but they tend to express an easy confidence that these risks will be relatively straightforward to manage. Accordingly, they wish to minimise how much attention is given to any potential dangers. Such attention, they argue, might:

1. Cause resources to be turned away from innovative technologies, delaying potential important breakthroughs
2. Encourage politicians and regulators to develop an interest in these technologies, and likely impose foolish restrictions, with little true understanding of the consequences of their meddling
3. Raise unhelpful calls for global cooperation in the face of potential global risks, making it more likely that problems with bureaucratic or self-serving restrictions will pass from a national level, where they already pose problems, up to an international level, where they would have an effect that is even more stultifying.

These concerns have some merit, but I see them as dangerous. We need an approach that appreciates the challenges of *both* risk prioritisation *and* risk management. That approach embodies both a "precautionary principle" and a "proactionary principle":

- The precautionary principle emphasises the downsides of *action* in areas of relative ignorance
- The proactionary principle emphasises the dangers of *inaction* in areas of relative ignorance
- The precautionary principle urges learning *before* action
- The proactionary principle urges learning *as a result* of action.

We need to take a closer look at the interplay between these two principles – and to appreciate how both can become distorted.

Precaution and proaction

Here's the formulation of the precautionary principle from the 1992 Rio Declaration on Environment and Development[701]:

> Where there are threats of serious or irreversible damage, lack of full scientific certainty shall not be used as a reason for postponing cost-effective measures to prevent environmental degradation.

In other words, if an action has a threat of damage that could not subsequently be reversed, and there is uncertainty over the science involved (so the threat cannot be ruled out), then any such action must be accompanied by the development of interventions ready to be used, if need be, to prevent that damage.

A simpler formulation is in the words of the common saying, "better safe than sorry".

However, as pioneering transhumanist philosopher Max More pointed out in an influential essay in 2010, "The Perils of Precaution"[702], that common saying can be countered with other time-honoured proverbs, such as "he who hesitates is lost" and "fortune favours the bold".

Indeed, alongside the drawbacks of *action*, we also need to appreciate the drawbacks of *inaction*. Countless technological innovations had safety concerns, including people dying (an example of "irreversible damage", surely). A blunt application of the precautionary principle, therefore, would have indefinitely delayed progress in areas such as railways, aeroplane flights, x-rays, new surgical techniques, agricultural improvements from the green crop revolution, radar, vaccines, and numerous new drugs.

Indeed, it's rarely a matter of choosing between two courses of action, one involving risks and the other being free from risk. In reality, both these courses of action typically involve risks. The important point, therefore, is to assess the comparative upsides as well as the comparative downsides of different courses of action, and to be ready to *manage* risks as they arise. Moreover, the amount of effort put into managing a risk should be related to the degree of damage expected. And the willingness to undertake a course of action, along with appropriate risk management, should be related to the degree of benefits expected.

With this understanding, the precautionary principle stated earlier makes good sense. If some geoengineering interventions in the stratosphere have a risk of pushing the whole earth into a much lower temperature, triggering catastrophic changes in weather, or perhaps disrupting the ozone layer, that's something which will need a great deal of scrutiny beforehand, and a great deal of risk management in parallel with the experiment. Likewise for actions that would allow easier access by seriously disgruntled groups of people to materials that could be assembled into weapons of mass destruction.

However, some governments have used the precautionary principle to block developments with technologies such as GMOs (genetically modified organisms) and next-generation nuclear reactors, even when scientific consensus seems strongly in favour of these developments. Slow-moving drug regulatory authorities, constrained by their own bureaucracies, have been blamed, in a similar way, for holding up novel therapeutics that might have saved millions of lives. In these cases, what prevailed was an *excess* of precaution.

Reacting to these excesses, a campaign to oppose the precautionary principle has developed momentum in some parts of the transhumanist community. According to this campaign, the precautionary principle is said in practice to mean "don't do anything for the first time". Or, more generously, it means "don't do anything if there are risks of harm associated". However, as noted above, the actual intent of the principle is "if there are risks *not just of harm, but of what could be called ruin*, then only go down this course of action if there are appropriate countermeasures ready to be applied".

It was as an envisioned alternative to excessive application of the precautionary principle that transhumanists have championed the proactionary principle. Here's a short definition from an essay Max More wrote in 2005[703]:

> The Proactionary Principle stands for the proactive pursuit of progress. Being proactive involves not only anticipating *before* acting, but learning *by* acting.

For a deeper dive into the meaning of the principle, here's More's summary from the beginning of that essay:

> People's freedom to innovate technologically is highly valuable, even critical, to humanity. This implies a range of responsibilities for those considering whether and how to develop, deploy, or restrict new technologies:
>
> - Assess risks and opportunities using an objective, open, and comprehensive, yet simple decision process based on science rather than collective emotional reactions.

- Account for the costs of restrictions and lost opportunities as fully as direct effects.
- Favour measures that are proportionate to the probability and magnitude of impacts, and that have the highest payoff relative to their costs.
- Give a high priority to people's freedom to learn, innovate, and advance.

Spelt out like that, the proactionary principle provides excellent advice. Where the principle becomes dangerous is when it, like the precautionary principle before it, becomes a blunt tool – when it is used to justify a disregard for existential risks, opposition to all regulation of new technology, and efforts to undermine potential international collaboration in the face of risks that have a global nature.

Indeed, the proactionary principle is sometimes combined with egocentric transhumanism. More than one transhumanist enthusiast has stated their personal philosophies to me as follows:

- They recognise that advanced AI could have disastrous consequences for humanity
- However, they also see that advanced AI provides the best chance to accelerate treatments for the reversal or aging, in the few decades that are left before they are likely to die of old age
- Without advanced AI, they estimate they have very little chance of personally remaining alive until anti-aging treatments are available
- Therefore, they judge that the risks of advanced AI going wrong (and, perhaps, destroying all of humanity) are worth it, since that development is likely the only hope for them personally to avoid the individual extinction of aging and death.

I believe similar lines of thought probably apply in other people's minds too – either consciously or subconsciously. These people tend to express annoyance when prominent transhumanists like Nick Bostrom keep drawing attention to the risks of advanced AI, as in his 2014 book *Superintelligence*[704]. They have suggested to me that this focus means Bostrom should no longer be considered a transhumanist. As you can tell, I take the contrary view. The sober assessment of risks is a core task of transhumanism.

For a stark contrast to the sober assessment of Nick Bostrom, consider the chirpy encouragement for risk-tasking offered by writer Steve Fuller, in his book *The Proactionary Imperative* (co-authored by Veronika Lipińska)[705]:

> A proactionary world would not merely tolerate risk-taking but outright encourage it, as people are provided with legal incentives to speculate with their bio-economic assets. Living riskily would amount to an entrepreneurship of the self.

Fuller continues, rather too breezily for my liking:

> Of course, society will need to be equipped to absorb the consequences of such risks, many of which are bound to be negative… Greater thought will need to be given to the uncomfortable topic of 'compensation' for injury, disability, and even death.

These injuries, disabilities, and even deaths, would be acceptable, in Fuller's view, because of the possibility there would be:

> …long-term benefits for survivors of a revolutionary regime that would permit many harms along the way.

The individuals who fall victim of these "many harms along the way" should nevertheless find a sense of purpose in:

> …voluntarily identifying with something larger than themselves and thereby consenting to serve as a means to that larger end.

It's little surprise that such sentiments have prompted reviewers to express distaste for Fuller's formulation of transhumanism. For example, this is from a review in the journal Sociology[706]:

> The life and well-being of the individual matters. No religious or crypto-religious belief in humanity's ultimate destination should prompt us to disregard them. In contrast to what the authors would have us believe, the end does *not* justify the means…
>
> What the authors embrace, and ask their readers to embrace, is the kind of ruthless optimism that… is not worried by any evil that might result from our actions because of the firm conviction that everything is for the best and cannot but turn out just fine. If you do not share that… conviction, then the proactionary principle has little to recommend it.
>
> And if Fuller and Lipińska are right that the transhumanist movement rests on the plausibility of the proactionary principle, then we can safely conclude that the whole philosophy of transhumanism lacks a coherent foundation.

In this case, I am entirely on the side of the critics. Any philosophy that is gung-ho about embracing risks, and doesn't mind sacrificing individuals in the service of a potential greater collective benefit, deserves to be opposed. Such a philosophy isn't transhumanism, but forms part of the shadow of transhumanism – and is something from which we need to move forward.

Beyond transhumanism

To take stock: the public assessment of transhumanism has been darkened by too much prominence being given, not to the essential features of the movement, but to what I've described as eight aspects of a transhumanist shadow – technological determinism, solution dogmatism, anti-regulation fundamentalism, solution hyping, egocentric transhumanism, monoculture transhumanism, loathing of biology, and risk complacency.

To heal this shadow – so that the positive impact of transhumanism can accelerate – it has been my goal, in this book and elsewhere, to flesh out a vivid, compelling, comprehensive picture of the true core of this philosophy.

In case a shorthand name is required, for the particular form of transhumanism that I am advocating, I suggest "active transhumanism".

Active transhumanism emphasises responsible real-world action. It highlights the pivotal role of human agency in determining whether the upsides or the downsides of new technologies are what prevail. It underlines inclusiveness and diversity, rather than egocentrism or monoculture. And it sees active politics as being vital to ushering in the profoundly better future in which the destructive limitations of human nature are left behind.

Having expressed some criticism of the thinking and practice of a number of transhumanist enthusiasts and supporters, it's time for me to switch direction. I have acknowledged some validity to the concerns raised by a number of the observers of transhumanism, but I now need to point out the ways in which other concerns raised by these observers are based on misunderstanding and, sometimes, deliberate distortion.

Indeed, by considering the viewpoints of various observers who assess transhumanism as being flawed or dangerous in a number of ways, we'll gain a deeper understanding of the likely future evolution of transhumanism, and why it is such an important development.

12. Antitheses

Antitheses, defined: Ideas that are opposed, or which are believed to be opposed, to a thesis previously propounded. Ingredients for reaching a deeper appreciation – a synthesis – of that previous thesis. In the case of transhumanism, a set of heartfelt but generally misplaced objections, grounded in instincts and fears that it is time to transcend.

Sometimes the best way to understand a worldview is to explore the criticisms of that worldview.

Transhumanism has attracted a minor industry of critics. Some of these critics raise a number of fair points – but only by focussing unduly on the conduct of subsets of the transhumanist community within what I've called the transhumanist shadow. These critics react, with some justification, against displays of personal weaknesses by various transhumanist enthusiasts: fatalism, dogmatism, fundamentalism, hype, egocentrism, monoculture, disdain of the physical body, and irresponsibility – all as covered in the previous chapter.

However, that's only the start of the criticisms levelled at transhumanism. I'll turn now to an array of criticisms that I believe to be unfair or confused.

My analysis of these confusions will hopefully provide answers to readers who find themselves conflicted about transhumanism – readers who have some sympathies with the core ideas of the subject, but who feel intimidated by the apparent strength of opposition raised by critics. Once that intimidation has been dispelled, these readers should find greater confidence to offer fuller support to transhumanist projects.

In parallel, the discussion in this chapter will shed extra light on a number of transhumanist scenarios that everyone seriously concerned about the future ought to bear in mind. That extra light should make it easier to assess the pluses and minuses of these scenarios – and to decide which actions are needed, as soon as possible, in light of these evaluations.

Eugenics

The first misplaced criticism is that transhumanism is essentially a repeat of eugenics.

Eugenics was a movement in the nineteenth and twentieth centuries that sought to control which humans interbred with each other. Weaker members of the species were to be discouraged from having children, or even prevented from doing so, via sterilisation. Otherwise, the eugenics movement feared, "better" groups of people would be outbred by "worse".

Prominent figures who offered various degrees of public support for aspects of eugenics included[707] US President Teddy Roosevelt, future UK Prime Ministers Winston Churchill and Arthur Balfour, Supreme Court Justice Oliver Wendell Holmes, inventor Alexander Graham Bell, birth control clinic pioneer Margaret Sanger, playwright George Bernard Shaw, social reformer William Beveridge, co-founder of the LSE Sidney Webb, suffragette campaigner Alice Lee Moqué, evolutionary biologist Julian Huxley, and economist John Maynard Keynes.

Eugenics took a particularly nasty form under the Nazi Third Reich. In July 1933 a statute known as the "Law for the Prevention of Offspring with Hereditary Diseases" was passed by the German government, advancing the sterilisation of people with various physical or mental disabilities that were deemed probable to be passed on to any children. The disabilities in question included types of schizophrenia, epilepsy, blindness, and deafness, as well as chronic alcoholism[708]. In 1935, the law was amended to withdraw the right of patients to appeal against their sterilisation. By that year, over 150 thousand sterilisations had already taken place under the statute.

"Racial hygiene", to use a term favoured by some of the scientists, doctors, and politicians involved in this programme, led on not just to sterilisation but to the mass "euthanasia" (murder) of the gas chambers, in which six million Jews perished[709].

The intent of the programme was summed up by German Minister for Propaganda, Joseph Goebbels:

> Our starting point is not the individual, and we do not subscribe to the view that one should feed the hungry, give drink to the thirsty, or clothe the naked… Our objectives are entirely different: we must have a healthy people in order to prevail in the world.

The alleged connection with transhumanism? I warn you in advance that it's ropey, but here goes:

- Nazism and transhumanism both seek improvements in the human condition

- Nazism and transhumanism both see genetics as influencing human nature
- Nazism and transhumanism both propose intervening upon the genetic arrangements that take place between one generation and the next, with improved outcomes in mind
- Therefore, (ahem) transhumanism is basically the same as Nazism.

That argument may have psychological appeal for someone who has a strong instinct against any attempts to change human society. If you think that the existing human condition is about the peak of what's possible, you'll fear any attempts at radical improvement. However, in that case, if you're being consistent, you should be opposing lots of other attempts to improve aspects of human society – including many medical treatments that take advantage of new insights from genetics.

In any case, transhumanism has profound differences from the eugenics initiatives mentioned earlier. These initiatives sought to restrict "weaker" or "undesirable" people from having children. Individuals would have to suffer, in service of the collectivist cause of a supposedly purer society. That's in stark violation of the transhumanist value "individuals as ends not means". In contrast, transhumanism looks forward to enabling *everyone* to enhance themselves – and any children they choose to have.

It's true that one person who advocated various forms of eugenics, Julian Huxley, was one of the first (see later in this chapter) to use the term "transhumanism". However, Huxley was strongly opposed to any elements of compulsion or enforcement[710]. He advocated the reform of laws on abortion, easier access for everyone to birth control, and the decriminalisation of homosexuality. Moreover, he staunchly rejected racism.

It's also true that transhumanism and eugenics have in common an interest in modifying human nature by modifying genetics. However, in a similar way, many initiatives share with Cambodia's Khmer Rouge regime an interest in modifying human nature by modifying education. It shouldn't be necessary to say that witnessing an excess in some quality X is no reason to forbid quality X altogether.

Just because the Khmer Rouge "Year Zero" re-education camps were amongst humanity's worst excesses, that's no reason for all subsequent societies to abandon any attempts at education. Just because Nazi eugenics experiments were humanitarian atrocities, that's no reason to ban the study of potential links between genetics and diseases. Just because some attempts to improve human nature have gone badly wrong, that's no reason to forbid all subsequent attempts to improve human nature. The lesson to take away, instead, is the critical importance of a society remaining open to criticism of its central guiding precepts – *open to disagreement and dissent* – as it explores methods for improving the human condition. The lesson to take away isn't to oppose attempts to enhance humanity; it's to oppose totalitarianism.

Totalitarianism

That takes us to the second misplaced criticism of transhumanism, which is that the philosophy is, supposedly, inherently totalitarian.

The criticism here is that people will be *forced* to upgrade themselves, notwithstanding their individual wishes, and regardless of any personal concerns that they might have. Allegedly, transhumanism will brook no dissent. Here's a comment from critic Susan Levin[711]:

> Transhumanism is a "totalizing vision": a comprehensive scientific position on what exists and can be known is supposed to reflect absolutely correct findings of reason and is treated, on that basis, as the rightful guide to how humanity should proceed henceforth.

In another article, the same critic argues that transhumanist concerns about destructive aspects of human character imply that moral upgrading would become compulsory in any society governed by transhumanists[712]:

> To avoid human extinction, bioenhancement of two moral attitudes, altruism and "a sense of justice," is morally required… What's more, to ensure that no one was psychologically primed to wreak disaster on humanity, the use of moral bioenhancement would have to be exceptionless.

That is, a "segue" would occur, "from a moral requirement to a legal obligation" – notwithstanding the habit of transhumanists to "vaunt autonomy".

Critic Benjamin Shane Evans paints a more vivid picture[713]:

> Imagine a society with no diversity of thought. People are told what to do and how to act based on ideologies held by those in power. Individuals are forced into professions based on "formulas" and "evidence," on "probabilities" and "statistics." In this society, the dreams and ambitions of citizens do not matter because they do not fit into mathematical formulas; their lives are structured around current scientific theory and popular rationality dictated by the state. Those in power decide only science,

> technology, mathematics, and engineering books are acceptable reading. History is rewritten; religions are increasingly labelled myths and disregarded as unenlightened or irrational (and irrationality is not tolerated because it cannot be explained by science). Mosques, temples, and churches – in fact, all religious symbols that are not hidden – are destroyed by the state. The government becomes an unalterable, unchallengeable, and tyrannical authority. It subjects its citizens to surveillance all of their lives, from the moment they are born until the moment they die, and can ruin their lives professionally or personally, or even kill them, if any of their thoughts conflict with the goals of the state.

Such a society, which Evans labels as "fascism and totalitarianism", is said to be implicit in the transhumanist declaration. The purported evidence (believe it or not) is the following clause in that declaration:

> We… need… a social order where responsible decisions can be implemented.

To be fair to Evans, I should acknowledge that he also refers to the novel *The Transhumanist Wager*[714] written by the media publicist and political campaigner Zoltan Istvan. The apparent hero of that novel, named Jethro Knights, sets up a community of transhumanist supporters that ultimately deploys a formidable arsenal of remote-controlled weaponry, with devastating effect. Is any more evidence needed of the totalitarian tendencies central to transhumanism?

For some counter-evidence, note that many members of the transhumanist community reacted with dismay to *The Transhumanist Wager*, comparing the character Jethro Knights to Joseph Stalin. According to these reviewers, Knights was *not* being true to transhumanist principles[715]. In any case, the book is a fictional thought-experiment[716], about a scenario that could develop if (as I said in my own review of the book) the development of transhumanism becomes "increasingly antagonised"[717]. It is by no means intended as the ideal blueprint to be followed.

Back to the wording of the transhumanist declaration. Is there anyone who can seriously object to the creation of "a social order where responsible decisions can be implemented"?

Susan Levin, the critic who complains about a segue from a moral requirement to a legal obligation, herself acknowledges the beneficial role that various legal obligations have played in improving public health:

- Laws that prohibit smoking in public areas

- Laws that mandate the wearing of seatbelts.

Her complaint about transhumanism is a matter of degree. She fears the "totalizing vision" that is said to overrule any dissident opinions out of a surfeit of over-confidence. Present-day laws to improve public health will be overtaken by a swathe of more comprehensive measures.

My response is to point to the transhumanist principles of openness and of respect for diversity – principles that are frequently championed in ongoing online transhumanist discussions.

Ah, but what if these principles fall by the wayside, in turbulent times ahead, once transhumanist ideas start having a greater influence on politics? Might it not be the transhumanist shadow that gains more power in practice – a bit like Lenin, Stalin, and Mao arguably left behind many of the enlightened aspects of Marxism as they seized and held onto power?

I don't deny there are risks ahead with politicians misusing power. But these risks are hardly exclusive to politicians that might listen to transhumanist ideas. The point is to keep emphasising openness, support for diversity, and, yes, a keen awareness of risks.

I therefore see it as unwarranted to suggest that transhumanism has inherent totalitarian tendencies. Any such tendencies are human tendencies, shared across the whole population, rather than being somehow peculiar to transhumanism. Transhumanism is correct to research ways to *counter* such tendencies. I encourage the critics to join in that research.

Scientism

A third misplaced criticism of transhumanism is that it is guilty of scientism. In other words, transhumanism is alleged to take science too seriously, and to hero worship it inappropriately.

The term "scientism" was defined by the economist Friedrich Hayek in 1942 as "slavish imitation of the method and language of science"[718]. Philosopher of science Karl Popper suggested in 1970 that a more useful definition would be "the aping of what is widely mistaken for the method of science"[719].

The related criticism of transhumanism has two aspects:

1. Some vital aspects of human life lie outside the understanding of present-day science, and stand to be trampled or destroyed by

transhumanists who take present-day science as their sole guide as to what should be done

2. Transhumanists think they are applying the best insights of science, but their thinking is actually dominated by ideas from "the hard sciences", such as physics (as exemplified by the adoption of the term "singularity"), and lacks awareness of other parts of science.

In response, I can point to the many statements by transhumanists that mention the importance of non-science factors alongside science itself. Here's one of the earliest definitions of transhumanism, dating to 1990, by Max More[720] (emphasis added):

> Transhumanism is a class of philosophies of life that seek the continuation and acceleration of the evolution of intelligent life beyond its currently human form and human limitations by means of science and technology, *guided by life-promoting principles and values.*

And this next definition, by Natasha Vita-More, also dates to the 1990s[721] (emphasis again added):

> Transhumanism is a commitment to overcoming human limits in all their forms including extending lifespan, augmenting intelligence, perpetually increasing knowledge, achieving complete control over our personalities and identities and gaining the ability to leave the planet. Transhumanists seek to achieve these goals through *reason*, science and technology.

Thus, the application of science and technology is to be guided by "life-promoting values and principles" and by "reason".

I acknowledge that certain people have a narrow conception of science. They are blind to the wide range of approaches used within and alongside science, and to the extensions possible in the set of phenomena that science describes and explains. Karl Popper was correct. Problems do arise when people are *mistaken* about what the methods of science involve, or when they apply these methods incorrectly. But that's not a problem of transhumanism.

Veteran transhumanist Giulio Prisco – who has spent time working as a theoretical physicist at CERN – frequently quotes Shakespeare:

> There are more things in heaven and Earth, Horatio,
>
> Than are dreamt of in your philosophy.

Prisco explains his admiration for that stanza as follows[722]:

> We live in a vast and mysterious universe, and contemporary science is not yet in touch with ultimate reality. Perhaps future science will unveil fundamental reality, or perhaps (more likely in my opinion) science will keep advancing and uncover new aspects of physical reality in an infinitely deep fractal zoom, without ever reaching the bedrock.

If anyone is still tempted to view transhumanists as having a closed mind as to the implications of science, they should take a look at the marvellous flights of ideas contained in the 2010 book *A Cosmist Manifesto* by current Humanity+ chair, Ben Goertzel[723].

Transhumanists readily acknowledge that scientific knowledge is provisional and incomplete. Indeed, to be scientific is to acknowledge that scientific theories can change.

Again, transhumanists recognise that methods that make good sense in some fields of science – such as double-blind trials, in which experimenters aren't aware which members of a sample are receiving a given treatment, as opposed to a placebo – aren't always feasible in other fields of science.

Moreover, it's true that some parts of the scientific community are experiencing their own inner struggles, such as a replication crisis over results that have been previously published[724], and a publication bias which leads to what science writer Ben Goldacre has called (in the titles of two of his books) "Bad science" and "Bad pharma"[725]. A detailed survey conducted by researchers at Vox in 2016 reported that many scientists perceive their careers as being "hijacked by perverse incentives"[726]:

> Our respondents told us… the process is riddled with conflict. Scientists say they're forced to prioritize self-preservation over pursuing the best questions and uncovering meaningful truths.

A particular shortcoming in the way some scientific research has been conducted is the excess prominence given to certain types of people as experimental subjects – so-called "WEIRD" people, that is, people from cultures that are western ('W'), educated ('E'), industrialized ('I'), rich ('R'), and democratic ('D'). By some estimates, such people make up only 12% of the world's population, but feature in up to 80% of experiments about social behaviour[727]. This throws doubts on the generality of the results obtained.

So, yes, there are issues over how science is practiced. But recognising these issues is a good first step toward fixing them. The right response here is not *less* science but *better* science.

Indeed, none of the issues raised above is a reason to throw caution to the wind and to turn our backs on science. Just because there are questions over the best way to apply various methods of science and rationality, that's no justification to accept every contrary instinct from every critic of transhumanism as having equal rational merit.

If a critic suspects that a core part of human life – whether it be creativity, responsibility, autonomy, acceptance, or whatever – is in danger of being misunderstood by transhumanists, on account of an over-narrow application by transhumanists of the methods of science, let's have an open discussion about that topic. The critic will discover that the transhumanist community has thought long and hard about all these topics. The accusation of scientism is without merit.

Technocracy

Just as scientism means giving too much respect to scientists – or to people practicing a particular type of science – technocracy means giving too much respect to people who believe themselves to be experts in the technology used in society.

Technocrats are often contrasted with democrats. The former group are said to apply their policies regardless of the ideas of the population as a whole, whereas the latter respect the collective insights of the entire population.

Technocracy is also contrasted with free market economics. Here's a definition from Patrick Wood, Editor-in-Chief of the website Technocracy News[728] (which, to be clear, is highly critical of the concept of technocracy):

> Technocracy is a replacement economic system for Capitalism and Free Enterprise… It proposes that all means of production and consumption would be controlled by an elite group of scientists and engineers (technocrats) for the good of mankind.

Wood (no relation of mine, so far as I know) is the author of a couple of books on technocracy, including *Technocracy Rising*.[729] Here's Wood's stark assessment of the dangers of technocracy, from the introduction to that book:

> The dark horse of the New World Order is not Communism, Socialism or Fascism. It is Technocracy.

He provides more details of what he expects to go wrong, in any society in which technocrats are able to dominate decision-making:

> [Technocracy] involves the gradual appearance of a more controlled and directed society. Such a society would be dominated by an elite whose claim to political power would rest on allegedly superior scientific know-how. Unhindered by the restraints of traditional liberal values, this elite would not hesitate to achieve its political ends by using the latest modern techniques for influencing public behaviour and keeping society under close surveillance and control.

Putting into words a sentiment that I find lurks in the minds of several critics of transhumanism, Wood talks about technocracy and transhumanism as being "Siamese twins"[730]:

> Technocracy and Transhumanism have always been joined at the hip. Technocracy uses its "science of social engineering" to merge technology and society. Transhumanism uses its field of NBIC to merge technology directly into humans.
>
> To put it another way, Technocracy is to society what Transhumanism is to the humans that live in it…
>
> Both are extremely dangerous for all of humankind and must be rejected before it is too late to stop them.

OK, let's unpack these ideas.

Other things being equal, it is surely sensible in general to pay attention to viewpoints from reputed domain experts. For example, in a sailing boat blown into unfamiliar turbulent waters by a storm, the recommendations of seasoned navigators generally deserve more attention than the panicked opinions of a first-time sailor. For matters of an individual patient's health, expert doctors are generally more trustworthy than lifestyle advice regurgitated by casual passers-by from mass distribution horoscope columns.

However, expertise has limits. Even experts occasionally make mistakes within their own specialist areas. Moreover, the fact that someone is an expert in one domain does not entail any special priority applies to their viewpoints in other domains. An expert sailing navigator gains no authority in a different field, such as medical treatments, just by virtue of their sailing proficiency. And if an expert doctor offers suggestions about how to steer an unfamiliar boat in the midst of a storm, we would be foolish to disregard all contrary opinions just because the doctor has an "MD" credential after their name.

What's more, decisions frequently involve the intersection of several different domains. A decision that appears sound from one perspective may be recognised as inadequate when other perspectives are introduced. If we listen only to experts from the first perspective, we risk reaching a bad decision.

Accordingly, there are major limitations to the concept of delegating hard decisions to domain experts. The recommendations of such experts need to be incorporated into a broader process that we can call "superdemocracy" – the involvement of representatives from the entire community in a deliberative process to reach decisions.

To be clear, in a superdemocracy, domain experts should remain respected and valued. Any society that ignores or denigrates the best insights of, for example, scientists, engineers, economists, project managers, or change management experts, risks major failures in the initiatives it pursues. But whilst these experts should *influence* the decisions, they shouldn't *dictate* any outcomes. The outcomes ought to be decided collaboratively, respecting the core transhumanist principles of openness and diversity.

Even when someone is an undoubted technical expert in a given domain, it's important to invest time and effort in explaining to the general public the reasoning behind their suggestions. Key recommendations should be communicated openly and collectively understood, rather than being forced onto uncomprehending recipients. The resulting consultation can have two types of key benefits:

1. Members of the wider community, as a result of their diverse perspectives, might draw attention to problems or opportunities that the original team missed – with the plan changing as a result
2. Members of the wider community, understanding what's proposed, are more likely to support it full-heartedly once it has been approved.

There's more to say about how a superdemocracy should operate. I'll come back to this topic in the next chapter. However, I can confidently affirm that there is no necessary implication from transhumanism to seeking "control by an elite group of scientists and engineers". There's plenty of room in transhumanist decision processes for poets, composers, artists, novelists, dancers, singers, explorers, gardeners, nurses, therapists, and, indeed, people from all walks of life. Everyone is invited. Everyone is welcome to help keep the experts on their toes. And everyone has the potential to become an expert in their own right, to share their new-found expertise as part of the superdemocracy, and to contribute in this way to the overall wellbeing of the wider community.

Utopianism

A fifth misplaced criticism of transhumanism is that the philosophy is utopian, that is, focused on attaining a fixed, unchanging state of perfection. However – the criticism runs – all visions of perfection are flawed. That's the message of countless novels, from Plato's *Republic* via Thomas More's *Utopia* to Aldous Huxley's *Brave New World.*

Critic of transhumanism Francois Zammit asserts the following[731]:

> Transhumanism presents itself as a utopia. It promises advancement and progress beyond imagination. However, the question is: Whose utopia would this be? ... Utopias for some might could mean a nightmare for others.

Michael Shermer, the well-known sceptical thinker, gives a list of problems with attempts to create a utopia[732]:

> Thomas More coined the neologism utopia for his 1516 work that launched the modern genre for a good reason. The word means "no place" because when imperfect humans attempt perfectibility – personal, political, economic, and social – they fail. Thus, the dark mirror of utopias are *dystopias* – failed social experiments, repressive political regimes, and overbearing economic systems that result from utopian dreams put into practice.
>
> The belief that humans are perfectible leads, inevitably, to mistakes when "a perfect society" is designed for an imperfect species. There is no best way to live because there is so much variation in how people want to live. Therefore, there is no best society, only multiple variations on a handful of themes as dictated by our nature.

Shermer goes on to point out the particularly deadly consequences when a mistaken utopian prescription for an ideal society is matched with closed-minded totalitarian governance that is unable to acknowledge the possibility that its vision is mistaken:

> Most... 19th-century utopian experiments were relatively harmless because, without large numbers of members, they lacked political and economic power. But add those factors, and utopian dreamers can turn into dystopian murderers. People act on their beliefs, and if you believe that the only thing preventing you and/or your family, clan, tribe, race, or religion from going to heaven (or achieving heaven on Earth) is someone else or some other group, then actions know no bounds. From homicide to genocide, the murder of others in the name of some religious or ideological belief accounts for the high body counts in history's conflicts, from the Crusades,

> Inquisition, witch crazes, and religious wars of centuries gone, to the religious cults, world wars, pogroms, and genocides of the past century.

Transhumanism agrees that the combination of totalitarianism and utopianism can be especially dangerous – regardless of whether the utopian vision comes from religious or secular sources.

There are two measures to avoid such an outcome. First, as reviewed earlier in this chapter, there's nothing essentially totalitarian in transhumanism. Regularly re-emphasising the needs for openness and diversity can help keep things that way. Second, it's simply mistaken to describe transhumanism as utopian, in the meaning of having in mind a fixed, unchanging state of perfection.

Shermer's article introduces an alternative concept instead of utopia: *protopia*, meaning "incremental progress in steps toward *improvement*, not perfection". The word had been coined by technology writer Kevin Kelly[733]:

> Protopia is a state of becoming, rather than a destination. It is a process. In the protopian mode, things are better today than they were yesterday, although only a little bit better. The "pro" in protopian stems from the notion of process and progress.

Shermer concludes by claiming that real societal progress has been driven by protopian incremental improvements:

> Protopian progress best describes the monumental moral achievements of the past several centuries: the attenuation of war, the abolishment of slavery, the end of torture and the death penalty, universal suffrage, liberal democracy, civil rights and liberties, same-sex marriage, and animal rights. These are all examples of protopian progress in the sense that they happened one small step at a time.
>
> A protopian future is not only practical, it is realizable.

Transhumanists have no objection to getting behind the concept of propotian improvements. However, they point to yet another word: "extropian", which appeared in core transhumanist literature long before either Kelly or Shermer drew attention to "protopian".

The term "extropian" first featured in the magazine "Extropy: Vaccination for Future Shock" launched by philosophers Tom Morrow and Max More in August 1988[734]. Before discussing "extropian", let's consider the root term "extropy". "Extropy" is itself positioned as a metaphorical opposite of entropy, which is a scientific measurement of the degree of disorder of a system. The celebrated Second Law of Thermodynamics states that the entropy of an isolated system never decreases over time. This gives mathematical expression to the observed general trend of matter and energy toward chaos and disorder.

For systems that are *not* isolated – where interchange of energy and matter can take place with the wider environment – it *is* possible for entropy to decrease. Living entities are an important example, with we humans having particular ability to remake our environment. Hence the term extropy, signifying "the extent of a system's intelligence, information, order, vitality, and capacity for improvement"[735].

Under the primary authorship of Max More, the statement of Extropian Principles evolved over the years, culminating in 2003 in version 3.11. This version lists seven principles[736]:

1. **Perpetual Progress**: Extropy means seeking more intelligence, wisdom, and effectiveness, an open-ended lifespan, and the removal of political, cultural, biological, and psychological limits to continuing development. Perpetually overcoming constraints on our progress and possibilities as individuals, as organizations, and as a species. Growing in healthy directions without bound.
2. **Self-Transformation**: Extropy means affirming continual ethical, intellectual, and physical self-improvement, through critical and creative thinking, perpetual learning, personal responsibility, proactivity, and experimentation. Using technology – in the widest sense to seek physiological and neurological augmentation along with emotional and psychological refinement.
3. **Practical Optimism**: Extropy means fuelling action with positive expectations – individuals and organizations being tirelessly proactive. Adopting a rational, action-based optimism or "proaction", in place of both blind faith and stagnant pessimism.
4. **Intelligent Technology**: Extropy means designing and managing technologies not as ends in themselves but as effective means for improving life. Applying science and technology creatively and courageously to transcend "natural" but harmful, confining qualities derived from our biological heritage, culture, and environment.
5. **Open Society – information and democracy**: Extropy means supporting social orders that foster freedom of communication, freedom of action, experimentation, innovation, questioning, and learning. Opposing authoritarian social control and unnecessary

hierarchy and favouring the rule of law and decentralization of power and responsibility. Preferring bargaining over battling, exchange over extortion, and communication over compulsion. Openness to improvement rather than a static utopia. Extropia ("ever-receding stretch goals for society") over utopia ("no place").

6. **Self-Direction**: Extropy means valuing independent thinking, individual freedom, personal responsibility, self-direction, self-respect, and a parallel respect for others.
7. **Rational Thinking**: Extropy means favouring reason over blind faith and questioning over dogma. It means understanding, experimenting, learning, challenging, and innovating rather than clinging to beliefs.

As well as the lexical contrast to entropy, the distinction between "extropia" and "utopia" was also deliberate. The extended description of the extropian principle of "Open Society" makes this clear:

> Open societies avoid utopian plans for "the perfect society", instead appreciating the diversity in values, lifestyle preferences, and approaches to solving problems. In place of the static perfection of a utopia, we might imagine a dynamic "extropia" – an open, evolving framework allowing individuals and voluntary groupings to form the institutions and social forms they prefer. Even where we find some of those choices mistaken or foolish, open societies affirm the value of a system that allows all ideas to be tried with the consent of those involved.
>
> Extropic thinking conflicts with the technocratic idea of coercive central control by insular, self-proclaimed experts. No group of experts can understand and control the endless complexity of an economy and society composed of other individuals like themselves. Unlike utopians of all stripes, extropic individuals and institutions do not seek to control the details of people's lives or the forms and functions of institutions according to a grand over-arching plan.
>
> Since we all live in society, we are deeply concerned with its improvement. But that improvement must respect the individual. Social engineering should be piecemeal as we enhance institutions one by one on a voluntary basis, not through a centrally planned coercive implementation of a single vision.
>
> We are right to seek to continually improve social institutions and economic mechanisms. Yet we must recognize the difficulties in improving complex systems. We need to be radical in intent but cautious in approach, being aware that alterations to complex systems bring unintended consequences. Simultaneous experimentation with numerous possible solutions and

> improvements – social parallel processing – works better than utopian centrally administered technocracy.

I've quoted these extracts at some length, since they present transhumanist principles in a particularly clear way, contradicting the crude simplifications often concocted by critics of the philosophy.

Returning to the topic of "from Utopia to Extropia" in the course of a 2009 essay, Max More sought to correct a number of popular misunderstandings about transhumanism. In each case, the correction sees transhumanism as being less utopian than various critics suppose[737]:

- Transhumanism is about continual improvement, not perfection or paradise.
- Transhumanism is about improving nature's mindless "design", not guaranteeing perfect technological solutions.
- Transhumanism is about morphological freedom, not mechanizing the body.
- Transhumanism is about trying to shape fundamentally better futures, not predicting specific futures.
- Transhumanism is about critical rationalism, not omniscient reason.

In summary: transhumanism supports protopian improvement and extropian transformation, but avoids the alleged utopian vice of targeting any fixed, unchanging future vision.

Divisive

Let's return to a question posed by Francois Zammit: "*whose* utopia?"

Even though transhumanist visions are extropian in character, rather than utopian, it remains a fair question as to whether the direction envisioned will actually benefit everyone in society, or just a subset.

This is the "broad sketch" that Zammit offers, of how a transhumanist future might turn out:

> The ruling class – the supreme owner of the new technology – will be able to control the manufacturing of goods and the provision of services without the input from the lower classes. By enjoying the access to biotechnology, the ruling classes will continuously enhance their abilities, health and longevity, thus gaining an enormous advantage over the rest. In such a society, the power will be concentrated in the hands of a small elite on the scale unprecedented in human history.

He asks this question:

> Will the advanced digital technology deliver a utopia for the majority, facilitating emancipation from routine, menial tasks? Or will it create a new underclass while helping the elite accumulate unprecedented power and wealth?

His answer:

> We simply do not know yet. But given the prevalent contemporary trends, the latter seems more plausible.

Along similar lines, historian Yuval Noah Harari foresees the possibility of an enormous division taking place in the near future[738]:

- Via their mastery of nanotech, biotech, infotech, and cognotech, one class of humans will become "near gods" with eternal youth, the keys to happiness, and the power to create life
- However, the majority of humans will become a "near useless" class, having nothing to contribute to society; they will have no economic value, and may even separate biologically from the "near gods" into a different species.

I find Harari's writing to be full of insight. The scenarios he describes for the future merit deep consideration. It is indeed possible that, in the not-too-distant future, billions of humans will find themselves to be without purpose, miserably alienated and depressed, and cut off from what they expected progress would deliver.

But that wouldn't be a consequence of transhumanism. It would be a consequence of the trajectory of technological change being insufficiently anticipated and insufficiently steered. That's the very opposite of what transhumanism seeks, with its focus on envisioning, evaluating, enhancing, and securing a positive future for everyone.

Harari makes that point too. He is clear that his purpose in describing various dystopian futures is to raise the probability of these futures *not* coming to reality. Instead, with greater wisdom, technology can deliver, *to everyone*, what he describes in his book as the three great projects of the twenty-first century: "immortality, boundless happiness, and divine powers of creation".

Francois Zammit is correct that, "given the prevalent contemporary trends", there's a strong likelihood of a dystopian future. But, of course, the point of transhumanism is to *disrupt and transform* the "prevalent contemporary trends" well before they reach such an outcome.

One additional eminent writer can be brought into this conversation – the political philosopher Francis Fukuyama. In a famous essay he wrote in 2009, he raised the following objection to transhumanism[739]:

> The first victim of transhumanism might be equality. The U.S. Declaration of Independence says that "all men are created equal," and the most serious political fights in the history of the United States have been over who qualifies as fully human. Women and blacks did not make the cut in 1776 when Thomas Jefferson penned the declaration. Slowly and painfully, advanced societies have realized that simply being human entitles a person to political and legal equality. In effect, we have drawn a red line around the human being and said that it is sacrosanct.
>
> Underlying this idea of the equality of rights is the belief that we all possess a human essence that dwarfs manifest differences in skin colour, beauty, and even intelligence. This essence, and the view that individuals therefore have inherent value, is at the heart of political liberalism. But modifying that essence is the core of the transhumanist project. If we start transforming ourselves into something superior, what rights will these enhanced creatures claim, and what rights will they possess when compared to those left behind? If some move ahead, can anyone afford not to follow? These questions are troubling enough within rich, developed societies. Add in the implications for citizens of the world's poorest countries – for whom biotechnology's marvels likely will be out of reach – and the threat to the idea of equality becomes even more menacing.

Fukuyama has a fair point. The greater the degree of enhancement that is adopted by some humans, the bigger the differential in capability will result. Unmodified humans will increasingly be unable to compete in various areas of life. Those humans who wish to exercise their fundamental right not to become enhanced might, therefore, perceive enhanced humans as threats.

You can probably anticipate my response. It is the goal of transhumanism to make "biotechnology's marvels" – and indeed all other technologies of enhancement – available to *anyone who wishes to access them*. It's true that, as different people choose different pathways to develop themselves, these technologies will likely result in a greater diversity of human form and experience than has been the case throughout human history. This greater diversity will bring its own set of challenges. But none of these should be seen as any fundamental reason to oppose the transhumanist project.

As a simple example, consider the technology of learning to read and write. For most of history, remaining illiterate was entirely compatible with the lifestyles of people in many walks of life. However, as society has changed, there are more and more personal drawbacks for someone choosing to avoid the enhancement (for that is what it is) of literacy. Does this mean we should ban literacy? *Of course not.* We encourage people to learn to read and write, but if we encounter people who lack these skills, we communicate with them in other ways. That illustrates, in a small way, some of the variety we can expect to coexist in a diverse society in the future.

For another comparison, consider the lifestyles of the Amish, a religious group whose members make the conscious choice to avoid using (or owning) certain items of modern technology[740]. Wider society respects the choice made by the Amish for themselves to reject the mainstream practice in which, for example, every family owns a motor vehicle or a television. Amish and non-Amish can happily coexist as neighbours and as work colleagues, despite very different lifestyles and attitudes.

The transhumanist core value of diversity – "we should cherish and nurture diverse opinions and lifestyles within the overall transhumanist framework" – anticipates in a similar way the coexistence of highly varied groups of humans and, yes, post-humans. And the transhumanist core value of the wellbeing of consciousness reiterates the importance of the wellbeing of all members of all such groups.

But perhaps you wonder whether this comparison is too quick. After all, the diversity of a transhumanist future will be altogether more radical – and potentially more disturbing and more dangerous – than these other examples of diversity I have briefly mentioned. If that's your concern, you would have Francis Fukuyama on your side. Accordingly, it's time to look at another part of his criticism of transhumanism – his view that transhumanists have a deeply irresponsible lack of humility.

Hubris

A seventh misplaced criticism of transhumanism is that transhumanists suffer from a dangerous degree of hubris – an excess of over-confidence. Transhumanist attempts to improve human nature are naive. The cure that transhumanists apply will be worse than the imagined disease of the apparent flaws in human nature.

Here's another extract from the 2009 essay by Francis Fukuyama:

> Transhumanism's advocates think they understand what constitutes a good human being, and they are happy to leave behind the limited, mortal, natural beings they see around them in favour of something better. But do they really comprehend ultimate human goods?
>
> For all our obvious faults, we humans are miraculously complex products of a long evolutionary process – products whose whole is much more than the sum of our parts. Our good characteristics are intimately connected to our bad ones: If we weren't violent and aggressive, we wouldn't be able to defend ourselves; if we didn't have feelings of exclusivity, we wouldn't be loyal to those close to us; if we never felt jealousy, we would also never feel love. Even our mortality plays a critical function in allowing our species as a whole to survive and adapt (and transhumanists are just about the last group I'd like to see live forever). Modifying any one of our key characteristics inevitably entails modifying a complex, interlinked package of traits, and we will never be able to anticipate the ultimate outcome.

Fukuyama therefore advocates humility in place of hubris:

> Nobody knows what technological possibilities will emerge for human self-modification. But we can already see the stirrings of Promethean desires in how we prescribe drugs to alter the behaviour and personalities of our children. The environmental movement has taught us humility and respect for the integrity of nonhuman nature. We need a similar humility concerning our human nature. If we do not develop it soon, we may unwittingly invite the transhumanists to deface humanity with their genetic bulldozers and psychotropic shopping malls.

Evolutionary psychologist Leda Cosmides makes a similar point[741]:

> Human nature is a collection of complex, functionally specialised mechanisms that are exquisitely designed to work well with one another and to function in certain ways given certain environments.

Cosmides asserts that transhumanists have

> …very little appreciation of how natural selection works and how it produces very exquisitely engineered functional mechanisms – not half-baked ones at all – that fit together in very precise ways.

She therefore asks,

> …what happens if you muck with some of them, yet they are designed to fit together in very precise ways with other ones?

There are, indeed, reasons to be humble and cautious, in the face of many remaining unknowns about the operation of the human mind. Attempted quick fixes risk reducing wellbeing, rather than enhancing it.

Nevertheless, these are not reasons for *inaction*. Nor for accepting the present human condition as being somehow ideal. Critics like Fukuyama and Cosmides presumably do support *some* methods to improve the human condition, including various approaches to improve education, healthcare, and agriculture. The question is *which* methods are appropriate. The transhumanist proposal is to follow careful scientific processes to analyse and review potential and actual interventions.

The arguments raised by Fukuyama and Cosmides could also be applied to attempts to improve human health, and to attempts to improve our economic and financial system. In all these cases, potential changes will act on an incredibly complicated body, with the potential for unintended side-effects. But such possibilities don't warrant us to adopt a complete "hands off" approach. They just warrant us taking a careful, thoughtful approach.

Extending healthy lifespan is a particularly relevant comparison. Geneticists used to argue that no modifications to the genome in a species could result in a longer lifespan, unless there were other, worse drawbacks from these modifications. Any such modifications that had no drawbacks, they used to claim, would have been found in advance by evolution.

Backing up such claims is the principle known as Orgel's Second Rule, articulated by the British biochemist Leslie Orgel in the 1960s[742]:

> Evolution is cleverer than you are.

The implied corollary: evolution is a better designer than any so-called "intelligent designer".

Distinguished evolutionary theorist George C. Williams had previously given a longer theoretical argument against the possibility of extending lifespan by a small number of changes in biological mechanism[743]. Here's one of his summary paragraphs from an article he published in 1957[744]:

> Basic research in gerontology has proceeded with the assumption that the aging process will be ultimately explicated through the discovery of one or a few physiological processes… Any such small number of primary physiological factors is a logical impossibility if the assumptions made in the present study are valid. This conclusion banishes the "fountain of youth" to the limbo of scientific impossibilities, like the perpetual motion machine…

> Such conclusions are always disappointing, but they have the desirable consequence of channelling research in directions that are likely to be fruitful.

Nearly two decades later, in 1978, another leading professor in the field of aging, George M. Martin of the University of Washington, reiterated the view that single changes in genes would not be able to significantly impact the longevity of organisms[745]:

> It is naïve to believe that a mutation at a single locus could be responsible for the determination of life-span and the various debilities of aging.

The blanket denouncements by these eminent professors – "the limbo of scientific impossibilities" and "naïve to believe" – helped to deter researchers from serious investigation of these possibilities. Arguably the field of anti-aging science was delayed by up to a couple of decades as a result.

The first clear evidence that these blanket assertions were wrong came in experiments published in 1982 by a pair of researchers from the University of Colorado, Boulder, namely Tom Johnson and Bill Wood, "Genetic analysis of life-span in *Caenorhabditis elegans*"[746]. Over time, as more researchers looked into the possibilities, yet more counter-examples were found. In a retrospective analysis published in 2002, husband and wife co-authors Leonid and Natalia Gavrilova lamented the consequences of earlier strong declarations that attempts to reverse aging should be banished "to the limbo of scientific impossibilities, like the perpetual motion machine". As the Gavrilovas expressed it, with heavy irony[747]:

> Evolutionary biologists were always very generous with gerontologists in providing advice and guidance on how to do aging research "in directions that are likely to be fruitful". Surprisingly, this generous intellectual assistance proved to be extremely injurious for aging studies in the past. This happened because evolutionary theory was interpreted in such a way that the search for single-gene mutations (or life-extending interventions) with very large positive effects on lifespan was considered a completely futile task, destined for failure for fundamental evolutionary reasons. Researchers were convinced by the forceful evolutionary arguments of George Williams…
>
> As a result of this triumphant evolutionary indoctrination, many exciting research opportunities for lifespan extension were squandered for half a century until the recent and astonishing discovery of single-gene mutants

> with profoundly extended longevity was ultimately made, despite all discouraging predictions and warnings based on evolutionary arguments.

After highlighting recent examples of single gene mutations that caused significant extensions, not only in lifespan, but in *healthy* lifespan for various organisms, the Gavrilovas concluded their review as follows:

> Gerontologists will have to learn a lesson from the damage caused by decades of misguided research, when the search for major life-extending mutations and other life-extension interventions was equated by evolutionary biologists to a construction of perpetual motion machine. Perhaps some wisdom from this lesson can be found in the title of a recent scientific review on the evolution of aging: "Evolutionary theories of aging: handle with care."

As for evolutionary theories of aging, so also with evolutionary theories of human nature. When these theories assert that it's impossible for human interventions to create results better than evolution, we should be sceptical.

The mistakes in both cases are to insist:

1. That natural selection will always find the best solutions to given biological problems
2. That natural selection has been able to try out all possible solutions
3. That human engineering will not be able to accomplish anything beyond the solutions that natural selection has been able to explore.

This is a bit like thinking that since natural selection did not put wings on humans, humans would never be able to fly.

On the contrary, natural selection is limited to solutions that:

- Can be reached in a step-by-step evolutionary manner from previous solutions
- Reflect the particular history of the environment experienced by the population.

With a different environment, new constraints apply. Indeed, with the present-day environment in which we humans find ourselves, the truly risky approach is to tie our hands and apply dark blinkers to our eyes, and to wishfully hope that, somehow, we'll get by fine as we are.

Transhumanist philosophers Julian Savulescu and Ingmar Persson draw attention to the serious risks posed to humanity of nuclear disaster and runaway climate change – risks that they argue are compounded by aspects of human psychology that were helpful for survival in the distant past, but which are highly dangerous in the present[748]. They continue their argument as follows:

> Our moral shortcomings are preventing our political institutions from acting effectively. Enhancing our moral motivation would enable us to act better for distant people, future generations, and non-human animals.
>
> One method to achieve this enhancement is already practised in all societies: moral education. Al Gore, Friends of the Earth and Oxfam have already had success with campaigns vividly representing the problems our selfish actions are creating for others – others around the world and in the future. But there is another possibility emerging.
>
> Our knowledge of human biology – in particular of genetics and neurobiology – is beginning to enable us to directly affect the biological or physiological bases of human motivation, either through drugs, or through genetic selection or engineering, or by using external devices that affect the brain or the learning process. We could use these techniques to overcome the moral and psychological shortcomings that imperil the human species.
>
> We are at the early stages of such research, but there are few cogent philosophical or moral objections to the use of specifically biomedical moral enhancement – or moral bioenhancement. In fact, the risks we face are so serious that it is imperative we explore every possibility of developing moral bioenhancement technologies – not to replace traditional moral education, but to complement it. We simply can't afford to miss opportunities.

That's *not* hubris. It's responsibility.

Wishful thinking

In passing, let me briefly address the frequent allegation that transhumanism suffers from an excess of wishful thinking.

These critics may concede the potential of science and technology to significantly improve the human condition at some far distant time in the future. Biological aging may, *eventually*, be brought under control, they acknowledge. Improvements in artificial intelligence may, *eventually*, allow the creation of ample material goods for everyone to enjoy a sustainably high quality of life, without the necessity to take part in a soul-destroying competitive marketplace for paid employment. But not any time soon, they insist. To imagine otherwise, runs this criticism, is to let wishful thinking override clear assessment.

I share with these critics a distrust of wishful thinking. In the turbulent times in which we live, clear assessments are essential. But it is the critics that frequently display wishful thinking. They wish, apparently, that society can continue roughly the same as before, with, perhaps, some greater attention to whatever moral principles these critics happen to prefer. They wish, apparently, to downplay any possibility of major disruptions arising in the next few decades – disruptions which cannot be managed simply by "business as usual", but which will require very different approaches to those used in the past.

Yes, clear assessment is vital. That's why I have taken considerable care, in preceding chapters, to draw attention to the various forces which have the potential to transform the human condition more drastically than any simple extrapolation of previous trends.

I've also given my reasons for why it is *conceivable* – though by no means *inevitable* – that, within just a few decades, major leaps forward will take place in areas such as rejuvenation biotechnology, the application of artificial intelligence to creativity, and the re-engineering of human consciousness. In my experience, critics of transhumanism often have only a vague understanding of the multiple factors that could propel these fields forward. Sadly, even apparent experts in various areas of research – such as artificial intelligence – can fall victim to a closed-mindedness about disruptive possibilities. They may be experts in their own particular waves of technology, without paying proper attention to potential new waves ahead.

I make no apology for wishing – preferring – certain future scenarios over others. But active transhumanism emphasises the uncertain nature of future developments. Something will not arise merely because we wish for it. In short, transhumanism is very far from being wishful thinking. It's a very serious matter indeed.

Utilitarianism

Some critics believe they can see a deeper problem with transhumanism. These critics accuse transhumanists of being utilitarian. The transhumanist goal of promoting wellbeing is said to be too vague; it fails to recognise virtues and higher values.

For example, consider a number of criticisms of transhumanism made in an essay by historian Hava Tirosh-Samuelson[749]. These criticisms all take as their starting point what she calls "The transhumanist approach to the pursuit of happiness". Here's Tirosh-Samuelson's first criticism:

> The transhumanist notion is an extension of the hedonic understanding of happiness characteristic of 19th century Utilitarianism. Focusing on self-fulfilment, transhumanists do not take the notion of virtue seriously enough... Transhumanists talk a lot about life satisfaction, self-fulfilment and self-realization, but they have not provided an analysis of the relationship between the subjective and objective aspects of happiness. A more rigorous analysis of the meaning of happiness which lies at the foundation of the transhumanist project is needed.

As it happens, the word "happiness" does not appear in the Transhumanist Declaration. The nearest equivalent is in clause 7:

> We advocate the well-being of all sentience, including humans, non-human animals, and any future artificial intellects, modified life forms, or other intelligences to which technological and scientific advance may give rise.

In the previous chapter, I offered this analysis of wellbeing:

> As for what wellbeing involves, how to measure it, and how to improve it, these are enquiries that remain open and ongoing. Wellbeing involves vitality, liberty, creativity, health, intelligence, awareness, happiness, collaboration, and bliss – but extends beyond these separate traits. Over time, our understanding of the conditions and possible expression of human wellbeing will surely evolve and improve. That's as it should be.

I claim, indeed, that transhumanists have long been engaged in attempts at the "more rigorous analysis of the meaning of happiness" which Tirosh-Samuelson claimed was needed. One noteworthy example is the book length analysis "The Hedonistic Imperative" by transhumanist philosopher David Pearce, which dates from 1995[750].

The only part of this criticism which might have some merit is in the claim that "transhumanists do not take the notion of virtue seriously enough". The term "virtue" refers to practices that have value in their own right, as opposed to contributing to a calculation of wellbeing.

Thus, in a later paragraph in her essay, Tirosh-Samuelson highlights aspects of human personality that she asserts are valuable, even though they're not associated with happiness:

> The most troubling aspect of the transhumanist approach to happiness is the notion that technology will allow us to produce pleasant sensations all the time. The ability to manipulate the molecules and electrical impulses in

> the brain is reaching a new sophisticated level due to precise brain scanning and soon neural implants which are now treating people with Parkinson's disease will someday jolt regions of the brain to induce or suppress specific emotions. It is this spectre of transhumanism which makes me most uneasy because it ignores the value of insecurity, anxiety, uncertainty which are very much part of being human.

Here's her worry. Chemical manipulation of the brains may well be able to remove insecurity, anxiety, and uncertainty. Such engineering, she says,

> …is not a prescription for cultural depth and creativity; it is a prescription for childish shallowness that regards having fun and feeling good above all other values.

At one level, this argument is clearly unfair. It keeps swapping out the broader term of "wellbeing" for more constrained notions such as "pleasant sensations all the time" and "having fun and feeling good". What she is criticising, therefore, isn't transhumanism. It's her own distorted reimagining of transhumanism.

But let's see where Tirosh-Samuelson takes her argument:

> Human culture (especially art and philosophy) could not have been possible without these allegedly negative aspects of being human. But if chemicals root out these human abilities, what will be the source of creativity?

The argument deserves another red card at this stage. Transhumanists see creativity as a key aspect of wellbeing. If various mental states – such as anxiety and insecurity – are truly necessary to enable profound creativity, then any transhumanist reengineering of the brain would need to retain the ability to experience such feelings. Again, what's being criticised isn't transhumanism, but a caricature of the philosophy.

In a sense, the mental states of anxiety and insecurity might still have utilitarian value. They have utility because they enable the desirable goal of creativity, which in turn is part of the larger goal of wellbeing. However, by referring to "virtue", Tirosh-Samuelson is implying that there are mental states which should be valued regardless of any such utilitarian calculation.

But where would any such value come from? From a supernatural being reaching into our intuitions, and telling us such-and-such a virtue should be paramount? By the human brain somehow connecting to transcendental truths in some other unspecified way? The problem with any claims of transcendental insight, of course, is that they are subject to rebuttal: *explain your reasoning.* After all, different philosophers claim different intuitions.

As it happens, transhumanism has no problem with the concept of virtue. Virtues can be endorsed as being important heuristics – that is, valuable aids in moral reasoning, or useful rules of the thumb. Certain types of state of mind – and certain types of action – gain value as virtues, and deserve to be respected, *on account of their likely consequences on human wellbeing.* Telling the truth is virtuous for that reason, as is the rule not to put someone to death, even if others might benefit as a result (for example, by harvesting organs from the deceased person). After all, a world with more lying, or with more people being put to death for narrow utilitarian reasons, would likely lead to a reduction in wellbeing overall. Therefore, transhumanists are happy to recommend respect for the virtues of (among many others) truth-telling and avoiding putting any individual to death.

Tirosh-Samuelson is still dissatisfied. Here's the next part of her argument:

> Beyond the philosophical lack of clarity, the hedonic understanding of happiness is problematic on scientific grounds, because it is materialistic and reductionist. Reducing mind to brain functions, transhumanists use the metaphor of the computer to explain how the mind works, but… this metaphor has serious shortcomings. The human brain is much more than a computational machine; it is part of a highly complex and integrated organism that requires to take into account not only the nervous system but also the immune system as well as the socio-cultural context in which we are embedded.
>
> If happiness concerns the flourishing of the individual as a whole, happiness cannot be reduced just to the functioning of the body, as we encounter in transhumanist literature. Nor can we reduce the human self just to brain functions of neurons that communicate using chemical messengers, neurotransmitters and neuromodulators via synaptic transmission. We need a more holistic understanding of the human self than the one presupposed by transhumanism.

The transhumanist response: "Bring it on!" Where there is real evidence of broader factors impacting human wellbeing, of course transhumanists will pay attention. However, we're going to need to hear something more tangible than vague claims that "materialism and reductionism" are "problematic".

What Tirosh-Samuelson does offer, later in her essay, as virtues to which transhumanists are oblivious, are aging and death. Here is her advocacy of the benefits of aging:

> There is a lot of wisdom that comes only with age and is directly related to encountering the challenges of growing frail and losing vigour. With aging comes the wisdom of compassion, acceptance, and forgiveness that is hard to attain when the good life is defined in terms of having fun or feeling pleasure.

The transhumanist response: there's no evidence that compassion and forgiveness can only be manifest in someone who has "encountered the challenges of growing frail and losing vigour". Even if it were true that some positive mental states are inaccessible without going through this personal decline, there's no evidence that the benefits of these states outweigh all the disbenefits of frailty.

As for death, here are complaints by Tirosh-Samuelson about the potential meaningless of lives that continue for multiple centuries:

> For what end? For what purpose should we extend human life indefinitely? What is human life going to be about for this extended duration? What will human beings engage in for the duration of 150 or 500 years? Will it be more consumerist activities, more entertainment, more "fun," more wars, more destruction of the natural environment? I wonder…
>
> The extension of human life cannot be divorced from a deeper reflection about the purpose of human life, and that reflection seems to be missing from transhumanist literature.

On the contrary, that reflection is *not* missing. Transhumanists are clear that the purpose of human life is something for humans to explore and define. We also expect our understanding of that purpose to evolve in the centuries ahead. If someone has a different idea, let them speak up, and the conversation will continue. If there truly are good arguments that human wellbeing (or conscious wellbeing) should be displaced by some other concept as the overarching goal for human activity, we're all ears.

Data-centrism

A tenth misplaced criticism of transhumanism is that its adherents give too much attention to various characteristics, such as data, or information, and thereby fail to respect some more important aspects of the human condition.

Variants of this criticism insist that transhumanism focuses too much on boosting intelligence, or on maximising efficiency.

For example, David North of the University of Chicago makes this claim[751]:

> The ideology of transhumanism seeks efficiency and optimization, concepts based in the historical project of Taylorism.

North goes on to explain his concerns:

> [Taylorism] studied labourers and sought to eliminate inefficiency within the workforce. Although this functioned at a collective level, this did not prevent the targeting of less intelligent people or workers with disabilities. In seeking to "trim the fat" of society, transhumanism creates a dangerous precedent of conformity coupled with social exclusion.

Later in his essay, North doubles down on his assertion, saying that transhumanism is an "ideology that demands productivity and efficiency from its followers".

I'm tempted to dismiss the whole essay as a piece of fantasy. It provides zero evidence to back up its characterisation of transhumanism. Transhumanism has no project to "trim the fat" of society, or anything remotely similar.

However, there's an underlying thought sequence that merits some attention. Intelligence can exist without there necessarily being any associated state of consciousness. A calculator presumably has no inner sentience when it is calculating the square root of an input number. Satnav systems that determine the quickest route between two points on a map can, again, perform that task without being conscious of that task. Even the human brain carries out lots of processing outside of conscious awareness. Might an increase in intelligence come at the cost of decreased consciousness – or, more generally, of decreased humanity?

Lutheran theologian Ted Peters highlights what he sees as a fundamental difference between machines with AI and humans with a soul – a difference to which he believes transhumanism is oblivious[752]:

> The transhumanists assume that our human mind is like software, lodged in our body as the hardware. This means, we could live in our minds without our bodies. In principle, we could upload our minds into the computer cloud and retain all our knowledge, wisdom, and selfhood. We could live everlastingly in digital form…

> Transhumanists invite us to increase our intelligence through intelligence amplification (…or deep brain computer chip implants) en route to uploading our minds into the computer cloud. Digital consciousness would be everlasting, eternal…
>
> [But] the first thing to note is that artificial intelligence isn't. That's right. Despite the advertising value of the word 'intelligence,' smart machines have not to date been developed that warrant this label. No lab has manufactured artificial general intelligence (AGI). Oh, yes, computers can calculate at breathtaking speed. But, in the end, a computer is just a bucket of code. It does not have a self. It does not possess a soul. There's nobody home. And any attempt at baptizing one might lead to a shorted circuit.

We can split out five parts to this argument:

1. Today's AI is far removed from the kinds of general intelligence displayed by humans
2. Even if a future AI could match the level of general intelligence of humans, there's no guarantee that such an AI would possess inner feelings or consciousness – a "self" or a "soul"
3. If a human mind could somehow be extracted from a biological body and instantiated on a computer cloud, there's no guarantee that the uploaded software would possess inner feelings or consciousness
4. Even if such software did possess some inner feelings or consciousness, it might be bereft of some other key aspect of humanity
5. Accordingly, any transhumanist focus on increasing intelligence is dangerous: the result could be a planet containing much more intelligence than at present, but devoid of key aspects of human life.

Sun Microsystems co-founder Bill Joy raised a similar concern in his famous 2000 essay, "Why the future doesn't need us"[753]:

> A… dream of robotics is that we will gradually replace ourselves with our robotic technology, achieving near immortality by downloading our consciousnesses; it is this process that… Ray Kurzweil elegantly details in [his 1999 book] *The Age of Spiritual Machines*…
>
> But if we are downloaded into our technology, what are the chances that we will thereafter be ourselves or even human? It seems to me far more likely that a robotic existence would not be like a human one in any sense that we understand, that the robots would in no sense be our children, that on this path our humanity may well be lost.

It is to the credit of Ted Peters that he assembles a number of quotations, in a 2011 essay deeply critical of transhumanism, that suggest increasing intelligence is of paramount interest to transhumanists[754]. Here's one:

> "The purpose of the universe reflects the same purpose as our lives: to move toward greater intelligence and knowledge… we will within this century be ready to infuse our solar system with our intelligence through self-replicating non-biological intelligence. It will then spread out to the rest of the universe."

And another:

> "Once AI achieves human levels, it will necessarily soar past it because it will combine the strengths of human intelligence with the speed, memory capacity, and knowledge sharing that nonbiological intelligence already exhibits."

But there are two snags with the approach taken by Peters:

1. The quotes are nearly all from just one writer, namely Ray Kurzweil – someone whose views are, as I have clarified earlier, by no means representative of active transhumanism (and, as has been ably pointed out by the transhumanist analyst Russell Blackford[755], the same applies for the other main source quoted by Peters)
2. Many of the quotes he uses are paraphrases, rather than direct copies of what Kurzweil has written; accordingly, the implications he draws from these passages are dubious.

Despite the claims Peters makes, there's nothing intrinsic in transhumanism which prioritises increasing intelligence above all other goals. To refer back to the thirteen core transhumanist values I listed in the previous chapter, what should be increased isn't intelligence but wellbeing – the wellbeing of humans and, more generally, the wellbeing of consciousness. In that discussion, I included intelligence as a *part* of wellbeing, but by no means the sole part:

> As for what wellbeing involves, how to measure it, and how to improve it, these are enquiries that remain open and ongoing. Wellbeing involves vitality, liberty, creativity, health, intelligence, awareness, happiness, collaboration, and bliss – but extends beyond these separate traits. Over time, our understanding of the conditions and possible expression of human wellbeing will surely evolve and improve.

An increase of "objective data" is included in the same statement of values, not as an end in itself, but as a "means to be adopted in pursuit" of the end goals:

> To improve our decisions, we should seek, publish, and review objective data, respecting the best scientific principles, rather than accepting the say-so of would-be pundits or celebrities.

What about the suggestion that transhumanism risks running headlong into a future in which there is more intelligence but less consciousness, on account of mistakenly assuming that consciousness will automatically emerge once systems of advanced intelligence are suitably configured? Is there a risk, indeed, that AIs in the future will tell us they experience inner feelings, but they are in fact mistaken (or deceiving us)?

My answer is that such a question arises frequently within transhumanist discussion groups and publications. Max Tegmark features such a possibility as one of the scenarios he includes in his mind-stretching look at future possibilities, the 2017 book *Life 3.0*[756]. Tegmark calls this "the zombie scenario":

> If a superintelligent zombie AI breaks out and eliminates humanity, we've arguably landed in the worst scenario imaginable: a wholly unconscious universe wherein the entire cosmic endowment is wasted. Of all traits that our human form of intelligence has, I feel that consciousness is by far the most remarkable, and as far as I'm concerned, it's how our Universe gets meaning. Galaxies are beautiful only because we see and subjectively experience them. If in the distant future our cosmos has been settled by high-tech zombie AIs, then it doesn't matter how fancy their intergalactic architecture is: it won't be beautiful or meaningful, because there's nobody and nothing to experience it – it's all just a huge and meaningless waste of space.

Transhumanist philosopher Susan Schneider puts this question centre stage in her 2019 book *Artificial You: AI and the Future of Your Mind*[757]. In that book, Schneider urges "metaphysical humility" regarding the relationship between intelligence and consciousness:

> Perhaps the best response to the ongoing controversy over the nature of persons is to take a simple stand of *metaphysical humility*. Claims about survival that involve one "transferring" one's mind to a new type of substrate or making drastic alterations to one's brain should be carefully scrutinised. As alluring as greatly enhanced intelligence or digital immortality might be…

there is much disagreement in the personal-identity literature over whether any of these "enhancements" would extend life or terminate it.

A stance of metaphysical humility says the way forward is public dialogue, informed by metaphysical theorising.

Both Tegmark and Schneider also consider scientific experiments which might throw further light on this question. They both consider the question to remain open.

Transhumanists welcome input on this question from critics too – including people from a theological background. We do ask, however, that these critics realise it's incorrect to assert that transhumanism prioritises intelligence, data, efficiency, or information above human wellbeing.

Ableism

Another way in which transhumanism might reduce human wellbeing is by curtailing or even eliminating a number of lifestyles which various people currently value and enjoy.

For example, should someone who was born deaf, and who finds satisfaction and value as part of a community in which there is frequent communication by sign language, be compelled to undergo surgery to restore their sense of hearing?

Some critics assume that transhumanists would be in favour of such compulsion. They go on to accuse transhumanism of ableism: having insufficient respect for the variety of ways in which people can find personal fulfilment[758].

An associated question is whether two parents, who were each born deaf, should be supported in a decision to select for implantation only embryos that carried the same genetic determinants of deafness, in order that their child would also be born deaf.

What's at stake here is whether deafness should be considered a disability, or instead as a different kind of ability.

Another example: suppose two people each suffered polio as children, losing the strength in their legs, and spend much of their time in wheelchairs. Suppose that they, too, wish to have a child that has the same state of "different ability" (that is, spending much of their time in a wheelchair) as themselves. They wish their child to have non-functional legs. Should such a decision be encouraged, discouraged, or even forbidden?

I raise these questions not in order to provide any quick answers. Rather, I'm drawing attention to a fear that some differently abled people may have: transhumanist encouragement of the notion of "transcending limitations" might invalidate the lived experience to which they have become accustomed, and may feel as being precious.

It's true that a single-minded drive toward transcending limits could reduce human diversity. Certain types of genius tend to be manifest in people who are "neurodiverse", with different mental makeup. If parents could routinely screen out genes for autism in their children, might society lose the benefits that neurodiverse children would have provided?

And regardless of questions of the benefit to society, what about the experiences of the individuals themselves? Who are transhumanists to decide that certain ways of living are intrinsically worse – or intrinsically better?

My answer is that each such issue deserves to be considered in its own right, rather than being squashed into a single rule. After all, active transhumanism advocates the cherishing and nurturing of diverse opinions and lifestyles. What's more, a vital part of human wellbeing is the liberty to choose, rather than being subject to unnecessary constraints.

At the same time, the principle of *mutual responsibility* reminds us of our obligation to "protect and elevate all members of society":

> Rather than keeping quiet about impending dangers about to befall someone, or major opportunities they are about to miss, we should find ways to speak up, just as we would ourselves like to be alerted to such dangers or opportunities in an equivalent circumstance.

Thus, choice should be *informed* choice – not a choice undertaken in circumstances when key information has been withheld. Imagine if someone born deaf had an experience with an early cochlear implant which distressed them, and led them to a firm conviction that such an "enhancement" was something they'd prefer to forego. But imagine, further, that cochlear implants have improved considerably in the meantime. Should we suggest to the deaf person that they reconsider their previous aversion to the technology? Should we highlight the fact that better versions of the technology are now available? I would say *Yes*. Should we then *insist* that the deaf person undergo the new treatment? *No*.

The complication is when choices have effects beyond the first person involved. There's an argument to restrict our freedoms when our actions would impact bystanders, family members, and other third parties. If a couple of parents decide to alter the genes of their baby-to-be so that the child will grow up without ordinary mobility, and will instead need to spend most of their time in a wheelchair, that impact on a third person – the child – is something that would alarm many observers.

What if a couple are told that their baby has been born as intersex, that is, neither fully male nor fully female? Suppose a doctor suggests to the parents that a medical procedure should take place, to resolve the apparent gender ambiguity? That choice would, of course, impact a third person – the child – in a way the child might conceivably come to deplore in later years. The child might complain that something unique about them had been removed, without their consent.

In several of the above examples, there are considerations that pull in different directions. It's by no means straightforward to decide which choices would increase human wellbeing, and which others would set wellbeing backward. But that's not any indictment of transhumanism. It's a reflection of genuine conflicts of opinion – and lack of clear data about the delta on human wellbeing expected to be caused by particular choices.

Similar dilemmas also apply when considering, not overall human wellbeing, but the narrower concept of physical health. Will a particular medical intervention be likely to improve physical health, or reduce it? Sometimes we don't know the answer. But that's not any indictment of the entire enterprise of medicine.

If criticism is to be made, it would apply, not to medicine, nor to transhumanism, but to particular close-minded attitudes that individual doctors (or individual transhumanists) might possess.

Neocolonialism

For a variant of the previous criticism – that transhumanism is ableist – consider the idea that transhumanism is neocolonial.

In this case, the allegation is that transhumanists may show insufficient respect for entire cultures – cultures that transhumanists fail to properly understand. Rather than arrogantly misunderstanding the circumstances of various individual humans (as the previous criticism asserted), this time the misunderstanding is said to involve a way of life practiced by a community, such as members of a tribe, or adherents of an indigenous religion.

The term "neocolonial" refers to the way in which aspects of the dominant culture of empires were imposed onto the lives of people who had been brought into economic relationship with the empire builders. By no means all of these influences were positive. Lives were ruined by the easy availability of alcohol and other addictive substances. Consumer materialism encouraged an aggressive "keep up with the Joneses" mentality which previously hadn't been present. Infamously, missionaries were said to arrive with a Bible in one hand and a gun in the other. Ways of life which had seen little change for centuries were disrupted: the wisdom of tribal leaders was ignored, in favour of whichever brand of soft drink or fast food was being most aggressively marketed by deep-pocketed multinationals. Mothers were persuaded to stop breast-feeding their children, and to purchase instead "formula" compounds with flashy packaging and a blizzard of scientific terminology. Land that had previously been used to grow crops for local consumption was converted into mines with miserable working conditions but, it seemed, better rates of pay.

Will it be the same with transhumanists? Might a clique largely consisting of white, educated, affluent males seek to impose their views on other groupings, with (as it were) a copy of the Transhumanist Declaration in one hand and a hypodermic syringe in the other? Might the transhumanist promise of radically improved wellbeing prove as dubious as earlier missionary promises of transformed eternal souls? Worse, might transhumanist apologists turn out to be mere tools of commercial forces, such as Big Tech or Big Pharma, much as various religious preachers can be seen as unwitting tools of western imperialist expansion?

My answer to this criticism mirrors my answer to the previous one:

1. *Diversity matters*: multiple different lifestyles and cultures can and should be incorporated into a transhumanist future
2. *Openness matters*: transhumanists need to be ready to learn from each encounter with each new subset of society, rather than just seeking to apply a pre-cooked formula
3. *Informed choice matters*: information should be made available, so that people in all walks of life can gain an appreciation of the opportunities and risks of new technology that is up-to-date but also realistic

4. *Wellbeing matters*: in some cases, it can be asserted, more forcefully, that certain lifestyles and cultures are actually *worse* for wellbeing than others.

Take the example of opposition to polio vaccinations. Some fringe groups in Afghanistan and neighbouring countries, associated with the Taliban and Islamic State, have decreed vaccinations to be un-Islamic. Vaccination workers have been murdered in order to obstruct the WHO campaign to immunise everyone against polio[759]. In view of this obstruction, should the campaign be terminated? Should the views of some self-declared Islamist health experts be treated as somehow sacrosanct? Should we say that these local people know better than western neocolonial do-gooders about the needs and circumstances of the nearby tribespeople? Might the actual scientific facts of the matter, regarding the biological effect of vaccinations on the health of the children involved, need to be set aside in respect of some kind of cultural wellbeing, in which extremist religious mullahs can maintain their thrall over communities?

Similar clashes exist over questions of female genital mutilation, child marriages, foot binding, and prohibition of girls' education. An absolute cultural relativist would avoid any condemnation of these practices. To my mind, that's taking a principle of respect for diversity far too far. The principle is diversity *within an overall transhumanist framework*, not an "anything goes" toleration.

Historically, some cultures practiced routine human sacrifice. Hearts were cut out of bodies while victims were still alive. It is thought that these cultures believed the practice was necessary to maintain the wellbeing of their overall society – satisfying the desires of gods, and supporting fundamental cycles of death and regeneration. There is evidence that many who were sacrificed were in a good state of health[760]. Perhaps the victims even imagined their souls would pass into an exalted status in the otherworld. Spanish conquerors were horrified by such customs as practiced by Mexican tribes that they encountered. If we had been present at these exchanges, what advice would we have offered? Might we tell the Spaniards not to be so neocolonial? After all, these invaders had only a limited appreciation of the intricate culture of the Aztecs. If the Aztecs chose to practice largescale human sacrifice, who were the Spanish to try to stop them? Perhaps the Aztecs had a better grasp of the fates of the eternal souls of people whose hearts were excised from bodies in this particular way?

For a less gruesome example, consider the prevalence of infectious diseases in various indigenous tribes worldwide. Routinely, significant fractions of people used to die (and, in some locations, still do die) from malaria, gastroenteritis, tuberculosis, and so on. People in these tribes have their own theories of sickness and medicine. It just turns out, however, that these theories are worse than the theories of so-called western medicine. An approach of extreme cultural relativism would be deeply inappropriate here – and, I would add, thoroughly immoral. The principle of mutual responsibility would forbid us from shrugging our shoulders and saying that we westerners have no right to impose our medical ideas on these non-western peoples. The same principle would forbid us, in the same way, from tolerating ongoing human sacrifices, no matter how indignantly the shamans of such tribes insisted that all victims were happy to embrace their gruesome fate. It also forbids us from giving anti-vaccination religious extremists the benefit of the doubt, when they assert that polio vaccinations might damage the divine standing of anyone who receives them.

In other circumstances, decisions are less clear cut. Indeed, in many of the harder cases, decisions are far from clear cut. How quickly and how widely should various potential therapies be trialled, with the potential to increase superlongevity, superintelligence, superhappiness, and superdemocracy? I've already mentioned that I consider such questions to be among the hardest ever faced by humanity. Going too slow could prove fatal, but so also could going too fast. We're going to need to draw upon the best of the collective wisdom of humanity in order to manage this entire process. And yes, that means a respect for diverse points of view. Yes, it means watching out for the dangers of monocultural transhumanism. But it does not mean to treat every point of view – every culture – as having equal validity. Accordingly, there's no need to become hung-up over the criticism that transhumanism is, somehow, inherently neocolonial.

Attachment

For those counting, we've now reached the thirteenth on the list of what I consider to be unfair, misplaced, or invalid criticisms of transhumanism. It's the criticism that the philosophy fails to understand and apply a core virtue of many eastern systems of thinking, namely, the importance of accepting one's fate with a spirit of humility and detachment. The criticism is that transhumanists are overly attached to life. They should learn to let go. That's how true inner peace can be attained.

According to this viewpoint, desire, grasping, and attachment are all signs of immaturity. The world already has too much desire, grasping, and attachment. Therefore, transhumanists are part of the problem, rather than part of any true solution.

Transhumanists should forget about striving to change the lives of individuals (as covered in the previous-but-one criticism) or to restructure societies of people (as covered in the previous criticism). Instead, these critics say, transhumanists should learn to appreciate life in all its richness.

These critics *seem* to have some highly respected thinkers on their side, including Gautama Buddha, 2nd century Stoic advocate Marcus Aurelius, and 20th century American Protestant theologian Reinhold Niebuhr.

Indeed, the "Four Noble Truths" at the heart of Buddhism[761] state that suffering arises from attachment to desires, and that suffering ceases only when attachment to desire ceases. To transcend the omnipresence of suffering, we have to learn to accept life as it is, and to set aside desire – such as the desire for better material possessions, pleasure, security, or long life.

The Stoic philosophy of life, developed in ancient Greece and Rome, likewise emphasises an attitude of acceptance. As Epictetus (55-135 CE) stated[762],

> Freedom is secured not by the fulfilling of men's desires, but by the removal of desire.

Stoic advocate Marcus Aurelius (121-180 CE), who was emperor of Rome for the last 19 years of his life, posed the following questions in his "Meditations"[763]:

> Why do you hunger for length of days? The point of life is to follow reason and the divine spirit and to accept whatever nature sends you. To live in this way is not to fear death, but to hold it in contempt. Death is only a thing of terror for those unable to live in the present. Pass on your way, then, with a smiling face, under the smile of him who bids you go.

A similar sentiment comprises the opening lines of Niebuhr's famous "serenity prayer"[764] (a prayer that everyone can appreciate, without any need to believe in a supernatural deity):

> God grant me
> *The serenity to accept the things I cannot change…*

This wisdom urges serenity and acceptance in the face of life's deep challenges. There's no merit in becoming unnecessarily agitated about an issue – such as the onset of aging, or the imminence of runaway climate change – if there's nothing that can be done about that issue. Why discuss a painful problem if you can't change the outcome? What's the point of complaining if there's no solution available?

But wait. What if a solution *is* available? Is passivity – detachment – still the most "mature" approach to take?

As it happens, there's a lot more to Buddhism than acceptance. Buddhist mindfulness coach Sunada Takagi comments as follows, in an essay entitled "Acceptance is the first step toward change"[765]:

> I recently had a couple people raise doubts to me about the Buddhist idea of "accepting what is." Isn't it too passive? What if we're in a situation that's really unacceptable?
>
> I've come across a few things recently that speak to this. Each makes a slightly different point, but they all basically say the same thing. "Accepting what is" does not mean passive acquiescence. Far from it, it's the first step in making real and lasting change…
>
> So "accepting what is" is not about passivity at all. It's about clear seeing… Paradoxically, it's when we take responsibility for our own failings and difficulties, or those of the world around us, that the real process of change can begin to take place. I see it as an essential starting point for anything we take on in life.

Many commentators on Stoic philosophy likewise adopt a strong action-orientation. For them, being stoical is far from being passive. It can, instead, be the prelude to urgency. Here's a call to action from Paul Jun[766]:

> What I particularly love and find challenging about Stoicism is that death is at the forefront of their thoughts. They realized the ephemeral nature of humans and how this is repeated in many facets of life.
>
> It provides a sense of urgency, to realize that you've lived a certain number of hours and the hours ahead of you are not guaranteed as the ones you have lived. When I think of this, I realize that everyday truly is an opportunity to improve, not in a cliché kind of way, but to learn to honestly appreciate what we are capable of achieving and how we are very responsible for the quality of our lives.
>
> This makes our self-respect, work ethic, generosity, self-awareness, attention, and growth ever more important. The last thing any of us wants

> to do is die with regret, hence why following principles of Stoicism puts your life into perspective. It humbles you and should also deeply motivate you.

That brings us back to the serenity prayer of Reinhold Niebuhr. Above, I quoted the first clause of that prayer – the so-called "acceptance clause". But there are two more clauses: an action clause and a wisdom clause. Here's the entirety:

> God grant me
> The serenity to accept the things I cannot change
> *The courage to change the things that I can*
> *And the wisdom to know the difference.*

Just as people can, rightly, be criticised for foolhardily attempting to change something that cannot be altered, so also can they, again rightly, be criticised for passively accepting some massive flaw or shortcoming which, it turns out, lay within their capacity to fix.

The most important clause in this prayer, arguably, is the "wisdom clause": if we can find out, objectively, whether something lies within our collective ability, it makes all the difference as to whether the right thing to do is to seek accommodation or to seek transformation.

For transhumanism, I have no doubt that the right thing to do is to seek transformation. Doing otherwise would be akin – to borrow another motif from Christian heritage – to walking past on the other side of the road, keeping well away from an unfortunate traveller who has been mugged, stripped of his clothing, and left half dead. When regarding the unfortunate state of everyone around the world that is already "half dead" due to the approach of diseases of old age, or vulnerable to other explosive landmines, who amongst us will prove to be a "good Samaritan" that sees the plight and provides tangible support? And who, in contrast, will be like the priest and the Levite of the biblical parable[767], rushing past with eyes averted, preoccupied with their de facto philosophy of resigned passivity?

Unnecessary

A fourteenth criticism of transhumanism changes tack. In this line of thinking, the wise development of NBIC technologies has vital importance. But there's no need for a *philosophy* or a *movement* to advocate for this development. Rather than wasting time talking about future possibilities, would-be transhumanists should just get on with the task of creating the necessary technological solutions.

These critics see the best transhumanists as those who don't bother to call themselves transhumanist, but who roll up their sleeves and contribute directly to building a better world.

Indeed, exotic talk about "transcending human nature" could *damage* the cause, frightening away potential investors with disturbing ideas. These critics would prefer symbols such as "H+" to disappear altogether. But if that symbol is to remain, it should refer to "more health" or "more happiness" rather than "going beyond human". More health and more happiness are causes which everyone can support, whereas the aspiration of "going beyond human" is bound to stir up divisions and confusion. Right?

What better evidence could there be, of the damage caused by the philosophy of transhumanism, than the long litany of criticisms that has been listed throughout this chapter? Even if it turns out (as I have argued) that the criticisms are misplaced, they still cause damage. Observers see the criticisms and think to themselves, "There's no smoke without fire". And that kind of apprehension could lead them to turn their back on the worthy causes supported by transhumanism: accelerating rejuvenation biotechnology, beneficial artificial general intelligence, technology for improved mental and emotional health, and so on.

But I disagree. My view is that big ideas – like transhumanism – have the power to unleash powerful action. Timely messages can inspire profound social reorientation. Chapter 8, "Creativity", provided examples, including John F. Kennedy's Apollo moonshot vision. The way to accelerate greater progress with rejuvenation biotechnology, beneficial artificial general intelligence, technology for improved mental and emotional health, and so on, involves *both* doing and envisioning. There's certainly a need for scientists, engineers, entrepreneurs, project managers, and other people directly involved with the development and deployment of new solutions. But there's *also* a need to raise awareness of credible, compelling visions of where these solutions can lead – and awareness of the set of transhumanist values that can guide the wise implementation of that vision.

Once more members of the public appreciate, and declare their support, for such visions and the associated sets of values, it will lead in turn to additional support from investors and even from politicians.

Would lesser visions suffice? Health+ and Happiness+ rather than Humanity+?

There's a *role* for such visions, to help open eyes to new possibilities. However, this issue is that these visions are inherently unstable. Once members of the public start to consider how Health+ or Happiness+ might be advanced with assistance of various NBIC technologies, they'll soon notice that these same technologies have many wider implications. They'll realise that scenarios in which most of life remains the same, but NBIC provides extra health or extra happiness, aren't credible. They will inevitably start to worry where NBIC will actually take humanity. If they hear no good answer, it will be no surprise that they expect bad answers. It's the role of the transhumanist community to be ready with good answers.

Transhumanism, therefore, is more than a belief in the radical positive consequences of NBIC technology. It is a belief in the radical positive consequences of more people making a declaration of support of that belief.

It's not just that profound progress can come from the wise development of NBIC. It's that profound progress can come from more people drawing attention to these possibilities of profound progress.

This particular "belief in belief", so to speak, was first put into words in an essay entitled "Transhumanism" published in 1957, in a book *New Bottles for New Wine* written by Julian Huxley[768]:

> The human species can, if it wishes, transcend itself – not just sporadically, an individual here in one way, an individual there in another way, but in its entirety, as humanity. We need a name for this new belief. Perhaps transhumanism will serve: man remaining man, but transcending himself, by realizing new possibilities of and for his human nature.
>
> "I believe in transhumanism": once there are enough people who can truly say that, the human species will be on the threshold of a new kind of existence, as different from ours as ours is from that of Peking man. It will at last be consciously fulfilling its real destiny.

The scale of what Huxley had in mind can be seen from preceding paragraphs in that essay:

> As a result of a thousand million years of evolution, the universe is becoming conscious of itself, able to understand something of its past history and its possible future. This cosmic self-awareness is being realized in one tiny fragment of the universe – in a few of us human beings. Perhaps it has been realized elsewhere too, through the evolution of conscious living

> creatures on the planets of other stars. But on this our planet, it has never happened before...
>
> Up till now human life has generally been, as Hobbes described it, "nasty, brutish and short"; the great majority of human beings (if they have not already died young) have been afflicted with misery in one form or another – poverty, disease, ill-health, over-work, cruelty, or oppression. They have attempted to lighten their misery by means of their hopes and their ideals. The trouble has been that the hopes have generally been unjustified, the ideals have generally failed to correspond with reality.
>
> The zestful but scientific exploration of possibilities and of the techniques for realizing them will make our hopes rational, and will set our ideals within the framework of reality, by showing how much of them are indeed realizable. Already, we can justifiably hold the belief that these lands of possibility exist, and that the present limitations and miserable frustrations of our existence could be in large measure surmounted. We are already justified in the conviction that human life as we know it in history is a wretched makeshift, rooted in ignorance; and that it could be transcended by a state of existence based on the illumination of knowledge and comprehension, just as our modern control of physical nature based on science transcends the tentative fumblings of our ancestors, that were rooted in superstition and professional secrecy.
>
> To do this, we must study the possibilities of creating a more favourable social environment, as we have already done in large measure with our physical environment...

The same book contains another essay, dating this time from 1951, which expresses probably the first public statement in favour of there being a philosophy named "transhumanism". Research by Peter Harrison and Joseph Wolyniak[769] has clarified that the essay in question, entitled "Knowledge, Morality, and Destiny", was originally presented in Washington DC over two evenings in April that year, before appearing in the journal Psychiatry a few months later[770]. The language in the essay might be viewed as dated in places, but the sentiment it expresses, from seven decades ago, holds true today:

> Never was there a greater need for a large perspective, in which we might discern the outlines of a general and continuing belief beyond the disturbance and chaos of the present...
>
> Every society, in every age, needs some system of beliefs, including a basic attitude to life, an organized set of ideas around which emotion and purpose may gather, and a conception of human destiny. It needs a philosophy and a faith to achieve a guide to orderly living - in other words, a morality...

> This brings me... to the emergent idea-system, the new organization of thought, at whose birth we are assisting. It takes account, first and foremost, of the fact that nature is one universal process of evolution, self-developing and self-transforming, and it includes us. Man does not stand over against nature; he is part of it. We men are that part of the process which has become self-conscious, and it is our duty and our destiny to facilitate the process by leading it on to new levels.
>
> Our chief motive, therefore, will derive from the exploration and understanding of human nature and the possibilities of development and fulfilment inherent in it, a study which will of course include the limitations, distortions, and frustrations to be avoided.
>
> Such a philosophy might perhaps best be called Transhumanism. It is based on the idea of humanity attempting to overcome its limitations and arrive at fuller fruition; it is the realization that both individual and social development are processes of self-transformation.

To summarise: for better or worse, in our present status, we humans are strongly influenced by the narratives that we tell ourselves. In the absence of a compelling, credible transcendental narrative, our minds will inevitably shrink, and we will be more likely to be overwhelmed by the tumultuous forces that are busy remaking society without our conscious attention. Transhumanism can be that countervailing narrative.

It's true that transhumanism has become accompanied by "smoke" – by a set of complaints and objections that threaten to obscure the core message of the philosophy. But it's my contention that the smoke can, and should, be dispelled. I trust that many who are reading these words will join the task of proclaiming, more clearly, the positive value of transhumanism, bringing and applying many new skills in the process.

Misnamed

But maybe the name "transhumanism" needs to be ditched.

That's the proposal of yet another group of critics of the philosophy. Actually, in this case, the critics are broadly sympathetic to the goals that I have been outlining. They also see the merit of drawing plenty of attention to the transhumanist vision. However, they think the term "transhumanism" carries too much baggage with it. Why not start over, with a new name? Or give more prominence to another word or phrase that already has some traction within the transhumanist community, such as "extropian", "technoprogressive", or "humanity plus"?

Another purported problem with the word "transhumanism" is that, when people hear "trans", their first thought, nowadays, is "transgender". Whilst transhumanists support the freedoms of choice and lifestyle advocated by transgender supporters, that connection shouldn't the first one that comes to someone's mind. The freedoms advocated by transhumanists extend beyond freedoms of gender identification and gender assignment.

But that's like saying we all need to stop using words like "transistor" or "transatlantic" or even "transcendent", in case people wrongly imagine we're talking about transgenders instead. There's room in the English language, thankfully, for more than one word starting with "trans".

I'm open to different ways to express transhumanist messages. A new word might, indeed, give the movement some additional impetus – like when the UK's "Ecology Party" changed its name in 1985 to the "Green Party", or when the description "gay" was embraced by homosexuals. That kind of reasoning lay behind the decision in 2008 to rebrand as "Humanity Plus" the organisation originally created as the World Transhumanist Association[771].

However, changing the terminology won't, by itself, eliminate the smoke of confusion and apprehension that hangs around the movement. That arises from three sources:

1. An almost inevitable "future shock" when the ideas of the philosophy are first encountered
2. The words and actions of the people I've described as the "shadow" of transhumanism – people who, as it happens, sometimes don't even use the word "transhumanist" to describe themselves
3. Lack of suitable responses, sufficiently repeated, to the misplaced criticisms that I have listed in this chapter.

These causes won't disappear merely with a name change for the philosophy and/or its associated community. Instead, what will cause them to lose force is:

1. Growing familiarity, in the public sphere, of the ideas of the philosophy, presented in ways that indicate continuity with various previous core traditions of humanity, alongside the need for some decisive breaks
2. More public prominence for what I've called active transhumanism, with the growing support of people who previously used, on occasion, to contribute to the shadow of the movement

3. When needed, robust answers to criticisms, that resolve the misunderstandings and, if relevant, highlight the inconsistencies, contradictions, or (on occasion) irresponsibilities of the critics.

Religion

I've left until last perhaps the most interesting of this list of criticisms: the claim that transhumanism is a "religion in disguise".

This criticism comes in two forms:

1. Some critics say that all religions are bad; therefore, since transhumanism is a sort of religion, it too is bad.
2. Others say that some "real" religions are good, but transhumanism is a flawed imitation, lacking the most important elements.

I accept that transhumanism has key similarities with religions. It provides a comprehensive view of life, history, possible futures, and the role of humanity. It highlights the possibility of modes of existence that far exceed those of current everyday living. It suggests that profound human fulfilment lies beyond what we can already see. There's also an analogue of the religious concept of sinfulness: transhumanism identifies our historical and prehistorical evolutionary history as giving rise to aspects of our condition – aspects of our biology, our psychology, our sociology, and our philosophy – which we now need to leave behind, via a process somewhat akin to the religious concepts of rebirth or salvation.

That brings us to the concepts of omnipotence, omniscience, and even immortality. Transhumanism foresees the possibility that, via NBIC technologies, humanity will have access to vast amounts of power and energy. Superintelligence won't deliver a full omniscience, but it will provide more information and more insight than ever before. Superlongevity isn't the same as immortality, but it will result in lives spent in a youthful state for an indefinite period of time. There's a sense, therefore, that transhumanism envisions the conquest of death.

Indeed, some transhumanists speculate, to my mind not unreasonably, about a future "technological resurrection". I'll say more about this in the final chapter. Briefly, such a scenario involves beings in the future with the god-like ability to bend space and time, in non-destructive ways. These future beings might be able to reach into the distant past to preserve someone's consciousness at the point of their death (whether they died by illness, by violence, or by accident), in order for that person to be able to continue living, in a different substrate, that we can hardly imagine at the present.

But although there are similarities between transhumanism and religion, there are also key differences.

First, there are no infallible scriptures in transhumanism, nor any rituals, nor any "pope" or "prophet" whose statements have some kind of transcendent reliability. Recall the transhumanist core value of openness:

> No book, thinker, or tradition should be given any absolute priority. Society needs to remain open to the possibility that our current favoured ideas and methods will be superseded. Of course, respect can be shown to books, thinkers, or traditions with good track records as sources of insight. But that respect should be tempered with caution. Runs of success can come to an end – especially in new circumstances or new contexts.

Second, whereas religions proclaim that the destiny of humanity lies in the hands of powers beyond our control, transhumanism sees the central importance of human agency: wise human thinking and concerted human action. We cannot sit back, think faithful thoughts, and just await some kind of transcendental intervention, like a messiah arriving "in the clouds".

It's true that the world contains loose forces that are *almost* beyond human control: pandemics, climate change, psychological malware, global corporations, and so on. It's also true that NBIC is likely to give rise to even stronger forces of change – forces that will be even harder for humans to steer. And if AI exceeds human capabilities in every field of thought, the challenge of control will intensify yet further. That latter scenario, known as the Singularity, will feature in the final chapter of this book. Some critics have labelled the idea of Singularity as "the rapture of the nerds"[772]. The nerds – clever people who probably lack common sense – are said to anticipate salvation coming from an ultraintelligent AI running on electronic clouds, rather than from Jesus Christ arriving on heavenly clouds.

It's a playful analogy, but it's an unfair description of transhumanism. The powerful forces mentioned, including NBIC technologies and potentially even a Singularity, provide no guarantee of any "salvation" – no guarantee of the paradise-like sustainable superabundance that transhumanists see as a desirable and, yes, *possible* scenario ahead. To increase the probability of such an outcome, humans need to take a firm grip, well before NBIC technologies attain their maturity.

To be clear, transhumanists are open to collaboration in projects with people from multiple religious communities – so long as the core principles of transhumanism are upheld. For example, don't expect us to give up on the fundamental importance of individual wellbeing, or to set aside openness in favour of dogmatism.

It's my view that people from diverse religious traditions will increasingly come to see transhumanism as part of the culmination of their faith[773]. That is, just as transhumanism transcends and fulfils humanism, as covered in the previous chapter, it also transcends and fulfils religion.

But for transhumanists, it's not a matter of waiting for "pie in the sky by and by". It's a matter of *here and now* actively managing technologies – and the environment in which technologies emerge.

Beyond antitheses

In this and the preceding chapter, I've set out the *vision* of transhumanism – thesis, antithesis, and synthesis.

That vision should provide the basis of what I've called the "supernarrative" that humanity badly needs at this time. That supernarrative foresees the arrival of superlongevity, superintelligence, and superhappiness. It also foresees what I've called "superdemocracy" – the repairing and the elevation of the social relationships we have with one another.

Just as transhumanism builds upon humanism, superdemocracy builds upon democracy – which Winston Churchill famously described[774] as "the worst form of government except for all those other forms that have been tried from time to time".

Can democracy survive in the tumultuous times ahead? Or will it become an even "worse form of government"?

One thing that's clear is that democracy won't survive merely by wishful thinking. It's going to take active involvement in politics to steer democracy to a better outcome. And it's unlikely to survive in any simple extension of its present form. To survive, democracy needs to transform into superdemocracy. That's the subject of the next chapter.

13. Politics

Politics, defined: The art of the possible. Claims to unique authority and the use of force in a society. Mechanisms to coordinate conflicting sources of power, and, in principle, to prevent excess dominance or exploitation of parts of society by malignant self-interested complexes.

"Government of the people, by the people, for the people."

These words from the conclusion of Abraham Lincoln's Gettysburg Address have provoked a variety of reactions over the decades.

Lincoln was commemorating all those who had fought in the American Civil War, including the many thousands who had died. The President urged his audience to resolve that "these dead shall not have died in vain". The result of the dedication and sacrifice of these soldiers should, he asserted, be "a new birth of freedom", namely "that government of the people, by the people, for the people, shall not perish from the earth".

In one piece of spectacular bad foresight from that day, the 19th of November 1863, the US correspondent of the London Times gave this scornful assessment of Lincoln's speech[775]:

> The inauguration of the cemetery at Gettysburg was… rendered… ludicrous by some of the luckless sallies of that poor President Lincoln.

That reporter failed to foresee that Lincoln's words – his apparent "luckless sallies" – would be inscribed in marble in a glorious memorial in the nation's capital city, constructed some fifty years later, between 1914 and 1922. Indeed, the sentiments of the speech would echo worldwide. For example, the phrase "gouvernement du peuple, par le peuple et pour le peuple" features as the stated "principe" (principal) of the French Republic, in the second article of that country's constitution, adopted in 1958 and still in force today[776].

But what does that phrase mean? And how relevant is it in a world where people are increasingly beleaguered? Let's look at the three sections of the phrase, one by one.

"Government of the people": the people are to be subject to some constraints. Our individual freedoms exist within a framework of agreements and restrictions, that is, *government.*

To use some twenty-first century examples, individuals have no inalienable right to decide by themselves how much alcohol they can consume before getting behind the driver's wheel of a car on a public highway. Nor to drive their car at double the mandated speed limit – whether or not they have imbibed spirits beforehand. Nor to emit whatever noxious fumes or other pollution or waste they individually judge as appropriate. Nor to carry any type of firearm wherever they please – and so on. No: the people are to be governed.

"By the people": decisions on limitations and restrictions – and on other aspects of collective governance, such as incentives – are to be taken *by representatives of the people as a whole*. The task of ensuring conformance to the decisions of government is, again, carried out by representatives of the people as a whole. Some of these representatives are appointed – such as police, judges, and civil servants. Others are elected. Critically, the elected representatives are subject to removal in elections, lest they cease to attend to the advice and requests from citizenry.

Veteran UK politician Tony Benn expressed it well in remarks in his farewell speech to the House of Commons in 2001, more than fifty years after first being elected a Member of Parliament[777]:

> In the course of my life, I have developed five little democratic questions. If one meets a powerful person – Adolf Hitler, Joe Stalin or Bill Gates – ask them five questions: "What power have you got? Where did you get it from? In whose interests do you exercise it? To whom are you accountable? And how can we get rid of you?" If you cannot get rid of the people who govern you, you do not live in a democratic system.

Benn developed the theme further[778]:

> Only democracy gives us that right [to ask these questions]. That is why no one with power likes democracy. And that is why every generation must struggle to win it and keep it – including you and me, here and now.

"For the people": the purpose of the government is to look after the wellbeing of the people – *all* the people, not just an elite. The limitations, restrictions, and incentives that are imposed, and revised from time to time, are for the people as a whole. Government does *not* exist to give primary privileges to any social complexes, such as the military, corporations, press barons, the political elite, or the ruling political party.

That's the theory. But that theory places a heavy responsibility on all "the people" carrying out the various tasks of government: the voters, politicians, civil servants, journalists, judges and lawyers, and so on. These individuals can fall short in many ways. They may lack personal autonomy, being too easily manipulated by pressures from vested interests. Their moral fibre may be weak. Skills in critical thinking may elude them. They may have only superficial understanding of matters of history and geography. Instead of keeping in mind the wellbeing of the citizenry as a whole, they may be preoccupied by the needs of a smaller group with whom they identify.

Winston Churchill is supposed to have expressed the following opinion about the dependency of democracy on "the average voter":

> The best argument against democracy is a five-minute conversation with the average voter.

Never mind that there is little evidence that Churchill ever uttered such a thought[779]. We have all, each of us, likely had a similar idea flit at least briefly through our minds when hearing a particularly thoughtless or brazen remark by a member of the public – an "average voter" who leaves us appalled.

When things work well, the various personal inadequacies we all manifest from time to time somehow balance each other out. A collective wisdom can, sometimes, emerge from the interactions of individuals who have limited awareness, short-sighted interests, fallible reasoning, and volatile attention. But by no means always. Democracies have made some terrible mistakes, even in countries with a long tradition of admirable scientific and cultural breakthroughs. In these cases, the electorate made truly bad decisions.

Democratic failures

Consider Germany. In March 1933, fourteen different parties contested a national general election for the 647 seats of the Reichstag parliament. Nearly 89% of the electorate cast votes[780]. Third place in the election was taken by the German communist party, winning 81 seats, with a popular vote of 12.3%. Second place went to the Social Democratic Party, winning 120 seats with a popular vote of 18.25%. The winners of the election were the Nazi Party, with 288 seats and a popular vote of 43.9%. Although not an absolute majority, this figure of 43.9% was the largest share gained by any party in any vote in the 14-year history of the German Weimar Republic (1919-1933)[781].

In August of the following year, the German President Paul von Hindenburg died. Already in the role of Chancellor, Adolf Hitler, leader of the Nazi Party, jumped at the opportunity to combine both roles. A national plebiscite took place, requesting democratic approval for this move. The question put to the electors was as follows[782]:

> The office of the President of the Reich is unified with the office of the Chancellor. Consequently all former powers of the President of the Reich are demised to the Führer and Chancellor of the Reich Adolf Hitler. He himself nominates his substitute.
>
> Do you, German man and German woman, approve of this regulation provided by this Law?

The plebiscite was passed, with 88.1% voting in favour, 9.9% against, and 2% spoilt ballots. Turnout was impressively high: 95.7%. In this way, Adolf Hitler's rise to absolute power in Germany received a fulsome democratic mandate. This was, it appeared, the clear will of the people.

It might be objected that neither the March 1933 election nor the August 1934 plebiscite were "free and fair" – that voters felt intimidated in those turbulent times. For example, the website Fact/Myth adjudicates as "myth" the claim that Hitler was elected President in a democratic election[783]:

> Yes, the Nazis were voted in, but it is hard to call the two general elections… "democratic" given the events surrounding the Machtergreifung (the Nazi seizure of power)…
>
> Perhaps it is best phrased as, "Hitler and the Nazi party seized power in a democratic system."

Nevertheless, this *was* an example of extreme politics taking advantage of a democratic system, and driving the government of a country in a direction that turned out to be deeply regrettable.

This is far from being the only example. You can doubtless supply your own additional illustrations from around the world.

The more power that technology places in the hands of unscrupulous politicians and their shadowy backers, the greater the danger of this kind of usurpation. On the other hand, the same general developments in technology could also allow citizenry to gain more autonomy, more knowledge, better skills in critical thinking, and more resilience against being misled.

One answer, accordingly, to the risk of worse politics at the hands of self-serving politicians with greater power, is that citizens as a whole, aided by education and technology, can become "better people":

- *Better journalists*, more able to highlight important issues
- *Better educators*, more able to impart key skills to greater numbers of students of all ages
- *Better voters*, more able to withstand devious twists, bribes, fear-mongering, and rabble-rousing
- *Better politicians*, able to coordinate coalitions in support of genuine improvements in overall wellbeing, and to win votes away from their more destructive political opponents.

That answer makes sense in its own way. Improving the people involved in all aspects of politics would be an important step forward.

But it's by no means the whole story. In parallel, we must also improve the *system* in which politics exists. Changing the system can produce faster results.

Let's look at two different ideas for what that might involve. Essentially, these ideas are to *reduce* government and to *rejuvenate* government. We might call these systems "minimal democracy" and "superdemocracy".

Minimalism

Here's a suggestion. If people aren't up to the task of government, shouldn't we have less government?

If politicians are generally ill-informed and self-serving, shouldn't we restrict the amount of influence politicians have over society?

Where cooperation is needed between people, can't we leave this, as far as possible, to other mechanisms, like the marketplace of buyers and sellers, alongside informal community arrangements and local judiciary, rather than any top-down imposition of rules by centralised politicians?

In this vision, we wouldn't actually need that much government. Society could function well enough, most of the time, without rulers.

Shouldn't we, therefore, replace Lincoln's Gettysburg Address description of how government should operate with the following phrase?

"As little government as possible."

Or perhaps like this instead?

"Politicians with as little power as possible."

My first objection to this suggestion is that it downplays all the positive accomplishments of governments and politicians. It sees only the negative aspects of politics, rather than their upsides. It disregards the history of successful political initiatives to advance healthcare, education, social justice, and peace-keeping.

My second objection is that, in the absence of an effective government, people throughout society will be vulnerable to the abuse of power by large corporations, mafia-style gangs, crime syndicates, guerrilla networks, and external armies from neighbouring states. As the eighteenth-century Anglo-Irish statesman Edmund Burke has been paraphrased as saying:

> The only thing necessary for the triumph of evil is that good men do nothing.

The full version of Burke's celebrated remarks emphasises the need not only for *action* but for *association*[784]:

> No man … can flatter himself that his single, unsupported, desultory, unsystematic endeavours are of power to defeat the subtle designs and united cabals of ambitious citizens. When bad men combine, the good must associate; else they will fall, one by one, an unpitied sacrifice in a contemptible struggle.

A remark from the other side of the Atlantic from roughly the same time, attributed to Benjamin Franklin, conveys the same thought in different language[785]:

> We must… all hang together, or assuredly we shall all hang separately.

Thus, whilst there are, indeed, reasons to worry about the misuse of power by politicians, there are also reasons to worry about the misuse of power by lots of other groups of people – groups that can expand their malign influence into any vacuum left by the absence of government.

My third and final objection to this vision of minimal government concerns the naivety of suggested alternatives to political institutions. Informal networks can work fine when stakes are low, and when there are kinship or other familiarity bonds between everyone involved. But when the number of people interacting grows larger, more formal structures of one sort or another become necessary. When they work well, these structures will guide everyone to contribute a fair share of effort to vital community projects, and to take no more than a fair share of community resources. Without these structures, what economists call "public goods" will suffer.

Examples of public goods include flood defence systems, networks of fire stations, transport infrastructure, a police force, the legal system, research into basic science, and a national currency. If everyone chips in to the effort of creating and maintaining these systems, everyone benefits. However, individuals can be tempted to become "free-riders" – making only token or zero contributions to these goods, but dipping into the benefits along with everyone else. So long as there are only a few free-riders, the public goods continue in place. But every society needs to take measures to prevent the number of free-riders from growing. And as the *size* of the society increases, systems of informal censures and commendations need to transition into more rigorous frameworks, where persistent or extreme free-riders are penalised by losing some of their liberties.

Within such frameworks, each individual person can reason to themself:

- It might be convenient if I could cheat the system from time to time – paying less tax than my fair share, driving faster than the specified speed limit, discarding litter rather than disposing of it tidily, or emitting excess greenhouse gases
- However, if lots of other people cheated in similar ways, public services would suffer, other drivers might crash into me or my loved ones, my neighbourhood would become despoiled, and the weather could become more extreme more often
- Therefore, it's in my interest that *everyone* is deterred from that kind of cheating
- These restrictions on my liberty – and on everyone else's liberty – means that we'll all actually have more liberty
- It's insufficient just to rely on everyone's good nature not to cheat when tempted to act in a socially irresponsible way; measures of compulsion play an important role in maintaining our overall state of increased liberty.

That line of reasoning might sound paradoxical, but it all makes sense.

This is *not* to say that political and legal measures are the only way to encourage the kind of positive collaboration from which we can all benefit.

Far from it. Informal measures have a big role too. As has the mechanism of *market coordination*, to which I'll turn shortly. But these other modes of collaboration ultimately depend upon the threat of more forceful sanction.

To restate my objection concerning the naivety of advocates of minimal government: I've not yet seen an explanation of "minimal government" which faces up to the threats that would be posed to social wellbeing by potential free-riders, cheats, bullies, and self-serving complexes – especially when these groups are well organised. In such a society, public goods would wither away, sooner or later. We might still feel *some* trust toward individuals that we recognise, but strangers would make us apprehensive. And we would be nervous even in the presence of people that we think we know, lest they harbour secret intentions to cheat us, bully us, steal our possessions, or maim us.

That observation was made by Thomas Hobbes in his 1651 book, *Leviathan*[786]:

> In the nature of man we find three principal causes of quarrel: first, competition; secondly, diffidence [that is, apprehension]; thirdly, glory.
>
> The first maketh man invade for gain; the second, for safety; and the third, for reputation. The first use violence, to make themselves masters of other men's persons, wives, children, and cattle; the second, to defend them; the third, for trifles, as a word, a smile, a different opinion, and any other sign of undervalue, either direct in their persons or by reflection in their kindred, their friends, their nation, their profession, or their name.

As I mentioned in Chapter 5, "Shortsight", the solution advocated by Hobbes – and many who have come after him – involves all members of society accepting a state of partial subservience to a "commonwealth", also known as a government.

Of course, governing systems have varied greatly in their effectiveness throughout history. Some "commonwealths" have brought peace and prosperity to their members, whereas others have brought increased suffering. But the fact that some governments have failed, does not imply that all governments should be resisted, or minimised. Rather, we need to understand the *difference* between bad government and good government.

Instead of a goal to minimise government, our objective, therefore, should be to revitalise government. Instead of relying on loose, informal mechanisms to somehow look after the important public goods upon which a society depends, we need to place these mechanisms onto a basis that is more stable and more reliable.

One of the most important public goods is the competitive free marketplace. In such a marketplace, when things go well, buyers and sellers interact with sustained mutual benefit. But like all public goods, the free market is vulnerable to becoming weak due to lack of support, in which case its outcomes can be far from mutually beneficial. Taking care of the free market is among the most essential – and also the most challenging – of the tasks facing governments. It is absolutely *not* the kind of thing that can happen simply by good intentions and informal relationships.

Markets and their failures

Before we talk about the spectacular ways in which markets can fail, let's remind ourselves of the profound positive results that markets can achieve.

A free market that is well-run and competitive can stimulate and facilitate remarkable innovation and enterprise. Free markets in goods and services have encouraged significant improvements in the utility, attractiveness, performance, reliability, and affordability of these goods and services. As an example, modern supermarkets are one of the marvels of the world, being stocked from the floor to the ceiling with all kinds of items to improve the quality of daily life. People around the world have access to a vast variety of all-round nourishment and experience that would have astonished their great grandparents.

In recent decades, there have been similar rounds of sustained quality improvement and cost reduction for personal computers, smartphones, internet access, flatscreen TVs, toys, kitchen equipment, home and office furniture, clothing, motor cars, airplane tickets, solar panels, and much more. The companies that found ways to improve their goods and services flourished in the marketplace, compelling their competitors to find similar innovations – or to go out of business.

It's no accident that the term "free market" contains the adjective "free". The elements of a free market which enable it to produce a stream of quality improvements and cost reductions include the following freedoms:

1. The freedom for companies to pursue profits – under the recognition that the prospect of earning profits can incentivise sustained diligence and innovation

2. The freedom for companies to adjust the prices for their products, and to decide by themselves the features contained in these products, rather than following the dictates of any centralised planner
3. The freedom for groups of people to join together and start a new business
4. The freedom for companies to enter new markets, rather than being restricted to existing product lines; new competitors keep established companies on their toes
5. The freedom for employees to move to new roles in different companies, rather than being tied to their existing employers
6. The freedom for companies to explore multiple ways to raise funding for their projects
7. The freedom for potential customers to *not* buy products from established vendors, but to switch to alternatives, or even to stop using that kind of product altogether.

What's more, the above freedoms are *permissionless*. No-one needs to apply for a special licence from central authorities before one of these freedoms becomes available.

Any political steps that would curtail the above freedoms need careful consideration. The result of such restrictions could include:

- A disengaged workforce, with little incentive to apply their inspiration and perspiration to the tasks assigned to them
- Poor responsiveness to changing market interest in various products and services
- Over-production of products for which there is no market demand
- Companies having little interest in exploring counterintuitive combinations of product features, novel methods of assembly, new ways of training or managing employees, or other innovations.

This is not to say that a free market dispenses with *all* constraints. Advocates of free markets generally understand the importance of setting and observing various rules:

1. *Protection of property*: goods and materials cannot simply be stolen, but require the payment of an agreed price

2. *Protection of intellectual property*: various novel ideas cannot simply be copied, but require, for a specified time, the payment of an agreed license fee
3. *Protection of brand reputation*: companies cannot use misleading labelling or other trademarked imagery to falsely imply an association with another existing company with a good reputation
4. *Protection of contract terms*: when companies or individuals enter into legal contracts, regarding employment conditions, supply timelines, fees for goods and services, etc, penalties for any breach of contract can be enforced
5. *Protection of public goods*: shared items such as clean air, usable roads, and general safety mechanisms, need to be protected against decay.

These protections all require the existence and maintenance of a legal system in which justice is available to everyone – not just to the people who are already well-placed in society.

These are not the only preconditions for the healthy operation of free markets. The benefits of these markets also depend on the existence of *viable competition*, which prevents companies from resting on their laurels. However, seeking an easier life for themselves, companies may be tempted to organise themselves into cartels, with agreed pricing, or with products with built-in obsolescence. The extreme case of a cartel is a monopoly, in which all competitors have gone out of business, or have been acquired by the leading company in an industry. A monopoly lacks incentive to lower prices or to improve product quality. A related problem is "crony capitalism", in which governments preferentially award business contracts to companies with personal links to government ministers. The successful operation of a free market depends, therefore, upon society's collective vigilance to notice and break up cartels, to prevent the misuse of monopoly power, and to avoid crony capitalism.

Further, even when markets do work well, in ways that provide short-term benefits to both vendors and customers, the longer-term result can be profoundly negative. So-called "commons" resources can be driven into a state of ruin by overuse. Examples include communal grazing land, the water flowing in a river, fish populations, and herds of wild livestock. All individual users of such a resource have an incentive to take from it, either to consume it themselves, or to include it in a product to be sold to a third party. As the common stock declines, the incentive for each individual person to take more increases, so that they're not excluded. But finally, the grassland is all bare, the river has dried up, the stocks of fish have been obliterated, or the passenger pigeon, great auk, monk seal, sea mink, etc, have been hunted to extinction. To guard against these perils of short-termism, various sorts of protective mechanisms need to be created, such as quotas or licences, with clear evidence of their enforcement.

A similar logic resulted in laws restricting the employment of children. When young boys and girls worked in factories, mines, or inside chimneys, there were often short-term economic benefits to the families of these children, as well as to the business owners or the gangs who provided chimney sweeping services. However, society resolved that the longer-term wellbeing of these children would be better improved by forbidding such employment. The existence of factory inspectors helped businesses resist any temptation to continue to exploit child labour in defiance of the new laws.

What about when suppliers provide shoddy goods? In some cases, members of a society can learn which suppliers are unreliable, and therefore cease purchasing goods from them. In these cases, the market corrects itself: in order to continue in business, poor suppliers need to make amends. But when larger groups of people are involved, there are three drawbacks with relying on this self-correcting mechanism:

1. A vendor who deceives one purchaser in one vicinity can relocate to a different vicinity – or can simply become "lost in the crowd" – before deceiving another purchaser
2. A vendor who produces poor quality goods on a large scale can simultaneously impact lots of people's wellbeing – as when a restaurant skimps on health and safety standards, and large numbers of diners suffer food poisoning as a result
3. It may take a long period of time before defects in someone's goods or services are discovered – for example, if no funds are available for an insurance payout that was contracted many years earlier.

It's for such reasons that societies often decide to augment the self-correction mechanisms of the free market with faster acting preventive mechanisms, including requirements for people in various trades to conform to sets of agreed standards and regulations. Such standards and regulations are controversial in some circles, being seen as opposed to the ideals of the free market. It's true that standards and regulations sometimes do act to limit innovation and the entry of new competitors. But that's no reason to dispense with all such systems. Instead, it's a reason to ensure such systems are implemented in ways that are more responsive to changing circumstances and new opportunities. As we'll see below, this is an area where technological innovation can provide assistance.

A final cause of market failure is perhaps the most significant: the way in which market exchanges fail to take "externalities" into account. A vendor and a purchaser may both benefit when a product is created, sold, and used, but other people who are not party to that transaction can suffer as a side-effect – if, for example, the manufacturing process emits loud noises, foul smells, noxious gases, or damaging waste products. Since they are not directly involved in the transaction, these third parties cannot influence the outcome simply by ceasing to purchase the goods or services involved. Instead, different kinds of pressure need to be applied: legal restrictions, taxes, or other penalties or incentives.

One economist who offered strong support in favour of the use of taxes in such circumstances was free market champion, Milton Friedman. In 1979, Friedman was asked by television interviewer, Phil Donahue, "Is there a case for the government to do something about pollution?" Here's Friedman's reply[787]:

> Yes, there's a case for the government to do something. There's always a case for the government to do something about it… when what two people do affects a third party... There is a case for the government protecting third parties, protecting people who have not voluntarily agreed to enter…
>
> But the question is: what's the best way to do it? And the best way to do it is not to have bureaucrats in Washington write rules and regulations saying a car has to carry this that or the other. The way to do it is to impose a tax on the cost of the pollutants emitted by a car and make an incentive for car manufacturers and for consumers to keep down the amount of pollution.

A video recording of this exchange was played for the audience at an event in October 2014 at the University of Chicago. The forum was entitled "What Would Milton Friedman Do About Climate Change?" Michael Greenstein, the Milton Friedman Professor of Economics at the University of Chicago, offered this commentary:

> What's happening when we turn on the lights, when the power is derived from a coal plant, or when we drive our car, is that carbon dioxide is emitted

> into the air, and that's sprinkling around damages in Bangladesh, London, Houston.
>
> And those costs are real, and they're not being reflected in the costs of that electricity or the tank of gas. Emitting carbon dioxide into the atmosphere does allow you to produce electricity more cheaply, but there's a whole other set of people who are being punished or penalized. It's a poor idea of economics.

Another professor attending, Steve Cicala from the Harris School of Public Policy, was even blunter:

> It is theft. That's a loaded term, but if anyone can come up with a better term for taking something from people without their consent and without compensating them, I'm happy to use that term.

These are strong words, from the successors to Milton Friedman. The present situation, lacking carbon taxes, is "a poor idea of economics". It is "theft". Greenstone commented further:

> The price system isn't working in the energy sector right now exactly because carbon is priced at zero.
>
> The problem isn't the U.S. has no carbon policy, but that it has a poor carbon policy, namely, that it's fine to pollute. By introducing a price on carbon, the government could create a market for free enterprise solutions.
>
> It would be very hard for companies to raise money for innovation when there's no market for it. And this is a case where the government can set the market and then get out of the way and let the private sector figure out what's the best way to get to low carbon energy.

Note in particular the phrase, "the government could create a market for free enterprise solutions". This acknowledges, once again, the way in which free markets depend on government.

It's not just *negative* externalities that can cause free markets to misbehave. Consider also *positive* externalities, where an economic interaction has a positive impact on people who do not pay for it. Some examples:

1. If a company purchases medical vaccinations for its employees, to reduce their likelihood of becoming ill with the flu, others in the community benefit too, since there will be fewer ill people in that neighbourhood, from whom they might catch flu

2. If a company purchases on-the-job training for an employee, the employee may pass on to family members and acquaintances, free of charge, some of the skills they learned
3. If a company pays employees to carry out fundamental research, which is published openly, people in other companies can benefit from that research too, even though they did not pay for it.

The problem here is that the company may decide *not* to go ahead with such an investment, since they calculate that the benefits *for them* will not be sufficient to cover their costs. The fact that society as a whole would benefit, as a positive externality, generally does not enter their calculation.

As you will realise, this brings us back to the concept of public goods. When there's insufficient business case for an individual investor to supply the funding to cover the costs of a project, that project will fail to happen – unless there's a collective decision for multiple investors to share in supporting it. Facilitating that kind of collective decision – one that would benefit society as a whole, rather than just a cartel of self-interested companies – is a core task of politics. When these decisions consider longer-term possibilities – in ways that, as noted, are problematic for a free market to achieve – they become known as *industrial strategy* or *social strategy*.

Fans of free markets often express a dislike for the concept of industrial strategy. Their argument is that politicians invariably do a poor job of long-term industrial thinking. Politicians lack the business acumen of business leaders, the technological acumen of technologists, and the engineering acumen of engineers. Innovation cannot be run from any central planning department. At least, that's what advocates for minimal government say.

However, what's needed is an appropriate *division of responsibility*. Politicians, acting on behalf of society as a whole, assisted by specially trained civil servants, and responsive to advice from business leaders, technologists, engineers, social scientists, futurists, and other experts, should set the overall direction. Given a clear direction, the free market, along with other methods for coordination, can work the appropriate wonders.

Dividing responsibility

Recall two examples from earlier chapters. When John F. Kennedy declared that astronauts would travel to the moon and back before the end of the 1960s, he did not specify whether the journey would involve "Direct ascent",

"Earth-orbit rendezvous", "Lunar-orbit rendezvous", or "Lunar surface rendezvous". That engineering question was something for the experts within NASA to address. Again, when Margaret Thatcher called for the phasing out of CFC chemicals from aerosols and refrigeration, she did not – despite her own background as a chemist – specify which alternative chemicals should be used in their place. That question was for something for chemical companies to address.

These examples illustrate aspects of a profound principle of political organisation: the division of responsibility. Politicians should tackle only the tasks which lie outside the capabilities of other groups or structures in society. Other tasks should be left to these other groups.

I've already looked at one famous statement from Abraham Lincoln about government – and I'll return to it later in this chapter. Here's another astute recommendation, which Lincoln made nine years earlier, in 1854[788]:

> The legitimate object of government, is to do for a community of people, whatever they need to have done, but can not do, at all, or can not, so well do, for themselves – in their separate, and individual capacities.
>
> In all that the people can individually do as well for themselves, government ought not to interfere.

In his remarks, Lincoln went on to identify two classes of "things which the individuals of a people can not do, or can not well do, for themselves":

1. Dealing with "crimes, misdemeanours, and non-performance of contracts"
2. Tasks which "require combined action… public roads and highways, public schools, charities, pauperism, orphanage, estates of the deceased, and the machinery of government itself".

The division of responsibility between the free market and political oversight, as it has evolved in the decades since Lincoln, is described particularly well in the writing of political scientists Jacob Hacker and Paul Pierson[789]. They offer fulsome praise to something they say "may well be the greatest invention in history". Namely, the *mixed economy*:

> The combination of energetic markets and effective governance, deft fingers and strong thumbs.

Their reference to "deft fingers and strong thumbs" expands Adam Smith's famous metaphor of the invisible hand which is said to guide the free market. Hacker and Pierson develop their idea as follows:

> Governments, with their capacity to exercise authority, are like thumbs: powerful but lacking subtlety and flexibility. The invisible hand is all fingers. The visible hand is all thumbs. Of course, one wouldn't want to be all thumbs. But one wouldn't want to be all fingers, either. Thumbs provide countervailing power, constraint, and adjustment to get the best out of those nimble fingers…
>
> The mixed economy… tackles a double bind. The private markets that foster prosperity so powerfully nonetheless fail routinely, sometimes spectacularly so. At the same time, the government policies that are needed to respond to these failures are perpetually under siege from the very market players who help to fuel growth. That is the double bind. Democracy and the market – thumbs and fingers – have to work together, but they also need to be partly independent from each other, or the thumb will cease to provide effective counterpressure to the fingers.

I share the admiration shown by Hacker and Pierson for the mixed market. I also agree that it's hard to get the division of responsibilities right. Just as markets can fail, so also can politicians fail. But just as the fact of market failures should not be taken as a reason to dismantle free markets altogether, so should the fact of political failures not be taken as a reason to dismantle all political oversight of markets. Each of these two sorts of fundamentalist approach – fundamentalist anti-market, and fundamentalist pro-market – is dangerously one-sided. The wellbeing of society requires, not so much the *reduction* of government, but the *rejuvenation* of government, in which key aspects of government operation are improved:

1. Smart, agile, responsive regulatory systems
2. Selected constraints on the uses to which various emerging new technologies can be put
3. "Trust-busting" – measures to prevent large businesses from misusing monopoly power
4. Industrial strategy – identifying directions to be pursued, and providing suitable incentives so that free market forces align toward these directions.

None of what I'm saying here should be controversial. However, the two fundamentalist outlooks that I mentioned, anti-market fundamentalism and pro-market fundamentalism, exercise a disproportionate influence over political discourse. Part of the reason for this is explained at some length in the book by the researchers Jacob Hacker and Paul Pierson which contained their praise for the mixed market. The title of their book is significant: *American Amnesia: Business, Government, and the Forgotten Roots of Our Prosperity.* It's not just that the merits of the mixed market have been "forgotten". They have been deliberately obscured by a sustained ideological attack. That attack serves the interest of various complexes that seek to limit governmental oversight of their activities:

- *Big Tobacco*, which tends to resist government oversight of the advertising of products containing tobacco
- *Big Oil*, which tends to resist government oversight of the emissions of greenhouse gases
- *Big Finance*, which tends to resist government oversight of "financial weapons of mass destruction" (to use a term coined by Warren Buffet)[790]
- *Big Agrotech*, which tends to resist government oversight of new crops, new fertilisers, and new weedkillers
- *Big Media*, who tend to resist government oversight of press standards
- *Big Money* – individuals, families, and corporations with large wealth, who tend to resist the power of government to levy taxes on them.

All these groups stand to make short-term gains if they can persuade the voting public that the power of government needs to be reduced. It is therefore in their interest to paint government as being systematically incompetent – and, at the same time, to paint the free market as being highly competent. However, it is in the *long-term* interest of *all of us*, to see that competent government is re-established.

Separation of power

To recap: human wellbeing can be advanced in many ways by the innovation and enterprise arising from a well-functioning free market. But free markets, left to themselves, can fail in several different ways, and damage human wellbeing. Accordingly, society needs a *separation of power*:

- Power for players throughout the free market, so they can take their own decisions and act on them, in order to create and improve products and services

- Power within the political state, to maintain the health of the free market via regulations, constraints, trust-busting, and incentives.

However, just as the free market can fail, so also can the political state fail. This leads in turn to a need for *another* separation of power:

- Power within the political state, to counter any malign effects of various complexes, such as business groupings, criminal syndicates, terrorist militia, and agents operating on behalf of other countries
- Power within the citizenry, to steer and constrain the political state via public scrutiny, legal reviews, independent opposition politicians, and democratic elections.

The point is to prevent too much power being centralised in any one person – or group of people. Without the checks and balances that characterise an effective democracy, any centralised power can flip over, in stages, from being a force for the overall good of society, into being a force with much smaller goals: self-preservation and aggrandization.

Importantly, these checks and balances aren't just a matter of having capable, socially-minded people in key roles throughout society. They're also a matter of having clear, compelling systems of procedures that:

1. Structure how people operate in different roles
2. Draw attention to instances where people are operating in violation of recognised best practices
3. Provide protection to "whistle blowers" who raise an alarm when they notice potentially injurious actions
4. Mandate not only the creation of contingency plans, ready for adoption in cases of disruption, but also – to guard against unwarranted overconfidence – *the careful testing of these plans* via suitable scenario exercises.

These operating procedures and agreed best practices are by no means static. As new opportunities and new threats become recognised, they will likely need to evolve. But any such evolution should not be left under the sole control of any one person – or group of people. The same principle of "separation of power" that applies for society as a whole also applies to the mechanisms to evolve the operating procedures for society:

- Acknowledged experts in various applicable fields should be given sufficient opportunity to express their views

- People holding alternative viewpoints – including radical and dissident opinions – should also have the opportunity to ask questions and to explain their own proposals
- In such a discussion, it should not be possible for the voices of the loud to drown out potentially more thoughtful viewpoints from quieter voices
- There is certainly a role for activists, who put a high priority on advancing a particular cause or principle that they deem as having fundamental importance
- There is also a role for academics, who put a high priority on establishing matters of fact, rather than championing any particular activist cause
- In such a discussion, there is a time for collecting ideas and debating their merits; but there is also a time for reaching a decision – potentially a compromise – and moving forward; subsequently, there is also a time to monitor the outcomes, to reflect on the overall process, and, potentially, to make a case to revisit the decision.

None of this is particularly easy. It requires skills within the community in areas such as facilitation, legal analysis, journalistic investigation, building consensus, and, yes, foresight. It requires a tolerance for diversity, and the ability to accept what appears to be an imperfect decision in the interest of moving forward together.

It's a system that encourages openness, but it's not a system of "anything goes". Different styles of thinking are encouraged, but not deliberate falsehoods or distortions. That's the general principle behind laws of libel and misrepresentation. Whilst each person has their own responsibility to check the validity of purported information that they encounter, in reality we absorb a great deal of what we hear and see without much scrutiny. Deceptive imagery and misleading communications can influence our actions, either immediately or some time afterward. Accordingly, legislation forbids:

1. Deliberate calls of, for example, "Fire!", that will provoke a dangerous panic in a crowded location, when no such fire exists, and there is no good reason for the first person to raise such an alarm
2. Advertising that makes false claims about a product's safety, effectiveness, provenance, or composition

3. Financial misinformation that is designed to mislead potential investors regarding the performance of a company
4. Speech that is liable to whip up hatred and incite violence against individuals, or against members of a particular community
5. Messages that damage someone's reputation by deliberately spreading incendiary misinformation.

In these cases, there is no punishment for honest mistakes, provided the person making the mistake took reasonable efforts to check what they were saying before spreading the message. The kinds of misinformation that can be prosecuted are when the speaker knew that the message was false, or when they *ought* to have known that the message was false.

Note the parallel. Society benefits from a free market for goods and services that thrives on openness, but these goods and services need to respect a number of standards and regulations, for the sake of society as a whole. Likewise, society benefits from free speech and open exchange of ideas and opinions, but, again, this exchange needs to respect a number of standards and regulations. In each case, naive and unhelpful fundamentalist positions are sometimes expressed:

- Pro-market fundamentalists argue against any regulation of the free market; anti-market fundamentalists argue that the entire economy must be centrally planned
- Anti-censorship fundamentalists argue against any regulation of what people can say; pro-censorship fundamentalists argue, in effect, that all speech on any contentious matter needs prior approval from a central "thought police".

In each case, what's needed is to avoid the extremes, and to accept the hard, hard task of finding – and regularly updating – an appropriate set of standards and regulations.

In all of the above, the good news is that *technology can help*. That brings us back to Abraham Lincoln's 1863 formulation of democracy, which we can now update to a formulation of *superdemocracy*.

Superdemocracy

"Government of the people, by the people, for the people."

All three of the clauses in Lincoln's statement can be updated. The result doesn't roll off the tongue quite so easily, but it's worth taking the time in each case to mention more than the simple word "people".

Let's start in the middle of the statement, and then move outward.

The middle clause becomes: **"by the people, aided by institutions and technology"**. I've already talked about some of the institutions: the legal system, a free press, the education system, alternative candidates in elections, the mixed economy, and, more generally, the separation of power. By taking advantage of new technology, including tools with elements of AI, additional mechanisms and institutions will grow in viability:

1. *Real-time fact checking*, which could highlight almost immediately whether there is evidence to contradict (or verify) a claim being made by a politician or their supporters
2. *Real-time logic checking*, that could highlight any invalid jumps in reasoning – or conversely, confirm the soundness of an argument
3. *Real-time source checking*, to verify whether a quotation, image, or video extract may have been altered before being presented, changing its meaning or any implications arising
4. *Reputation systems*, that keep track of the reliability of people's past contributions to particular topics
5. *The creative generation of new proposals*, that can combine key elements from previous suggestions in ways that address earlier concerns
6. *Simulations*, in huge computational models, of potential consequences of envisioned legislative changes, to help the identification and evaluation, ahead of time, of possible real-world risks and benefits of these changes
7. *Improved electoral systems*, involving elements of proportional representation as well as ranked preference votes, to avoid the present situation in which far too many people feel that their votes will be essentially meaningless, or that they ought to cast a tactical vote for a candidate different from their actual first preference
8. *Liquid voting*, in which citizens can temporarily assign their voting rights in specified topic areas to people they trust to vote on their behalf regarding these topics

9. *Facilitated citizens' assemblies*, that act in similar ways to jury trials, with representative groups of citizens being selected at random, and supported in a task to evaluate possible solutions to given social issues, ahead of the conclusions of these assemblies being forwarded to society as a whole for wider consideration
10. *A "House of AI" revising chamber of government*, that applies AI reasoning to provide feedback on proposed legislation, as well as offering possible revisions to that legislation.

The first clause of Lincoln's 1863 phrase becomes **"Government of the people, resources, institutions, and technology"**. The point is to emphasise that selected constraints and restrictions should be applied, not just to what people do, but also to:

1. The usage of particular resources, for example, aspects of the environment
2. The institutions that are a key part of society, but which, individually, cannot be allowed to become too powerful
3. Any technology which could, in some cases, have huge negative consequences, unless appropriate limitations are imposed.

That leaves the third clause – the "for" clause which specifies for who (or what) the government exists. Although I added "institutions and technology" into new expressions of the first and second clause, and "resources" into the new expression of the first clause, I do not propose to add these terms into the third clause. Government does not exist for any of them. Instead, government exists for the same end targets as stated in the "Transhumanist Values" proposed in Chapter 11: human wellbeing, and generalised to the wellbeing of consciousness.

Accordingly, the third clause becomes **"for the people, and for consciousness in general"**.

Putting everything together gives the following summary of superdemocracy:

"Government of the people, resources, institutions, and technology,
by the people, institutions, and technology,
for the people, and for consciousness in general."

Given this statement, we can consider four types of criticism of the concept of superdemocracy. It could be contended that:

1. People are inherently too unreliable, even with technological support
2. Institutions can hinder political progress rather than enable it
3. Technology will make politics worse rather than better
4. Existing political forces will oppose any useful reforms.

My answer is: yes, this is challenging. Don't expect an overnight miracle. But if the overall vision is kept in mind, if the best insights of diverse participants are carefully considered, and if changes are implemented with due caution and reflection, superdemocracy can emerge over the course of the next decade or so. This will happen due to the following parallel changes:

1. People with clearer thinking, fewer biases, and greater compassion, becoming more involved in all aspects of political life
2. Social and political institutions evolving, speedily where needed, to serve the present and the future rather than the past, and with stronger support from the populace as a whole
3. Trials of different technological tools, such as those listed earlier – different systems being trialled in different parts of the world – and the systems with the best results being adopted more widely
4. Constructive political alliances and coalitions, which transcend earlier divisive factionalism – as explored in the next section.

Party politics

Although I disagree with any recommendation to minimise *politics*, I strongly support the related recommendation to minimise *party politics*.

Political parties made sense in the past, but nowadays are more of an impediment than an aid to effective government. Political parties multiply mistrust: people in different parties profoundly mistrust each other.

Political parties provided the support for people interested in becoming involved in politics, including training, networks of potential connections, financial assistance, and help with the key task of becoming elected. In turn, politicians were expected to show loyalty to their parties, such as:

1. Voting for policies chosen by party leaders, regardless of their own personal assessments of these policies
2. Joining with party colleagues to pour scorn on opposing parties.

Now, thoughtful disagreement is a necessary part of life, especially when circumstances are complex. To help clarify the strengths and weaknesses of different ideas, groups of people can usefully take on the task of debate, exploring and advocating different positions. Such disagreement features regularly in science, and science is the better for it. It's the same with politics. However, *party* politics damages the nature of these debates:

1. Rather than focusing on which *policy* is best, the debate often becomes, in effect, which *party* is best – with attention drawn to purported errors made in the past by the different parties, even if these errors have little direct relevance to the current policy debate
2. Disagreements are often magnified, for theatrical purposes, rather than compromises being sought
3. Even when politicians are aware of particular pluses or minuses of a given policy, they often keep silent about these points, since they would run counter to their party's official position
4. When politicians perceive that a point someone is making is damaging to their cause, they often attempt to suppress that voice, or to misrepresent or ridicule it, or to damage the reputation of the people involved – rather than engaging honestly with the substance of the point.

When circumstances are *particularly* complex, with fast-changing possibilities – as in the present day, with the consequences of NBIC technologies becoming ever more prominent – it's especially important to rescue political dialogue from the rancour and distortions of partisanship. The drawbacks of entrenched partisan politics may have been a tolerable weakness in past decades, but are nowadays becoming ever more dangerous. It's time, therefore, for the dominance of parties to recede.

Happily, many of the forms of support for prospective politicians, which used to be available only from political parties, are nowadays available from non-party sources, including online networks, and non-partisan think tanks.

In this vision, there will still be a role for political parties to fulfil, but these parties will be more fluid than before. It will become much more common for:

- People who are associated with one party, to nonetheless support a different party on one or more specific policy areas
- People to move between parties
- New parties to form

- Parties to split and merge, creating new groupings
- Governments to include people from multiple different parties.

Countries vary in the extent to which they are already entering the era of post-partisan politics. Factors which aid that kind of politics include:

1. Voting systems, such as proportional representation, that make it easier for new parties to enter parliament, rather than being squeezed out by electors' fears that any votes for new parties will be "wasted"
2. A tradition of parties forming coalitions, with a clear understanding of the best practice in such relationships
3. A tradition of coalitions working in partnership with individuals from other parties that remain formally outside the coalition
4. Public dissatisfaction with any media that is highly partisan
5. A growing general recognition of the drawbacks of "groupthink" – of which partisan politics is an evident troubling example
6. A reduction in the importance of large financial funding for political parties – due to limits being imposed on political expenditure, and due to less expensive ways for politicians to spread their messages.

In countries like the US and the UK with a particularly strong tradition of unpleasant partisan politics, including the dominance of first-past-the-post elections, the following developments should provide extra pressure to overcome existing inertia and to experiment with post-partisan politics:

1. Growing comfort level with the kinds of technological assistance that support more sophisticated voting methods
2. Evident successes of post-partisan politics in other countries
3. Evident successes of post-partisan politics at local, state, or regional levels
4. Evident successes of citizens' assemblies, convened to address tough issues, but with their members (hopefully) able to transcend the blinkers of their initial political affiliations as the assemblies proceed.

Beyond national politics

Local and national politics involve collective decisions on constraints and incentives. In the 1854 words from Abraham Lincoln quoted earlier in this chapter:

> The legitimate object of government, is to do for a community of people, whatever they need to have done, but can not do, at all, or can not, so well do, for themselves – in their separate, and individual capacities… all which… requires combined action, as public roads and highways, public schools, charities, pauperism, orphanage, estates of the deceased, and the machinery of government itself.

A very similar set of considerations applies for *international* politics. Freedoms which make good sense for individual countries, when assessed individually, make less sense if applied more widely.

Thus, nations can prepare to defend themselves against violent aggressors, but should, ideally, be constrained not to carry out certain kinds of tests of nuclear weaponry. Nations have the freedom to exploit the natural resources at their disposal, but should, ideally, be constrained not to unduly damage the international environment as a side-effect. Nations can use measures such as targeted tax relief to support businesses working in their countries, but within constraints so as not to unfairly distort international market dynamics. Nations can determine their own policies on research and development of new products, but are constrained by international moratoria to exercise great care in particularly risky fields of investigation, such as "gain of function" research with infectious viruses.

Just as for the constraints imposed by local politics, these international constraints cause annoyance and frustration from time to time. Nevertheless, most countries recognise that, in principle, greater safety, stability, and prosperity would follow from adoption of *appropriate* constraints on sovereignty. Just as for local politics, the dilemma is how to agree these constraints – and how to ensure they are fairly enforced.

The extra complication for international politics is that, unlike the level of the nation state, there is no overall governing structure for global relationships. There is no global police force to track down violators to ensure compliance. There is no process of worldwide democracy whereby one set of global politicians can be voted out of office, if they are perceived as having failed in their leadership roles. Existing international bodies, such as the United Nations, and the International Criminal Court located in The Hague, have limited powers, which individual countries seem to be able to ignore with impunity.

Some critics express gratitude for this lack of an international government. Prime sovereignty, they argue, should remain at the level of the nation state. No international government could be trusted to operate in a way that gains and keeps the assent of the various leading countries of the world. Any such body would be inclined to add extra layers of bureaucracy and interference. It would likely mandate policies that would be an anathema to national self-determination. It would suck up extra taxes, away from local jurisdiction, to serve the needs of globe-trotting administrators and their far-flung interventionist projects. Therefore – according to these critics – any moves to an international government should be resisted.

Similar opposition is often expressed to the idea of "super-state" conglomerations of neighbouring countries. The notion of a European Union committed to "ever closer integration" alarms many observers, who fear the imposition of alien values and the usurpation of local autonomy. These observers believe that citizens could never feel as much loyalty to the European Union as to their nation state (such as Germany, Spain, or the United Kingdom). Thank goodness, they say, for the supposed failures of super-states. It's time for these super-states to unravel, with, for instance, more countries in the EU following the "Brexit" example of the UK.

I say, in contrast, that any such unravelling should be regretted. Without effective, trustworthy mechanisms of global coordination, countries will be driven to take matters into their own hands. We risk ending up in a race to the bottom. This makes the world a more dangerous place for all of us.

For one more time in this chapter, my theme is the need to avoid each of two extremes. In this case, the two extremes are:

1. To reject all initiatives in which individual countries give up some portion of their national sovereignty to an international body
2. To call for a global government that has paramount authority over all decisions in all the countries of the world.

Instead of these extremes, we should, once again, look for an appropriate separation of powers.

In other words, rather than *minimal international democracy*, or any *global centralisation of power*, I look forward to *international superdemocracy*. The next chapter explores how that might work.

14. Geopolitics

Geopolitics, defined: The art of the possible, in a world without a global government. Achieving international cooperation in the service of common causes despite long-established distrust. Communications that transcend national rivalries to create an international climate for positive change.

"In all that countries can individually do as well for themselves, international politics ought not to interfere."

These are words that a modern-day Abraham Lincoln might have said, as an international analogue of the warning the real Lincoln had offered in 1854:

> In all that the people can individually do as well for themselves, government ought not to interfere.

The European Union has its own version of that principle, which is known by the rather inelegant term "subsidiarity"[791]:

> The principle of subsidiarity… aims to ensure that decisions are taken as closely as possible to the citizen and that constant checks are made to verify that action at EU level is justified in light of the possibilities available at national, regional or local level.
>
> Specifically, it is the principle whereby the EU does not take action… unless it is more effective than action taken at national, regional or local level. It is closely bound up with the principle of proportionality, which requires that any action by the EU should not go beyond what is necessary to achieve the objectives of the [EU] Treaties.

That's a principle that even critics of the EU ought to be able to support.

In other words, bodies that govern matters that transcend the boundaries of individual countries should restrict themselves to precisely these matters. No more and no less.

Thankfully, there are some examples from which we can take inspiration. Consider the processes to agree rules for international sports competitions. When the nations of the world meet to compete in the Football World Cup, they all need to accept the same rules about offside, substitutes, yellow card offences, red card offences, penalty kicks, and so on. Regardless of which kind of political system applies in its own country, a team at the World Cup cannot unilaterally decide to have two goalkeepers on the pitch at the same time, each allowed to handle the ball – or a total of thirteen players, instead of the usual eleven. And when new technologies enable a change in the playing conditions, such as Video Assisted Referees to help adjudicate contentious on-field decisions, the different countries in any one competition all need to accept whatever new rules are agreed regarding adoption of these technologies.

Rules governing international football competitions are overseen by FIFA (Fédération Internationale de Football Association), which describes itself as[792] "the international governing body of football". FIFA was formed in 1904 when representatives of seven countries met together in Paris[793]: Belgium, Denmark, France, Netherlands, Spain, Sweden, and Switzerland. At the time of writing, the association has grown to 211 countries[794]. But despite its evident authority in the sport of football, FIFA, rightly, has no authority over other sports such as cricket, golf, rugby, snooker, or tennis.

In a broadly similar way, the International Civil Aviation Organization (ICAO) oversees international cooperation in matters such as air traffic control, airline identification codes, communications between different aircraft, aircraft safety, flight inspections, air accident investigations, and maintaining sets of recognised best practice for civil aviation. The ICAO can trace its history back to a meeting in Berlin in 1903 involving eight countries; today it is backed by 193 national governments[795]. One recent example of an initiative assisted by ICAO support was a modernisation of rules governing air cargo in Latin America, in order to speed up the transport of vaccines by international flights[796].

For a different kind of example, with more complications, let's take some time to consider the evolution of international rules about chemical weapons.

Chemical warfare

As long ago as 1899, at an international convention in The Hague, twenty-three countries signed up to a "Declaration concerning the Prohibition of the Use of Projectiles with the Sole Object to Spread Asphyxiating Poisonous Gases"[797]. By 1907, at a second convention also held in The Hague, four more countries had joined the agreement. The signatories included countries that, nevertheless, went on to use poison gas during the First World War, with the kinds of horrific consequences the declaration had been intended to prevent. It is estimated that, over the course of that war, weapons containing chlorine, phosgene, and mustard gas resulted in more than 1.3 million casualties, including around 90,000 deaths[798]. The particular distress caused by these attacks was vividly conveyed in poems written by soldiers fighting on the front line, such as *Dulce et Decorum Est* by Wilfred Owen[799]:

> Guttering, choking, drowning…
>
> The white eyes writhing in his face, his hanging face, like a devil's sick of sin…
>
> Obscene as cancer, bitter as the cud of vile, incurable sores on innocent tongues…

In the aftermath of these horrors, thirty-six countries agreed and signed in 1925 the Geneva Protocol "for the Prohibition of the Use in War of Asphyxiating, Poisonous or other Gases, and of Bacteriological Methods of Warfare"[800]:

> WHEREAS the use in war of asphyxiating, poisonous or other gases, and of all analogous liquids, materials or devices, has been justly condemned by the general opinion of the civilised world; and
>
> WHEREAS the prohibition of such use has been declared in Treaties to which the majority of Powers of the world are Parties; and
>
> TO THE END that this prohibition shall be universally accepted as a part of International Law, binding alike the conscience and the practice of nations;
>
> [We] DECLARE:
>
> That the High Contracting Parties, so far as they are not already Parties to Treaties prohibiting such use, accept this prohibition, agree to extend this prohibition to the use of bacteriological methods of warfare and agree to be bound as between themselves according to the terms of this declaration.
>
> The High Contracting Parties will exert every effort to induce other States to accede to the present Protocol.

The bad news is that two of the signatories, Japan and Italy, disregarded the treaty commitments in subsequent years, deploying poisonous gas in China and Abyssinia respectively. What's more, the treaty allowed the development and accumulation of chemical weapons; it was only their actual use that was prohibited. Participants in the Second World War prepared stockpiles of such weapons, and considered using them. Apart from an accidental but deadly discharge of mustard gas from an American ship targeted by German bombers at the port of Bari, Italy, in 1943[801], these stockpiles remained unused. What deterred their use, however, was a simple calculation of likely retaliation and escalation, rather than any sense of obligation to the Geneva Protocol. Closer to the present time, chemical weapons have been used in Iraq, Iran, and Syria.

It might seem, therefore, that international attempts to control chemical weapons have failed. As an example of international cooperation, this is not encouraging.

Nevertheless, out of each failure, the international community has the opportunity to reconsider, and to try again. Just as the 1925 Geneva Protocol arose from the failures of the First World War, the Chemical Weapons Convention (CWC) of 1997 sought to address the failures of subsequent decades. Since that date, 193 countries have signed the convention[802]. But that's only the start of the significance of this convention. Compared to earlier treaties, this was much further reaching:

- It prohibited not just *use* but also the *production* of such weapons
- It committed signatories to destroying their existing stockpiles; indeed, it is reported that more than 98% of previous stockpiles of chemical agents have been destroyed since the convention was agreed
- It created an impartial inspections system, empowered to enter into countries to investigate instances of the production of chemicals that could potentially be used in chemical weapons.

The inspections system, along with general monitoring of adherence to the terms of the CWC, are handled by an international organisation set up for that purpose, namely the Organisation for the Prohibition of Chemical Weapons (OPCW). As a mark of the success of that organisation, and in recognition of "its extensive efforts to eliminate chemical weapons", the OPCW was awarded the 2013 Nobel Peace Prize[803].

The inspections capability of OPCW is particularly noteworthy. It includes a mixture of routine and "challenge" (non-routine) inspections, with inspection teams able to visit any regions inside member states where there are allegations of the usage, or the storage, of chemical weapons[804].

Accordingly, *some* progress can be celebrated. On the other hand:

- Usage of chemical weapons continues, including the 2017 assassination by VX nerve agent of North Korean Kim Jong-nam in Kuala Lumpur airport, and usage of Novichok nerve agent against

Alexei Navalny in Russia and against the Skripal family in Salisbury, England

- It took nearly a century of diplomatic effort, from the first Hague Convention in 1899, before the CWC came into being
- Alongside the task of controlling the spread of chemical or biological weapons, the international community is facing a growing number of new major risks.

Can the process to reach – and monitor – such international agreements be speeded up? Or will an apparent inherent slowness in such a process lead more countries to fall back to unilateral actions – actions which make a sort of sense for each individual country, but which, in aggregate, make the world an even more dangerous place?

Recall from Chapter 8, "Creativity", the analysis which I shared from Harvard professor John Kotter about the three biggest reasons why major change initiatives fail. These reasons apply to international politics as well as to corporate transformations:

1. Lack of a sufficient sense of urgency
2. Lack of an effective guiding coalition
3. Lack of a credible appealing vision of the desired new state of affairs.

The first reason is that, although people are aware of a sense of danger, the level of danger doesn't seem that dramatic, for the time being at least.

The second reason is that, although lots of people in different countries around the world might wish something could be done about the perceived problem, there are no good mechanisms to aggregate these individual concerns into a tangible action plan.

The third reason is that ideas about a better operating model remain vague, idealistic, or unconvincing.

In short, these reasons mean there's no *positive climate for change.*

In principle, the way to escape this bind is to do at least one of the following:

1. Increase the sense of urgency, by clarifying the risks if events accelerate in an unmanaged way
2. Create and strengthen a guiding coalition, by forging greater mutual trust, and by noticing and filling gaps in it

3. Sharpen the positive vision, so that it is arresting, challenging, plausible, and memorable.

For a simple but important example, consider an opportunity brought to the world's attention in the late 1950s: the possibility to eliminate smallpox.

International health

In 1946, sixty-one countries had signed the constitution of the World Health Organisation, affirming the following principles as being "basic to the happiness, harmonious relations and security of all peoples"[805]:

> Health is a state of complete physical, mental and social well-being and not merely the absence of disease or infirmity.
>
> The enjoyment of the highest attainable standard of health is one of the fundamental rights of every human being without distinction of race, religion, political belief, economic or social condition.
>
> The health of all peoples is fundamental to the attainment of peace and security and is dependent upon the fullest co-operation of individuals and States.
>
> The achievement of any State in the promotion and protection of health is of value to all.
>
> Unequal development in different countries in the promotion of health and control of disease, especially communicable disease, is a common danger…

The sixty-one signatories included both the USA and the USSR. At the founding conference, an American was elected Chairman, along with Vice-Chairmen from France, the UK, the USSR, China, and Brazil. However, geopolitical tensions soon disrupted the intended collaboration. Politicians in the USSR and their allies accused the WHO and the US of failing to provide much-needed medical assistance in Eastern Europe. Moreover, they accused the WHO of adopting a "capitalist" approach to healthcare, rather than recognising the social and economic roots of many health problems[806]. Accordingly, the USSR boycotted the WHO from 1949 to 1958.

Despite hostilities between politicians, various medical practitioners in both the USA and the USSR established and maintained personal relationships. One such relationship was to prove pivotal in accelerating the adoption of a polio vaccine throughout the USSR[807]. By 1954, Albert Sabin, a medical researcher in Cincinnati Ohio, had developed a vaccine for polio that could be administered orally, that is without an injection, and which was in due course proven to be effective with just a single dose – in contrast to the more famous vaccine developed by Jonas Salk. In parallel, doctors in the USSR were alarmed by growing numbers of polio cases in their country. A group of virologists, led by Mikhail Chumakov, visited the USA at the start of 1956. Chumakov and Sabin soon established a warm rapport.

Sabin, it turns out, had been born in 1906 in Bialystok, a city which was part of Russia at that time. His family had emigrated to the USA in 1921, but Sabin could still speak some Russian in the 1950s. Chumakov had grown up in a provincial region in the Caucuses. The two found common interests – especially in ideas on how to accelerate testing and adoption of an oral vaccine. Sabin received US State Department approval to share some of his vaccines with Chumakov, and travelled to the USSR several times in the years that followed, meeting with scientists and helping to deepen their confidence in his approach. After successful trials, Chumakov oversaw widespread vaccination adoption within the USSR. The resulting vaccine was subsequently exported from the USSR to some sixty other countries. The success of the vaccine in the USSR also persuaded American authorities that it was safe and effective to use in the USA too.

It's understandable, therefore, that Chumakov is heralded on some Russian websites as[808] a "great Soviet virologist, [who] saved the world from poliomyelitis".

That stellar status of Mikhail Chumakov might, however, be eclipsed by the striking achievements of Viktor Zhdanov, a virologist from the Ukraine, who lived from 1914 to 1987. Zhdanov has been nominated, by Oxford University philosophy professor William MacAskill[809], in answer to the question "Out of everyone who ever existed, who has done the most good for humanity?"

Zhdanov was the head of the delegation from the USSR when that country returned, in 1958, to participating in the World Health Assembly events of the WHO, for the first time since 1948. Soviet Premier Nikita Khrushchev was pursuing a post-Stalin "peaceful coexistence" policy of greater engagement with the west; the following year, he would himself visit the USA for two weeks. In 1958, it was Zhdanov that took the lead, as the WHO event was in Minneapolis that year.

This was no token appearance. Zhdanov surprised attendees by presenting a detailed proposal on how smallpox could be eradicated from the earth within ten years. According to MacAskill, Zhdanov

> Conveyed his message with passion, conviction, and optimism.

As evidence that he knew his subject, Zhdanov described his involvement in the successful containment of smallpox in the USSR in the 1930s. His message was accompanied by a bold offer: the USSR would provide 25 million smallpox vaccine doses, along with assistance to poorer countries to deploy these doses. The message was also accompanied by a clever reference to the history of the USA. Zhdanov recalled a letter written in 1806 by the US President of that time, Thomas Jefferson, to smallpox vaccine pioneer Edward Jenner in England[810]:

> I avail myself of this occasion of rendering you a portion of the tribute of gratitude due to you from the whole human family. Medicine has never before produced any single improvement of such utility… Future nations will know by history only that the loathsome small-pox has existed and by you has been extirpated.

Accordingly, Zhdanov was inviting the American members of WHO, as well as others throughout the world, to cooperate with a project that would fulfil the ambition of one of that country's most renowned historical figures.

Jefferson had been overly optimistic about the timescale for the "extirpation" of smallpox. Zhdanov, too, suggested a timescale that was on the short side – just ten years. It took the WHO until 1966 to agree a framework for their "Global Smallpox Eradication Campaign". But by 1977, the task was complete. Thanks to careful targeting, smallpox had, indeed, been removed from any natural occurrences. It nowadays exists only in a small number of carefully controlled medical laboratories.

For a while in the 1960s, it seemed that the initiative would stall, due to the sheer difficulty of coordinating international resources. Again, it was some key personal relationships that kept the project moving forward, including a powerful rapport between the American doctor, Donald Henderson, charged with running the whole project, and the Soviet deputy health minister, Dimitri Venediktov[811].

How bad a disease was smallpox? It is estimated that, during the twentieth century, some 300 million people died from the disease[812]. That's three times as many people as all those who died from military conflict in the century.

No one contested the claim that this disease was a scourge on humanity, especially in developing countries. However, what was unclear to many people in the 1950s and 1960s – including many members of the WHO community – was whether sufficient action could be taken to actually eliminate the disease from the entire planet. Victor Zhdanov deserves huge credit for his forceful, intelligent advocacy of that possibility. And the world as a whole deserves credit too, for the establishment of the sets of relationships within WHO that turned the possibility into a reality – despite the geopolitical environment of deep suspicion between the world's largest two nuclear armed superpowers. Despite their entrenched enmity, the two foes could recognise that they shared a common enemy, and that it was in their mutual interest to annihilate it.

Might a similar approach allow distrustful competitors to nevertheless cooperate, in the next decade, on challenges that could be even larger in scale? Let's consider the example of impending nuclear holocaust.

International tension

"One of the foremost authorities on Communism in the world today said we have 10 years. Not ten years to make up our minds, but ten years to win or lose. By 1970, the world will be all slave or all free."

The speaker was a famous actor. In July 1961, he was giving a talk to the Orange County California Press Club, in which he returned again and again to the theme of a titanic life-and-death struggle between Communism and Capitalism. The paragraph I've just quoted came near the end of his speech. This is from near the beginning[813]:

> Karl Marx established the cardinal principle that Communism and Capitalism cannot co-exist in the world together. Our way of life, our system, must be totally destroyed; then the world communist state will be erected on the ruins. In interpreting Marx, Lenin said, "It is inconceivable that the Soviet Republic should continue to exist for a long period side by side with imperialistic states. Ultimately, one or the other must conquer."
>
> Last November, the communist parties of 81 countries held a convention in Moscow; and on December 6, re-affirmed this principle of war to the death. In a 20,000-word manifesto, they called on Communists in countries

where there were noncommunist governments to be traitors and work for the destruction of their own governments by subversion and treason.

Such circumstances, the speaker warned, were no occasion for America to cut back on military expenditure:

Only in that phase of the war which causes our greatest fear are we ahead – the use of armed force. Thanks to the dedicated patriotism and realistic thinking of our men in uniform we would win a shooting war. But this isn't a decisive factor in the Communist campaign. They never really intended to conquer us by force unless we yielded to a massive peace campaign and disarmed. Then, the Russians would resort to armed conflict if it could shortcut their time table with no great risk to themselves.

The reason to pay attention to these remarks by an actor – despite his piece of manifest bad foresight about the year 1970 – is because that actor, Ronald Reagan, went on, twenty years later, to become the 40th President of the United States, entering the White House in 1981. Ever since his 1961 speech, he had remained an implacable foe of Soviet Communism. He maintained a fierce resolve against lowering the defences of the western allies – against disarming in response to any misguided "massive peace campaign".

Thus, in a speech in the UK House of Commons in June 1982, Reagan declared[814],

We must continue our efforts to strengthen NATO… Our military strength is a prerequisite to peace.

Reagan anticipated a resounding victory for NATO:

The march of freedom and democracy… will leave Marxism-Leninism on the ash heap of history.

His language reached a controversial rhetorical zenith in March 1983 when he labelled the Soviet Union "an evil empire"[815]:

If history teaches anything, it teaches that simpleminded appeasement or wishful thinking about our adversaries is folly. It means the betrayal of our past, the squandering of our freedom.

I urge you to speak out against those who would place the United States in a position of military and moral inferiority… So, in your discussions of the nuclear freeze proposals, I urge you to beware the temptation… [to] label both sides equally at fault, to ignore the facts of history and the aggressive impulses of an evil empire, to simply call the arms race a giant misunderstanding…

Rather than any "giant misunderstanding", the arms race, according to Reagan, was a necessary part of a "struggle between right and wrong and good and evil".

Reagan was no believer in the "peaceful coexistence" that Nikita Khrushchev and subsequent Soviet leaders had been advocating, on and off, since 1956. In Reagan's view, an ideological conflict between the two superpowers was inevitable.

Just two weeks after his "Evil Empire" speech, Reagan returned to the same theme in a television address live from the Oval Office[816]:

> For 20 years the Soviet Union has been accumulating enormous military might. They didn't stop when their forces exceeded all requirements of a legitimate defensive capability. And they haven't stopped now. During the past decade and a half, the Soviets have built up a massive arsenal of new strategic nuclear weapons – weapons that can strike directly at the United States.

But on this occasion, Reagan had a new idea to introduce. The initiative came to be known, formally, as the Strategic Defence Initiative (SDI), and informally – usually by critics[817] – as "Star Wars".

In its own terms, it seemed an admirable concept. As Reagan described it, it was a way to evade the dreadful threat of "mutual assured destruction":

> My predecessors in the Oval Office have appeared before you on other occasions to describe the threat posed by Soviet power and have proposed steps to address that threat. But since the advent of nuclear weapons, those steps have been increasingly directed toward deterrence of aggression through the promise of retaliation.
>
> In recent months, however, my advisers, including in particular the Joint Chiefs of Staff, have underscored the necessity to break out of a future that relies solely on offensive retaliation for our security…
>
> What if free people could live secure in the knowledge that their security did not rest upon the threat of instant U.S. retaliation to deter a Soviet attack, that we could intercept and destroy strategic ballistic missiles before they reached our own soil or that of our allies?

In this concept, incoming missiles could be shot out of the sky, long before they came near their intended targets. Creating such a defence system would require "a comprehensive and intensive effort"; therefore, Reagan issued this grand invitation:

> I call upon the scientific community in our country, those who gave us nuclear weapons, to turn their great talents now to the cause of mankind and world peace, to give us the means of rendering these nuclear weapons impotent and obsolete…
>
> Tonight… I am directing a comprehensive and intensive effort to define a long-term research and development program to begin to achieve our ultimate goal of eliminating the threat posed by strategic nuclear missiles.

There were echoes of the moonshot declaration, twenty-two years earlier, by John Kennedy – and of the declaration by Richard Nixon, twelve years earlier, of a war on cancer.

But almost immediately, forecasters warned that the initiative could have unintended awful consequences. Recall the saying which I suggested, in Chapter 8, summed up the analysis of nuclear war strategist Herman Kahn: "To create nuclear peace, we have to prepare scenarios involving nuclear war." Here's another unwelcome twist on that disturbing idea: "If we anticipate scenarios involving nuclear weapons being rendered impotent and obsolete, we increase the likelihood of these weapons being used before these scenarios become viable."

Imagine Soviet military leaders observing fast progress by NATO toward a potentially impregnable missile defence system. Imagine these leaders also reading speeches from NATO political leaders, like Reagan, anticipating Marxism-Leninism being pushed onto "the ash heap of history". Imagine, moreover, the reaction of these leaders to hearing what was described at the time as an inopportune joke:

> My fellow Americans, I'm pleased to tell you today that I've signed legislation that will outlaw Russia forever. We begin bombing in five minutes.

These words were an off-the-cuff remark by Reagan on 11 August 1984 ahead of the proper start of recording his weekly radio address[818]. The president was apparently unaware that the microphone was live and that the recording had already started. When the recording was leaked several days later, the reaction from USSR spokespeople was highly critical. Reagan's remarks were condemned[819] as being "unprecedentedly hostile" and as a "monstrous statement". They seemed to confirm suspicions that Western official statements in favour of détente were just a cover for darker, more belligerent aspirations.

That describes an important part of the context in which, in March 1985, Mikhail Gorbachev became General Secretary of the Communist Party of the Soviet Union – the de facto leader of that country. Within a few days of assuming power, Gorbachev had conveyed his thinking on nuclear weapons in an interview with Pravda. These weapons were not only "dangerous" but also "irrational". His strongest criticism targeted Reagan's Strategic Defence Initiative, which "threatened to undermine the nuclear balance and unleash a new race in offensive missiles"[820].

Western politicians were unsure how to assess Gorbachev. The UK Prime Minister, Margaret Thatcher, had met Gorbachev during a visit to London a few months earlier. In a BBC TV interview shortly afterward, she had expressed her "cautious optimism" about the prospects of collaboration with the Soviet politician[821]:

> I like Mr. Gorbachev. We can do business together.

In that same interview, Thatcher had underscored the desirability of disarmament talks succeeding in reducing the levels of nuclear armaments, but she had avoided expressing any opinion about SDI. She also forecast that the two leaders would remain ideologically opposed to each other:

> We both believe in our own political systems. He firmly believes in his; I firmly believe in mine. We are never going to change one another.

Reagan, likewise, was wary, noting in his diary shortly after Gorbachev's ascension to the position of General Secretary[822],

> Gorbachev will be as tough as any of their leaders. If he wasn't a confirmed ideologue, he would never have been chosen by the Politburo.

Gorbachev had, indeed, inherited nearly seventy years of Soviet ideological hostility toward what was perceived as "western imperialism". His predecessors as Soviet leader had placed a high priority on achieving and maintaining at least parity with the west in terms of nuclear arsenals. In parallel, they had built up large superiority in ground troops in Europe, backed by INFs: intermediate-range nuclear forces, that is, ballistic missiles with ranges of up to five thousand kilometres.

At the direction of previous Soviet premier Leonid Brezhnev, several hundred SS-20 INFs had been deployed throughout Eastern Europe from 1976 onward. They could be fired from mobile launching sites, with minimal preparation time required. Each missile carried three separately targetable warheads. Various political leaders from NATO countries increasingly expressed alarm. *Why were so many SS-20s needed?*

These countries eventually agreed on a countermeasure. It was publicly announced in 1979 that, in four years' time, 1983, several hundred "cruise missile" INFs would be added to NATO forces throughout Western Europe. The delay was in order to provide encouragement to the USSR to remove their SS-20s beforehand, in which case no cruise missiles would be deployed. But neither Brezhnev nor his successor from 1982, Yuri Andropov, backed down. Therefore, the cruise missiles arrived on schedule in 1983[823].

It was a period of high public distress. I was doing postgraduate research in the philosophy of science at the time. But, along with many others, I was distracted by a vigorous public discussion about the pros and cons of different approaches to disarmament. The future seemed bleak. One scenario often discussed was that a nuclear holocaust might be triggered by accident. A careless joke, perhaps, might be misinterpreted, causing an opposing military leader to panic.

If anything, matters had become even more intense due to the shooting down on 1st September 1983 of Korean Airlines flight KAL007. On account of a navigational error made by the flight crew, the airplane had inadvertently strayed into restricted airspace over the Kamchatka Peninsula of far eastern Russia. Soviet reconnaissance assumed the craft was a US spy plane, fired some warning shots (which it is presumed the civilian aircrew did not see), and then downed the plane with a direct hit. All 269 personnel on board perished. At first, the USSR denied all knowledge of the incident. Then it claimed the KAL007 was actually taking part in a secret spy mission, and therefore deserved to be shot down[824]. These explanations were *not* well received by the US. Ronald Reagan condemned what he called the "Korean Air massacre"[825]:

> There was absolutely no justification either legal or moral for what the Soviets did. This crime against humanity must never be forgotten.

It was not publicly known at the time, but one aftermath of the KAL007 incident almost *was* an accidental nuclear war. Look up the account of how Lieutenant-Colonel Stanislav Petrov used his own human judgement, on 26th September 1983, to override the official Soviet policies on promptly alerting senior leaders about perceived threats from incoming nuclear missiles[826]. The systems being overseen by Petrov used some rudimentary artificial intelligence to monitor satellite signals about intercontinental ballistic missiles on a trajectory toward the USSR. That morning, loud sirens and flashing red lights indicated that the system had detected trouble. Petrov's team frantically checked and rechecked the data, but the answer seemed robust: a deadly nuclear warhead was en route from Montana, USA, to the Soviet Union.

A few minutes later, the stakes raised even higher. Additional warning sounds indicated that the number of incoming nuclear missiles was actually five. The rules were clear: Petrov, the most senior officer at the site, should notify higher command immediately.

However, as a civilian, who had previously noticed teething problems with the recently installed automated alarm system, Petrov hesitated. He later reflected that it seemed to him implausible that the USA would commence an attack with just five missiles, given the vast size of their overall arsenal. *Thank goodness his intuition prevailed, and was proven correct.* Analysis eventually identified the cause of the mistaken attribution, which included an unusual combination of satellite position, sun position, and cloud cover – as well as the fact that fewer than the specified number of satellites were operational.

If Petrov had followed orders, in similar fashion to the air defence team members who shot down the KAL007 over the Kamchatka Peninsula a few weeks earlier, what would have happened next? The Soviet leader at the time, Yuri Andropov, is known to have believed that Ronald Reagan really was contemplating a pre-emptive nuclear strike against the USSR[827]. Much earlier in his career, the young Andropov had watched Joseph Stalin disregard intelligence information in 1941 alerting him to the imminent "Operation Barbarossa" invasion of the USSR by Adolph Hitler – an incident I discussed in Chapter 3. Andropov was determined not to make a similar mistake during his own time as premier[828]. Bitter memories cast long shadows. If data had come his way suggesting a surprise attack was underway, that morning in September 1983, Andropov may well have unleashed a retaliatory strike. And, quite possibly, none of us would be here today.

Although that particular near-miss example was unknown to the public in the mid-1980s, there was plenty of speculation about similar possibilities. In view of these fears, perhaps it was, after all, "better to be red than dead". Others – including me at the time – protested that these two poles, "red" (under the domination of Soviet communism) and "dead", were by no means the only scenarios to consider.

But in all these animated discussions, with all their twists and turns, I don't remember anyone suggesting that the Berlin Wall might be dismantled by the end of the decade, leading to the reunification of East and West Germany under a multi-party democracy. Nor that the Soviet Union would dissolve itself peacefully by 1991, reducing, for a while, most of the worries about the prospect of catastrophic nuclear war. Such titanic possibilities seemed, in the mid-1980s, too far-fetched to even start to imagine.

So, what changed? And what can we learn from this example for the urgent task of envisioning better international politics for the near future?

A climate for change

The most profound transformations usually involve not just one trend in isolation but the interactions between multiple trends.

That was a principle I introduced in Chapter 6, "Disruptions". Let's now see how that principle plays out in the extraordinary geopolitical transformation between 1985 and 1991.

Part of the credit for that transformation goes to two remarkable international leaders: Mikhail Gorbachev and Ronald Reagan. Despite their very different backgrounds, they were eventually able to establish a deep personal rapport. They were both also able to transcend many of the ideological assumptions that had served them well earlier in their careers. Other leaders, thrust into the same circumstances, may well have conformed more closely to their previous typecasting.

Accordingly, I answer the question, "Do individuals matter", with an emphatic "yes". Actions by a single person, at critical junctures of history, can reconfigure the track lines of humanity. In Chapter 1, I gave credit to both Nelson Mandela and FW de Klerk for reconfiguring the track lines of South African history. Other individuals who had a lion-sized impact on global history, where contemporary alternative choices for national leader would likely have done things very differently, include Napoleon Bonaparte, Abraham Lincoln, Adolf Hitler, and Winston Churchill – and, yes, Gorbachev and Reagan. Numerous other examples exist at local or regional levels of business, religion, or politics

But individuals don't operate in isolation. In the case of the geopolitical transformation between 1985 and 1991, at least four other factors deserve attention.

The first factor contributed to a sense of deepening national crisis within the USSR – prompting the leaders there to seek alternative ways to operate. This was the debacle of the Soviet invasion of Afghanistan.

Leonid Brezhnev had sent 75,000 Soviet troops into Afghanistan in December 1979, with the goal to prevent loss of Soviet influence in that country. Brezhnev had apparently overruled concerns raised by other members of the Politburo, including his successor-to-be Yuri Andropov, and long-time Minister of Foreign Affairs, Andrei Gromyko, that such an intervention would be fraught with difficulties[829].

Brezhnev was being loyal to a policy that was internationally known by his own name – "the Brezhnev doctrine" – which he had articulated back in 1968 to justify the intervention of Soviet tanks in Czechoslovakia[830]:

> When external and internal forces hostile to socialism try to turn the development of a given socialist country in the direction of restoration of the capitalist system, when a threat arises to the cause of socialism in that country – a threat to the security of the socialist commonwealth as a whole – this is no longer merely a problem for that country's people, but a common problem, the concern of all socialist countries.

The policy was motivated by a fear that was the mirror image of what the USA had feared about the war in Vietnam: If Vietnam became communist, it was thought likely to trigger a cascade of "dominos" – neighbouring countries also becoming communist, such as Cambodia, Laos, Thailand, and the Philippines. For Brezhnev, if Afghanistan were to slip outside of Soviet influence, it might trigger a wider unravelling of Soviet control. That's why he sent in the troops in such numbers.

Paradoxically, that action probably accelerated the outcome it was intended to prevent. Over the next decade, nearly one million Soviet soldiers took part in the resulting war, with, perhaps, up to fifty thousand of these soldiers being killed. The number of civilian casualties were many times higher. With deep-pocketed support from numerous organisations around the world, various groups of Afghan Mujahideen proved every bit as resilient against conscript Soviet forces as the Viet Cong guerrillas had been against conscript American forces in the Vietnam war. In both cases, the return home of large numbers of war veterans, scarred physically and psychologically, had wide repercussions – especially among the many non-Russian states within the Soviet Union that saw little reason for that war.

Political science researchers Rafael Reuveny and Aseem Prakash have identified four overlapping ways in which the drawn-out conflict altered Soviet politics[831]:

(1) Perception effects: it changed the perceptions of leaders about the efficacy of using the military to hold the empire together and to intervene in foreign countries;

(2) Military effects: it discredited the Red Army, created cleavage between the party and the military, and demonstrated that the Red Army was not invincible, which emboldened the non-Russian republics to push for independence;

(3) Legitimacy effects: it provided non-Russians with a common cause to demand independence since they viewed this war as a Russian war fought by non-Russians against Afghans; and

(4) Participation effects: it created new forms of political participation, started to transform the press/media before *glasnost*, initiated the first shots of *glasnost*, and created a significant mass of war veterans (*Afghansti*) who formed new civil organizations weakening the political hegemony of the communist party.

This ongoing war was one of the issues Gorbachev inherited when he became Soviet leader in 1985. He increasingly realised there was little likelihood of the intervention having a successful outcome. Inside the Politburo, he was not alone in that thinking. Slavishly following the Brezhnev Doctrine, along with other principles from previous decades, no longer made much sense. New ways of operating needed to be found.

That brings me to a second factor responsible for changing the climate within the Soviet Union. It was the spread of new ideas among a growing underground of dissidents.

What happened next can be described by a famous quote from the economist Milton Friedman, in the preface to his book *Capitalism and Freedom*.[832]:

> There is enormous inertia – a tyranny of the status quo – in private and especially governmental arrangements. Only a crisis – actual or perceived – produces real change. When that crisis occurs, the actions that are taken depend on the ideas that are lying around. That, I believe, is our basic function: to develop alternatives to existing policies, to keep them alive and available until the politically impossible becomes politically inevitable.

Ideas that were increasingly "lying around" within the Soviet bloc, from the mid-70s onward, included the contents of "Basket III" of the international agreement signed in Helsinki in 1975 at the Conference on Security and Cooperation in Europe (CSCE).

The CSCE was the outgrowth of an international attempt to bring greater stability to Europe following the disruption of the Soviet clampdown in Czechoslovakia in 1968. The goal, shared by both superpower blocs, was to take some of the tension out of the Cold War. In due course, 35 heads of state gathered in Helsinki in August 1975, including, for the first time at such a conference, the heads of both East and West Germany, as well as the heads of all European countries apart from Albania and Andorra. The assembled leaders put their signatures on a declaration that contained four "baskets":

I. "Questions relating to security in Europe" – including confidence-building measures such as observation of each other's military exercises

II. "Co-operation in the fields of economics, of science and technology, including commercial exchanges, industrial co-operation and projects of common interest"

III. "Co-operation in humanitarian and other fields, including human contacts, information, culture, and education"

IV. "Follow-up to the conference".

The agreement went on to list a number of basic principles, including "Respect for human rights and fundamental freedoms, including freedom of thought, conscience, religion or belief" and "Equal rights and self-determination of peoples"[833].

Several parts of the final text had been strongly resisted by the Soviet Union – particularly in Basket III. Nevertheless, the overall text also gave Leonid Brezhnev, the Soviet leader, much of what he wanted, including a commitment to "Inviolability of borders" and "Non-intervention in internal affairs". Andrei Gromyko, the Soviet Foreign Minister, apparently advised Brezhnev, "Don't worry, we are masters in our own house." But in the aftermath of the Soviet invasion of Afghanistan, western leaders, including US President Jimmy Carter, gave more prominence to the themes of that agreement. And many people throughout the Soviet bloc paid attention.

Researchers have analysed the influence of Basket III on various dissident movements which grew in scale as the years passed, such as:

- Solidarity headed by Lech Walesa in Poland
- Charter 77 headed by Vaclav Havel in Czechoslovakia
- Echo Glasnost in Bulgaria
- Activities organised by East German Lutheran churches

Hence, the title of a book that provides further details: *The Helsinki Effect: International Norms, Human Rights, and the Demise of Communism*, written by Daniel C. Thomas, professor of political science and international relations.

Just as I answered affirmatively, earlier, to the question of whether *individual people* can make a difference, so do I now assert that *ideas* can make a difference. The difference made by ideas can be a lot larger than expected by practitioners of so-called "realpolitik" such as US Secretary of State Henry Kissinger, who was present at the Helsinki CSCE negotiations and who had given informal personal assurances to his Soviet counterparts that the high-sounding words in the agreement would have little lasting impact.

Kissinger eventually admitted his lack of foresight in a passage in the final volume of his memoirs[834]:

> Turning points often pass unrecognised by contemporaries…
>
> [This] was the case with the European Security Conference… Proposed by the Soviets in 1954 and intended as a manoeuvre to undermine the Atlantic Alliance, it was hesitantly accepted by the democracies and concluded amongst bitter controversy. Yet, with the passage of time, it came to be appreciated as a political and moral landmark that contributed to the progressive decline and eventual collapse of the Soviet system over the next decade and a half.
>
> Rarely has a diplomatic process so illuminated the limitations of human foresight.

Anatoly Dobrynin, the Soviet ambassador to the U.S., subsequently commented as follows regarding the CSCE agreement[835]:

> Its very publication in *Pravda* gave it the weight of an official document. It gradually became the manifesto of the dissident and liberal movement, a development totally beyond the imagination of the Soviet leadership.

People's willingness to give serious attention to new ideas depends on the degree to which they are dissatisfied with current prevailing systems of thought. That takes us to a third key factor responsible for changing the ideological climate within the Soviet Union, namely, the meltdown that occurred at the Chernobyl nuclear power station in April 1986. This made a heavy impression on Gorbachev himself.

Due to faults in both the design of the reactor and the administration of a test of some of the capabilities of the reactor under stress conditions, a runaway nuclear chain reaction occurred, generating huge temperatures. An explosion in the resulting superheated cooling water destroyed the protective casing around the reactor. For the next nine days, as authorities tried to manage the crisis, a raging fire spewed deadly radioactive contamination high into the atmosphere. The day after the explosion, 53,000 people were hurriedly evacuated from the area around the reactor. The number of people subsequently permanently displaced exceeded 300,000.

In his book *Russia and the Idea of the West: Gorbachev, Intellectuals, and the End of the Cold War*, historian Robert English summarised as follows the impact of Chernobyl on the thinking of the Soviet leadership[836]:

> The impact of Chernobyl on the new thinking, and on the broader evolution of perestroika, is difficult to overestimate; its effect on both domestic and foreign policy was tremendous.
>
> The disaster consumed the leadership for nearly three months. The government – with a Politburo crisis committee, constant meetings and reports, and a summoning of all available civilian and military resources – was on a virtual wartime footing. Participants recall mobilization of a frantic pace and grave intensity seen only in the years of the Great Patriotic War.
>
> More than just another economic setback, Chernobyl gave a broader impetus to domestic reforms by further exposing the backwardness and corruption of the Stalinist system, particularly the failures of central planning with its haste, sloppiness, and disregard of "the human element."

Moscow-born professor of international history Vladislav Zubok put it like this[837]:

> The lessons of Chernobyl called for abrogation of secrecy and xenophobia, for fundamental rethinking of security in the nuclear age. In political terms, Gorbachev used Chernobyl to undercut the very basis of the nuclear orthodoxy: the heroic and romantic image of Soviet nuclear power.
>
> The catastrophe for the first time induced the Soviet leadership to look at the task of nuclear disarmament as a moral imperative independent of political calculations… For the first time, the Soviet leadership allowed the media to pursue serious public debates about nuclear dangers…

Immediately after Chernobyl, Gorbachev decided to achieve a breakthrough in strategic arms control.

All this time, one more factor had been at work – a growing realisation that a nuclear war would not just be *terrible*, something like a rerun of the Second World War, but could be *civilisation-ending*. For that growing realisation, we should give thanks to a futurist.

Contemplating extinction

What caused the extinction of the dinosaurs, some sixty-six million years ago, after they had dominated the earth for the previous one hundred and thirty million years?

Nowadays, most people are quick to mention the impact on the earth of an asteroid (or, perhaps, a comet) as large as Mount Everest. That impact is thought to have had an explosive force more than one billion times that of the Hiroshima and Nagasaki atomic bombs[838]. It generated such a huge cloud of debris in the atmosphere that global temperatures plummeted for several years. Without light from the sun, photosynthesis would have stopped. In turn, herbivores and then carnivores would have run out of food, and died in vast numbers. Upward of three quarters of all species living at that time were rendered extinct[839].

But such an idea entered the public consciousness only four decades ago. Father and son Luis and Walter Alvarez had proposed it in 1980, as a result of detecting a fine layer of the chemical iridium in sedimentary deposits all around the world, at precisely the geological boundary beyond which dinosaur fossils cease to be found. Over time, more evidence in favour of the hypothesis grew[840]. I remember watching famed palaeontologist Stephen Jay Gould give an exhilarating guest lecture on the subject in a large lecture theatre in Cambridge in the early 1980s. The audience, who had come from multiple different faculties of the university, were fascinated.

The stinger of that talk, however, veered from past geological epochs to the possible near future. Could a fate similar to that of the dinosaurs befall humans? Due, not to an extra-terrestrial object, but to collective human malfeasance?

The idea was that of *nuclear winter*. When nuclear weapons were first conceived, it was their immediate explosive blast that commanded attention. Any buildings and, yes, people, anywhere within several miles of the blast, would be destroyed by a combination of extreme heat and the pressures arising from the explosion. It also quickly became apparent that people would, in addition, die in large numbers from diseases caused by the ionising radiation emitted by the bomb. Estimates of the total number of deaths caused at Hiroshima and Nagasaki range around one hundred thousand to two hundred thousand[841]. Military planners contemplating a larger scale nuclear war scaled these numbers up by a factor of around ten thousand, taking into account larger bombs being used in greater numbers. In other words, perhaps one to two billion people might die. Terrible, but not the end of the world – as war strategist Herman Kahn had been keen to emphasise, as we noted in Chapter 8. But scenarios involving nuclear winter upturned these calculations.

It wouldn't be heat, or blast, or ionising radiation that would cause most of the deaths. In a kind of replay of the death of the dinosaurs, it would be the blocking out of the sun on account of the dust clouds kicked up into the atmosphere from the explosion and from numerous resulting wildfires. Vegetation would fail, and entire populations would starve to death.

A mini example of this had already been seen in 1816, the "year without a summer" briefly mentioned in Chapter 2, in which crop yields in many parts of the Northern Hemisphere fell by up to 90%. The cause: the largest volcanic explosion of the last millennium, in April of the previous year, 1815, on the Indonesian island of Sumbawa. Around ten thousand Indonesians died in the direct aftermath of that Mount Tambora explosion and the accompanying tsunami floods. Researchers have estimated that perhaps eighty thousand Indonesians died in outbreaks of diseases following the resulting social breakdown[842]. But the worldwide impact was due to the vast amounts of sulphur dioxide thrown into the atmosphere, causing a worldwide cooling of around two degrees Centigrade. In the eastern states of North America, 1816 was known as "the year of 1800-and-froze-to-death". Professor of history John Dexter Post called the period 1816-1819 "the last great subsistence crisis in the western world" in a book of the same name[843]. And that "great crisis" resulted from just one explosion. Imagine what hundreds of such explosions could achieve – especially if they were accompanied by numerous uncontrollable fires.

The first academic article on this possibility appeared in late 1982: "The Atmosphere after a Nuclear War: Twilight at Noon", by Paul J. Crutzen and John W. Birks[844]. With the context of heightening international tensions, and

Reagan's announcement of the Strategic Defence Initiative, other scientists were motivated to dig deeper quickly.

Five scientists who had all done work modelling the climatic consequences of atmospheric events on other planets, Venus and Mars, applied their expertise to this new scenario. Their research would be published in Science in December 1983[845]. One member of that team, Richard Turco, coined the term "Nuclear winter", which was used in the title of the article, "Nuclear Winter: Global Consequences of Multiple Nuclear Explosions". The article received coverage in the New York Times[846]:

> Detailed arguments for the hypothesis that a catastrophic "nuclear winter" might result from concerted missile attacks on major cities and be followed by the annihilation of much, if not all, of the human species have been presented for the first time in a scientific journal.
>
> Two articles on the subject written by teams of authors representing many specialties appear in the Dec. 23 issue of Science. They elaborate on arguments presented at a conference held in Washington on Oct. 31 and Nov. 1.
>
> An article on biological effects states: "In any large-scale nuclear exchange between the superpowers, global environmental changes sufficient to cause the extinction of a major fraction of the plant and animal species on the earth are likely. In that event, the possibility of the extinction of Homo sapiens cannot be excluded."

Another member of that team of five had already taken the decision to draw greater public attention to the implications of this research, even before it had been formally published. That team member switched from relying on his long-established formidable skills as a *scientist* to utilising his equally formidable skills as a *science communicator*. His name was Carl Sagan.

Profound communication

Carl Sagan's 13-episode TV show *Cosmos*, which first aired in 1980, was for many years the most widely watched series in the history of American public television. Even today, out of all the series produced over the years by the Public Broadcasting Service (PBS), it has the largest viewing figures worldwide, having been broadcast in over sixty countries and watched by some six hundred million viewers[847]. Previously, Sagan had won a Pulitzer Prize for his book *The Dragons of Eden*.[848] He was the superstar science communicator for his generation. And he was deeply alarmed at the prospect of nuclear war.

Realising that the concept of nuclear winter tilted the scales even further away from there being any credible military use of nuclear weapons, Sagan decided he needed to reach a larger audience quickly. The popular weekly magazine *Parade*, with a circulation of ten million, carried an article by him as their cover story for 30th October 1983, presented as "A special report by Carl Sagan"[849]: The text on the cover was dramatic:

> Would nuclear war be the end of the world?
> In a major 'exchange', more than a billion people would instantly be killed. But the long-term consequences could be much worse.

Sagan followed up with TV appearances. With his knack for memorable language, his messages caused many people to re-evaluate their stances on arms control negotiations. For example, here's a comparison he offered on an interview on ABC[850]:

> Imagine, a room, awash in gasoline. And there are two implacable enemies in that room. One of them has 9,000 matches. The other has 7,000 matches. Each of them is concerned about who's ahead, who's stronger. Well, that's the kind of situation we are actually in. The amount of weapons that are available to the United States and the Soviet Union are so bloated, so grossly in excess of what's needed to dissuade the other that if it weren't so tragic, it would be laughable.

More scientists did their own analysis. There was by no means universal agreement, but it seemed undeniable that there was at least a significant risk of something like a nuclear winter resulting from even a limited exchange of nuclear missiles. A so-called "nuclear autumn" would be bad enough, even if some humans survived to try to restart civilisation. Senior members of the military in both superpower blocs paid attention – lots of attention.

In due course, having listened to their advisers, both Reagan and Gorbachev became convinced that the threat of nuclear winter, whilst not certain, was too serious for them to risk continuing along previous lines of negotiation. At a summit in Reykjavik in October 1986, the two leaders came close to agreeing a dramatic reduction in nuclear warheads. Although an agreement eluded them on that occasion, they each realised that the other was much more serious than they had previously thought about the possibility of what Gorbachev called the "ultimate liquidation of nuclear weapons". Gorbachev later acknowledged that the discussions had produced in him a psychological impact that was "comparable to Chernobyl". An American assessment shortly after the discussion concluded that Gorbachev had offered more concessions in that one round of negotiations than they had received from his predecessors in total over the previous 25 years[851].

High-level discussions continued via multiple channels after the Reykjavik summit, addressing numerous details. By December the following year, 1987, enough progress had been made for Reagan and Gorbachev to sign a comprehensive "Intermediate-Range Nuclear Forces Treaty" at a summit in Washington DC. This committed both sides to eliminating the much-feared SS-20 and Cruise INF missiles. In parallel, the US significantly cut back on its expenditure on SDI, in part because of recognition of severe technical difficulties with the plan, and in part because the political will behind the initiative had been much reduced.

These developments would be followed, after Reagan left office, by:

- Further downscaling of the SDI project
- The "START" Strategic Arms Reduction Treaty of 1991, which imposed lower limits on the numbers of intercontinental ballistic missiles each side could deploy, mandating elimination of significant fractions of existing stockpiles.

Gorbachev and Reagan held their last summit together in Moscow in late May and early June 1988. During these discussions, Gorbachev specifically mentioned Carl Sagan as having had a major influence on the ending of nuclear proliferation. Just as palaeontologist Stephen Jay Gould had electrified an audience in Cambridge (including me) with his discussion of dinosaur extinction and nuclear winter, Carl Sagan had helped provide a similar understanding at the very highest levels of international politics.

Both these scientists acted as first-class futurists in the sense of vividly portraying a forthcoming scenario that they could highlight as being *credible* but, at the same time, deeply *undesirable*. And both of them encouraged actions to lower the probability of that scenario actually becoming true.

That can serve as a model, in the 2020s, for altering the trajectory of various deeply entrenched antagonistic forces that are, alas, strongly suspicious of one another. Once these global adversaries understand that they face common challenges that threaten something broadly comparable to nuclear winter – namely, the panoply of global risks covered in the chapter on "Landmines" – then they should be ready, at least for a while, to contemplate radical changes in outlook. Equally, if they can understand the potential huge upsides of wisely and safely harnessing NBIC technologies, this should enable them to set aside some of their present dogmas and doctrines that are seriously limiting their future wellbeing.

It all depends, evidently, on the clarity of their perception of these future possibilities. That is what will determine their response, once they start to experience some major short-term shocks – akin to the debacles of Afghanistan and Chernobyl. With sufficient vital foresight, they will find the appropriate ideas "lying around", ready to guide constructive responses. But without such clarity of thought, the responses these great powers take have every chance of making matters worse, rather than better.

Beyond politics

The ideas from Basket III of the Conference on Security and Cooperation in Europe – ideas about human rights, freedom of thought, and self-determination – had faced some strong resistance within the Soviet bloc. Although similar principles were already written into the national constitutions of the Warsaw Pact countries, these principles were in practice often opposed by state functionaries who viewed loyalty to public officials as having a higher priority than those somewhat abstract concepts. Thus, these potentially liberating ideas had to contend with muscular obstruction – censorship, imprisonment, and other manipulation.

But whilst individual dissidents and activists were imprisoned, their ideas continued to circulate and exert influence, even winning elements of support in high places. In time, sufficiently many minds were turned.

Fast forward to the 2020s. In the present time, vital ideas are facing obstruction, not just from censorship and imprisonment, but from tidal waves of contrary thinking. If we don't keep our wits about us, we can fall victim to all manner of intellectual sabotage. Just as our bodies can be hijacked by biological viruses or bacterial infections, our minds face a blizzard of powerful mental distortion.

Some of these antagonistic memes have been deliberately concocted to deceive us and lead us into distraction, confusion, or despair. Many others have arisen by processes involving blind natural selection. In both cases, regardless of the origins of these memes, many people who are stricken by them honestly think they have good reasons to believe in them. Vast networks of supportive "rationale" have been created to bolster these beliefs.

Of course, ideological conflict is nothing new. Ideas have faced contrary opinions all throughout history. Thank goodness. Out of the struggle between ideas, key new insights have arisen that have gradually provided humanity with ever greater technological mastery.

But never before has so much energy been unleashed onto the task of designing and maintaining networks of arguments in support of all kinds of contrary concepts. A potent combination of human creativity, AI tools, and marketing expertise, mashed up by global connectivity operating at the speed of light, is constantly generating and regenerating enormous sets of arguments – arguments that can redirect the thinking processes of people on the receiving end, often without them realising what's happening. The resulting clouds of confusion badly complicate the quest to elevate truly vital foresight above the noise of ideas that are mediocre or, worse, destructive.

In principle, the answer is straightforward: let's improve education, so that the clouds of confusion are, well, less confusing.

In practice, education suffers from the same kinds of inertia that hold up lots of the other kinds of positive changes that have been discussed in previous chapters.

But as appreciation grows of the crises facing humanity, it's time to give greater focus to the project to uplift education – to make education fit for the 2020s. That's the subject of the next chapter.

15. Education

Education, defined: The sharing of key insights and skills, to help citizens of all ages to grow toward their full potential. Guidance for all citizens in a diverse, fast-changing, complex society. Systems of knowledge acquisition and character formation that, alas, often hark backward more than they face forward, and which are, accordingly, overdue their own transformation.

As a transhumanist, just as I look forward to profound upgrades of aspects of our individual human nature, I also look forward to profound upgrades of aspects of our educational systems.

The most important change will be in the basic *purpose* of education. That purpose used to be to help children to become adults who were well adapted to the risks and opportunities of a human society whose general shape was mainly fixed. But from now on, education needs to help prepare everyone for the *swiftly changing* risks and opportunities of *an increasingly fluid, transhuman* society – a society whose general shape *is very far from being fixed.*

Indeed, whereas education used to be something that mainly happened in the earlier phases of people's lives, it should, from now on, be something that happens *continually*, at all stages of life.

That might sound expensive or impractical. But the same technologies that will drive so many other changes in our lives have the ability to provide an upgraded education to everyone, for essentially zero cost. Let's take a look.

Out with the old

Education used to be straightforward. Youngsters needed to be prepared for a career. A standard combination of general skills and some specific skills had to be imparted. In this way, people leaving school would be ready for employment as, for example, soldiers, sailors, butchers, bakers, cleaners, cooks, farmers, fishers, tailors, weavers, joiners, builders, domestic servants, nurses, craftspeople, shopkeepers, merchants, accountants, lawyers, writers, artists, entertainers, teachers, doctors, chemists, engineers, or clergy. There weren't *that* many career choices. Life was simpler in those times. The syllabus didn't change much from year to year, or even from decade to decade.

But nowadays, there's a growing sense of crisis and confusion. Careers, which were once relatively static, are experiencing lots of uncertainty and potential disruption.

Consider the occupation of radiologist: someone who studies medical images such as x-rays or ultrasound scans. That occupation didn't exist until the early twentieth century. By 2019, there were just under four thousand consultant radiologists employed in the UK; there was, moreover, enough hospital demand for *at least another one thousand* of them. According to the Clinical Radiology UK Workforce Census Report[852],

> The number of NHS radiologists is falling desperately short of demand, with survey respondents confirming staff shortages are now resulting in delayed cancer diagnoses and inadequate emergency diagnostic and interventional services.

It might look as though picking radiologist as your career would be a shrewd move. However, not everyone agreed. AI Deep Learning pioneer Geoffrey Hinton – one of the so-called three godfathers of that subject – had already issued a warning that it was *a bad idea* for anyone to train as a radiologist. He issued the following vivid warning at the Machine Learning and Market for Intelligence Conference in November 2016 in Toronto[853]:

> If you work as a radiologist, you're like the coyote that's already over the edge of the cliff but hasn't yet looked down, so it doesn't realise there's no ground underneath him. People should stop training radiologists now. It's just completely obvious that within five years, deep learning is going to do better than radiologists, because it's going to be able to get a lot more experience.

After a momentary pause, Hinton softened his prediction:

> It might be ten years…

Five years after these remarks, the radiology profession is still in a state of not having enough humans to do all the work it receives. AI systems that use deep learning are able to do *parts* of that job, but for the time being, by no means all of it.

What decision should a potential student of radiology take, in the light of that conflicting advice? Is it safe to disregard the prediction of Geoff Hinton, as being naive and unfounded? However, bear in mind more recent research findings, such as the performance of software by Google Health that analyses mammogram scans. As reported in January 2020[854], that software was trained on 91,000 mammograms, which had each been labelled as to whether they contained a cancerous tumour. The software was subsequently tested on 30,000 additional scans. It performed significantly better than expert human counterparts who had also evaluated those additional scans:

- In mammograms containing cancerous tumours, the AI missed 9.4% fewer tumours, compared to the human radiologists
- In mammograms *not* containing cancerous tumours, the AI had 5.7% fewer false alarms (identifying tumours when none existed).

Simultaneously scoring lower on *both* types of error is particularly impressive. So perhaps Hinton's forecast will prove correct after all, though with a timescale more like ten years than five years. The existing shortage of radiologists might, by then, start to turn into a surplus.

Similar considerations apply to many other professions: retail assistants, food preparation, drivers, secretaries, paralegals, proof readers, language translators, bank clerks, accountants, and so on[855]. AI will be able, sooner or later, to do many tasks in these professions systematically better than human workers – without tiring, or becoming distracted, bored, or depressed.

There's room for debate about *timescales* for AIs and robots to acquire the requisite skills, and also about the extent to which *some* humans will still operate in these occupations – though focussing on a different mix of tasks than at present[856]. Where there's little debate is that these professions will change. By 2030, the training to prepare people to work in these professions will likely be significantly different from the corresponding training in 2010.

Training for individual professions builds upon general skills that students have learned in schools. For centuries, these general skills included "the three Rs" of reading, writing, and arithmetic. Along the way, skills in rote memorisation and regurgitation were meant to be inculcated too. But these general skills are also being transformed by new technologies:

- In the early 1970s, I learned at secondary school how to use a clever but tedious technique called logarithms to do long multiplication and division. But the advent of electronic calculators soon led – hurrah! – to the elimination of logarithm tables.
- The importance of being able to commit huge bodies of disparate facts to memory has been diminished by the convenient accessibility of digital memories and online search systems.

- The task of creating written articles has been altered considerably by software for word processing, with its built-in support to improve spelling, grammar, and style.

However, these changes are only part of a broader set of reconfigurations of both the content and the methods of education. To remain relevant in the fast-moving decades ahead, education will need to keep on changing.

Six upgrades

The requirements for upgrading education can be split into six groups.

First, whereas previous educational models tended to assume that most change is linear (incremental), transhumanist education will raise awareness of exponential change and accelerating feedback cycles. It will focus attention on the potential for emerging disruptive technology to transform human experience in multiple ways that are hard to predict. In particular, it will cover skills of anticipatory foresight and scenario design and evaluation, including (as covered in Chapters 6 and 7 in this book) the identification and management of both disruption and contingency.

Second, whereas previous educational models assumed a broadly static cultural background, transhumanist education will prepare students for ultra-diversity. People's interactions with each other nowadays aren't just more *numerous* than in the past, but are much more *varied* – because of greater global travel, and because groups of people are increasingly adopting new lifestyles, new bodily modifications, new social structures, and new philosophies. Moreover, transhumanist education will prepare us to coexist, not just with diverse other people, but also with advanced AIs and robots.

Third, whereas previous educational models tended to prioritise the memorisation of facts, transhumanist education will focus on critical thinking and collaborative intelligence. The goal, in effect, will be to inoculate all of us, in advance, against the damaging mental pathogens that are increasingly bombarding us. Indeed, we all are coming into contact with ever-greater amounts of information, in rapidly evolving formats – with much of that information being *designed* to mislead or confuse, and lots more being *unintentionally* misleading or confusing. We must learn to handle all that better.

Fourth, many of the assumptions behind traditional frameworks for ethics and morality are being challenged by new ideas that are circulating, and by unprecedented new possibilities that technology puts in our hands. It will remain important for people to be able to listen to their intuitions, but these intuitions will likely prove misguided more frequently than before. That's a reason for improved fluidity and clarity of thinking. It's also a reason for transhumanist education to elevate not only IQ (measures of raw intellectual power) but also EQ, including emotional resilience and mental agility.

Fifth, whereas most of history has witnessed a competitive struggle for scarce resources, NBIC technologies will increasingly enable a post-scarcity society, in which the majority of the products and services needed for a good standard of living will be available in abundance. Accordingly, transhumanist education will highlight the management of abundance alongside the management of scarcity – noting that both skills will be needed in parallel.

Sixth, as a special case of transitioning from scarcity to abundance, society will need to be ready for a transition in what it is assumed most people will be doing with their time – a transition *from* the assumption that most people should seek and gain paid employment, *to* the assumption that most people will be "post-employment".

Of the six challenges that I have listed, it's the final one that tends to cause the most controversy. There are several arguments raised to counter it. It's worth looking more closely at them.

Whither employment?

The threat to employment from automation has long been foretold. Up till now, these predictions seem to have been premature. People who have lost jobs in one occupation, due to automation, have often been able to retrain to acquire jobs in new occupations. People who were no longer needed to work on farms found new jobs in factories. As automation took over more roles inside factories, employees learned to become personal coaches, website designers, project managers, and Uber drivers. As AI systems powered by deep learning increasingly outperform human radiologists at scanning large sets of medical images, these human radiologists can spend more of their time doing the parts of their job which are beyond the capabilities of AIs.

Accordingly, there's an argument from history which says that paid employment won't disappear; instead, it will transform. That argument maintains, further, that the total number of jobs *created by automation* will likely exceed the number of jobs *eliminated by automation*:

- By allowing some tasks to be done more efficiently and more cheaply, automation generates more revenues for companies
- These additional revenues can be invested in expanding the scope of the business, providing additional employment opportunities.

The conclusion of this particular argument is that, yes, education must change, but in such a way that it prepares people to continually adapt to new work situations. NBIC will cause more frequent updates in work conditions than in previous times. Accordingly, education must equip people:

1. To learn how to learn – to quickly pick up whatever new skills turn out to be needed
2. To be emotionally ready for changes in work conditions.

I accept these conclusions, but they're not the whole story. The argument from history is hazardous. It depends on the assumption that humans can continue to tap into a reservoir of skills that lie forever beyond the reach of robotic automation. Such skills are thought to involve, for example, creativity, compassion, common sense, or the kind of subtle dexterity of plumbers, gardeners, or massage therapists. However, developments in AI are addressing all four of these areas. Some examples:

1. Systems involving GANs – Generative Adversarial Networks – are producing creative pieces of arts that can pass various "Turing tests", meaning that even a skilled observer cannot easily determine which work was produced by a human, and which was produced by an AI
2. Affective computing can increasingly respond to signs of emotions, and can convey the appearance of its own emotional state[857]
3. The GPT-3 software from OpenAI that analyses and generates text, whilst far from having "true" common sense, is able to provide a surprising simulation of understanding common sense over a series of interactions
4. Numerous manufacturers of robots – among them Boston Dynamics, Amazon Robotics, Sarcos Robotics, Ghost Robotics, Agility Robotics, and Unitree Robotics – are continuing to achieve progress in motor control and dexterity.

As reviewed in Chapter 10, "NBIC", numerous other lines of research are being conducted into enhancing the capabilities of AI. The general pattern is that these lines of research *underperform* expectations, most of the time, but a smaller number of them occasionally achieve breakthrough results *which jolt the field forward.* It's when these results turn out to possess "overhang", as described in Chapter 9, "Technology", that the most dramatic progress takes place. Creativity, compassion, common sense, and dexterity, may elude machine emulation for a while, but *only* for a while.

At this stage in the discussion, other counter arguments may be heard:

1. It may be asserted that there are fundamental limits to energy efficiency of AI, or to the connectivity between different parts of an extended AI system. Attempts to replace more human workers with automated systems will, in this line of thinking, run up against barriers of energy consumption or communications bandwidth.
2. It may be asserted that a combination of a human worker and an AI will always be able to outperform an AI working by itself. Thus, AI will be said to "augment" human powers, rather than to replace them.
3. It may be asserted that, if humans don't earn money by working, the resulting society will be morally defective. In this line of thinking, paid employment has important merits beyond simply providing financial income.

To counter the first counter: Improvements in AI systems don't necessarily involve consuming more resources. They often involve achieving "more with less", when smarter algorithms or designs are used. There is no fundamental reason why artificial systems cannot achieve at least the efficiency levels of human brains. That's the kind of result targeted by the field of neuromorphic computing, with encouraging progress[858].

To counter the second counter: It's true that, in an initial phase, a "cyborg" combination of human-plus-AI may achieve better performance than either a human or an AI in isolation. But, again, this depends upon the human having skills which an AI can never reach. However, in time, a standalone AI will be able to outperform any system which is slowed down by the inclusion of a human. Accordingly, the initial phase of "humans augmented" is likely to be superseded by a subsequent phase of "humans rendered redundant after all"[859].

The third counter is the most significant of the three. It's the one that brings us back to the need to upgrade our education system. At issue is the question of which of two visions of society should be preferred:

1. From each according to their ability, to each according to their *work*
2. From each according to their ability, to each according to their *need.*

The second of these statements was emphasised by Karl Marx, and is sometimes called "the basic principle of communism"[860]. In contrast, the first was emphasised by Vladimir Lenin as summarising an earlier, "lower" form of communism – described by Lenin as "socialism". Thus the 1936 constitution of the USSR contains the following[861]:

> The Union of Soviet Socialist Republics is a socialist state of workers and peasants…
>
> In the U.S.S.R. work is a duty and a matter of honour for every able-bodied citizen, in accordance with the principle: "He who does not work, neither shall he eat."
>
> The principle applied in the U.S.S.R. is that of socialism: "From each according to his ability, to each according to his work."

There's no contradiction here between the visions of Marx and Lenin. Both eagerly looked forward to a society characterised by the second principle. Both recognised that such a principle could fully operate only once technologies of abundance had been put in place. Here's Marx writing on that subject, from 1875[862]:

> In a higher phase of communist society, after the enslaving subordination of the individual to the division of labour… has vanished; … after the productive forces have also increased with the all-around development of the individual, and all the springs of co-operative wealth flow more abundantly – only then can the narrow horizon of bourgeois right be crossed in its entirety and society inscribe on its banners: "From each according to his ability, to each according to his needs!"

This so-called "basic principle of communism" has been widely criticised. If people receive all that they need, without working for it, won't they become lazy and irresponsible? They won't have any incentive to take care of what they receive, and will let it fall into disrepair and ruin. If something they receive stops working, due to lack of care, they can expect it to be replaced – since their need for it remains.

Another objection against that principle is that, once people become reliant on the state as the provider of all their basic needs, the state will acquire too much power.

However, if the accelerating abilities of automation mean that more and more people find themselves unable to earn money by paid employment – since they cannot out-compete robots and AIs – does that mean such people should starve, or otherwise lack provisions for a good standard of life?

Active transhumanism foresees a different future. Paid employment will no longer be the centrepiece of our lives. In that future, one aspect of social philosophy that has been paramount throughout history, up to the present, will be deprioritised – namely, the strong encouragement provided to everyone to make regular diligent contributions to the economy.

Until now, that strong encouragement has been central to the success of effective economies. It found voice in Lenin's admonition, "He who does not work, neither shall he eat". Earlier, writing in 1905, the German sociologist Max Weber had coined the term "Protestant Work Ethic"[863]; his work, along with that of other scholars, pointed out various positive reinforcements from the ideas of religious thinkers worldwide upon people's willingness to embrace a culture of hard work and enterprise. That encouragement has been further reinforced by the structure and content of education. We can all be grateful for the effects of that encouragement, namely, the wide provision of goods and services of increasing quantity and quality. But that's no reason to keep in place, indefinitely, the same systems of incentives and encouragements.

Google founder Larry Page expressed it like this[864]:

> The idea that everyone should slavishly work so they do something inefficiently so they keep their job – that just doesn't make any sense to me. That can't be the right answer.

It would be far better, Page said, for more and more humans to stay out of the workplace altogether, once robots and automation can do their jobs better than these humans.

What about the fear that people will, in that case, become lazy and irresponsible? Indeed, there's plenty of evidence that human nature includes some tendencies toward behaviour that is lazy and irresponsible. However, laziness isn't an entirely bad attribute: many innovations have arisen from a desire to reduce the amount of human effort required in a task. In any case, human nature can be shaped by social circumstances, and, yes, by education.

As well as tendencies toward laziness and irresponsibility, we also have tendencies toward immersing ourselves in states of "flow" – states where we become absorbed in activity. Historically, such activity has often been in workplaces. Historically, a prime motivation to enter into such states has been the financial reward that is expected, or hoped, to result. However, that same positive psychological state of flow can be achieved even without any prospects of links to financial reward. Consider hobbies, sports, games, quests, causes, explorations, and creativity in general. That is how more of our time will be spent in the transhuman future. And education needs to prepare all of us for that.

And let's be clear. The fact that an idea was advocated by any particular thinker – such as Karl Marx – is no reason, by itself, to reject that idea.

Changing attitudes

"For many ages to come the old Adam will be so strong in us that everybody will need to do some *work if he is to be contented... Three-hour shifts or a fifteen-hour week may put off the problem for a great while. For three hours a day is quite enough to satisfy the old Adam in most of us!"*

Another giant figure from the past who expressed views about the reducing need for people to work for a living was the economist John Maynard Keynes. A talk he gave in Madrid in 1930 was entitled "Economic Possibilities for our Grandchildren"[865]. The above quote predicting a fifteen-hour work week is taken from that talk. It is sometimes highlighted as a supposed case of bad foresight. I disagree.

First, Keynes was using the term "grandchildren" loosely. The actual timescale he had in mind is mentioned several times in his remarks. This is from close to the start:

> What can we reasonably expect the level of our economic life to be a hundred years hence?

Keynes then offered some ballpark calculations:

> If capital increases, say, 2 per cent per annum, the capital equipment of the world will have increased by a half in twenty years, and seven and a half times in a hundred years. Think of in terms of material things – houses, transport, and the like...
>
> I would predict that the standard of life in progressive countries one hundred years hence will be between four and eight times as high as it is today. There would be nothing surprising in this even in the light of our present knowledge. It would not be foolish to contemplate the possibility of a far greater progress still...

> I draw the conclusion that… the *economic problem* will be solved, or be at least within sight of solution, within a hundred years. This means that the economic problem is not – if we look into the future – *the permanent problem of the human race.*

One reason I particularly like this essay by Keynes – contrary to the opinion of some short-sighted detractors – is that Keynes moves on to point out the dramatic psychological challenge that will arise:

> Why, you may ask, is this so startling? It is startling because – if, instead of looking into the future, we look into the past – we find that the economic problem, the struggle for subsistence, always has been hitherto the primary, most pressing problem of the human race – not only of the human race, but of the whole of the biological kingdom from the beginnings of life in its most primitive forms.
>
> Thus we have been expressly evolved by nature – with all our impulses and deepest instincts – for the purpose of solving the economic problem. If the economic problem is solved, mankind will be deprived of its traditional purpose.

That's why Keynes referred, in the quote given earlier, to "the old Adam" – to our instincts (both individual and social) to *want* to continue working, even if for shorter lengths of time.

Such instincts, Keynes observed, continue to find support from "pseudo-moral principles" – which he hoped would retreat in their power:

> When the accumulation of wealth is no longer of high social importance, there will be great changes in the code of morals. We shall be able to rid ourselves of many of the pseudo-moral principles which have hag-ridden us for two hundred years, by which we have exalted some of the most distasteful of human qualities into the position of the highest virtues. We shall be able to afford to dare to assess the money-motive at its true value. The love of money as a possession – as distinguished from the love of money as a means to the enjoyments and realities of life – will be recognised for what it is, a somewhat disgusting morbidity, one of those semi-criminal, semi-pathological propensities which one hands over with a shudder to the specialists in mental disease.

Keynes looked forward with optimism to an *eventual* overthrow of the influence of these "pseudo-moral principles":

> All kinds of social customs and economic practices, affecting the distribution of wealth and of economic rewards and penalties, which we now maintain at all costs, however distasteful and unjust they may be in

> themselves, because they are tremendously useful in promoting the accumulation of capital, we shall then be free, at last, to discard…
>
> But beware! The time for all this is not yet. For at least another hundred years we must pretend to ourselves and to everyone that fair is foul and foul is fair; for foul is useful and fair is not. Avarice and usury and precaution must be our gods for a little longer still. For only they can lead us out of the tunnel of economic necessity into daylight.

In the meantime – before "the greatest change which has ever occurred in the material environment of life for human beings" – some important preparations can be laid. In the conclusion of his presentation, Keynes made this plea:

> Meanwhile, there will be no harm in making mild preparations for our destiny, in encouraging, and experimenting in, the arts of life as well as the activities of purpose.
>
> But, chiefly, do not let us overestimate the importance of the economic problem, or sacrifice to its supposed necessities other matters of greater and more permanent significance.

That change of attitude is among the most essential tasks of the present time – with an upgraded, reconfigured education playing a vital part in enabling that change.

The vital syllabus

To recap: the overall requirement for an upgraded education system is to prepare people of all ages to handle the risks and take advantage of the opportunities of a society that:

1. Is changing rapidly, in ways that are difficult to anticipate
2. Is ultra-diverse – with a growing variety of transhumans and AIs
3. Is awash with irrationality and destructive tendencies
4. Has lost its confidence in traditional moral principles
5. Is approaching a state of "post-scarcity", characterised by abundance
6. Is approaching a state of "post-work".

This is no time to try to establish a fixed, unchanging syllabus. However, it's important to set out a potential framework to address the above requirements. That's what I offer in the next few pages – as a starting point for further evolution. This suggested "vital syllabus" consists of twenty-two areas, each illustrated by a number of example topics:

(1) *Learning how to learn* – how to pick up new skills quickly and reliably:

- The strengths and weaknesses of various online search tools
- Finding online courses that are best suited to individual needs
- Finding learning communities that can improve understanding
- Skills in evaluating the reliability of sources and communities
- The Dunning Kruger effect (overestimation of self-expertise)
- Learning by listening, learning by discovery, and learning by doing
- Learning via playfulness and retrospectives
- How to consolidate new learning
- How to set aside previous learning that no longer pertains
- Knowing oneself better in order to learn in the best way

(2) *Communications* – with a variety of different kinds of audiences:

- The importance of narrative (story-telling) as well as facts
- Skills in graphic and video design
- Skills in immersive communications
- Skills in building empathy
- Skills in listening as well as skills in speaking
- Ways to convert negative critics and trolls into constructive partners

(3) *Agility* – how to manage uncertainty by:

- Dividing up tasks into a series of short sprints
- Obtaining useful feedback at the end of each sprint
- Updating plans based on new information obtained
- Combining a series of short sprints into lasting positive change

(4) *Creativity and exploration* – going beyond existing methods and solutions:

- Methods for generating innovative new ideas
- Methods of evaluating innovative new ideas
- Methods for transforming new ideas into actual solutions
- Methods to decide between innovation and the status-quo

(5) *Intelligence augmentation* – technology and tools to boost thinking skills:

- Traditional methods to boost memory, concentration, etc
- Uses of personal, wearable, and embedded technologies
- Roles for brain-computer interfaces

- Tools that can act like a "personal guardian angel"
- Tools and techniques to strengthen critical thinking
- Tools and techniques to boost creativity
- Tools and techniques to widen or deepen perspective
- Biofeedback mechanisms, to monitor and manage mental state
- The impact of various "consciousness raising" practices

(6) *Collaborative intelligence* – becoming wiser together:

- Addressing individual blind-spots by collective analysis
- Designing teams to promote synergies rather than cancellation
- Forms of play and other team activities that boost mutual learning
- Strengths and weaknesses of wikis and other open systems

(7) *Emotional health* – nurturing emotional strength:

- Mindfulness
- Playfulness and recreation
- The benefits of a growth mindset
- The strengths and weaknesses of positive thinking
- Not being slaves to inner anxieties and other "demons"
- Not being afraid to fail, provided that good learnings can arise
- Skills in dealing with underperformance in oneself and others
- Failing forward and failing fast (associated with Agility)
- Ways to take beneficial advantage of positive emotions
- Social skills and perceptiveness
- Understanding, supporting, and valuing diversity
- Distinguishing eustress ("good stress") from harmful distress
- Links between emotional health and social circumstances
- Links between emotional health and physical health

(8) *Physical health* – factors impacting physical health:

- Opportunities for all-round "better than well" health
- Opportunities for lives in a state of permanent youthful vitality
- Anticipating social changes due to greatly extended healthspans

(9) *Foresight* – anticipating the unexpected:

- Identifying trends that have the potential to cause disruptive changes
- The factors behind potential exponential change

- Identifying potential accelerators – and brakes – for trends
- Establishing "canary signals" for advance warning of tipping points
- How trends can combine to form scenarios
- Examples of interconnections producing unforeseen scenarios
- Using imagination to anticipate novel scenarios
- Methods to evaluate the credibility of imagined scenarios
- Methods to evaluate the desirability of imagined scenarios
- Methods to assess actions to influence the actual course of scenarios
- Precautionary and proactionary approaches to risk and opportunity

(10) *Leading change* – inspiring and maintaining transformations:

- The factors which often cause major change initiatives to fail
- Positive methods to manage major change initiatives
- Cultivating a sense of urgency instead of complacency or resignation
- Building and managing a coalition to guide vital change
- Identifying and addressing misaligned incentives

(11) *Technologies* – in history, the present, and the future:

- The structure of industrial revolutions
- Technologies and overhang
- Energy systems – green and non-green sources of energy
- Security and privacy
- Technologies for food, clothing, shelter, and beyond
- Nanotech
- Biotech
- Infotech
- Cognotech
- Virtual and Augmented Reality tech
- Robotics
- Collaboration technology

(12) *Economics* – in history, the present, and the future:

- The positive accomplishments of free markets
- The various failure modes of free markets
- The roles of money and banking
- Opportunities and risks from cryptocurrencies

- Solutions to "the tragedy of the commons"
- The "mixed model": selective government oversight of the economy

(13) *Governance* – in history, the present, and the future:

- Regulating the use of new technologies, tools, and therapies
- Issues and opportunities with "trustable monitoring"
- Options with "lean regulations" and "self-regulating" technologies
- Public incentives for the development and deployment of new tech
- Models for redistribution of wealth within society
- Strengths and weaknesses of social safety nets and social contracts
- Strengths and weaknesses of "minimal governance"
- Strengths and weaknesses of centralisation vs. decentralisation

(14) *Democracy* – in history, the present, and the future:

- Potential interplay of technocracy and democracy
- The importance of the separation of powers
- Avoiding overconfidence by distributing checking of plans
- Failure modes of democracy – and how to manage them
- Methods of deliberative democracy, including citizens' assemblies
- Augmenting human deliberations with AI tools
- Moving beyond party politics

(15) *Politics* – influencing political processes, nationally and internationally

- Evidence-based approaches vs. ideology-based approaches
- Bridge-building and the management of alliances and partnerships
- Options for self-governing virtual states
- Scenarios to rejuvenate the Bretton Woods institutions
- The importance of the international separation of powers

(16) *Numeracy* – arithmetic for the modern age

- A better understanding of probability and statistics
- A better understanding of exponentials
- Use and misuse of the Normal distribution

(17) *Science* – distinguishing "good science" from "bad science":

- The structure of scientific revolutions
- Strengths and weaknesses of scientific methods

- Identification and management of cognitive biases
- Identification and management of social pressures on science
- Potential limits of science

(18) *Philosophy* – thinking about thinking:

- Practical examples of the impact of philosophical decisions
- The potential large impact of transcendent thinking
- Awareness of philosophical biases and fallacies
- Approaches to determine ultimate priorities
- Implications of modern science and tech for traditional worldviews
- Strengths and weaknesses of religions
- Strengths and weaknesses of varieties of transhumanist philosophy
- Options for evolving a framework for ethics fit for the 2020s

(19) *Culture* – the basis for extended flourishing:

- Models for societies with increasingly diverse subcultures
- Varieties of transhumanist culture
- Coexistence with AIs and robots – in the workplace, and at home
- Coexistence with pets and other animals with uplifted capabilities

(20) *The environment* – the context in which humanity exists

- Models of environmental independence and interdependence
- The evolution of life and mind: past, present, and future
- Options for de-extinction
- Options for re-wilding
- Options for exploring the wider universe
- Alien life and the Fermi paradox

(21) *Landmines and solutions* – anticipating the biggest transformations ahead:

- Assessing the set of existential risks facing humanity
- Assessing the set of existential opportunities facing humanity
- The best ways to monitor existential canary signals

(22) *Ultimate futures* – beyond the event horizon:

- Thinking beyond the unthinkable
- Ultimate physics: births and deaths of universes
- Beyond human death: cryonics and reanimation

- Space-time engineering and technological resurrection
- Parallel multiverse branches: communication beyond base reality
- AGI or not AGI: fundamental choices
- The singularity principles (see the final chapter of this book)

Free education for all

It's one thing to suggest an extended set of topics, as above, to be covered in an upgraded educational system. It's another thing to foresee how these concepts and skills can be shared, in practice, with a huge population of potential students worldwide. Educational facilities have been steadily raising their costs over recent decades.

However, the technologies of abundance can come to our aid. Rather than the costs of education rising, they can instead shrink, toward zero.

This is the active transhumanist vision of free world-class education for all, regardless of background or circumstance.

The technologies to deliver this kind of education are sometimes called "edtech". They include:

- An expansion of online materials and online courses
- Tech-supported collaborative learning – so that communities of students can support and assist each other
- AI systems, including automated essay marking, which can improve the evaluation of the areas in which each student would benefit from further study or alternative approaches
- "Precision personalised education" – akin to "precision personalised medicine"
- Use of biofeedback to monitor and manage mental states while learning
- Opportunities with gamification and "serious games"
- Immersive virtual reality learning environments
- Time-shifted education, to counteract the "social jet lag" experienced by teenagers
- Empirical measurements of the effectiveness of different approaches to education.

Thanks to ongoing improvements in edtech, there is no reason for education to be anything like as expensive as at present.

Edtech can transform, not only how educational materials are delivered and received, but also the content and structure of those educational materials, and, therefore, the ease of updating that material. The greater agility enabled by edtech will allow any one generation of educational material to be replaced more quickly by newer material whose relevance has become clear.

In parallel with increased use of edtech, the main role of human teachers will change from knowledge conduit to mentor – as captured by the somewhat hackneyed (but nevertheless insightful) phrase "from the sage on the stage to the guide on the side".

The evaluation of edtech solutions is complicated by inflated claims made on behalf of specific methods and products. That should come as no surprise: it's the same as for many other areas of emerging technologies. Trials of various edtech solutions will, therefore, result in a mix of disappointments alongside positive results.

Happily, judicious use of various skills listed in the vital syllabus – in sections such as "learning how to learn", "augmented intelligence", and "collaborative intelligence" – can accelerate the process of distinguishing between effective and ineffective edtech solutions. Bear in mind, also, that a solution which proves disappointing during one trial may well be improved – by the application of skills from sections such as "Agility" and "Creativity and exploration" – so that subsequent upgrades of that solution could prove highly effective after all.

Beyond today's academia

What I've just described is a disruption – actually a series of disruptions, since they won't all happen at once. Like all disruptions, the likelihood is that they will tend to be resisted by existing institutions. We may therefore expect that breakthrough uses of edtech will tend to be pioneered in groups and organisations outside of the educational mainstream.

The biggest changes may come from the replacement of profit-driven organisations by those operating on a non-profit basis. Groups of people with broad transhumanist motivation can help take the lead, designing and delivering increasing numbers of educational modules in service of the topics in the above "vital syllabus". There is a need for a variety of different approaches, which assume different amounts of background knowledge and different prior expectations.

What will accelerate the development of such modules is an increased appreciation of the positive impact these modules could have:

- Impacts on the individual lives of people who absorb the material
- Impacts on the overall probability for humanity to successfully navigate the existential juncture that lies ahead.

The next chapter looks in more detail at that juncture – the choice between actions likely to trigger the existential landmines reviewed in earlier chapters, and actions likely to bring about, instead, the sustainable superabundance also described.

16. Juncture

Juncture, defined: The critical choices that demand a response. The decisions that separate two roads: one paved with good intentions but weak foresight, which lurches toward a bleak subterranean destination, and one less travelled, which has truly stellar possibilities. The actions that can tame the essential challenges of our time and obtain unprecedented liberty for humanity.

Here's an opinion that's held widely. The world in 2050 won't be especially different from today. Most things in 2050 will be broadly the same as the present time. Software will be a bit smarter on the whole, most cars will be electric, and the weather may be slightly warmer from time to time. But the majority of people will still have jobs, and will get married and have children, before growing old and dying. Seasonal flus will keep varying, and annual flu vaccinations will remain controversial. Football fans in England in 2050 will still look back fondly at the World Cup of 1966 and wonder when England might finally repeat the glory of winning that quadrennial tournament. There will still be arguments over the offside law, hand balls, and the appropriate use of video-assisted referees. Disagreements will still rumble on over the use by sportspeople of performance enhancement stimulants, and over the best ways to detect cheating. There will be more constancy than change.

That's an example of what can be called the "business-as-usual" view of the future. It's what most people tend to have in their mind as the kind of changes that are likely to unfold over the next few decades.

But scenarios like that are, in my view, *very* unlikely to come to pass. They vastly underestimate the instabilities introduced by combinations of NBIC technologies. These technologies are providing humanity with god-like powers. They're letting some awesome genies out of the flask.

Therefore, software, mid-century, won't just be *a bit* smarter than today, but could be millions of times smarter. Cars won't just be electric but will be fully autonomous, resulting in numerous changes in urban landscapes. The additional energy usage of people all around the world will, in the absence of significant changes in trajectory, more than double the heating effects of greenhouse gases. Effective biomedical interventions won't just address new infectious threats more quickly, via faster-developed vaccines, but could comprehensively reverse aging. Body enhancement technologies won't just make athletes ten percent stronger than today, but will more than double people's capacities. As for country loyalties, people's attachments to traditional national identities are likely to fragment, with the creation of all kinds of new self-governing states seceding from parent countries and then regrouping. In any case, rather than countries calling the shots in global discussions, major corporations might hold the upper hand.

That's only the start of the kinds of changes that might take place. Bear in mind that the biggest upsets often involve combinations and intersections of trends. That's why, in the chapter on landmines, I pointed out that some particularly troublesome developments could operate as "meta-landmines" – as factors that increase the difficulties in devising and implementing sensible policies to respond to the other landmines.

The default outcome, over the next few decades, therefore, will be for at least one of these landmines to explode cataclysmically. That's likely to happen, even if people all around the planet are aware of the risks, and call out warnings. Even if we're careful most of the time, it might take only a single misstep to lead us over the edge. It would be like observing sensible social distancing measures nearly all of the time, during an infectious pandemic, but then momentarily lapsing, *fatally*, into an over-close face-to-face conversation with someone you wrongly presumed to be noncontagious.

The road forward that is paved with good intentions, so to speak, but which lacks the active steering of vital foresight, won't just lead to "more of the same" as today. It's more likely to lead us into a *much* worse situation.

To put some rough numbers to these predictions, I estimate the chance of humanity in 2050 being in some kind of "business-as-usual" extrapolation of today's situation as less than 10%. The chance of humanity being in a much bleaker situation is at least 30%.

That leaves around 60%, as the chance of something significantly different. That's the chance of humanity rousing from our sleepwalking, navigating our way along "the road less travelled", and reaching a state broadly corresponding to the sustainable superabundance I've been describing throughout the previous chapters of this book.

Prima facie, these numbers – 60% versus 30% – make me more of an optimist than a pessimist. However, I need to stress two important caveats:

1. The 30% number is *far* too high for any comfort. Would you board an airplane if you were told there was a 30% chance of it plummeting

out of the sky mid-flight, before reaching your intended destination? *Not if you could help it.*

2. The 60% number assumes that humanity will do more than "become aware" of the risks we collectively face. As I mentioned, that awareness, by itself, won't keep us safe from danger. Instead, we're going to need to organise ourselves into major transformational projects, so that we can take profound positive advantage of the disruptive possibilities of NBIC technologies.

As for what this might involve, let's revisit one-by-one the list of eleven landmines from Chapter 4. Let's see how the active transhumanist approach advocated in earlier chapters could make a sufficient difference in each case.

The "left behinds"

"The world has enough for everyone's needs, but not everyone's greed."

That famous saying by Mahatma Gandhi, already mentioned in passing in Chapter 11, has often been contested. The seemingly simple concepts of "need" and "greed" turn out to be more controversial in practice. Who is to judge whether a desire is for a legitimate need, or whether it crosses over into being illegitimate greed? Who will deny individuals' pursuit of "more"?

After all, the more we have, the more we often *perceive* ourselves as needing. As our standard of living rises, our desires seem to grow for:

- Multiple sets of fine clothing
- Cosmopolitan variety in cuisine
- Multiple long-haul holidays each year
- Secure housing with comfort and privacy
- Swift access to the latest healthcare solutions
- Anything else that our neighbours seem to be enjoying.

Any suggestion that limits might be imposed, from on high, on the fulfilments of such desires, provokes anxiety. Developing countries fear that their citizens will have to survive using much less energy, on average, than citizens in the US and the EU. People unable to find employment with high salary fear that their quality of life will be unfairly constrained – compared to that of others who often chanced on their wealth as much by luck, or even by exploitation, as by genuine merit. People's lives may come to a premature end on account of an illness for which no treatments are available *to them*, due to lack of healthcare insurance. For them, the world does *not* provide even the basic needs of life.

However, the vision of active transhumanism is that, within just a few decades, there truly *will* be enough to provide for a rich quality of life for everyone – regardless of age, location, or employment status. That is the vision of sustainable superabundance. Intelligent automation will generate ample clean energy, fresh water, food, clothing, shelter, material goods, health treatments, education, entertainment, and opportunities for creativity, exploration, and social engagement. In short, *everyone* will have access to the means for flourishing at ever deeper levels.

This won't just be a better life for people who are currently in the bottom 50% – or the bottom 90% – of the spectrum of wealth. It will also be a better quality of life for those who are currently in the top 10%, 1%, and even 0.1% of wealth. There will be a great lifting of the enormous psychic stresses that accompany today's inequality of opportunities. And there will no longer be any need for gated security compounds or constant vigilance against attacks.

However, to reduce the current pandemic of "deaths of despair", and the associated growth of bitterly angry people ready to wreak destruction on what they perceive as a warped or evil society, two other breakthroughs will be necessary, beyond the sheer *vision* of sustainable superabundance.

First, that vision must become widely recognised, not just as being attractive, but as being *credible* and *attainable.*

Second, it must also become widely recognised that, in the interim period ahead of the tangible realisation of sustainable superabundance, sufficient assistance will be available, to defend people against the powerful social complexes who presently threaten to exploit them, abuse them, and leave them behind.

The first of these breakthroughs involves transhumanist education. The second involves transhumanist politics. The first provides answers to all sorts of questions about the generation and distribution of abundance. The second provides confidence that the state will be powerful enough to take action against cancerous social complexes, *and* that society as a whole will be powerful enough to constrain the political state against overreach.

These breakthroughs cannot be secured merely by propounding theories. They will need support from visible practical examples:

- Examples of all the basic ingredients of a good life reducing in price and increasing in distribution
- Examples of groups, regions, and countries that are moving closer to the transhumanist political ideals of superdemocracy
- Examples of powerful social complexes becoming less threatening, losing their power to wield WMDs (weapons of mass destruction).

WMD proliferation

Here's the problem with proliferation of WMDs. Even if the vast majority of alienated individuals lose their sense of alienation, and come to feel at ease with the direction in which society is moving, that will not be enough. It only requires a small number of people to remain deeply disgruntled, for the risk of acquisition and usage of WMDs to be alarming.

The issue was stated in a semi-humorous form by rationality advocate Eliezer Yudkowsky at the Stanford "Accelerating Change" conference in 2005[866]:

> Moore's Law of Mad Scientists: The minimum IQ required to destroy the world drops by one point every 18 months.

The reference, here, is to the original "Moore's Law", which can be stated loosely as "The hardware computing power of silicon chips doubles, for a given price point, every 18 months". The "Mad Scientists" variant highlights the fact that advanced technologies are increasingly easy to find, configure, and deploy.

One example of destructive technology spreading more widely is "ransomware as a service" (RaaS). Ransomware prevents victims from using their computer until they have paid a fee – often via a cryptocurrency that is hard to trace. Some developers of ransomware have taken the process a step further, packaging up their malicious software into a kit that is:

- Advertised via YouTube videos
- Available on the "dark web" portions of the Internet
- Well documented, allowing purchasers of the system to customise it
- Accessible to people with minimal programming skills – people sometimes called "script kiddies".

As philosopher Nick Bostrom has pointed out, it was deeply fortunate that nuclear weapons require considerable sophistication to produce[867]:

> Making an atomic weapon requires several kilograms of plutonium or highly enriched uranium, both of which are very difficult and expensive to produce. However, suppose it had turned out otherwise: that there had been some really easy way to unleash the energy of the atom – say, by sending an electric current through a metal object placed between two sheets of glass.

If it had turned out to be easier to create atomic weapons, it would very likely have increased the chances of them being used more frequently. Thankfully, humanity escaped that particular bullet, so to speak. But as science and technology progresses, new options for easy access to vastly destructive forces remain a matter of grave concern. New WMDs might not require any fundamental breakthrough; instead, the mere convergence of existing technologies, combined in an unexpected way, could be all that it takes to place terrible weaponry within the grasp of people with the adverse psychological disposition to wield it in anger.

Reducing the likelihood of wide use of WMDs therefore involves four projects:

1. Making it clear to as many people as possible that a bright future awaits them, in a future sustainable superabundance, in which case their motivation should diminish to initiate mass destruction
2. Keeping track of the set of possible WMDs which recalcitrant members of society might be able to utilise – noting that this set will grow in size over time, as science and technology evolve
3. Developing counter measures to deploy against potential WMDs
4. Monitoring for signs of any plans to use WMDs.

The last of these projects is potentially controversial. It involves part of society surveilling citizens in ways that could be considered deeply intrusive. Such surveillance could enable state authorities to place undue constraints on members of the public. In other words, if not overseen carefully, *legitimate* surveillance could be accompanied by *illegitimate* surveillance.

The answer is to develop systems of "trustable monitoring". This would be somewhat similar to the way in which society trusts medical doctors with sensitive medical information. Doctors found to have misused such information – or to have been careless with it – are subject to fines, loss of privileges, or other penalties. Likewise, in a corporation, members of the IT department have privileged access to some of the company's key information stores, and are, again, required to make sparing use of such powers. Again, all commercial aircraft carry cockpit voice recorders, with the recordings being accessed only in case of accident. As one final example, lawyers often see information that is kept out of the public eye.

To avoid abuse, trustable monitoring requires an agreed separation of powers. Each of us might individually dislike the idea that our actions could be monitored, on the off-chance that we are preparing to acquire and deploy WMDs. However, that's a freedom we may agree to give up, as part of *a collective social agreement*, in order to reduce the chance that WMDs are acquired and deployed anywhere within our society. The degree to which we are comfortable to accept that trade-off will depend on the degree to which we can trust the part of society that is doing the monitoring. In turn, that depends on the overall quality of the social infrastructure within our society.

To be clear, there's a significant difference between the kind of trustable monitoring I'm proposing, and the earlier examples of restricted access to private data by doctors, IT technicians, aircraft crash analysts, and lawyers. In these earlier examples, the surveillance has the approval of the people being surveilled. Patients might not want their medical records released to friends or work colleagues, but acknowledge that their doctors should have sight of that information. However, a would-be mass bomber will take steps to prevent *anyone* from finding out about their plans. Accordingly, to be effective, the monitoring system will presumably need to keep secret some aspects of its methods of gathering information. Critics who have a deep distrust of public officials will be alarmed at any such measures of secrecy. They'll wonder: *what else is being concealed?*

That's why a separation of powers is so important. There will be "watchers" – units of the state that keep a look out for activities potentially involving WMDs. And there will be "watchers of the watchers" – a separate unit that oversees the operation of the surveillers. Next, the watchers of the watchers will themselves be subject to democratic supervision. Moreover, the entire process is subject to criticism from journalists, analysis by independent researchers, and legal challenges in courtrooms. As one example, agents of the UK's MI5 security service are subject to review by:

- Internal MI5 supervision
- The Investigatory Powers Commissioner's Office (IPCO)[868]

- The Intelligence and Security Committee (ISC) of Parliament[869].

Public support for these surveillance systems depends on confidence that what is happening behind the scenes is in line with the external description of these systems. Saying one thing but doing something very different under the cloak of secrecy is a recipe for damaging public trust. Any such duplicity could cause "trustable monitoring" to switch, instead, to "contested, despised monitoring". It's all the more reason to insist on the highest standards of integrity in the conduct of such activities. The people involved, especially at senior management level, must be beyond suspicion: they should be recognised as carrying out their tasks, not for political or other ulterior purposes, but in line with principles that command bipartisan support.

Biotech hazards

Systems of trustable monitoring, as just described, can play an important role to prevent the creation or distribution of deadly new biological infections. However, no surveillance system can be completely watertight, especially as the tools to edit biological organisms become more widespread. Sadly, we cannot rule out the possibility of a disaffected group of individuals unleashing a new viral or bacterial contaminant on the world. For this reason, another line of defence needs to be prepared as a matter of high priority: more powerful medical interventions.

The example of COVID-19 provides an indication of what is possible:

- The genetic material of the virus was sequenced within just a few days of the disease being noticed
- Whereas vaccines for new diseases had previously taken several years to be developed, a number of COVID-19 vaccines were developed and deployed within twelve months
- Various other treatments to increase the chances of survival were developed over the course of that year.

The same example also highlights the need for proactive public preparations for any future pandemics, whether natural in origin or engineered by human malcontents:

- Large private corporations had seen little business case, in advance of any new outbreak, to increase their competence in the swift development of vaccines against novel pathogens

- Supply chains for protective clothing and other medical items had lacked resilience, having been over-optimised for "just-in-time" deliveries that were deemed to involve lower costs
- Discussion of possible cures for COVID-19 were bedevilled by political undertones and the spread of pseudoscience
- Political wrangling, as well as smouldering international rivalries, complicated options for accelerating processes for testing and approving new vaccines.

Accordingly, a number of actions need to be prioritised:

1. Public funding to develop generic vaccine platforms, that will allow any new virus outbreaks to be treated more quickly
2. Public funding to develop new antibiotics, to guard against the growing risk of bacteria that are resistant to all existing antibiotics
3. Reviews of ideas for swifter testing and approval of new medical treatments
4. Educational initiatives, aimed at people of all ages, to deepen understanding, not only of the specifics of medical interactions, but also of the general methods of science in the face of uncertainty
5. Powerful penalties against anyone who knowingly or carelessly spreads false medical information.

Infotech hazards

As for biotech hazards, so also for infotech hazards: trustable monitoring can help reduce the risks, but is far from sufficient to remove all dangers. In both cases, more attention needs to be given to mechanisms to resist attacks.

Just as biotech hazards take advantage of weaknesses in human biology, infotech hazards take advantage of weaknesses in our shared software infrastructure. These weaknesses include software being written without sufficient focus on security, and software kept in use even though it is known to be insecure.

Unfortunately, vulnerabilities in software platforms are often kept secret by groups that discover them, rather than being reported to the manufacturer. Hackers can make lots of money by selling their discoveries to the highest bidder. In this way, shadowy groups develop and stockpile software exploits, with a view to making offensive use of them against perceived enemies.

However, the same vulnerabilities can be discovered and utilised by these enemies as well, in what New York Times security writer Nicole Perlroth has labelled a "boomerang" effect[870].

To reduce these software vulnerabilities, a number of public initiatives need to be accelerated:

1. Improved software update processes, so that older, insecure versions of software can be replaced more easily by newer, secure versions
2. Wider education in methods to design software that is secure from the ground up
3. Wider education in methods to systematically test software for potential vulnerabilities
4. Penalties imposed on software vendors when their software is found to have security flaws
5. Penalties imposed on software vendors that prioritise speed of delivery over product security
6. Rewards given when people report new software vulnerabilities that they have found
7. Improved alternatives developed to replace the use of passwords to confirm the identity of users – since humans all-too-often type their passwords into windows that appear to be familiar but which are actually created by adversaries
8. Strong discouragement of the stockpiling of software vulnerabilities.

In case it's not clear, I'll emphasise that these initiatives necessarily involve elements of legal regulation. They're not something that an unconstrained free market can develop and adopt of its own volition.

Of course, any time it is proposed that regulations are imposed on fast-changing technological products, some critics object that government regulators will cause worse problems than the ones they are intended to solve. It is said that:

- Regulators are frequently out-of-touch with the latest technological possibilities
- Regulations impose delays and inefficiencies on a market, resulting in companies being out-performed by competitors from other countries with laxer regulatory systems

- Regulators can be "captured" by vested interests representing today's most dominant companies, to the detriment of smaller, less powerful companies that have more innovative ideas.

These concerns all have merit. But they're not a reason to abandon regulations, or to accept the continuation of today's highly insecure software systems. They're a reason to ensure that highly talented people are attracted into the roles of regulator – people with skills and experience in both technical and legal matters.

Renowned security expert Bruce Schneier puts it like this[871]: "We need more public-interest technologists". Among many other credentials, Schneier is Lecturer in Public Policy at the Harvard Kennedy School, and a Fellow at the Berkman-Klein Center for Internet and Society. He raised his concerns in a New York Magazine article entitled "Click Here to Kill Everyone". He spells out his recommendation on "public-interest technologists" as follows:

> The historical divide between Washington and Silicon Valley – the mistrust of governments by tech companies and the mistrust of tech companies by governments – is dangerous.
>
> We have to fix this. Getting… security right depends on the two sides working together and, even more important, having people who are experts in each working on both.
>
> We need technologists to get involved in policy, and we need policy-makers to get involved in technology. We need people who are experts in making both technology and technological policy. We need technologists on congressional staffs, inside federal agencies, working for NGOs, and as part of the press. We need to create a viable career path for public-interest technologists, much as there already is one for public-interest attorneys. We need courses, and degree programs in colleges, for people interested in careers in public-interest technology. We need fellowships in organizations that need these people. We need technology companies to offer sabbaticals for technologists wanting to go down this path. We need an entire ecosystem that supports people bridging the gap between technology and law. We need a viable career path that ensures that even though people in this field won't make as much as they would in a high-tech start-up, they will have viable careers.

As Schneier emphasises, the stakes are sky-high:

> The security of our computerized and networked future – meaning the security of ourselves, families, homes, businesses, and communities – depends on it.

Financial instabilities

Another area where skilled, knowledgeable, agile-minded regulators are sorely needed is that of the regulation of finance – including the regulation of money.

An active transhumanist account of the future of money starts with the recognition that money is a technology – a powerful, sophisticated technology. Like other technologies, money is a mechanism that:

1. Allows humans to do things that would not otherwise be possible (or to do these things more fully)
2. Has experienced many innovations in its operation over the years – consider developments such as paper money, cheques, insurance contracts, limited liability companies, mutual investment funds, credit cards, deposit insurance guarantees, and cryptocurrencies
3. Can interact with other technologies in multiple ways – some hard to anticipate in advance
4. Can have both good and bad societal impact.

The final point just noted deserves underscoring. Despite the harsh criticisms they often receive, money and its related institutions, such as banking and investment mechanisms, have enabled profound advances in the human condition.

It's not just that money enables a more efficient sharing of produce than simple barter mechanisms. It's that money enables and encourages people to become involved in enterprises which would otherwise scarcely have been possible. Rather than just trying to rely on good will from family and friends when you need extra resources to start a project, you can obtain investment from far-distant sources. Financial risks can be spread out in ways that make them more tractable. Rather than a single business person being liable for all the downside if, say, a ship carrying lots of cargo is sunk by an unseasonable storm – and the person in question therefore being deterred from commencing the project in the first place, for fear of such an accident – insurance can provide the incentive to take the plunge.

Indeed, the Industrial Revolution would probably not have taken place, or would have proceeded much more slowly, in the absence of financial innovations such as joint stock companies. The Economist magazine suggested[872] in 1926 that the unknown person who had devised the idea of the limited liability company deserved "a place of honour with Watt [the steam engine trailblazer], Stephenson [the railways innovator] and other pioneers of the industrial revolution". I agree.

Business development initiatives have been facilitated by a growing network of commercial banks and other financial intermediaries. These banks have, in turn, been facilitated by central banks that were prepared to act, with government backing, as the "lender of last resort".

The American humourist Will Rogers is said to have quipped[873] that "There have been three great inventions since the beginning of time: fire, the wheel, and central banking". Many a true word is said in jest (albeit in exaggeration). The institutions of central banking – such as the Federal Reserve in the United States and the Bank of England in the United Kingdom – have provided significant extra stability to financial systems, compared to before their introduction. These institutions intervene from time to time to loan funds to commercial banks, to prevent the failure of these banks.

But there are plenty of dissenting views. The New Testament in the Bible warns us that "The love of money is the root of all evil"[874]. Many religions have declared it sinful to charge interest ("usury") on loans. Contemporary critics use lots of choice insults to describe bankers. Celebrity chef Mario Batali of the Food Network opined, in a 2011 Time Magazine Person of the Year debate, that bankers had the same moral standing as Stalin and Hitler[875]:

> [The institution with] the largest effect on the whole planet without us really paying attention… is the entire banking industry and their disregard for the people that they're supposed to be working for... The ways the bankers have… toppled the way money is distributed and taken most of it into their hands is as good as Stalin or Hitler and the evil guys.

An area of particular controversy is the ability of banks to create money out of nothing – by so-called "fiat". This money has no direct backing from any material "gold standard" or other tangible set of goods. Nor does it correspond to money loaned to the bank by investors. Instead, a bank simply adds extra credit into the balance of a borrower. The borrower is expected in due course to repay that loan, thereby cancelling out the fiat creation. In the meantime, the bank earns interest from the loan.

Fiat money creation takes place at two levels: from commercial banks to business investors (as well as to private households); and from central banks to commercial banks. In both cases, the extra money has the potential to distort the economy: with more money chasing the same quantity of real-world goods, prices could rise, resulting in inflation, which would in turn diminish the value of savings.

To some critics, fiat money creation seems an absurd state of affairs. These critics have in the back of their mind the idea that money is some kind of substitute for a fixed scarce commodity, like gold bars.

However, there is nothing fundamentally wrong with these money-creation mechanisms. Banning these mechanisms completely would be akin to governments banning the creation of all new cryptocurrencies – an unwarranted intrusion on economic liberty.

Of course, money creation does have drawbacks as well as benefits. As mentioned, too much money creation can result in inflation, or a declining public respect for a currency. And as reviewed in Chapter 4, too much private debt can be a prelude to a spiralling financial downturn.

Moreover, the very perception that a central bank will be ready to loan new money to troubled commercial banks, with government backing, encourages a "moral hazard" in which banks act recklessly. These banks see themselves as "too big to fail". For these reasons, it's important that frameworks putting limits on money creation are agreed, and are then regularly updated as new technological and societal possibilities emerge.

In turn, these regulatory frameworks are part of a vital wider review of the envisioned benefits and the potential risks of financial technology.

Financial technology, also known as fintech, should be treated similarly to other major technological innovations, such as artificial intelligence:

1. Whilst innovation should be encouraged, it is important to agree the desired outcomes of such innovation – not "ultra-efficient AI" but "beneficial AI", and not "ultra-efficient fintech" but "beneficial fintech"
2. A vigilant safety culture needs to be developed and supported
3. Ongoing toleration of unstable situations should be challenged as being thoroughly irresponsible
4. Reassuring words from industry insiders should be viewed with scepticism
5. Scenarios should be drawn up for how to address the accumulation of underlying toxic problems, such as excess private indebtedness.

The good news is that discussions along such lines have already been taking place in multiple forums, such as the International Monetary Forum, the World Bank, and the Basel Committee on Banking Supervision. The bad news is that these discussions face many obstacles, including the following:

1. Proposals for "debt forgiveness" are controversial: critics believe any such forgiveness will act as an encouragement for a repetition of financially irresponsible borrowing
2. Any ideas on reforming the Eurozone are politically contentious
3. Participants in these discussions are frequently constrained by powerful system inertia – as vividly chronicled in the disclosures by former Greek Finance Minister Yanis Varoufakis about his numerous dialogues with leading financial professionals[876]
4. Participants clash on their different theories of economics.

To move beyond this impasse, a stronger vision is needed. That's the vision of the profound social transformations which lie ahead – both the profoundly bad transformations which new financial crises could trigger, and the profoundly good transformations of sustainable superabundance. Contemplation of both these transformations should concentrate minds more effectively than before.

A central part of this vision is mechanisms to direct the financial markets away from investments that are likely to produce long-term or medium-term damage, toward investments that may play a key role in overcoming the various landmines. The tendency of financial markets to prioritise investment with shorter-term paybacks needs to be resisted. For an important example, let's consider actions to reduce the risks of runaway climate change.

Environmental instabilities

In principle, it is well understood what needs to be done, in order to reduce the risks of a dramatic destabilisation of the global climate system[877]. Human activities that presently emit greenhouse gases need to be transformed so that they no longer cause such emissions. In parallel, activities that presently remove greenhouse gases from the atmosphere need to be intensified and augmented.

On the emissions side of the ledger, significant changes are needed in:

1. How we manufacture various items that are in wide usage, such as cement, steel, glass, fertilisers, and plastics – since our present

methods of manufacturing emit, by some estimates, around 31% of all greenhouse gases

2. How we generate electricity (27% of greenhouse gases)
3. How we use land for agriculture and forestry (17%)
4. How we power transportation, including cars, trucks, trains, ships, and aircraft (16%)
5. How we heat – and cool – our buildings (7%).

On the removal side of the ledger, options include planting more trees, planting various crops on soil which would otherwise be bare, spreading algae on oceans, and chemical methods to extract CO2 directly from the air.

On both sides of the ledger, many *potential* approaches are known. Some are being adopted with impressive speed, including solar and wind energy. Reasons why adoption isn't proceeding faster, and across all required categories, include:

1. The high costs of several of these alternatives
2. Challenges in scaling up these alternatives from local usage into country-sized applications that require much greater quantities of land and raw materials
3. General human discomfort with change, and a preference to keep on doing things in ways that are viewed as "tried and tested"
4. Various arguments over the desirability of some of the proposed alternatives, such as nuclear power, synthetic ("lab-grown") meat, and geoengineering approaches that would reflect back into space some of the energy being received by the earth from the sun
5. Other arguments over whether solutions to climate change require "degrowth" – lower levels of economic activity, reduced travel, fewer possessions, and so on, *and perhaps even the dismantling of capitalism* – or whether, instead, a notion of "green growth" is feasible, along with what has been called "Climate capitalism"[878]
6. A final set of arguments over *the degree of urgency* of fully adopting these alternatives, in order to prevent possible acceleration of climate change – or whether more effort should be prioritised into, for example, improving the *adaptability* of society to changes in climate.

Several of these arguments have created polarisation, in which support or opposition to particular ideas becomes subordinated to general political or ideological stances, rather than the ideas being evaluated on their own merits. Groups that are opposed to action to address climate change – groups labelled as "climate *inactivists*" by geophysicist and climatologist Michael Mann[879] – have been taking deliberate steps to manipulate the public discussion in ways that multiply mistrust and slow down any decisive actions.

With the current rate of adopting new solutions, and the current rate of *increase* in adoption, greenhouse gases are likely to keep accumulating in the atmosphere, pushing the global climate system further into conditions not experienced at any time in human history. If that happens, all bets are off.

To accelerate the acceleration of adoption of suitable new solutions, active transhumanism highlights the following steps:

1. Champion a more rational, open-minded, dispassionate evaluation of all the options, rather than allowing political or ideological pressures to distort dialogue. Groups or individuals that deliberately mislead the discussion should be forcefully prosecuted
2. Accelerate scientific and engineering research of different options, by encouraging increases in both public and private financing of the relevant research; this research should cover both incremental and disruptive forms of innovation
3. By stages, apply increased taxes to all activities that generate greenhouse gases; this will help correct the present dangerous price differentials that favour these activities. Part of the tax revenues raised can be distributed to the members of society who are most impacted by climate change; other parts can be deployed in support of the scientific and engineering research mentioned above
4. Provide more transparency of the steps that are being taken by different companies and organisations toward net zero carbon emissions. Add levies to any use of finance by companies and organisations with plans that are unclear or inadequate
5. Provide support for civil court cases for members of the public to obtain compensation from companies whose activities can be assessed as more likely than not as being a significant contributor to damages from extreme weather events. (This will be similar to the legal cases mounted against tobacco companies for the costs incurred by the healthcare system from diseases such as lung cancer whose prevalence was increased by products from these companies.)

6. Encourage financial disinvestment from the companies whose present high share price valuations presume that their vast oil and other reserves will all be burned[880]
7. Further encourage market adoption of climate-friendly alternatives to existing products, by mandating their adoption in contracts controlled by government, and by providing subsidies when needed
8. Continue the process of building international consensus about the necessity of coordinated action, in which countries stage by stage voluntarily agree global carbon taxes, limits on greenhouse gas emissions, and greater reporting transparency, recognising the greater security and other benefits these steps will bring
9. Emphasise the compatibility of the goal of net-zero greenhouse gas emissions with the vibrant operation of a free-market economy and with an increased degree of human flourishing – so long as that free market is subject to the kind of democratic "mixed market" oversight covered in Chapter 13, "Politics". That will ensure that both positive and negative externalities have their prices included in economic calculations.

Can these steps be taken by democratic governments? Or are matters already so serious that elements of democracy must be sacrificed, giving governments authoritarian powers to take the actions that are deemed necessary? My answers, which I'll develop further in the next section, are that:

1. Democratic processes can indeed take the right decisions
2. The imagined "cure" of an authoritarian government will likely be *worse* than the problems it is supposed to solve.

Democracy under threat

The reason why democracy has been losing its appeal is because it is increasingly perceived as producing poor outcomes:

1. To remain in power, political parties need to promise, and deliver, results in the short-term, that is, before the date of the next election. The consequence is often to stack up problems for the longer-term, with difficult decisions repeatedly being "kicked down the road"
2. Politicians in a democracy often prioritise "playing to their base", that is, saying and doing things that appeal to the subset of the

electorate who are most likely to vote for them, rather than addressing the needs of the electorate as a whole

3. Lots of energy is devoted to oppositional politics, with parties trying to make each other look bad, rather than finding ways to work together constructively on matters of shared concern
4. Within individual parties, leaders often come to power with the assistance of extreme wings of the party – the party members who have strong passions for particular causes – with the result that cooperation between different parties becomes harder
5. To maintain their electoral support in times when national progress falters, political leaders are inclined to assign blame to scapegoats, such as foreign adversaries, international conspiracies, or imagined "enemies within" – rather than giving sufficient attention to the actual causes of discontent or alienation.

Given these tendencies, it is understandable that alternative "strong man" models of government start to seem attractive. With no need to seek re-election, political leaders can devote more attention to long-term decisions, and have no need to hand out bribes to keep their own voting base happy. Without a cacophony of competing political parties, energy can be devoted to tasks of national importance, rather than to internecine battles. With government control of the media, news stories that would distract or confuse the public can be quashed. With the judiciary subordinated to the dictates of the ruling party, there is no need for the time-wasting inconvenience of independent legal review. *The appeal of such a system is clear.*

On the other hand, the drawbacks of authoritarian government are equally well known. Political leaders who start out as "benevolent dictators" morph over time, all too often, into tyrannical dictators. Without independent reviews of decisions, and a landscape of alternative proposals, the state can become blinkered, seeing only what it wants to see. Having risen to power with a promise of taking hard decisions in the national interest, autocrats in reality often prioritise maintaining their own internal support base; they persecute anyone who dares to suggest that the national interest may require different policies, or, heaven forbid, a new person in the top role.

Given the growing availability of technologies of extreme surveillance and societal manipulation, there's increased potential for autocratic governments to cause even more harm – perpetuating their own position of power, hiding or distorting inconvenient facts, suppressing discussion of variant ideas, and denying citizens any rights to alternative views, alternative lifestyles, or alternative political structures. Using a mixture of distraction and fear, autocratic governments can steer and coerce citizens into compliance with actions that preserve the existing authority structure. Society will be encouraged to sleepwalk, without any attention to potential landmines other than those mentioned by the country's political leaders. *Despite any superficial appeal, it would be a perilous state of affairs.*

To prevent a slide into authoritarian government, it is imperative that democracy is seen to succeed. But I have little confidence in "democracy as usual". A continuation of the troubled democratic systems of the recent past is unlikely to win back wide trust in such systems. Instead, what is more likely to change the public assessment will be steps toward the concept of superdemocracy described in previous chapters:

1. The reduction of significance of individual political parties, with much greater fluidity of party makeup and party membership
2. Less focus on *who* is correct, and more on *what* is correct
3. Representation at the highest levels of government – that is, a senior cabinet position – for advocates for the medium-term future
4. The growth of influence of groups throughout society that, likewise, emphasise flourishing in the medium and longer term, to help counter pressures toward short-termism
5. Appropriate levels of respect for experts, even when the recommendations from these experts are "politically incorrect" or "politically inconvenient". Note that this also requires a better understanding of the *limits* of expertise, and the complications arising when decisions involve intersections of multiple disciplines
6. Protection for the separation of power: independent press, judiciary, civil service, and diverse political groupings
7. Support from real-time artificial intelligence to improve the calibre of analysis of potential political policies.

Cancers within society

If one dangerous response to the challenges experienced by democracies is the embrace, as discussed in the previous section, of a move toward authoritarian government, another dangerous response is to try to avoid government and politics altogether. The attraction in this case is the idea that, without meddling politicians, everyone will be able to get along fine.

However, it's a naive idea. When government is weak, many other forces can step forward, including crime syndicates, mafiosi dynasties, apocalyptic fantasists, armed militia, and powerful corporations. These forces would wreak havoc on the rest of us as they battle for dominance.

Indeed, there's a risk of a downward spiral. Once a government loses some authority, it will have less ability to raise taxes: the richer portions of society will be able to evade scrutiny. With a poorer financial position, the institutions of the state will be cut back further, ceding even more authority to the various cancerous complexes that are exerting increasing power.

As described in earlier chapters, the answer is a combination of an active, capable state kept in check by an active, capable society – that is, by a successful implementation of the principle of separation of power. Under such a system, no group – and no individual – is above the law. No group can expand its power without check. Cancers can be handled in their early stages, before they damage society's overall wellbeing.

That process applies relatively straightforwardly within individual countries. At the international level, matters are more complicated. Let's take a closer look.

Divided nations

International bodies such as the United Nations Security Council suffer from logjams: key decisions can be delayed indefinitely by vetoes. As a result, the most powerful people in various countries appear to be able to accumulate huge wealth and power for use by themselves and their families. They can even have their critics killed, with, it seems, little response from the justice system. The investigative journalist Oliver Bullough describes some depressing examples in his well-researched 2018 book *Moneyland: Why Thieves and Crooks Now Rule the World and How To Take It Back*[881].

Nevertheless, despite the challenges, a dual track process can be applied that reduces the potency of these international cancers. Veteran human rights lawyer Geoffrey Robertson outlines what he calls "Plan A" and "Plan B" to deal with such outrages[882].

Plan A is possible when the world's most powerful countries agree. Plan B becomes necessary when some of these countries thumb their noses at international courts.

Examples of Plan A include:

1. The international trials in Nuremberg and Tokyo at the end of World War Two, prosecuting the instigators of the worst war crimes
2. Trials by the International Criminal Tribunal for the former Yugoslavia, set up by the United Nations, of individuals for crimes committed during the Balkan wars that took place from 1991 to 2001
3. Trials by the International Criminal Court, located in The Hague, of Congolese rebel leaders Thomas Lubanga and Germain Katanga, as well as the politicians Koudou Laurent Gbagbo of the Ivory Coast and Jean-Pierre Bemba of the Democratic Republic of the Congo.

Plan B requires individual countries, or groups of countries, to apply targeted economic sanctions against people that flagrantly violate agreed human rights standards. Such sanctions are sometimes called "Magnitsky sanctions", referring to the Russian tax lawyer, Sergei Magnitsky, who died in a Moscow prison in 2009.

Magnitsky had accused Russian officials of large-scale theft of assets owned by the state and by private companies, such as Hermitage Capital Management. Details of Magnitsky's appalling mistreatment were publicised by the co-founder of Hermitage, the American businessman Bill Browder[883]. Browder subsequently lobbied US politicians to pass what was known as the Magnitsky Act. This gives the US government the power to sanction individuals who are adjudged to be egregious violators of human rights, such as those involved in the mistreatment and death of Magnitsky. Such sanctions can include:

1. Freezing of assets owned by the individual or by their family
2. Prevention of the individual or their family from entering the United States
3. Forbidding US nationals from carrying out business with the individual.

Since the original Magnitsky Act in the United States, similar legislation has been passed in Canada (2017), the United Kingdom (2018), the European Union (2020), and an increasing number of other jurisdictions. Individuals targeted by sanctions enabled by this legislation operate from Russia, Belarus, Saudi Arabia, Venezuela, China, Sudan, and Burma, amongst other countries.

These targeted sanctions avoid penalising entire countries. In contrast, general trade restrictions would likely increase economic hardship for the poorest citizens of these countries – citizens who had not been involved in any of the human rights abuses. (Indeed, they may even have been human rights victims themselves, at the hands of state officials.) It's their selectivity that gives Magnitsky sanctions additional bite.

Angry reactions to Magnitsky sanctions, by state officials in the impacted countries, indicate their effectiveness: they are hitting where it hurts. Boris Nemtsov, who had been Deputy Prime Minister of Russia under Boris Yeltsin, and who subsequently became a persistent critic of Vladimir Putin, expressed his support for targeted actions:

> You will only stop Putin assassinating enemies in the UK if you stop his oligarch friends from sending their children to Eton.

Another Russian critic of Putin, Alexei Navalny, made a similar plea[884]:

> There is no sense to sanction colonels or generals or people who are definitely not travelling a lot or have bank accounts in Europe… Just target Russian oligarchs.

Navalny urged that, so long as human rights continued to be routinely violated by Russian state officials – in defiance of the Russian constitution – oligarchs with close ties to the regime should no longer be able to moor their luxurious yachts in glamorous Western European locations such as Barcelona or Monaco, or otherwise enjoy the delicacies of life in such cities.

Of course, targeted sanctions are something that can be misused. Politicians can apply such sanctions, not out of a genuine respect for human rights and democracy, but for their own convenience. That's why the global community needs an ongoing discussion, to draw attention to examples of the two sorts of usage, giving praise or opprobrium as appropriate.

Moreover, a set of sanctions from one country (such as the United States) against officials in another (such as China) can never come to define the entirety of the relationship between those two countries. Antony Blinken explained it as follows in March 2021 in his first public speech in the role of US Secretary of State, in which he defined his approach to foreign policy[885]:

> Our relationship with China will be competitive when it should be, collaborative when it can be, and adversarial when it must be.

For example, in areas such as combatting global climate change, collaboration between these two superpowers will be essential.

Blinken's speech had the broader vision of renewing and defending democracy, at home and abroad:

> We will renew democracy, because it's under threat…
>
> Strong democracies are more stable, more open, better partners to us, more committed to human rights, less prone to conflict, and more dependable markets for our goods and services. When democracies are weak, governments can't deliver for their people, or a country becomes so polarized that it's hard for anything to get done, they become more vulnerable to extremist movements from the inside and to interference from the outside.

Blinken was clear that a battle is underway, between competing models of governance. But the way to fight such a battle cannot involve military conflict:

> Shoring up our democracy is a foreign policy imperative. Otherwise, we play right into the hands of adversaries and competitors like Russia and China, who seize every opportunity to sow doubts about the strength of our democracy…
>
> But we will not promote democracy through costly military interventions or by attempting to overthrow authoritarian regimes by force. We have tried these tactics in the past. However well intentioned, they haven't worked. They've given democracy promotion a bad name, and they've lost the confidence of the American people. We will do things differently.

Rather than military power, Blinken sang praise, rightly, for "the power of example":

> The more we and other democracies can show the world that we can deliver, not only for our people, but also for each other, the more we can refute the lie that authoritarian countries love to tell, that theirs is the better way to meet people's fundamental needs and hopes. It's on us to prove them wrong…
>
> We will use the power of our example. We will encourage others to make key reforms, overturn bad laws, fight corruption, and stop unjust practices. We will incentivize democratic behaviour.

Although these words were spoken by a member of the Democrat party, they deserve to command the support of members of the Republican party too, as well as people from across the political spectrum in any countries committed to democracy and human rights. To the extent that these countries coordinate their actions, in bodies such as the G7 or its anticipated enlargement, the D10 or D12[886], it will keep in check forces in other countries that would otherwise act as international cancers. It will also provide greater encouragement to the forces inside those countries that wish to be true to what their own constitutions say about the protection of human rights.

To be clear, this is not just a matter for political leaders. It's a matter for the world's judiciary systems: it's essential that courts can speak clearly and compellingly about the rationales for individual decisions they make. It's a matter for the integrity of business leaders, as they elevate principles of human rights above short-term profit motives, and as they choose to respect international sanctions rather than seek to work around them. And it's a matter for independent researchers and journalists, as they labour to uncover the circumstances behind abuses of power and the illicit accumulation of wealth, and as they bring such issues out of the murky depths of deceit into the public light of scrutiny.

On that last point – identifying the objective truth regarding points of contention – winning the battle for rationality over irrationality will be especially important. That brings us to the solutions for one more landmine – actually to the *meta-solutions for a meta-landmine.*

Reason under threat

"Disinformation is rampant."

That's another comment from the March 2021 speech by Antony Blinken that I've just been reviewing. As Blinken explained, rampant disinformation is part of the reason why democracy is under threat. It's part of the reason why, as a result, society is at increasing risk of domination by various cancerous elements – elements which, despite their accumulation of power, are ill-equipped to guide humanity through the tumultuous challenges and opportunities of the coming decade.

If we are unable to think clearly, we are unlikely to make the correct decisions. Factors promoting widespread irrationality at this time include:

1. Our inherited psychological predispositions to take short-cuts in reasoning, and to give undue credence to factors that have no intrinsic merit – as discussed in Chapter 5, "Shortsight"

2. Shortcomings in our educational system, which pays insufficient attention to improving our capabilities in critical thinking – as discussed in Chapter 15, "Education"
3. Distortions that are deliberately crafted by self-interested complexes so as to cause confusion and to weaken resistance to the growth of power of these complexes – as discussed in Chapter 4, "Landmines"
4. Feelings of pain and distress – also discussed in Chapter 4 – which lead people to clutch onto beliefs that strike them as providing meaning and validation; these systems of belief, whether old or new, seem to offer a kind of purpose and redemption in a world that otherwise appears bleak.

These factors can be countered in various ways, that complement and support each other:

1. Our inherited psychological defects can be addressed, in part, by the cognotech solutions which were covered in Chapter 10, "NBIC"
2. Improvements in educational systems, as covered in Chapter 15, can strengthen our critical thinking capabilities
3. Specific items of disinformation can be tackled and debunked, ahead of spreading widely, by vigilant monitoring carried out by online systems of fact-checking and logic-checking
4. The positive transhumanist vision of sustainable superabundance for all, covered throughout this book, *as well as tangible signs of progress toward that vision*, can give people more power to resist the siren attractions of conspiracy theories, millenarian religious fantasies, ultra-nationalist illusions, and other destructive narratives.

Evidently, technology has important roles to play in these solutions. This includes systems of:

1. *Collective intelligence*, where people help each other to reason more thoughtfully
2. *Artificial intelligence*, with automated reasoning and data analysis.

These tools interact, raising additional possibilities for aiding our rationality[887]. At the same time, we need to be aware that these tools are capable of bad outcomes too. Collective intelligence can produce collective stupidity. And AI systems are prone to various amounts of bias, misunderstanding, quirks, and other faults. People who use these tools sometimes put too much trust in them, without independently assessing their recommendations[888].

A related risk, identified by writer Jamie Bartlett as "the moral singularity"[889], is that our ability to take independent hard decisions will atrophy, through lack of practice, on account of us delegating more and more of these decisions to AI systems. With withered moral intuitions, we would unthinkingly become dominated by the moral decisions made on our behalf by machine intelligence. When the occasion arises that machine intelligence makes a *bad* decision on a matter with huge consequences, we might not notice the decision was flawed, until too late. Accordingly, to anticipate a discussion from this book's final chapter, we need to keep human rationality actively in the loop at all times. So, whilst human rationality can, and should, be *strengthened* by technological tools, it must not be *displaced* by them.

Divided aging

The final landmine from the list of eleven is the potential for unprecedented chaos arising once larger numbers of people grasp the shocking fact that technologies for substantial human enhancement are arriving fast. When that realisation spreads, the sorts of topic that dominate today's public discussions will be displaced by intense dialogue regarding the prospects for superlongevity, superintelligence, superhappiness, and superdemocracy.

In principle, these wider discussions should be welcomed. Ideally, the public will say: *these prospects are highly desirable: let's do everything in our power to encourage their swift arrival.* Accordingly, these discussions should lead to a greater share of humanity's talents and resources being applied to accelerate the development and deployment of these technologies.

However, what will cause problems is if groups of people come to believe that they will be excluded from receiving these radical benefits. Their fear will be that only the rich and powerful in society will receive:

1. The health treatments that enable extended youthful vitality and, indeed, the end of aging
2. The undistorted real-time information flows that enable accurate understanding and effective decisions
3. The general flow of goods and services perceived as enabling profound happiness
4. The means to steer democratic processes and to hold onto power.

In such a case, many people will view themselves as being "left behind" from the greatest opportunities ever available. They may lash out as never before against a society that appears to be treating them deeply unfairly.

Of all the concerns that I hear people expressing about transhumanism, it is this potential for extreme inequality that arises most often, and with the greatest force. Rational counters to this concern seem to make little headway. From my observations over the years, this concern grows out of something deeper than intellectual analysis. It arises from narratives that people hold tightly, about the apparent fundamental unfairness of the human experience – narratives that are reinforced by the examples that people notice regarding the excesses perpetrated by the powerful against those with less power.

Rather than showing any shame for these apparent excesses, those who benefit from wealth often provide justifications for their behaviour. Conservative analyst George Will wrote[890] that "income inequality in a capitalist system is truly beautiful… The best way to spread the wealth around is to leave it in the hands of the wealthy". Scott Winship from the Manhattan Institute maintained[891] that "Income inequality is good for the poor". The composite fictional character Gordon Gekko from the film *Wall Street* put it even more bluntly[892]:

> Greed… is good. Greed is right. Greed works.

Characters in the musical *Finian's Rainbow* reflect, in song, on the hypocritical attitudes of society toward the rich and the poor[893]:

> When a rich man doesn't want to work, he's a bon vivant, yes, he's a bon vivant. But when a poor man doesn't want to work, he's a loafer, he's a lounger, he's a lazy good for nothing, he's a jerk.
>
> When a rich man loses on a horse, isn't he the sport, oh, isn't he the sport. But when a poor man loses on a horse, he's a gambler, he's a spender, he's a lowlife, he's a reason for divorce.
>
> When a rich man chases after dames, he's a man about town – a man about town. But when a poor man chases after dames, he's a bounder, he's a rounder, he's a rotter, and a lotter dirty names.

Economist Brooke Harrington gave more examples of this hypocrisy[894]:

> When the wealthy are revealed to be drug addicts, philanderers, or work-shy, the response is – at most – a frisson of tabloid-level curiosity, followed by a collective shrug.

> Behaviours indulged in the rich are not just condemned in the poor, but used as a justification to punish them, denying them access to resources that keep them alive, such as healthcare and food assistance. Discussion of poverty has become almost impossible without moral outrage directed at lazy "welfare queens", "crackheads" and other drug addicts, and the "promiscuous poor" (a phrase that has cropped up again and again in discussions of public benefits over more than a century).

Harrington goes on to observe:

> These disparate perceptions aren't just evidence of hypocrisy; they are literally a matter of life and death. In the US, the widespread belief that the poor are simply lazy has led many states to impose work requirements on aid recipients – even those who have been medically classified as disabled. Limiting aid programs in this way has been shown to shorten recipients' lives: rather than the intended consequence of pushing recipients into paid employment, the restrictions have simply left them without access to medical care or a sufficient food supply. Thus, in one of the richest counties in America, a boy living in poverty died of a toothache; there were no protests, and nothing changed.

It's no wonder that many are concerned about an unjust distribution of access to healthcare. This is not a concern that can be dissolved by words alone. It's a concern that will remain in people's minds until they see *repeated practical illustrations* of the wide distribution of transhumanist benefits and societal justice. Examples that will help change minds and hearts can include:

1. Vaccinations and other treatments for pandemic infections being available to all people throughout the planet, regardless of country, social class, or wealth
2. World-class educational material – including online courses with AI tutors – available free-of-charge to all people throughout the planet
3. Political systems that prioritise reducing the costs of all the requirements for a good quality of life, rather than increasing measures such as GDP which add up the total monetary value of all economic transactions in the country, destructive and constructive alike
4. Appropriate penalties for misdeeds by people in powerful positions – in other words, no-one should be "above the law".

In short, steps of progress toward superlongevity, superintelligence, and superhappiness need to be accompanied by visible progress toward superdemocracy. That's how the transhumanist supernarrative will come to be seen, not as wishful thinking or naive aspiration, but as increasingly credible and reliable. And that's how more and more people will rise to the task of accelerating sustainable superabundance for all.

Beyond juncture

At the start of this chapter, I assigned a probability of roughly 30% to humanity being in a much worse situation in 2050 than at present, and a probability of roughly 60% to humanity being in a much better situation. My relative optimism, despite all the landmines that I have described, reflects my views as to the strengths and capabilities of humanity. Yes, various inherited characteristics predispose us to actions that will be deadly destructive in today's world. But we also have characteristics that predispose us to conceive and attain constructive solutions. At our best, we can be truly ingenious, compassionate, enterprising, and painstaking. Provided our best can come to the fore, we can avoid the treacherous landmines in our midst.

But to be clear, that will *not* signal any kind of *end of human history*. Even once these landmines have all been defused, humanity will still face some dramatic choices. The disruptions of the fourth industrial revolution, powered by NBIC technologies, huge though they are, might be dwarfed by even larger disruptions arising more quickly than expected.

Indeed, these forthcoming *singularity* disruptions (for that's what they are) could arise well before 2050 – that is, well before humanity has finished responding to the challenges of the fourth industrial revolution. Just as the fourth industrial revolution started disrupting society well before the third industrial revolution had finished unrolling, a kind of *fifth* industrial revolution could arrive in the midst of our collective struggles to take best advantage of NBIC. That could transform everything, even more radically. That's the subject of the final chapter of this book.

17. Singularity

Singularity, defined: Where foresight breaks down. A transformation in which humanity risks being left far behind, but which could also propel humanity to unimaginable heights. The crescendo of all the perceptions, assessments, and steering that precedes it.

"The accelerating progress of technology and changes in the mode of human life… gives the appearance of approaching some essential singularity in the history of the race beyond which human affairs, as we know them, could not continue."

The eminent mathematician John von Neumann expressed that sentiment to his long-time friend Stanislaw Ulam in a conversation in the 1950s[895]. Time magazine had described[896] von Neumann as having "the best brain in the world". As well as making numerous breakthroughs in physics, mathematics, and computer science, von Neumann had an encyclopaedic knowledge of history. He apparently used to embarrass history professors at Princeton by knowing more about aspects of history than they did[897]. Therefore, his opinion about the impact of technology on human history deserves attention.

The term "singularity", used by von Neumann, has its roots in mathematics. It describes a situation where a formula breaks down, such as the formula $y=1/(2045-x)$ when x approaches 2045, and when, correspondingly, y approaches infinity[898]. Mathematical theories of physics feature singularities too, such as at the heart of a black hole.

The distinguished nineteenth century physicist James Clerk Maxwell had also spoken about singularities[899]: points at which "influences whose physical magnitude is too small to be taken account of by a finite being, may produce results of the greatest importance". Maxwell had given some examples from the natural world and from human experience:

> The rock loosed by frost and balanced on a singular point of the mountain-side, the little spark which kindles the great forest, the little word which sets the world a fighting, the little scruple which prevents a man from doing his will, the little spore which blights all the potatoes, the little gemmule which makes us philosophers or idiots.

Almost sounding like a modern lifestyle guru, Maxwell had offered the following advice:

> All great results produced by human endeavour depend on taking advantage of these singular states when they occur.

As we might say it in the 2020s: the key to success in life is anticipating and managing disruptions.

However, an essential aspect of these singularities, as Maxwell pointed out, is the impossibility of predicting the outcome. If we are perched at a "singular point" between two valleys, "on a physical or moral watershed, where an imperceptible deviation is sufficient to determine into which of two valleys we shall descend", then "prediction… becomes impossible".

The impossibility of foresight was on the mind of one more writer, Vernor Vinge, in 1983, when he likewise drew attention to the notion of a "singularity" in human history. Vinge was a professor of computer science and mathematics, and also the author of a series of well-regarded science fiction novels. Here's an extract from his 1983 essay[900]:

> There is a stone wall set across any clear view of our future, and it's not very far down the road. Something drastic happens to a species when it reaches our stage of evolutionary development – at least, that's one explanation for why the universe seems so empty of other intelligence. Physical catastrophe (nuclear war, biological pestilence, Malthusian doom) could account for this emptiness, but nothing makes the future of any species so unknowable as technical progress itself…
>
> We are at the point of accelerating the evolution of intelligence itself. The exact means of accomplishing this phenomenon cannot yet be predicted – and is not important. Whether our work is cast in silicon or DNA will have little effect on the ultimate results. The evolution of human intelligence took millions of years. We will devise an equivalent advance in a fraction of that time. We will soon create intelligences greater than our own.

This is when Vinge introduces his version of the concept of singularity:

> When this happens, human history will have reached a kind of singularity, an intellectual transition as impenetrable as the knotted space-time at the centre of a black hole, and the world will pass far beyond our understanding. This singularity, I believe, already haunts a number of science fiction writers. It makes realistic extrapolation to an interstellar future impossible.

If creatures (whether organic or inorganic) attain levels of general intelligence far in excess of present-day humans, what kinds of goals and purposes will occupy these vast brains? Will their motivations be just the same as our own present goals and purposes? Or might the immense scale of these new minds prove alien to our comprehension? Might they appear as unfathomable to us, as human preoccupations appear to the dogs and cats and other animals that observe us from time to time?

One additional twist to the concept of singularity needs to be mentioned. It's not just that the *consequences* of passing the point of singularity are deeply unpredictable. It's that the *timing* of reaching the point of singularity may be unpredictable too. That makes a difference from the simple mathematical example given earlier.

For a simple formula such as y=1/(2045-x), there's no question as to the location of the singularity: it's when x attains the value 2045. But the timing of the advent of a technological singularity may catch us all by surprise. For example, we might reassure ourselves that present-day artificial intelligence lags significantly behind the capability of human level general intelligence. But recall the notion of "overhang" from Chapter 9. As I said then, inventions sometimes turn out to be surprisingly fruitful. A new technique might prove itself much more widely useful than originally envisioned. In the case of AI, a new AI technique might prove capable of improving AI itself. Software assigned the task to improve its own performance could be run several times over, improving itself again and again, taking extra advantage each time of its newly enhanced powers of comprehension and analysis.

This scenario was conceived as long ago as 1959 by IJ Good, who had been a close collaborator of Alan Turing at both Bletchley Park and Manchester University. Good included these remarks in a lecture given at IBM in New York in 1959[901]:

> Once a machine is designed that is good enough…, it can be put to work designing an even better machine…
>
> There will only be a very short transition period between having no very good machine and having a great many exceedingly good ones.

Good briefly mentioned two scenarios for what could happen next:

> At this point an "explosion" will clearly occur; all the problems of science and technology will be handed over to machines and it will no longer be necessary for people to work. Whether this will lead to a Utopia or to the extermination of the human race will depend on how the problem is handled by the machine.

Hence Good's conclusion:

> The important thing will be to give them [the machines] the aim of serving human beings.

Writing at almost the same time – 1960 – another pioneer of the field of machine intelligence, Norbert Wiener, emphasised a similar piece of advice[902]:

> If we use, to achieve our purposes, a mechanical agency with whose operation we cannot efficiently interfere once we have started it, because the action is so fast and irrevocable that we have not the data to intervene before the action is complete, then we had better be quite sure that the purpose put into the machine is the purpose which we really desire and not merely a colourful imitation of it.

Wiener had developed an argument that would reappear in other forms in subsequent decades. We can call it the "bottle maximiser" argument, in anticipation of more recent "paperclip maximiser"[903] arguments:

> When a machine constructed by us is capable of operating on its incoming data at a pace which we cannot keep, we may not know, until too late, when to turn it off. We all know the fable of the sorcerer's apprentice, in which the boy makes the broom carry water in his master's absence, so that it is on the point of drowning him when his master reappears. If the boy had had to seek a charm to stop the mischief in the grimoires of his master's library, he might have been drowned before he had discovered the relevant incantation. Similarly, if a bottle factory is programmed on the basis of maximum productivity, the owner may be made bankrupt by the enormous inventory of unsalable bottles manufactured before he learns he should have stopped production six months earlier.

The risk posed by uncontrollable AI whose objectives are misaligned with those of humanity far exceeds factory owners being rendered bankrupt. In the words of IJ Good, the risk is "the extermination of the human race" – with the events leading up to that catastrophe taking place outside of the conscious awareness of the vast majority of the human population.

Why I am a singularitarian

John von Neumann was right. In their various ways, so were James Clerk Maxwell, Vernor Vinge, IJ Good, and Norbert Wiener. Technology is taking humanity along a trajectory with the potential for a sudden transition into a state that defies our prior comprehension. Therefore, to paraphrase Norbert

Wiener, "we had better be quite sure" that the methods by which we develop technology will lead to an outcome "which we really desire and not merely a colourful imitation of it".

Around twenty years ago, when I first came across a version of IJ Good's "intelligence explosion" argument – taken from an article he published in 1964[904] – I felt straight away that I had encountered something truly significant:

> Let an ultraintelligent machine be defined as a machine that can far surpass all the intellectual activities of any man however clever. Since the design of machines is one of these intellectual activities, an ultraintelligent machine could design even better machines; there would then unquestionably be an "intelligence explosion," and the intelligence of man would be left far behind. Thus the first ultraintelligent machine is the *last* invention that man need ever make, provided that the machine is docile enough to tell us how to keep it under control.

It took me some time, but in due course I added the designation "singularitarian" to my personal business card, alongside the designations "futurist" and "catalyst" which date back longer.

The argument advanced by IJ Good is by no means watertight. You can probably think of a number of issues with it. Other writers such as James Barrat[905], Nick Bostrom[906], Roman Yampolskiy[907], and Stuart Russell[908] have made it more robust. Suffice it to say that I am confident that the possibility of an AI singularity deserves much more attention than it presently receives. That's what I mean when I describe myself as a singularitarian[909].

In more detail, I maintain that:

1. There is no magical or metaphysical reason why AI cannot in due course reach and surpass the level of general intelligence possessed by humans.
2. There is no magical or metaphysical reason why an ultraintelligent AI will intrinsically care about the continuation of human flourishing. (Indeed, it's possible it would conclude the opposite.)
3. A system which is much more intelligent (and therefore more powerful) than we can currently comprehend may well decide to deviate from whatever programming we have placed in it – just as we humans have decided to deviate from the instinctual goals placed in us by the processes of biological evolution.

4. Even if an "ideal" ultraintelligent AI would act to support the continuation of human flourishing, the systems that we end up creating (by our own effort, and with the help of AI systems with intermediate levels of capability) may fail to match our intention; that is, they may fall short of the ideal specification that we had in mind.
5. The dangers that may be posed by a misconfigured ultraintelligent AI are by no means dependent on that AI possessing some kind of malevolent feeling, spiteful streak, or other negative emotions akin to those which often damage human relationships. Instead, the dangers will arise from divergent goals. (The goals in question could be either explicit or implicit; in both cases, there are risks of divergence.)
6. The timescales for the arrival of ultraintelligent AI are inherently uncertain; we cannot categorically rule *in* any date as an *upper* boundary, but nor can we categorically rule *out* any date as a *lower* boundary. We cannot be sure what is happening in various AI research labs around the world, and what the consequences of any breakthroughs there might be.
7. Just as the singularity could turn out to be catastrophically dreadful, it could also turn out to be wonderfully beneficial. Although there are no guarantees, the result of a well-designed ultraintelligent AI could be hugely positive for humanity.
8. Although the advent of an ultraintelligent AI is the version of a technological singularity that most deserves our attention, there are other types of technological singularity that we should also consider – some of which I introduce later in this chapter.

Singularity shadow

If anything, the concept of a technological singularity receives even more scorn than the concept of transhumanism. When people hear that I describe myself not only as a transhumanist but also as a singularitarian, it gives them a double reason to steer away from me. If I had wanted an easy life, I would have purged both words from my biography long ago.

Just as for transhumanism, the set of criticisms of the technological singularity split into two types:

1. Those that have some validity, but which apply to a set of "shadow" distortions of the main concept, rather than to the core subject itself
2. Those that are unfair or confused, and which arise (at least in part) from psychological unease experienced by the critics.

As I explained in Chapter 11, "Transhumanism", every movement has a shadow – a dark underbelly which can cause it problems. Singularitarianism is no exception.

The Singularity shadow has a lot in common with the transhumanist shadow. Here are its key components:

1. *Singularity timescale determinism* – an insistence that narrow date ranges can be confidently predicted for the emergence of ultraintelligent AI
2. *Singularity outcome determinism* – an insistence that the outcome of the singularity is bound to be overwhelmingly positive for humanity
3. *Singularity preoccupation* – an insistence that shorter-term issues deserve little attention, since they pale in significance compared to the magnitude of changes arising from the technological singularity
4. *Singularity anti-regulation fundamentalism* – an insistence that governments be prevented from passing regulations which might slow down progress toward the kinds of advanced AI that could lead to the singularity
5. *Singularity hyping* – uncritical enthusiasm for particular tools or techniques whose advocates claim are well on the way to delivering ultraintelligent AI, but which lack any substantive supporting evidence
6. *Singularity risk complacency* – a willingness to overlook the risks of possible existential disaster, out of a fervent hope that the singularity will arrive as quickly as possible – early enough to deliver cures for age-related diseases that would otherwise cause specific individuals to die.

If you've read all the preceding chapters, you will anticipate that I personally plead "not guilty" to each of these shadow transgressions. For example, on the subject of "singularity preoccupation", you'll note that I have dedicated the sixteen previous chapters of this book to discussing scenarios for developments *before* the question of a singularity arises. After all, the explosion of any of the eleven landmines featured in these previous chapters could terminate the progress of human technology. Deprioritising attention for these landmines would, therefore, be supreme folly.

In Chapter 11, I suggested the name "active transhumanism" for transhumanism that sidesteps the flaws that lurk within the transhumanist shadow. In a similar way, we could use the name "active singularitarian" for someone that, likewise, sidesteps the flaws of the singularity shadow. An active singularitarian:

1. Recognises the uncertainties in the timescales for the advent of ultraintelligent AI, the uncertainties regarding the methods that are most likely to bring about that advent, and the uncertainties about the consequences of that advent
2. Takes actions to reduce the above uncertainties – and, in particular, to ensure that the outcome is truly beneficial
3. Takes actions to avoid humanity being catastrophically disrupted by any metaphorical landmines, or similar dangers, even before the singularity can be approached
4. Recognises the positive role of well-designed governmental regulation in steering the development and deployment of the technologies that can give rise to the singularity
5. Avoids putting undue reliance on the singularity itself as a solution for all the problems of human existence; instead, solutions to these problems can often involve less advanced technology and, indeed, use approaches other than technology.

Unsound criticisms

Let's now turn to the second type of criticism of singularity thinking – the type that would presume it has a point even against active singularitarians.

One such criticism is the claim that artificial intelligence can *never* reach the levels attained by humans. In some cases, that claim is motivated by a conviction that can be described as religious or spiritual. These critics assert they have grounds for faith that the human soul, or spirit, or whatever, has an origin outside of the operations of the realms of physics, chemistry, and biology. In other cases, that claim is defended by observing that all attempts *so far* to create artificial general intelligence have failed; therefore (the argument runs) all future attempts are going to fail too. Notably, people who make such claims often refer to their own young children. They are deeply impressed, as parents, by the problem-solving skills, or the curiosity or creativity, that these young humans display. *No mere machine can ever match this*, they exclaim, with great pride.

Needless to say, none of these arguments hold water. For example, even if someone insists that intelligence has an irretrievably non-material aspect, they ought to acknowledge the possibility, in that case, that a similar non-material aspect could arise as the result of interactions in (suitably configured) silicon. And even if all attempts up to a given time fail to create a particular technology, such as heavier-than-air powered flight, or AGI, that's no reason to insist that all future attempts will likewise fail.

At this point, the argument is likely to shift. Rather than stating that ultraintelligent AI is an impossibility, the critic will insist that any such breakthrough is too far into the future for us to worry about in the present. These critics may draw some comfort from the comments by some leading AI developers that AGI won't arise until around the end of this century.

My first answer to this is that leading AI developers have been wrong in the past. We shouldn't treat their judgements as infallible. For example, in their 1969 book *Perceptrons*,[910] Marvin Minsky and Seymour Papert maintained that neural networks would be unable to carry out all but the simplest kinds of calculation. This criticism from renowned members of the AI community helped to dissuade researchers from carrying out any serious work on neural networks[911]. The few researchers who kept faith with neural networks at various times in the following decades were viewed as irresponsible mavericks – until the power of their approach had become blatantly clear even to the most trenchant of AI traditionalists.

My second answer here is to point out that some leading AI researchers have an interest in *under*-hyping their work. That's because they fear, with some justification, the damage that could be inflicted on their industry by poorly informed politicians who might seize on the subject of AGI, if they happen to hear that these AI researchers actually believe AGI could arise within, say, just a couple of decades. Accordingly, these AI researchers have learned to guard their words carefully.

My third answer here refers back to the possibilities of overhang: an apparently small breakthrough might turn out to be the key to unlocking much faster progress across a range of problems.

Once critics acknowledge that AGI might not be that distant after all, they often advance other arguments – ones that I consider to be equally unsound. For example, they claim that it would be *easy* to control an AGI: all that's needed, they say, is to unplug the power source. Or they claim that it will be *easy* to avoid placing into the AGI anything akin to human desires for self-preservation. Finally, they claim that an AGI that is sufficiently intelligent will be able to notice if any action it takes would harm humans, and that it would, therefore, avoid such an action. After all, say the critics, an AGI with abundant intelligence is bound at the same time to be abundantly ethical.

I'll answer these points in reverse order:

- There's no fundamental guarantee that an "abundantly ethical" AGI would agree that humans need to be preserved in large numbers; that would be like insisting that an abundantly ethical human would always avoid actions that could have a side-effect of killing some ants
- In any case, our lesson from the world of humans is that greater intelligence by no means implies a higher ethical standard
- Even if no self-preservation instinct is programmed into an AGI, that AGI might develop such an instinct as a subgoal of whatever its main goal is. For example, an AGI with the goal to generate hugely interesting immersive virtual reality worlds will resist being switched off, since if that happens, it is no longer able to generate such worlds
- Pulling out a power cord will only switch off an AGI if that AGI is restricted to a single source of power, rather than being distributed over a cloud of processors. Note also that any AGI will have at least an *implicit* motivation to improve its own security by spreading its operation over multiple power sources, thereby making itself less vulnerable to any hacking.

To be clear, I'm *not* saying that all attempts to design an AGI that will remain under human control, or to ensure the AGI has a motivational system deeply aligned with human flourishing, are doomed to failure. Instead, I'm saying that these projects are *deeply difficult*, and that many ideas for solving them, whilst well-intentioned, are actually naive.

The fact that it's *deeply difficult* to guarantee a positive outcome is, indeed, one reason why the technological singularity is, well, a singularity.

I'll come back shortly to some recommendations to make that deeply difficult task at least a bit easier. First, though, let's broaden our minds to consider other types of singularity that could dramatically impact humanity.

A physics singularity

Discussion of the concept of "singularity" often references the physical object known as a black hole. My own introduction to this subject, at the beginning of this chapter, conformed to that pattern. A black hole results from the collapse of a sufficiently large star. The resulting object is so dense that not even light can escape from it.

Might black holes arise in other ways? For example, might particle collisions at the CERN large hadron collider (LHC) near Geneva be so energetic that a new type of black hole would be created – and then proceed to devour the entire earth?

That was one of the possibilities that occupied a number of minds in the first few months of 2008. For example, the subtitle of an article in the Guardian[912] was "This summer, the earth could be sucked into a black hole". The occasion was the drawing close of a long-planned increase in the energy at which various particle collisions would take place at the LHC. Two people with training in physics, Walter Wagner and Luis Sanchos, had filed legal proceedings to forbid CERN from increasing the energy levels. Here's part of an affidavit submitted to the court by Sanchos[913]:

> I was initially in favour of funding the Large Hadron Collider – the biggest, most technologically advanced machine ever built. It is a superconductive, superfluid ring in which bundles of heavy atoms are to be accelerated to almost the speed of light and smashed together to replicate the awesome energies of the Big Bang and to create showers of heavy-mass particles found only in those first seconds when the universe was destroyed and re-created.
>
> Unfortunately, theoretical calculations show that the LHC could produce two kinds of dark matter – black holes and strange, ultradense quark matter – that are extremely dangerous, as both have been theoretically proven to swallow in a chain reaction the entirety of Earth. Thus, a cosmological bomb billions of times more powerful than the atomic bomb might be created at the European Organization for Nuclear Research…

> The director of CERN has said, "The LHC will be the closest we will ever be to God," as the Big Bang is the violent beginning and end of the universe. I hope he is wrong.

Sanchos offered some additional comparisons:

> The LHC experiment would be, technically, the largest holocaust in history. It would also be the biggest environmental crime in history, far more harmful than global warming, as it would mean the destruction of all life-forms on the planet.

That would be quite a singularity!

CERN fought back. Numerous experts had calculated, again and again, the probability of any such disaster. The probability was too small to register on any meaningful scale. CERN's experts argued that the calculations offered by Wagner and Sanchos were deeply flawed.

The court, which was based in Hawaii, dismissed the suit. The plaintiffs had failed to demonstrate any reason for concern. In any case, courts in the USA had no legal authority over CERN, which operated in Europe. A subsequent appeal was dismissed on the same grounds in 2010[914].

At this point, it would be easy to become lost in detailed discussions about high energy physics. However, what's more important is to consider the general form of arguments about potential singularity-type disasters.

For example, here's a *bad* argument. One of the plaintiffs in the case against the LHC, Walter Wagner, had a poor track record[915]. He had raised similar concerns about an earlier, less powerful particle collider, namely the Relativistic Heavy Ion Collider (RHIC) at Brookhaven National Laboratories on Long Island in New York state. Judges in 1999 and 2000 had rejected his suits at that time[916]. The RHIC had been switched on and… the world was not destroyed. Wagner also had a dubious past as a campaigner against supposedly dangerous radioactive tiles, and evidently inflated his credentials in various CVs he used. His poor grasp of the basics of probability theory were, memorably, lambasted by political commentator (and comedian) John Oliver during an interview on the Daily Show[917]:

> John Oliver: So, roughly speaking, what are the chances that the world is going to be destroyed? One-in-a-million? One-in-a-billion?
>
> Walter Wagner: Well, the best we can say right now is a one-in-two chance.
>
> JO: 50–50?
>
> WW: Yeah, 50–50… It's a chance, it's a 50–50 chance.

JO: You come back to this 50–50 thing. What is it, Walter?

WW: Well, if you have something that can happen and something that won't necessarily happen, it's going to either happen or it's gonna not happen. And, so, it's kind of… best guess at this point.

JO: I'm… not sure that's how probability works, Walter.

However, predictions that fail to come true in a set of previous forecasts can, of course, come true in a later event, when circumstances are different, or when more energy is applied. People who are outsiders, with unusual career trajectories, and eccentric personality quirks, may well perceive important issues that mainstream thinkers miss. And just because a critic makes a mistake in one line of argument – such as the foundations of probability theory – it does not mean all their other arguments are likewise mistaken. No, when the stakes are sky high – such as the possible destruction of the entire earth when novel physical interactions are invoked for the first time since the Big Bang – we need higher standards of scrutiny.

Here's another *bad* argument: the weight of authority. CERN has a webpage[918] carrying statements from well-known physicists such as Stephen Hawking, Roger Penrose, and Martin Rees, all declaring that "The LHC is absolutely safe" or similar. Here's the first quote on that list, attributed to "Academician Vitaly Ginzburg, Nobel Laureate in Physics, Lebedev Institute, Moscow, and Russian Academy of Sciences":

> To think that LHC particle collisions at high energies can lead to dangerous black holes is rubbish. Such rumours were spread by unqualified people seeking sensation or publicity.

However, history has many examples when the established experts in a field collectively joined ranks against discomforting objections by outsiders – but the outsiders were subsequently vindicated. History also has examples of defenders of an industry turning a blind eye to evidence that would question the appropriateness of various products delivered by that industry.

Therefore, we all should be grateful for unconventional thinkers who suggest new ways of interpreting evidence, and who propose alternative scenarios for how things might develop. Equally, we should all be grateful for the analysts who dispassionately review these novel suggestions, and who turn, not a blind eye, but an open mind, to potential early warning signals of surprise developments. That's the case for possible physics singularities, as well as for other types of singularity.

The *good* arguments for why the LHC is safe point out that the collisions in this equipment aren't as unprecedented as CERN's rhetoric sometimes implied. Similar ranges of energy are involved when cosmic rays impact the earth's atmosphere. As Stephen Hawking pointed out,

> Collisions releasing greater energy occur millions of times a day in the earth's atmosphere and nothing terrible happens.

Edward Kolb, a professor in astrophysics at the University of Chicago, concurs:

> Nature has already done this experiment... Cosmic rays have hit the moon with more energy and have not produced a black hole that has swallowed up the moon.

But might there be something different about the types of collision inside the LHC? That's where a more detailed analysis is required. And that's what CERN has undertaken, at several different times over its history[919]. Importantly, this analysis is open for all to inspect, rather than being hidden away from public scrutiny. That analysis was reviewed in turn by a subcommittee of members of the American Physical Society, who endorsed the conclusions[920].

Nevertheless, the critics of high energy physics experiments do raise a general point that we need to keep in mind. Here's another extract from the legal affidavit submitted by Luis Sanchos:

> As we close Chernobyl-like plants for security reasons and forbid the reproduction of the Ebola virus in an open environment (though some specialized virologists would like to study it for research purposes), so should we forbid the reproduction of free, uncontrolled dark matter, even if its theorists would like to study it at CERN.

In other words, curiosity, by itself, is no reason to permit a particular scientific experiment, even if benefits might arise from that experiment. We definitely need to consider whether unexpected large downsides might arise instead. Only once we are satisfied that a careful, thorough analysis has been carried out of potential large downsides should we proceed with the experiment. Naivety and wishful thinking cannot be permitted to enable any such negative singularity.

That brings us to another contentious scientific experiment: the attempt to bring the existence of human civilisation to the attention of any aliens on other planets who might be scanning the heavens.

Shouting into the cosmos

"Where is everybody?"

With that famous question, voiced during a lunchtime discussion at the Los Alamos National Laboratory in the summer of 1950[921], physicist Enrico Fermi originated what has become known as "Fermi's paradox". There are reasons to believe the galaxy has huge numbers of planets capable of giving rise to intelligent life. So why don't we notice any evidence of "ETIs" – that is, extra-terrestrial intelligences? *Where is everybody?*

Some of the most plausible answers are the following:

1. The evolution of complex life forms is an almost impossibly rare event. For example, perhaps the emergence of multicellular life forms depended on a very rare set of circumstances
2. The evolution of life forms with human-level intelligence is an almost impossibly rare event. Creatures that can build space-faring technology, therefore, might almost never come into existence
3. Species that can build space-faring technology are highly likely to destroy themselves, via something similar to the landmines or singularities described in this book
4. Species that can build space-faring technology take great care, as a kind of courtesy, to hide their existence from more primitive species, such as Earth's humans – this is sometimes called "the zoo hypothesis"
5. Species that can build space-faring technology take great care to hide their existence from *any* other intelligent species in the cosmos, out of an abundance of caution for what these other intelligent species might do to them
6. Species that can build space-faring technology quickly become more interested in living in a "transcended" state which, as it happens, leaves almost no visible trace in the wider universe.

Of these answers, I see the sixth as having considerable merit. This idea was proposed by futurist John Smart under the title "the transcension hypothesis"[922]:

> The transcension hypothesis proposes that a universal process of evolutionary development guides all sufficiently advanced civilizations into what may be called "inner space," a computationally optimal domain of

> increasingly dense, productive, miniaturized, and efficient scales of space, time, energy, and matter, and eventually, to a black-hole-like destination. Transcension as a developmental destiny might also contribute to the solution to the Fermi paradox, the question of why we have not seen evidence of or received beacons from intelligent civilizations.

But before we can conclude that intelligent species in the universe always travel on a trajectory toward inner space rather than to outer space, we need to evaluate the preceding option on that list of possible solutions to the Fermi paradox – the scenario in which intelligent species are all deeply afraid of each other. It's a disconcerting scenario. We could even call it ugly. It suggests that at least some species of superintelligent aliens might choose to destroy other intelligent life that they notice. That thought seems so… unenlightened. But we must beware the trap of assuming that a species with abundant intelligence is bound at the same time to display what we humans might wish to consider as abundant ethics.

Our difficulty here is one mentioned earlier: the near-impossibility of anticipating what will motivate intelligences that significantly exceed our own.

However, we can consider a range of potential scenarios. Here's one. Imagine that something similar to the "physics singularity" of the previous section is actually possible – but with the resulting physical interactions leading to the destruction, not just of the planet where the interaction took place, but of a significant part of the entire cosmos. For example, that interaction might trigger something like the inflationary expansion that took place shortly after the big bang. Physicists have spoken of "vacuum decay" as "a quick, clean and efficient way of wiping out the Universe"[923]:

> The walls of the true vacuum bubble would expand in all directions at the speed of light. You wouldn't see it coming. The walls can contain a huge amount of energy, so you might be incinerated as the bubble wall ploughed through you. Different vacuum states have different constants of nature, so the basic structure of matter might also be disastrously altered…
>
> Vacuum decay is the ultimate ecological catastrophe; in a new vacuum there are new constants of nature; after vacuum decay, not only is life as we know it impossible, so is chemistry as we know it.

Imagine also that any intelligent species that gains sufficient technological prowess – perhaps only a few decades more advanced than us at present – might undertake experiments that, unknown to the perpetrators, risk causing such a physics singularity. Next, imagine that another intelligent species, which has become yet more advanced – let's call them the A-species – has itself avoided carrying out such a universe-threatening experiment, and is now on the active lookout to prevent any other species in the galaxy from running such an experiment. Finally, imagine that, for whatever reason, the A-species has decided on a policy of a rapid first-strike attack on any other technologically-capable species that it detects. ('A' stands for advanced, or attack, or aggressive.) *Better safe than sorry*, the A-species might say.

If there is any chance that a scenario like that could happen, would it be wise for us humans to actively advertise to the cosmos as a whole that we are on the point of becoming a space-faring species? Shouldn't we do our best to keep quiet?

You might reply that you find my scenario implausible. If a far-remote intelligence notices our existence, it would probably take them thousands of years to reach Earth, even if travelling at the speed of light. But perhaps such an A-species has already spread probes throughout the galaxy, in order to react more quickly to any signs that it would regard as an existential danger.

In that case, you might reply that our existence has probably *already* been noticed, on account of the radio signals we have been generating in large quantities for many decades. Is actively trying to send a focused message to extraterrestrial intelligences, as proposed by METI[924], any more dangerous than the radio signals that have already been winding their way from the Earth into interstellar space?

My answer is that *it is too early to be sure*. And that's just looking at one possible scenario. There could well be other scenarios, even more troubling, which we have not yet properly explored.

That thought matches the view of a significant group of scientists and other public figures, who have signed an open statement warning of the existential dangers of METI[925]:

> METI has been conducted sporadically in the past, but recently a surge of individuals and organizations have initiated or suggested new METI programs, both academic and commercial in nature. METI programs carry unknown and potentially enormous implications and consequences. We feel the decision whether or not to transmit must be based upon a worldwide consensus, and not a decision based upon the wishes of a few individuals with access to powerful communications equipment. We strongly encourage vigorous international debate by a broadly representative body prior to engaging further in this activity...

> ETI's reaction to a message from Earth cannot presently be known. We know nothing of ETI's intentions and capabilities, and it is impossible to predict whether ETI will be benign or hostile…
>
> *Intentionally signalling other civilizations in the Milky Way Galaxy raises concerns from all the people of Earth, about both the message and the consequences of contact. A worldwide scientific, political and humanitarian discussion must occur before any message is sent.*

One of the signatories, the distinguished science fiction writer David Brin, has described METI as "shouting into the cosmos"[926] and, more recently, as "shouting into a jungle"[927]:

> We are the youngest of all technological races in the cosmos, like an orphan child who suddenly finds herself wandering a strange jungle that's quiet – *too quiet.* So quiet that the simplest, parsimonious explanations appear rather daunting. Almost as if the creatures and natives *know something that we don't know*, and are keeping silent for a reason.
>
> Or else, something is keeping the *number* of creatures and natives low – too low. If you found yourself in such a situation, would you listen a while? Maybe talk things over with your fellow orphans? Especially when you are already learning at a rapid pace, and may have more of the clues you need soon, with a little more listening? And patience?
>
> Perhaps you have the kind of personality that says: "What the heck! I might as well shout and see what happens!"
>
> That's all very well if the only one you are putting at risk is yourself. But when that risk is also imposed upon our children – all of humanity and our planet – is it too much to ask that we *discuss it first*?

Physics communicator Michio Kaku makes a similar point. Even if we believe any aliens are *likely* to be friendly, we need to beware of the probability that they are unfriendly[928]:

> We all know what happened to [Aztec emperor] Montezuma when he met [Spanish Conquistador] Cortés in Mexico so many hundreds of years ago. Now, personally, I think that aliens out there would be friendly but we can't gamble on it.

Terminating the simulation

Alongside the question whether we can be sure of the motivation of any superintelligent aliens, we also need to consider the question of how sure we can be of the fundamental structure of what we perceive as the universe.

Most scientists operate nowadays on the assumption that the universe arose from factors that are mindless. Few take seriously the idea common in previous centuries that the universe was conceived by a conscious deity, and that the continued existence of the universe depends on the will of that transcendent mind. However, a striking new version of this creator hypothesis has emerged in recent decades, and has been endorsed by Elon Musk and Neil deGrasse Tyson, among others.

One upshot of this new conception, as I'll explain shortly, is that we may have more to worry about than aliens discovering our existence and deciding to annihilate us in an act of pre-emptive caution. We may have to worry about the creator of our universe deciding to terminate our entire cosmos – or, maybe, to restart it, like we humans can decide to restart a game we are playing. This would be an extraordinary singularity in the history of humanity.

The argument has a number of stages to it:

1. There already exist a number of immersive virtual reality video games, with new games regularly exceeding their predecessors in scale, graphics realism, and an ability to cause participants to want to spend more and more time in these games
2. These games often contain simulated characters that display aspects of intelligence, powered by AI algorithms; new games typically contain better AI
3. At some point, these simulated characters will manifest not only simple emotions (as is already the case) but a kind of consciousness
4. Although such characters would be conscious, it would not be obvious to them that they had been created by a games designer external to their own universe (game); nor would it be obvious that some of their interactions inside their world were with entities (players) that originated outside their universe
5. A civilisation that is significantly more capable than humans – on account, for example, of existing in a technologically advanced state for several centuries longer – will have the ability to create large numbers of simulated universes, each containing large numbers of conscious characters
6. The total number of conscious characters in simulated universes will vastly exceed the number of conscious characters in what might be called "base reality"

7. If we select one of these conscious characters at random – for example, ourself – the odds are high that we are in a simulated universe rather than base reality
8. If we dislike that conclusion, we need to find fault in one of the preceding steps in the argument; for example, perhaps technologically advanced civilisations always self-destruct before creating large numbers of simulated worlds that contain conscious characters.

This argument was the subject of a 2003 article by Oxford philosopher Nick Bostrom, "Are You Living in a Computer Simulation?"[929] Although Bostrom's article did not mention it, the 1999 film *The Matrix* had already brought to popular attention the idea that what looks to us like reality may actually be an enormous simulation created by an ultraintelligent AI[930]. But what could easily be dismissed as science fiction fantasy in *The Matrix* found a compelling logic in Bostrom's hands.

At a conference in 2016, Elon Musk commented in response to an audience question "Is life a video game?" that he had thought a great deal about the simulation theory[931]:

> Forty years ago, we had Pong – two rectangles and a dot. That was what games were. Now, forty years later, we have photorealistic 3D simulations with millions of people playing simultaneously, and it's getting better every year…
>
> Given that we're clearly on a trajectory to have games that are indistinguishable from reality, and those games could be played on… billions of computers… it would seem to follow that the odds that we're in base reality is one in billions.

Although more measured in his enthusiasm than Musk, science populariser Neil deGrasse Tyson has also expressed support for the simulation hypothesis, saying the odds were "better than 50-50" that the conclusion was true. He went on[932]:

> I wish I could summon a strong argument against it, but I can find none.

Of all the arguments that I have included in this book, the simulation theory might be the one that generates the greatest disgust. Hostile critics scornfully label it pseudoscience[933], nonsense[934], and a throwback to religious creationism[935]. But note that many of the critics' points are anticipated *and answered* in Bostrom's 2003 paper, or in an associated FAQ[936] – which includes a rebuttal of any claim that the argument is designed to support something akin to traditional religion. Bostrom urges us to "keep in mind that the simulation argument does not imply the simulation-hypothesis."

Various objections against the simulation argument work, in my view, only against constrained versions of the hypothesis, but not against a more general form. For example, the simulation has no need to include every subatomic particle in every distant galaxy – something which would require truly astronomical computing power. It only needs to model the parts of the universe at which the conscious participants are looking.

As for the objection that the simulation hypothesis is entirely metaphysical, with no hopes for any experiment being possible to test it, that may be wrong too. It might be possible to conduct searches for what are semi-humorously described as "glitches in the matrix"[937].

Another, more dramatic demonstration of the validity of the simulation hypothesis would be if actions by humans caused the external observers of the simulation to intervene – perhaps appearing within our universe as new characters with apparently miraculous powers, or by causing actions that we would calculate as having zero probability based on our prior assumptions, or, in the worst case, by terminating the game (in which case we probably wouldn't experience anything at all, since we would cease to exist). But what kind of human action might provoke such a reaction? Since we can have only a dim comprehension of the motivation of the hypothesised external observers, any suggestions here are necessarily highly speculative.

Responding to an early draft of Nick Bostrom's article, the philosopher Robin Hanson offered a set of suggestions for "How To Live In A Simulation"[938]:

> While you probably cannot learn much detail about the specific reasons for and nature of the simulation you live in, you can draw general conclusions by making analogies to the types and reasons of simulations today. If you might be living in a simulation then all else equal it seems that you should care less about others, live more for today, make your world look likely to become eventually rich, expect to and try to participate in pivotal events, be entertaining and praiseworthy, and keep the famous people around you happy and interested in you.

Hanson's rationale for these suggestions was that they would increase the likelihood that the operators of the simulation will wish to keep you in existence.

Another possibility is that a "simulation singularity" will be triggered once the consciousnesses inside the simulation manage to infer sufficient information about the likely nature of the level of reality beyond the simulation. At that point, some humans may try to break out of our own level of reality, by taking something akin to the "red pill" of the film *The Matrix*.

Of course, this discussion has strong echoes of religious themes. Philosopher David Pearce has provided this comment[939]:

> The Simulation Argument is perhaps the first interesting argument for the existence of a Creator in 2000 years.

Despite what some critics imply, these echoes are no reason, by themselves, to reject the hypothesis. For example, we cannot simply rerun the traditional "argument from the problem of evil" to conclude that no such creator can exist. That argument depends on the hypothesised creator having a number of characteristics: divine omnipotence, divine omniscience, and divine omnibenevolence. The simulation hypothesis can accept creator omnipotence (complete control over what happens inside the simulation) and creator omniscience (complete awareness over what happens), but can deny creator omnibenevolence. We can make no assumption over the moral characteristics of the operator(s) of the simulation.

Whereas traditional religions typically try to exude conviction regarding future outcomes – based on claims to deep insights into the motivation of the divinities postulated by these religions – the simulation hypothesis offers no such certainties. Instead, it just says: *let's take care.*

Note that Bostrom says he maintains an open mind on the implications of his simulation hypothesis argument. In his FAQ, here's how he answers the question "Do you really believe that we are in a computer simulation?":

> No. I believe that the simulation argument is basically sound. The argument shows only that at least one of three possibilities obtains, but it does not tell us which one(s). One can thus accept the simulation argument and reject the simulation hypothesis (i.e. that we are in a simulation).
>
> Personally, I assign less than 50% probability to the simulation hypothesis – rather something like in 20%-region, perhaps, maybe. However, this estimate is a subjective personal opinion and is not part of the simulation argument.

Even if there's only a 1% chance, say, that we are living in a computer simulation, with our continued existence being dependent on the will of external operator(s), that would be a remarkable conclusion – something to which much more thought should be applied.

That additional thought is something I expect to be applied in increased quantity if and when humanity pulls clear of the existential risks covered in earlier chapters.

Becoming gods

There's one more type of extraordinary intervention in human affairs that we ought to discuss. Instead of intervention by aliens, or by simulation operators, it's intervention by our own future descendants, who may achieve god-like powers in the decades and centuries ahead. These powers may include the ability to perform space-time engineering, including reaching back through time to make a copy of our consciousness.

The person who has thought hardest about this possibility is retired physicist Giulio Prisco. He argues that many of the traditional functions of religion – even including a belief in an afterlife – can be fulfilled by what he calls "enlightening science" and "awakening technology". In the second (2020) edition of his remarkable book *Tales of the Turing Church*, Prisco takes nearly 600 pages to build his case[940]. This is from the start of the Introduction to that book:

> This isn't your grandfather's religion.
>
> Future science and technology will permit playing with the building blocks of space, time, matter, energy, and life, in ways that we could only call magic and supernatural today.

What does this mean? Prisco explains:

> Someday in the future, you and your loved ones will be resurrected by very advanced science and technology. Inconceivably advanced intelligences are out there among the stars. Even more God-like beings operate in the fabric of reality underneath spacetime, or beyond spacetime, and control the universe. Future science will allow us to find them, and become like them.
>
> Our descendants in the far future will join the community of God-like beings among the stars and beyond, and use transcendent "divine" technology to resurrect the dead and remake the universe.

In case of any doubt, Prisco clarifies what he has in mind:

> Science? Spacetime? Aliens? Future technology? I warned you, this isn't your grandmother's religion.

> Or isn't it?
>
> Simplify what I said and reword it as: God exists, controls reality, will resurrect the dead and remake the universe. Sounds familiar? I bet it does. So perhaps this *is* the religion of our grandparents, in different words.

Later pages of his book provide a number of possible mechanisms by which our descendants might take advantage of advanced "space-time engineering" to recreate us, after our physical deaths, in a new state, alongside our families and friends. Our personal consciousness, therefore, might take a singular leap from the point of death of our physical body, into a transformed body in what we might describe as a heavenly realm.

Prisco is well aware he can offer no firm proof of his conjectures. But he maintains that his conjecture, whilst "undecidable", is "plausible".

I regard these ideas as having ballpark similarity to those of each of the two previous sections. In all three cases – alien intervention, simulation interruption, and an afterlife enabled by spacetime engineering by god-like descendants – I see the idea as having a low degree of likelihood to impact my own life: perhaps between one in a hundred and one in a million. But in all three cases, the idea deserves more thought. A potential event with extraordinary consequences deserves attention and analysis even if the probability for it to occur is initially judged very small.

I suspect, however, that wiser humans of, say, 2050 – assuming we survive that long – will take a very different view of forthcoming "singularity" possibilities. The few options that I have listed in this chapter may well look quaint by that time. As we discover more about the universe, we are likely to appreciate vast whole new areas of risk and opportunity. These new possibilities may be as unthinkable to us, today, as were ideas such as "vacuum decay" or "nuclear winter" to people living in the middle ages.

The one type of singularity that will likely *not* look quaint at that time, however, is the transition from "narrow" AI to "general" AI (AGI) that exceeds human capabilities in every field of thought. That's the singularity for which we have the most evidence accumulated. If we mishandle the approach to that singularity, we very probably won't be around to find out anything about the other types.

Therefore, in the closing pages, let me bring together what can be called "the singularity principles" – my recommendations for increasing the probability that the AGI singularity will be beneficial rather than disastrous.

The singularity principles

Happily, my recommendations for managing the approach to the AGI singularity are closely aligned with my recommendations for handling the NBIC disruptions. That's good news. It means that we don't have to choose between "managing the fourth industrial revolution" (NBIC) and "managing the fifth industrial revolution" (AGI). The same approaches are needed in both cases.

My recommendations arise from a number of observations:

1. The more powerful technology becomes, the more powerful are the results it can produce – including powerfully good results and powerfully bad results
2. Results that are evaluated as "good" from one standpoint, such as an increase in profits or in market share, can also be evaluated as "bad" from other standpoints, for example when externalities are factored into calculations
3. Breakthroughs in technological capability may be dramatic and unexpected, both in terms of timing (such as a sudden breakthrough following a long period of slow progress) and in terms of impact (with the breakthrough being more widely applicable than was previously anticipated)
4. Complex interactions between multiple developments in different fields – including disruptive breakthroughs as well as incremental progress – make outcomes even harder to predict
5. Although there are many technological failures from which it's possible to recover, some failures may have such a large scale that subsequent recovery would be extremely hard or even impossible
6. The mere fact that a piece of technology has delivered a string of good results does not guarantee, by itself, that the technology will deliver good results in altered circumstances in the future
7. It's insufficient to rely on the good intentions of individuals or companies to ensure the avoidance of any very bad outcomes
8. Due to wishful thinking, providers of potential solutions are often motivated to turn a blind eye to problematic features that may arise

9. Although competition can often accelerate progress, it can also result in dangerous corner-cutting and other reckless risk-taking; hostile arms races are particularly hazardous
10. There's no need to regard human institutions, human attitudes, and human intentions as fixed and unchangeable; changes in all these aspects of the human outlook can be part of wise responses to technological risks and opportunities.

The response to these observations can be stated in short form, in medium form, or in long form. Here's the short form.

Be sure we know:

- *What we're hoping to accomplish*
- *The products and methods that are most likely to serve these goals well*
- *How we will manage any surprises arising.*

The long form, as you probably guessed, is the entirety of this book.

The medium form comprises the following twenty-one principles, which are intended to provide the basis for practical policy recommendations:

1. *Question desirability*: Challenge assumptions about which outcomes are desirable, and be ready to update these assumptions in the light of improved understanding. Avoid taking for granted that agreement exists on what will count as a good outcome.
2. *Clarify externalities*: Draw attention to possible wider impacts (both positive and negative) from the use of products and methods, beyond those initially deemed central to their operation, and ensure that these externalities are included in cost/benefit calculations.
3. *Promote peer reviews*: Avoid trusting the opinion of any one individual, no matter how talented, or any one group, no matter their good track record. Instead, bring in external analysts to conduct independent peer reviews.
4. *Involve multiple viewpoints*: Assessments on the desirability of products and methods should involve a diversity of perspectives drawn from multiple backgrounds; this should include expertise in law, economics, and human factors, as well as scientists and engineers.

5. *Take a whole-system point-of-view*: Explore options for using new products and methods in combination with parallel changes in various aspects of the environment in which they will operate. This will deepen understanding of potential upsides and downsides.
6. *Anticipate fat tails*: Pay particular attention to any possibility of results beyond those which would be expected from a normal distribution, given an estimated mean and estimated variance. In other words, prioritise "potential ruin" more highly than mere "potential harm".
7. *Reject opacity*: Avoid "black box" products and methods whose internal operations are unclear, and where the reasons for individual successes and failures are poorly understood.
8. *Promote resilience*: Prioritise products and methods that make systems more robust against shocks and surprises.
9. *Promote verifiability*: Prioritise products and methods where it is possible to ascertain in advance that the system will behave as specified – and where it is possible to ascertain in advance that there are no significant holes in the specification.
10. *Promote auditability*: Prioritise products and methods where the performance can be monitored in real-time, in such a way that alarms are raised promptly in case of any deviation from expected behaviour.
11. *Clarify risks to users*: Ensure that users of products and methods are made aware, in advance, of:
    - Potential limits and biases in the data sets used to train these systems
    - Any latent weaknesses in the algorithms used (including any potential for the system to reach unsound conclusions in particular circumstances)
    - Any potential security vulnerabilities, such as risks of the system being misled by adversarial data, or having some of its safety measures being edited out or otherwise circumvented.
12. *Clarify trade-offs*: Draw attention to any trade-offs between different measures of fairness in the use of products and methods – bearing in mind the counter-intuitive point that different ideas on fairness are often impossible to satisfy at the same time.

13. *Insist on accountability*: When problems arise from any product or method, the provider of the solution should not be allowed to shrug their shoulders of any responsibility for the mishap, for example by hiding behind get-out clauses in one-sided license agreements.
14. *Penalise disinformation*: Communications that deliberately distort or misrepresent features of a product or method should result in sanctions, proportionate to the degree of damage that could ensue.
15. *Design for cooperation*: Prefer products and methods that encourage collaboration between different parties, and which deter any risk-laden "race to the bottom" competition.
16. *Analyse via simulations*: Create environments such as virtual reality simulations in which products and methods can be analysed in advance of real-world deployment, with a view to uncovering potential surprise developments that may arise in stress conditions.
17. *Maintain human oversight*: Although recommendations for next steps in developing products and methods will increasingly originate from software or AI, control needs to remain in human hands. We must ensure that such proposals arising from automated systems are reviewed and approved by an appropriate team of human overseers.
18. *Provide incentives to address gaps*: Where any of the above principles cannot be carried out adequately, prioritise measures to make available the additional resources or suitably trained personnel that can fill these gaps.
19. *Delay development when these principles cannot be followed*: In case any of the above principles cannot be carried out adequately, and measures to make amends are blocked, delay any further development until such time as the principles can once again be observed.
20. *Build consensus*: Discuss this set of principles widely, to ensure wide buy-in, with conformance in spirit as well as in letter. Be ready to update these principles if discussion makes such a need clear, provided the potential change is widely reviewed beforehand.
21. *Consolidate progress*: Embed aspects of the above principles in legal frameworks, to increase the chance that they will be followed. Be ready to update these legal statutes promptly if it becomes clear that they need amending, following appropriate review.

Two non-solutions

Perhaps you have heard of two other solutions that have been proposed, for the possibility that misconfigured or mis-specified AI might veer horribly out of control as it becomes more powerful. On the face of things, both solutions are considerably simpler than the list of singularity principles I have just outlined. However, I see both these solutions as being "non-solutions".

The first non-solution is the idea of *humanity establishing a backup colony on another planet*, such as Mars. Then if something goes wrong on Earth, the community on Mars will avoid destruction. It will live on, safe and sound.

It's true that some kinds of planetary disaster, such as runaway climate change, would impact only the original planet. However, other types of existential landmine are likely to cast their malign influence all the way from Earth to Mars. For example, a superhuman AI that decides that humanity is a blight on the cosmos will likely be able to track down and neutralise any humans that are hiding on a different planet.

In any case, this whole approach seems to make its peace far too easily with the awful possibility that all human life on Earth is destroyed. That's a possibility we should work a lot harder to avoid, rather than escaping to Mars.

Therefore, whilst there are good arguments for humans to explore other planets and create settlements there, creating a secure solution against existential threats isn't one of these arguments.

The second non-solution is that, by means of *humans merging with AI*, humans could remain in control of AIs, even as these AIs rapidly become more powerful. With such a merger in place, human intelligence will automatically be magnified, as AI improves in capability. Therefore, we humans wouldn't need to worry about being left behind.

One problem with this idea is that, so long as human intelligence is rooted in something like the biology of the brain, the mechanisms for any such merger may only allow relatively modest increases in human intelligence. If silicon-based AIs were to become one thousand times smarter over a period of time, humans whose brains are linked to these AIs might experience only a tenfold increase in intelligence. Our biological brains would constrain the speed of progress. The human-AI hybrid would, after all, be left behind in this intelligence race. *So much for staying in control.*

A considerably bigger problem with this idea is the realisation that a human with superhuman intelligence is likely to be just as dangerous as an

AI with superhuman intelligence. The magnification of intelligence will allow that superhuman human to do all kinds of things with great vigour – settling grudges, acting out fantasies, demanding attention, pursuing vanity projects, and so on. Just think of your least favourite politician, terrorist leader, crime lord, religious fanatic, media tycoon, or corporate robber baron. Imagine that person with much greater power, due to being much more intelligent. Such a person would be able to destroy the earth. Worse, they might *want* to do so.

That's an argument that we need to do considerably more than enable greater intelligence. We also need to accelerate greater wisdom – so that any beings with superhuman intelligence will operate truly beneficently. And that involves the systematic application of the singularity principles.

Final words

I accept that the singularity principles comprise a tall order. However, the stakes are extraordinarily high, and we should be especially wary of any suggestions that a few vague "magic bullet" principles would be sufficient.

Although they *are* a tall order, there are plenty of people who can help out. Nearly eight billion – although they won't all come at once.

Indeed, as the singularity principles start to be put into practice, it should help to generate an ever-stronger spirit of transnational cooperation.

I expect that, despite their bitterness, existing fierce geopolitical rivalries will be transcended – due to the spread of a shared global awareness of the enormous threats and, yes, opportunities, that humanity is collectively facing.

As more and more people come to anticipate and appreciate the profoundly positive transhumanist scenarios that lie within our grasp, momentum will build in support of actions to accelerate these scenarios. It's a project with the potential to unite and uplift all of humanity.

But if humanity remains in "business as usual" mode, just giving lip service to the needs for deep transformation, the chances increase of chaos and tragedy. Indeed, if humanity keeps making excuses rather than insisting on fundamental reforms to our collective management of new technology, we should not be surprised if our technology ends up misconfigured, hacked, bug-ridden, unruly, ungovernable, and acutely dangerous.

The choice is ours.

Acknowledgements

I'm deeply grateful to everyone who provided helpful comments on drafts of *Vital Foresight*. This includes (in alphabetical order) Ashish Manwar, Catarina Lamm, Chris Monteiro, David Shumaker, Didier Coeurnelle, Keith Mansfield, Kim Solez, Martin Sondergaard, Natasha Vita-More, and Yates Buckley. The errors and inelegancies that remain are my own responsibility.

The ideas in *Vital Foresight* have arisen from my reflections on a large number of inspiring books and articles that I have read over the years. I have acknowledged many of these in endnotes. For these, and all the others that I omitted to mention explicitly, I offer my profound thanks.

Vital Foresight has also benefited enormously from literally thousands of discussions I have enjoyed within the broad community of supporters and friends of transhumanism and foresight. Video recordings of a couple of hundred of these discussions are available on the London Futurists YouTube channel[941], but these are just the tip of the iceberg. I have learned a great deal from my interactions with that community.

The cover of *Vital Foresight* incorporates elements of a graphic design from Pixabay user Fruity-Paws[942], used with gratitude.

Acknowledgements

Endnotes

Note: For the convenience of readers, the online page https://transpolitica.org/projects/vital-foresight/endnotes/ provides an easily clickable version of the following list of endnotes.

---

1 "Definitions of Transhumanism" collected by Anders Sandberg, 1997 https://web.archive.org/web/19970712091927/http://www.aleph.se/Trans/Intro/definitions.html

2 "Humanity+: What We Do" https://humanityplus.org/

3 "Natasha Vita-More PhD" https://natashavita-more.com/

4 One example is from August 2001: "Towards the 100 millionth Symbian OS phone" available at https://deltawisdom.com/insight/august-2001/

5 As covered in my 2014 book *Smartphones and Beyond: The remarkable rise and fall of Symbian* https://smartphonesandbeyond.com/

6 In *Technology, Management and Society* by Peter F. Drucker, Harper and Row, 1970

7 "Welcome to London Futurists" https://londonfuturists.com/

8 "Futurism Is Dead" by Hope Cristol, Wired, 2003 https://www.wired.com/2003/12/futurism-is-dead/; "Bullshit Jobs – Futurist, Thought Leader, Leader... if you call yourself this, you're most probably not" by Donald Clark, 2018 http://donaldclarkplanb.blogspot.com/2018/09/bullshit-jobs-forget-technology-and.html; "Predictions are shit (& calling yourself a Futurist is silly)" by Bruce McTague, Enlightened Conflict, 2019 http://brucemctague.com/tag/futurists-are-just-full-of-shit

9 For the importance of narrative in transforming our future, see *The Myth Gap: What Happens When Evidence and Arguments Aren't Enough* by Alex Evans, Transworld Digital, 2017, and "ReWriting the Human Story: How Our Story Determines Our Future" by Nikola Danaylov, Singularity Weblog, 2021 https://www.singularityweblog.com/rewriting-the-human-story-how-our-story-determines-our-future/

10 "The Mont Fleur Scenarios" by Adam Kahane, Pieter le Roux, Vincent Maphai, et al, Deeper News, Global Business Network, 1992 https://reospartners.com/wp-content/uploads/old/Mont%20Fleur.pdf

11 "Mont Fleur Conference Centre" https://www.montfleur.co.za/about/

12 Excerpt from *Transformative Scenario Planning* by Adam Kahane, Penguin Random House, 2012 https://www.penguinrandomhouse.ca/books/575191/transformative-scenario-planning-by-adam-kahane/9781609944902/excerpt

[13] "Bio: Adam Kahane" https://reospartners.com/reos-management/adam-kahane/
[14] *Rabble-Rouser for Peace: The Authorised Biography of Desmond Tutu* by John Allen, Free Press, 2006
[15] *Breaking the Mould, The Role of Scenarios in Shaping South Africa's Future* by Nick Segal, Sun Press, 2007
[16] The scenarios can be viewed in video format: "Mont Fleur Scenarios" https://www.youtube.com/watch?v=f92RYCZMwEk
[17] "The Icarus Scenario" by Clem Sunter, News 24, 2010 https://www.news24.com/news24/columnists/clemsunter/The-Icarus-Scenario-20100120
[18] "Statement by Mr Mboweni at his inauguration as new Governor of the Reserve Bank of South Africa", Bank for International Settlements, 1999 https://www.bis.org/review/r990812c.pdf
[19] "An Essay on Criticism" by Alexander Pope, 1711, in Eighteenth-Century Poetry Archive https://www.eighteenthcenturypoetry.org/works/o3675-w0010.shtml
[20] "A Little Learning", Poets' Graves https://www.poetsgraves.co.uk/Classic%20Poems/Pope/a_little_learning.htm
[21] "The Neuroses of the Railway" by Ralph Harrington, History Today, July 1994 https://www.historytoday.com/archive/neuroses-railway
[22] "There is No Reason for Any Individual To Have a Computer in Their Home" by Garson O'Toole, Quote Investigator, 2017 https://quoteinvestigator.com/2017/09/14/home-computer/
[23] Association of Professional Futurists https://www.apf.org/
[24] The Foresight Institute https://foresight.org/
[25] The Millennium Project http://www.millennium-project.org/
[26] The Institute for Ethics and Emerging Technologies (IEET) https://ieet.org/
[27] Chapter 29, verse 18, in the King James translation
[28] The reference is to the interpretation by Joseph of the dreams of the Pharaoh, from Chapter 41 of the Book of Genesis
[29] "Social cycle theory", Wikipedia https://en.wikipedia.org/wiki/Social_cycle_theory
[30] *The Year Without Summer: 1816 and the Volcano That Darkened the World and Changed History* by William K. Klingaman and Nicholas P. Klingaman, St. Martin's Press, 2013
[31] "Ignaz Semmelweis and the birth of infection control" by M Best and D Neuhauser, BMJ Quality and Safety, 2004 https://qualitysafety.bmj.com/content/13/3/233
[32] "Continental Drift: Theory & Definition" by Becky Oskin, Live Science, 2017 https://www.livescience.com/37529-continental-drift.html

[33] "Shape the future: Our vision" https://web.archive.org/web/20200930041646/https://www.cisco.com/c/en/us/about/careers/working-at-cisco/executive.html
[34] "Be moved" http://corporate.sony.ca/html/sonyinfo/index.html
[35] "The mission and history of Dell Computers" https://www.thebalancesmb.com/dell-computer-company-profile-2892813
[36] "A computer in every home: How a crazy 'shared mission' drove Microsoft's early days" from *Microsoft Secrets: An Insider's View of the Rocket Ride from Worst to First and Lessons Learned on the Journey* by Dave Jaworski, Tech In Asia, 2018 https://www.techinasia.com/computer-home-crazy-shared-mission-drove-microsofts-early-days
[37] "From the garage to the Googleplex" https://about.google/our-story/
[38] "About Tesla" https://www.tesla.com/about
[39] "BHAG – Big Hairy Audacious Goal" from *Built to Last: Successful Habits of Visionary Companies* by Jim Collins and Jerry Porras, 1994 https://www.jimcollins.com/article_topics/articles/BHAG.html
[40] "We have 12 years to limit climate change catastrophe, warns UN" by Jonathan Watts, The Guardian, 2018 https://www.theguardian.com/environment/2018/oct/08/global-warming-must-not-exceed-15c-warns-landmark-un-report
[41] *Human Extinction: A History of Thinking About the End of the World* by Phil Torres, forthcoming, 2021
[42] *Population Bomb* by Paul R. Ehrlich, Ballantyne Books, New York, 1968, revised 1971 and 1978. Later editions of the book changed "in the 1970s" in that quote to "in the 1970s and 1980s"
[43] "Lifeboat Ethics: The Case Against Helping the Poor" by Garrett Hardin, Psychology Today, 1974 https://www.garretthardinsociety.org/articles/art_lifeboat_ethics_case_against_helping_poor.html
[44] *What to Expect when No One's Expecting: America's Coming Demographic Disaster* by Jonathan V. Last, Encounter Books, 2013, page 7
[45] "The Real Causes of Famine" by Jeffrey Sach, Time Magazine, 1998 https://www.earth.columbia.edu/sitefiles/file/Sachs%20Writing/1998/Time_1998_TheRealCausesofFamine_10_26_98.pdf
[46] *More from Less: The Surprising Story of How We Learned to Prosper Using Fewer Resources* by Andrew McAfee, Scribner, 2019
[47] "The Father of the Green Revolution" by Henry I. Miller, Hoover Institution, 2012 https://www.hoover.org/research/father-green-revolution
[48] *How Innovation Works* by Matt Ridley, 4th Estate, 2020, section "Dwarfing Genes from Japan"
[49] "The Population Bomb Revisited" by Paul R. Ehrlich and Anne H. Ehrlich, The Electronic Journal of Sustainable Development, 2009 http://www.populationmedia.org/wp-

content/uploads/2009/07/Population-Bomb-Revisited-Paul-Ehrlich-20096.pdf
[50] "The Swine Flu Panic of 2009" by Philip Bethge et al, Spiegel International, 2010 https://www.spiegel.de/international/world/reconstruction-of-a-mass-hysteria-the-swine-flu-panic-of-2009-a-682613.html
[51] "2009 swine flu pandemic by country", Wikipedia summary of official reports
https://en.wikipedia.org/wiki/2009_swine_flu_pandemic_by_country
[52] "Director-General Statement following the first meeting of the Emergency Committee", World Health Organization, 2009 https://www.who.int/news/item/25-04-2009-director-general-statement-following-the-first-meeting-of-the-emergency-committee
[53] "World now at the start of 2009 influenza pandemic" by Margaret Chan, World Health Organization, 2009 https://reliefweb.int/report/world/world-now-start-2009-influenza-pandemic-statement-press-who-director-general-dr
[54] "The Swine Flu Panic of 2009" by Philip Bethge et al, Spiegel International, 2010 https://www.spiegel.de/international/world/reconstruction-of-a-mass-hysteria-the-swine-flu-panic-of-2009-a-682613.html
[55] "Global Estimates of 2009 H1N1 Pandemic Mortality Released by CDC-Led Collaboration", CDC, 2012 https://www.cdc.gov/flu/spotlights/pandemic-global-estimates.htm
[56] "Interview: Dr. Richard Schabas" by Meagan Fitzpatrick, Canwest News Service, 2009 https://web.archive.org/web/20091214081830/http://www.canada.com/health/interview+richard+schabas/2221030/story.html
[57] "Council of Europe will investigate and debate on 'Faked Pandemic'" by Wolfgang Wodarg, 2010 https://web.archive.org/web/20100215080904/http://www.wodarg.de/english/2948146.html
[58] "Conflicts of interest and pandemic flu" by Fiona Godlee, BMJ, 2010 http://www.bmj.com/content/340/bmj.c2947.full
[59] "We Go From Hysteria to Hysteria" by Dennis Prager, Real Clear Politics, 2020
https://www.realclearpolitics.com/articles/2020/03/03/we_go_from_hysteria_to_hysteria_142552.html
[60] "Exercise Cygnus uncovered: the pandemic warnings buried by the government" by Paul Nuki and Bill Gardner, Daily Telegraph, 2020 https://www.telegraph.co.uk/news/2020/03/28/exercise-cygnus-uncovered-pandemic-warnings-buried-government/
[61] "Revealed: the secret report that gave ministers warning of care home coronavirus crisis" by David Pegg, Robert Booth, and David Conn, The Guardian, 2020

https://www.theguardian.com/world/2020/may/07/revealed-the-secret-report-that-gave-ministers-warning-of-care-home-coronavirus-crisis

[62] *COVID-19: The Pandemic that Never Should Have Happened and How to Stop the Next One* by Debora MacKenzie, Hachette Books, 2020

[63] "What were climate scientists predicting in the 1970s?" SkepticalScience https://skepticalscience.com/ice-age-predictions-in-1970s-intermediate.htm

[64] "Newsweek's 'Global Cooling' Article From April 28, 1975" by Peter Gwynne https://www.scribd.com/doc/225798861/Newsweek-s-Global-Cooling-Article-From-April-28-1975

[65] "The Editor's Desk", Newsweek, 2007 https://www.newsweek.com/editors-desk-98979

[66] "From Global Cooling to Global Cooling" by Steve Taylor, The View From Mid-America, 2010 http://viewfrommidamerica.blogspot.com/2010/09/from-global-cooling-to-global-cooling.html

[67] "Sorry, a TIME Magazine Cover Did Not Predict a Coming Ice Age" by Bryan Walsh, Time, 2013 https://science.time.com/2013/06/06/sorry-a-time-magazine-cover-did-not-predict-a-coming-ice-age/

[68] "The Myth of the 1970s Global Cooling Scientific Consensus" by Thomas C. Peterson et al, Bulletin of American Meteorological Society, 2008 https://journals.ametsoc.org/bams/article/89/9/1325/59455/THE-MYTH-OF-THE-1970s-GLOBAL-COOLING-SCIENTIFIC

[69] "Reid Bryson: University of Wisconsin Climatologist and Meteorologist", by Bill Hanley, Mother Earth News, 1976 https://www.motherearthnews.com/nature-and-environment/reid-bryson-zmaz76mazraw

[70] "My 1975 'Cooling World' Story Doesn't Make Today's Climate Scientists Wrong" by Peter Gwynne, Inside Science, 2014 https://www.insidescience.org/news/my-1975-cooling-world-story-doesnt-make-todays-climate-scientists-wrong

[71] "Alan Turing to be the face of new £50 note", Bank of England, 2019 https://www.bankofengland.co.uk/news/2019/july/50-pound-banknote-character-announcement

[72] "This Is Only a Foretaste of What Is To Come, and Only the Shadow of What Is Going To Be", Quote Investigator, 2019 https://quoteinvestigator.com/2019/10/12/ai-shadow/

[73] "The Turing Digital Archive" http://www.turingarchive.org/browse.php/b/4

[74] "Computing Machinery and Intelligence" by Alan Turing, Mind, 1950 https://www.csee.umbc.edu/courses/471/papers/turing.pdf

[75] "A proposal for the Dartmouth summer research project on Artificial Intelligence" by J. McCarthy et al, August 31, 1955 http://raysolomonoff.com/dartmouth/boxa/dart564props.pdf
[76] "Heuristic Problem Solving: The Next Advance in Operations Research" by Herbert Simon and Allen Newell, Operations Research, 1958 https://pubsonline.informs.org/doi/abs/10.1287/opre.6.1.1
[77] "Allen Newell, 1975" by Hunter Heyck, ACM Awards https://amturing.acm.org/award_winners/newell_3167755.cfm
[78] "Press Release", The Nobel Prize, 1978 https://www.nobelprize.org/prizes/economic-sciences/1978/press-release/
[79] "Chess Championship: Machines Play, People Watch" by Craig Stinson, Softline, January 1982 http://www.cgwmuseum.org/galleries/issues/softline_1.3.pdf
[80] *Computer Chess* by Monroe Newborn, Academic Press, 1975
[81] *Artificial Intelligence: A Modern Approach* by Stuart Russell and Peter Norvig, Prentice Hall, 1995
[82] "The Drosophila of AI", Chess Programming Wiki article about Stephen Coles https://www.chessprogramming.org/L._Stephen_Coles#The_Drosophila_of_AI
[83] "The Mystery of Go, the Ancient Game That Computers Still Can't Win" by Alan Levinovitz, Wired, 2014 https://www.wired.com/2014/05/the-world-of-computer-go/
[84] "What the AI behind AlphaGo can teach us about being human", by Cade Metz, Wired, 2016 https://www.wired.com/2016/05/google-alpha-go-ai/
[85] "Mastering Chess and Shogi by Self-Play with a General Reinforcement Learning Algorithm", David Silver et al, arXiv, 2017 https://arxiv.org/abs/1712.01815
[86] "No plan survives contact with the enemy", Boot Camp & Military Fitness Institute https://bootcampmilitaryfitnessinstitute.com/military-and-outdoor-fitness-articles/no-plan-survives-contact-with-the-enemy/
[87] "Plans Are Worthless, But Planning Is Everything", Quote Investigator, 2017 https://quoteinvestigator.com/2017/11/18/planning/
[88] https://books.google.co.uk/books?id=ooFGl74WbXsC&pg=PT209
[89] "The Maginot Line – 11 Fascinating Facts About France's Great Wall" Military History Now, 2017 https://militaryhistorynow.com/2017/05/07/the-great-wall-of-france-11-remarkable-facts-about-the-maginot-line/
[90] See references quoted in Wikipedia https://en.wikipedia.org/wiki/Battle_of_France#Popular_reaction_in_Germany
[91] "Mein Kampf", Wikiquote https://en.wikiquote.org/wiki/Mein_Kampf

[92] "Stalin's Intelligence", by Niall Ferguson, New York Times, 2005 https://www.nytimes.com/2005/06/12/books/arts/stalins-intelligence.html
[93] "The Eastern Front", The National WW2 Museum https://www.nationalww2museum.org/war/articles/eastern-front
[94] "Fooling Hitler: The Elaborate Ruse Behind D-Day" by Christopher Klein, History Stories, 2014 https://www.history.com/news/fooling-hitler-the-elaborate-ruse-behind-d-day
[95] "Famous Deceptions of World War 2" by Stephanie Huesler, History Undusted, 2014 https://historyundusted.wordpress.com/2014/06/07/famous-deceptions-of-world-war-2/
[96] *The Great Illusion* by Norman Angell, G.P. Putnam's Sons, 1910
[97] "World War One: First war was impossible, then inevitable" by Anatole Kaletsky, Reuters, 2014 https://web.archive.org/web/20140701010006/http://blogs.reuters.com/anatole-kaletsky/2014/06/27/world-war-one-first-war-was-impossible-then-inevitable/
[98] Quote included in "A mirror on the crisis" by Hamish McRae, The Independent, 2008 http://www.independent.co.uk/arts-entertainment/books/reviews/the-ascent-of-money-by-niall-ferguson-980013.html
[99] "Flight 8969: GIGN's Greatest Hour" by Mike Perry, SOFREP, 2012 https://sofrep.com/news/flight-8969-gign/
[100] "Swatting Hijackers Away: The Hijacking of Air France 8969 and the GIGN Intervention" by Massimo Catusi and Daniela Tardo, Aviation Security International, 2019 https://www.asi-mag.com/swatting-hijackers-away-the-hijacking-of-air-france-8969-and-the-gign-intervention/
[101] "Operation Bojinka's bombshell" by Matthew Brzezinski, The Star, 2002 https://web.archive.org/web/20020614124327/http://www.thestar.com/NASApp/cs/ContentServer?pagename=thestar%2FLayout%2FArticle_PrintFriendly&c=Article&cid=1009926464027
[102] "Echoes of '95 Manila Plot" by Terry McDermott, Los Angeles Times, 2006 https://www.latimes.com/archives/la-xpm-2006-aug-11-na-manila11-story.html
[103] "Yousef bombs Philippines Airlines Flight 434", Global Security https://web.archive.org/web/20061128034427/https://www.globalsecurity.org/security/profiles/yousef_bombs_philippines_airlines_flight_434.htm
[104] "The Sociology and Psychology of Terrorism: Who Becomes a Terrorist and Why?" by Rex A. Hudson, Library of Congress, 1999 https://www.loc.gov/rr/frd/pdf-files/Soc_Psych_of_Terrorism.pdf
[105] "A Review of the FBI's Handling of Intelligence Information Prior to the September 11 Attacks, Chapter 3", Office of the Inspector General, 2004

https://web.archive.org/web/20051205061924/http://www.justice.gov/oig/special/0506/chapter3.htm
[106] "What the CIA knew before 9/11: New details" by Chris Whipple, Politico, 2015 https://www.politico.eu/article/attacks-will-be-spectacular-cia-war-on-terror-bush-bin-laden/
[107] "The Twentieth Hijacker" by Jason Zengerle, New York Magazine, 2011 https://nymag.com/news/9-11/10th-anniversary/twentieth-hijacker/
[108] "The FBI's Handling of the Phoenix Electronic Communication and Investigation of Zacarias Moussaoui Prior to September 11, 2001" by Eleanor Hill, 2002 https://fas.org/irp/congress/2002_hr/092402hill.html
[109] "Damning evidence highlights FBI bungles" by Jerry Markon and Timothy Dwyer, Washington Post, 2006 https://www.smh.com.au/world/damning-evidence-highlights-fbi-bungles-20060322-gdn7hz.html
[110] "Government Terrorist Trackers Before 9/11: Higher Ups Wouldn't Listen" by Sean Naylor, History, 2017 https://www.history.com/news/government-terrorist-trackers-before-911-higher-ups-wouldnt-listen
[111] "Traces of Terrorism: The Warnings, F.B.I. Knew for Years About Terror Pilot Training" by Philip Shenon, New York Times, 2002 https://www.nytimes.com/2002/05/18/us/traces-of-terrorism-the-warnings-fbi-knew-for-years-about-terror-pilot-training.html
[112] "Proof that life is getting better for humanity, in 5 charts" by Max Roser, Vox, 2016 https://www.vox.com/the-big-idea/2016/12/23/14062168/history-global-conditions-charts-life-span-poverty
[113] "Global Inequality of Opportunity", Our World In Data by Max Roser, 2019 https://ourworldindata.org/global-inequality-of-opportunity
[114] "Top 1% net personal wealth share, United Kingdom, 1896-2012", World Inequality Database, https://wid.world/country/united-kingdom/
[115] "Top 1% net personal wealth share, USA, 1913-2016", World Inequality Database, https://wid.world/country/usa/
[116] "Trends in income and wealth inequality" by Juliana Menasce Horowitz, Ruth Igielnik, and Rakesh Kochhar, Pew Research Center, 2020 https://www.pewresearch.org/social-trends/2020/01/09/trends-in-income-and-wealth-inequality/
[117] "Statement from the new Prime Minister Theresa May", 13 July 2016 https://www.gov.uk/government/speeches/statement-from-the-new-prime-minister-theresa-may
[118] "Social care services: funding cuts are biting hard" by Simon Bottery, The Kings Fund, 2020 https://www.kingsfund.org.uk/blog/2020/01/social-care-funding-cuts-are-biting-hard

[119] "'Deaths of despair': The deadly epidemic that predated coronavirus" by Roge Karma, Vox, 2020 https://www.vox.com/2020/4/15/21214734/deaths-of-despair-coronavirus-covid-19-angus-deaton-anne-case-americans-deaths
[120] *The Precariat: The New Dangerous Class* by Guy Standing, Bloomsbury Academic, 2011
[121] "Germanwings crash: Who was co-pilot Andreas Lubitz?", BBC News, 2017 https://www.bbc.co.uk/news/world-europe-32072220
[122] "An Accurate Look at Timothy McVeigh's Beliefs" by Bruce Prescott, Good Faith Media, 2010 https://goodfaithmedia.org/an-accurate-look-at-timothy-mcveighs-beliefs-cms-15532/
[123] "Aum Shinrikyo: The Japanese cult behind the Tokyo Sarin attack", BBC News, 2018 https://www.bbc.co.uk/news/world-asia-35975069
[124] "The Next Wave of Extremists Will Be Green" by Jamie Bartlett, Foreign Policy, 2017 https://foreignpolicy.com/2017/09/01/the-green-radicals-are-coming-environmental-extremism/
[125] "Accidental Nuclear War: A Timeline of Close Calls", Future of Life Institute http://futureoflife.org/background/nuclear-close-calls-a-timeline/
[126] "Mike Pompeo, Trump's pick for secretary of state, talks about politics as a battle of good and evil", by Tara Isabella Burton, Vox, 2018 https://www.vox.com/identities/2018/3/15/17117298/mike-pompeo-trump-secretary-of-state-politics-battle-evangelical-holy-war-christian
[127] "Reasons for the increase in emerging and re-emerging viral infectious diseases" by Eric Ka-Wai Hui, Microbes and Infection, 2006 https://www.ncbi.nlm.nih.gov/pmc/articles/PMC7110580/
[128] "'Wet markets' likely launched the coronavirus. Here's what you need to know" by Dina Fine Maron, National Geographic, 2020 https://www.nationalgeographic.co.uk/science-and-technology/2020/04/wet-markets-likely-launched-coronavirus-heres-what-you-need-know
[129] "Biologists are trying to make bird flu easier to spread. Can we not?" by Kelsey Piper, Vox, 2019 https://www.vox.com/2019/2/17/18225938/biologists-are-trying-to-make-bird-flu-easier-to-spread-can-we-not
[130] "How smallpox claimed its final victim" by Monica Rimmer, BBC News, 2018 https://www.bbc.co.uk/news/uk-england-birmingham-45101091
[131] "Threatened pandemics and laboratory escapes: Self-fulfilling prophecies" by Martin Furmanski, Bulletin of the Atomic Scientists, 2014 https://thebulletin.org/2014/03/threatened-pandemics-and-laboratory-escapes-self-fulfilling-prophecies/
[132] "How deadly pathogens have escaped the lab – over and over again" by Kelsey Piper, Vox, 2019 https://www.vox.com/future-

perfect/2019/3/20/18260669/deadly-pathogens-escape-lab-smallpox-bird-flu

[133] "Taiwan's new SARS case raises questions about sloppy procedures" USA Today, 2003 http://usatoday30.usatoday.com/news/health/2003-12-17-singapore-sars_x.htm

[134] "How a Cult Used Salad Bars to Orchestrate the Worst Bioterror Attack in US History" by Mayukh Sen, Vice, 2018 https://www.vice.com/en_us/article/kzp4n9/wild-wild-country-netflix-salad-bar-bioterror-attack

[135] "Bacillus anthracis Bioterrorism Incident, Kameido, Tokyo, 1993", by Hiroshi Takahashi et al, Emerging Infectious Diseases, 2004 https://wwwnc.cdc.gov/eid/article/10/1/03-0238_article

[136] "How North Korea got away with the assassination of Kim Jong-nam" by Hannah Ellis-Petersen and Benjamin Haas, The Guardian, 2019 https://www.theguardian.com/world/2019/apr/01/how-north-korea-got-away-with-the-assassination-of-kim-jong-nam

[137] *Cyber Wars: Hacks that Shocked the Business World* by Charles Arthur, Kogan Page, 2018

[138] "WH: Kim Jong Un behind massive WannaCry malware attack" by Joe Uchill, The Hill, 2017 https://thehill.com/policy/cybersecurity/365580-wh-kim-jong-un-ordered-release-of-disastrous-wannacry-malware

[139] "U.S. to give ransomware hacks similar priority as terrorism" by Christopher Bing, Reuters, 2021 https://www.reuters.com/technology/exclusive-us-give-ransomware-hacks-similar-priority-terrorism-official-says-2021-06-03/

[140] *Countdown to Zero Day: Stuxnet and the Launch of the World's First Digital Weapon* by Kim Zetter, Crown, 2014

[141] "The inside story of the biggest hack in history" by Jose Pagliery, CNN Business, 2015 https://money.cnn.com/2015/08/05/technology/aramco-hack/index.html

[142] "Sony Cyberattack, First a Nuisance, Swiftly Grew Into a Firestorm" by Michael Cieply and Brooks Barnes, New York Times, 2014 https://www.nytimes.com/2014/12/31/business/media/sony-attack-first-a-nuisance-swiftly-grew-into-a-firestorm-.html

[143] "More deaths linked to Ashley Madison hack as scammers move in" by Iain Thomson, The Register, 2015 https://www.theregister.com/2015/08/24/death_toll_ashley_madison/

[144] "Equifax data breach FAQ: What happened, who was affected, what was the impact?" by Josh Fruhlinger, CSO, 2020 https://www.csoonline.com/article/3444488/equifax-data-breach-faq-what-happened-who-was-affected-what-was-the-impact.html

[145] "A new data leak hits Aadhaar, India's national ID database" by Zack Whittaker, ZDNet, 2018 https://www.zdnet.com/article/another-data-leak-hits-india-aadhaar-biometric-database/

[146] "When cyberwar struck its first civilian target" by Brian Nussbaum, Nature, 2019 https://www.nature.com/articles/d41586-019-03457-9

[147] *Dawn of the Code War: America's Battle Against Russia, China, and the Rising Global Cyber Threat* by John P. Carlin and Garrett M. Graff, Public Affairs, 2018

[148] "Venezuela data offer rare glimpse of economic chaos" by Gideon Long, Financial Times, 2019 https://www.ft.com/content/5cb83c1c-821b-11e9-b592-5fe435b57a3b

[149] "IMF sees Venezuela inflation at 10 million percent in 2019", Reuters, 2018 https://in.reuters.com/article/venezuela-economy-idINKCN1MJ1YX

[150] "On the Measurement of Zimbabwe's Hyperinflation" by Steve H. Hanke and Alex Kwok, Cato Journal, 2009 https://papers.ssrn.com/sol3/papers.cfm?abstract_id=2264895

[151] *This Time Is Different: Eight Centuries of Financial Folly* by Carmen Reinhart and Kenneth Rogoff, Princeton University Press, 2009

[152] "1927-1933 Chart of Pompous Prognosticators" by Colin J. Seymour, Gold-Eagle, 2001 http://www.gold-eagle.com/article/1927-1933-chart-pompous-prognosticators

[153] "The Mississippi Bubble of 1718-1720" by Jesse Colombo, The Bubble Bubble, 2012 https://web.archive.org/web/20120623001540/http://www.thebubblebubble.com/mississippi-bubble/

[154] "The Plot Between Ignorance and Arrogance" by Catherine Rampell, New York Times, 2009 https://economix.blogs.nytimes.com/2009/09/30/the-plot-between-ignorance-and-arrogance/

[155] "1929 Stock Market Crash: Did Panicked Investors Really Jump From Windows?" by Christopher Klein, History, 2019 https://www.history.com/news/stock-market-crash-suicides-wall-street-1929-great-depression

[156] "Macroeconomic Priorities" by Robert Lucas, The American Economic Review, 2003 http://pages.stern.nyu.edu/~dbackus/Taxes/Lucas%20priorities%20AER%2003.pdf

[157] "Global economy can withstand U.S. downturn, IMF says", New York Times, 2007 https://www.nytimes.com/2007/04/11/business/worldbusiness/11iht-imf.4.5239924.html

---

[158] "GDP Growth (annual %)", The World Bank https://data.worldbank.org/indicator/NY.GDP.MKTP.KD.ZG?end=2019&start=1961&view=chart

[159] "The economic forecasters' failing vision" by Chris Giles, Financial Times, 2008 https://www.ft.com/content/50007754-ca35-11dd-93e5-000077b07658

[160] "The 2008 recession 10 years on", The Office of National Statistics, 2018 https://www.ons.gov.uk/economy/grossdomesticproductgdp/articles/the2008recession10yearson/2018-04-30

[161] "The euro could be nearing a crisis – can it be saved?" by Joseph Stiglitz, The Guardian, 2018 https://www.theguardian.com/business/2018/jun/13/euro-growth-eurozone-joseph-stiglitz

[162] "Lord King says UK 'fortunate' as he savages eurozone as huge 'threat to EU stability'" by Svar Nanan-Sen, Daily Express, 2020 https://www.express.co.uk/news/uk/1281153/Brexit-News-EU-monetary-union-Germany-banks-Lord-Mervyn-King-latest-update

[163] "Disintegration of the eurozone has begun. Austerity will be worse than in 2011" by Hugo Neutel, TSF, 2020 https://www.tsf.pt/portugal/economia/disintegration-of-the-eurozone-has-begun-austerity-will-be-worse-than-in-2011-12080552.html

[164] *Can We Avoid Another Financial Crisis? (The Future of Capitalism)* by Steve Keen, Polity Press, 2017

[165] "Private debt hyperinflations and the prospect of renewed crisis" by Geoff Tily, Prime Economics, 2018 http://www.primeeconomics.org/articles/private-debt-hyperinflations-and-the-prospect-of-renewed-crisis

[166] "China's Debt Bomb" by Enda Curran, Bloomberg, 2018 https://www.bloomberg.com/quicktake/chinas-debt-bomb

[167] "China's banking debt crisis is a ticking time bomb that must be defused with urgent financial-sector reforms" by Hans Yue Zhu, South China Morning Post, 2020 https://www.scmp.com/comment/opinion/article/3044148/chinas-banking-debt-crisis-ticking-time-bomb-must-be-defused-urgent

[168] "Flash Crash – Don't Fall for Market 'Spoofers'" by Ted Bauman, Value Walk, 2017 https://www.valuewalk.com/2017/05/flash-crash-dont-fall-for-market-spoofers/

[169] "The Coming Cryptocurrency Crash" by Robert C. Wolcott, Forbes, 2017 https://www.forbes.com/sites/robertwolcott/2017/07/07/the-coming-cryptocurrency-crash-and-why-its-a-good-thing/

[170] "The Historical Impact of Epidemic Typhus" by Joseph M. Conlon, https://www.montana.edu/historybug/documents/TYPHUS-Conlon.pdf

[171] "Who was Anne Frank?", Anne Frank House https://www.annefrank.org/en/anne-frank/who-was-anne-frank/
[172] "The Truth About DDT and Silent Spring" by Robert Zubrin, The New Atlantis, 2012 https://www.thenewatlantis.com/publications/the-truth-about-ddt-and-silent-spring
[173] "Paul Müller Facts", The Nobel Prize https://www.nobelprize.org/prizes/medicine/1948/muller/facts/
[174] "Earth Day Reflections, Land Indicator: Protected Land" by Berks Nature, BCTV, 2020 https://www.bctv.org/2020/04/29/earth-day-reflections-land-indicator-protected-land/
[175] "The Case of the Thinning Eggshells" by Matthew Wills, JSTOR Daily, 2019 https://daily.jstor.org/the-case-of-the-thinning-eggshells/
[176] "DDT Linked to Abnormal Sperm" by Brian Bienkowski, Scientific American, 2015 https://www.scientificamerican.com/article/ddt-linked-to-abnormal-sperm1/
[177] "Study Links DDT Residues to Early Miscarriages" Harvard School of Public Health, 2005 http://archive.sph.harvard.edu/press-releases/archives/2005-releases/press09142005.html
[178] "Cancer Risk Lingers for Long-Banned DDT" by Kelli Miller, WebMD, 2008 https://www.webmd.com/men/news/20080428/cancer-risk-lingers-for-long-banned-ddt
[179] "DDT exposure tied to breast cancer risk for all women through age 54", Science Daily, 2019 https://www.sciencedaily.com/releases/2019/02/190213124347.htm
[180] "Chlorofluorocarbons and Ozone Depletion", American Chemical Society, 2017 https://www.acs.org/content/acs/en/education/whatischemistry/landmarks/cfcs-ozone.html
[181] "James Lovelock" by Philip Ball, Prospect, 2000 https://www.prospectmagazine.co.uk/magazine/jameslovelock
[182] "The Nobel Prize in Chemistry 1995" https://www.nobelprize.org/prizes/chemistry/1995/summary/
[183] "Large losses of total ozone in Antarctica reveal seasonal ClOx/NOx interaction" by J. C. Farman, B. G. Gardiner, and J. D. Shanklin, Nature, 1985 https://www.nature.com/articles/315207a0
[184] "Joe Farman obituary" by Fiona Harvey, The Guardian, 2013 https://www.theguardian.com/environment/2013/may/16/joe-farman
[185] "Opinion: Montreal Protocol on CFCs holds lessons for climate action" by Sébastien Jodoin and Hamish van der Ven, Montreal Gazette, 2017 https://montrealgazette.com/opinion/opinion-montreal-protocol-on-cfcs-holds-lessons-for-climate-action
[186] "There's money in the air: the CFC ban and DuPont's regulatory strategy" by James Maxwell and Forrest Briscoe, Business Strategy and the

Environment, 1997 https://eng.ucmerced.edu/people/awesterling/SPR2014.ESS141/Assignments/DuPont

[187] "Microplastics in freshwater and soil", The Royal Society, 2019 https://royalsociety.org/topics-policy/projects/microplastics-in-freshwater-and-soils/

[188] "A scientific perspective on microplastics in nature and society", Science Advice for Policy by European Academies, 2019 https://www.sapea.info/topics/microplastics/

[189] "Baby fish have started eating plastic. We haven't yet seen the consequences" by Laura Parker, National Geographic, 2019 https://www.nationalgeographic.com/magazine/2019/05/microplastics-impact-on-fish-shown-in-pictures/

[190] "Microplastics in the soil environment: Occurrence, risks, interactions and fate – A review" by Baile Xu et al, Critical Reviews in Environmental Science and Technology, 2019 https://www.tandfonline.com/doi/abs/10.1080/10643389.2019.1694822

[191] "Planetary Boundaries – an update", Stockholm Resilience Centre, 2015 https://www.stockholmresilience.org/research/research-news/2015-01-15-planetary-boundaries---an-update.html

[192] "Scientists Say Planetary Boundaries Crossed", United Nations Climate Change, 2015 https://unfccc.int/news/scientists-say-planetary-boundaries-crossed

[193] *Climate Change: The Facts 2017* edited by Jennifer Marohasy, Connor Court Publishing, 2017

[194] *False Alarm: How Climate Change Panic Costs Us Trillions, Hurts the Poor, and Fails to Fix the Planet* by Bjorn Lomborg, Basic Books, 2020

[195] "Climate emergency: world 'may have crossed tipping points'" by Damian Carrington, The Guardian, 2019 https://www.theguardian.com/environment/2019/nov/27/climate-emergency-world-may-have-crossed-tipping-points

[196] *The Uninhabitable Earth: Life After Warming* by David Wallace-Wells, Tim Duggan Books, 2019

[197] *Requiem for a Species: Why We Resist the Truth about Climate Change* by Clive Hamilton, Earthscan Publications, 2010

[198] "Climate tipping points – too risky to bet against" by Timothy M. Lenton et al, Nature, 2019 https://www.nature.com/articles/d41586-019-03595-0

[199] "Past perspectives on the present era of abrupt Arctic climate change" by Eystein Jansen et al, Nature Climate Change, 2020 https://www.researchgate.net/publication/343298299_Past_perspectives_on_the_present_era_of_abrupt_Arctic_climate_change

[200] *Under a Green Sky: Global Warming, the Mass Extinctions of the Past, and What They Can Tell Us About Our Future* by Peter Ward, Smithsonian, 2007

201 *The Ends of the World: Volcanic Apocalypses, Lethal Oceans and Our Quest to Understand Earth's Past Mass Extinctions* by Peter Brannen, Harper Collins, 2017

202 "How Understanding What Killed The Dinosaurs Can Help Us Prepare For Climate Change", High Plains Public Radio, 2017 https://www.hppr.org/post/how-understanding-what-killed-dinosaurs-can-help-us-prepare-climate-change

203 "Who Should We Fear More: Biohackers, Disgruntled Postdocs, or Bad Governments? A Simple Risk Chain Model of Biorisk" by Anders Sandberg and Cassidy Nelson, Health Security, 2020 https://www.liebertpub.com/doi/pdfplus/10.1089/hs.2019.0115

204 *The Formation Of National States In Western Europe* edited by Charles Tilly, Princeton University Press, 1975

205 "Rwanda genocide: 100 days of slaughter", BBC News, 2019 https://www.bbc.co.uk/news/world-africa-26875506

206 "A Century After Armenian Genocide, Turkey's Denial Only Deepens" by Tim Arango, New York Times, 2015 https://www.nytimes.com/2015/04/17/world/europe/turkeys-century-of-denial-about-an-armenian-genocide.html

207 "Khmer Rouge: Cambodia's years of brutality", BBC News, 2018 https://www.bbc.co.uk/news/world-asia-pacific-10684399

208 "World War II: The Holocaust" by Alan Taylor, The Atlantic, 2011 https://www.theatlantic.com/photo/2011/10/world-war-ii-the-holocaust/100170/

209 "Holodomor: The Ukrainian Genocide", University of Minnesota Holocaust and Genocide Studies https://cla.umn.edu/chgs/holocaust-genocide-education/resource-guides/holodomor

210 "Mao's Great Leap Forward 'killed 45 million in four years'" by Arifa Akbar, The Independent, 2011 https://www.independent.co.uk/arts-entertainment/books/news/maos-great-leap-forward-killed-45-million-in-four-years-2081630.html

211 "Who Killed More: Hitler, Stalin, or Mao?" by Ian Johnson, New York Review of Books, 2018 https://www.nybooks.com/daily/2018/02/05/who-killed-more-hitler-stalin-or-mao/

212 "Lord Acton Quote Archive", Acton Institute https://www.acton.org/research/lord-acton-quote-archive

213 "Report: Global Satisfaction with Democracy 2020" by RS Foa et al, Bennett Institute for Public Policy, 2020 https://www.bennettinstitute.cam.ac.uk/media/uploads/files/DemocracyReport2020.pdf

214 *How Markets Fail: The Logic of Economic Calamities* by John Cassidy, Farrar Straus & Giroux, 2009

[215] "Transcript of Bayer CEO Marjin Dekkers quote at the December 3, 2013 FT Event" by Claire Cassedy, Knowledge Ecology International, 2014 https://www.keionline.org/22414
[216] "About DNDi" https://dndi.org/about/
[217] *An Inquiry into the Nature and Causes of the Wealth of Nations* by Adam Smith, 1776
[218] "Greenspan - I was wrong about the economy. Sort of" by Andrew Clark and Jill Treanor, The Guardian, 2008 https://www.theguardian.com/business/2008/oct/24/economics-creditcrunch-federal-reserve-greenspan
[219] *Adam Smith: What He Thought, and Why it Matters* by Jesse Norman, Allen Lane, 2018
[220] "Financial Secretary to the Treasury", UK Government https://www.gov.uk/government/ministers/financial-secretary-to-the-treasury
[221] *Adam Smith: What He Thought, and Why it Matters*, Penguin https://www.penguin.co.uk/books/307560/adam-smith/9780141987118.html
[222] "Launch Presentation, 30th October 2006" by Sir Nicholas Stern, HM Treasury, 2006 https://webarchive.nationalarchives.gov.uk/20100407173721/http://www.hm-treasury.gov.uk/d/stern_speakingnotes.pdf
[223] "Stern Review on the Economics of Climate Change", HM Treasury, 2006 https://webarchive.nationalarchives.gov.uk/20100407173719/http://www.hm-treasury.gov.uk/sternreview_index.htm
[224] "The Economics of Healthcare" by N. Gregory Mankiw, Harvard University, 2017 https://scholar.harvard.edu/mankiw/publications/economics-healthcare
[225] "U.S. Health Care from a Global Perspective, 2019: Higher Spending, Worse Outcomes?" by Roosa Tikkanen and Melinda K. Abrams, The Commonwealth Fund, 2020 https://www.commonwealthfund.org/publications/issue-briefs/2020/jan/us-health-care-global-perspective-2019
[226] "Eisenhower's Farewell Address to the Nation", Marquette University, 1961 http://mcadams.posc.mu.edu/ike.htm
[227] *Republic of Lies: American Conspiracy Theorists and Their Surprising Rise to Power* by Anna Merlan, Metropolitan Books, 2019
[228] "X Prize Founder Peter Diamandis Has His Eyes on the Future" by Ted Greenwald, Wired, 2012 https://www.wired.com/2012/06/mf-icons-diamandis/
[229] "A Genocide Incited on Facebook, With Posts From Myanmar's Military" by Paul Mozur, New York Times, 2018

https://www.nytimes.com/2018/10/15/technology/myanmar-facebook-genocide.html
[230] "Assessing Russian Activities and Intentions in Recent US Elections", National Intelligence Council, 2017 https://en.wikisource.org/wiki/Assessing_Russian_Activities_and_Intentions_in_Recent_US_Elections
[231] "Here's Everything The Mueller Report Says About How Russian Trolls Used Social Media" by Ryan Broderick, BuzzFeed News, 2019 https://www.buzzfeednews.com/article/ryanhatesthis/mueller-report-internet-research-agency-detailed-2016
[232] "Political Lying" by Jonathan Swift http://www.bartleby.com/209/633.html
[233] "'I think the people of this country have had enough of experts'" by Richard Portes, London Business School, 2017 https://www.london.edu/think/who-needs-experts
[234] "How to Destroy Surveillance Capitalism" by Cory Doctorow, OneZero, 2020 https://onezero.medium.com/how-to-destroy-surveillance-capitalism-8135e6744d59
[235] "The Truth About Tonkin" by Lieutenant Commander Pat Paterson, Naval History Magazine, 2008 https://www.usni.org/magazines/naval-history-magazine/2008/february/truth-about-tonkin
[236] "How a False Flag Sparked World War Two: The Gleiwitz Incident Explained" by Cassie Pope, History Hit, 2018 https://www.historyhit.com/gleiwitz-incident-explained/
[237] "When Continental Drift Was Considered Pseudoscience" by Richard Conniff, Smithsonian Museum, 2012 https://www.smithsonianmag.com/science-nature/when-continental-drift-was-considered-pseudoscience-90353214/
[238] "'Einstein: His Life and Universe' by Walter Isaacson" by Len Barcousky, Pittsburgh Post-Gazette, 2007 https://www.post-gazette.com/ae/book-reviews/2007/04/20/Einstein-His-Life-and-Universe-by-Walter-Isaacson/stories/200704200408
[239] "The Doctor Who Drank Infectious Broth, Gave Himself an Ulcer, and Solved a Medical Mystery" by Pamela Weintraub, Discover, 2010 https://www.discovermagazine.com/health/the-doctor-who-drank-infectious-broth-gave-himself-an-ulcer-and-solved-a-medical-mystery
[240] "Opium of the people", Wikipedia https://en.wikipedia.org/wiki/Opium_of_the_people
[241] "Conspiracy theories as part of history: The role of societal crisis situations" by Jan-Willem van Prooijen and Karen Douglas, Memory Studies, 2017 https://journals.sagepub.com/doi/10.1177/1750698017701615
[242] "Conspiracy Theory Entrepreneurs, Movements and Individuals" by Jaron Harambam, Taylor & Francis Group, 2020

https://www.taylorfrancis.com/books/e/9780429452734/chapters/10.4324/9780429452734-3_2

243 "Master of false news gives right-wing Americans headlines they believe", Agence France-Presse, 2020 https://www.france24.com/en/20200216-master-of-false-news-gives-right-wing-americans-headlines-they-believe

244 "Conspiracy theories are dangerous – here's how to crush them" interview with Nancy Rosenblum and Russell Muirhead, The Economist, 2019 https://www.economist.com/open-future/2019/08/12/conspiracy-theories-are-dangerous-heres-how-to-crush-them

245 "The Union of Soviet Socialist Republics (USSR) and the Anti-Apartheid Struggle", South Africa History Online https://sahistory.org.za/article/union-soviet-socialist-republics-ussr-and-anti-apartheid-struggle

246 "Over Where? Cuban Fighters in Angola's Civil War" by Ron Soodalter, History Net, 2016 https://www.historynet.com/cuban-fighters-angolas-civil-war.htm

247 "Dictatorships and Double Standards" by Charles Krauthammer, CNN Inside Politics, 2002 https://edition.cnn.com/2002/ALLPOLITICS/09/16/time.standards/index.html

248 *The End of History and the Last Man* by Francis Fukuyama, Free Press, 1992

249 "Foreign Affairs Big Mac I" by Thomas Friedman, New York Times, 1996 https://www.nytimes.com/1996/12/08/opinion/foreign-affairs-big-mac-i.html

250 *The World Is Flat: A Brief History of the Twenty-first Century* by Thomas Friedman, Farrar, Straus and Giroux, 2005

251 "Have Two McDonald's-Containing Countries Ever Been at War with Each Other?" by Alex Kasprak, Snopes, 2018 https://www.snopes.com/fact-check/mcdonalds-countries-war/

252 "'Whoever leads in AI will rule the world': Putin to Russian children on Knowledge Day", RT, 2017 https://www.rt.com/news/401731-ai-rule-world-putin/

253 "'Fundamental Existential Threat': Lawmakers Warned of the Risks of Killer Robots" by Julia Conley, Common Dreams, 2017 https://www.commondreams.org/news/2017/07/19/fundamental-existential-threat-lawmakers-warned-risks-killer-robots

254 "Life expectancy gap between rich and poor in England widens" by Gareth Iacobucci, BMJ, 2019 https://www.bmj.com/content/364/bmj.l1492.full

255 "Is inequality about to get unimaginably worse?" by Yuval Noah Harari, BBC News, 2017 https://www.bbc.co.uk/news/world-39706765

256 "Costs for orally administered cancer drugs skyrocket", Science Daily, 2016 https://www.sciencedaily.com/releases/2016/04/160428132130.htm

[257] "Expenditures and Prices of Antihyperglycemic Medications in the United States: 2002-2013" by Xinyang Hua et al, JAMA, 2016 https://jamanetwork.com/journals/jama/fullarticle/2510902
[258] "What does the Bible say about Geocentrism", OpenBible https://www.openbible.info/topics/geocentrism
[259] "Pareidolia: Why we see faces in hills, the Moon and toasties" by Lauren Everitt, BBC News, 2013 https://www.bbc.co.uk/news/magazine-22686500
[260] "Exploring the natural foundations of religion" by Justin Barrett, Trends in Cognitive Sciences, 2000 http://behavioralhealth2000.com/wp-content/uploads/2017/12/Exploring-the-natural-foundations-of-religion.pdf
[261] *Religion Explained: The Evolutionary Origins of Religious Thought* by Pascal Boyer, Basic Books, 2001
[262] "Evolution's Sweet Tooth" by Daniel E. Lieberman, New York Times, 2012 https://www.nytimes.com/2012/06/06/opinion/evolutions-sweet-tooth.html
[263] "Obesity and overweight", World Health Organisation, 2020 https://www.who.int/en/news-room/fact-sheets/detail/obesity-and-overweight
[264] "From Diabetes to Athlete's Foot, Our Bodies Are Maladapted for Modern Life" by Jeff Wheelwright, Discover Magazine, 2015 https://www.discovermagazine.com/the-sciences/from-diabetes-to-athletes-foot-our-bodies-are-maladapted-for-modern-life
[265] "The Evolution of Cognitive Bias" by Martie G. Haselton, Daniel Nettle, and Damian R. Murray, The Handbook of Evolutionary Psychology, 2015 https://onlinelibrary.wiley.com/doi/full/10.1002/9781119125563.evpsych241
[266] "List of Cognitive Biases", Wikipedia https://en.wikipedia.org/wiki/List_of_cognitive_biases
[267] "The Cognitive Biases Tricking Your Brain" by Ben Yagoda, The Atlantic, 2018 https://www.theatlantic.com/magazine/archive/2018/09/cognitive-bias/565775/
[268] "Drowning", World Health Organization, 2021 https://www.who.int/news-room/fact-sheets/detail/drowning
[269] "Road traffic injuries", World Health Organization, 2020 https://www.who.int/news-room/fact-sheets/detail/road-traffic-injuries
[270] *Crossing the Chasm: Marketing and Selling High-Tech Products to Mainstream Customers* by Geoffrey Moore, Harper Collins, 1991
[271] "Father of the cell phone", The Economist, 2009 https://www.economist.com/technology-quarterly/2009/06/06/father-of-the-cell-phone

272 "Moore's Law: Transistors per microprocessor", Our World In Data, 2017 https://ourworldindata.org/grapher/transistors-per-microprocessor
273 "Cooper's Law", ArrayComm, 2019 https://web.archive.org/web/20200921033012/http://www.arraycomm.com/technology/coopers-law
274 "De Méré's paradox and the birth of probability theory" by Peter Mander, Carnot Cycle, 2018 https://carnotcycle.wordpress.com/2018/07/02/de-meres-paradox-and-the-birth-of-probability-theory/
275 "A formula for justice" by Angela Saini, The Guardian, 2011 https://www.theguardian.com/law/2011/oct/02/formula-justice-bayes-theorem-miscarriage
276 "Improve statistics in court" by Norman Fenton, Nature, 2011 https://www.nature.com/articles/479036a
277 "How Statisticians Found Air France Flight 447 Two Years After It Crashed Into Atlantic", MIT Technology Review, 2014 https://www.technologyreview.com/2014/05/27/13283/how-statisticians-found-air-france-flight-447-two-years-after-it-crashed-into-atlantic/
278 "Man Vs Maths and a Ship Filled with Gold" by Timothy Revell, The Gist, 2016 https://the-gist.org/2016/09/man-vs-maths-and-a-ship-filled-with-gold/
279 "Bayesian Search for Missing Aircraft" by Lawrence Stone, Metron Scientific Solutions, 2017 https://www.nps.edu/documents/103424533/106018074/Bayes+Search+for+Missing+Aircraft+NPS+20+Apr+2017.pdf
280 "How the Korean War Almost Went Nuclear" by Carl A. Posey, Air & Space Magazine, 2015 https://www.airspacemag.com/military-aviation/how-korean-war-almost-went-nuclear-180955324/
281 "The Doomsday Clock: A timeline of conflict, culture, and change", Bulletin of Atomic Scientists https://thebulletin.org/doomsday-clock/past-statements/
282 "Who will win the presidency?" FiveThirtyEight, 2016 https://projects.fivethirtyeight.com/2016-election-forecast/
283 "The Real Story Of 2016" by Nate Silver, FiveThirtyEight, 2017 https://fivethirtyeight.com/features/the-real-story-of-2016/
284 "Why FiveThirtyEight Gave Trump A Better Chance Than Almost Anyone Else" by Nate Silver, FiveThirtyEight, 2016 https://fivethirtyeight.com/features/why-fivethirtyeight-gave-trump-a-better-chance-than-almost-anyone-else/
285 "The trouble with overconfidence" by Don A. Moore, & Paul J. Healy, Psychological Review, 2008 https://web.archive.org/web/20141106041057/http://repository.cmu.edu/cgi/viewcontent.cgi?article=1340&context=tepper

[286] "Overconfidence, Overoptimism, Halo Effect, and Anchoring" by Lee Merkhofer http://www.prioritysystem.com/reasons1ba.html
[287] "Are we less risky and more skillful than our fellow drivers?" by Ola Svenson, Acta Psychologica, 1981 https://www.sciencedirect.com/science/article/abs/pii/0001691881900056
[288] *The (Honest) Truth About Dishonesty: How We Lie to Everyone – Especially Ourselves* by Dan Ariely, Harper Collins, 2012
[289] "The evolutionary logic of overconfidence" by Max Beilby, Darwinian Business, 2019 https://darwinianbusiness.com/2019/10/12/the-evolutionary-logic-of-overconfidence/
[290] "The evolution of overconfidence" by Dominic Johnson and James Fowler, Nature, 2011 http://fowler.ucsd.edu/evolution_of_overconfidence.pdf
[291] "Queen Elizabeth's finest hour" by Indira Rajaraman, Business Standard, 2012 https://www.business-standard.com/article/opinion/indira-rajaraman-queen-elizabeth-s-finest-hour-112062600065_1.html
[292] "Upton Sinclair" https://en.wikiquote.org/wiki/Upton_Sinclair
[293] "What we have learned 10 years after Chuck Prince told Wall St to keep dancing" by David Wighton, Financial News London, 2017 https://www.fnlondon.com/articles/chuck-princes-dancing-quote-what-we-have-learned-10-years-on-20170714
[294] "This is how we let the credit crunch happen, Ma'am" by Heather Stewart, The Guardian, 2009 https://www.theguardian.com/uk/2009/jul/26/monarchy-credit-crunch
[295] "68–95–99.7 rule", Wikipedia https://en.wikipedia.org/wiki/68%E2%80%9395%E2%80%9399.7_rule
[296] "Goldman pays the price of being big" by Peter Thal Larsen, Financial Times, 2007 https://www.ft.com/content/d2121cb6-49cb-11dc-9ffe-0000779fd2ac
[297] "A Black Swan in the Money Market" by John B. Taylor and John C. Williams, Federal Reserve Bank of San Francisco Working Paper, 2008 https://www.frbsf.org/economic-research/files/wp08-04bk.pdf
[298] "The dangerous disregard for fat tails in quantitative finance", Systematic Risk and Systematic Value, 2018 https://www.sr-sv.com/the-dangerous-disregard-of-fat-tails-in-quantitative-finance/
[299] "Biosecurity Vulnerabilities in Crop Monocultures" by Sam Raasch, Propagate Research, 2017 https://www.propagate.org/research/2017/9/4/biosecurity-vulnerabilities-in-crop-monocultures
[300] "Employment in Agriculture" by Max Roser, Our World In Data, https://ourworldindata.org/employment-in-agriculture

301 "Demographic history of the United States", Wikipedia https://en.wikipedia.org/wiki/Demographic_history_of_the_United_States
302 "Employment in agriculture", The World Bank, 2020 https://data.worldbank.org/indicator/SL.AGR.EMPL.ZS
303 "Anomalies: The Winner's Curse" by Richard H. Thaler, Journal of Economic Perspectives, 1988 https://www.researchgate.net/publication/4719439_Anomalies_The_Winner%27s_Curse
304 "What a 'Lemon' Product Is, and How to Avoid Purchasing One" by Barclay Palmer, Investopedia, 2019 https://www.investopedia.com/articles/pf/11/solutions-to-lemon-problem.asp
305 "Writing the 'The Market for "Lemons"': A Personal Interpretive Essay" by George A. Akerlof, The Nobel Prize, 2001 https://www.nobelprize.org/prizes/economic-sciences/2001/akerlof/article/
306 "How Infection Shaped History: Lessons from the Irish Famine" by William G. Powderly, Transactions of the American Clinical and Climatological Association, 2019 https://www.ncbi.nlm.nih.gov/pmc/articles/PMC6735970/
307 "The Curious Case of Phineas Gage and Others Like Him" by Margarita Tartakovsky, Psych Central, 2018 https://psychcentral.com/blog/the-curious-case-of-phineas-gage-and-others-like-him/
308 "Rambler #134" by Samuel Johnson, 1751 https://www.samueljohnson.com/ram134.html
309 "Works and Days" by Hesiod http://www.perseus.tufts.edu/hopper/text?doc=Perseus:abo:tlg,0020,002:410
310 "The Tyranny of Procrastination: On the origins, mechanics, and defeat of our least favorite trait" by Taylor Mitchell Brown, Medium, 2018 https://medium.com/s/story/the-tyranny-of-procrastination-cfe58511cc22
311 As in *The Ministry for the Future* by Kim Stanley Robinson, Orbit, 2020
312 "What is GAAP?", Corporate Finance Institute https://corporatefinanceinstitute.com/resources/knowledge/accounting/gaap/
313 "Are you ready for these 4 major changes to the accounting rules?", Baker Tilly, 2017 https://www.bakertilly.com/insights/are-you-ready-for-these-4-major-changes-to-the-accounting-rules
314 "The Golden Rule: Treat Others the Way You Want to Be Treated", Effectiviology https://effectiviology.com/golden-rule/
315 Leviticus 19:18
316 Exodus 21:20-21

317 "Measuring the Value of Slaves and Free Persons in Ancient Law" by James Lindgren, Chicago-Kent Law Review, 1995 https://scholarship.kentlaw.iit.edu/cgi/viewcontent.cgi?article=3017&context=cklawreview

318 "Boney M. – Rivers Of Babylon Lyrics", Metrolyrics https://www.metrolyrics.com/rivers-of-babylon-lyrics-boney-m.html

319 "Did God command genocide in the Bible?" by Jonathan Merritt, Religion News Service, 2015 https://religionnews.com/2015/01/12/god-command-genocide-bible/

320 "The Columbian Exchange: A History of Disease, Food, and Ideas" by Nathan Nunn and Nancy Qian, Journal of Economic Perspectives, 2010 https://www.kellogg.northwestern.edu/faculty/qian/resources/NunnQian JEP.pdf

321 "The Behavioral Immune System Shapes Political Intuitions" by Lene Aarøe, Michael Bang Petersen, and Kevin Arceneaux, American Political Science Review, 2017 https://www.cambridge.org/core/journals/american-political-science-review/article/behavioral-immune-system-shapes-political-intuitions-why-and-how-individual-differences-in-disgust-sensitivity-underlie-opposition-to-immigration/AB22952FCB7F270E0D296378D2E330C7

322 "The Tragedy of the Commons" by Garrett Hardin, Science, 1968 https://science.sciencemag.org/content/sci/162/3859/1243.full.pdf

323 "Leviathan Chapter 13: Of the natural condition of mankind as concerning their felicity and misery" by Thomas Hobbes, 1651 http://studymore.org.uk/xhob13.htm

324 "Leviathan Chapter 17: Of the Causes, Generation, and Definition of a Commonwealth" by Thomas Hobbes, 1651 http://studymore.org.uk/xhob17.htm

325 *The Narrow Corridor: States, Societies, and the Fate of Liberty* by Daron Acemoglu and James A. Robinson, Penguin Books, 2019

326 "The scientific background of the International Sanitary Conferences, 1851-1938" by Norman Howard-Jones, World Health Organization, 1975 https://apps.who.int/iris/bitstream/handle/10665/62873/14549_eng.pdf

327 *COVID-19: The Pandemic that Never Should Have Happened and How to Stop the Next One* by Debora MacKenzie, Hatchette Books, 2020

328 "Lodge Reservations", Wikipedia https://en.wikipedia.org/wiki/Lodge_Reservations

329 "Palestine and the Fate of the UN" by Lawrence Davidson, Counterpunch, 2010 https://www.counterpunch.org/2010/11/15/palestine-and-the-fate-of-the-un/

330 "It Takes A Village To Determine The Origins Of An African Proverb" by Joel Goldberg, NPR, 2016

https://www.npr.org/sections/goatsandsoda/2016/07/30/487925796/it-takes-a-village-to-determine-the-origins-of-an-african-proverb
331 *Unweaving the Rainbow: Science, Delusion and the Appetite for Wonder* by Richard Dawkins, Houghton Mifflin, 1998
332 "How the Science of 'Blue Lies' May Explain Trump's Support" by Jeremy Adam Smith, Scientific American, 2017 https://blogs.scientificamerican.com/guest-blog/how-the-science-of-blue-lies-may-explain-trumps-support/
333 "Does This Photograph Document Mike Pence's 'Gay Past'?" by Dan Evon, Snopes, 2016 http://www.snopes.com/mike-pences-gay-past/
334 *Red Teaming: Transform Your Business by Thinking Like the Enemy* by Bryce G. Hoffman, Piatkus, 2017
335 "CEO Forum: Microsoft's Ballmer having a 'great time'" by David Lieberman, USA Today, 2007 http://usatoday30.usatoday.com/money/companies/management/2007-04-29-ballmer-ceo-forum-usat_N.htm
336 "What People Don't Understand About Steve Ballmer" by Matt Rosoff, Business Insider, 2011 https://www.businessinsider.com/what-people-dont-understand-about-steve-ballmer-2011-1
337 "IDC: Mobile Phone Market Q2 2012 – Samsung, Apple top Smartphone vendors by shipments" by Srivatsan Sridhar, Fone Arena, 2012 https://www.fonearena.com/blog/52728/idc-mobile-phone-market-q2-2012-samsung-apple-top-smartphone-vendors-by-shipments.html
338 "Mobile Vendor Market Share Worldwide, Jan - Dec 2017", Stat Counter https://gs.statcounter.com/vendor-market-share/mobile/worldwide/2017
339 "Windows 10 Mobile gets its final death sentence" by Claire Reilly, CNET, 2017 https://www.cnet.com/news/windows-10-mobile-features-hardware-death-sentence-microsoft/
340 "Bill Gates ditches Windows Phone for Android" by Jessica Dolcourt, CNET, 2017 https://www.cnet.com/news/bill-gates-uses-android-phone/
341 "Smartphones and Beyond: Lessons from the remarkable rise and fall of Symbian" by David Wood, 2014 https://smartphonesandbeyond.com/
342 "Time Travel Tuesday: Nokia N95 vs iPhone (Crickey, the N95 was sooo good!)" by Jay Montano, My Nokia Blog, 2013 http://mynokiablog.com/2013/08/13/timetraveltuesday-nokia-n95-vs-iphone-crickey-the-n95-was-sooo-good/
343 "Ballmer Laughs at iPhone", YouTube, 2007 https://www.youtube.com/watch?v=eywi0h_Y5_U
344 "Steve Ballmer finally explains why he thought the iPhone would be a flop" by Chris Smith, BGR, 2016 https://bgr.com/2016/11/04/ballmer-iphone-quote-explained/
345 *The Perfect Thing: How the iPod Shuffles Commerce, Culture, and Coolness* by Stephen Levy, Simon & Schuster, 2006

---

[346] "What you see is what you get" by David Thomas, Daily Telegraph, 2005 https://www.telegraph.co.uk/culture/tvandradio/3637246/What-you-see-is-what-you-get.html

[347] "20 bestselling mobile phones of all time", Daily Telegraph, 2017 https://www.telegraph.co.uk/technology/2016/01/26/the-20-bestselling-mobile-phones-of-all-time/motorola-razr-v3/

[348] "Today in Apple history: Steve Jobs unveils Rokr E1, the first iTunes phone" by Luke Dormehl, Cult of Mac, 2020 https://www.cultofmac.com/444315/apple-history-motorola-rokr-e1/

[349] "Motorola ROKR iTunes phone 'may have flopped' with six times the returns versus normal rate", Mac Daily News, 2005 https://macdailynews.com/2005/10/21/report_motorola_rokr_itunes_phone_may_have_flopped/

[350] "Motorola CEO Ed Zander heads for the exit" by Jack Schofield, The Guardian, 2007 https://www.theguardian.com/technology/blog/2007/nov/30/motorolaceoedzanderheadsf

[351] "Towards the 100 millionth Symbian OS phone" by David Wood, 2001 https://deltawisdom.com/insight/august-2001/

[352] "Forecasting Symbian success" by David Wood, 2014 https://smartphonesandbeyond.com/chapters/part-i/forecasting-symbian-success/

[353] "HMV: Did streaming cause retailer to fail?" by Rory Cellan-Jones, BBC News, 2018 https://www.bbc.co.uk/news/technology-46703208

[354] "The Hemingway Law of Motion: Gradually, then Suddenly" by Timothy Taylor, Conversable Economist, 2015 http://conversableeconomist.blogspot.co.uk/2015/01/the-hemingway-law-of-motion-gradually.html

[355] *The End of Alchemy: Money, Banking, and the Future of the Global Economy* by Mervyn A. King, W. W. Norton, 2016

[356] "Interview with Dr. Rudi Dornbusch" Frontline, 1998 http://www.pbs.org/wgbh/pages/frontline/shows/mexico/interviews/dornbusch.html

[357] *The Road Ahead* by Bill Gates, with Nathan Myhrvold and Peter Rinearson, Viking Penguin, 1995

[358] "Bye-bye Bill" by Rory Cellan-Jones, BBC News, 2008 https://www.bbc.co.uk/blogs/technology/2008/06/byebye_bill.html

[359] "Summary: The Road Ahead, by Bill Gates" by Allen Cheng, https://www.allencheng.com/the-road-ahead-bill-gates-summary-pdf/

[360] "The worst things Bill Gates ever said" by Matt Weinberger, The Independent, 2016 https://www.independent.co.uk/news/people/worst-things-bill-gates-ever-said-a6990046.html

[361] "'Road Ahead': Gates and Our PC Future" by Paul Andrews by Seattle Times, 1995 https://archive.seattletimes.com/archive/?date=19951122&slug=2153890
[362] "Netscape: The IPO that launched an era" by John Shinal, Market Watch, 2005 https://www.marketwatch.com/story/netscape-ipo-ignited-the-boom-taught-some-hard-lessons-20058518550
[363] "May 26, 1995: Gates, Microsoft Jump on 'Internet Tidal Wave'", Wired, 2010 https://www.wired.com/2010/05/0526bill-gates-internet-memo/
[364] "Sept. 28, 1998: Internet Explorer Leaves Netscape in Its Wake" by Michael Calore, Wired, 1998 https://www.wired.com/2009/09/0928ie-beats-netscape/
[365] The more common word for this substance in America is "molasses".
[366] "Smartphones and Beyond: Lessons from the remarkable rise and fall of Symbian" by David Wood, 2014 https://smartphonesandbeyond.com/
[367] "Steve Jobs left designer Jony Ive more power than anyone at Apple" by Sam Oliver, Apple Insider, 2011 https://appleinsider.com/articles/11/10/21/steve_jobs_left_designer_jony_ive_more_power_than_anyone_at_apple
[368] "Back to the future: Dusting off Bill Gates' 'The Road Ahead'" by Sean Gallagher, Ars Technica, 2014 https://arstechnica.com/information-technology/2014/02/back-to-the-future-dusting-off-bill-gates-the-road-ahead/
[369] "Microsoft Names Harel Kodesh and Moshe Lichtman as Vice President", Microsoft, 1998 https://news.microsoft.com/1998/08/27/microsoft-names-harel-kodesh-and-moshe-lichtman-as-vice-president/
[370] *Breaking Windows: How Bill Gates Fumbled the Future of Microsoft* by David Bank, Free Press, 2001
[371] "Who Fatally Wounded Microsoft? It Was Bill Gates" by Mike Cane, iPad Test, 2010 https://ipadtest.wordpress.com/2010/03/11/who-fatally-wounded-microsoft-it-was-bill-gates/
[372] "Disruptive Technologies: Catching the Wave" by Joseph L. Bower and Clayton M. Christensen, Harvard Business Review, 1995 https://hbr.org/1995/01/disruptive-technologies-catching-the-wave
[373] "The Scorpion and the Frog", Wikipedia https://en.wikipedia.org/wiki/The_Scorpion_and_the_Frog
[374] "First look at MS 'Stinger'-based phone" by Richard Shim, ZDNet, 2000 https://www.zdnet.com/article/first-look-at-ms-stinger-based-phone/
[375] "Microsoft's masterplan to screw phone partner – full details" by Andrew Orlowski, The Register, 2003 https://www.theregister.com/2003/01/06/microsofts_masterplan_to_screw_phone/

[376] "Bill Gates' Open Letter to Hobbyists", by William Henry Gates III, Homebrew Computer Club Newsletter, 1976 http://www.digibarn.com/collections/newsletters/homebrew/V2_01/gatesletter.html
[377] "What would you like to see most in minix?" by Linus Benedict Torvalds, comp.os.minix, 1991 https://groups.google.com/forum/#!msg/comp.os.minix/dlNtH7RRrGA/SwRavCzVE7gJ
[378] "An Introduction to Apache Software" by Maximilian Michels, 2017 https://maximilianmichels.com/2017/an-introduction-to-apache-software/
[379] "The Halloween Documents", by Eric S. Raymond, The Cathedral and the Bazaar http://catb.org/~esr/halloween/index.html
[380] "Let's Get This Straight: Microsoft's Halloween scare" by Scott Rosenberg, Salon, 1998 https://www.salon.com/1998/11/04/straight_39/
[381] "The Cathedral and the Bazaar" by Eric S. Raymond, First Monday, 1998 https://firstmonday.org/article/view/578/499
[382] "Highlights/memories of LinuxWorld Spring 1999" by Doran L. Barton, YouTube, 2013 https://www.youtube.com/watch?v=k41nZJp3hDA
[383] "Towards the 100 millionth Symbian OS phone" by David Wood, 2001 https://deltawisdom.com/insight/august-2001/
[384] "100 million Symbian smartphones shipped", Symbian Press, 2006 https://web.archive.org/web/20061127040414/http://www.symbian.com/news/pr/2006/pr20068610.html
[385] "Symbian CEO pitches middle ground between iPhone, Android" by Tom Krazit, CNet, 2008 https://www.cnet.com/news/symbian-ceo-pitches-middle-ground-between-iphone-android/
[386] "1.5 billion Series 40 phones, plus half a billion Symbian too" by Steve Litchfield, All About Symbian, 2012 http://www.allaboutsymbian.com/news/item/14132_15_billion_Series_40_phones_pl.php
[387] "Android activations surpass 500 million, growth rate keeps increasing" by Chip, GSM Arena, 2012 http://blog.gsmarena.com/android-activations-surpass-500-million-growth-rate-keeps-increasing/
[388] "Without Much Fanfare, Apple Has Sold Its 500 Millionth iPhone" by Mark Rogowsky, Forbes, 2014 https://www.forbes.com/sites/markrogowsky/2014/03/25/without-much-fanfare-apple-has-sold-its-500-millionth-iphone/
[389] "Google makes its entry into the wireless world" by Miguel Helft and John Markoff, New York Times, 2007 https://www.nytimes.com/2007/11/05/technology/05iht-05cndgphone.8194320.html

[390] "I, Robot: The Man Behind the Google Phone" by John Markoff, New York Times, 2007 https://www.nytimes.com/2007/11/04/technology/04google.html
[391] "Android just another Linux platform, says Symbian CEO" by Martyn Williams, Washington Post, 2007 https://www.washingtonpost.com/wp-dyn/content/article/2007/11/06/AR2007110600600.html
[392] "Symbian dismisses Google Android" by Darren Waters, BBC News, 2007 http://news.bbc.co.uk/1/hi/technology/7082414.stm
[393] "We're At Mobile World Congress, But Where Is Android?" by Casey Chan, Android Central, 2009 https://xcomputer.website/2016/11/22/were-at-mobile-world-congress-but-where-is-android/
[394] "Google's Mobile-Handset Plans Are Slowed" by Jessica E. Vascellaro and Amol Sharma, Wall Street Journal, 2008 https://www.wsj.com/articles/SB121418837707895947
[395] *Crossing the Chasm: Marketing and Selling Technology Products to Mainstream Customers* by Geoffrey A. Moore, Harper Collins, 1991
[396] *Diffusion of Innovations* by Everett M. Rogers, Free Press of Glencoe, 1962
[397] "The 5 Customer Segments of Technology Adoption", On Digital Marketing https://ondigitalmarketing.com/learn/odm/foundations/5-customer-segments-technology-adoption/
[398] "Smartphones and Beyond: Lessons from the remarkable rise and fall of Symbian" by David Wood, 2014 https://smartphonesandbeyond.com/
[399] "Can a Butterfly in Brazil Really Cause a Tornado in Texas?" by Natalie Wolchover, Live Science, 2011 https://www.livescience.com/17455-butterfly-effect-weather-prediction.html
[400] "How far out can we forecast the weather? Scientists have a new answer" by Paul Voosen, Science, 2019 https://www.sciencemag.org/news/2019/02/how-far-out-can-we-forecast-weather-scientists-have-new-answer
[401] "How a Lunar Eclipse Saved Columbus" by Joe Rao, Space, 2008 https://www.space.com/2729-lunar-eclipse-saved-columbus.html
[402] "Regiomontanus" by Adam Mosley, Cambridge History and Philosophy of Science, 1999 http://www.sites.hps.cam.ac.uk/starry/regiomontanus.html
[403] "The Fourth Voyage of Christopher Columbus" by Christopher Minster, Thought Co, 2019 https://www.thoughtco.com/fourth-new-world-voyage-christopher-columbus-2136698
[404] "Investor lessons from a market bubble that cost Isaac Newton a bundle" by Barbara Kollmeyer, Market Watch, 2016 http://www.marketwatch.com/story/investor-lessons-from-a-market-bubble-that-cost-isaac-newton-a-bundle-2016-08-25

[405] "How Isaac Newton went flat broke chasing a stock bubble" by Tim Price, Sovereign Man, 2013 https://www.sovereignman.com/finance/how-isaac-newton-went-flat-broke-chasing-a-stock-bubble-13268/
[406] "Excerpt from the 'Special Message to the Congress on Urgent National Needs'" by President John F. Kennedy, NASA, 1961 https://www.nasa.gov/vision/space/features/jfk_speech_text.html
[407] "Concept to Apollo: Beginnings through July 1960" by Ivan D. Ertel and Mary Louise Morse, NASA, 1979 https://www.hq.nasa.gov/office/pao/History/SP-4009/v1p1.htm
[408] "Destination Moon", IMDb https://www.imdb.com/title/tt0042393/
[409] "The British Interplanetary Society" https://www.bis-space.com/what-we-do/the-british-interplanetary-society
[410] "First dog in space died within hours" by David Whitehouse, BBC News, 2002 http://news.bbc.co.uk/1/hi/sci/tech/2367681.stm
[411] "Sputnik Reconsidered: Image and Reality in the Early Space Age" by Kim McQuaid, Canadian Review of American Studies, 2007 http://hsci3331spaceracefinalproject.weebly.com/uploads/1/2/7/1/12719548/kim_mcquaid_sputnik_reconsidered_image_and_reality_in_the_early_space_age.pdf
[412] *Sputnik: The Shock of the Century* by Paul Dickson, Walker & Company, 2001
[413] "Wunderwaffen: The History of Rocketry – Race For Space" by Walther Johann von Lopp, 2010 http://v33v.tripod.com/ww3.html
[414] "The Feasibility Studies" by Courtney G Brooks, James M. Grimwood, Loyd S. Swenson, NASA, 1979 https://www.hq.nasa.gov/office/pao/History/SP-4205/ch1-7.html
[415] "Address To Joint Session Of Congress May 25, 1961", John F. Kennedy Presidential Library and Museum, https://www.jfklibrary.org/learn/about-jfk/historic-speeches/address-to-joint-session-of-congress-may-25-1961
[416] "Enchanted Rendezvous: John C. Houbolt and the Genesis of the Lunar-Orbit Rendezvous Concept" by James R. Hansen, NASA, 1999 https://history.nasa.gov/monograph4.pdf
[417] "John F. Kennedy Moon Speech – Rice Stadium", NASA, 1962 https://er.jsc.nasa.gov/seh/ricetalk.htm
[418] "'We have a fire in the cockpit!' The Apollo 1 disaster 50 years later" by Sarah Larimer, Washington Post, 2017 https://www.washingtonpost.com/news/speaking-of-science/wp/2017/01/26/50-years-ago-three-astronauts-died-in-the-apollo-1-fire/
[419] "How Luck Made Neil Armstrong the First Man on the Moon" by Amy Shira Teitel, Discover, 2019 https://www.discovermagazine.com/the-sciences/how-luck-made-neil-armstrong-the-first-man-on-the-moon

[420] "The Moon Landing: An Undelivered Nixon Speech", by Bill Safire, Presidential library, 1969 https://watergate.info/1969/07/20/an-undelivered-nixon-speech.html
[421] "The Rendezvous That Almost Wasn't" by Kathy Barnstorff, NASA, 2004 https://www.nasa.gov/vision/space/features/apollo_lor.html
[422] "Remarks on Signing the National Cancer Act of 1971" by Richard Nixon, The American Presidency Project https://www.presidency.ucsb.edu/documents/remarks-signing-the-national-cancer-act-1971
[423] "Milestone 1971", National Cancer Institute https://dtp.cancer.gov/timeline/flash/milestones/M4_Nixon.htm
[424] "The Long War on Cancer: Transcript" by Jill Rosenbaum, Olivia Katrandjian, and Anne Alvergue, Retro Report, 2013 https://www.retroreport.org/transcript/the-long-war-on-cancer/
[425] "Cancer deaths in 1970 and in 1997" by Gilbert Ling, 1997, https://www.gilbertling.org/lp2.htm
[426] "Sidney Farber, MD", Dana-Farber Cancer Institute https://www.dana-farber.org/about-us/history-and-milestones/sidney-farber,-md/
[427] "A tribute to Sidney Farber – the father of modern chemotherapy" by Denis R. Miller, British Journal of Haematology, 2006 https://onlinelibrary.wiley.com/doi/full/10.1111/j.1365-2141.2006.06119.x
[428] "Cancer Wars", US National Library of Medicine https://profiles.nlm.nih.gov/spotlight/tl/feature/cancer
[429] "The War on Cancer, 40 years later", Dana-Farber Cancer Institute, 2011 https://blog.dana-farber.org/insight/2011/12/the-war-on-cancer-40-years-later/
[430] "The Lasker Awards: A history of 'America's Nobels'" by David N. Keegan, Cell Mentor, 2018 http://crosstalk.cell.com/blog/the-lasker-awards-a-history-of-americas-nobels
[431] "Notable New Yorkers: Mary Lasker", Columbia University, 2006 http://www.columbia.edu/cu/lweb/digital/collections/nny/laskerm/transcripts/laskerm_1_7_183.html
[432] "Mr. Nixon: You Can Cure Cancer" by Citizens Committee for the Conquest of Cancer, Washington Post, 1969 https://profiles.nlm.nih.gov/spotlight/tl/catalog/nlm:nlmuid-101584665X20-doc
[433] *The Emperor of All Maladies: A Biography of Cancer* by Siddhartha Mukherjee, Scribner, 2010
[434] "Cancer Wars", US National Library of Medicine https://profiles.nlm.nih.gov/spotlight/tl/feature/cancer
[435] *The Emperor of All Maladies: A Biography of Cancer* by Siddhartha Mukherjee, Scribner, 2010

[436] *Rebel Cell: Cancer, Evolution and the Science of Life* by Kat Arney, Weidenfeld & Nicolson, 2020
[437] "Is the war on cancer an 'utter failure'?: A sobering look at how billions in research money is spent" by Tom Blackwell, National Post, 2013 https://nationalpost.com/news/war-on-cancer
[438] "Fifty years in fusion and the way forward" by J. Jacquinot, Nuclear Fusion, 2009 https://www.researchgate.net/publication/231115363_Fifty_years_in_fusion_and_the_way_forward
[439] "Homi Bhabha and how World War II was responsible for creating India's nuclear future" by Taran Deol, The Print, 2019 https://theprint.in/theprint-profile/homi-bhabha-and-how-world-war-ii-was-responsible-for-creating-indias-nuclear-future/312842/
[440] "Forever 20 years away: will we ever have a working nuclear fusion reactor?" by Michael Brooks, New Statesman, 2014 https://www.newstatesman.com/sci-tech/2014/11/forever-20-years-away-will-we-ever-have-working-nuclear-fusion-reactor
[441] "Nuclear Fusion: Holy Grail of Energy" by Quamrul Haider, Nuclear Fusion, 2019 https://www.researchgate.net/publication/330947985_Nuclear_Fusion_Holy_Grail_of_Energy
[442] "Fusion history beyond the fiascos" by Jean Jacquinot, Nature, 2009 https://www.nature.com/articles/457265a
[443] "Fusion energy pushed back beyond 2050" by Edwin Cartlidge, BBC News, 2017 https://www.bbc.co.uk/news/science-environment-40558758
[444] "We've Long Waited for Fusion. This Reactor May Finally Deliver It – Fast" by Caroline Delbert, Popular Mechanics, 2020 https://www.popularmechanics.com/science/energy/a34224299/nuclear-fusion-compact-reactor-sparc-timeline/
[445] "Two British companies confident of nuclear fusion breakthrough" by Clive Cookson, Financial Times, 2019 https://www.ft.com/content/a8d0a7e4-20e3-11ea-b8a1-584213ee7b2b
[446] "Nuclear fusion project leader laments 'uncontrollable' political forces" by Carmen Rodríguez, Euractiv, 2016 https://www.euractiv.com/section/energy/news/nuclear-fusion-project-leader-laments-uncontrollable-political-forces/
[447] "The ITER story", Iter, https://www.iter.org/proj/iterhistory
[448] "5 Big Ideas for Making Fusion Power a Reality" by Tom Clynes, IEEE Spectrum, 2020 https://spectrum.ieee.org/energy/nuclear/5-big-ideas-for-making-fusion-power-a-reality
[449] "1986: Coal mine canaries made redundant", BBC News http://news.bbc.co.uk/onthisday/hi/dates/stories/december/30/newsid_2547000/2547587.stm

[450] Chapter 3 of *Taking the Medicine: A Short History of Medicine's Beautiful Idea, and our Difficulty Swallowing It* by Druin Burch, Chatto & Windus, 2009
[451] "Karl Popper on The Line Between Science and Pseudoscience", Farnam Street blog, 2016 https://fs.blog/2016/01/karl-popper-on-science-pseudoscience/
[452] "Science and Pseudo-Science", Stanford Encyclopedia of Philosophy, 2017 https://plato.stanford.edu/entries/pseudo-science/
[453] "Lunar orbit rendezvous", Wikipedia https://en.wikipedia.org/wiki/Lunar_orbit_rendezvous
[454] "Why companies fail - the rise and fall of HMV" by Philip Beeching, 2012 http://www.philipbeeching.com/2012/08/why-companies-fail-rise-and-fall-of-hmv.html
[455] "Harry Truman vs. The Volcano" by John Jennings, The IFOD, 2020 https://www.theifod.com/harry-truman-vs-the-volcano/
[456] "1980 eruption of Mount St. Helens", Wikipedia, https://en.wikipedia.org/wiki/1980_eruption_of_Mount_St._Helens
[457] "Thomas Kuhn", Stanford Encyclopedia of Philosophy, 2018 https://plato.stanford.edu/entries/thomas-kuhn/
[458] "Cholera epidemics in Victorian London", The Gazette, 2016 https://www.thegazette.co.uk/all-notices/content/100519
[459] "Celebration: William Farr (1807–1883) – an appreciation on the 200th anniversary of his birth" by DE Lilienfeld, International Journal of Epidemiology, 2007 https://academic.oup.com/ije/article/36/5/985/775018
[460] "Death and miasma in Victorian London: an obstinate belief" by Stephen Halliday, BMJ, 2001 https://www.ncbi.nlm.nih.gov/pmc/articles/PMC1121911
[461] "A 'disease mist… an angel of death'" by Stephen Halliday, UCLA Department of Epidemiology http://www.ph.ucla.edu/epi/snow/farr/farr_mist.html
[462] "John Snow and the Broad Street Pump" by Kathleen Tuthill, Cricket, 2003 https://www.ph.ucla.edu/epi/snow/snowcricketarticle.html
[463] "Reverend Henry Whitehead" by Ralph R. Frerichs, UCLA Department of Epidemiology http://www.ph.ucla.edu/epi/Snow/whitehead.html
[464] "Index case at 40 Broad Street" by Ralph R. Frerichs, UCLA Department of Epidemiology https://www.ph.ucla.edu/epi/snow/indexcase.html
[465] "The Broad Street Pump: An Episode in the Cholera Epidemic of 1854" by Henry Whitehead, Macmillan's Magazine, 1865 https://books.google.com/books?id=iSiFb2ANrG8C&pg=PA113
[466] "Dr John Snow and Reverend Whitehead" by Peter Daniel and David Markoff, Cholera and the Thames http://www.choleraandthethames.co.uk/cholera-in-london/cholera-in-soho/

467 "The changing assessments of John Snow's and William Farr's cholera studies" by John M. Eyler, Soz.- Präventivmed, 2001 https://web.archive.org/web/20180728035635/http://www.epidemiology.ch/history/papers/eyler-paper-1.pdf

468 "Sir Joseph Bazalgette (1819-1891)" by Jacqueline Banerjee, Victorian Web, 2011 http://www.victorianweb.org/technology/engineers/bazalgette.html

469 "How Bazalgette built London's first super-sewer" by Alwyn Collinson, Museum of London, 2019 https://www.museumoflondon.org.uk/discover/how-bazalgette-built-londons-first-super-sewer

470 "Death and miasma in Victorian London: an obstinate belief" by Stephen Halliday, BMJ, 2001 https://www.ncbi.nlm.nih.gov/pmc/articles/PMC1121911

471 "Joseph Bazalgette", History https://www.history.co.uk/biographies/joseph-bazalgette

472 "Contesting the Science of Smoking" by David Heath, The Atlantic, 2016 https://www.theatlantic.com/politics/archive/2016/05/low-tar-cigarettes/481116/

473 "Addendum to 'Assessing ExxonMobil's climate change communications (1977–2014)'" by Geoffrey Supran and Naomi Oreskes, Environmental Research Letters, 2020 https://iopscience.iop.org/article/10.1088/1748-9326/ab89d5

474 "The EPA is meant to protect us. The Monsanto trials suggest it isn't doing that" by Nathan Donley and Carey Gillam, The Guardian, 2019 https://www.theguardian.com/commentisfree/2019/may/07/epa-monsanto-round-up-trial

475 "The greatest steps towards the discovery of Vibrio cholerae" by D. Lippia and E. Gotuzzo, Clinical Microbiology and Infection, 2014 https://www.sciencedirect.com/science/article/pii/S1198743X14608557

476 "Multiple Nobel Laureate: Linus Pauling", Nobel Prize, https://www.nobelprize.org/laureate/217

477 *The scientific 100: a ranking of the most influential scientists, past and present* by John G. Simmons, Citadel Press, 1996

478 "The Vitamin Myth: Why We Think We Need Supplements" by Paul Offit, The Atlantic, 2013 https://www.theatlantic.com/health/archive/2013/07/the-vitamin-myth-why-we-think-we-need-supplements/277947/

479 "Vitamin C", NHS https://www.nhs.uk/conditions/vitamins-and-minerals/vitamin-c/

480 "Is it possible to take too much vitamin C?" by Katherine Zeratsky, Mayo Clinic, 2020 https://www.mayoclinic.org/healthy-lifestyle/nutrition-and-healthy-eating/expert-answers/vitamin-c/faq-20058030

[481] *Vitamin C, the Common Cold and the Flu* by Linus Pauling, W.H.Freeman & Co, 1976
[482] "How Linus Pauling duped America into believing vitamin C cures colds" by Megan Thielking, Vox, 2015 https://www.vox.com/2015/1/15/7547741/vitamin-c-myth-pauling
[483] "The Vitamin Myth: Why We Think We Need Supplements" by Paul Offit, The Atlantic, 2013 https://www.theatlantic.com/health/archive/2013/07/the-vitamin-myth-why-we-think-we-need-supplements/277947/
[484] "Why vitamin pills don't work, and may be bad for you", BBC Future https://www.bbc.com/future/article/20161208-why-vitamin-supplements-could-kill-you
[485] "The Loss of Vitamin C: One More Proof for Evolution" by Bruno Van de Casteele, Skeptoid Blog, 2014 https://skeptoid.com/blog/2014/08/17/the-loss-of-vitamin-c-one-more-proof-for-evolution/
[486] Discussed in Chapter 7 of my 2016 book *The Abolition of Aging*
[487] "High Doses of Vitamin C Are Not Effective as a Cancer Treatment" by Stephen Barrett, Quackwatch, 2011 https://quackwatch.org/related/cancer/c/
[488] "The Founding of the Institute of Orthomolecular Medicine", Pauling Blog, 2013 https://paulingblog.wordpress.com/2013/03/13/the-founding-of-the-institute-of-orthomolecular-medicine/
[489] "High dose vitamin C and cancer: Has Linus Pauling been vindicated?" by David Groski, Science-Based Medicine, 2008 https://sciencebasedmedicine.org/high-dose-vitamin-c-and-cancer-has-linus-pauling-been-vindicated/
[490] "De re militari", Wikipedia https://en.wikipedia.org/wiki/De_re_militari
[491] "Fat Man: Herman Kahn and the nuclear age" by Louis Menand, The New Yorker, 2005 http://www.pages.drexel.edu/~ina22/301/hnrs301-text-fat_man.htm
[492] "America's Nuclear Triad" https://www.defense.gov/Experience/Americas-Nuclear-Triad/
[493] "Multiple Independently-targetable Reentry Vehicle (MIRV)", Center for Arms Control and Non-Proliferation https://armscontrolcenter.org/multiple-independently-targetable-reentry-vehicle-mirv/
[494] *Future Shock* by Alvin Toffler, Random House, 1970
[495] *Thinking about the Unthinkable* by Herman Kahn, Horizon Press, 1962
[496] "America's Greatest Movies", American Film Institute, 1998 https://web.archive.org/web/20110313150543/http://www.afi.com/Docs/100Years/movies100.pdf

[497] "Herman Kahn: The physicist, nuclear-war strategist, and Cold War 'scenario planner' who inspired Kubrick's 'Dr. Strangelove'" by Boban Docevski, Vintage News, 2017 https://www.thevintagenews.com/2017/12/03/dr-strangelove-inspiration/

[498] *The Seven Sisters: The Great Oil Companies and the World they Shaped* by Anthony Sampson, Viking Press, 1975

[499] "Historical Crude Oil prices, 1861 to Present", ChartsBin http://chartsbin.com/view/oau

[500] "Sisters Under Stress" by Anthony Sampson, Journey to Forever, http://journeytoforever.org/biofuel_library/sevensisters/7sisters9.html

[501] "Brief History", OPEC https://www.opec.org/opec_web/en/about_us/24.htm

[502] "Libya and Britain: A Study of the History of British-Libyan Relations 1969-1979" by Ali Abdussalam Abdulla Ali, Nottingham Trent University, 2014 https://core.ac.uk/download/pdf/30624181.pdf

[503] Chapter "Mystics" in *The Age of Heretics: Heroes, Outlaws, and the Forerunners of Corporate Change* by Art Kleiner, Nicholas Brealey, 1996

[504] "Promoting American leadership and global engagement for a secure, free, and prosperous future", Hudson Institute https://www.hudson.org/about

[505] *The Year 2000: A Framework for Speculation on the Next Thirty-three Years* by Herman Kahn and Anthony J. Wiener, Macmillan, 1967

[506] *The Emerging Japanese Superstate: Challenge and Response* by Herman Kahn, Prentice Hall, 1970

[507] "What Can Past Technology Forecasts Tell Us About the Future?" by Richard E. Albright, Technological Forecasting and Social Change, 2002 http://www.albrightstrategy.com/papers/Albright_Past_Forecasts.pdf

[508] "Pierre Wack", The Economist, 2008 https://www.economist.com/news/2008/08/29/pierre-wack

[509] "The man who saw the future" by Art Kleiner, Thought Leaders, 2003 https://www.strategy-business.com/article/8220?gko=4447f

[510] "Scenarios: Uncharted Waters Ahead" by Pierre Wack, Harvard Business Review, 1985 https://hbr.org/1985/09/scenarios-uncharted-waters-ahead

[511] "Forty Years of Shell Scenarios", Shell, 2012 https://www.shell.com/promos/forty-years-of-shell-scenarios/_jcr_content.stream/1448557479375/a0e75f042fee5322b72780ee36e5ba17c35a4fc6/shell-scenarios-40yearsbook080213.pdf

[512] "The scenario approach to possible futures for oil and natural gas" by Jeremy Bentham, Energy Policy, 2014 https://www.sciencedirect.com/science/article/pii/S0301421513008124

[513] "Exploring Alternatives to the War on Drugs" by Adam Kahane, Stanford Social Innovation Review, 2013 https://ssir.org/articles/entry/exploring_alternatives_to_the_war_in_drugs

[514] "Adam Kahane", Reos Partners https://reospartners.com/reos-management/adam-kahane/
[515] "How to Change the Future" by Adam Kahane, RSA video, 2012 https://www.youtube.com/watch?v=XiGS9Vq0FGA
[516] Chapter 8, "New Stories Can Generate New Realities" in *Transformative Scenario Planning: Working Together to Change the Future* by Adam Kahane, Berrett-Koehler Publishers, 2012
[517] Chapter 4, "Unconventional, Stretch Collaboration Is Becoming Essential" in *Collaborating with the Enemy: How to Work with People You Don't Agree with or Like or Trust* by Adam Kahane, Berrett-Koehler Publishers, 2017
[518] "Destino Colombia 1997-2000: A Treasure to be Revealed" by Alfredo de León and Elena Díez Pinto, Democratic Dialogue Network, 2000 http://www.democraticdialoguenetwork.org/files/documents_bk_marzo_7/271/attachment/CivicDialogueWorkshop-English.pdf
[519] "The Nobel Peace Prize for 2016", Nobel Prize, 2016 https://www.nobelprize.org/prizes/peace/2016/press-release/
[520] "President Juan Manuel Santos' prologue to the Spanish language edition of Adam Kahane's book *Collaborating with the Enemy*" by Juan Manuel Santos, Reos Partners, 2018 https://reospartners.com/prologue-to-the-spanish-language-edition-of-adam-kahanes-book-collaborating-with-the-enemy-how-to-work-with-people-you-dont-agree-with-or-like-or-trust/
[521] *Leading Change* by John Kotter, Harvard Business Review Press, 1988
[522] "Brent Spar", Wikipedia https://en.wikipedia.org/wiki/Brent_Spar
[523] "Case Study: Brent Spar", Fisheries Research Services https://www2.gov.scot/Uploads/Documents/AE07Brent2004.pdf
[524] "Lessons from Exxon Valdez, 25 years later" by Richard Steiner, Greenpeace, 2014 https://www.greenpeace.org/usa/lessons-from-exxon-valdez-25-years-later/
[525] "Predictable Surprises: The Disasters You Should Have Seen Coming" by Michael D. Watkins and Max H. Bazerman, Harvard Business Review, 2003 https://hbr.org/2003/04/predictable-surprises-the-disasters-you-should-have-seen-coming
[526] "Greenpeace: A history of confrontation" by Martin Koch, DW, 2013 https://www.dw.com/en/greenpeace-a-history-of-confrontation/g-17119321
[527] "The Brent Spar Fight" by Jack Doyle, Pop History Dig, 2020 https://www.pophistorydig.com/topics/greenpeace-shell-brent-spar/
[528] "Greenpeace vs the Brent Spar (From Crude Britannia: The Story of North Sea Oil)", ricjl, YouTube, 2019 https://www.youtube.com/watch?v=0INCoJvEFdw
[529] "Brent Spar Greenpeace vs. Shell", Planet Film International, YouTube, 2010 https://www.youtube.com/watch?v=KToV-c8uvPc

[530] "Giant Outsmarted: How Greenpeace Sank Shell's Plan to Dump Big Oil Rig in Atlantic" by Bhushan Bahree, Kyle Pope, and Allanna Sullivan, Wall Street Journal, 1995 http://www.pitt.edu/~mitnick/EBEweb/Greenpeace7_7_95.html

[531] "Brent Spar Revisited, 10 Years On" by Thomas Mösch, DW, 2005 https://www.dw.com/en/brent-spar-revisited-10-years-on/a-1621883

[532] "Pipe Dreams: Ken Saro-Wiwa, Environmental Justice, and Micro-Minority Rights" by Rob Nixon, Black Renaissance, 1996 https://web.archive.org/web/20141220005732/http://english.wisc.edu/rdnixon/files/pipe_dreams.pdf

[533] "Shell pays out $15.5m over Saro-Wiwa killing" by Ed Pilkington, The Guardian, 2009 https://www.theguardian.com/world/2009/jun/08/nigeria-usa

[534] "Seeds of NGO Activism: Shell Capitulates in Saro-Wiwa Case" by Jon Entine, NGO Watch, 2009 https://web.archive.org/web/20150508150554/http://www.aei.org/publication/seeds-of-ngo-activism-shell-capitulates-in-saro-wiwa-case/

[535] "It took five tries to hang Saro-Wiwa" by Frank Aigbogun, The Independent, 1995 https://www.independent.co.uk/news/world/it-took-five-tries-to-hang-saro-wiwa-1581703.html

[536] "Bio" https://www.sas.upenn.edu/tetlock/bio

[537] *Superforecasting: The Art and Science of Prediction* by Philip E. Tetlock and Dan Gardner, Crown, 2015

[538] "Frequently Asked Questions (FAQ)", Good Judgement Open, 2019 https://www.gjopen.com/faq

[539] "Welcome to Good Judgment® Open" https://www.gjopen.com/

[540] *The Hedgehog and the Fox: An Essay on Tolstoy's View of History* by Isaiah Berlin, Weidenfeld & Nicolson, 1953

[541] *Good to Great: Why Some Companies Make the Leap and Others Don't* by Jim Collins, Random House Business, 2001

[542] "The Hedgehog Concept", Jim Collins https://www.jimcollins.com/concepts/the-hedgehog-concept.html

[543] "Scanning the Environment: PESTEL Analysis", Business To You, 2017 https://www.business-to-you.com/scanning-the-environment-pestel-analysis/

[544] Classic articles on transhumanism are collected together in *The Transhumanist Reader: Classical and Contemporary Essays on the Science, Technology, and Philosophy of the Human Future* edited by Max More and Natasha Vita-More, Wiley-Blackwell, 2013. For a thorough account of the history (and prehistory) of transhumanism, see "A History of Transhumanism" by Elise Bohan, PhD thesis, Macquarie University, 2018 https://www.researchgate.net/publication/332289738_A_History_of_Transhumanism

[545] "An Excerpt From *The Singularity Is Near*" by Ray Kurzweil, Penguin, 2005 https://www.penguin.com/ajax/books/excerpt/9780143037880
[546] *The Age of Spiritual Machines: When Computers Exceed Human Intelligence* by Ray Kurzweil, Viking Press, 1999
[547] "Singularity Q&A" by Ray Kurzweil, Kurzweil AI, 2005, https://www.kurzweilai.net/singularity-q-a
[548] "The Immortal Ambitions of Ray Kurzweil: A Review of *Transcendent Man*" by John Rennie, Scientific American, 2011 https://www.scientificamerican.com/article/the-immortal-ambitions-of-ray-kurzweil/
[549] "The six epochs of evolution" by Jason Silva, YouTube, 2012 https://www.youtube.com/watch?v=KNkW353QkxU
[550] "The Singularity is Near: How Kurzweil's Predictions Are Faring" by Paul Feakins, Antropy, 2017 https://www.antropy.co.uk/blog/the-singularity-is-near-how-kurzweils-predictions-are-faring/
[551] "Assessing Kurzweil: the results" by Stuart Armstrong, Less Wrong, 2013 https://www.lesswrong.com/posts/kbA6T3xpxtko36GgP/assessing-kurzweil-the-results
[552] *Collapse: How Societies Choose to Fail or Succeed* by Jared Diamond, Viking Press, 2005
[553] "Bibliography of Works Providing Estimates of Life Expectancy at Birth" by James C. Riley, Life Table, 2005 https://www.lifetable.de/RileyBib.pdf
[554] "Life expectancy per country from 1543 to 2019" by Alberto Maria Falletta, Kaggle, 2020 https://www.kaggle.com/albeffe/life-expectancy-per-country-from-1543-to-2019
[555] For a graphical representation see Our World in Data, https://ourworldindata.org/grapher/life-expectancy?tab=chart&country=~GBR
[556] Our World in Data, https://ourworldindata.org/grapher/life-expectancy?tab=chart&country=~SWE
[557] "US life expectancy is still on the decline. Here's why" by Jen Christensen, CNN, 2019 https://edition.cnn.com/2019/11/26/health/us-life-expectancy-decline-study/index.html
[558] Section "Moore's Law Was Not the First, but the Fifth Paradigm To Provide Exponential Growth of Computing" in "The Law of Accelerating Returns" by Ray Kurzweil, Kurzweil AI, 2001 https://www.kurzweilai.net/the-law-of-accelerating-returns
[559] "Change: The beguiling nature of exponential curves" by Nic Brisbourne, The Equity Kicker, 2017 http://www.theequitykicker.com/2017/05/31/change-the-beguiling-nature-of-exponential-curves/

[560] "What is happening to life expectancy in the UK?" by Veena Raleigh, The Kings Fund, 2020 https://www.kingsfund.org.uk/publications/whats-happening-life-expectancy-uk

[561] "GDP per capita in England", Our World in Data, 2020 https://ourworldindata.org/grapher/gdp-per-capita-in-the-uk-since-1270

[562] "Average years of schooling", Our World in Data, 2018 https://ourworldindata.org/grapher/mean-years-of-schooling-long-run?tab=chart&country=~GBR

[563] "History of Energy in the United States: 1635-2000", Energy Information Administration (EIA), 2008 https://web.archive.org/web/20100107032323/http://www.eia.doe.gov/emeu/aer/eh/frame.html

[564] "Harnessing the Void: How the Industrial revolution began in a Vacuum" by Robert O. Woods, American Society of Mechanical Engineers, 2003 https://asmedigitalcollection.asme.org/memagazineselect/article/125/12/38/379686/Harnessing-the-VoidHow-the-Industrial-revolution

[565] "Industrial Revolution", Wikipedia https://en.wikipedia.org/wiki/Industrial_Revolution

[566] "We're living through a new industrial revolution" by Andrew McAfee, Financial Times, 2014 https://www.ft.com/content/e6218eaa-0675-3ee2-8d54-3599d7560386

[567] "The Unreasonable Effectiveness of Mathematics in the Natural Sciences" by Eugene Wigner, Communications in Pure and Applied Mathematics, 1960 https://www.dartmouth.edu/~matc/MathDrama/reading/Wigner.html

[568] "GCHQ pioneers on birth of public key crypto" by Tom Espiner, ZDnet, 2010 https://www.zdnet.com/article/gchq-pioneers-on-birth-of-public-key-crypto/

[569] "The Golden Age of Theoretical Physics: P.A.M. Dirac's Scientific Work from 1924 to 1933" by Jagdish Mehra, 1972 https://www.osti.gov/servlets/purl/4661346

[570] "Nothing in Biology Makes Sense Except in the Light of Evolution" by Theodosius Dobzhansky, The American Biology Teacher, 1973 https://www.pbs.org/wgbh/evolution/library/10/2/text_pop/l_102_01.html

[571] "10 Reasons Countries Fall Apart" by Daron Acemoglu and James A. Robinson, Foreign Policy, 2012 https://foreignpolicy.com/2012/06/18/10-reasons-countries-fall-apart/

[572] "The Second Industrial Revolution, 1870-1914" by Ryan Engelman, U.S. History Scene, https://ushistoryscene.com/article/second-industrial-revolution/

[573] "The Fourth Industrial Revolution: what it means, how to respond" by Klaus Schwab, World Economic Forum, 2016

https://www.weforum.org/agenda/2016/01/the-fourth-industrial-revolution-what-it-means-and-how-to-respond/

574 "Technological Revolutions and the Shape of Tomorrow" by Carlota Perez, Baillie Gifford, 2020 https://www.bailliegifford.com/en/uk/individual-investors/funds/scottish-mortgage-investment-trust/insights/ic-video/2020-q2-paradigm-shifts-with-carlota-perez-ind-we-1682

575 "Kondratiev wave", Wikipedia https://en.wikipedia.org/wiki/Kondratiev_wave

576 "The Kondratieff Cycle: Real or Fabricated?" by Murray Rothbard, Investment Insights, 1984 https://www.lewrockwell.com/1970/01/murray-n-rothbard/business-cycles-real-and-fabricated/

577 "On Computable Numbers, with an Application to the Entscheidungsproblem" by Alan Turing, Princeton University, 1936 http://www.cs.virginia.edu/~robins/Turing_Paper_1936.pdf

578 "History of programming languages" by Justin Lestal, Devskiller, 2020 https://devskiller.com/history-of-programming-languages/

579 "Why Software Is Eating the World" by Marc Andreessen, The Wall Street Journal, 2011 https://a16z.com/2011/08/20/why-software-is-eating-the-world/

580 "How Zynga is rising from the dead" by Dawn Kawamoto, San Francisco Business Times, 2019 https://www.bizjournals.com/sanfrancisco/news/2019/10/31/how-zynga-is-rising-from-the-dead.html

581 "You May Have Forgotten Foursquare, but It Didn't Forget You" by Paris Martinea, Wired, 2019 https://www.wired.com/story/you-may-have-forgotten-foursquare-it-didnt-forget-you/

582 "Metcalfe's Law Recurses Down the Long Tail of Social Networks" by Robert Metcalfe, VC Mike's blog, 2006 https://vcmike.wordpress.com/2006/08/18/metcalfe-social-networks/

583 "Predicting the Internet's catastrophic collapse and ghost sites galore in 1996" by Bob Metcalfe, InfoWorld, 1995 https://web.archive.org/web/19990913041024/http://www.infoworld.com/cgi-bin/displayNew.pl?/metcalfe/bm120495.htm

584 *The Cuckoo's Egg: Tracking a Spy Through the Maze of Computer Espionage* by Clifford Stoll, Doubleday, 1989

585 "25 years on, here are the worst ever predictions about the internet" by Amelia Tait, New Stateman, 2016 https://www.newstatesman.com/science-tech/internet/2016/08/25-years-here-are-worst-ever-predictions-about-internet

586 "Why the Web Won't Be Nirvana" by Clifford Stoll, Newsweek, 1995 https://www.newsweek.com/clifford-stoll-why-web-wont-be-nirvana-185306

[587] "Sage who warned of Net's collapse eats his words" by W. John MacMullen, Reuters, 1997 http://www.ibiblio.org/pjones/ils310/msg00259.html
[588] "Newsweek in 1995: Why the Internet will Fail" by Zee M. Kane, The Next Web, 2010 https://thenextweb.com/shareables/2010/02/27/newsweek-1995-buy-books-newspapers-straight-intenet-uh/
[589] "We'd Better Watch Out" by Robert M. Solow, New York Times, 1987 http://www.standupeconomist.com/pdf/misc/solow-computer-productivity.pdf
[590] "Robert M. Solow: Facts", The Nobel Prize Organization, 1987 https://www.nobelprize.org/prizes/economic-sciences/1987/solow/
[591] "Technical Change and the Aggregate Production Function" by Robert M. Solow, The Review of Economics and Statistics, 1957 https://www.semanticscholar.org/paper/TECHNICAL-CHANGE-AND-THE-AGGREGATE-PRODUCTION-Solow/42607bb3d65c74eb44364a379d5496e69567e323
[592] "The PC: Personal Computing Comes of Age" IBM https://www.ibm.com/ibm/history/ibm100/us/en/icons/personalcomputer/impacts/
[593] "Time's Top Man? The Personal Computer" by Tony Long, Wired, 2007 https://www.wired.com/2012/12/dec-26-1982-times-top-man-the-personal-computer/
[594] "The Productivity Paradox of Information Technology: Review and Assessment" by Erik Brynjolfsson, Communications of the ACM, 1993 http://ccs.mit.edu/papers/CCSWP130/ccswp130.html
[595] See for example, the chapter "Computing Bounty" in *The Second Machine Age: Work, Progress, and Prosperity in a Time of Brilliant Technologies* by Erik Brynjolfsson and Andrew McAfee, W. W. Norton Company, 2014
[596] "GDP per capita, 1870 to 2016", Our World In Data https://ourworldindata.org/grapher/average-real-gdp-per-capita-across-countries-and-regions?country=~USA
[597] "The Dynamo and the Computer: An Historical Perspective on the Modern Productivity Paradox" by Paul A. David, The American Economic Review, 1990 http://www.dklevine.com/archive/refs4115.pdf
[598] "Does the 'New Economy' measure up to the Great Inventions of the past?" by Robert J. Gordon, National Bureau of Economic Research, 2000 https://www.nber.org/system/files/working_papers/w7833/w7833.pdf
[599] *The Rise and Fall of American Growth: The U.S. Standard of Living Since the Civil War* by Robert J. Gordon, Princeton University Press, 2016
[600] "Perspectives on The Rise and Fall of American Growth" by Robert J. Gordon, American Economic Review, 2016

https://www.researchgate.net/publication/302973038_Perspectives_on_The_Rise_and_Fall_of_American_Growth
601 *The Digital Doctor: Hope, Hype, and Harm at the Dawn of Medicine's Computer Age* by Robert M. Wachter, McGraw-Hill Education, 2015
602 "How journals like Nature, Cell and Science are damaging science" by Randy Schekman, The Guardian, 2013 https://www.theguardian.com/commentisfree/2013/dec/09/how-journals-nature-science-cell-damage-science
603 *Deep Medicine: How Artificial Intelligence Can Make Healthcare Human Again* by Eric J. Topol, Basic Books, 2019
604 "Google is using AI to design chips that will accelerate AI" by Karen Hao, MIT Technology Review, 2020 https://www.technologyreview.com/2020/03/27/950258/google-ai-chip-design-reinforcement-learning/
605 "A logical calculus of the ideas immanent in nervous activity" by Warren S. McCulloch and Walter H. Pitts, Bulletin of Mathematical Biophysics, 1943 http://www.cse.chalmers.se/~coquand/AUTOMATA/mcp.pdf
606 "Rosenblatt's Contributions" by Charles C. Tappert, Pace University http://csis.pace.edu/~ctappert/srd2011/rosenblatt-contributions.htm
607 "ImageNet Classification with Deep Convolutional Neural Networks" by Alex Krizhevsky, Ilya Sutskever, and Geoffrey E. Hinton, Communications of the ACM, 2017 https://dl.acm.org/doi/10.1145/3065386
608 "Found in translation: More accurate, fluent sentences in Google Translate" by Barak Turovsky, Google Blog, 2016 https://www.blog.google/products/translate/found-translation-more-accurate-fluent-sentences-google-translate/
609 "The Heroes of CRISPR" by Eric S. Lander, Cell, 2016 https://www.broadinstitute.org/files/news/pdfs/PIIS0092867415017055.pdf
610 "Genetic scissors: a tool for rewriting the code of life", Nobel Prize Organization, 2020 https://www.nobelprize.org/prizes/chemistry/2020/popular-information/
611 "Clearance of $p16^{Ink4a}$-positive senescent cells delays ageing-associated disorders" by Darren J. Baker et al, Nature, 2011 https://www.nature.com/articles/nature10600
612 "The new science of ageing", Royal Society, 2010 https://royalsociety.org/science-events-and-lectures/2010/science-ageing/
613 "We Know How You Feel" by Raffi Khatchadourian, The New Yorker, 2015 https://www.newyorker.com/magazine/2015/01/19/know-feel
614 *Girl Decoded: My Quest to Make Technology Emotionally Intelligent – and Change the Way We Interact Forever* by Rana el Kaliouby, Penguin Business, 2020

[615] "0.18-micron Technology" TSMC https://www.tsmc.com/english/dedicatedFoundry/technology/logic/l_018micron
[616] "IBM, Intel wrangle at 90 nm" by David Lammers, EE Times, 2002 https://www.eetimes.com/ibm-intel-wrangle-at-90-nm
[617] "Forget 5nm, TSMC already has its eyes on 2nm chips" by Georgi Zarkov, Phone Arena, 2020 https://www.phonearena.com/news/TSMC-2nm-chip-research-development-ongoing_id124111
[618] "Intel's Manufacturing Roadmap from 2019 to 2029: Back Porting, 7nm, 5nm, 3nm, 2nm, and 1.4nm" by Ian Cutress, Anand Tech, 2019 https://www.anandtech.com/show/15217/intels-manufacturing-roadmap-from-2019-to-2029
[619] "Cramming more components onto integrated circuits" by Gordon E. Moore, Electronics, 1965 https://newsroom.intel.com/wp-content/uploads/sites/11/2018/05/moores-law-electronics.pdf
[620] "Beyond Moore's Law: 3D Silicon Circuits Take Transistor Arrays Into the Third Dimension" by University of Michigan, Scitech Daily, 2019 https://scitechdaily.com/beyond-moores-law-3d-silicon-circuits-take-transistor-arrays-into-the-third-dimension
[621] "The future of electronics is light" by Arnab Hazari, The Conversation, 2016 https://theconversation.com/the-future-of-electronics-is-light-68903
[622] "We're not prepared for the end of Moore's Law" by David Rotman, MIT Technology Review, 2020 https://www.technologyreview.com/2020/02/24/905789/were-not-prepared-for-the-end-of-moores-law/
[623] "Quantum computing for the qubit curious" by Cathal O'Connell, Cosmos, 2019 https://cosmosmagazine.com/physics/quantum-computing-for-the-qubit-curious/
[624] "Quantum Machine Learning", EdX https://www.edx.org/course/quantum-machine-learning
[625] "IBM promises 1000-qubit quantum computer – a milestone – by 2023" by Adrian Cho, Science, 2020 https://www.sciencemag.org/news/2020/09/ibm-promises-1000-qubit-quantum-computer-milestone-2023
[626] "China Stakes Its Claim to Quantum Supremacy" by Tom Simonite, Wired, 2020 https://cosmosmagazine.com/physics/quantum-computing-for-the-qubit-curious/
[627] "Nobody agrees on how to build a quantum computer" by Michael Brooks, Protocol, 2020 https://www.protocol.com/manuals/quantum-computing/nobody-agrees-on-how-to-build-quantum-computer
[628] "Ribosome", British Society for Cell Biology https://bscb.org/learning-resources/softcell-e-learning/ribosome/

[629] *Engines of Creation: The Coming Era of Nanotechnology* by K. Eric Drexler, Doubleday, 1986
[630] "Press release: The Nobel Prize in Chemistry 2016", Nobel Prize Organization, 2016 https://www.nobelprize.org/prizes/chemistry/2016/press-release/
[631] "Against Transhumanism: The delusion of technological transcendence" by Richard A.L. Jones, Soft Machines, 2016 http://www.softmachines.org/wordpress/wp-content/uploads/2016/04/Against_Transhumanism_1.0_small.pdf
[632] "Deep learning godfathers Bengio, Hinton, and LeCun say the field can fix its flaws" by Tiernan Ray, ZDNet, 2020 https://www.zdnet.com/article/deep-learning-godfathers-bengio-hinton-and-lecun-say-the-field-can-fix-its-flaws/
[633] *Nano Comes to Life: How Nanotechnology Is Transforming Medicine and the Future of Biology* by Sonia Contera, Princeton University Press, 2019
[634] "Room-Temperature Superconductivity Achieved for the First Time" by Charlie Wood, Quanta Magazine, 2020 https://www.quantamagazine.org/physicists-discover-first-room-temperature-superconductor-20201014/
[635] "Press release", Nobel Prize Organization, 2010 https://www.nobelprize.org/prizes/physics/2010/press-release/
[636] "Nanosensors: Latest Research and Reviews", Nature Research, 2020 https://www.nature.com/subjects/nanosensors
[637] "DNA Data Storage Is Closer Than You Think" by Sang Yup Lee, Scientific American, 2019 https://www.scientificamerican.com/article/dna-data-storage-is-closer-than-you-think/
[638] "Delivering DNA origami to cells" by Dhanasekaran Balakrishnan, Gerrit D. Wilkens, and Jonathan G. Heddle, Future Medicine, 2019 https://www.futuremedicine.com/doi/full/10.2217/nnm-2018-0440
[639] "Deciphering the Genetic Code", American Chemical Society, 2009 https://www.acs.org/content/acs/en/education/whatischemistry/landmarks/geneticcode.html
[640] "Marshall W. Nirenberg", Nobel Prize Organization, 1968 https://www.nobelprize.org/prizes/medicine/1968/nirenberg/facts/
[641] "Public Reactions to the Genetic Code, 1961-1968", The Marshall W. Nirenberg Papers, U.S. National Library of Medicine https://profiles.nlm.nih.gov/spotlight/jj/feature/publicreaction
[642] Available as a chapter in *The Next Fifty Years: Science in the First Half of the Twenty-First Century* edited by John Brockman, Vintage Books, 2002
[643] "DNA Sequencing Costs: Data", National Human Genome Research Institute https://www.genome.gov/about-genomics/fact-sheets/DNA-Sequencing-Costs-Data

644 "The Man Behind Next-Generation Sequencing" by Clara Rodríguez Fernández, LabIOtech, 2019 https://www.labiotech.eu/interviews/next-generation-sequencing-nick-mccooke/
645 "Next-Generation Sequencing Methods" by T. Rajesh and M. Jaya, Current Developments in Biotechnology and Bioengineering, 2017 https://www.sciencedirect.com/science/article/pii/B9780444636676000079
646 "Press release", Nobel Prize Organization, 2012 https://www.nobelprize.org/prizes/medicine/2012/press-release/
647 "The Hallmarks of Aging" by Carlos López-Otín et al, Cell, 2013 https://www.ncbi.nlm.nih.gov/pmc/articles/PMC3836174/
648 *Ageless: The New Science of Getting Older Without Getting Old* by Andrew Steele, Doubleday Books, 2020
649 *The Abolition of Aging: The forthcoming radical extension of healthy human longevity* by David W. Wood, Delta Wisdom, 2016
650 "The Burden of Disease and the Changing Task of Medicine" by David S. Jones et al, New England Journal of Medicine, 2012 https://www.nejm.org/doi/full/10.1056/NEJMp1113569
651 "Juvenescence raises another $100m to invest in longevity" by Clive Cookson, Financial Times, 2019 https://www.ft.com/content/ddec6a10-c046-11e9-b350-db00d509634e
652 "Computers Are Useless. They Can Only Give You Answers", Quote Investigator, 2011 https://quoteinvestigator.com/2011/11/05/computers-useless/
653 "Is artificial intelligence set to become art's next medium?" Christies, 2018 https://www.christies.com/features/A-collaboration-between-two-artists-one-human-one-a-machine-9332-1.aspx
654 "How AI-Generated Music Is Changing The Way Hits Are Made" by Dani Deahl, The Verge, 2018 https://www.theverge.com/2018/8/31/17777008/artificial-intelligence-taryn-southern-amper-music
655 "An album in the style of The Beatles, generated by OpenAI Jukebox" YouTube, 2020 https://www.youtube.com/watch?v=yZu24pddzwk
656 "Alpha Zero's 'Alien' Chess Shows the Power, and the Peculiarity, of AI" by Will Knight, MIT Technology Review, 2017 https://www.technologyreview.com/2017/12/08/147199/alpha-zeros-alien-chess-shows-the-power-and-the-peculiarity-of-ai/
657 "AlphaZero: How Intuition Demolished Logic" by Carloz Perez, Intuition Machine, 2017 https://medium.com/intuitionmachine/alphazero-how-intuition-demolished-logic-66a4841e6810
658 "Meet GPT-3. It Has Learned to Code (and Blog and Argue)" by Cade Metz, New York Times, 2020

https://www.nytimes.com/2020/11/24/science/artificial-intelligence-ai-gpt3.html
659 "It seems that GPT-3 has its own sense of humor, more of an anti-humor in fact" By nullc, Y Combinator Hacker News, 2020 https://news.ycombinator.com/item?id=24007784
660 "18 Impressive Applications of Generative Adversarial Networks (GANs)" by Jason Brownlee, Machine Learning Mastery, 2019 https://machinelearningmastery.com/impressive-applications-of-generative-adversarial-networks/
661 "Combining GANs and reinforcement learning for drug discovery" by Insilico Medicine, EurekAlert, 2018 https://www.eurekalert.org/pub_releases/2018-05/imi-cga050918.php
662 "The incredible life of DeepMind founder Demis Hassabis" by Sam Shead, Business Insider, 2017 https://www.businessinsider.com/the-incredible-life-of-deepmind-cofounder-demis-hassabis-2017-5
663 "Neuroscience-Inspired Artificial Intelligence" by Demis Hassabis et al, DeepMind, 2017 https://deepmind.com/research/publications/neuroscience-inspired-artificial-intelligence
664 *A Thousand Brains: A New Theory of Intelligence* by Jeff Hawkins, Basic Books, 2021
665 "Why Is the Human Brain So Efficient?" by Liqun Luo, Nautilus, 2018 http://nautil.us/issue/59/connections/why-is-the-human-brain-so-efficient
666 "Neuromorphic Computing", Intel https://www.intel.co.uk/content/www/uk/en/research/neuromorphic-computing.html
667 "Quantum computing should supercharge this machine-learning technique" by Will Knight, MIT Technology Review, 2019 https://www.technologyreview.com/2019/03/13/136628/quantum-computing-should-supercharge-this-machine-learning-technique/
668 "How may quantum computing affect Artificial Intelligence?", BBVA, 2020 https://www.bbva.com/en/how-may-quantum-computing-affect-artificial-intelligence/
669 *The Hidden Spring: A Journey to the Source of Consciousness* by Mark Solms, WW Norton Company, 2021
670 *Artificial You: AI and the Future of Your Mind* by Susan Schneider, Princeton University Press, 2019
671 *The Book of Why: The New Science of Cause and Effect* by Judea Pearl and Dana Mackenzie, Allen Lane, 2018
672 "Probabilistic Programming and the Art of the Possible" by Michael Kozlov and Ashish Kulkarni, World Quant, 2019

https://www.weareworldquant.com/en/thought-leadership/probabilistic-programming-and-the-art-of-the-possible/
[673] "The next wave: Probabilistic programming" by Stuart Russell, CogX YouTube, 2021 https://www.youtube.com/watch?v=YYFbPQiLlxk
[674] "About SingularityNET" https://singularitynet.io/aboutus/
[675] "Mark Zuckerberg on Facebook's Future" by Steven Levy, Wired, 2014 https://www.wired.com/2014/04/zuckerberg-f8-interview/
[676] *Human Compatible: Artificial Intelligence and the Problem of Control* by Stuart Russell, Viking, 2019
[677] "Jean M. Hebert, Ph.D." Albert Einstein College of Medicine https://www.einsteinmed.org/faculty/9069/jean-hebert
[678] "How the Catholic Church came to oppose birth control" by Lisa McClain, The Conversation, 2018 https://theconversation.com/how-the-catholic-church-came-to-oppose-birth-control-95694
[679] Proverbs 13:24
[680] *A Rumor of Angels: Modern Society and the Rediscovery of the Supernatural* by Peter L. Berger, Doubleday, 1969
[681] Leviticus 20:9
[682] "The relevance of Gandhi in the capitalism debate" by Oliver Balch, The Guardian, 2013 https://www.theguardian.com/sustainable-business/blog/relevance-gandhi-capitalism-debate-rajni-bakshi
[683] "Red in tooth and claw" by Gary Martin, The Phrase Finder https://www.phrases.org.uk/meanings/red-in-tooth-and-claw.html
[684] "To Asa Gray, 22 May" by Charles Darwin, 1860 https://www.darwinproject.ac.uk/letter/DCP-LETT-2814.xml
[685] "All Things Dull And Ugly Lyrics", Lyrics Depot http://www.lyricsdepot.com/monty-python/all-things-dull-and-ugly.html
[686] "About Humanists International" https://humanists.international/about/
[687] "What is humanism?" Humanists International https://humanists.international/what-is-humanism/
[688] *The Righteous Mind: Why Good People are Divided by Politics and Religion* by Jonathan Haidt, Pantheon, 2012
[689] *The Moral Landscape: How Science Can Determine Human Values* by Sam Harris, Free Press, 2010
[690] "The Transhumanist FAQ, v2.1" by Nick Bostrom, World Transhumanist Association, 2003 https://www.nickbostrom.com/views/transhumanist.pdf
[691] "Transhumanist Values" by Nick Bostrom, Ethical Issues for the 21st Century, 2003 https://www.nickbostrom.com/ethics/values.html
[692] "Overpopulation and Near-Future Tech" by Nicola Bagalà, Lifespan IO, 2021 https://www.lifespan.io/news/lifextenshow-overpopulation-and-near-future-tech/

[693] "Transhumanist Declaration", Humanity+, 2009 https://humanityplus.org/philosophy/transhumanist-declaration/
[694] This banner has been removed from that particular site, but a Google image search for the phrase "Victory of transhumanism is inevitable" will find other examples. See also the commentary in "Transhumanism has never been modern" by Richard Jones, Soft Machines, 2014 http://www.softmachines.org/wordpress/?p=1549
[695] "Kurzweil Claims That the Singularity Will Happen by 2045" by Christianna Reedy, Futurism, 2017 https://futurism.com/kurzweil-claims-that-the-singularity-will-happen-by-2045
[696] "Transhumanist FAQ", Humanity+ https://humanityplus.org/transhumanism/transhumanist-faq/
[697] "Reject the Deadly Precautionary Principle: Approve All Covid-19 Vaccines Immediately!" by Gennady Stolyarov II, U.S. Transhumanist Party, 2020 https://transhumanist-party.org/2020/12/15/reject-precautionary-principle/
[698] *Extra Life: A Short History of Living Longer* by Steven Johnson, Riverhead, 2021
[699] "In Praise of Industrial Policy" by Francis Fukuyama, American Purpose, 2021 https://www.americanpurpose.com/blog/fukuyama/in-praise-of-industrial-policy/
[700] "What Would It Mean for Humans to Become Data?" by Joelle Renstrom, Slate, 2019 https://slate.com/technology/2019/07/years-and-years-finale-bethany-transhumanist.html
[701] "Principle 15", Rio Declaration on Environment and Development 1992 https://www.jus.uio.no/lm/environmental.development.rio.declaration.1992/15.html
[702] "The Perils of Precaution" by Max More, 2010 https://web.archive.org/web/20101208083349/http://www.maxmore.com/perils.htm
[703] "The Proactionary Principle, Version 1.2" by Max More, 2005 https://web.archive.org/web/20110709213137/http://www.maxmore.com/proactionary.htm
[704] *Superintelligence: Paths, Dangers, Strategies* by Nick Bostrom, Oxford University Press, 2014
[705] *The Proactionary Imperative: A foundation for transhumanism* by Steve Fuller and Veronika Lipinska, Palgrave Macmillan, 2014
[706] "Book Review Symposium: Steve Fuller and Veronika Lipińska, *The Proactionary Imperative: A Foundation for Transhumanism*" by Matthew David and Dora Meredith, Sociology, 2015 https://journals.sagepub.com/doi/10.1177/0038038515611312

[707] "21 Historical Figures You Didn't Know Supported the Eugenics Movement" by Kara Goldfarb, All That's Interesting, 2018 https://allthatsinteresting.com/eugenics-movement
[708] "Law for the Prevention of Offspring with Hereditary Diseases (July 14, 1933)", German History in Documents and Images http://germanhistorydocs.ghi-dc.org/pdf/eng/English30.pdf
[709] "Deadly Medicine: Creating the Master Race", United States Holocaust Memorial Museum, https://encyclopedia.ushmm.org/content/en/article/deadly-medicine-creating-the-master-race
[710] "Julian Huxley and the Continuity of Eugenics in Twentieth-century Britain" by Paul Weindling, Journal of Modern European History, 2012 https://www.ncbi.nlm.nih.gov/pmc/articles/PMC4366572/
[711] "The irrationality of transhumanists" by Susan B. Levin, IAI News, 2021 https://iai.tv/articles/the-irrationality-of-transhumanists-auid-1701
[712] "Playing to lose: transhumanism, autonomy, and liberal democracy" by Susan B. Levin, OUP Blog, 2021 https://blog.oup.com/2021/01/playing-to-lose-transhumanism-autonomy-and-liberal-democracy-long-read/
[713] "Beyond Transhumanism: The Dangers of Transhumanist Philosophies on Human and Nonhuman Beings" by Benjamin Shane Evans, Iowa State University, 2017 https://lib.dr.iastate.edu/cgi/viewcontent.cgi?article=6307&context=etd
[714] *The Transhumanist Wager* by Zoltan Istvan, self-published, 2013
[715] "Book review | The Transhumanist Wager" by Giulio Prisco, Kurzweil AI, 2013 https://www.kurzweilai.net/book-review-the-transhumanist-wager
[716] "NEWS FLASH: The Transhumanist Wager is NOT Zoltan Istvan's Political Manifesto" by Chris T. Armstrong, Continuity of Consciousness, 2016 https://carmstrong1959blog.wordpress.com/2016/02/12/news-flash-the-transhumanist-wager-is-not-zoltan-istvans-political-manifesto/
[717] "A muscular new kid on the block" by David Wood, dw2blog, 2013 https://dw2blog.com/2013/12/22/a-muscular-new-kid-on-the-block/
[718] "Six Signs of Scientism" by Susan Haack, Logos and Episteme, 2012 https://philpapers.org/rec/HAASSO
[719] "Steven Poole takes issue with linguist Steven Pinker's language" by Steven Poole, The Guardian, 2013 https://www.theguardian.com/books/2013/aug/23/steven-pinker-language-poole
[720] "Philosophy", Humanity+ https://humanityplus.org/philosophy/
[721] "Definitions of Transhumanism" collected by Anders Sandberg, https://www.aleph.se/Trans/Intro/definitions.html

---

[722] "I'll speak at TransVision 2019, July 6–7 in London" by Giulio Prisco, Turing Church, 2019 https://turingchurch.net/ill-speak-at-transvision-2019-july-6-7-in-london-f033ea85377f
[723] Available at https://goertzel.org/CosmistManifesto_July2010.pdf
[724] "Psychology's Replication Crisis Is Running Out of Excuses" by Ed Yong, The Atlantic, 2018 https://www.theatlantic.com/science/archive/2018/11/psychologys-replication-crisis-real/576223/
[725] *Bad Pharma: How Drug Companies Mislead Doctors and Harm Patients* by Ben Goldacre, Fourth Estate, 2012
[726] "The 7 biggest problems facing science, according to 270 scientists" by Julia Belluz, Brad Plumer, and Brian Resnick, Vox, 2016 https://www.vox.com/2016/7/14/12016710/science-challeges-research-funding-peer-review-process
[727] "Are your findings 'WEIRD'?" by B. Azar, American Psychological Association, 2010 https://www.apa.org/monitor/2010/05/weird
[728] "FAQ: Technocracy" by Patrick Wood, Technocracy News https://www.technocracy.news/faq-2/
[729] *Technocracy Rising: The Trojan Horse of Global Transformation* by Patrick M. Wood, Coherent Publishing. 2014
[730] "The Siamese Twins of Technocracy and Transhumanism" by Patrick Wood, Technocracy News, 2020 https://www.technocracy.news/the-siamese-twins-of-technocracy-and-transhumanism/
[731] "Transhumanism & AI: Utopia or a Nightmare in the Making?" by Francois Zammit, Isles of the Left, 2018 https://www.islesoftheleft.org/transhumanism-ai-utopia-or-a-nightmare-in-the-making/
[732] "The problem with utopias" by Michael Shermer, Aeon, 2018 https://theweek.com/articles/760689/problem-utopias
[733] *The Inevitable: Understanding the 12 Technological Forces That Will Shape Our Future* by Kevin Kelly, Viking, 2016
[734] "Extropy Magazines" https://hpluspedia.org/wiki/Extropy_Magazines
[735] "The Extropian Principles version 3.0" https://web.archive.org/web/20170415055109/http://vency.com/EXtropian3.htm
[736] "Principles of Extropy version 3.11" https://web.archive.org/web/20110806105153/http://www.extropy.org/principles.htm
[737] "H+: True Transhumanism" http://www.metanexus.net/essay/h-true-transhumanism
[738] *Homo Deus: A Brief History of Tomorrow* by Yuval Noah Harari, Harvill Secker, 2016

[739] "Transhumanism" by Francis Fukuyama, Foreign Policy, 2009 https://foreignpolicy.com/2009/10/23/transhumanism/
[740] "Do Amish use technology?" Amish America https://amishamerica.com/do-amish-use-technology/
[741] "Prospects for a transhuman mind?" Leda Cosmides in conversation with Natasha Mitchell, ABC All in the Mind, 2007 https://www.abc.net.au/radionational/programs/allinthemind/prospects-for-a-transhuman-mind/3391110
[742] "Leslie E. Orgel Biographical Memoirs" by Jack D. Dunitz and Gerald F. Joyce, Nasa Online, 2007 http://www.nasonline.org/publications/biographical-memoirs/memoir-pdfs/orgel-leslie.pdf
[743] Reviewed in Chapter 4 of my 2016 book *The Abolition of Aging*
[744] "Pleiotropy, Natural Selection, and the Evolution of Senescence" by George C. Williams, Evolution, 1957 https://www.jstor.org/stable/2406060
[745] "Genetic syndromes in man with potential relevance to the pathobiology of aging" by George M. Martin, Birth Defects Original Article Series, 1978 https://pubmed.ncbi.nlm.nih.gov/147113/
[746] "Genetic analysis of life-span in *Caenorhabditis elegans*" by Thomas E. Johnson and William B. Wood, Proceedings of the National Academy of Sciences, 1982 http://sageke.sciencemag.org/cgi/reprint/2001/1/cp6.pdf
[747] "Evolutionary Theories of Aging and Longevity" by Leonid A. Gavrilov and Natalia S. Gavrilova, The Scientific World, 2002 http://longevity-science.org/Evolution.htm
[748] "Unfit for the future: The urgent need for moral enhancement" by Julian Savulescu and Ingmar Persson, Philosophy Now, 2012 https://blog.oup.com/2012/08/unfit-future-moral-enhancement/
[749] "Facing the Challenges of Transhumanism: Philosophical, Religious, and Ethical Considerations" by Hava Tirosh-Samuelson, Metanexus, 2007 https://www.metanexus.net/facing-challenges-transhumanism-philosophical-religious-and-ethical-considerations/
[750] "The Hedonistic Imperative" by David Pearce https://www.hedweb.com/
[751] "Transforming Transhumanism" by David North, University of Chicago Philosophy Review, 2019 https://web.archive.org/web/20201128013418/https://ucpr.blog/2019/06/06/transforming-transhumanism/
[752] "Artificial intelligence, transhumanism, and rival salvations" by Ted Peters, Lutheran Alliance for Faith, Science and Technology, 2019 https://luthscitech.org/artificial-intelligence-transhumanism-and-rival-salvations/
[753] "Why the Future Doesn't Need Us" by Bill Joy, Wired, 2000 https://www.wired.com/2000/04/joy-2/

754 "H-: Transhumanism and the Posthuman Future: Will Technological Progress Get Us There?" by Ted Peters, Metanexus, 2011 https://www.metanexus.net/h-transhumanism-and-posthuman-future-will-technological-progress-get-us-there/
755 "H+: Trite Truths About Technology: A Reply to Ted Peters" by Russell Blackford, Metanexus, 2011 https://metanexus.net/h-trite-truths-about-technology-reply-ted-peters/
756 *Life 3.0: Being Human in the Age of Artificial Intelligence* by Max Tegmark, Knopf, 2017
757 *Artificial You: AI and the Future of Your Mind* by Susan Schneider, Princeton University Press, 2019
758 "The New Eugenics of Transhumanism: A Feminist Assessment" by Nikila Lakshmanan, Gender Forum, 2018 http://genderforum.org/wp-content/uploads/2018/05/5_Lakshmanan_Transhumanism.pdf
759 "Killings of police and polio workers halt Pakistan vaccine drive" by Lucy Lamble, The Guardian, 2019 https://www.theguardian.com/global-development/2019/apr/30/killings-of-police-and-polio-workers-halt-vaccine-drive-in-pakistan
760 "Feeding the gods: Hundreds of skulls reveal massive scale of human sacrifice in Aztec capital" by Lizzie Wade, Science, 2018 https://www.sciencemag.org/news/2018/06/feeding-gods-hundreds-skulls-reveal-massive-scale-human-sacrifice-aztec-capital
761 "The Four Noble Truths", BBC, 2009 https://www.bbc.co.uk/religion/religions/buddhism/beliefs/fournobletruths_1.shtml
762 *Discourses of Epictetus*, https://archive.org/stream/epictetus02epicuoft#page/140/mode/2up/search/freedom
763 https://en.wikipedia.org/wiki/Meditations
764 https://en.wikipedia.org/wiki/Serenity_Prayer
765 "Acceptance is the first step toward change" by Sunada Takagi, Mindful Purpose, 2010 http://www.mindfulpurpose.com/personal-change/acceptance-is-the-first-step-toward-change
766 "The Stoic: 9 Principles to Help You Keep Calm in Chaos" by Paul Jun, 99u http://99u.com/articles/24401/a-makers-guidebook-9-stoic-principles-to-nurture-your-life-and-work
767 Luke 10:25-37
768 *New Bottles for New Wine* by Julian Huxley, Chatto and Windus, 1957 https://archive.org/details/NewBottlesForNewWine
769 "History of 'transhumanism'" by Peter Harrison and Joseph Wolyniak, Notes and Queries, 2015 https://www.academia.edu/13997038/History_of_transhumanism

770 "Knowledge, Morality, and Destiny" by Julian Huxley, Psychiatry, 1951 https://www.tandfonline.com/doi/abs/10.1080/00332747.1951.11022818?journalCode=upsy20

771 "WTA changes its image" by Russell Blackford, 2008, Metamagician and The Hellfire Club http://metamagician3000.blogspot.com/2008/07/wta-changes-its-image.html

772 "Rapture of the nerds: will the Singularity turn us into gods or end the human race?" by Ben Popper, The Verge, 2012 https://www.theverge.com/2012/10/22/3535518/singularity-rapture-of-the-nerds-gods-end-human-race

773 Two examples are the Christian Transhumanist Association, https://www.christiantranshumanism.org/, and the Mormon Transhumanist Association, https://transfigurism.org/

774 "Democracy is The Worst Form of Government" by Richard M. Langworth https://richardlangworth.com/worst-form-of-government

775 "We didn't think much of Lincoln at Gettysburg" by Rose Wild, The Times, 2017 https://www.thetimes.co.uk/article/we-didn-t-think-much-of-lincoln-at-gettysburg-b9tptwfvw

776 "Constitution du 4 octobre 1958" https://www.legifrance.gouv.fr/loda/article_lc/LEGIARTI000006527453/

777 "10 of the best Tony Benn quotes – as picked by our readers" by James Walsh, The Guardian, 2014 https://www.theguardian.com/politics/2014/mar/15/10-of-the-best-tony-benn-quotes-as-picked-by-our-readers

778 "Tony Benn and the Five Essential Questions of Democracy" by John Nichols, The Nation, 2014 https://www.thenation.com/article/tony-benn-and-five-essential-questions-democracy/

779 "Famous Words Churchill Never Said" by Michael Richards https://www.winstonchurchill.org/publications/finest-hour/finest-hour-141/history-detectives-red-herrings-famous-words-churchill-never-said

780 "German federal election, March 1933" https://en.wikipedia.org/wiki/German_federal_election,_March_1933

781 "Was Hitler democratically elected?" by Eike Pierstorff, Die Beste Aller Zeiten, 2009 http://diebesteallerzeiten.de/blog/2009/02/19/was-hitler-democratically-elected/

782 "German referendum, 1934" https://en.wikipedia.org/wiki/German_referendum,_1934

783 "Hitler Was Elected President in a Democratic Election: Myth" by Thomas DeMichele, Fact/Myth, 2016 http://factmyth.com/factoids/hitler-was-elected-in-a-democratic-election/

[784] "The Only Thing Necessary for the Triumph of Evil is that Good Men Do Nothing" by Garson O'Toole, Quote Investigator, 2010 https://quoteinvestigator.com/2010/12/04/good-men-do/
[785] "Benjamin Franklin", Wikiquote https://en.wikiquote.org/wiki/Benjamin_Franklin
[786] "Leviathan", Chapter XIII: http://www.bartleby.com/34/5/13.html
[787] "What Would Milton Friedman Do About Climate Change? Tax Carbon" by Jeff McMahon, Forbes, 2014 https://www.forbes.com/sites/jeffmcmahon/2014/10/12/what-would-milton-friedman-do-about-climate-change-tax-carbon
[788] "Fragment on Government (July 1, 1854)" by Abraham Lincoln, Lincoln's Writings http://housedivided.dickinson.edu/sites/lincoln/fragment-on-government-july-1-1854/
[789] *American Amnesia: Business, Government, and the Forgotten Roots of Our Prosperity* by Jacob S. Hacker and Paul Pierson, Simon & Schuster, 2016
[790] Letter "To the Shareholders of Berkshire Hathaway Inc" by Warren E. Buffett, 2003 https://www.berkshirehathaway.com/letters/2002pdf.pdf
[791] "Glossary of summaries: Subsidiarity", EUR-Lex https://eur-lex.europa.eu/summary/glossary/subsidiarity.html
[792] "FIFA" https://www.fifa.com/
[793] "History of FIFA – Foundation" https://www.fifa.com/news/history-fifa-foundation-447
[794] "FIFA Member Associations" https://www.fifa.com/associations/
[795] "About ICAO" https://www.icao.int/about-icao/
[796] "New ICAO-LACAC air cargo liberalization agreement to bolster regional vaccine transport long-term recovery" ICAO, 2020 https://www.icao.int/Newsroom/Pages/New-ICAO-LACAC-air-cargo-liberalization-agreement-to-bolster-regional-vaccine-transport-long-term-recovery-.aspx
[797] "Declaration concerning the prohibition of the use of projectiles with the sole object to spread asphyxiating poisonous gases", Dutch Ministry of Foreign Affairs https://web.archive.org/web/20130831162027/http://www.minbuza.nl/en/key-topics/treaties/search-the-treaty-database/1899/7/002422.html
[798] "Chemical Warfare and Medical Response During World War I" by Gerard J. Fitzgerald, American Journal of Public Health, 2008 https://www.ncbi.nlm.nih.gov/pmc/articles/PMC2376985/
[799] "Dulce et Decorum Est" by Wilfred Owen, The War Poetry Website http://www.warpoetry.co.uk/owen1.html
[800] "Protocol for the Prohibition of the Use in War of Asphyxiating, Poisonous or Other Gases, and of Bacteriological Methods of Warfare" United Nations Office for Disarmament Affairs http://disarmament.un.org/treaties/t/1925

[801] "Air raid on Bari", Wikipedia https://en.wikipedia.org/wiki/Air_raid_on_Bari
[802] "OPCW by the Numbers", OPCW, https://www.opcw.org/media-centre/opcw-numbers
[803] "The Nobel Peace Prize for 2013", Nobel Prize Organisation, https://www.nobelprize.org/prizes/peace/2013/press-release/
[804] "Preventing the Re-Emergence of Chemical Weapons" OPCW https://www.opcw.org/work/preventing-re-emergence-chemical-weapons
[805] "Chronicle of the World Health Organization", United Nations, 1947 https://web.archive.org/web/20070809031008/http://whqlibdoc.who.int/hist/chronicles/chronicle_1947.pdf
[806] "At the Roots of The World Health Organization's Challenges: Politics and Regionalization" by Elizabeth Fee, Marcu Cueto, and Theodore M. Brown, American Journal of Public Health, 2016 https://www.ncbi.nlm.nih.gov/pmc/articles/PMC5055806/
[807] "A Cold War Vaccine: Albert Sabin, Russia, and the oral polio vaccine" by James L. Franklin, Hektoen International, 2020 https://hekint.org/2020/05/11/a-cold-war-vaccine-albert-sabin-russia-and-the-oral-polio-vaccine/
[808] "Mikhail Chumakov", Russia-IC http://russia-ic.com/people/general/c/375
[809] "The best person who ever lived is an unknown Ukrainian man" by William MacAskill, Boing Boing, 2015 https://boingboing.net/2015/07/30/the-best-person-who-ever-lived.html
[810] "A Pox on Your Narrative: Writing Disease Control into Cold War History" by Erez Manela, Diplomatic History, 2010 https://academic.oup.com/dh/article/34/2/299/432057
[811] "At the height of the Cold War, the US and Soviet Union worked together to eradicate smallpox" by Sean B. Carroll, World Economic Forum, 2016 https://www.weforum.org/agenda/2016/07/at-the-height-of-the-cold-war-the-us-and-soviet-union-worked-together-to-eradicate-smallpox/
[812] "Smallpox: Eradicating an ancient scourge", WHO https://www.who.int/about/bugs_drugs_smoke_chapter_1_smallpox.pdf
[813] "Encroaching Control: Keep Government Poor and Remain Free" by Ronald Reagan, Orange County California Press Club, 1961 https://cdn.cnsnews.com/documents/Encroaching%20Control-Keep%20Government%20Poor%20And%20Remain%20Free-Ronald%20Reagan-07-28-61.pdf
[814] "President Reagan: Speech to the House of Commons, June 8, 1982" Fordham University https://sourcebooks.fordham.edu/mod/1982reagan1.asp

815 "Ronald Reagan, 'Evil Empire Speech' (8 March 1983)" Voices of Democracy http://voicesofdemocracy.umd.edu/reagan-evil-empire-speech-text/
816 "Address to the Nation on Defense and National Security", Ronald Reagan, 1983, Ronald Reagan Presidential Library https://www.reaganlibrary.gov/archives/speech/address-nation-defense-and-national-security
817 "'Star Wars': How the Term Arose" New York Times, 1985 https://www.nytimes.com/1985/09/25/world/star-wars-how-the-term-arose.html
818 "The Famous 'We Begin Bombing' Audio" by Corey Deitz, Radio About, 2004 https://web.archive.org/web/20130403121932/http://radio.about.com/od/funradiothingstodo/a/aa060503a.htm
819 "Soviets Assail Reagan for 'Monstrous' Joke," Pittsburgh Post-Gazette, 1984 https://news.google.com/newspapers?nid=1129&dat=19840816&id=6NVRAAAAIBAJ&sjid=Hm4DAAAAIBAJ&pg=3722,4149076&hl=en
820 "Telling the Soviet Redemption Story: Ronald Reagan's Changing Soviet Rhetoric" by Mark W. Lavoie, University of Illinois at Urbana-Champaign, 2016 https://www.ideals.illinois.edu/bitstream/handle/2142/95488/LAVOIE-DISSERTATION-2016.pdf
821 "TV Interview for BBC ('I like Mr. Gorbachev. We can do business together')" Margaret Thatcher Foundation, 1984 https://www.margaretthatcher.org/document/105592
822 *An American Life* by Robert Lindsay and Ronald Reagan, Simon & Schuster, 1990
823 "1979: The Soviet Union deploys its SS20 missiles and NATO responds" by Jamie Shea, NATO, 2009 https://www.nato.int/cps/en/natohq/opinions_139274.htm
824 "Korean Air Lines Flight 007", Wikipedia https://en.wikipedia.org/wiki/Korean_Air_Lines_Flight_007
825 "Declaring 'this crime against humanity must never be forgotten'" by Jack Reed, UPI, 1983 https://www.upi.com/Archives/1983/09/05/Declaring-this-crime-against-humanity-must-never-be-forgotten/3399431582400/
826 "The Day the World Didn't End" by John Bull, Medium Lapsed Historian, 2016 https://medium.com/lapsed-historian/the-day-the-world-didnt-end-76b9deececcc
827 "In 1983 'war scare,' Soviet leadership feared nuclear surprise attack by U.S." by David E. Hoffman, Washington Post, 2015 https://www.washingtonpost.com/world/national-security/in-1983-war-

scare-soviet-leadership-feared-nuclear-surprise-attack-by-us/2015/10/24/15a289b4-7904-11e5-a958-d889faf561dc_story.html
[828] "A Cold War Conundrum: The 1983 Soviet War Scare" by Benjamin B. Fischer, CIA, 1997 https://www.cia.gov/static/4f74a357a4372cc542944cd39e5e30bc/Cold-War-Conundrum.pdf
[829] *Memoirs* by Andrei Gromyko, Doubleday, 1989
[830] "The Khrushchev/ Brezhnev Doctrine at Helsinki" by Harry Schwartz, The New York Times, 1975 https://www.nytimes.com/1975/08/05/archives/the-khrushchevbrezhnev-doctrine-at-helsinki.html
[831] "The Afghanistan war and the breakdown of the Soviet Union" by Rafael Reuveny and Aseem Prakash, Review of International Studies, 1999 http://faculty.washington.edu/aseem/afganwar.pdf
[832] *Capitalism and Freedom* by Milton Friedman, University of Chicago Press, 1962
[833] *The Helsinki Effect: International Norms, Human Rights, and the Demise of Communism* by Daniel C. Thomas, Princeton University Press, 2001
[834] *Years of Renewal* by Henry Kissinger, Simon & Schuster, 2012
[835] *In Confidence: Moscow's Ambassador to America's Six Cold War Presidents (1962-1986)* by Anatoly Dobrynin, Times Books, 1996
[836] *Russia and the Idea of the West: Gorbachev, Intellectuals, and the End of the Cold War* by Robert D. English, Columbia University Press, 2000
[837] "How the Soviet leader became a nuclear abolitionist" by Vladislav M. Zubok, Boston Review, 2000 https://bostonreview.net/forum/eliminating-danger/vladislav-m-zubok-gorbachev%E2%80%99s-nuclear-learning
[838] "The Chicxulub Asteroid Impact and Mass Extinction at the Cretaceous-Paleogene Boundary" by Peter Schulte et al, Science, 2010 http://doc.rero.ch/record/210367/files/PAL_E4389.pdf
[839] "Cretaceous–Paleogene extinction event", Wikipedia https://en.wikipedia.org/wiki/Cretaceous%E2%80%93Paleogene_extinction_event
[840] "Asteroid dust linked to Chicxulub crater confirms dinosaur extinction theory" by Rhys Blakely, The Times, 2021 https://www.thetimes.co.uk/article/asteroid-dust-linked-to-chicxulub-crater-confirms-dinosaur-extinction-theory-nz0fdpr2q
[841] "Counting the dead at Hiroshima and Nagasaki" by Alex Wellerstein, Bulletin of the Atomic Scientists, 2020 https://thebulletin.org/2020/08/counting-the-dead-at-hiroshima-and-nagasaki/
[842] "Why a volcanic eruption caused a 'year without a summer' in 1816" by Ashley Strickland, CNN, 2019

https://edition.cnn.com/2019/09/17/world/tambora-eruption-year-without-summer-scn/

843 *The Last Great Subsistence Crisis in the Western World* by John D. Post, Johns Hopkins University Press, 1977

844 "The Atmosphere after a Nuclear War: Twilight at Noon" by Paul J. Crutzen and John W. Birks, Ambio, 1982 https://www.researchgate.net/publication/236736050_The_Atmosphere_after_a_Nuclear_War_Twilight_at_Noon

845 "Nuclear Winter: Global Consequences of Multiple Nuclear Explosions" by R. P. Turco et al, Science, 1983 https://science.sciencemag.org/content/222/4630/1283

846 "Specialists Detail 'Nuclear Winter'" by Walter Sullivan, New York Times, 1983 https://www.nytimes.com/1983/12/26/us/specialists-detail-nuclear-winter.html

847 "Cosmos (1979)" Cosmo Learning https://cosmolearning.org/documentaries/cosmos/

848 "The 1978 Pulitzer Prize Winner in General Nonfiction" The Pulitzer Prizes https://www.pulitzer.org/winners/carl-sagan

849 "When Carl Sagan Warned the World About Nuclear Winter" by Matthew R. Francis, Smithsonian Magazine, 2017 https://www.smithsonianmag.com/science-nature/when-carl-sagan-warned-world-about-nuclear-winter-180967198/

850 "How the threat of nuclear winter changed the Cold War" by T.J. Raphael, The World, 2016 https://www.pri.org/stories/2016-04-05/how-threat-nuclear-winter-changed-cold-war

851 "How the Soviet leader became a nuclear abolitionist" by Vladislav M. Zubok, Boston Review, 2000 https://bostonreview.net/forum/eliminating-danger/vladislav-m-zubok-gorbachev%E2%80%99s-nuclear-learning

852 "The NHS does not have enough radiologists to keep patients safe, say three-in-four hospital imaging bosses" Royal College of Radiologists, 2019 https://www.rcr.ac.uk/posts/nhs-does-not-have-enough-radiologists-keep-patients-safe-say-three-four-hospital-imaging

853 "Geoff Hinton: On Radiology", Creative Destructive Lab, YouTube, 2016 https://www.youtube.com/watch?v=2HMPRXstSvQ

854 "AI system outperforms experts in spotting breast cancer" by Ian Sample, The Guardian, 2020 https://www.theguardian.com/society/2020/jan/01/ai-system-outperforms-experts-in-spotting-breast-cancer

855 *The War on Normal People: The Truth About America's Disappearing Jobs and Why Universal Basic Income Is Our Future* by Andrew Yang, Hachette Books, 2018

856 *A World Without Work: Technology, Automation, and How We Should Respond* by Daniel Susskind, Metropolitan Books, 2020

[857] *Heart of the Machine: Our Future in a World of Artificial Emotional Intelligence* by Richard Yonck, Arcade Publishing, 2017
[858] "Neuromorphic computing: The long path from roots to real life" by William Van Winkle, Venture Beat, 2020 https://venturebeat.com/2020/12/15/neuromorphic-computing-the-long-path-from-roots-to-real-life/
[859] See the argument in Chapter 10, "Towards Abundant Creativity", of *Sustainable Superabundance* by David W. Wood, Delta Wisdom, 2019
[860] "From each according to his ability, to each according to his needs", Wikipedia
https://en.wikipedia.org/wiki/From_each_according_to_his_ability,_to_each_according_to_his_needs
[861] "1936 Constitution of the USSR" Bucknell University http://www.departments.bucknell.edu/russian/const/36cons01.html
[862] "Critique of the Gotha Programme" by Karl Marx, 1875 https://www.marxists.org/archive/marx/works/1875/gotha/ch01.htm
[863] "The Protestant Ethic and the Spirit of Capitalism" Wikipedia https://en.wikipedia.org/wiki/The_Protestant_Ethic_and_the_Spirit_of_Capitalism
[864] "FT interview with Google co-founder and CEO Larry Page" by Richard Waters, Financial Times, 2014 https://www.ft.com/content/3173f19e-5fbc-11e4-8c27-00144feabdc0
[865] "Economic Possibilities for our Grandchildren" by John Maynard Keynes, 1930, Panarchy http://www.panarchy.org/keynes/possibilities.html
[866] "Accelerating Change 2005" by P. Jammer, Live Journal, 2005 https://web.archive.org/web/20060327005000/http://pjammer.livejournal.com/151502.html
[867] "The Vulnerable World Hypothesis" by Nick Bostrom, Global Policy, 2019 https://nickbostrom.com/papers/vulnerable.pdf
[868] https://www.ipco.org.uk/
[869] https://isc.independent.gov.uk/
[870] *This Is How They Tell Me the World Ends: The Cyberweapons Arms Race* by Nicole Perlroth, Bloomsbury, 2021
[871] "Click Here to Kill Everyone" by Bruce Schneier, New York Magazine, 2017 https://nymag.com/intelligencer/2017/01/the-internet-of-things-dangerous-future-bruce-schneier.html
[872] "The key to industrial capitalism: limited liability", The Economist, 1999 http://www.economist.com/node/347323
[873] "Monetary metamorphosis", The Economist, 1999 http://www.economist.com/node/242113
[874] 1 Timothy 6:10
[875] "Celebrity Chef Mario Batali Says Bankers as Bad as Hitler, Stalin" by Jeff Bercovici, Forbes, 2011

https://www.forbes.com/sites/jeffbercovici/2011/11/08/celebrity-chef-mario-batali-says-bankers-as-bad-as-hitler-stalin
876 *Adults in the Room: My Battle With Europe's Deep Establishment* by Yanis Varoufakis, Random House, 2011
877 *How to Avoid a Climate Disaster: The Solutions We Have and the Breakthroughs We Need* by Bill Gates, Allen Lane, 2021
878 *The Case for Climate Capitalism: Economic Solutions for a Planet in Crisis* by Tom Rand, ECW Press, 2020
879 *The New Climate War: The Fight to Take Back Our Planet* by Michael E. Mann, Public Affairs, 2021
880 *The Burning Question: We can't burn half the world's oil, coal and gas* by Mike Berners-Lee and Duncan Clark, Profile Books, 2013
881 *Moneyland: Why Thieves and Crooks Now Rule the World and How To Take It Back* by Oliver Bullough, Profile Books, 2018
882 *Bad People: And How to Be Rid of Them: A Plan B for Human Rights* by Geoffrey Robertson, Biteback Publishing, 2021
883 *Red Notice: A True Story of High Finance, Murder, and One Man's Fight for Justice* by Bill Browder, Simon Schuster, 2014
884 "Alexei Navalny calls for EU sanctions on Russian oligarchs" by Shaun Walker, The Guardian, 2020 https://www.theguardian.com/world/2020/nov/27/alexei-navalny-calls-for-eu-sanctions-on-russian-oligarchs-abramovich-usmanov
885 "A Foreign Policy for the American People" by Antony J. Blinken, U.S. Department of State, 2021 https://www.state.gov/a-foreign-policy-for-the-american-people/
886 "Africa's democracies deserve an invite" by Nicholas Westcott, Financial Times, 2021 https://www.ft.com/content/1622a950-3f92-4eaa-b4a5-a43c0943e05d
887 *Superminds: The Surprising Power of People and Computers Thinking Together* by Thomas W. Malone, Little, Brown and Company, 2018
888 *The Alignment Problem: Machine Learning and Human Values* by Brian Christian, W. W. Norton Company, 2020
889 *The People Vs Tech: How the Internet Is Killing Democracy (and How We Save It)* by Jamie Bartlett, Ebury Press, 2018
890 "How income inequality benefits everybody" by George F. Will, Washington Post, 2015 https://www.washingtonpost.com/opinions/how-income-inequality-benefits-everybody/2015/03/25/1122ee02-d255-11e4-a62f-ee745911a4ff_story.html
891 "Income Inequality Is Good For The Poor" by Scott Winship, The Federalist, 2014 https://thefederalist.com/2014/11/05/income-inequality-is-good-for-the-poor/

892 "Movie Speech", American Rhetoric, 1987 https://www.americanrhetoric.com/MovieSpeeches/moviespeechwallstreet.html
893 "Finian's Rainbow (1968)", IMDb https://www.imdb.com/title/tt0062974/characters/nm0000001
894 "The bad behaviour of the richest: what I learned from wealth managers" by Brooke Harrington, The Guardian, 2018 https://www.theguardian.com/us-news/2018/oct/19/billionaires-wealth-richest-income-inequality
895 "Tribute to John von Neumann" by Stanislaw Ulam, Bulletin of the American Mathematical Society, 1958 https://www.ams.org/journals/bull/1958-64-03/S0002-9904-1958-10189-5/S0002-9904-1958-10189-5.pdf
896 "A Beautiful Theory" by Tim Harford, Forbes, 2006 https://www.forbes.com/2006/12/10/business-game-theory-tech-cx_th_games06_1212harford.html
897 *Prisoner's Dilemma: John Von Neumann, Game Theory, and the Puzzle of the Bomb* by William Poundstone, Anchor Books, 1992
898 The choice of the constant 2045 in this particular formula is a nod to predictions made by Ray Kurzweil. See for example "Kurzweil Claims That the Singularity Will Happen by 2045" by Christianna Reedy, Futurism, 2017 https://futurism.com/kurzweil-claims-that-the-singularity-will-happen-by-2045
899 "James Clerk Maxwell, essay on Determinism and Free Will (1873)" by Greg Hammett, Princeton Plasma Physics Laboratory https://w3.pppl.gov/~hammett/Maxwell/freewill.html
900 "When Vernor Vinge Coined the Technological Singularity" by Nikola Danaylov, Singularity Weblog, 2012 https://www.singularityweblog.com/when-vernor-vinge-coined-the-technological-singularity/
901 "Speculations on perceptrons and other automata" by I.J. Good, IBM Research Report, 1959 http://domino.research.ibm.com/library/cyberdig.nsf/papers/58DC4EA36A143C218525785E00502E30/$File/rc115.pdf
902 "Some Moral and Technical Consequences of Automation" by Norbert Wiener, Science, 1960 https://science.sciencemag.org/content/131/3410/1355
903 "Paperclip Maximizer", Less Wrong https://www.lesswrong.com/tag/paperclip-maximizer
904 "Speculations Concerning the First Ultraintelligent Machine" by Irving John Good, 1964 http://web.archive.org/web/20010527181244/http://www.aeiveos.com/~bradbury/Authors/Computing/Good-IJ/SCtFUM.html

[905] *Our Final Invention: Artificial Intelligence and the End of the Human Era* by James Barrat, Thomas Dunne Books, 2013
[906] *Superintelligence: Paths, Dangers, Strategies* by Nick Bostrom, Oxford University Press, 2014
[907] *Artificial Superintelligence: A Futuristic Approach* by Roman V. Yampolskiy, Chapman and Hall, 2017
[908] *Human Compatible: Artificial Intelligence and the Problem of Control* by Stuart Russell, Viking, 2019
[909] For background to the terms "Singularitarian" and "Singularitarianism" see "The Singularitarian Principles" by Eliezer S. Yudkowsky, 2001 https://web.archive.org/web/20081229202843/http://yudkowsky.net:80/obsolete/principles.html and "Singularitarianism", Wikipedia https://en.wikipedia.org/wiki/Singularitarianism
[910] *Perceptrons: An Introduction to Computational Geometry* by Marvin Minsky and Seymour Papert, The MIT Press, 1969
[911] *Genius Makers: The Mavericks Who Brought AI to Google, Facebook, and the World* by Cade Metz, Dutton Books, 2021
[912] "Precautionary principles" by David Cox, The Guardian, 2008 https://www.theguardian.com/commentisfree/2008/apr/19/precautionaryprinciples
[913] "Fear Review" by Luis Sanchos, Harper's Magazine, 2008 https://harpers.org/archive/2008/06/fear-review/
[914] "LHC lawsuit case dismissed by US court" by Lisa Zyga, Phys Org, 2010 https://phys.org/news/2010-09-lhc-lawsuit-case-dismissed-court.html
[915] "The Return of Radiation Man" by R. Eric Van Newkirk, Standing on the Shoulders of Giant Midgets, 2008 https://web.archive.org/web/20110708062855/http://shouldersofgiantmidgets.blogspot.com/2008/10/return-of-radiation-man.html
[916] "Asking a Judge to Save the World, and Maybe a Whole Lot More" by Dennis Overbye, The New York Times, 2008 https://www.nytimes.com/2008/03/29/science/29collider.html
[917] "Could the Large Hadron Collider make an Earth-killing black hole?" by Ethan Siegel, Medium, 2016 https://medium.com/starts-with-a-bang/could-the-large-hadron-collider-make-an-earth-killing-black-hole-1da6ee2bd7d9
[918] "The Safety of the LHC" https://home.cern/science/accelerators/large-hadron-collider/safety-lhc
[919] "Review of the Safety of LHC Collisions" by John Ellis et al, LHC Safety Assessment Group, 2008 http://lsag.web.cern.ch/LSAG-Report.pdf
[920] "Statement by the Executive Committee of the DPF on the Safety of Collisions at the Large Hadron Collider", Division of Particles and Fields, American Physical Society, 2008

https://web.archive.org/web/20080909231642/http://www.aps.org/units/dpf/governance/reports/upload/lhc_saftey_statement.pdf
[921] "'Where is everyone?' – an account of Fermi's question" by Eric M. Jones, Los Alamos National Laboratory, 1985 https://web.archive.org/web/20070629174738/http://www.fas.org/sgp/othergov/doe/lanl/la-10311-ms.pdf
[922] "The transcension hypothesis: Sufficiently advanced civilizations invariably leave our universe" by John M. Smart, Acta Astronautica, 2012 https://www.sciencedirect.com/science/article/abs/pii/S0094576511003304
[923] "Vacuum decay: the ultimate catastrophe" by Katie Mack, Cosmos, 2015 https://cosmosmagazine.com/physics/vacuum-decay-ultimate-catastrophe/
[924] METI = Messaging extra-terrestrial intelligence: http://meti.org/mission
[925] "Regarding messaging to extraterrestrial intelligence (METI) / active searches for extraterrestrial intelligence (active SETI)" by Armando Azua-Bustos et al, SETI at home https://setiathome.berkeley.edu/meti_statement_0.html
[926] "Shall We Shout Into the Cosmos?" by David Brin, 2006 https://www.davidbrin.com/nonfiction/setisearch.html
[927] "The Search For Extra-Terrestrial Intelligence: Should We Message ET?" by David Brin https://www.davidbrin.com/nonfiction/meti.html
[928] "String theorist Michio Kaku: 'Reaching out to aliens is a terrible idea'" by Andrew Anthony, The Guardian, 2021 https://www.theguardian.com/science/2021/apr/03/string-theory-michio-kaku-aliens-god-equation-large-hadron-collider
[929] "Are You Living in a Computer Simulation?" by Nick Bostrom, Philosophical Quarterly, 2003 https://www.simulation-argument.com/simulation.html
[930] "20 years after 'The Matrix' hit theatres, another sequel is in the works. Many scientists and philosophers still think we're living in a simulation" by Aylin Woodward, Business Insider, 2019 https://www.businessinsider.com/the-matrix-do-we-live-in-a-simulation-2019-4
[931] "Is life a video game? | Elon Musk | Code Conference 2016" Recode on YouTube https://www.youtube.com/watch?v=2KK_kzrJPS8
[932] "Elon Musk says we may live in a simulation. Here's how we might tell if he's right" by Corey S. Powell, NBC News, 2018 https://www.nbcnews.com/mach/amp/ncna913926
[933] "The Simulation Hypothesis is Pseudoscience" by Sabine Hossenfelder, Backreaction, 2021 http://backreaction.blogspot.com/2021/02/the-simulation-hypothesis-is.html

934 "Simulated Universe Nonsense (The Penguin Argument)" by Singularity Utopia, Hplus Magazine, 2012 https://hplusmagazine.com/2012/11/09/simulation-nonsense/
935 "Digital Physics vs. The Simulation Argument" by Eray Özkural, Examachine, 2013 https://examachine.net/blog/digital-physics-vs-simulation-argument/
936 "The Simulation Argument FAQ" by Nick Bostrom, 2008 https://www.simulation-argument.com/faq.html
937 "On testing the simulation theory" by Tom Campbell et al, Quantum Physics, 2017 https://arxiv.org/abs/1703.00058
938 "How To Live In A Simulation" by Robin Hanson, Journal of Evolution and Technology, 2001 https://www.jetpress.org/volume7/simulation.pdf
939 Quoted on https://www.simulation-argument.com/
940 *Tales of the Turing Church: Hacking religion, enlightening science, awakening technology* by Giulio Prisco, independently published, 2020
941 https://www.youtube.com/c/Londonfuturists/videos
942 "Ring of Fire" https://pixabay.com/illustrations/ring-of-fire-circle-blue-fire-2141192/

www.ingramcontent.com/pod-product-compliance
Lightning Source LLC
Chambersburg PA
CBHW071308150426
43191CB00007B/539
* 9 7 8 0 9 9 5 4 9 4 2 5 1 *